John Smyth

The Berkeley Manuscripts

Vol. III

John Smyth

The Berkeley Manuscripts
Vol. III

ISBN/EAN: 9783337194840

Printed in Europe, USA, Canada, Australia, Japan

Cover: Foto ©ninafisch / pixelio.de

More available books at **www.hansebooks.com**

THE BERKELEY MANUSCRIPTS

A DESCRIPTION

OF THE

Hundred of Berkeley

IN THE COUNTY OF GLOUCESTER

AND OF

Its Inhabitants

BY JOHN SMYTH, OF NIBLEY

VOL. III

Edited by Sir JOHN MACLEAN, F.S.A., etc.

FOR THE BRISTOL AND GLOUCESTERSHIRE ARCHÆOLOGICAL SOCIETY

GLOUCESTER: PRINTED BY JOHN BELLOWS
FOR THE SUBSCRIBERS
MDCCCLXXXV

PREFACE TO VOLUME III

It is with much gratification we lay before the Subfcribers the Third and laft Volume of the firft feries of Smyth's Berkeley Manufcripts which the Council of the Briftol and Gloucefterfhire Archæological Society, with the obliging permiffion of Lord Fitz Harding, has caufed to be printed for the members of the Society. We fay the firft feries, for thefe three volumes form but a fmall portion of Smyth's voluminous works, extending to twenty-fix volumes, moft of them folio, as defcribed by himfelf in a fchedule at the end of this volume. Unfortunately few of thefe are now extant. At Berkeley Caftle is one of them. It would feem to be one of thofe numbered 7 and 8 in Smyth's fchedule referred to above, probably No. 7. The title-page ftates it to be "A Regifter of all fuch Tenures by Knight's Service as are belonginge either to the Baronyes of Berkeley and Brufe in the County of Gloucefter; or, To the Baronyes of Mowbray and Segrave in the County of Leicefter; or, Which are holden of any Manors in the Countyes of Gloucefter, Somerfet, Leicefter, Warwicke, Rutland, Northampton and Suffex, or which lye in any of them; being the inheritance of the right honourable Henry Lord Berkeley, or of Thomas Berkeley knight, fonne and heire apparent of the faid Lord Berkeley. Collected by the labours of John Smyth, a profeffed follower of theire unattaynted family, and finifhed in Anno tercio Regis Jacobi Primi Anno que Dñi 1605." It extends, altogether, to about 440 pages, fome few of which are blank The other volume, No. 8, appears to be loft.

In the poffeffion of Reginald Cholmondeley, of Condover Hall, County Salop, Efq., Smyth's heir-at-law, are two other volumes. One of the fet numbered 14, 15 and 16 in Smyth's fchedule. The title of this

volume

volume is "The Names and Surnames of all the able and sufficient men in body fitt for his Maties service in the warres in the Dyvision of the fforest, within the County of Glouc^r, wherein are contayned the hundreds of St. Brevils, Westbury, Bedsloe, Botloe, and the Duchy of Lancaster, with their ages, personal statures, and armours, viewed by the right honorable Henry Lord Barkley lord Lieutenant of the said County by direction from his Matie in the month of September 1608. Anno que Sexto Regni Regis Jacobi Anglie &c." The volume contains also the names of the Lords of the Manors as stated in the schedule before mentioned. The two missing volumes embrace, of course, the particulars for the remainder of the County.

The other volume at Condover is a folio of great interest and value. It is numbered 19 in Smyth's schedule, and contains Abstracts of all the Offices, or Inquisitions post mortem, and of Ad quod damnum, in the County of Gloucester from 10th Henry III. to 28th Henry VIII.

The special volumes mentioned under No. 26 of Smyth's schedule are not now to be found. They might possibly have been handed over to the purchasers, with the title deeds, when the estates to which they refer were sold by Henry Lord Berkeley.

I hope the Council will be able to see its way to print, as a *second series*, all the volumes now extant, or so many of them as may be permitted by the owners, with as little delay as possible.

The preparation of these volumes was manifestly a labour of love with the writer, and few can estimate the vastness of that labour. "Great indeed," he says, "had not a continued delight of 40 yeares haled mee alonge," he is thus bearing testimony to the absorbing attraction which historical researches have for a student who once gives himself to the subject. Smyth loved his books as his children, and the manner in which he takes leave of them on the conclusion of his labours is quite pathetic. The subscribers cannot fail, however, to have noticed that this
volume

PREFACE

volume has been written in haſte. It is not, the author tells us, caſt in the mould which he intended, for he purpoſed it ſhould have contained a review of a book of the lord Berkeley's tenures by knight ſervice in this hundred of Berkeley, finiſhed in the year 1605, but his "withered age" prevented it. This, however, is not the point to which we more particularly allude. The volume is, generally, left in a leſs perfect condition than his previous works. There are many blanks, which, perhaps, in the proceſs of writing his defect of memory did not enable him readily to fill up, and therefore he reſerved for further reſearches, which poſſibly he was never afterwards able to make. He evidently thought that the time was faſt approaching when he muſt reſt from his labours, as he well deſerved to do, for concluding this volume on the 21ˢᵗ December, 1639, in the 73ʳᵈ year of his age, he died on the 25ᵗʰ February, 1640-1. The loſs of the great bulk of the contents of the Muniment Room in Berkeley Caſtle in the Civil War renders it now impoſſible to complete what Smyth unfortunately left unfiniſhed.

We cannot conclude our connection with the three moſt important volumes which we have had the pleaſure of paſſing through the preſs, without expreſſing our obligations to Mr. J. H. Cooke, F.S.A., now Steward of the Berkeley Eſtates, for his great kindneſs in collating the text with that of the reviſed and improved copies which Smyth preſented to George Lord Berkeley, which has rendered the volumes as printed more perfect than they otherwiſe could have been. We deſire alſo to thank Mr. J. A. C. Vincent for the very careful manner in which he prepared the tranſcripts, which has confiderably lightened the editorial labour; and laſtly the Printer, for the attention beſtowed upon the typographical portion of the work, which has added greatly to its attractive appearance.

J. M.

The Hundred of Berkeley

A Description of the Hundred of BERKELEY, and of the Inhabitants thereof, in the County of Glouc͠ ; The Remaines of a greater worke, collected and disposed by the indeavors of — JOHN SMYTH.

My residence wherein, for more then forty yeares, emboldeneth mee: ffirst in generall, And after in perticuler, by way of ALPHABET, to make my observations legible.

In generall thus;

This hundred of Berkeley with the residue of the County of Gloucester was anciently inhabited by the Brittaines called Dobuni, somtimes in ancient authors, by transplantinge of the two first consonants, called Boduni; And when by the Conquest of the English Saxons, that name was worne out, The Inhabitants of this hundred, (as others round about it,) were called by newe Saxon name, Wiccij: The Relickes of which appellation, aswell in this hundred as in other parts of this County, yet seeme to live in the name of Wicke; whereby divers villages are called, whose scituation is not disagreeinge to the Etimology of that name, A creeke, cove, or reach of a ryver, or necke of land: But after such time as Ceaulin kinge of the West Saxons, had, about the yeare of Grace 566, put the Brittaines at Durham [Dyrham] not farre from this hundred, to flight, and dispossessed them of Durham, Gloucester, Cirencester, and other adioyninge places, It was for many yeares subiect to the West Saxons; Vpon whom, though the Mercian a succeedinge kingdome in the time of the Saxon heptarchy prevailed, yet afterwards Penda, kinge of the Mercians, was dispossessed againe by Cineglise, then raigninge over the West Saxons; Howbeit, aswell those Townes as this hundred, with all the territories therabouts, came againe vnder the subiection of the Mercians, and so continued till Egbert, kinge of the West Saxons, reduced the wholl Heptarchy into one English Monarchy, about the yeare—800, And gave to the wholl the name of England.

But

Hundred of Berkeley

But it muſt bee conceived, that the word (hundred,) till kinge Egbert had divided this kingdome, was not in vſe, but diſtinguiſhed in ſmall regions, by Hides of land, eſpetially in theſe parts, as after will appeare; Each Hide, generally contraininge, 160 acres. That is, 4. yard land, at 40. acres to each yard land, which to this day, is the vſuall content of a yard land in the ritcher ſoile of this hundred; But in the wolds, or hilly part therof, a yard land is ſomwhat more.

In the kingdome of the Weſt Saxons, or of Mercia, when at the largeſt, were reckoned one hundred thouſand hides, whereof in this hundred of Berkeley, as the booke of Domeſdei ſheweth, were 123 hides, beſides certaine Carucates, and yard lands, as after perticulerly followeth: And in truth this name (hundred) or this diviſion by Hundreds was not fully eſtabliſhed till the raigne of kinge Aelfrid als Alured, after hee became ſole Monarche, about the yeare of our Lord—890.

And in that firſt age after the Saxons converſion to Chriſtianity, or the age that followed, (ages of much piety,) It ſeemes that a Nunry was founded by one of thoſe princes, in that part of this hundred, where the Caſtle of Berkeley (the center-place of the hundred) now ſtandeth, but by whom, I could never finde; nor, doe I thinke that, that which for ſix hundred yeares hath byn loſt, will bee found heerafter; and the ſame largely endowed, if not with all yet with the greateſt part of the poſſeſſions of this Hundred; And ſo continued till about the beginninge of the raigne of kinge Edward the Confeſſor, Anno 1043, when by the wily and wicked plot of Earle Goodwin, recorded by Walter Mape in his manuſcript hiſtory of that time, it was by that king diſſolved, And all the poſſeſſions therof given to that Earle; who left the ſame to Harold his ſonne, who after the death of that kinge vſurped the Crowne of this land; whom William Duke of Normandy, called the Conqueror, ſlewe in battle, in Anno 1066, wherby this his paternall poſſeſſion eſcheated,[1] And, with what elſe hee had, veſted in the Crowne: And ſo continued about 85 yeares, lett in feefarme to that noble family of the Berkeleis, called of Dureſly, till toward the end of the raigne of kinge Stephen, as after more perticulerly followeth.

Which wily and wicked plot of the ſaid Earle Goodwin to gaine thereby this tract of ground, Mape thus delivereth.

Berkeley

---

[1] This does not agree with the Domeſday record in which Berchelai appears under *Terra Regis*, that is land in the hand of King Edward the Confeſſor. [ED.]

General Description

Berkeley neere vnto Severne is a towne of 500ˡⁱ revenue; in it there was a nunnery, and the Abbeſſe over theis Nunnes was a noble woman and beautifull: Earle Goodwyn, by a cunninge and ſubtile witt deſiringe not her ſelfe but hers, as hee paſſed that way, leaft with her a nephew of his, a very proper and beautifull yonge gentleman, (pretending that hee was ſickely,) vntill hee returned backe. Him hee had given this leſſon, that hee ſhould keepe his bed, and in no wiſe ſeeme to bee recovered, vntill hee had got both her, and as many of the Nunnes as hee could, with child, as they came to viſit him: And to the end the younge man might obtaine their favour and his full purpoſe, when they viſited him, the Earle gave vnto him pretty ringes | and fine girdles, to beſtowe for favours vpon them, and therby to deceive them: Hee therfore beinge gladly and willingly entred into this courſe of libidinous pleaſure, (for that the way downe to hell is eaſy,) was taught his leſſons, and wiſely playeth the foole in that which ſeemed wiſe in his owne conceipt: with him were reſtant all thoſe thinges which the fooliſh virgins could wiſh for, beauty, dainty delicates, ritches, faire ſpeach; and carefull hee was nowe to ſingle them alone; The Devill therfore thruſt out Pallas, brought in Venus, and made the church of our Saviour and his ſaints an accurſed temple of all idolls, and the ſhrine a very ſtewes: And ſo of pure lambes hee made them ſoule ſhee wolves, and of pure virgins filthy harlots; now when as many of their bellies bare out bigge and round, this youth beinge by this time over-wearied with conqueſt of pleaſure, getteth him gone, And forthwith bringeth home vnto his lord and maiſter a victorious enſigne, worthy to have the reward of iniquity, and to ſpeake plainly, relateth what was done: Noe ſooner heard hee this, but hee hieth him to the kinge, informeth him how the lady Abbeſſe of Berkeley and her Nunnes were great with childe, and comonly proſtitute to every one that would, ſendeth meſſengers on purpoſe for enquiry therof, proveth all that hee had ſaid; hee beggeth Berkeley of the kinge his lord, after the Nunnes were thruſt out, and obtaineth it at his hands, And hee left it to his wife Gweda; but becauſe ſhee her ſelfe would eat nothinge that came out of this Manor, for that the Nunrye was deſtroied, hee purchaſed for her, Woodcheſter, that therof ſhee might live, ſo longe as ſhee made her abode at Berkeley.[1]

Thus Mape.

Howbeit, ſuch ſeemes to have byn the ſtruglinge, at leaſt of the chaſter Nunnes, if not of the wantons alſo, that ſome of them held a kinde of footinge there till the end of kinge Stephen's raigne, Anno. 1154; for in the great roll of the pipe, in an

accompt

---

[1] See Ante, "Lives of the Berkeleys," Vol. II., p. 26.

Hundred of Berkeley

accompt made for the laſt yeare of that kinge, in the firſt of his ſucceſſor, kinge Henry the ſecond, William Berkeley of Dureſly had an allowance of three pounds, by him laid out for the garments of three Nunnes heere: which as it is the firſt accompt that at this day remaines in any of the kings Courts vnconſumed by time, ſoe it is the laſt wherin any memoriall is of theſe Nunnes.

Parkes.   Nor Hundred in this county of Glouc̄, nor ſcarce in this kingdome, hath in ſoe ſmall a tract of ground beene better ſtored with deere, both redd and ſallowe, Till huſbandry of late daies turned many of thoſe parkes and chaſes into better profitt; ffor in this hundred were the parkes called the Worthy, or Caſtle parke of Berkeley, Whitcliffe parke, Newparke, Oakley parke, Shepnaſh parke, Hawe-Parke | by Wotton, Beverſton parke, Hill parke, Owſelworth parke, Almondeſbury parke, Cromhall parke, Ewley parke, with ſome others, as after appeareth in this deſcription; And the Chaſes of Michaelwood and Redwood.

Scite.   Geographers meaſure the poſition or ſeite of Berkeley towne, (the hart of this hundred,) by the longitude of twenty degrees and 25. ſcruples, and by the latitude of fifty two degrees and 5 ſcruples, or very neere therto.

And this hundred ſeemes ſoe evenly devided, by one part therof ſtandinge high in the wolds, and the other in the vale at the foote of thoſe hills, That it is not eaſily diſcerned whether of the two is the greater part: By reaſon of which ſcituation, many hundreds, even thouſands, of ſprings breake forth at the ſydes, knees, and feete of thoſe hills, begettinge divers delicate ſmall Rivers, neither knowinge want of water in ſoier, nor ſo increaſinge their chanell in winter, that the trade of clothinge which heere aboundeth, is neither in drought not wett wether hindred: A principall cauſe of the multitude of Tuckmills, and fullinge mills, which heere abound.

Soile.   The Soile is for moſt part bountefull; ritch in paſture and meadow, fruitfull in procreation of divers and different kindes of trees, (whereof I have numbred many hundreds,) every where delightinge the beholders with their beautifull verdancy. And that which hath of old beene written ſeemes true, that the eaſy and free increaſe of fruit doth nouriſh ſloth in the comon people. The lowe and fat grounds doe yeild ſuch abundance of paſture for kyne and oxen, as ſufficeth the greedines of thoſe beaſts, and covetouſnes of their owners: And in the hilly part where the ground is dryer and the graſſe ſhorter, it feedeth innumerable numbers of ſheepe, excuſinge the barrennes of the ſoile with a large profit drawne from them.

For

General Description

Precedence. For the State and eminency of the yeomanry, this hundred is allowed the preheminence before any of the other thirty hundreds of the County: challenginge this further prerogative by ancient vſage, to bee firſt ranked in all Subſidy rolls, Muſter Rolls, and the like: And to bee firſt called and diſpatched in the generall aſſemblies of the county: which my ſelfe hath knowne the high Baily and high Coneſtables of this hundred to have publikely challenged, and conteſted for, as an honorable right and preheminence, derived to them from ages paſt; which hath accordingly bene allowed to them.

Fifteenes. In the Collection of the ffifteenthes and tenthes, this hundred in the kings Courts is charged at—135^{li} 16^s 11^d, wherout for decaied villages is deducted—26^{li} 18^s 10^d ob. q$_{b}$: And then remaines payable into the kings Exchequer—108^{li} 17^s 11^d q$_b$, beſides 20^s paid by 5 ſubtaxors. Whence note, that this payment which comonly at this day wee call the ffifteene, was anciently and truly named the Tenth and ffifteene: The Tenth for ſo much therof, as was paid out of Cities and Burrowes, in the name of the Tenth of their goods and moveables: And fifteene, for the reſidue therof, which was originally and properly due out of the vplandiſh and country townes or villages, as a fifteenth part of their goods or moveables; Of the wholl ſome of which ffifteenth and Tenth, there was Six thouſand pounds abated in the time of kinge Henry the ſixt, by parliament, in reſpect of the poverty of ſundry decaied cities and townes in every part of the Realme.

Liberties. Within this hundred, the lord therof hath by divers grants and Confirmacõns from kinge Henry the ſecond and his ſucceſſors kings of this Realme, The Liberty of ſervinge all writts and proceſſe with returne therof, by their owne baylies: A viewe of franke pledge and what ſoever therto belongeth: All felons goods of what kind ſoever, whether felons of them ſelves, or otherwiſe: All wayved goods, Eſtreyes, Treſure trove, Deodands, yeare, day, and waſt, Eſtrepements,[1] The goods of fugitives and of convict, attainted, outlawed, and waived perſons, before what Judge ſoever or in what court ſoever ſuch goods ſhall come to bee forfeited: And all iſſues and amerciaments loſt or forfeited by any perſons within the ſaid hundred: And all whale fiſhes, Sturgeons, and all other great and royall fiſhes, in whatſoever free fiſhings of other men within the ſaid hundred in the Ryver of Severne: And free warren in all his demeſne lands, and in all other places where his Anceſtors have vſed

---

[1] Spoil made in lands and woods by a tenant for life to the damage of him in reverſion. See Ante, "Lives of the Berkeleys," Vol. II., p. 435 n. [Ed.]

vsed to have free warren, within the said hundred, with whatsoever to free warren appertaineth: And also a Court of pleas for triall of all actions, bee they of debt, trespas, trover, Detinue, assault, battery, of the case, or other, where the dett or damage is accompted vnder forty shillings, holden each Munday three weekes at Berkeley: And also the grantinge of Replevins, for all distresses taken or impounded within the said hundred, with the awardinge of proces of Returno habendo, Second deliverance, Capias in withernam,[1] and whatsoever to such acc̄ons of Replegiare appertaineth: And the makinge of processe of Subpena ad testificandum, betweene party and party in each of the said actions; with divers other liberties specified in my three volumes of the history of this Berkeleian family: And to conclude; In Berkeley Castle is a Deed in 5. E. 2. wherby Phillip Coby granted to Thomas then lord Berkeley, two acres of land in Alkington (a manor in the parish of Berkeley,) quas recuperasset per breve d̄ni Regis de recto, in hundredo de Berkeley.

Nomina villarum.

The booke in the Exchequer called Nomina villarum compiled in the nynth yeare of kinge Edward the second, Anno. 1315, declareth that in this County of Glouc̄, are thirty hundreds, (naminge them,) one wherof is this hundred of Berkeley, wherof Thomas lord Berkeley the elder, is owner: And that in this hundred are two Burrowe townes, viz̄ᵗ, Berkeley, wherof Thomas lord Berkeley is lord; And Dursley, wherof John the sonne of William de Berkeley, is lord; And the village of Newenton, whereof the said John Berkeley is lord; The Villages of Hame, Came, and Wotton, whereof the said Thomas de Berkeley the elder, is lord: The Villages of Kingsweston and Beverston, wherof Thomas ap Adam is lord: The village of Hull wherof John fitz Nicholl is lord: The villages of Almondesbury and Ashelworth, wherof the Abbot of Sᵗ Augustine's by Bristoll is lord. Thus the booke.

Fifteene peny booke

The booke called the Fifteene peny booke compiled in the third yeare of kinge Henry the fifth, Anno. 1415, declareth that in this hundred of Berkeley are theis villages. vzᵗ; Hame—9ˡⁱ 15ˢ 6ᵈ. Wotton forinececa—13ˡⁱ 13ˢ 4ᵈ. Wotton narincita—4ˡⁱ ob., Hull and Nyndesfeild—8ˡⁱ 7ˢ 2ᵈ q, Cromhale—3ˡⁱ 10ˢ 5ᵈ ob. q, Came—11ˡⁱ 9ˢ 11ᵈ Covely. 5ˡⁱ 14ˢ 6ᵈ Newinton Bagpath, Owselworth—4ˡⁱ 2ˢ Vley and Wodemancote—3ˡⁱ 14ˢ 7ᵈ Dursley—6ˡⁱ 15ˢ 5ᵈ Beverston—5ˡⁱ 2ˢ 9ᵈ Kingescote and Oulepenne.—4ˡⁱ 2ᵈ ob. Kingesweston and Ailberton. 10ˡⁱ 13ˢ 4ᵈ ob. q. Horfeild and ffilton—3ˡⁱ 10ˢ 6ᵈ q. Almondesbury. 3ˡⁱ 2ˢ Erlingham—9ˡⁱ Ashelworth—4ˡⁱ Slimbrugg.—11ˡⁱ 8ˢ 5ᵈ ob. q, Berkeley—3ˡⁱ 11ˢ 8ᵈ q,. Sum̄.—132ˡⁱ 1ᵈ Thus the booke.

A Quo

---

[1] Explained Ante, "Lives of the Berkeleys," Vol. II., p. 344 *n*. [Eᴅ.]

General Description

A Quo warranto in the Receipt of the Exchequer Court brought by kinge Edward the firſt, in the fifteenth yeare of his raigne againſt Thomas lord Berkeley, layeth downe the names of Villages and Townſhips within this hundred, and the liberties of the lord therof in the ſame, more perticulerly then the former bookes; As that the ſaid lord Berkeley had free warren in the Townes of Berkeley, Hame, Clapton, Bevington, Pedington, Stone, Swanhunger, Wanefwell, Egeton, Alkington, Newport, Woodford, Swanley, Wike, Hineton, Rockhampton, Came, Hurſt, Kingeſton, Goſington, Stinteſcombe, Stancombe, Cleyhunger, Matteſdon, Cowley, Hulmancote, Slimbridge, Wotton, Simondſale, Combe, Wortley, Bradley, Nybley, and Bircheley: Denyinge that the townſhips of Beverſton, Ailberton, Kingfweſton, Hill, Nymesfeild, Horfeild, ffilton, Almondeſbury, Cromhall, Aſhelworth, Durfeley, Vley, Kingſcote, Oulpen, Newenton, Owſelworth, Huntingford and Erlingham, though all of them within the hundred of Berkeley, yet in none of them hee claimeth to have free warren at all.

Pʼlita de Quo warranto. 15. E. 1. Rot. 12. in recepi Scĉij.

Which excellent record, (a little inlarged with theſe other here marginald,) doth give vs further to knowe, That that ancient family of the Berkeleis of Durfeley ſhortly after William the Conquerors daies, (if not in his time,) rented the whole manor of Berkeley, wherto this hundred is appendant, of the Crowne, at the yearly farme rent of—500ˡⁱ etc. vntill kinge Henry the ſecond in the firſt of his raigne, granted the ſame, with all the herneſſe, that is with all the nookes and corners therof, to Robert the ſonne of Hardinge, Or rather, vntill the attonement made at Briſtoll by that kinge, (then but Duke of Normandy,) and kinge Stephen; betweene the ſaid Robert, and Roger Berkeley then lord of Durfeley, not fully two yeares before: whereby the ſaid Roger releaſed to the ſaid Robert and his heires, All his claime and intereſt in the ſaid Manor and hundred of Berkeley, as more largely I have written in my hiſtory | of this Berkeleian family, in the life of the ſaid Robert, called Robert the firſt: And as followeth fol: 325.

From this Robert the ſonne of Harding, the firſt lord Berkeley who died in 17. H. 2. this manor and hundred diſcended and came to the lord Maurice his ſonne and heire, who dyed in 1. R. 1. And from him to the lord Robert his ſonne and heire; And from him, (dyinge without iſſue in 4. H. 3.,) to the lord Thomas his brother and heire, who dyed in 28. H. 3. And from him to the lord Maurice his ſonne and heire, who dyed in 8. E. 1. and from him to the lord Thomas his ſonne and heire, (which is hee that is mentioned in the foreſaid Quo warranto, And in the ſaid booke, called Nomina villarum,) who dyed in 14. E. 2. And from him to

Berkeley Pedigree

the

the lord Maurice his sonne and heire, who dyed in 20. E. 2. and from him to the lord Thomas his sonne and heire, who augmented his liberties in this hundred of Berkeley by a grant from kinge Edward the third in the fourth of his raigne, and after, in the xxiijth of that kinge, entailed the same vpon the heires males of his body, and dyed in 35. E. 3. And from him to the lord Maurice his sonne and heire, who dyed in 42. E. 3. and from him to the lord Thomas his sonne and heire, who dyed without issue male in 5. H. 5. And from him to the lord James his nephewe and heire male, sonne of Sir James, brother of him the said lord Thomas, who dyed in 6. H. 4. and from the said lord James who dyed in 3. E. 4. to the lord William his sonne and heire, who was first created Viscont Berkeley, afterwards Earle of Nottingham, and afterwards Marquesse Berkeley, with the offices of Earle Marshall and great Marshall of England, who in the fourth yeare of kinge Henry the seaventh conveyed (inter alia) this Manor and hundred of Berkeley for defalt of issue of his owne body, to that kinge and the heires males of his body, and for default of such heires males, to remaine to the right heires of him the said Marques Berkeley: wherby, from the xiiijth day of ffebruary in the vijth yeare of that kings raigne Anno. 1491. when the said Marques dyed, till the death of kinge Edward the sixth, (the space of 61. yeares, 4. monthes and 20. daies,) the same remained in the Crowne, And then reverted to Henry lord Berkeley, as right heire of the said Marques Berkeley: vizt, sonne and heire of Thomas lord Berkeley, who dyed in 26. H. 8. sonne and heire of Thomas lord Berkeley, who dyed in 24. H. 8. brother and heire of Maurice lord Berkeley, who dyed without issue in 15. H. 8. sonnes of Maurice lord Berkeley who dyed in 22. H. 7. brother and heire of the said William Marques Berkeley; And from the said lord Henry Berkeley who dyed in 11. Jacobi, to George nowe lord Berkeley, sonne of Sir Thomas Berkeley, who dyed in 9. Jac: sonne and heire apparant, whilest hee lived, of the said lord Henry; which lord George in the xiiijth yeare of the raigne of kinge James, much repayred the defects, and inlarged his liberties in this manor and hundred of Berkeley by a new grant obtained from that kinge, more to bee prised then all the former. Theis for | the space of one thousand one hundred and fifty yeares, or neere thereabout have beene the flittings and removes of this Manor and hundred of Berkeley, and such the owners as aforesaid. See this pedegree also, fol: 77. 78.

Domesday booke. **The** booke called Domesday, remaininge in the receipt of the Exchequer at Westminster compiled in the xiiijth yeare of the raigne of William the Conqueror, hath of this Manor and hundred of Berkeley theis words, thus englished: Hæ Bercw, &c. Theis villages appertaine to Berkeley; In Hill are 4. hides; In Almintune

General Description

Almintune 4. hides; In Hinetune 4. hides; In Came 6. hides, and 11. other hides; In Gofintune 4. hides; In Derfilege 3. hides; In Covelege 4. hides; In Euuelege 2. hides; In Nimdesfelle 3. hides; In Vittune, 15. hides; In Simondeſhall half an hide; In Chingefcote 4. hides; In Beureſtane 10. hides; In Oſteuuorde halfe an hide; An Almondefberie 2. hides; In Horefelle 8. hides; In Weſtune 7. hides and one yard land; In Eldbertone 5. hides; In Cromale 2. hides; In Erlingehame 9. hides; In Efceleuuorde 3. hides. Denotinge vnto vs, That the Demefne lands of the Conqueror were fuch in each of thofe townſhips; And concludes Hæc fupradicta membra omnia pertinent ad Berchelai; All theis Villages are members belonginge to Berkeley.

At a generall Mufter of all the able men for the warre taken by Henry Lord Berkeley for the County of Glouc̃ by fpeciall direction from kinge James in the fixt yeare of his raigne, hee then lord Leiutenant of the Shiere; there appeared before him—2064 able men fitt for martiall fervice, then dwellinge in this hundred, whofe names with their feverall ages and ſtatures, were (with all the refidue of the County) written in three bookes in folio, the labor of my felfe and of William Archer my Clarke, which now remaine in Berkeley Caſtle; befides many that made default in this hundred and appeared not.[1] *Able men.*

Of Trained foldiers this yeare 1639, vnder their three Captaines, Edward Stephens, Thomas Veel and William Thorpe, Efq:̃, are men well difciplined; And 18. light horfe, parcell of 50. vnder the comaund of Sir Gabriell Loe knight, wherof one with the furniture is charged vpon my felfe. *Trained foldiers.*

In the laſt Subfedy affeffed before Sir Robert Pointz and my felfe, Comiffioners, in the fifth yeare of king Charles, were—404. fubfedy men in this hundred, who then paid the kinge—164^{li}. *Subfedy men.*

Towards the Purveyance, or provifion for the kings houſhold, this County of Glouc̃ paies by compofition—440^{li}. in money; Therof the Divifion of Berkeley (accompted a fourth part of the Shire) paieth—110^{li}. And this hundred (accompted a third part of that Divifion) paies—33^{li}. 3^{s}. And this hundred for the releife of the prifoners in the kingefbench and Marſhalfey, paies yearly | 9^{li}. 6^{s}. 4^{d} And for releife of the poore | prifoners in the Gaole of Glouc̃, by the yeare—7^{li}. 16^{s}. 8^{d}. And to the Muſtermaſter for his wages for this hundred yearly—4^{li}. 9^{s}. And to the Treaforer *Purveiance and other payments.*

towards

---

[1] This Book is now at Condover Hall, Co. Salop. [ED.]

towards the pentions of maymed fouldyers, cafuall fires, and the like, yearly out of this Hundred—17ˢ. 6ᵈ. 8ᵈ.

Spirituall promotions.

The Rectories, Parfonages, Vicarages, and other fpirituall promotions togeather with the Impropriations within this hundred, doe appeare perticulerly in my feverall defcription of each townfhip, with the Deanery called of Durfeley.

Sports.

The large and levell playnes of Slimbridge warth and others in the vale of this hundred: And the downes or hilly playnes of Stintefcombe, Weftridge, Tickruydinge, and others in the hilly or Cottefwold part, doe witnes the inbred delight, that both gentry, yeomanry, rafcallity, boyes and children, doe take in a game called Stoball, The play whereat each child of 12. yeares old, can (I fuppofe) afwell defcribe, as my felfe: And not a fonne of mine, but at 7. was furnifhed with his double ftoball ftaves, and a gamfter therafter.

Marches of Wales

The wholl County lyeth vnder the goverment of the Comiffion for the Marches of Wales, as beinge within the fame: Howbeit, thefe Records, which in my fearches in the kings Courts, I have curfarily obferved, will evince, that neither this hundred of Berkeley, nor any part of this County, are within the Marches of Wales: viz!; The parliament roll.—16. R. 2. number. 34. The pliam! roll. 13. H. 4. number 3. And the pliament roll. 20. H. 6. And the pliament roll—27. H. 6. membrana. 10. with fome others.

The 3. fteppes.

In the body of this hundred are obferved three fteps or degrees, obvious to every obferver: The firft from the chanell of Severne halfe way towards the hills, which hath wealth without health. The fecond, from thence neere towards the tops of thofe hills, which hath wealth and health: And the third fteppe or degree, from thence forward, called the weald or Cotfall part, affordeth health in that fharpe aire, but leffe wealth, And feemes to take name of the barren wooddy parts: Into the beft wherof, the mercifull goodnes of almighty God hath caft my lott, beyond my hopes or defires. |

10
Court of pleas, or, three weekes Court.

At the Yeald hall or Both hall in Berkeley Towne is holden each Munday three weekes throughout the yeare, a Court of Pleas, for tryall of accons betweene party and party, fuch as formerly are mentioned: vnles (which feldome happeneth) the fame bee adiourned for fix weekes or more, at the difcretion of the Steward and freefutors, vpon reafonable caufe by them approved of: wherat theis cuftomes

and

and proceedings have of mine owne knowledge byn vſed 46. yeares, (my ſelfe ſo
longe havinge byn Steward there:) And, as I confidently beleive, time out of
minde, before. viz!

1. The Court holdeth not plea, were the dett, damage, or ſõme in demaund, is, or
is alleadged to bee, of the value of—40ˢ or above.

2. The proceſſe in the ſaid Court, is made forth by the Steward, by ſõmons, Attachment, and Diſtringas, accordinge to the courſe of the cõmon lawe.

3. The high bayly of the hundred, and not the Steward, granteth 𝕽𝖊𝖕𝖑𝖊𝖛𝖎𝖓𝖌, for
the delivery of any goods or Chattells repleviable, impounded in any place
within the hundred: But proceſſe of 𝕽𝖊𝖙𝖔𝖗𝖓𝖔 𝖍𝖆𝖇𝖊𝖓𝖉𝖔, and of Second deliverance, and of 𝕮𝖆𝖕𝖎𝖆𝖘 𝖎𝖓 𝖂𝖎𝖙𝖍𝖊𝖗𝖓𝖆𝖒 are made by the Steward of the Court.

4. No perſon is admitted to bee an Atturney either for plt. or defendᵗ vnles ſuch
pſon ſhew forth a warrant in writinge vnder the ſeale of the ſaid plt. or defᵗ
to ſuch effect: But the plt. or defᵗ beinge p͠ſent in court, may appoint his
Atturney by word only, ſo it bee entred accordingly by the Steward.

5. If an executor or adminiſtrator bee plt. in any action, and the ſame paſſe for the
defᵗ, yet hee hath noe coſts of ſuite vnles it evidently appeare to the Court
That the ſute was comenced for vexation only. The like is vſed if the executors executor, or the adminiſtrators adminiſtrator bee pᵗ.

6. If any inhabitant within the hundred bee ſuppoſed to bee fugitive, that is, likely
to be removed out of the hundred before the next Court, againſt whom
another hath cauſe of action: Vpon ſuch Action entred in the Stewards booke,
either ſedente Curia or out of the ſame, the Steward vſeth to grant an
Attachment, called an Attachmᵗ fugitive, authoriſinge therby the Baily of the
hundred to attach ſuch goods of the party as hee can finde within the hundred,
and the ſame to put in ſafety to anſwere the dett or damage, if the accõn
vpon triall paſſe againſt him that is ſuppoſed fugitive.

7. The like attachmᵗ is vſed to bee granted, if any perſon dwellinge without the
hundred havinge goods within the hundred, againſt whome another hath cauſe
of accõn, and entred as aboveſaid. And the like alſo is vſed if both parties
dwell

dwell out of the hundred, the def: having goods within the hundred, to attach such goods, therby to drawe the def: to answere ; which goods soe in theis and the former cases attached, are liable to satisfy the plt. if hee recover against the def: ; Howbeit, the plt. putteth in pledges dwellinge within the hundred of sufficiency to satisfy the def: his costs and damages if the sute passe against the plt. vpon triall. |

8. If vpon entry of any action (except in Replevins) the def: after somons appeareth not, hee is for such his default, at the first court amerced iij^d—ffor his second default at the next court vj^d—ffor his default at the third court ix^d—ffor his default at the fourth court xij^d—And so for every default at every court day after xij^d—vntill such def: doe appeare ; But the plt. at the second court may, if hee will, sue forth an Attachment, And at the third court a Distringas ; And if the def:^{s} goods bee thervpon attached or distreyned, and hee vpon returne of the processe, appeare not, such goods are forfeited to the lord of the liberty.

9. The custome of the Court is, to allowe the ordinary costs of sute expended in court, either by p^{lt} or def: without diminucõn, vnles the p^{lt} sue as executor or administrator, and then, as is aforesaid : But for costs and charges susteyned either by p^{lt} or def: in diet, losse of worke, neglect of busines at home, or in wages or diet given to Witnesses produced by either party, therin the court vseth liberty and discretion, accordinge to the circumstances of the persons, quality of the sute, and distance of place.

10. If any def: bee awarded to wage his lawe, with one or more hands, and either offereth soe to doe, or else doth himselfe accordingly performe his lawe, but one or more of his hands refuse : In such case, the Court vseth to give Judgem^t against such def: for that hee performed not the wholl rule and order of the Court.

11. Where the plt. declareth in Trespas, or the like, and the def: pleades not guilty, the plt. is alwaies enioyned to prove his trespas, and damages at the next court by Witnesses produced before the freesutors (which are called benchers,) who vpon hearinge of the evidence assesse damages accordinge to their discretions : ffor there is not nor ever hath byn in any age, as most ancient Court rolls doe witnesse, any trialls by Jury in the said Court, vpon any plaint or action

or action whatsoever; The freesutors, (more then 400,) and seldome or never lesse then 20 at each Court, (comonly many more,) supplyinge the tryall by Jury, sittinge vpon their oathes of sealty, first once taken when their first service is done, with more vnderstandinge then comon Jurors can doe.

12. Vpon each accōn entred (other then in Replevyns) is paid iij^d,—termed pro licentia concordandi; And in Replevins, xij^d,—to the lord of the liberty, which is thus paid: If the action bee agreed out of Court, then it is paid by the def^t: if tryed in Court, then if it passe against the def^t, hee also paies it, If it passe against the plt., then hee payeth it pro falso clamore: Or, if the p^{lt} withdrawe his accōn after entry hee payeth it, and so if hee become nonsuite: But in Replevins, if the sute bee agreed out of Court, then the xij^d is paid by the plt., because the Court intends That the def^t would not have impounded without iust cause.

13. Noe def^t may bee essoined of his lawe, present or not present in Court, at the day when hee is to doe the same.

14. If vpon returne of a Replevin, the plt. therin appeare not nor declare, The def^t shall vpon his apparance and praier, have returne of the cattell or goods formerly replevied, by a **retorno habendo** from the Steward directed to the Baily; And the def^t to goe without further day, and the p^{lt} to bee amereed xij^d for his desalt of not appearinge. But if the plt. appeare and declare, and the def^t make desalt, the def^t shall at every Court bee amereed xij^d—vntill his apparance, and avowry to bee made; and in that sort the action to remaine: But the plt. may notwithstandinge (if hee will) sue forth afterwards from the Steward a Replevyn of second deliverance, And the cause to proceed therevpon by Declaracōn and avowry as aforesaid.

15. If vpon callinge of any action in Court, neither p^{lt} nor def^t themselves or their Atturnies, doe appeare, the Court vseth for that day only to continue the accōn till the next court in the same estate it standeth, without preiudice to either party: But if at the Court next followinge neither party by themselves or their Atturnies doe appeare, but make like desault as before, Then the accōn is wholly discontinued; The Court intendinge that the double negligence of both parties implieth that the action is agreed; And therefore the Court is neither willinge to give Judgement for either party when none praieth it;

nor

nor by holdinge the cause in Court to amerce the said parties to the benefit of the lord, when they are perswaded the same is compounded; and that the negligence of some one put in trust to have signified the agreement of the parties, is the cause that notice was not given accordingly.

16. The Steward hath vsed time out of minde to award proces in the nature of a Subpena ad testificandum, either for p̃t or dẽft witnesses dwellinge within the hundred to testify in the matter of question; who, if they appeare not, havinge had their competent charges tendred vpon an accõn brought against such witnes, recovery in damages shall bee had, to the value of what the plt. or deft was damnified for want of such testimony. |

13. The ffees of the Steward and other ministers belonginge to the said hundred Court, or three weekes Court of pleas, time out of minde have beene, as followeth, And none other, vizt:

ffor the entry of any action (other then Replevyns) and against fugitive persons - - - - - - - - - - - - ij^d
ffor entry of a plaint in a Replevin, or against a person supposed to bee fugitive - - - - - - - - - - - - iiij^d
ffor entry of every essoigne - - - - - - - j^d
ffor an Attachment (other then against the goods of persons supposed fugitive iiij^d
ffor an Attachment against a person fugitive - - - - - xij^d
ffor every Distringas for apparance - - - - - - - iiij^d
ffor the drawinge and entry of every declaraçõn - - - - iiij^d
ffor the entry of every Imparlance other then in Replevins - - j^d
ffor the entry of an Imparlance in a Replevin - - - - iiij^d
ffor the drawinge and entry of the answere or plea to every declaraçõn - ij^d
ffor the drawinge and entry of every Replicaçõn and Reioynder other then in Replevins - - - - - - - - - - ij^d
ffor the drawinge and entry of every plea in barre of the avowry, and for every replicaçõn to the said barre in a Replevin - - - - iiij^d
ffor entringe of every Judgment - - - - - - - iiij^d
ffor every processe of Execuçõn - - - - - - - iiij^d
ffor entry of the continuance of any action - - - - - j^d
ffor the entry of every warrant of atturney other then in replevins - j^d
ffor the entry of every warrant of Atturney in Replevins - - iiij^d

ffor

General Description

ffor the allowinge and certifyinge of any plaint to bee removed by Recordare, or Accedas ad Curiam	ij^s vj^d
ffor miniftringe oath in a wager of lawe, for the defendant and his hands	j^d
ffor miniftringe oath to every deponent for evidence in triall of any Acçon	ij^d
ffor the awardinge and makinge of a Retorno habendo	ij^s
ffor the awardinge and makinge of a Second deliverance	ij^s vj^d
Vpon returne of every Replevin into the Court, after the goods or chattells have by force therof beene delivered	iiij^d
ffor every proceffe of Subpena for Witneffes to teftify betweene party and party, for every name	ij^d
ffor allowinge and certifyinge of every Writt wherein falfe iudgement is fuppofed to bee given	ij^s vj^d
ffor allowance and executinge of every writt de execuçõne iudicij iffueinge out of any the Courts at Weftminfter	xij^d
ffor allowance of any warrant out of the county court, vpon a writt of Jufticies,[1] to attach any inhabitant within this hundred by his goods and chattells for his apparance therat	xij^d

ffor foṁoninge of every defend^t to appeare at the firft court after the acçon entred againft him	ij^d	Bailies fees
ffor the fervinge or executinge of an Attachment	iiij^d	
ffor the fervinge or executinge of a diftringas	iiij^d	
ffor the delivery of an Execuçõn after Judgement	iiij^d	
ffor the levyinge of any dett or damage, or cofts of fuite, recovered after Judgement, for every twelve pence foe recovered, one penny, called penny fhilling	j^d	
ffor the executinge of an Attachment vpon the goods of any perfon fuppofed to bee fugitive	xij^d	
ffor executinge the warrant of the high Sheriffe vpon a Juftices, to caufe the def^t dwellinge in this hundred to appeare at his county court	xij^d	
ffor the makinge of a Replevin, and the obligaçõn for returne therof	ij^s vj^d	

The Conestable, Tithingman or other officer of the townfhip for deliveringe of goods or Chattells by replevyn, there impounded	iiij^d	Conestable or Tithingmans fees
	The fee	

---

[1] This is a Writ directed to a Sheriff, in fpecial cafes, to enable him to hold a plea of debt in his County Court for a large fum, ordinarily it being limited to 40^s. It is called *Jufticies* becaufe it is a Commiffion to the Sheriff to do a man Juftice and Right, and begins with the word Jufticies. [ED.]

Atturnies fees. The fee of every Atturney retained for p^{lt} or def^t, for the wholl caufe, prove it fhort or depend it longe - - - - - - - - vj^d

All which fees were collected into a table, in the xljth yeare of the raigne of Queene Elizabeth, and hanged vp in the Court houfe by confent of the Steward, freefutors, and bayly, ffor the direction of every client, and futor; A Court that doubtleffe doth determine at leaft 30. caufes each Court day in the yeare, if not more: As alfo were the faid Cuftomes in the proceedings in fuch actions, then fet downe, and generally agreed vpon, as formerly is expreffed.

The names of all which ffreefutors, and for what lands, fuch fervice by fuite of Court, is by them feverally done, fhall hereafter perticulerly appeare, As I write of each townfhip in this hundred by it felfe, wherein fuch lands doe lye.

And when, vpon difcent, or purchafe, any freeholder doth his firft fute to this Court, the Stewards entry, is thus. Ad hanc Curiam venit J. S. et fecit primam fectam, et folvit vinum. Which wine hee beftowes (claimed by ancient vfage) vpon his fellow benchers, And paieth alfo iiij^d—to the cryer of the Court for the cufhion hee that day fitts vpon, brought him by the Cryer.

Alfo I fhall expreffe the true tenure of each manor and freeholders land within this hundred, whether holden of the kinge or of a comon perfon, by knight fervice, or in foccage; And what manors or lands have efcheated to kinge or fubiect; And how the ftate and tenure of them ftandeth at this day, with other like perticulers. |

15
Cuftomes in Copyhold lands

The Cuftomary or Copihold lands yet remaininge to this ancient family of their Manor of Berkeley, (befides Indenture holds, Demefnes, parkes, and eftates at will,) in the derivative petty or Submanors of Hame, Alkington, Hinton, Hurft, Slimbridge, Sages, Came, Cowley, Canonbury, Wotton fforren, Wotton and Berkeley burrowe townes, members and parcells of the faid Manor of Berkeley, Are by the yeare, 394^{li}. 9^s. 4^d.— wherin are theis cuftomes followinge approved of betweene them and their Landlord; And which alfo for 46. yeares I have knowne in frequent vfe amongft themfelves. And to have beene at feverall Courts holden for the faid Manor of Berkeley prefented to bee the ancient cuftomes therin; efpecially in July in 40 Eliz. Regina, by 92. of the moft able cuftomary tenants therof, And fince by 104. in [?]

1. **Imprimis,**

Manorial Customs

1. **Imprimis,** That estates may bee granted of any Copihold messuages or lands for three lives or vnder, And that the wife of every such copihold tenant dyinge seized and in possession, shall, after the decease of her husband hold the same so longe as she shall live chast and vnmarried; And that for such lands as are herietable, the best quicke beast that the tenant hath at his death shall bee paid the lord for an heriot: And if such tenant have noe quicke beast then the best good which hee hath shall bee paid for the heryott.

2. **Item,** That the lord of the manor for the time beinge, beinge seized of any estate of Inheritance or freehold therof, may grant estates in Revertion at his pleasure to any person or persons, not exceedinge three lives, to begin after the expiracõn of the former copy in beinge: And that the same are good by the custome against those that shall have any estate afterwards in the manor.

3. **Item,** That if there bee any default of reparacõns in any Mess or houses, or if any spoile or wast bee done vpon the same, That it ought to bee presented by the homage at the next Court, And such tenant to bee amced for the same from time to time till it bee repaired and amended: And that if any default of raparcõn bee, and the same not presented by the homage, wherby the same falleth into decay and becometh ruinous, That then the customary tenants of that manor shall repaire the same at their owne costs and charges: And that if any customary tenant fell or cut downe any wood or timber, and by himselfe or his executors carry it away or fell the same from of the land, hee shall therefore bee amced treble damages.

4. **Item,** That all the Copiholders may take vpon the severall Tenements at all seasonable times, housboote, hedgeboote, ploughboote, and fireboote, without wast makinge; And if any wast bee committed, they shall be amerced for the same by the homage.

5. **Item,** That any customary or copihold tenant for 2. or 3. lives, beinge the first taker, may surrender into the hands of the lord or of the Steward for the time beinge, Or otherwise sell his estate; And then the second life and third life shall bee vtterly void vpon any such surrender; or vpon | such sale beinge found a forfeiture; Neither in such case availeth it whether the second or third life paid all or any part of the Lords fine, or not.

6. **Item,** That any Copiholder holdinge in his owne right may by his tre of Attorney, vnder his hand and seale, and delivered as his Deed, surrender and

deliver

deliver vp into the hands of the lord by the hands of the Steward for the time beinge, All or any part of such lands or Tenem^{ts} as hee soe holdeth, And the same surrender to bee as good to all intents and purposes as though such surrender had byn made by the customary tenant in person in open court there personally present.

7. **Item**, the custome is, That if any man take of the lord by copy of Court roll any lands or tenements for terme of three lives or vnder in maniï followinge, That is, To him selfe, A. his wife, and B. his childe, or to any other person, (hee beinge then maryed to his wife,) In this case the wife shall have but her widowes estate, and not her life, after her husbands deceafe, though shee bee named in the Copy by her Christian name: But if shee bee named in such copy before her husband, That then shee shall have the same for her life, though shee doe marry afterwards.

8. **Item**, If any customary tenant dye after the ffeast of St Michaell and Arch- angell, It shall bee lawfull for his executor or administrator to hold all such messuages and lands which hee held, vntill the feast of the Anunciac͠on of our lady then next followinge, and then the next life or taker to take it, payinge for the feed and one earth, if any of the land bee sowen or plowed; But the same next life or taker may before the said Anunciac͠on fallowe the arrable land for barly, and sowe beanes and peafe: And the said executor or administrator shall pay the lords rent for the whole halfe yeare then endinge.

9. **Item**, If any Customary tenant dye after the feast of the Anunciac͠on of our lady, It shall bee lawfull for his executor or administrator to hold such messuages and lands which hee held vntill Michaelmas day then next followinge, The same executor or administrator permittinge the next life or taker to enter, and take to the meadowe and fallowe; And the same to occupy to his owne vse accordinge to his estate then in beinge; And the said executor or administrator to pay the lords rent for the wholl halfe yeare then endinge: And that (by the custome) is to bee reputed for meadowe, that hath most vfually byn mowed for fifty yeares then last past: But if vpon such tenants death the same doe fall in hand to the lord, Then noe executor or administrator is to hold the same at all, but the lord presently to enter.

10. **Item**, If the first life or name named in the copy shall or doe sell his or her estate, by word or writinge, without licence of the lord or his Steward, hee or shee

or shee shall forfeit his or her estate, and all the rest of the estates mentioned in the said copy, vnles it bee a woman vnder Co̅u̅rt baron : But noe other life named in the copy shall forfeit thereby, but his owne estate only.

11. **Item**, If any person havinge a Revertion copy for two or three lives, doe sell or grant over the same to any person by paroll or writinge without licence, If such person were the first life named in such revertion copy, comonly called the taker, The same, by the custome is a forfeiture of the rest of the lives named in such copy, | And also of their wives widowes estates.

12. **Item**, By the custome of the Manor, any Copiholder may by word or writinge let his copihold lands for three yeares, soe that the same bee one day in each yeare actually in his hands and occupacõn, And duringe such time may dwell from of the same ; But to let of set the same in any other sort, without licence, is a forfeiture of his estate.

13. **Item**, The custome is, That if any customary tenant dye, and heriot bee paid after his death : And if before entry or admittance of the next life that by the copy is to hold the same, the said next life also deceafe ; That heriot notwithstand-inge shall bee paid, And that the widowe of such Tenant soe dead before entry or admittance shall have her widowes estate, and heriot to bee paid, if shee also should deceafe before admittance.

14. **Item**, the custome is, That if any copiholder dye seised of any copihold lands or tenem̅t̅s̅, the next life which by the copy is to have the same, beinge within one and twenty yeares and vnmaryed, That the lord by his Steward shall comit the custody of the body and of such Customary lands, vntill the infant (male or female) come to the age of 21. yeares, at such rate as in the discretion of the Steward, to the infants vse, shall seeme fittinge : And such comittee not to bee further answer-able to the infant, then the Rent and conditions agreed vpon, in open court.

15. **Item**, the Custome is, That if a Cowe happen to bee an heriot, which hath a calfe : Or a mare that hath a fole, or an ewe that hath a lambe, or a Sowe that hath pigs, That such younge shall goe with the dam for heriot, and bee as parcell of her, so longe as they are vnweaned, and vnsevered from the dam.

16. **Item**, the custome is, That if any customary tenant dye seized of any customary lands which suffice for the breedinge of an horse beast or Rother[1] beast,
havinge

[1] Horned Cattle. [ED.]

havinge noe such beast of his owne at the time of his death, That either the best beast of his vndertenant occupyinge the land, or the value of such an heriott out of the tenants estate, or from the next in Remainder, as the case requireth, shall bee paid for an heriott. Then which noe one point of custome hath more often happened.

17. **Item** the custome is, That if vpon the death of any customary tenant in possession, Clayme bee not made by the next in Remainder or Revertion, or by the widowe for her free bench or widowes estate, within three generall courts next followinge, such party after proclamacõns made at such courts is barred by the custome; vnlesse such party bee an Infant, ffeme cov̾t, in prison, of non-sane-memory, or beyond seas in the kings service.

18. **Item**, the Custome is, That if any man lyinge vpon his death bed, or in time of extreame sicknes, when death followeth, where true ends of holy wedlocke, cañot bee intended to bee, shall take a wife, and dye, That such widowe wife or woman shall have noe freebench or widowes estate; As presumed also not to stand with the first institution of the custome, with the ordinance of God or honour of religion.

19. **Item**, The custome is, That a Lease for yeares made by any customary tenant by licence, reservinge a rent, is good against his widowe duringe the terme, and shee only to have the rent; ffor, if such customary tenant may by licence of the lord surrender, and so altogeather barre his widowe, which is the greater: hee may by like licence of the lord make such a lease, which to doe is lesser then to surrender away his whole estate altogeather: Neither can the wife by the death of her husband, have from him a greater interest then what was in him at the time of his death, wch was the rent reserved; | and the possibillity of survivinge the terme.

20. **Item**, the custome is, That neither the executor nor administrator of a customary tenant may after his death sell or withdrawe the dounge or soile that was at his death vpon the ground, nor timber, tallet poles, or the like, that were felled for the repaire or vse of the houses, But to remaine for the vsage of the next life: ffor the Act of God in the tenants death shall not preiudice any man, either the lord of the Manor, or the next life in remainder or revertion: ffor the copiholder had such things only to the vse of his tenement; And if hee could not by the custome have sold them away in his lifetime, his executor or administrator cañot after his death; for they can have from the dead noe greater power or interest after his death then what was in him at his death.

21. **Item**,

Manorial Customs

21. **Item,** The custome is, That if any copiholder shall not dwell vpon his copihold house: or haveinge for somtime dwelled thervpon, shall recede or goe from the same, and dwell out of the Manor, That the same is a forfeiture of his estate, after publike proclamacõns at three Courts made for his returne.

22. **Item,** by the custome, the widowe of a copihold tenant may im̃ediately after her husbands death waive or forsake her widowes estate, and soe pay noe heriot: But if shee once take the profitts, it is otherwise, though but for a short time: And haveinge once taken any profitt, though shee dye before the next court, or her admittance, yet shee shall pay heriott: And the like custome for payment of heriott is for the second or third life in the copy, though such person dye before admittance in court.

23. **Item,** the custome is, That if a Copiholder dye leavinge his house in decay and not sufficiently repaired, that the next life after him shall repaire it, and not the homage of the manor, because the remainder-man or next life might have complained therof before them in court, and soe have had it repaired: But if it soe fall into the lords hands, by the death or forfeiture of the last life, haveinge not byn presented or payned by the homage at the last court, Then the homage, vizt. the whole customary tenants of that perticuler manor, shall repaire the same at their charges, for that it comes ruinous to their lord by their default.

24. **Item,** The custome is, That the lord of the manor, may for ffynes for contempt, treble damage for wast, and the like am̃ciaments imposed in open court vpon any Copihold tenant, distraine any Cattle goinge vpon such copihold lands, either of the copiholders owne or his vndertenants, because the same was adiudged by the Homage themselves to bee iust and right: Which received a tryall at Lent assises Anno. 14. Regis Caroli, betweene Tyler p^lt and ffillimore def^t.; And then were three presidents fresh in memory vouched and proved by 28. copiholders produced as witnesses for the def^t, out of each manor three, or fower, wherof the Judge vpon hearinge of 7. only was soe satisfied, that hee bid the p^lt. bee nonsuite; vizt, one president 20. y^rs agone in the manor of Alkington, when Thomas Bailies cattle were taken and impounded for treble damage in wast comitted by Clutterbooke the Copiholder; The second in the Manor of Came about 17. years agone, when Tylers cattle were taken, tenant to Parker the copiholder, who had com̃itted wast, and amerced in treble damages. The third in the manor of Cowley, when the treble damage was levied about 5. yeares agone vpon the Cattle of Richard Woodward

who

19 who | rented the copihold of Widowe ffords, who comitted the waft: And they all affirmed That the lord was at his eleccōn, whether hee would take the cattle of the Copiholder or of his leffee for any amerciam', which beinge impounded, were not to bee replevied by their cuftome, becaufe the cuftome was in favour of the Copiholder, who otherwife forfeited his eftate for waft; And for that the waft was valued by themfelves vpon oath at the lords Court, which the lord was tyed to accept of; and not to take the forfeiture of the copihold forfeited by the Comon lawe. The like prefident was in Hinton manor, betweene Lewes and Jofeph Hopton.

25. **Item**, By the Cuftome, noe widow holdinge by her widowes eftate can alter or change the nature of her land, but to continue it in the fame quality and condicōn as the grounds were, when her hufband dyed: And not to convert that into arrable which fhee found pafture, or the like, But in all things to continue fuch her holdinge in the fame plight as it was left vnto her, without any preiudice to thofe in remainder or revertion; ffor that fuch widowes eftate is only by the curtefy of the cuftome, and not by any grant by her name made to her in the copy.

26. **Item**, the generall cuftome throughout the whole hundred and Barony of Berkeley, is, That afwell vpon alienations of freehold lands as vpon difcents, Releeves are paid which in all ancient rolls are entred fecundum confuetudinem patriæ, And foe for heriots fervice.

What the Cuftomes are amongft Copihold tenants of other manorˢ within this hundred, not the inheritance of the lord Berkeley, fhall after appeare in the defcription of each of thofe Manors.

Reeves of Manors. **And** heere I will note in generall for all the feverall Manors within this hundred, That each Manor had its proper **Reeve** or Præpofitus, whofe office and authority was not only to levy the lords rents, to fet to worke his fervants and tenants in hufbandinge his demefnes to his beft profitt, But alfo to governe his tenants in peace, And as fome have faid, to lead them forth to warre, when neceffity within the land foe required. |

20
Phrafes and proverbs of fpeach proper to this hundred.

In this hundred of Berkeley are frequently vfed certaine words proverbs and phrafes of fpeach, which wee hundreders conceive, (as we doe of certaine market moneyes,) to bee not only native but confined to the foile bounds and territory therof; which if found in the mouthes of any forraigners, wee deeme them as leapt

over

Gloucestershire Proverbs and Phrases

over our wall, or as ſtrayed from their proper paſture and dwellinge place: And doubtles, in the handſome mouthinge of them, the dialect ſeemes borne of our owne bodies and naturall vnto vs from the breaſts of our nurſes: with ſome fewe of which diſhes I will heere feaſt my reader and ſport my ſelfe, viz:.

1. A native hundreder, beinge aſked where hee was borne, anſwereth, where ſhu'd y bee y bore, but at Berkeley hurns, And there, begis, each was y bore. Or thus, Each was 'geboren at Berkeley hurns.

2. So naturall is the dialect of pronouncinge the lre (y) betweene words endinge and beginninge with conſonants, that it ſeemes droppinge from the aire into our mouthes: As, John y Smyth: John y Cole: Sit y downe: I can y finde it: her has y milkt: come y hither: well y ſaid my Tomy: It's a good y white pott: Each ha kild a ferry vat y hogg: Our ſowe does not well y fatt y: hur may y ſerve for lard y: moder cut y mee ſome meat: my mal is a good y wench: Watt y ge Tom y ſome nin y wel y din'd: hur is y gone: I will y goe: Come y my ſweet y will y: Th'art my pretty dick y: With thouſands the like, accomptinge our ſelves by ſuch manner of ſpeach to bee true patryots, And true preſervers of the honored memory of our old forefathers, Gower, Chauſer, Lidgate, Robert de Glouc̄, and others of thoſe and former ages.

3. The letter (ff) is frequently vſed for v. As fewed for viewed: ſowe for vowe: ſeniſon for veniſon: farniſh for varniſh: and others the like.

4. The lre (v) is alſo frequently vſed for (f.) as vethers for fethers: vaſtinge for faſtinge: vowlar for fowlar: venne for fenne: a varthinge for a farthing token: vire for fire: vat for fat veniſon; So powerfull a prerogative of tranſplantacōn, have wee hundreders over the Alphabet.

5. G is often alſo uſed for C. As guckowe for cuckowe; grabs for crabs: A guckold for a Cuckhold, and the like.

6. ffor duſt, wee ſay, douſt: rowſty, for ruſty: fouſty, for fuſty, youſe for vſe: and the like.

7. Thicke and thucke, for this and that, ruſh out with vs at every breath. As, d'ont thick way; d'ont thuck way: for, doe it on this way: doe it on that way.

8. Putton vp, for put it up: putton on thick way: putton on thuck way: fetton vp, for fet it vp: cutton of, for cut it of; And many the like.

9. I wou'd it was hild, for I would it were flead, or the ſkyn of.

10. y w'ood t'wert hild: for, I would thou were hanged.

11. Hur

11. Hur goes too blive for mee: i.e. fhee goes too faft for mee.
12. filippant. i.e. flippery, quicke, nimble.
13. Neighboriden; for neigbourhood in all fenfes.
14. Wenchen, for wenches, or girles. |
21 15. Axen, for afhes.
16. Hur ligs well y bed y this morne; i. fhee fleepes a napp of nyne houres.
17. I can beteeme fhee any thinge. i.e. I can deny her nothinge.
18. What? wil't y piffe a bed. i.e. what will you piffe your bed:
19. Sheeme bene heere a numbers while. i.e. mee feemes I have byn heere a longe while.
20. Beanes thick yeare are orribly hong'd. i.e. Beanes this yeare are horribly codded.

Hur is dothered. i.e. fhee is amazed aftonifhed.
An attery, or thwartover wench. i. An angry or croffe natur'd wench.
H'eel take it fery hugey. i.e. hee will take it in evill part. H'eel growe madd y.
gaa. i.e. come, let us goe: If you'l goe, gaa. i.e. If you will goe, then come let vs goe.
A fhard. i. a gapp or broken place in an hedge.
A loppertage. i. A lowe place where a hedge is trodden downe.
Hembles. i. a dead fhard or gap, neere to a gate: A frequent word in bylawes at our Courts.
y wud and y cud. i.e. I would doe it if I could.
you fpeake dwelth. i.e. you talke you know not what.
Each'ill warrant you. i.e. I will bee your warrant.
Each ha'nnot wel y din'd. i. I have not well dyned.
The tre (v) is frequently vfed for (i.) As gurdle, for girdle; Threfcall for threfhold.
Harrouft, for harveft.
To hint. i.e. to end. hintinge, a word in hufbandry.
A wize acre. i. a very foole.
Lick many. i. like many.
To hite abroad. i.e. To ride abroad on pleafure.
To tett. i.e. to chafe. Hee tet my fheepe. i.e. chafed them.
To veize, and veizinge. i. to chafe: chafinge violently vp and downe.
Loome, loomer, i. often and oftner. And loomer. i. fafter.
To loxe. i.e. to convey away privately. A loxer. i.e. A fecret purloyner. Loxinge. i.e. private pilferinge.

To Vocket

Gloucestershire Proverbs and Phrases

To vocket, vockater, vockatinge: In like fenfe as to loxe, a loxer, & loxinge, laſt mentioned.

The pugg. i.e. the refufe corne left at winnowinge.

Shoon. i. ſhoes; The naturall ideome of my whole family, my felfe fcarce free from the infection.

A penſton, a coine or Jameſtone.

Thick cole will y not y tind. i. This cole will not burne.

Wee ſhim all huſh at home i.e. wee are all quiet at home.

meeve. i.e. move. As, meeve them a lich. i.e. move them a like.

grannam. i.e. grandame, a grandmother. good gramere. i.e. good grandmother.

Twit. i.e. vpbraid.

gait. i.e. all in haſt; or heddy.

A grible. i.e. A crabſtocke to graft vpon.

Howe fare fader and moder · when fawe you fader and moder; fader and moder will bee heere to morrowe. Altogeather without the pronoune poſſeſſive.

This hay did well y henton. i.e. dry or wither well. |

Each am well y fritt. i.e. I am well filled.

Ch'am w'oodly agreezd. i.e. I am wonderfully agreived.

In the familiar difference of the vfuall words, gay and goe, confiſteth halfe the thrift of my huſbandries. gaye, is let vs goe, when my felfe goes as one of the company: But, goe, is the fendinge of others when my felfe ſtaies behinde.

A gofchicken. i. a goſlin or younge goofe.

Ourne, for ours; theirn, for theirs: hurne for hers, and many the like.

A piſſe glaſſe. i.e. an vrinall.

A flaterne, i.e. a rude ill bred woman. An haytrell, the like.

An hoytrell, i.e. a loofe idle knave.

Hur will bee bedlome anoae. i.e. ſhee will bee by and by mad.

A Dowd, i.e. An vnfeemely woman, vnhandfome in face and foote.

Dunch, i.e. deafe. Hurts, i.e. bilbaries. Solemburies, i.e. fervice berries; wized. i.e. wiſhed.

Hee makes noe hoe of it. i.e. hee cares not for it.

Hee is an haſtis man, i.e. haſty or angry.

Come a downe, i.e. get yee downe. Come y vp. i.e. come vp. I pray fet a downe. i.e. I pray fit downe.

Hite, i.e. Comely. vnhity, i.e. vncomely. you diſhite mee, i.e. you ſhame mee.

Tyd, i.e. wanton. Hee is very tyd, i.e. very wanton. A tyd bit, i.e. a fpeciall morfell referved to eat at laſt.

Each

Each ha fongd to a childe, i.e. I have byn godfather at a childes chriſtninge. Hee did fange to mee, i.e. hee is my godfather.

To fonge, i.e to receive.

The cowes white, i.e. butter and cheefe.

A voulthay, i.e

To gale, A galer, The galefiſhinge ; wherof read after, in my defcripçōn of Severne.

Wone, twa, three, voure, vive, id eſt. 1. 2. 3. 4. 5.

Hee n'eer blins, i.e. hee never ceafeth.

Meefe, meefy, i.e. moſſe, moſſy.

Hee wants boot a beame, i.e. Hee wants money to fpend : or mony in his purſe.

Thuck vire don't y bran, i.e. this fire doth not burne.

It war y gold, that war y gam y ; i.e. That was gold wch was given mee.

ga'as zo'm of thuck bread, i.e. give mee fome of that bread.

Hur ha's weil y tund her geer to day. i. ſhee hath applied her booke to day.

Moder, gyn, will not y waſhen' the diſhen'. i. Mother, Jone, will not waſh the diſhes.

Gyn y com y and tyff y the windowes. i. Jone, come, and trim vp the windowes, (meaninge with flowers.)

Eefee, and eaffee. i. waighty.   Eefeer and eeſteer. i. waightier.   Its eefee corne in hond.

Camplinge, i. brawlinge, chidinge.

Pilſteers, i. pillow beers.

But, Claudite jam rivos pueri, fat prata liberunt. |

23
Proverbs peculiar to this Hundred.

1. **Hee's** like an Aprill ſhoure, that wets the ſtone 9 times in an houre.   Hee's like a feather on an hill.—Applyed to an vnconſtant man.

2. **Hee** is an hughy proud man, hee thinkes himſelfe as great as my lord Berkeley. —Our fimple ancient honeſties knewe not a greater to make compariſon by, when this proverbe firſt arofe.

3. **Hee'l** proove, I thinke, a man of Durfeley, i.e. A man that will promife much but performe nothinge.—This (now difperſed over England,) tooke roote from one Webb a great Clothier dwellinge in Durfeley in the daies of Queen Mary, as alfo was his father in the time of kinge Henry the viijth; vſinge to buy very great quantities of wooll out of moſt counties of England ; At the waighinge wherof, both father and fonne, (the better to drawe on their ends,) would ever promife out of that parcell a gowncloth peticote cloth apron or
the like,

Proverbs peculiar to the Hundred

the like, to the good wife or her daughters, but never paid any thinge: Old Edward Greene vicar of Berkeley, in the firſt of kinge James, vſinge this proverbe in his ſermon there, whereat many of Durſley were preſent, had almoſt raiſed a tumult amongſt his auditory, wherof my ſelfe was one.

4. **Hee** ſeekes for ſtubble in a ſallowe feild, i.e. hee looſeth his labour. Or, as wee otherwiſe ſpeake, ſeekes for a needle in a bottle of hay.

5. **No** pipe noe puddinge: In the like ſenſe as, No penny no pater noſter. Or as, Carmina ſi placeant, fac nos gaudere palato. Now thou my penny haſt, of the muſicke let mee taſt.

6. **Hee** that feares every graſſe muſt never piſſe in a meadowe. In like ſenſe as, A faint hart never won a faire lady.

7. **Hee** that's cooled with an Apple, and heated with an egge. Over mee ſhall never ſpread his legg.—A widowe's wanton proverbe.

8. **Neighbor**, w'are ſure of faire weather, each ha beheld this morne, Abergainy hill.—A frequent ſpeach with vs of the hilly part of this hundred; and indeed that little picked hill in Wales over that Towne is a good Alminake maker; wherof my ſelfe have often made vſe in my huſbandry.

9. **Hee** is very good at a white pott.—By white pot, wee weſterne men doe meane a great cuſtard or puddinge baked in a bagg, platter, kettle, or pan: Notinge heerby, a good trencher man, or great eater.

10. **J muſt** play Benall with you. A frequent ſpeach when the gueſt, immediately after meat, without any ſtay departeth.

11. **A great** houſkeeper is ſure of nothinge for his good cheare, ſave a great Turd at his gate. I wiſh this durty proverbe had never prevailed in this hundred, havinge from thence baniſhed the greater halfe of our ancient hoſpitallity.

12. **My** catt is a good mouſhunt.—An vſuall ſpeach when wee huſbands commend the diligence of our wives. Wee hundreders maintaininge as an orthodox poſition, That hee that ſomtimes flattereth not his wife cañot alwaies pleaſe her.

13. **Quicklye prickes** the tree, that a ſharpe thorne will bee.—In like ſence, as elſewhere.—Soone crookes the tree, that a good cambrell will bee. Contrary to that wicked one—A younge ſaint an old Devill.

14. **Day** may bee diſcerned at a little hole.—Diverſly and not vnaptly applied. |

15. **The** gray mare is the better horſe.—meaninge, that the moſt maſter goeth breechleſſe: i. when the ſilly huſband muſt aſke his wife, whether it ſhall bee a bargaine or not.

16. **Money** is noe foole, if a wiſe man have it in keepinge.—Alludinge to the old common ſayinge,—That a foole and his money are ſoone parted.

17. When

17. **When** wheat lies longe in bed, it riſeth with an heavy head. When wheat is ſowne in October or November, and by reaſon of an heavy furrowe caſt vpon it, or other accident of nyppinge wether, ſhewes not above ground till December or January. Our plowmen ſay It will at harveſt have the greater care; But, (by the leave of my fellow ploughmen and their proverbe,) I thinke both they and my ſelfe bury neere halfe the ſeed wee ſowe in that manner, that never riſeth.

18. **Dip** not thy finger in the morter, nor ſeeke thy penny in the water.—Lord Coke, cheife Juſtice, in the yeare 1613, brought this into that hundred at the maryage of the lady Theophila Berkeley to Sir Robert his eldeſt ſonne, which ſince is growne frequent. A prudent dehortation from buildings and water-workes. ffor my follies in both, I may iuſtly bee indited.

19. **Hee's** like the maſter Bee that leades forth the ſwarme.—Alludinge to the prime man of a pariſh, to whoſe will all the reſt agree.

20. **Hee** mends like ſowre ale in ſomer. i.e. Hee growes from nought to worſe.

21. **Hee** hath offered his candle to the divell.—This (now comon) thus aroſe; Old fullimore of Cam, goinge in Anno 1584, to pſent Sr Tho. Throgm: of Tortworth with a ſuger loſe, met by the way with his neighbor S. M: who demanded whither and vpon what buſines hee was goinge, anſwered, **To offer my candle to the Divill**: which cominge to the eares of Sr Tho: At the next muſter hee ſent two of fullimores ſonnes ſouldiers into the Low countries, where the one was ſlayne and the other at a deere rate redeemed his returne.

22. **Be-gis**, be-gis, it's but a mans fancy.—A frequent ſpeach which thus aroſe: William Bower of Hurſt ffarme, had each ſecond yeare one or more of his maidſervants with childe, whom, with ſuch portions as hee beſtowed vpon them, hee maryed either to his menſervants, (perhaps alſo ſharers with him,) or to his neighbors ſonnes of meaner ranke: Some yeares paſt, it was demaunded of A: Cl: why hee beinge of an eſtate in wealth well able to live, would marry one of Bowers double whores, (for by her hee had had two baſtards,) wherto A. Cl: ſoberly replyed, Begys, Begys, its but a mans fancy, Its but a mans fancy: meaninge, &c. take which of the conſtructions you pleaſe; In both ſenſes it's comon with vs hundreders.

23. **Gett** him a wife, get him a wife. W. Quinten of Hill havinge a peſtilent angry and vnquiet wife, much more inſulting over his milde nature then Zantippe over Socrates, was oft enforced to ſhelter himſelfe from thoſe ſtormes, to keepe his chamber; whence, hearinge his neighbors complayninge of the vnrulines of their towne bull, whom noe mounds would keepe out from ſpoilinge of their

corne

corne feilds, the bull then bellowing before them, and they then in chafinge him towards the comon pound; peepinge out of his chamber windowe, cryed to them: Neighbors, Neighbors, gett him a wife, gett him a wife; meaninge, That by that meanes hee would bee made quiett and tamed as himselfe was: from whence this proverbe (nowe frequent) first arose. |

24. Jf once againe I were Jacke Tomfon or John Tomfon, I would never after bee good man Tomfon while I lived: Hence this, thus: This Jacke Tomfon foe called till fixteene, and after John Tomfon till hee maryed at 24, was the only jovyall and frolicke younge man at merry meetings and Maypoles in all Beverfton, where hee dwelled: After his maryage, (humors at home not well fettlinge betweene him and his wife,) hee loft his mirth and began to droope, which one of his neighbors often obfervinge, demanded vpon a fit opportunity, the caufe of his bad cheare and heavy lookes; wherto, hee fighing gave this anfwere: Ah neighbor, if once againe I were either Jacke Tompfon or John Tomfon, I would never bee goodman Tomfon while I lived: This ftory I derived from Willm Bower the elder, the old Bayle of this hundred, vpon whofe kinfman the inftance was; And from whome his owne cafe diffented but little.

25. Hee drew it as blith as a Robin reddocke: viz!, As a robin redbreft.

26. Ch'am woodly agreezd. vz!, I am wonderfully greived.

27. When Weftridge wood is motley, then its time to fowe barley.

28. Hee's well ferved, for hee hath oft made orts of better hay; Orts is the coarfe butt end of hay which beafts leave in eatinge of their fodder: This proverbe is applyed to man or woman who refufinge many good offers in maryage, either in greatnes of portion or comlines of perfon, At laft it makes choice of much leffe or worfe.

29. Hee hath fold a beane and bought a peaze; } Reproaches
    Hee hath fould a pound and bought a penny; } to an vnthrifty
    Hee hath fold Briftoll and bought Bedminfter; } man.

30. Beware, Clubs are trumps; Or clubs will prove trumps. A caution for the maids to bee gone for their Miftreffes anger hath armed her with a cudgell: Or, to the filly hufband to bee packinge, for his wife draweth towards her altitude.

31. Hee's a true chipp of the old blocke. Like fonne like father.

32. All the maids in Wanfwell may dance in an egg fhell. I hold this a lying proverbe at this day, it flandereth fome of my kindred that dwell there.

33. Hee has met with an hard Winter. Alludinge to one recov̄ed from a pinchinge ficknes: or to a beaft caft down with hardnes of fare.

34. Simondfall

34. **Simondsall sauce**, vsuall To note a guest bringinge an hungry appetite to our table : Or when a man eates little, to say hee wants some of Simondsall sauce: The farme of Simondsall stands on the highest place and purest aire of all that country : If any scituacōn could promise longe and healthy daies I would thence expect it : provided I have a good woodpile for winter.

35. **Simondsall newes.** The clothiers horscarriers and wainmen of this hundred who weekely frequent London, knowinge by ancient custome, That the first question, (after welcome home from London,) is What newes at London ; Doe vsually gull vs with seigned inventions, devised by them vpon those downes ; which wee either then suspectinge vpon the report, or after findinge false, wee cry out, Simondsall newes. A generall speach betweene each coblers teeth.

36. **Hee** is as milde as an hornett. Meaninge a very waspe in tongue or trade ; This proverbe I have from my wife, a true Cowleian, and naturall bred hundredor ; A proverbe as frequent with her, as chidinge with her maides. |

37. **Poorly** sitt, ritchly warme ; when on an high chaire wee sit before the fire the legs are only warmed : but sittinge on a poore lowe stoole, then thighes belly breast & bosome face & head take benefitt & are warmed. Howbeit wee hundredors somtimes metaphorize this proverbe into a prudent counsell, directinge our worldly affaires.

38. **ffaire** fall nothinge once a yeare. It needs no coment.

39. **J'le** make abb or warp of it. If not one thinge yet another.

40. In little medlinge is much ease.
    Of much medlinge, comes no sound sleepinge.

41. **An** head that's white to mayds brings noe delight : or An head that's gray serves not for maydens play : In which state my constituciōn now stands.

42. **When** the daies begin to lengthen the cold begins to strengthen.—meaninge the coldest part of Winter is after the winter Solstice. Alludinge also to the rule of husbandry : That at Candlemas a provident husbandman should have halfe his fodder, and all his corne remaininge.

43. **All** is well save that the worst peece is in the midst. Noe speach more true, when the taylor first puts on our wives new gownes.

44. **A** man may love his house well though hee ride not vpon the ridge : Or, Love well his cowe though hee kisse her not.

45. **As** nimble as a blinde cat in a barne.

46. **J** w'ud I c'ud see't, ka' blind Hugh. for I would I could see it.

47. **Lide** pilles the hide : meaninge that March (called by vs lide) pinches the poare man's beast. 48. **Two**

Proverbs peculiar to the Hundred

48. **Two** hungry meales makes the third a glutton. In like fence as, Hungry dogs eat durty puddings.
49. **If** thou lov'ft mee at the hart, thou'lt not loofe mee for a fart. Often varied into divers applicacions.
50. **When** the crow begins to build then fheepe begin to yeald: meaninge, that the fall of rotten fheepe is principally in February or March, wherin that bird gathereth fticks to make her neft: Alludinge to that other proverb, Michaelmas rott comes fhort of the pott: Intimatinge, that thofe fheepe which by wett fomers hony dewes, or like caufes of rott, which when comonly comes in Auguft or September, Rottinge at Michaelmas, dye in Lent after, when that feafon of the yeare permitted not the poore hufbandman to eat them.
51. **Smoke** will to the fmicker: meaninge, If many goffips fit againft a fmokey chimney the fmoke will bend to the faireft; A proverbe which doth advantage a merry goffip to twitt the foule flutt her neighbour.
52. **A mifty** morne in th'old o'th moone doth alwaies bringe a faire poft-noone. An hilly proverbe about Simondfall.
53. **The** more beanes the fewer for a penny. Meaninge, When beanes prove beft wheat and barley prove worft, wherby the price of pulfe is raifed.
54. **When** thou doft drinke beware the toft, for therein lyes the danger moft.
55. **My** milke is in the Cowes horne, now the zunne is 'ryv'd at Capricorne: meaninge, when the dayes are at fhorteft, the cowe comonly then fed with ftrawe and neere the calvinge, gives little or no milke.
56. **Bones** bringe meat to towne: meaninge, Difficult and hard things are not altogether to bee reiected, or things of fmall confequence.
57. **A poore** mans tale may now bee heard: viz', When none fpeakes the meaneft may.
58. **Store** is noe fore; Plenty never rings it's mafter by the eare.
59. **In** defcripcōn of our choiceft morfells, wee fay; The backe of an hearinge, the poll of a tench. The fide of a falmon, the belly of a wench. |
60. **fitch** doth proove the man who hath the hand, To bury wives, and t'have his fheepe to ftand.
61. **A fowe** doth fooner then a cowe, bringe an oxe to the plowe: meaninge, more profit doth arife to the hufbandman by a fowe then a cowe.
62. **As** bawdy as a butcher: meaninge, that filthines ftickes to his conditions, as vifibly as greafe to the butchers apron.
63. **Hee** that will thrive muft rife at five: But hee that hath thriven may lye till feaven.

64. Hee that smells the first savour, is the faults first father. This proverbe admits many applicacōns: The homlyest is, That hee first smels the fart that lett it.
65. Hee is tainted with an evill guise,
Loth to bed, and lother to rise.
66. Hee that worst may, must hold the candle. Or, the weakest goes to the wall.
67. If two ride vpon an horse one must sit behinde; meaninge, That in each contention one must take the foile.
68. See the counsell better, bee it worse,
ffollow him, that beares the purse.
69. Many esteeme more of the broth, then of the meat sod therein. Divsly applied.
70. The Crowe bids you good morrow. A phrase wherby wee figuratively call a man a knave.
71. Barley makes the heape, but wheat the cheape: Meaninge, that a good wheat yeare pulles downe the price of its selfe and of all other graines, which noe other graine doth.
72. Hee bites the eare, yet seemes to cry for feare: meaninge, hee doth the wronge yet first complaines.
73. Neerest to the well furthest from the water. Like, neerest to the church furthest from God.
74. Hee never hath a bad day that hath a good night: not much vnlike, Hee never hath a bad lease that hath a good landlord.
75. Hee hath eaten his rost meat first: diversly applyed.
76. Norlie anew, nocke anew. i.e. Try againe.
77. Boad a bagg, and bearn'. i. An ill hap falles where it is feared.
78. Need and night make the lame to trott.
79. The owners foot doth fatt the soile: Or the masters eye doth feed the horse.
80. The cup and cover will hold togeather: Birds of a feather will flocke togeather; Like will like; The Dyvell likes the collier.
81. Faire is the weather where cup and cover doe hold together: vizt, where husband and wife agree.
82. Things ne'ere goe ill where Jacke and Gill pisse in one quill.
83. A woman, spaniell, and a walnut tree, } Sed quere de hoc.
The more they are beaten, better they bee.
84. Much smoke little fire; much adoe about nothinge.
85. Hee that wreakes himselfe at every wronge,
Shall never singe the ritch mans songe.
86. A style toward, and a wife forward, are vneasy companions.

87. As

Dedication

87. **As** the good man faies, fo it fhould bee,
But as the good wife faies, foe it muft bee.
88. **As** proud as an Ape of a whip; vz. not proud at all; rather in diflike of ye thinge.
89. **On** St Valentines day caft beanes in clay, But on St Chad fowe good and badd. —So that wee hundredors lymit the feed time of that lenten crop between the 14th of ffebruary and the fecond of March.
90. **As** proud as a dog in a dublett. i.e. very proud.
91. **Patch** by patch is yeomanly; but patch vpon patch is beggerly. |
92. **Winter** never dies in her dams belly. Our climate is fure of frofts or fnowes firft or laft.
93. **Botch** and fit, build and flit. I befhrew this proverbe, wherby the tenant is kept from a comly repairinge of his houfe, for doubt of havinge it taken in revertion over his head.
94. **Its** merry in the hall when beards wagg all. i.e. when men are eatinge, and women dancinge.
95. **The** mice will play when the catt is away. i.e. Servants will loyter when the mafter is abfent: This my experience in my longe abodes abroade, all my life longe, hath prooved too true for my profitt.
96. **Lill** for loll: Id eft, one for another: As good as hee brought:
97. **When** Wotton hill doth weare a cap, Let Horton towne beware of that. i.e. That foggy mift comonly turnes that way into raine.
98. **Better** a bit then noe bread. i.e. Somthinge is better then nothinge. Nothinge hath noe favour.
99. **Many** feames many beanes. An hufbandly proverbe checkinge great and broad furrowes, too frequent with our hynde fervants.
100. **Beware** the fox in a fearne bufh. i.e. Old fearne of like colour keepes often the fox vnperceived. Hypocrify often clokes a knave.
—— Sat lufimus iftis.

I have now ended what I intended in generall, in fport or earneft, in the defcription of this hundred. I nowe fall vpon a perticuler defcription of each Towne, parifh, village, hamblet, Ryver, hill, dale, or other remarkeable place, As by Alphabet they prefent themfelves before mee; Dedicatinge what followeth,

To you my beloved fonne John Smyth, and to you my ancient and honeft fervant William Archard; Thus tellinge you, That,

I had caft what followeth into a mould farre otherwife cut out then now you fee it:

it: I had also purposed in a volume by it selfe the reviewe of a booke of the lord Berkeleys tenures by knights service in this hundred of Berkeley finished in the yeare 1605, and then presented to Henry lord Berkeley, in acknowledgm^t of the dett which I owed from the place of Stewardship I held, (as still I doe,) vnder his fee and patent: In this space of thirty and sower yeares, (my desires still pushinge mee that way,) I have finished the three volumes of the history of that family, lately copied out by one of you: ffrom my endeavors wherin are a remaine of that perticuler worke, (great indeed, had not a continued delight of 40. yeares haled mee alonge,) I found least in my rough pap^rs, such store of materialls as seemed sufficient, both for this description of the hundred of Berkeley, And also for a reviewe of my said booke of tenures; which, as my second thoughts told mee, could not well bee divided into severall volumes, as I first intended: At least, my withered age, (become a freind to ease,) prepared mee soe to thinke, suggestinge that I more fitly might, (as the proverbe is,) make vp both those gaps with one bush and the same flakes; which I have heerein essayed to doe, the cause of the newe fashioned garment | wherwith I have now apparelled this followinge Description.

In this space, yee two, havinge beene in many sallies abroad and serches at home my helpers and Amanuenses, and withall most likely after my daies to hold vnder that noble family the place I yet doe, I offer then to your viewe and amendment, if in any thinge I have erred; the rather also for that your future daies, treadinge in the same waies wherin I have walked, may both iudge of my stepps and inlarge the path which I have trodden in, much by mee desired, for the benefitt of that noble lord and his ever honored family, vnder which I have growne vp to bee what I am; and vnder mee, yee to bee what you now are, with future hopes conceived of you both. God Almighty blesse yee: The affectionate prayer of

John Smyth the elder.

December. 1639.
Anno 15. Regis Caroli. |

Alkington

Alkington.

Alkington, in Domesday booke, Almintune: And in the time of kinge Henry the third written Alcrinton, but erroniously: is a Manor lo^{pp} or tithinge within the parish of Berkeley, consistinge of these small hambletts or petty villages; vizt, Nuport, Woodford, Swanly, Wike, Goldefwike, Dangervilswike, Baynham, Rugbagge, Holts, Heathseild, and Alkington, which last giveth name to the whole manor; Of all which George lord Berkeley is owner, holden of the kinge by knights service in Capite, and parcell of his Barony and great Manor of Berkeley; whereof himselfe and his Ancestors in a lineall discent of 20 generations, the space of—550. yeares, have byn owners, without attainder; Whose Discent from Hardinge the Dane to the lord Robert his sonne and heire, And from him to the said lord George, is before laid downe in fol: 7. And after fol: 109; Of each of which eleaven small hambletts somthinge is after written in perticuler. — 30

This Manor of Alkington is accompted a fourth part of the parish of Berkeley, and contributeth after that rate in all parish payments; The demesnes wherof in the time of William the Conqueror consisted of sower hides of land, As by Domesdei booke appeares.

In the said hamblett called Alkington is halfe the parke called the Worthy or Castle parke; And in other parts of this Manor or tithinge are the parks called Oakeley parke, and Mychaelwood park or chase: In which Chase is the shewe of an ancient and spatious campe, deeply entrenched, called at this day the ffortreffe, or old castle; but when cast vp, or vpon what occasion, I have not found. — Parkes. ffortreffe.

Betweene the hamblets of Wike and Nuport, is a little meade called Riam, whither on Sunday next after Whitsunday resorted the youthes of both sexes from many Villages adioyninge, spendinge the afternoone in dancinge, leapinge, Wrastlinge, and the like exercises; A day knowne in all the quarters therabouts by the matronimicall name of Riam-mead sunday; A meetinge of late years omitted. Whereof read more fol: 344. — Riam-mead.

In a feild neere therto, by the gravell pitts, are often digged and ploughed vp divers dead mens bones and sculls; but when buried or how there laid vp I have not found; Neither can more probably conjecture then of the vrnes or empty earthen — Vrnes or pitchers earthen pitcher that have likewife there byn digged vp, fome of them covered with maffy broad ftones.

Tithe barne   **In** this hamblet of Wike ftandeth one of the eight tythe barnes belonginge to the parifh of Berkeley, worth per Anñ—xxxij^{li}.

Michaelwood   **Wherin** alfo I rather place the Chace of Michaelwood then in Woodford, which hath longe byn honored with a Ranger and two keepers ; But vpon an agreement in the Tenth yeare of kinge James betweene Henry lord Berkeley and the inhabitants of this lordfhip of Alkington havinge Comon of pafture in this Chace, It was by a Decree in the Court of Chancery foe fetled by confent That 400 acres at 18 foote to the perch was enclofed into a paled parke, And the refidue vpon that decree, was left to bee the free comon of the faid inhabitants, | And the Deere from thenceforwards for ever excluded ; And theron 1000 oakes to bee left for the maft and fhadowe of the Cattle of the Comoners, which at noe time after fhould bee felled or otherwife difpofed of : Howbeit it longe foe remained not, ffor George lord Berkeley grandchilde and heire of the faid lord Henry did in the Third of kinge Charles difparke the fame, and lett it to 12 feverall men at an improved rent, caryinge the pales for repaire of his three other parks of Whitcliffe, Newparke, and the Worthy, then in much decay : Which foe continueth to this day, 1639.

Places in Mukelwood.   **The** moft remarkeable parts of which Chace are knowne by the names of Sandridge, Harehills, Blakemore, Redford, the pikes, the fortreffe, the lodge quarter, the gully, and Campden Hill : Of which diftinguifhable names good vfe was made in a fuite in the court of Wards and Liveries in 42. Eliz. profecuted by Anne Counteffe of Warwicke widowe, againft Henry lord Berkeley and others

Affarts defendants, for the greater halfe thereof, wherein fhee prevailed not. Much of which Chace hath almoft round about byn cut out pared and affarted by feverall grants made in fee and fee taile, by the lords therof, in feverall kings times ; And amongft others, **Thomas** lord Berkeley the fecond of that name, by Deed without

Foxles grove date granted to Richard de Wike and his heires, Vnum claufum in bofco fuo de Mukelwood de quodam affarto quod Willus ffowell quondam tenuit quod continet fex acras et fexaginta perticatas terræ et bofci, quod iacet inter clum Pucellæ de Haggely et viam quæ ducit per medium de Mukelwood verfus Eccliam de Nubbeley ; To hold of him and his heires by knights fervice, and the yearly rent of three fhillings, which is paid at this day by John Purnell of Wike, whofe father Thomas Purnell in quarto Jacobi, purchafed the fame of Willm Gibbs and Henry Hathway,

as they

as they in co^{tt} anno Jacobi of Will'm Baffet Efq., fonne of Edward, fonne of Will'm, fonne of Robert, fonne of Gyles, fonne of Robert fonne of John, fonne of Edmond brother and heire of John and Maurice, who both dyed without iffue, the three fonnes of Sir Simon Baffet knight, who dyed in 37. E. 3. fonne of Sir Edmond, brother and heire of Sir John Baffett, fonnes of Anfelme Baffet and Margaret his wife, daughter of Thomas lord Berkeley the firft of that name ; Which name of ffoules grove continueth to this day, anno 1639, from the poffeffion of the faid Will'm ffowell, and lieth bounded as of old is mentioned in the Deed ; And came firft into the family of the Baffetts by the faid S^r. Simon Baffett, a very remarkeable fcholler and Souldier, and many yeares Efcheator and Sheriffe of this county in the raigne of kinge Edward the third ; Of whom read more in the defcription of Ewly, fol. 185. 190.

The like grant or Affart of another part of this Mukelwood was made by Robert lord Berkeley the fecond of that name, in the time of kinge Richard the firft, who by his Deed without date, dedit Galfrido vitulo et heredibus fuis, diverfas parvas peellas terræ in Huntingford, Et totum | affartum illud in orientali bofci fui de Muelwood, quod Radus Scai affartavit, Reddendo—15^s p añ ad fefta S^{ti} Michis et Pafche pro omnibus fervitijs et demandis, Salvo regali fervicio quando ad vnam virgatam terre pertinet : Et etiam conceffit viginti porcos quieftos de pannagio in bofco fuo de Muclewood p̄d̄e̅o̅ five claufus fuerit, five non. And alfo by this deed in another parcell of Muclewood affarted, granted to the faid Geffry Veel and his heires, bounded to lye next Woodycates on the north part, and the Meadowe ground called Wingefmore on the eaft pte, And the ground called Hinctall on the fouth part ; and is divided from other grounds parcell of the ferme of Huntingford by a little brooke on the eaft and fouth parts, called Camylham, and containeth about eight acres, knowne by the name of the Woodleys, which yealdeth fix pence of ancient cuftome, towards the fifteenth and Tenth affeffed vpon this Manor of Alkington, when it is granted by parliament, as lyinge within the fame : And is now the inheritance of Thomas Graile by a late purchafe made by him from John Dutton of Shirborne Efq, who purchafed the fame (inter alia) of Sir Henry Baynton knight who purchafed the fame of Sir William Throkmerton, fonne and heire of Sir Thomas Throkmerton, who died in the fixt of kinge James, in whofe office the fame is perticulerly mentioned : wherof alfo, fee more in Huntingford, fol :—235.

Affarts.

32

In the yeare 1605. vpon controverfies arifinge betweene the Inhabitants of this manor of Alkington and of Stinchcombe adioyninge, touchinge Com̄onage, It was by the

Com̄onage fetled betweene Stinch^e. and Alkington.

by the mediation of Robert Hale Efq, a Barryfter of Lincolnes Inne and myfelfe thus fetled by the affent of both townfhips ; vz!, That the Inhabitants of Alkington Stincheombe and Stancombe fhall entercom̄on togeather from the lake or grip in Crefway which divideth the waft grounds of thofe Lo?.' vnto Crefway head containinge in length   perches, and in bredth as the hedges on either fide confine the fame, without difturbance on either fide: And if any of the cattell of the inhabitants of Alkington come over the faid lake or gripp into the waft grounds of Stinchcombe, and noe man prefent to returne them backe, then it fhall bee lawfull for them of Stinchcombe to impound them as Trefpaffors : And likewife if any cattell of Stincheombe or Stancombe fhall come or depafture beyond Crefway head into the waft grounds of Alkington, and noe man prefent to returne them backe, then it fhall bee lawfull for them of Alkington to impound them as trefpaffors : Which Agreement continueth to this day . A? 1639.

Holts

Holts, one of the little hambletts, wherof this Manor or lordfhip of Alkington is faid to confift, is memorable for the many longe and troublefome fuits in lawe which of old in the time of kinge Henry the fifth, Henry the fixt, and kinge Edward the fourth, And of late in the times of Queene Elizabeth and kinge James have arifen about the title thereof, in moft of the kings Courts, if not in all, continuinge till the vij*th* of kinge James ; wherof to write at large would tire a patient reader, but nowe are fallen afleepe in peace ; **And** vnwillinge I am to ravell a thread, or awaken any fence of them. |

33
Newport Chantry

In Newport (which I have in the time of kinge Edward the third feene written, novus portus,) one of the little hamblets of this Lo?. or Tithinge of Alkington, feated in the midd, and highway betweene the Cities of Glouc̄. and Briftoll, wherby it feemes a pretty through-fare towne, beautified with three or fower Innes for travellers ; Thomas lord Berkeley in the xvij*th* and xx*th* yeares of kinge Edward the third founded two Chantries, and endowed them with two meffuages, two yard land and five pounds rent, lyinge in Berkeley, Wotton, Hill, and Alkington, for two Chapleins to celebrate in the Chapple of Saint Maurice there, licenced by the kinge, and confirmed by Wolftan Bifhop of Worcefter: And by his Charter of foundation appointed what kindes of Maffes and praiers fhould bee funge vpon vfuall dayes, ordinary holydayes, and vpon fpeciall feftivalls, in foe decent and holy a manner, that vnles hee had byn a fcholler to John Wickecliffe, (who now lived,) hee could not have come neerer to the doctrine of theis prefent dayes in the church of England ; forbiddinge theis his preifts to take money of any

man,

Alkington

man, or to bee servant or chaplein to any person but to God only in spiritualities, and to himselfe in honest and necessary temporalities; And that they should live chastly and honestly, and not come to markets alehouses or tavernes, neither should frequent playes or vnlawfull games: In a word, Hee made theis preists by theis ordinances to bee two of those honest men whom wee mistake and call puritans in theis our times: In which condition theis Chanteries and their Chaple continued, (reputed a manor by the additions of other lands by his posterity,) till its fatall blowe was given by parliament in the first yeare of kinge Edward the sixt: Out of which possessions the lord George Berkeley, heire male to the said lord Thomas the founder, receiveth a fee rent of—xliiij^s. viij^d at this day, saved to him by the said act of Dissolucōn. And afterwards in July in the Third of kinge Edward the Sixt, the kinge granted the same to Matthew White and Edward Burry and their heires, And they by Deed inrolled in the same month conveyed to Anthony Burchier and his heires, And hee againe the same month to Thomas ffransom and his heires, with other lands; who scattered those possessions into many hands, And amongst others, by his Deed dated 26. ffebr. 4. E. 6. aliened the chantry house and Chaple, with the ground adioyninge to John Goodrugge and Agnes his wife, and his heires, whose sonne Thomas aliened the same to Thomas Gibbens and his heires, who by his will dated 24. Aprill: A^o. 18. Jacobi, (inter alia,) devised the same to John his second sonne and his heires, who by his Deed dated 23. Octobr. Anno 3° Caroli, sold the same to ffortune Came widowe and her heires, By whose death in 14to regis Caroli, the same discended to Thomas Came her sonne and heire, As an office found the same yeare after her death sheweth; Holden (as the rest of those possessions of the kinge as of his manor of Wakefeild in the county of Yorke, in free soccage, by fealty only and not in Capite, for all services. |

The second of December, kinge Edward the third in the xxjth yeare of his raigne, granted to Thomas lord Berkeley (the third lord of that name) and his heires, To have two faires yearly to bee holden in his towne of Newport, the one on the vigill, day, and morrow of the translacōn of St Thomas Becket, which is also the day of St Marcialis, vsually the vijth day of July: And the other on the vigill, day, and morrow of St Maurice, which is also St Mathewes day, vsually the xxjth day of September; with all liberties to such faires appertaininge, which later is a iust weeke after the faire at Wotton. The choice of which two Saints daies may seeme to bee in an honorable memoriall of his owne name, and of the lord Maurice his eldest sonne, who succeeded him: And of the Chantries hee had there a little before founded to the honor of St Maurice: ffor which ffaires, see the Charter roll

34 Faires in Newport

roll in the tower of London, 22. E. 3. membr. 11. And the Record in banco Cĕi, in Hillary terme. 1. H. 4. Rot. 187. Glouĕ.

Scatteringly in every of the hamblets within this manor or Tithinge of Alkington, hath much Marle been anciently digged, of divers colours and temperatures, for the compostinge and inritchinge both of arrable and pasture ground; the frequent vse wherof in 7 or 8 places of remarkeable note and greatnes, now called Marle pitts and Marle pooles, continued till the times of H. 6. and E. 4. who almost, in their contentions about the Crowne, desolated and laid wast a great part of this parish of Berkeley; As also did the contentions in the same times, betweene the heires generall and the heires male of the family of the lord Berkeley, vnhappily meetinge togeather in the same age, (wherof read more in the Description of Berkeley towne,) since which time, that husbandry, neither in this nor other manors round about, hath byn recontinued, to the great hindrance of the husbandman.

Marle

And in Sandridge, a parcell of the great chace or wood called Michaelwood, was one called Wylotts marlepitt, Out of which Thomas lord Berkeley the second of that name, in the time of kinge Edward the first, and in the 2, 8, 10, and other yeares of kinge Edward the second, sold and granted great quantities of marle to such donees as hee gave lands vnto in tayle, and enfeoffed in fee simple, (wherof I have written elsewhere in the life of that lord,) for amendment of such their lands soe conveyed, both for betteringe the grasse, and breedinge of corne; As the Deeds and Reeves accompts of those times doe witnes: The like hee and other lords his ancestors and successors did also in this and other their Manors in this hundred, As by like testimony in Berkeley Castle appeareth: And to speake in this place of this title of Marle all I doe intend in this description, (to which I shall after referre what properly in other Manors was to have byn written,) when that lord Thomas in the time of kinge Edward the first aliened a marle pitt in his manor of Cowley, nowe called the Marle poole, to one William Hathermare and his heires, hee referred such a quantity of Marle to bee therout digged, (though hee had | others in the same manor,) as should yearly suffice for his owne demesne lands.

Sandridge.

35

And however many men of lesse iudgement may thinke otherwise, yet the wisest sort of men and best naturalists are perswaded, that there scarce is a manor in England, either subsistinge wholly of barren grounds, or in part, (which is the condicon of this hundred,) but hath in it a Marle as they terme it: That is, a satt earth as I terme it: bee it of what kinde or colour soever; bee it Chalke, sand, clay, turfe, stone, or otherwise, either to bee burned or vnburned; which will helpe

and

and inritch the ground, as much or more then dunge, to be digged out of its proper bed and ground, at one fadome, 2. 3. 4. or 5. or perhaps fomwhat deeper in the wombe of the earth; fome of which by the revolucōn of time have in fome places byn turned to lyme or lymeſtone; And againe this lyme in fome places is growne to a finer mould, even to chalke, which is the perfection of all marle: And where none of theis as yet feeme to appeare or abound, (nature havinge not as yet wrought her felfe to her fulnes,) I would advife that the ingenious landed man would with an augur borer or percinge worme, (as once my felfe did in the village wherin I live,) fearch in the deepeſt part of his earth where the fame lyeth hid, for moſt men are perfwaded, and I with them, that ſhallow or deepe, hee may finde marle vpon his land: If it bee vnctious and clammy then it is fat and ritch: And as marles are of fundry colors, fo different likewife in their goodnes: Of colours, fome marles are red, fome yealowe, fome gray, fome blewe; All which (of what colour foever) are good, if they bee oily and ſlippery as fope, and mixed with earth; as alfo weake, if it bee incorporated with gravell, ſtone, or fand: The red marle generally is the worſt, vnles it lye neere vnto the blewe; for the beſt I fuppofe that is in this hundred is the blewe for operacōn; which, when the huſbandman hath met withall, as vndoubtedly hee may if the fault bee not in himfelfe, let him glory that hee hath mett with a treafure, able to fupply his owne and countries neceſſities: And let God have the honor by his acknowledgement.

But let him take this as a Caveat, that at the firſt marlinge of his ground that hee plowe not with broad or deepe furrowes, but narrowe, leaſt hee throwe his marle into the dead mould; ffor the nature of marle is, as the wifeſt have obſerved and written, to fend all its goodnes downwards, and for that caufe muſt not bee buried too deepe, but ſtill kept aloft vpon the vpper mould: And in this it differeth much from dunge or mucke, which fpend their vertue vpwards and will afcend by their miſty vapour fpringinge vp to the face on the ground, though they bee buried deeper then they ought to have beene. **ffor** the hartninge of out-worne grounds I have obferved other remedies, wherof my felfe have made fome vfe, not without profit, as one of you knoweth; As with the foyle of old ditches, and with fand; | and by transferringe and temperinge freſh earth brought from lay grounds with my overfpent mould, as I have heard they vfe in Devonſhire; And to add tough clay to the tender fandy ground; for the one is life and fprightfull to the other, beinge foe incorporated, fpecially moiſt with the dry.

One of you, then my fervant, may remember that finkinge of a broad well in the bafe court where I dwell, not farre from my ſtable doore, about the Tenth yeare
of

of kinge James, That at fower fathom deepe or thereabouts, (havinge before paffed through a fmall blewifh rocke,) I drew vp a blew clay or marle, which beinge afterwards caft vpon a parcell of poore arrable land in the feild called Peckam, proved foe rich that my cropp for more then ten yeares after, without any helpe or additament, was more then treble in value and goodnes to any other part of that feild, foe farre as that blew marle was fpread.

Shortly after which I preured divers colliers from Coventry city fide with their borers and other inftruments, to come to Nibley, who affayinge in that this and other villages adioyninge, found in divers places of each of them, at different depthes, fuch flimy oyly and vnctuous earthes, that I affured my felfe they would proove ritch marles: But for cole, (the principall obiect I then looked after,) I received noe comfort at all. Howbeit, fuch hath ever fince beene my conftrayned imployments and troubles of life, enforcinge my abfences from home moft parts of each yeare, That to this day 1639 I have not purfued the fame; which is foe knowne, that one of you lately verifyed in a pleafant manner thofe my abfences, by my plantinge of a cherry orchard a fewe yeares before I digged that well, (the trees wherof are now growne paft their ftrength and in decay,) and yet I have not byn any one yeare at home in the time of their ripenes to taft that fruit, to this day, as one of you obferved, and affirmed: To which hufbandry, of plantinge tillage and manuringe of the ground, as the only vocation wherein Innocency remaineth, I willingly would perfwade and encourage; bringinge alfo more pleafure quiet and reft in that cuntry life, by takinge the benefit of the ground, then any other, payinge alfo her creditor with foe profitable an vfury, when others in other callings in Cities and market townes, doe but feeke meanes and bufy themfelves how to deceive and beguile one another, as though it were the perfection of their tradinge.

Neither would I have any hufbandman ignorant, but that much good is to bee done and profitt rayfed in corne and graffe, by water frefh and falt: And by obfervinge alfo the difference of Earthes, in makinge the earth of one clofe or feild to fupply the defect of another, and fo interchangeably tempered to an excellent benefitt, wherof I have in a fmall quantity made a fufficient tryall; Theis and the like hufbandries, this tillage of the ground, I accompt the beft and moft harmleffe of all bodily exercifes, defpifed of none fave fooles; ever by the wifeft fort held the moft noble, as fuftayninge the life of all men: which hath drawne mee alonge, (from the title of marle plentifully vfed of old, and ftill in this tithinge of | Alkington to bee found,) to this conclufion, with little or noe digreffion; Referringe my reader

for

Alkington

for more heerof to that which is afwell, or better written in Mr Markams bookes of hufbandry, wherto in this place, I was not willinge to bee beholdinge.

Bond fervants or Villeins

In this Manor or Tithinge alfo, and in all or moft of this Hundred, the lords therof have had divers villeins or bondfervants imployed in the hufbandries therof vnder the overfight of the Reeve of the Manor, who was their principall hufbandman, vntill the time of our laft civill warres betweene the houfes of Yorke and Lancafter; Of whom I have feene many fales and grants by divers Deeds, fome of whom continued till the end of kinge Edward the fourth and beginninge of kinge Henry the vijth, when the laft manumiffion was by William lord Berkeley in this manor, that I have obferved. And I conceive, (which alfo a learned writer hath lately publifhed,) that the lawes concerninge Villenage are ftill in force, of which the lateft are the fharpeft; But nowe, faith hee, and that moft truly in mine opinion, fince flaves were made free which were of great vfe and fervice, there are growne vp a rabble of Rogues cut purfes and the like mifcheivous men, flaves in nature though not in lawe: And if any thinke this kind of dominion not to bee lawfull, yet furely it is naturall; And certainly wee finde not fuch a latitude of difference in any creature, as in the nature of man; wherin the wifeft excell the moft foolifh of men by farre greater degree then the moft foolifh of men doth furpaffe the wifeft of beafts; And therfore when comiferacōn hath given way to reafon, wee fhall finde that nature is the ground of mafterly power, and of fervile obedience which is therto correfpondent; and a man is animal politicum, apt even by nature to comaund or to obey every one in his proper degree; Take this alfo as a fmall or noe digreffion, wherof I intend to write noe more in any other Manor.

Fifteene, or Kingfilver

In payment of the ffifteene or Kingeffilver, (when it runneth,) the Manor of Alkington is rated with Hineton; And the onus or charge of both in the kings Exchequer is 9^{li} 10^s 6^d The deduction is—3^{li} 3^s 4^d The Remanet which is paid into the exchequer is,—6^{li} 7^s 2^d of which this manor or Tithinge of Alkington paies, —3^{li} 3^s 7^d And that of Hineton, iuft fo much more; And heere note, for altogeather, throughout this wholl defcription of this Hundred, That theis ffifteenthes and Tenthes at the firft were only raifed and levied vpon Corne, goods, and beafts; But now in moft places are raifed vpon land: The cuntry people payinge the ffifteenth part, And the Inhabitants of Cities and Townes the Tenth part, of their goods, wherupon they are called Tenths and ffifteenthes, And that the deduction of—3^{li} 3^s 4^d formerly mentioned, is part of Six thoufand pounds deducted for the decayes which the Civill warres had made in Citties and country villages, in moft parts of the land, whereof fee more before, pag: 5

And

Subsedy men.	**And** at the ratinge of the Subsedy in A.º 5.º Regis Caroli were in this tithinge fourteene Subsedy men, which paid—4ˡⁱ 17ˢ 4ᵈ
Able men.	**And** of able men for the warres, betweene 20. and 60. yeares old, were in 6.º Rᵉ Jacobi, which appeared before Henry lord Berkeley then Lieutenant of the County at a generall Muster.—106.
Soldiers.	**And** now are of trayned Souldiers vnder Wiłłm Thorpe Esq̨, their Captaine —21, whereof 7. Corsletts, and 14. musketts.

And if the wholl Devision of Berkeley, accompted a fourth part of the county, bee rated in any tax for the kinge or comon welth at—100ˡⁱ, This hundred of Berkeley paies thereof—33ˡⁱ 3ˢ. And this Manor or tithinge—15ˢ. And so after that proportion bee the tax more or lesse.

ffreeholds in the Tithinge of Alkington.

In this tithinge are many auncient freeholds, the severall Inheritances of sundry men, which with their tenures doe ensue; which to ascertaine hath proved my longest labour, viz̄,

Purnells land cls Dangervills.	**In** the hamblet called Dangervills Wicke, aunciently written, de Angervill, and de Angervillis, Is an ancient messuage with divers lands therto belonginge, containinge about 52. acres, some parts whereof (as also the messuage it selfe,) are in Nybley, the inheritance of John Purnell, whose father Thomas Purnell in Eliz. purchased the same of Richard Warner and Wiłłm his father, And hee in of Nicholas Snell Esq̨.; And were before the lands of John sonne of Richard Dangervill, and before of Henry sonne of Roger Dangervill, lyinge for most parts by Clay pitts greene; and are holden of this Manor of Alkington by the ffiftieth part of a knights fee, sute of court, and the yearly rent of—2ˢ 6ᵈ, which Thomas lord Berkeley the second of that name by his Deed in the Eighth yeare of kinge Edward the second gave to Nicholas Dangervill and the heires of his body, reservinge the said rent and services. ffrom the sirname of which family of the Dangervills, this place lyinge in Wike, hath taken it's name.

ffor somwhat more of this land see the will of the said Thomas Purnell in 22. Jac: 1620. And the office found after his death shortly after, Anno p̄d. Co: roll of Alk. 36. H. S. Johes Dangervill obijt.   Rent 2ˢ 6ᵈ   Walter est sil et heres !

In

Alkington

In this tithinge is an ancient meſſuage and divers lands therto belonginge contayninge 60. acres, anciently reputed one yard land, comonly called Motuns land, wherof Robert lord Berkeley in the time of kinge Richard the firſt by Deed enfeoffed Adam Motun in fee: And after in the time of kinge Henry the third, the land of Walter Motun, And in the time of kinge Edward the firſt, of Geffry Motun, And after of Sundry others of the ſame firname, from whoſe ſeizin the name of **Motuns land** is faſtned vpon it to this day, 1639.

Motuns land, nowe Curnocks, Popes, and Smythes.

At length it diſcended vpon fower daughters, wherof one called Ellen, who died in 22. H. 7. was maryed to Thomas Curnocke, who had iſſue betweene them Thomas, who dyed 16. H. 8, leavinge iſſue Nicholas Curnocke, who dyed   Eliz. levinge iſſue William yet livinge 1639. aged, 87, who ſtill holds the ſame; Which Willm Curnocke alſo in 39. Eliz. by fyne purchaſed one other fourth part therof of Walter May, ſonne of Robert, who dyed 23. Eliz. before his father Walter May, who dyed 27. Eliz. ſonne of Thomas May who dyed   H. 8. ſonne of Edmond May and of Jone his wife, one other of the aforeſaid 4. daughters and coheires; And the ſaid Thomas May ſonne of Edmond in 8. H. 8. ſold his ſaid fourth part to Thomas Hetkins, which afterwards hee again repurchaſed. And the other halfe of the ſaid yard land, is now the inheritance of Thomas Pope, which hee in   Caroli, purchaſed of William Trotman of Buckover, ſonne and heire of Thomas Trotman of Durſley, who dyed in 4°. Jacobi, havinge before in 29. Eliz. repurchaſed the ſame of one other Thomas Curnocke (ſonne of Robert, ſonne of Thomas Curnocke) which Thomas Curnocke alſo, in 40. Eliz. purchaſed 2. acres in Achinton parcell of this moity of Anthony Huntley, who purchaſed the ſame of the ſaid Thomas Curnocke, ſonne of Robert; And three other acres of land in Achinton, and halfe an acre in Wickam meadowe, parcell alſo of this halfe yard land, was by Thomas Pegler purchaſed in 29. Eliz. of the ſaid Thomas Curnocke, which now is the inheritance of John Smith ſonne of John Smith of Heathſeild, who purchaſed the ſame of Richard Pegler ſonne and heire of the ſaid Thomas. Which whole yard land is holden of George lord Berkeley as of his Manor of Alkington, by knight ſervice, ſuite of court, and the yearly rent of xxiiij^s. wherof the ſaid William Curnocke paies—xij^s and Thomas Pope other xij^s.

Heere alſo in the Hamblet called Goldeſwike, and in other places in this Manor not farre from Clay pits greene, are divers lands and tenements containinge about   acres, anciently, called Withes lands, denominated from the ſomtimes owners therof: wherof John With, written John le vith, lived in the beginninge of kinge Edward

Withes lands, now Curnocks; and

40 Edward the third, And was a feoffee in | trust to Thomas lord Berkeley the third of that name, in those conveyances wherby hee entailed this and his other manors in this hundred, with his Barony, to the heires males, in the xxiijth of that kinge: In the end of whose raigne lived James With: After whom, Thomas With of Thornbury in the time of kinge Henry the Sixt: who was father of John With, father of Richard, father of Thomas With, (written also Wight,) who left issue Cicely, married to Wiłłm Lauerence,) somtime Steward of this and divers other Manors to Henry lord Berkeley, A place hee held till the xixth of Qu: Eliz: when hee died:) who by his said wife, (an inheritrix of divers faire lands in that parish of Thornbury,) left issue James Laverence, who by fyne and other conveyances in 27. Eliz. sold the same to William Curnocke of Nybley, who yet lives and holds the same, 1639. And are holden by suite of Court to this Manor, and by the yearly rent of—xij^s: ffor which lands see the Records of Triñ terme in the xxixth of Queene Eliz: with the Remembrancer to the lord Treforer, in the Exchequer, Rot: discharginge them from a tenure of the kinge.

Cromes lands now Halls.

Deere also in the hamblet of Wodford, (soe called from the sourd or passage over the water by the wood called Michaelwood,) are divers lands containinge about nyne acres, vsually called Cromes lands, now the inheritance of William Hall iuñ, in minority, sonne of Wiłłm Hall, sonne of Edward, brother of William Hall thelder, lately deceased; which Wiłłm Hall thelder purchased of Richard Crome, sonne of Thomas Crome who died 39. Eliz: sonne of Richard Crome, who purchased the same of Robert Harrold, sonne of John Harrold, who died 3. Eliz. who purchased the same of John Heyward, who had them from the heires of Toyte, And to Walter Toyte and Johan his wife, and the heires of their bodies, did Thomas lord Berkeley the second of that name, by two Deeds, the one in the eleaventh the other in the 14th of kinge Edward the second, give the same; Reservinge the yearly rent of—viij^s: vj^d and six capons, which are paid at this day, or xviij^d in money in lieu of the capons, And a tenure by knights service: and though the said rents were the full value of the said 9. acres at the time of the said guift in taile, yet the owners pay—13^s. 4^d more, as a rent secke[1] to Christopher Purnell second sonne of Thomas; ffor which sute in the court of Wards of late was in the minority of John Purnell elder brother of the said Christopher, against the said Wiłłm Hall th'elder, which set the said rent asoote.

Co:

[1] Rent sect, or dry rent, is where a man by deed passeth his Estate to another and reserves to himself and his heirs. [ED.]

Alkington

Co: roll of Alk. 30. H. 8. John Toite died seized of divers lands. Releefe for doble rent,—18ˢ 6ᵈ And Alice Toite the daughter of Walter Toite brother of the said John his heire. |

Also in the said hamblet of Woodford are divers lands and tenemᵗˢ containinge about 23. acres called Davis lands, now the inheritance of Thomas Came, holden by knight service, sute of court, to the manor of Alkington, and the yearly rents of —17ˢ and of 12ᵈ, which Arthur Cam father of the said Thomas and ffortune his wife, by Deed and other Conveyances in 5ᵗᵒ Jacobi Regis, (as the Court roll of Alkington of that yeare sheweth,) purchased to them and their heires (perticulerly named and bounded in the Deed,) of Edward Davis, sonne of Thomas Davis, brother of John Davis, sonnes of John Davis thelder, who died in 27. H. 8. as by an Office after his death, and by his Will therein found, appeareth: And as by another office after the death of the said ffortune Came in 14. Rᵉ Caroli, which derive the title and tenure as above; As also the death of Arthur Came, and the survivinge of his wife: Togeather with the perticuler names of the closes and lands. — *41 Davis land, now Cames*

The said Thomas Came holds also to him and his heires, one Messuage and nyne acres of land in Nuport aforesaid, which hee in   Rᵉ Caroli, purchased of John Atkins a yonger sonne of Robert Atkins, who in the vijᵗʰ of kinge James purchased the same of mee John Smyth, and I the same of James Laverence in the 40ᵗʰ of Qu: Eliz: who was sonne of Willm Laverence, who died in 19ᵗʰ Eliz., sonne of Richard Laverence, who purchased the same of John Dosie, sonne of Robert Dosie; And were before the lands of Richard Allien, And before of Roger Mortimer, And before of Walter le gripp, and of Alice his wife, daughter of Maud, daughter and heire of Roger Nattocke, who lived in the time of kinge Henry the third; And are holden of George now lord Berkeley as of his Manor of Canonbury, by knight service, suit of Court to that Manor, by heryot service, And the yearly rent of—4ˢ to that manor of Canonbury, and 12ᵈ to this manor of Alkington; Of theis lands (as the Court roll in 18. R. 2. sheweth,) Isable Dosy dyed seized, held by knight service, And —4ˢ 8ᵈ rent to this manor of Canonbury, and paid an heriott, And 3ˢ 4ᵈ for a Releese, whose sonne and heire was Willm Dosye then 30. yeares old. Of which Canonbury, and the lord Henry Berkeleis purchase thereof, see after in fol: 145. — *Cams land, late Atkins, olim Dosies*

In Dangervils Wike aforesaid, at Clay pits greene, vpon kite hill, are certaine closes of pasture ground called Cutcrofts, now the inheritance of Willm Cole gent, and — *Cutcrofts, late Taylors land, now Coles.*

and late of Robert Evans als Taylor, who about 36. Eliz. purchased the same of Mathew Legg, sonne of John Legg and Jone his wife daughter and heire of Dollinge als Jobbins, whose Anceſtor Richard Dollinge in the ffifteenth yeare of kinge Edward the second purchased the same of John of ffrouceſter, sonne of Thomas of Cowley and of Margaret de Hagely his wife; And are holden of this manor of Alkington by knight service, sute of court, and the yearly rent of—ij.d ffor which see the court roll of Alkington. 37. Eliz. |

<small>42
q:
Coles land late Dangervills.</small>

And this William Cole aforesaid holdeth also by knight service, sute of court and the yearly rent of—ob., three acres of land in Clayfeild within this manor of Alkington, late Thomas Coles of Briſtoll, somtimes the land of John Parsons, and before of Merricke, And before of David Dangervill, and of Isable his wife; To whom and the heires of their bodies, Thomas lord Berkeley the second of that name in   E.   gave the same.

<small>Coles land, late Hoopers.</small>

In Wike aforesaid, within this Tithinge of Alkington, is an ancient meſſuage with 12 acres of land by eſtimaćon therto belonginge, coṁonly called and knowne by the name of Hoopers, now the inheritance of Richard Cole gent, sonne of Thomas Cole, late the land of Arthur Cam of Wike, and by him in the 44th yeare of Qu: Eliz: purchased of Richard Crome sonne of Richard and of Jone his wife daughter of John Doofy, who vpon maryage of the said Jone in 21. Eliz. as her maryage portion conveyed the same to her in fee; which by an anceſtor of his of the same name of John Doofy was in 37. H. 6. purchased of John Hooper sonne of   Hooper.

And are holden of George lord Berkeley as of his Manor of Canonbury by knight service, sute of Court, to that Manor, and the yearly rent of—3^s 4^d And by heriot service. Out of which also ij^d is yearly paid to this manor of Alkington.

And because the familyes of the firname of Cole held in this and other tithings in this hundred divers faire poſſeſſions, take heere their pedegree, which I conceive to bee true.

William Cole lived at Avonscourt within this tithinge of Alkington in the time of kinge Henry the fixt: And had iſſue Thomas Cole who there also lived, and left iſſue Maurice Cole; which Maurice had iſſue three sonnes, viz.t 1 Edmond, 2 John, and 3 Thomas, which Thomas dyed without iſſue. The said Edmund had iſſue Thomas and Maurice.

Thomas

Alkington

Thomas had iſſue Richard, who had iſſue ffortune maryed to Willm Knight of fframpton vpon Severne. And of the ſaid Maurice brother of the ſaid Thomas are divers iſſues.

John Cole ſecond brother of Edmond had iſſue Thomas, and Richard Cole; which Thomas Dyed 1607. A°. 5. Jacobi, levinge iſſue Willm Cole of Briſtoll, and ffortune married to Arthur Came late of Wike, who have iſſue Thomas Came, and others.

And the ſaid Willm had iſſue Richard, Thomas, Willm, and Joſeph, and two daughters.

The ſaid Richard Cole brother of Thomas ſonnes of John, died in 41. Eliz. without iſſue. q: if any. |

In Wike in this Tithinge of Alkington, neere to Nuport, is an ancient Meſſuage with divers lands therto belonginge of old eſteemed halfe a yard land, now the inheritance of Thomas Trotman, ſonne of Willm Trotman of Buckover in the pariſh of Thornbury; And of Thomas Pope of Stinchcombe, and others. Which by Thomas Trotman of Durſley father of the ſaid Willm, were in Anno   purchaſed of Thomas Curnocke, of old written Crannoc, ſonne of Thomas, ſonne of   Curnocke: And were before the lands of John Dooſy. And are holden of George lord Berkeley as of his Manor of Canonbury, by ſute of Court, And by the yearly rent of 13ˢ. 4ᵈ. wherof Thomas Pope for   acres therof, which hee lately purchaſed of the ſaid William Trotman, is apportioned to pay—
And Simon Munday als Munden for 7. yeares [ſic? acres] therof incloſed called Pennings purchaſed of   Trotman paieth   . And Samuell Belcher holdeth acloſe called Charlecroft with an houſe theron built, containinge 3 acres: And 2 acres of paſture in a cloſe called Howcroft by Bolgrove in 2. peells, And two other peells in the ſame cloſe containinge halfe an acre; which hee by Deed dated 1. Novembr̃. A°. 15. Rᵉ Caroli purchaſed of William Curnocke the elder: And is apportioned to pay—

43
Trotmans land late Curnocks. olim Doſies.

Also in the foreſaid hamblet of Woodford is an ancient meſſuage and 14. acres of land called Heſkens, the inheritance of William Beale of Nibley, which hee purchaſed of Richard Bridges late of Combe, ſomtime the lands of John Smyth als Barnſdall, who died in   , and before of James Smyth als Barnſdall father of the

Beales lands late Bridges olim Heſkins.

the said John, who died 1ᵉ. Eliz. sonne of   , holden of this manor of Alkington by sute of Court, and the yearly rent of—xˢ. viijᵈ.

Hospitall of Bedminstre lands late Nevills.

Also in the hamblet of Wike and in other places within this tithinge of Alkington, and in Wanswell, are certaine lands and tenements late parcell of the possessions of the hospitall of Sᵗ. Katherine in Bedminstre by Bristoll, founded by Robert lord Berkeley the second of that name in the beginninge of the raigne of kinge Henry the third, as in his life I have elswhere written. To which lands, supposed to bee concealed, Queene Elizabeth was entitled by Inquisiĉon, and granted the same away in fee: which afterwards by attainder againe returned to her: who againe first granted the same to hold of her by knights service in Capite; And after againe To hold in coṁon Soccage: Theis lands whereof I heere write, (whereof John Knight of Wike holds 25 acres in Wike for his life, And Thomas Hody of Bristoll 100. acres in Wanswell in fee,) came to Thomas Sackvile created lord Buckhurst and after Earle of Dorset, and his Co-feoffees, who aliened a great part of the possessions of that hospitall, And after conveyed the residue to ffrancis

44 Nevill Esq̃, who by his further sales | hath much also dispersed the same: And theis are now the inheritance of the said Thomas Hody, cozen and heire of Thomas Hody, who purchased the same of the said ffrancis Nevill as aforesaid.

Maurice lord Berkeley the first of that name, in the time of kinge Henry the second, gave to the Abbot of Sᵗ. Augustines by Bristoll (inter alia) one yard land in Alcrinton, (foe written,) which was afterwards confirmed to the Monastery by the lord Thomas his sonne, about the 4ᵗʰ of H. 3. which confirmaĉon see after fol: [64.] This continued with the Monastery till the dissoluĉon therof in 31. H. 8, And was after, in   , granted in fee to

ffreames lands.

In this Manor also are divers lands neere the place called Claypitts greene, the inheritance of Thomas ffreame of Lipiatt, wherof read more in the descripĉon of Halmer. fol: 220.

Thorps lands.

Heere also are divers lands and tenements late the inheritance of George Thorpe Esq̃, And were of late in the vnderholdinge of John Windowe, and are nowe the severall inheritances of George Haynes of Rockhampton, Thomas Tindall now the kings Ward, for three acres of land in Achinton, and of John Smyth of Heathsfeild for   , all late parcell of Wanefwell Court. wherof read more in Hame and Wanefwell fol: 209. et 367. 368.

Heere

Ailberton alias Aylberton—Almondesbury

Heere also in Woodford and Swanley Thomas Came of Newport holdeth one close called Kingcraft and three acres in little Ryam, which ffortune Came his mother, (whose heire hee is,) by Deed dated 10 Octobr̃. 14. Jač, Rc̃ purchased of James Baily, who lately before (inter alia) purchased the same of Edmond Pyke. And hee theis and others in Stone and other places, of John Ady the younger, sonne of John, who had the same of   , And were part of Stone Chantry, wherof read in fol : 356. — *Chantry lands in Woodford and Swanley.*

Matford, A spacious plaine and fertile meadowe of an 100 acres or more, the trayninge place of the disciplined or trayned soldiers of the Villages therabouts, within the tithinge of Alkington : The inhabitants wherin pretend their ill custome, viz! hand over head, pell mell, on Lammas day, to thrust in all manner of their Cattell, whether they have any ground therin or not ; wherby the herbage to the small benefit of any one is in one weeke or sooner eaten vp and consumed ; The breakinge day wherof of ancient vsage as they say, is Lammas day the first of August. | — *Matford mead.*

Michaelwood als Mucklewood : Is a vast wood neere 1000 acres, of old much more ; A meere solitude vninhabited and vncultivated place it was, as also were the parts of this Cuntrey next adioyning ; But from the time of kinge R. 1. industry and inclosings of many peells therof on every side havinge soe prevailed in each age since, As at this day through the husbandries stockings grubbings and other cultivatinges therof, and soe replenished with houses and people round about the skirts and in the body therof, as it may probably bee defended, That there is noe weald, woody part or michaelwood at all : Which I had rather vndertake to doe, then certainly to pronounce, either when of old it began, or when it made an end. | — *45 Michaelwood*

46 blank

Ailberton als Aylberton.
See Elberton. fol : 182.

Almondesbury. 47

Almondesbury : In Domesday booke written Almodesberie, Id est Almodes Court or the place of Assembly ; A manor wherof Thomas Chester Esq̃, is lord, holden

holden by knight fervice in Capite, viz¹, the ffortieth part of a knights fee; The demefnes wherof as that booke fheweth confifted in the time of Willm the Conqueror of two hides of land.

This Townfhip or Manor was amongft divers others given by kinge Henry the fecond in the firft yeare of his raigne to Robert the fonne of Hardinge and his heires, vnder the grant of Berkelai et totam Berkelai herneffe manerium, cum omnibus appendicijs fuis: Howbeit that Robert had the fame by a former grant from the faid kinge Henry in the time of kinge Stephen, when the faid Henry was but Duke of Normandy.

Vpon Eafter day then the xjth of Aprill in the xiijth yeare of the raigne of kinge Stephen, in the yeare of our lord 1148, the fower Bifhops of Worcefter, Exceter, Landaffe, and St Afaph, confecrated the Church and buildings which the faid Robert had built neere to the Towne of Briftoll, dedicatinge them to God and to St Auguftine the Englifh Apoftle; then newly by the faid Robert built vpon his manor of Bilefwike, at the place fince called St Auguftines greene, and then inductinge the Abbot and Cannons; And (amongft other poffeffions,) then endowed that Church and Monaftery by his Deed, which hee laid downe vpon the Aulter there, with this manor of Almondefbury, the manor of Horfeild, the manor of Afhelworth, the manor of Cromall, (fince called Cromall Abbotts,) and with divers lands and tenements in Arlingham, with halfe of his fifhings there, and the Tyth of the other halfe, with the Churches and Advowfons of Berkeley, of Wotton, of Cromall, of Beverfton, of Afhelworth, and of this Almondefbury, and of all other his Churches and advowfons of Berkeley herneffe, with all their Chaples and lands in the county of Glouc̄, To hold in ffrankalmoigne; And wills in his faid deed that the fame vpon his bleffinge fhould quietly bee enioyed; wherof fee a confirmac̄on fol: 64.

The firft Abbot now ftalled vpon the foundac̄on was **Richard**, who dyed 4 Septembr̄. 1186.

John was the fecond Abbot, who dyed 12. ffebr̄. 1215.

Joseph was the third Abbott, who lived but 31. weekes after his elecc̄on; And becaufe hee dyed 17 Sept. 1216 before his inftalment, is not reckoned as one of the Abbotts in fome old collections.

David was the fourth Abbot, who refigned and after dyed 5. Julij 1253.

William

Almondesbury

William de Bradston was the 5th Abbot, elected the 21th of May 1234, vpon his predecessors resignacōn; who also resigned the 10th of August 1242. And after dyed the 20th of May. 1252.|

William Longe was the sixt Abbot, elected vpon the resignacōn of Bradston, and dyed 17. Maij. 1264.

Richard of Malmesbury was the seaventh Abbott, who dyed the 13th of September 1276.

John de Marina was the 8th Abbot, who dyed the 21th of ffebr̃: 1286.

Hugh de Dodington was the 9th Abbot, who died the 26th of November, 1294.

James Barry was the 10th Abbot, who died the xijth of Novembr: 1306.

Edmond de Knoll was the 11th Abbot, who of new builded the Church and Vestiary from the foundacōn; Hee procured from the Crowne a Confirmacōn of all the possessions belonginge to the Monastery, As by the Charter Rolls, 18. E. 1. membr. 69. And 6. E. 2. membr. 7. And 10. E. 2. ps. 2. membr. 29. in the tower of London appeareth; And dyed 9º. Junij. 1332.

John Snowe was the 12th Abbot, who dyed 12. Julij. 1341.

Raph Ashe was the 13th Abbot, who dyed 1. mcij. 1353.

William was the 14th Abbot, who resigned 1. Octobr̃. 1365, And dyed 8. Apr̃: 1366. In whose time it was found by Inquisicōn what lands the Monastery was seized of: As by Escaet. 45. E. 3. numero. 72. in the Tower of London appeareth.

Henry Shalingford als Blebury was the 15th Abbot, who dyed 2. Decembr̃. 1388.

John Cerney was the 16th Abbot, who dyed 5. Octobr̃. 1393.

John Daubeny was the 17th Abbot, who dyed 16. Januar̃. 1428.

Walter Newbury was the 18th Abbot, who was fraudulently deposed for 5. yeares space, and then restored: And afterwards new built the Manor house of the Lot of Almondesbury; And dyed 3. Sept. 1463.

Thomas

Thomas Sutton was the 19th Abbot, (if to bee numbred in this Catalogue,) A man noted subtilly to have vsurped for five years, and then cast out vpon the restoringe of Newbery; noted also to have wasted the goods of the Monastery; ffor which and other his misdeeds noe memoriall of his death time or place of buriall was preserved.

William Hunt was the 20th Abbot, who died 14. mcij. 1481.

John Newland was the 21th Abbot, elect the 6th of Aprill 1481, Ruled his Monastery 38 yeares and two months, And died 2. Junij 1515. A°. 7. H. 8. This is that Abbot that made that remarkeable collection and pedegree of his founders, drawinge downe the same from William the Conquerors daies to the 5th yeare of kinge H. 7. where hee ended; more then 20. times by mee vouched in all the three volumes of my Berkeleian history. |

was the 22th Abbot, who dyed in the   yeare of kinge Henry the viijth

Burton was the 23th Abbot, who made the lease of the Tithes of Hinton and Oldminster barne to Anne lady Berkeley widowe, mother to Henry late lord Berkeley; About which that great and tedious suite was moved by Sir Thomas Throkmerton, who in the end carried it against the said lord Henry, wherof I have at large written in the life of that lord vnder the title of his Lawe suits; And died 1536, the same yeare after hee had made the said lease, Anno. 28. H. 8. [fo. 765.]

Morgan Gwillm was the 24th and last Abbot, In whose time, after hee had ruled three yeares, the Monastery in 31. H. 8. was dissolved, And this Manor by that Act of Parliament given to that kinge; who 15. Apr. in the 36th yeare of his raigne granted the same in fee to Myles Partridge, And from him to Arthur Darcy, and from him and his brothers vnto Thomas Chester Esquire, father of William, father of the said Thomas Chester, an eminent gent of much remarkeablenes in this hundred; who therin hath a parke well stored with fallow deere, And in the same a neate and well compacted lodge the seate of the owner; who beautifieth it and it him, since the death of his father in 4. Jac:

This Manor as it were by an equall poize pertaketh with hill and dale; vpon which hilly part hath lead in good plenty byn digged, To which the faire Castle of Berkeley for part of her coveringe doth acknowledge her selfe beholdinge.

The

Almondesbury

The wholl parish is within the Diocesse of the Bishop of Bristoll, and not of Glouc̄; As also of that Deanary. The Church wherof I take to bee a mother Church, honored with her two Chappells of ffilton and Elberton.

Kinge Edward the first, the second of January in the 13th yeare of his raigne, then at Bristoll (as by Rot. Cart. in 18. E. 1. in arce London appeareth,) granted to the foresaid John de Marina then Abbot of the Monastery of Sᵗ Augustines by Bristoll, and to the Covent there, to have free warren in all their demesne land within this manor of Almondesbury, And in their manors of Horsfeild and Cromall in the County of Glouc̄: And the 8th of May followinge in the same yeare of his raigne, granted to the said Abbot and Covent to have a market each Wednesday, and a faire each whitsonmunday, to endure for six daies, in this their manor of Almondesbury. Which grant was by king Edward the fourth the first of ffebr̄: in the 12th of his raigne recited and confirmed to Walter Hunt aforesaid the Abbot, as by the Patent roll of that yeare ps. 2. membr. 16. appeares.

In payment of the ffifteene or Kingsilver (when it is granted by parliament,) this manor of Almondesbury paieth for a wholl—3ˡⁱ. 2ˢ — *Fifteene or Kingsilver.*

And at the ratinge of the last Subsedy in the 5th of kinge Charles, were in this Tithinge eight subsedy men, who (besides the lord therof) paid—56ˢ | — *Subsedy men.*

And of able men for the warres, betweene 20. and 60. yeares old, were in the sixth of kinge James which appeared before Henry lord Berkeley then Leiutenant of this county at a generall muster,—27. — *50 Able men.*

And now are of trayned souldiers vnder Thomas Chester Esq̄, their Captaine . wherof   Corslets, and   muskets. — *Souldiers.*

And if the whole Division of Berkeley accompted a fourth part of the county, bee rated in any taxe, for the kinge or comonwealth at—100ˡⁱ. This hundred of Berkeley paies therof 33ˡⁱ. 3ˢ. And this manor or Tithinge—20ˢ And so after that proportion, bee the tax more or lesse. — *Rates.*

In this parish was an ancient and remarkeable Chantry, obvious in many records in the kings courts, called Brokenbury chantry, dedicated to the service of the blessed Virgin Mary, variously tumbled and tossed in divers ages; which blessed virgin — *Brokenbury chantry.*

virgin by the Charter roll in the Tower of London in 5. H. 5. seemes to bee the tutelary saint and protectrix of this parish church of Almondsbury also, wherin this Chantry was founded.

By an Inquisicōn vpon an Ad quod damnum in the Tower of London in the Nynth yeare of kinge Henry the ffifth, it is found that William Turner and Alice his wife had byn seazed time out of minde of the manor of Brokenborrowe, (soe called, as indeed it anciently was,) vntill Henry Croke with violence eiected them.

In the 13. of H. 6. James lord Berkeley, (amongst other lands,) conveied the moity of the said manor of Brokenburgh with the alternate course of presentinge to the Chantry of our lady in Almondesbury to Thomas Berkeley his youngest sonne, and to the heires of his body with divers Remainders over.

Afterwards the same part came to Maurice lord Berkeley the sixt Baron of that name. who in 15. H. 8. dyed seized of the 4th part of the Manor of Brokenburrowe with the Advowson of the said Chantry; which discended to the lord Thomas his brother and heire, and from him to the lord Thomas his sonne and heire, And from him to Henry lord Berkeley his sonne and heire, who in the sixth yeare of Queene Elizabeth for 200^{li} sold to John Hollister, Thomas Harper, and Margarett Wade of ffilton in the parish of Almesbury, and their heires, All those his Messuages lands and Tenements in the hambletts or parishes of Brokenburrow and Almesbury accompted a fourth part of that manor: And covenants them to bee worth 4^{li} p Añū.

By Inquisicōn in 4. H. 8, Thomas Ive is found to dye seazed of the Manor of Brokenborow within the parish of Almondsbury, which discended to Richard his sonne and heire, then 22. y^{rs} old.

How when and by whom the church of Almondesbury was first given to the said monastery of St Augustines, and after appropriated for the feedinge of the Abbot and monks there, by the Bishop of Worcester, in whose Diocese the same then and till 34. H. 8., was; See after in | Berkeley fol :

By Inquisicōn in aº 5. R^{c} Jacobi, William Chester Esquire is found to dye seized of the Manor of Almondesbury, holden of the kinge in Capite by the 40th part of a knights fee, And that Thomas Chester then within age was his sonne and heire yeares old.

Which

Apleridge

Which Manor by the ffeodaries survey in the Court of Wards the same yeare, is found to extend into the Townships of Almondsbury, Hempton, Patchway, and Compton. |

Apleridge.

Apleridge, als Appulrugge, comonly knowne by the name of the ffarme of Apleridge, Is at this day reputed parcell of the Manor of Hame within the parish of Berkeley, the inheritance of George lord Berkeley, holden by knight service in Capite. A great part of this ffarme, (somtime called the Manor of Apleridge,) hath since the time of kinge Edward the second byn inclosed within the parke called Newparke; And the residue lyeth betweene that parke and the Village of Stone.

This parcell of ground I conceive to have byn parcell of the manor of Berkeley, and granted by kinge Henry the second to the lord Robert and his heires, as parcell therof; Who not longe after aliened the same in fee, which in the space of 30 yeares or therabouts was repurchased by the lord Maurice sonne of the said Robert, in the later end also of the raigne of that kinge, for the said Maurice dyed in the first yeare of kinge R. 1. And soe ever since hath gone alonge with the said manor of Hame, and reputed, (as it may well bee said to bee,) parcell of the manor of Hame at this day; Howbeit the Inquisicōn in 42. E. 3. found after the death of the lord Maurice Berkeley, distinguisheth it from the manor of Hame, and saith that in the manor of Aplerugge (inter alia) est vnus parcus inclusus vocat le Newparke, qui nil valet vltra clausuram, quia herbagium inde depascitur cum feris bestijs. In which reputacōn of a Manor it is conveyed by Willm Marques Berkeley to kinge Henry the seaventh and the heires males of his body in the ffowerth of his raigne. And after the said Marques death, was by Thomas Goodman Receivor and Supervisor to that kinge the 4th of ffebr: in the 21th of his raigne demised at 3li rent and heriot to Thomas Butler of Bristoll Marchant, by the name of the Manor of Appulrugge in Hame, for 61 yeares from the death of Edith Corbet widowe, which ended about the 12th yeare of Queene Elizabeth, what time a newe lease for 21 yeares was by Henry then lord Berkeley, (the estate taile of kinge Henry the seaventh then spent in the death of kinge Edward the sixth,) granted to the said Thomas Throkmerton; whom the said lord in few yeares after by the instigacōn of his Officers Grantham and Huntley questioned somwhat harshly for wast supposed to bee comitted by the lessee, in a coppice peell therof; wherof and of the ill effects which that sute after
drew

drew on continuinge 7. yeares at leaſt, I heere forbeare to write, havinge blotted many leaves in the relation thereof, in my third volume of the hiſtory of the family of the Lords of Berkeley, writinge of that lords life, in the title of his Lawe ſuites. |

Arlingham

Arlyngham als Erlingham, In Domeſdei booke written Erlingehame, is one of thoſe five inferior manors or hamblets (parcell of the great Manor of Berkeley,) that adioyne to the river of Severne, And on that part or ſide extendeth to the middle of the Channell wherſoever for the time the chanell is, which often changeth its courſe, as after in the deſcription of Slimbridge I ſhall have fitter occaſion to write.

It is a pariſh of rich ground and faire extent, wherin till of late yeares have byn ſeverall manors, the inheritances of ſeverall lords, as after appeares; The principall whereof is now the freehold of Richard Yate Eſquire, ſonne and heire of Thomas Yate an aged gent lately deceaſed; All of them within the Leet or Law-day of the Hundred of Berkeley, holden at Berkeley towne twice every yeare, wherat all the male inhabitants of this pariſh above twelve yeares old make their appearance.

The demeſnes of this manor in the time of William the Conqueror and before, as by Domeſdei booke appeares, conſiſted of Nyne hides of land; And was (with many other Manors,) granted by kinge Henry the ſecond in the firſt of his raigne to Robert the ſonne of Hardinge, (wherby alſo hee was created Lord, and a Peere of the Realme,) to him and his heires: ffrom which lord Robert, who dyed in the 17th of that kinge, this manor of Arlingham (inter alia) diſcended to the lord Maurice his ſonne and heire, By whoſe death in the firſt yeare of kinge R. 1. the ſame (inter alia) diſcended to the lord Robert his ſonne and heire, called Robert the ſecond: And from him, who died without iſſue in the 4th yeare of kinge Henry the third, to the lord Thomas his brother and heire, And from the ſaid lord Thomas, who dyed in the 28th yeare of the ſaid kinge, to the lord Maurice his ſonne and heire, called Maurice the ſecond; who by a fine levyed in the third yeare of kinge Edward the firſt, gave this Manor of Arlingham to his two younger ſonnes, Robert and Simon and their heires ioyntly, to hold of him and his heires by the yearly rent of of one penny for all services and demaunds; ffor which alienacŏn thus made without licence, And held by the said lord Maurice by knight service in Capite, a pardon was had threescore and five yeares after, As by Rot. finiũ. 6. E. 3. membr. 16. in the tower of London, And by Original cum Reñi Thesaur̃ in Sc̃cio. 6. E. 3. Rot. 34. appeareth, Which Records till that yeare doe lay downe the Discents as aforesaid.

The said Simon dyed not longe after the grant, without issue, wherby this wholl Manor survived and came to the said Robert called Robert de Berkeley, then a knight, who by Jone his first wife had issue John, Thomas, Robert and Isable, of which three yonger children mention will bee made in other places of this hundred; And after died about the 28th of kinge Edward the first.

The said John Berkeley, eldest sonne of the said Sr Robert, dyed in the Tenth yeare of kinge Edward the second, leavinge issue sower daughters, Elizabeth, ffelicia, Leticia, and Margaret, which were thus maryed; vizt, Elizabeth (often also written Isable) first to James Wilton, | After to   Thornhill, And thirdly to   , yet left noe issue by any of them; ffelicia, I finde not to have byn maryed; Leticia was maryed to John Westmancote, who died 12 E. 3. and by him had issue William Westmancote, who by Margery his wife had issue John and Willm; John sonne of John maryed Margery, and dyed about 8. H. 4. without issue, And the said Margery was after remaryed to Michaell Ap-Ithell, and dyed about 12. H. 6. And the said Willm Westmancote brother and heire of the said John dyed also without issue in the time of king Henry the ffifth, in whom ended the issue of the said Leticia.

Margaret the ffowerth and yongest daughter was maryed to John atte Yate, an ancient gent dwellinge in Arlingham, who dyed in 36. E. 3. And after his death shee was remaryed first to Richard Aston, and after to Richard Staverton, but had noe issue by either of them: And after dyed as I conceive in the time of kinge Richard the second, leavinge issue John Atte Yate, who dyed about the ffifteenth of kinge Henry the sixt, leavinge issue William Yate, (Atte left out of the name,) who was in ward to Richard Beauchampe Earle of Warwicke for a messuage and a Carucate of land in Arlingham, the old inheritance of his Ancestors, holden of that manor by knights service, which the said Earle then held as tenant by the curtesy of England, after the death of Elizabeth his first wife, daughter and sole heire to Thomas lord Berkeley, who about the end of kinge Henry the fourth had gotten into the possession of Westmancotes part of this manor.

The

The said William Yate dyed about   of kinge   , leavinge issue John Yate who dyed without issue, And Richard Yate brother and heire of John; which Richard dyed in 22. H. 8. leavinge issue Walter Yate, who by Jone his wife daughter and heire of John de Boxe had issue Richard, and after dyed in 38. H. 8. Which Richard dyed in   , leavinge issue Thomas Yate, who in extreame old age dyed in 14. Regis Caroli, levinge issue Richard Yate, a gent of much remarkeablenes in Arlingham, possessinge there the seate of his Ancestors, with opulent possessions, and an hopeful posterity likely to succeed him.

Yates manor.
Westmancotes manor.

The last mentioned Thomas Yate, by deed dated 20. Novembr: A⁰ 8. Regis Jacobi, in consideracõn of 700ˡⁱ purchased of Henry lord Berkeley, an other Manor in Arlingham called Westmancotes manor, and which in the partition betweene the said daughters of John Berkeley was allotted to Lettice the wife of John Westmancote, wherby hee seemed to make the wholl againe intire, this his purchase then beinge—5ˡⁱ 12ˢ 8ᵈ in cheefe rents paid by divers ffreeholders, And—9ˡⁱ 9ˢ 6ᵈ in Copihold and Indenture hold Rents; Togeather also with the said lands, severall and free fishings as farre as the manor or parish of Arlingham doth reach and extend, And all felons goods Estrayes &c. to the said manor of Arlingham belonginge, or reputed to belonge, (savinge to the said lord and his heires) the liberty of all Royall fishes in Severne, and savinge sute to his Leete and to his hundred Court of Berkeley for all persons inhabitinge vpon the granted premisses, other then the said Thomas Yate his heires and assignes concerninge the suite to the hundred Court of Berkeley, for or in respect of any lands then in the proper occupacõn or manurance of the said Thomas Yate his lessees and farmors, And savinge the liberty of servinge of Writts processes and precepts; And also the liberty of makinge and doeinge all manner of Execucõns, either in the hundred Court of Berkeley or elsewhere; And all amciam̃ issues and ffynes either in the Leete or hundred court of Berkeley, and power to levy the same; And also savinge and exceptinge the yearly rents and services heertofore accustomed or due to bee paid or done by the said Thomas Yate or his Ancestors, for the manor or reputed Manor of Arlingham, the ancient inheritance of the said Thomas Yate and his auncestors: All which said pmisses the said Henry lord Berkeley and Robert Viscount Lisle by their Deed dated 27. Novembr: A⁰ 7. Jac̃. R͡ did convey to William Dutton and John Smyth and their heires, saith the Deed.

And to theis two manors heertofore parted in copcinery, now againe vnited in the said Richard Yate, belonge all the wast grounds, and not to any of the petty Manours followinge.

In

Arlingham

¶ In this parish the Abbot of St Auguſtines by Briſtoll had a manor, rayſed in length of time out of divers lands and tenements which the lord Berkeleys of Berkeley, aſwell when the lord Robert firſt founded that Monaſtery as other Lords after, As alſo ſome other ffreeholders, gave vnto them at ſeverall times ; which cominge to the Crowne by the Diſſoluc͠on of that Monaſtery in 31. H. 8. was by the ſame kinge in the 34ᵗʰ of his raigne againe with other poſſeſſions conferred vpon the Deane and Chapiter, then by him with a Biſhoppricke there of new erected, where the ſame yet continues; which erection both of the Biſhoppricke and of the Deane and Chapter, is to bee ſeene in the Rolls Chappell of that yeare : And is alſo inrolled entred and pleaded in the Exchequer with the Remembrancer to the lord Treſorer in Trinity Terme 36. H. 8. inter memorand ibm. To hold in pure and perpetuall Almes, payinge for all their poſſeſſions 85ˡⁱ· 10ˢ p Añu. at Michas only.

The Abbot of St Auguſtines manoʳ. Now the Deane & Chapiter of Briſtoll

¶ In this pariſh alſo, the Abbot of the Monaſtery of fflaxley had a little Manor, raiſed like as the former by the guifts at ſeverall times of the lord Berkeleys and other ffreeholders, which likewiſe cominge to the Crowne by the diſſoluc͠on of that Monaſtery in 31. H. 8. was forthwith after given by that kinge to Sir Anthony Kingſton, (at that time one of the knights of this Shire for that parliament, And then high Steward of Berkeley hundred,) and his heires. By whoſe death in the firſt of Qu: Mary, it came to Edmond Kingſton, father of Anthony, father of Wiłłm Kingſton of fflaxley that nowe is, who is ſaid to have lately either ſold the fee or to have made longe Leaſes equivalent therto, to Robert Longney, Henry Wintle, Richard ſfryer of Hockerhill, Walter Carter, and   . The tenure wherof is of the kinge by knight ſervice in Capite ; And for moſt part, or altogeather, lye in the hamblet called Sloo, in the furtheſt part northward of the pariſh. |

Flaxley Manor. now Kingſtons.

¶ In this pariſh alſo in another little manor called Wike als Arlinghams Wike, the inheritance of the foreſaid Richard Yate ſonne of Thomas, holden of the kinge by knight ſervice in Capite, which of old were the lands of Peter de Wike, And by purchaſe came to Thomas lord Berkeley the fourth of that name ; And by his death in 5. H. 5. diſcended to Elizabeth his daughter and heire then wife of Richard Beauchampe Earle of Warwicke, And from her death in the firſt yeare of kinge Henry the ſixt, to Margaret Eleanor and Elizabeth the three daughters and co-heires of the ſaid Counteſſe Elizabeth : And in partition betweene them three in the ſixt yeare of kinge Edward the fourth, was allotted (inter alia) to the ſaid Margaret, then the widowe of John Talbot Earle of Shroeſbury, who dyed the yeare after the ſaid partition, in the 7ᵗʰ of E. 4. wherby this manor diſcended to her

56 Wike manor.

her grandchilde and heire, Thomas Talbot Viscont Lisle, by whose death without issue, in 10. E. 4. slayne at Nybley greene by William Lord Berkeley, it discended to Elizabeth his sister and heire maryed to Edward Gray Viscont Lisle in her right, And by her death in 7. H. 7. two yeares after her husband, to John Gray viscont Lisle, and by his death in 19. H. 7. to Elizabeth Gray his daughter and heire, maryed to Henry Courtney Earle of Devon, And by her death in 12. H. 8. without issue to Elizabeth her aunt, sister of the said John Gray Viscont Lisle, who was first maryed to Sir Edmond Dudley, by whom shee had issue John Dudley, by kinge E. 6. created Duke of Northumberland, And second to Arthur Plantaginet base sonne to kinge Edward the fourth, in whose right hee was Viscont Lisle; and by her death in 33. H. 8. the same was to have discended to the said John Dudley her sonne; howbeit it seemes hee had it by conveyance from her (inter alia) in her life time; ffor by ffine and other assurances in 31. H. 8. hee aliened the same to William Popely and his heires, who shortly after aliened the same to Walter Yate, By whose death in 38. H. 8. the same discended to Richard Yate his sonne and heire, By whose death in   , it came to Thomas Yate his sonne and heire, And by his death in 14. Regis Caroli, to Richard Yate his sonne and heire formerly mentioned.

Of which little Manor of Wike more may bee read in theis Records. vizt,
Inquisitio 5. H. 5. post mortem Thomæ Dñi Berkeley.
Inq: 7. E. 4. post mortem Margaretæ Comitissæ Salop.
Inq: 7. H. 7. post mortem Edw: Gray, visc Lisley.
ffinis in banco. 31. H. 8. pro Popely.
Pasch: rec: 35. H. 8. Rot 60 in Sccio cum Reñi Thesaur.
Inqu: 38. H. 8. post mortem Walteri Yate. |

57
Le Berrowe.

In this parish are divers ancient freehold lands, contayninge about   acres somtimes also reputed a Manor, called Le Berewe, als the Berowes, esteemed as a Carucate of land, which by an Inquisicõn taken in 33. E. 1. after the death of Richard de la Berewe, remaininge in the Tower of London, are found, vizt, That hee dyed seized of two parts of a messuage and of a carucate of land at the Berew in Arlingham, holden of the heire of William Berkeley of Dursley, per servitium ponendi primũ ferrulam coram eo die natalis dni apud Dursley: And of one acre of land in Arlingham holden of the heire of Robert de Berkeley in Ward to Thomas Lord Berkeley, by the yearly rent of—ob., And John atte Berue was his brother and heire, 11. yeares old. Theis lands are now the inheritance of Thomas Bycke gent..

Arlingham

genī., Goffe Chin, William Clutterbooke genī., and of the forefaid Richard Yate, ftill retaininge the name and mentioned in very many old Deeds both before and fince the faid Inquifiçŏn, which I have read. As also in an Inquifiçŏn in 2. H. 8. in the Chaple of the Rolls, found after the death of John Roberts, who (inter alia) dyed feized of 8. acres of arrable land and of 35. acres of pafture called Berrue, holden of Edward Wikes lord of Durfley.

The two records in the Tower of London of Rot. finiū. 10. E. 2. membr. 16. and of Rot. Clauſ. 14. E. 2. membr. 2. fhewe that the forementioned John de Berkeley, when hee dyed in 10. E. 2, held noe land of the kinge: And that Elizabeth, ffelicia, Thomafia, (not Leticia,) and Margaret, all of them within age, were his daughters and heires, To whom the kinge reftored the meane profits, that had for three yeares byn vniuftly taken.

By Deed (with Thomas Bicke) Thomas fonne of Thomas late lord Berkeley granted in 2. E. 3. to Thomas de Bradfton and Ifable his wife, and to his heires, All that his meffuage with all lands meadowes and paftures therto belonginge, which Ifable de Wike fomtimes held in Arlingham, To bee held of the cheife lord by the fervices accuftomed; Which by the Record of Rot. Clauſ. 43. E. 3. mem : 6. are there faid to bee a third part of the Manor of Arlingham. And theis are now the inheritance of John Dryver, fonne of Gyles Dryver, fecond fonne of Robert Dryver, and which the faid John of late purchafed of his Cozen Gyles Dryver fonne and heire of Thomas Dryver, eldeft fonne of the faid Robert Driver, who purchafed the fame of   , but not held to containe fo much, by much, as the faid record of 43. E. 3. doth make them.

Bradftons lands. now Dryvers, late Thomas lord Wentworths.

In what fort theis lands difcended from the faid Thomas de Bradfton to Thomas lord Wentworth, who in 4. Eliz. aliened them, fee in the defcription of Bradfton and Stinchcombe at large. |

Deere alfo in Arlingham, is an auncient meffuage with 4. cottages and 212. acres of land therto belonginge, comonly called Roberts lands, adioyninge to the lands called the Berrewe, with 8. acres of the Berrewe, wherof John Roberts by Inquifiçŏn in 2. H. 8. is found to dye feized, and of a fifhinge in Severne called Roberts putts in Arlingham, Overton and Middleton, The one moity wherof (faith this Inquifiçŏn) is holden of the Manor of Berkeley by—4ˢ 6ᵈ rent for all fervices, And the other moity of Richard Yate, (then Efcheator,) And Walter Roberts was his

Roberts lands. now Chins, Bickes, and others.

his sonne and heire; Howbeit theis lands were entayled as the Inquisicōn sheweth vpon Richard Roberts, eldest sonne of the said John by Jone Davis his second wife; And theis are nowe the inheritance of Thomas Bicke, sonne of Thomas, and of William Clutterbooke and of Richard Yate, sonne of Thomas, and of Goffe Chin, and are called Roberts and Rogers : Of whom Goffe Chin is in by discent from one of the heires of Roberts: The other three, by the purchases of their Ancestors. Which Thomas Bicke dyed in Anno 14º Regis Caroli, leavinge his sonne and heire   yeares old. Of whom see after fol : 60.

Rowles land.   Deere also, is another ancient messuage with 100. acres of land therto belonginge. the inheritance of William Rolls, brothers sonne and heire of William Rolles, who dyed   , sonne of   Rolls, who died   , who in his life time purchased the same of   , somtime the land of R. Knight, And pte also somtime the land of   Scott.

Walls land.   Jn this parish of Arlingham are divers lands and tenemᵗˢ comonly called Walls lands, holden of the lord Berkeley by sute to his hundred Court of Berkeley from 3. weekes to 3. weekes and by   ; somtimes the land of William Wall, father of   Wall, who died   , father of Walter Wall who dyed in the 24. H. 8. and was father of Richard, Roger, and Walter Wall; which Richard dyed in 2. E. 6. and by Margaret his wife left issue Walter and John Wall, Which Walter by severall ffines and other assurances in the 3. 5. 6. 12. and other yeares of the raigne of Queene Elizabeth, aliened most of these lands to severall persons, as followeth ; And after dyed without issue in 33. Eliz. And are nowe the severall inheritances of Richard Yate sonne of Thomas Yate gen̄, John Cage gen̄ in right of his wife, John Dryver, John Kinge, Thomas Daniell, John Carter, Richard Yate | gent., Walter Croft, Richard Willis, Richard ffryer of Midleton als Milton-end, Richard Carter of ffriday streete, Thomas Bicke geii, John Lyes, John Carswell, Willm Rolls, Richard Carter of   , ffrancis Croft, Thomas Butt, and John Wall sonne of Richard, sonne of John, brother of the last mencōned Walter Wall ; To which John Wall only remaineth one Cottage with an orchard adioyninge : from the longe seizin of whose ancestors theis lands have taken and still retaine the name of Walls lands, though now in the severall hands of   ffreeholders.

Of theis lands see a ffine in the Comōn pleas in Easter terme 17. H. 6. by William Wall, to whom the fee was lymitted.

The

Arlingham

The Court of Canonbury als Berkeley in 18. H. 6. hath thus; viz', Adhuc preceptum eſt diſtringere Wiłłm Wall iuñ, ad faciend̃ D̃no homagium, et ad ſatiſfaciend̃ Releviũ pro terris et teñtis quæ de D̃no tenet in Erlingham per ſervicium militare.

Deere alſo is a meſſuage and about 15. acres of land knowne by the name of Bailies, which in the time of H. 6. were the inheritance of John Weſtmancote, who entayled the ſame vpon John Bayly and Jone his wife, and the heires of their bodies; who had iſſue Robert and William, which Robert Bayly had iſſue Jone, who after dyed without iſſue in 17. H. 7. then the wife of Lawrance Hamond; After whoſe death the ſame diſcended and came to Richard Bayly ſonne of John, ſonne of the ſaid Wiłłm Bayly, brother of the ſaid Robert, who was 60. yeares old at the takinge of an Inquiſicõn in 2. H. 8. found after the death of the ſaid Jone wife of the ſaid Lawrance Hamond, wherin all the ſame appeareth; And that the ſame are holden of the heire of John Weſtmancote by fealty and a capon, by reaſon of the ſaid guift in tayle. And are now, Anno. 1639, the inheritance of Webbe of Glouc̃, an Apothecary. — Bailies land.

Deere alſo is an ancient capital meſſuage with an 100. acres of land therto belonginge, the inheritance of John ffryer of Overton in Arlingham, ſonne of Richard, who died in   , ſonne of John ffryer who dyed in 28. Éliz. Rent. 10ˢ ſonne of   , ſonne of Henry ffryer. — ffriers land of Overton

Which in the time of kinge E. 4. were the lands of Kenelme Digas, And before of Richard Mead, whoſe name ſoe ſetled in theſe lands that they retaine the name of Meads lands to this day.

This John ffryer is lately dead, and hath left   his ſonne and heire, very younge.

Deere alſo is a meſſuage and divers lands and fiſhings therto belonginge, contayninge about 80. acres, the inheritance of John Hodges, now in minority, ſonne of Thomas, who died 3ᵃ R͏̃ Caroli, ſonne of Wiłłm, ſonne of John Hodges, who in the 28ᵗʰ of Eliz. purchaſed the ſame of William Bridgeman ſonne of John Bridgeman Eſquire of Micheldeane; who in 28. of H. 8. in conſideracõn of 200. m̃ks purchaſed the ſame of Thomas Tame then of Stowell Eſq, by the name of all that his manor, meſſuage, lands, tenements, and fiſhings in Arlingham, wherof a fine in Michas terme, 30. H. 8. was levyed to John Bridgeman, and to the ſaid Wiłłm his — 60 Hodges lands late Bridgemans.

his sonne, by the said Thomas Tame and Jone his wife, and Edmond Horne and Eliz. his wife, aswell of this messuage and lands in Arlingham, As of the manor of Gosington and of divers lands and tenements in Gosington, Slimbridge, Came, Cowley, Hurst and Hame: And theis are holden of Richard Yate Esq. as of his manor of Arlingham, in Soccage, by suite of Court and the yearly rent of 23ˢ 8ᵈ, whereof two Inquisiĉons after the death of the said Thomas Hodges were of late in 13º et 14º Rℯ Caroli found, And a wardship pretended for the kinge vpon a suppofed incroachment to have byn made by the said Thomas, of a small parcell of ground alleadged to bee held by knights service in Capite; But ffinch the prosecutor prevayled not.

Bickes land, late Bridgemans.

Heere also in an ancient messuage called the ffarme, with divers lands and tenements therto belonginge continuinge by estimaĉon   acres, the inheritance of Thomas Bicke gent (said to bee dead this present October. 1638. as I am in my last reviewe of this description,) eldest sonne of Thomas Bicke by   his second wife, daughter of   , borne after the death of his said father, whose issue male by his first wife yet also remaineth; which the said Thomas the father (inter alia) purchased in   Eliz. of   Bridgeman, sonne of   Bridgeman, holden   . And dyed in 31. Eliz., whose office was found in 12º. Regis Jacobi.

Of which Thomas Bicke see before fol: 58. And this Thomas Bicke hath left issue Thomas Bicke 12. yeares old, as by an office found in October 1639. 15. Caŕ, appeareth; The tenures of whose lands appeare in the two foresaid Inquisiĉons in 12. Jaĉ. and 15. Caroli, if the first (found before Adam Bainham Escheator by vertue of a writt of Mandamus,) bee not perished, as I have byn told it is. |

61
Fryers lands of Middleton als Milton end in Arl:

Heere also is an ancient messuage with divers lands therto belonginge, lyinge in Midleton end als Milton end aforesaid, late the inheritance of Richard ffryer of Milton end aforesaid, which hee purchased of Simon Ludby and Jane his wife, John Huntley and Margaret his wife, and of Edward Molyneux and Vrsula his wife, daughters and coheires of John Sydenham Esq. And which the said Richard ffryer hath of late conveyed in tayle to Walter ffryer his eldest sonne, reservinge to himselfe an estate for his owne life, which walter is dead, levinge the said Richard his father, and hath left issue   , to whom the inheritance in taile is discended.

In this parish the Pryor of Stanley als Leonard Stanley, a Cell to the great Monastery of Sᵗ Peter of Glouĉ, had divers lands, which cominge to the Crowne by

Arlingham

by the suppreſſion of that monaſtery in 31. H. 8. were afterwards granted to   , and now the inheritance of   , holden

The moſt remarkeable hamletts or names of places within this pariſh, which in the ſituaćōn is as a necke of land Iſtmos or peninſula, are Wike, als Arlingham Wike, the Berue, the Slo als Sloo, Overton, i.e. the overtowne, Middleton, als Milton, als Milton end; i.e. the middleſt of the Towne, or the end of the midle towne; And South end.

Names of Places

Heere alſo have beene within the pariſh in the river of Severne divers weres putts and fiſhinge places, called Rodleis were, Garons were, Puthouſe, and others of very great remarkeableneſ and ancient continuance in the eldeſt records in the kings courts; from before the time of Wiłłm the Duke of Normandies Conqueſt, As by the booke in the Exchequer called Domeſdei, and other moſt ancient Pipe rolls, and the private Deeds of many men, and leidger booke of Monaſteries and Biſhopricks, wherof I have ſeene many, doe appeare; Some of which croſſed the wholl river; wherof ſome have yet their continuance, and ſome were deſtroyed by vertue of a Comiſſion of Sewers in the time of kinge Henry the 8th, wherof I ſhall write more largely in the deſcription of the pariſh of Slimbridge, and of the River of Severne.

Weres or fiſhinge places.

And (as more then 100. accompts and other evidences as yet remaininḡ in Berkeley Caſtle have informed mee,) It was a conſtant courſe held by the S. firſt lords of Berkeley, in the times of Lent, to abide at their manor of Wike aforeſaid in Arlingham, now the inheritance of Richard Yate ſonne of Thomas, And to feed themſelves with ſuch ſalmon lamprey ſhads herings ſoles plais flounders eeles and other fiſh, which theſe weres in thoſe times in great abundance afforded; And then to returne to one of their houſes, of Berkeley Caſtle or | Wotton Vnderedge: But nowe a licentious liberty havinge almoſt baniſhed thoſe politicall obſervations of meates and ſeaſons, Heaven ſeemes for to have withdrawne her bleſſings that thoſe Weares are growne ſcarce worth the watchinge and repairinge.

The Rectory or Perſonage is impropriate, and was before the diſſoluc̄ōn of that Monaſtery belonginge to St. Peters of Glouc̃, as to their Cell of Stanley: And cōminge to the Crowne in 31. H. 8. was
And is nowe the inheritance of Sir John Bridgeman by his late purchaſe of Thomas Bicke:

Rectory and Vicaridge.

Bicke: Which Sir John hath alfo the Advowfon of the Vicaridge there, wherof John Giles is nowe the incumbent; And by a compoficōn remaininge within the office of the Regifter to the Bifhop of Worcefter, in whofe Dioceffe the fame then was, made with the affent of Gervais Bifhop of Worc̃, about the 21th yeare of kinge E. 3. A^o 1347, betweene the Pryor of Leonard Stanley, a Cell belonginge to the Monaftery of St Peters in Glouc̃, of the one part, And the Vicar of Arlingham on the other part; wherby it was fetled that the Vicar for the time beinge fhould have the fifth of the tythe of all grayne fowne within this parifh, except of the corne growinge vpon the glebe land of the Rectory, from whence nothinge fhall bee taken: And that the Vicar fhould have halfe the tyth hay, except of the glebe land and of the meadowes called the Leficke and Valemore, the tythes wherof fhall bee to the faid Pryor although they fhould bee fowne with grayne: And that the Vicar fhould have all manner of the tythes of the Curtelages, except of the corne growinge, The tythes wherof fhall bee devided as before, except for the curtelages and clofes of Bertrand and Jones, wherwith the Vicar fhall not meddle. And that the Vicar fhould have the fifth part of the corne called Breteorne; And the Vicar alfo fhould have the tithes of all fifh taken in Severne in the putts, (the tithes in Garnewere and Rodleis were for fifh taken in them excepted, which fhall bee to the faid Pryor;) Alfo that the Vicar fhould have the Tyth of Silva cædua, and of what is comprehended under the name of Alterage, All other tythes remayninge to the faid Pryor; And alfo that all the tythe corne of the whole parifh fhall bee brought into the Pryors barne at Arlingham, for caryage wherof the vicar to finde one plowe or teeme and three men to gader and carry; And the divifion of the tyth corne to bee made betweene the Pryor and Vicar in the Pryors barne aforefaid. And that the Vicar fhould pay to the Pryor 2^s yearly, as of old hath byn accuftomed: And alfo that the vicar fhould have curam animarum of all the inhabitants of the parifh; and fhall pay all procurations and alfo all other charges ordinary and extraordinary, fave that the pryor fhall pay procuracõns to the Archdeacon only, and other charges accordinge to the proportion of the fruite hee receiveth. All which continueth in vfe to this day betweene the impropriate perfon, and the Vicar. |

63
Chantry lands.

In this parifh alfo were divers lands and tenements dedicated to the fervice of the bleffed virgin Mary, to whom alfo I thinke the parifh church was dedicated; which lands in the time of kynge Henry the fourth were vnder the difpofinge and lettinge of procuratores fervicia beatæ Mariæ virginis de Arlingham, the houfe the preift then before dwelt in, and after, was and yet is called our Ladies preifts houfe: And however theis lands were conceived not to bee given to the Crowne by the Statute

Arlingham

Statute of Chantries made in the first yeare of kinge Edward the sixth, yet by an Inquisicōn found in the 13th yeare of Queene Elizabeth, shee was by virtue of that Act intituled vnto them, And accordingly in the 14th yeare of her raigne granted them to Percivall Gonston in fee, And from him they came to Robert Dryver, and others; Howbeit those lres patents and grant through defects therein beinge avoided, the same were againe of new granted by the said Queene in the 29th of her raigne to Sir ffrancis Walsingham and to ffrancis Mills and their heires, from whom the same are now in the hands of divers persons; But not without a kinde of reluctacōn of the generall inhabitants of this parish at this day, suppofinge the same ought not to have come to the Crowne by that statute.

In Berkeley castle is a Deed made in 46. E. 3. betweene John de Yate and 17. others the cheife Inhabitants of Arlingham on the one part, And Nicholas Wishonger, cementarium[1] de Glouc̄, of the other part, which pticularly shewes their composicōn made with him In the buildinge of the tower or Belfree wherin the bells doe hange, And of the most part if not of all the church of Arlingham.   *Arlingham church new built.*

In the sixth yeare of kinge Charles, a Bill in the Exchequer chamber was by Heath Attorny generall exhibited against the foresaid Thomas Bicke and eight other ffreeholders and inhabitants in Arlingham, chargeing them to have intruded vpon certaine newe grounds called Arlingham warth, lately cast togeather by the flowe and reflowe of the river of Severne, which shuld belonge to the kinge, &c. wherto all the defendᵗˢ made their ioynt and severall answeres very perticulerly, which seemed soe farre forth to satisfy that noe further proceedinge followed, but soe resteth to this day: But in the 13th yeare of kinge Charles, whilest I am in my last reviewe heereof, an Inquisicōn was first found in this County to entitle the kinge to the said Warth, as beinge somtimes parcell of the said river of Severne; And after an Informacōn of Intrusion was exhibited against Thomas Bicke, Richard Yate aforesaid, and others, by Banks Atturny generall, which is not yet come to tryall. But see more heerof, and of Slimbridge warth in the description of Slimbridge. | *Warth.*

In payment of the ffifteenth or kingsilver, when it is granted by Parliament, The onus or charge in the Exchequer is—9ˡⁱ. The deduction for the decayes in this parish is—3ˡⁱ, The remanet paid into the Exchequer is 6ˡⁱ; Of which payment see before in Alkington fol: 37. and also fol: 4.   *64 Fifteenth*

In the last Subsedy in the ffifth of kinge Charles were in this parish 24 subsedy men, who paid 9ˡⁱ 3ˢ 4ᵈ to the kinge.   *Subsedy*

And

---
[1] From the Latin Cæmentarius—a rough mason, a waller or builder of walls.

Hundred of Berkeley

Able men.
And of able men for the Warre betweene 20. and 60. yeares of age, were in 6º. Jacobi, which appeared at a generall muster before Henry lord Berkeley then Leiutenant of the County,—98.

Trained soldiers.
And now are of trayned soldiers vnder Willm Thorpe Esq, their Captaine 4. corsletts and 12. musketts.

Rates.
And if the whole Division called Berkeley Division, esteemed a 4th part of the county of Glouc, bee rated in any taxe for kinge or Comonwealth, to pay—100^{li}, Then this hundred of Berekeley payeth towards the same—33^{li} 3^s, And this parish of Arlingham— 36^s 8^d. And soe after that rate.

Deanry.
This wholl parish is within the Deanry of Glouc, As by the Roll of Taxaćon in the tower of London in 20. E. 1. appeareth.

Confirmaćon.
And heere for once and for all, I will incert the Cofirmaćon of Thomas lord Berkeley the first of that name, made betweene 4. H. 3. when hee entred vpon his Barony and 28. H. 3. when hee dyed, entendinge hither to referre all the Townships and lands therin mentioned . viz̵,

Omnibus sc̄e matris Eccliæ filijs ad quos p̄sens scriptum pveñit, Thomas de Berket filius Mauricij de Berket, salm̄ in Dño. Nov̄int univ̄sitas ūra me pro salute anime mee, Avi mei Robti filij Hardingi, Patris mei Mauricij de Berket, et f̄ris mei Robti de Berket, necnon et Johanne vxoȓ mee sȝ, et omniū anteceſſorū et ſucceſſoȝ meoȝ, dediſſe et conceſſiſſe et hac p̄senti carta mea confirmaſſe Deo et Eccliæ Sc̄i Augusti de Bristoll et canonicis regulaȓ ibm deo servientibus, Omnia illa quæ avus meus Robtus filius Hardingi, Mauricius de Berket pater meus, et Robtus de Berket frater meus eisdem dederunt et cartis suis confirmaverunt, vz̵, ex dono avi mei, Almodesbuȓ, Horesfeld, Aſſelesword, Cromat cū eoȝ ptineñ, Dimidias etiam piscarias de Erlingeham, et alterius medietatis decimam totam, Item fishidam in Dorseta, Legam que fuit manerium de Bedmenistria, Et terram apud sc̄a Katherinā de feod portbiȓ. Silter et sex libratas terræ apud Cernay, Et terram quam habuit apud Blakenesword. Ex dono autem et concensu Mauricij de Berket patris mei, Dimidiam hidam terræ apud Hineton, et vnā virgatā terre apud Alerinton, Decimam etiam de toto pannagio meo de Muelewde, de Appelrugḡ, de Acle, et de Wttoñ, et pastuȓ apud Berket, bobus vnius carucæ cū dnicis bobus meis. Ex dono etiam Robti de Berket quatuor virgatas terræ apud Erlingeham, et decem puchias et dimidiā et vnū
liberū

Ashelworth

liberū palū in gurgite de Rodleg. cum meſſuagijs et pratis | et omnibus alijs ad dcas **65**
terras ptinentibᵖ. Et dimidiā virgatā terre apud Riham quā Radulſus Mattoch tenuit :
Molendinū etiā de Berkel quod novum molendinum appellatur, cum confuetudine
molture caſtelli mei et totius fequele, ficut vnquam melius folebat fieri ; Et vnā
virgatā terre iuxta idem molendinum, quā Reginaldus carucarius et Aluredus de
findleford tenere confuerunt, Necnon et Hugonem piſtorē cum illa virgata terre quam
tenet apud Hulmanecote ; Et vnā virgatā terre apud Swanhangre quā Reginaldus
Luffinge tenuit : Silter et terras et pratum et ōia quæ Wiltus Cobi dc̄is canonicis
dedit, et dc̄us Robtus de Berkel frater meus eiſde confirmavit ; Et boſcum quod
vocatur Ewecumbe. f3, et infup totā terrā quā dc̄us frēr meus Robtus de Berkel
habuit infra muros Briſtoll, et ōia burgagia quæ Robtus avus meus, vel Mauricius
pater meus, vel Aeleiſia mater infra murū Briſtoll vel extra eiſdem contulerunt : Ī
terras illas quæ fuer̄ de purchaſio Mauricij frīs mei ; Et terram de Baggrugge, quā
idem frater meus Robtus de Berkel emit de Willo de leſromonte et eiſdem canonicis
dedit et carta fua confirmavit. Hec et cetera ōia que in eccliaſticis bāficijs feu terris
et rebus alijs dc̄is canonicis a memorato avo meo, patre, vel fratre meo caritativē funt
collata, cū coɀ libtatibus et liberis confuetudinibᵖ eiſdem dedi, conceſſi, et hac p̄nti
carta mea cofirmavi, ficut in corū cartis et confirmac̄onibus plenius et melius contine-
tur ; Ita vt dc̄i canonici imunes ſint et quieti ab omni demanda et fervicio feculari,
excepto folo murdro, et excepto regali fervicio quantū ptinet ad vnā virgatā terre in
Swanhungre, et ad vnā virgatā terre pro terra de Baggerugḡ. Inſuper conceſſi vt
ecclefiæ in terris meis que ad canonicos pertinent omnes habeant libertates et liberas
confuetudines in comunis paſturaɀ et ōibus alijs rebus quas habuerunt tempore regis
Henrici et fuprādc̄i Robti avi mei, et Mauricij patris mei ; Preteria omnia que in
tenementis meis diĉtis canonicis recte data ſunt, vel dabuntur in poſterum, eis hac
preſenti carta mea in ppetuā durac̄one et conceſſione confirmavi. Hijs teſtibus, Dn̄o
Robto filio Ric tunc feneſchallo meo, Dn̄o Petro de Stinteſcumb, Rogero Aillard,
Mauricio filio Nigelli et Roberto filio eius, Philippo de Cromhat, Radulfo de Stanes,
Ricardo portar̄, Reginaldo de Pennard et multis alijs. |

Ashelworth.   **66**

Ashelworth, In Domefdei booke Efceluuorde : And in the times of R. 1. and
of kinge John written Effelefwrd, is a manor and parifh not farre from the Citie of
Glouc̄, belonginge to the Bifhop of Briſtoll.

Anciently

Anciently this manor was part of the great manor of Berkeley and of Berkeley herneſſe, And was by Robert the ſonne of Hardinge given amongſt other manors to the Abbot and Covent of the Monaſtery of S:t Auguſtines by Briſtoll, when hee firſt founded the ſame: wherof read more in the deſcription of Almondeſbury fol. 47, and in fol : 64. 65. And continued, as that did, in the poſſeſſion of thoſe Abbots there ſucceſſively mentioned, till the diſſolucōn of that monaſtery in 31. H. 8. And vpon that kings erectinge of newe the Biſhoppricke of Briſtoll in the 33th of his raigne, was deſigned to bee part of the poſſeſſions of the Biſhoppricke ; In which tres patents this and all other the Biſhops lands are perticulerly mentioned.

The Demeſnes of this manor in the time of Willm the Conqueror conſiſted of three hides of land, as by the booke in the Exchequer called Domeſdei appeares : which, though held by the ſaid lord Robert by knight ſervice in Capite, yet his grant therof to that Monaſtery was to hold in frank almoigne : I referre you for more heerof to my hiſtory of the family of the lords of Berkeley, lately by mee finiſhed and given to the lord George Berkeley : to bee read in the life of the ſaid lord Robert therin called Robert the firſt.

The Capitall meſſuage and almoſt the wholl manor was new builded whileſt Walter Newbury was Abbot of that Monaſtery, who died in a:o Dñi. 1463. 13. E. 4. And are within the Deanry of Glouc̄, as that of Arlingham laſtly deſcribed.

Bounds or Comōns.

After many yeares contention betweene the Abbots of this monaſtery and Sir John Pauncefoot knight, who was ſonne of Hugh, ſonne of Adomarus, ſonne of Grymbald, ſonne of Richard Pauncefoot, (a family of great antiquity in this county,) touchinge the bounds and Comōns betweene this the Abbotts Manor of Aſhelworth and that of his of Hasfeld, an agreement followed the 20th of ffebruary in 21. H. 6, which for a perpetuall quietnes in ages followinge they inrolled in Chancery ; As by the Rot. Clauſ. 21. H. 6. mem : 24. in dorſo, in the tower of London appeares.

Derivacōn of the name.

The Etimon or derivacōn of the name of this pariſh or townſhip, take whether of theis two wayes you pleaſe ; Either from the word **worth**, now ſpoken **woorth**, a baſe court or yard, ſuch as is comōnly before the better ſort of houſes : Or from the German word, **werd**, which is a poole.

Alſo, in this Towne the ancient family of the Berkelies of Durſley had halfe an hide of land, as the Certificate of | Roger Berkeley to kinge Henry the ſecond,

ſet

set downe verbatim in the red booke in the Exchequer, doth shewe, wherof read after in Dursley fol: 177. which I suppose came shortly after to the Abbot and Covent of S.t Augustines aforesaid.

In payment of the ffifteene or kingessilver, when it runneth, the onus or charge in the Exchequer is—4.ˢ. The deduction for the decayes within this Manor is—20.ˢ The Remanet paid into the Excheq.ʳ—3.ˡⁱ *ffifteenes*

In the last subsedy rated in the 5.º Caroli, were in the parish 8. subsedy men, who paid 3.ˡⁱ 6: 8.ᵈ *Subsedy*

Of able men for the warres between 20. and 60. yeares of age, who appeared at a generall muster before Henry lord Berkeley lord Lieutenant of this County in 6.ᵗᵒ R.e Jacobi, were 71. *Able men.*

Of trayned souldiers vnder Will.m Thorpe Esq, their Captaine nowe are—4: viz.t 2. corslets and 2. muskets. *Souldiers.*

And if Berkeley Division esteemed a 4.ᵗʰ part of the county of Gloū bee rated in any tax for kinge or comōn welth to pay—100.ˡⁱ the hundred of Berkeley paies thereof—33.ˡⁱ 3.ˢ and this township 20.ˢ *Rates.*

ffor this Church and the inpropriatinge therof, see at large in Berkeley fol: 81. 82. 83. And in Almondesbury fol: 47. |

Avonscourt.

See Bainham fol: 71. And Pedington. fol: 313.

Bagpath.

Bagpath; called also Newton als Newenton Bagpath, because Newton als Newenton, is within the parish of Bagpath.

Of this Manor of Bagpath Ambrose Webb Doctor of Divinity is Lord, and also patron of the Church. And M.r ffeilding his sonne in lawe Incumbent; whose presentacōn is said to have byn his maryage portion with Doctor Webs daughter.

Though

Church.	**Though** fcarce any church (worthy the name of a church) can bee leffe or worfe built, yet within the parifh therof is both Newenton, Caldcote, and Owlpen: And though the manor houfe or capitall meffuage of Laffeborrowe, (the feate of Sir Thomas Eftcourt late deceafed,) bee without the compaffe of this parifh and alfo of this Hundred of Berkeley, yet within both parifh and hundred is the garden ground adioyninge, And a great part of the parke alfo, inclofinge (as it were) both houfe and garden.
Newenton.	**Newton** als Newenton is a poare hamblet, of 3. or 4. dwellinge houfes, feated neerer that church welnigh by halfe a myle then that of Bagpath; often in old records written (as iuftly it may) Coldnewenton, from which quallity and conftitucōn of aire is Coldcoate its neighbour, now called Caldcote; A farme heertofore parcell of the poffeffions of the Abby of Kingfwood, and now of the Lords of Laffeborrow adioyninge.
	This Newenton was part of the old lands of the ancient family of the Berkeleis of Durfeley, longe before the Conqueft, as was his hide of land in Durfley where his dwellinge houfe and place of abode was; Soe noe part of the Manor of Berkeley nor of Berkeley herneffe at any time, noe more then the Manor of Slimbridge, another part of their old poffeffions: for which fee the Certificate of Roger Berkeley to kinge Henry the fecond, after in fol: 177.
	In Newton Bagpath is a place obvious in many evidences called Nutgarfhall, als Lurgefhall, a
Turners land.	**In** Newton als Newington are two freeholds of ancient daies, the one the inheritance of Robert Turner, containinge about 60. acres, fonne of John Turner, who died in 19. R^e Jacobi, And as I conceive is holden of the Manor of Kingfwood in Soccage by the yearly rent of—4^s 4^d And was by the faid John Turner in the 29th of Qu: Eliz: purchafed of Nicholas Pointz Efq, after knight. And was before the land of Ralph Higs.
Harris land.	**The** other ffreehold is the inheritance of Harris, of a leffe quantity then the former, holden of |
69	**Theis** 2. ffreeholds were before the time of kinge H. 3. the lands of Shokerwicke, and in the 50th yeare of that kinge of Willm Mauduit, who by an Inquifiĉōn then

Bagpath

then taken remaininge in the tower of London 50. H. 3. numero. 48. is found to have byn contra regem in municione caftri de Merlebge. (Marleburrowe,) et in bello de Lewes; And then held a carucate of land in Beoly, and a yard land in la planch, And a yard land in Bagpath, (this whereof I nowe write.)

And by another Inquisicōn in the tower of London, found in the first yeare of kinge Edward the first, six yeares after the former, theis lands are found to bee holden of Wiłłm Shokerwike, and to have byn in the kings hands a yeare and a day.

This land in the time of kinge Edward the third was the inheritance of John Rede, who left two daughters, Maud married to   , and Edith, married to

Jn 15. E. 1. Henry Berkeley of Durſley is by Inq: found to dye seized (inter alia) of the manor of Newenton, holden of the kinge in Capite. And by a booke of knights fees in the Exchequer, fomwhat more ancient then the foresaid Inquisicōn, remaininge with the Remembrancer to the lord Treaforer, Henry de Berkeley of Durſley holds Durſley and Newenton of the kinge in Capite by two knights fees.   *Newenton.*

Jn the Court of Pleas at Weſtm̃, Term̃ pasche 26. H. 3. Rot. 1. in dorso, (elder then either of the 2. former records,) the Church of Newton is said to have beene questioned by Roger de Berkeley, grandfather of John de Berkeley: from which record in haſt I tooke my notes too ſhort.   *Church.*

By Rot. patēn. 15. E. 3. ps. 2. in dorso. John de Berkeley de Durſley and Hawifia his wife arraigned an Aſſife againſt the Abbot of Kingſwood and others for lands and tenements in Coldnewenton.

Jn Trin̄ Terme, 14. E. 4. rot. 353. in the Court of comōn pleas at Weſtm̃, John Wikes Eſq. (then lord of Durſley) demaunds againſt Edmund Berkeley ſonne and heire of John Berkeley, als dict John Planch, (of whom are the families of the Berkeleys of Shropſhire,) the Manors of Durſley, Newenton Bagpath, and Stanley.

And the yeare before, by Inquisicōn 13. E. 4. Thomas Wikes Eſq. is found to dye seized of the Manors of Durſley, with Coldnewenton and Bagpath, beinge pcells of the manor of Durſley, holden in Capite, by halfe a knights fee; And that John Wikes, ſonne of John, ſonne of the ſaid Thomas Wikes, is his heire, 30. yeares old.

And

And by Inquificon in 1. H. 7. it is found That John Wikes dyed feized of the Manor of Durfley, with Coldnewenton and Bagpath, peells therof, as in the Inq: 13. E. 4. And that Edmond Wikes was his fonne and heire 17. yeares old; Alfo there is another Inquificon in 3. H. 7. Virtute officij, after the death of the faid John. |

70 Church. Afwell by a writt called Ad quod damnum, 10 April. 35. E. 1. As by an Inquificon taken by vertue therof the fame yeare, It appeares, That the Abbot of Kingfwood purchafed of the Abbot of Glouc. one acre of land in Bagpath, with the Advowfons of the churches of Owfelworth and of Weftnewenton, (foe this is called,) by way of exchange betweene them, for ten pounds rent in Hafelden and Culkerton given by the faid Abbot of Kingfwood to the Abbot of S! Peter of Glouc. And that the faid churches are holden of John fonne of Willm de Berkeley of Durfley, in ward to the kinge. in pure Almes; And that the faid 10^{li} rent is holden of Peter de Breoufe in pure Almes alfo.

Fifteene. In payment of the ffifteene or Kingefilver, when it is given to the crowne by parliament, Bagpath and Newton are rated togeather with Owfelworth, a fmall parifh alfo adioyninge; The onus or charge of all, in the kings records and bookes of the Excheq^r—4^{li} 2^s. The deduction—10^s. The remanet paid into the Excheq^r—3^{li} 12^s.

Subfedy. In the laft Subfedy in 5. R^e Caroli, heere were in Bagpath and Newton and Owfelworth, which are rated and goe togeather 11. fubfedy men, who paid—6^{li} 17^s 4^d.

Able men. And of able men for the warre, at a generall Mufter in 6to Jacobi, aged betweene 20. and 60. yeares old who appeared, were—47. in theis three places of Bagpath, Newton, and Owfelworth.

[Trained Soldiers] And now are of trayned fouldiers in Newton and Bagpath vnder Edward Stephens of Sodbury their captaine, are— |

Baynham.

71

Rugbagge. Bainham ats Baynham farme is in Rugbagg, a place of ten habitations, And before in the defcription of Alkington, faid to bee one of the hambletts or petty villages

villages of that manor: The moſt principall meſſuage or dwellinge houſe wherin
was of old called Avenſcourt from the old owners therof, ſuch as John de Avone   Avenſcourt.
and Hugh de Avone, ſonne of John, whom the ffeoffments of the ancient lords of
Berkeley in the times of R. 1. kinge John and kinge Henry the third, had made
owners therof, and of divers other lands in the pariſh of Berkeley, in ffee. And
they in proceſſe of time drewe that ſirname of Avone to them from the water or
ſmall ryver runninge neere vnto it: And was anciently held of the lords of Berkeley by knight ſervice, and the yearly rent of—40ˢ. which was the true worth and
improved yearly value at the firſt grant and reſervacōn therof: As I ſhall after
write in other poſſeſſions which they had in Pedington, Wike, and other places:
ffrom this name of Avone theis lands whereof I nowe write called Bainham farme
were in the times of kinge Edward the third the lands of John Walton, by maryage
of the heire of Avone: And after a fewe diſcents fell into the name of Treſray,
and after to the name of Kendall, And by the Attainder of John Kendall of high
treaſon in the firſt yeare of kinge Henry the ſeaventh for takinge part with kinge
Richard the third, who then did weare the Crowne, and then ſlayne at Boſworth
feild. The ſame came to the family of Dineley als Dingley, by the grant of kinge
Henry the 8ᵗʰ, wherof ſee much more at large in Pedington, and Wike, hamblets
within the manor of Hame; fol: 313. and fol: 386. And is nowe the inheritance
of ffrancis Dingley holden of the kinge by knight ſervice in Capite. |

Beckets-burie.   72

Beckets-burp is a fortreſſe or Campe place, fortified with double trenches, at
the browe of a ſteepe and precipitious hill in Weſtridge wood within the pariſh of
Wotton vnderedge, caſt vp as traditions goe in the time of kinge Henry the ſecond,
what time contention raged and many comotions were raiſed in many parts of this
kingdome in favour of Thomas Becket then Archbiſhop of Canterbury, done to
death by the meanes of that kinge as was then beleived in his Metropolitan Church
of Canterbury; the ſtory wherof is at large delivered in moſt of our coīnon Engliſh
Chronicles, whither I ſend my reader. Of this place, ſee after fol: 404. |

Benecombe.   73

Benecombe als Bencombe: An ancient farme houſe coīnonly called Bencombe
place, and Claviles place, which though it bee within the pariſh of Ewley yet is in
the

the tythinge of Combe, one of the hamblets of the manor of Wotton fforren; And appeareth at the Leet of Berkeley hundred, (which alfo Ewley doth,) holden yearly at Berkeley, not as an inhabitant of Ewley but as of Combe; And is (as turne cōmeth,) chofen Tythingman of and for Combe: And is holden of George lord Berkeley as of his manor of Wotton fforren afore faid, by knight fervice, fuite to his hundred court of Berkeley from three weekes to three weekes, and by the yearly rent of—x! And hath had the reputacōn of a fmall Manor, with fome cheife rents in Cowley and other places belonginge vnto it.

It was of old in the times of R. I. and kinge John the land of Peter de Ewley and other of his name, as Walter de Ewl and others, but by the grant of what lord of Berkeley I have not found, though doubtles of one of the firft of thofe lords: About the begininge of H. 3. time, Peter de Ewley gave the fame in franke maryage to Matilda als Maude his daughter, then maryed to Walter de Bencombe, who had iffue Robert de Bencombe, who by Maud his wife had iffue John Bencombe, who had iffue Agnes his daughter and heire maryed to John Clavile in the time of E. 3, who, betweene them had iffue Robert Clavile a Burgeffe of Briftoll, By whofe death in 19. R. 2, the fame difcended to William Clavile, father of Robert, father of Richard, father of Robert, father of Willm, father of Giles Clavile; by whofe death in 43. Eliz. the fame difcended to William his fonne and heire, then aged about 70. yeares, and a batcheler: But the fame yeare, maryinge with Elizabeth a younge gentlewoman, daughter of Edward Baffett Efquire then dwellinge at Ewley, did by his Deed dated the 21ᵗʰ of May Anno 43. Eliz. ƥd, convey to her vfe the ffee fimple of this, and all other his lands; And fhortly after dyed, leavinge her (as talke comonly was) both a widowe and maid; who in January after, A° 44. Eliz. maryed with Thomas Pointz, fecond fonne of Mathew Pointz Efq, then of Alderley, who have a plentifull pofterity and are ftill livinge, inhabitinge vpon this ancient farme place or Capitall Meffuage.

What time this laft Willm Clavile did his firft fuite at the three weekes Court of pleas for the hundred of Berkeley holden at Berkeley after the death of his father, for this land then lately difcended vpon him, hee ferioufly complained to mee of his fortune, farre worfe then of other men; enforced | through the old age of his father to ftay for his fathers lands, till himfelfe was now become above 70. yeares old; The next newes of him I heard, was firft of his maryage, and next of his death, and his wives inheritinge of his land from all kindred, wherof hee had many of his name.

In

In the great Pipe roll in the Exchequer, in 46. H. 3. Robertus filius Walteri de Benecombe et Matilda vxor eius debent vnam mr̃ca pro habenda aſſiſa. And by Roť Pateñ the ſame yeare in 46. H. 3. in dorſo, in the tower of London, An Aſſiſe was tryed betweene the ſaid Walter Bencombe and Maud his wife, and Willm Berkeley of Durſley, for lands at Bencombe.

By an old rentall of the Manor of Wotton in the time of kinge E. 1. Robertus de Benecumb tenet vnã virgatã terre p redd̃ p anñ ad 4. term̃—x? et ſectam Curiæ de 3. in 3. ſept, et ſervicium regale, et denarios ſc̃i Petri.

As for proofes for the tenure, And of 2. or 3. wardſhips which in ſeverall ages have thervpon byn had, I have therof elſwhere written in another booke.

The ſaid William Clavile left two brothers, ffrancis and Robert, who pretended title to theis lands after their brother William his death, but in vaine : who after releaſed by their ſeverall Deeds to the ſaid Thomas Pointz and his heires in A° 5. Jacobi 1607. By the name of a Capitall meſſuage and farme houſe called Bencombs place, with all lands therto belonginge in Vley, Bagpath, Wotton vnderedge, Cowley, and Slimbridge.

Beoley.

Beoley, written alſo Beleigh, and Beele, is an ancient capitall Meſſuage called Beoley farme, or the farme of Beoley, with 100. acres of ground or therabouts therto belonginge, in the pariſh of Berkeley and tithinge of Came, which hath heertofore beene in ſome records reputed and called a manor, but was not nor is ; nowe the inheritance of Edward Try gent̃ and wheron hee dwelleth, by a late purchaſe by him made of Willm Trye of Hardwicke Eſq, his eldeſt brothers ſonne and heire, in 7. Caroli, as after followeth ; holden of the Caſtle of Berkeley by knight ſervice and ſute of court to the hundred of Berkeley from 3 weekes to 3 weekes, whereat one halfe peñy cheife rent is yearly accuſtomably received by the lord Berkeleys reeve of his manor of Hurſt, neereſt to which manor Beoly is, And as I take it, ſome ſcattered parts therof within Hurſt.

This Meſſuage and land with certaine other lands called Inwoods in Stinchcombe within the pariſh of Came, were by Maurice lord Berkeley the ſecond lord

of

of that name, about the third yeare of kinge Edward the firſt, given to Sir Robert Berkeley knight ſecond ſonne of him the ſaid lord Maurice, and to his heires ; As alſo at or neere the ſame time was the manor of Arlingham, as before I have written fol : 53. See more in fol : 347, 345.

This Sir Robert Berkeley who dyed about 28. E. 1. left this land of Beoley to Thomas Berkeley his ſecond ſonne, and his heires, comonly therby called Thomas of Beoly, who (as an Inquiſicõn in the Tower of London in 15. E. 2. concerninge rebells lands ſheweth,) was found to have adhered and taken part with Maurice lord Berkeley his cozen againſt that kinge and Hugh Earle Spenſer, wherby his land of Beoly came to that kinge by Eſcheate, and ſoe continued for about 5. yeares, till by the revoluc̃on of time that kinge was taken and brought priſoner to Berkeley caſtle, where hee was moſt barbarouſly murdered, as in the life of that lord Maurice and of the lord Thomas his ſonne and heire, I have more largely written in my hiſtory of their family ; And in 1. E. 3. this Thomas was reſtored to theis lands with the meane profitts, to hold as before of old hee did, as by a generall Act of parliament in 1. E. 3. appeares.

This Thomas Berkeley of Beoley, by Maud his wife, had iſſue John and Margaret, and dyed about 6. E. 3. which John dyed in his minority without iſſue in 20. E. 3. then in ward to the ſaid Thomas lord Berkeley for this land, leavinge the ſaid Margaret his ſiſter and heire ; who was firſt maryed to Walter Shoile, by whom thee had noe iſſue, and after remaryed to Raph Try (written ſomtimes Rawlyn,) who had iſſue William who dyed in the life of his father without iſſue, and John Try who dyed in   , leavinge iſſue John Trye, (for by Willm his elder brother was noe iſſue ;) And the ſaid John by Katherine his wife daughter and heire of Nicholas Tuſſely, had iſſue William Try, who by Iſable his wife daughter of James lord Berkeley and ſiſter of William Marques Berkeley, (whom hee maryed in 16. E. 4.) had iſſue William Trye, and dyed in 13. H. 7. (the ſaid Iſable dead 6. yeares before,) which William ſonne of William, by Anne his wife daughter of Thomas Baynham Eſquire, and widowe of Mr. Clifford, had iſſue Edward Trye, and dyed in 16. H. 8. The ſaid Edward dyed in 18. H. 8. within 3. yeares after the death of his father, and by Sibill his wife left iſſue John Trye, who dyed 33. H. 8. levinge iſſue John Trye, by Elizabeth his wife daughter and coheire of Mr. Gurney of Suffolke ; which John ſonne of John dyed in 33. Eliz. and by Margaret his wife daughter of Mr. Skipwith, left iſſue Willm Trye, who dyed in 8. Jacobi. And by Mary his wife daughter of William Tirrell had iſſue William Trye, before menc̃oned

to

to have alyened to the said Edward his vncle in fee. Of this pedegree see fol: 345. 362.

More of this ancient farme or Capital Messuage is to bee read in theis Records, vz,

  Inquisitio. 37. E. 3. de feodis de Berkeley in Scēio. per serviē militare.
  Inq : 13. H. 7. post mortem Willi Trye.
  Inq : 16. H. 8. post mortem Willi Trye.
  Inq : 18. H. 8. post mortem Edŕi Trye.
  Inq : 33. H. 8. post mortem Johis Trye. 2 ps in Coñi Lincolñ.
  Inq : 8. Jacobi, post mortem Willi Trye.
  Inq : 17 Caroli post mortem Edŕi Try : tenť de Georgio Dño Berkeley et p Secta Cuŕ et p quod serviciū ignorant.

An Inquisicōn in 50. H. 3. nº 48. And another in 1. E. 1. finde, That Willm Mauduit held a Carucate of land in Beoley of the lord Berkeley, and halfe a yard more there of the lord of Kingston in Hurst in the parish of Slimbridge : which halfe yard land came shortly after to the Abbot of Kingswood, and is nowe the fee of

And more, 9. acres of land and 3. acres of meadowe in Beoley of Peter of Stintescombe. And more, 1. messuage and 1. yard land in Beley of Henry Berkeley de Dursley : And was attainted of felony and hanged, for beinge against the kinge in the seidge of Marleborowe and in the battell of Lewes, And that the kinge had had the yeare, day, and wast. This came shortly to the Abbot of Kingswood, and is nowe the fee of

By deed about 12. H. 3. Tho : lord Berkeley gave to Henry his sonne in fee, totā rudiggam Suam de Buleia, quæ fuit de dominico suo de Cam, et tendit de regali strato de longo in longum vsq, ad pontem de Beleia : Salvo regali servicio, tantū selt quantū ad dimidiam virgatam terræ ptinet. Redđ—8ᵈ p añ. In Berkeley Castle |

Berkeley.

Berkeley: In the booke called Domesdei written Berchelai, And in the Saxon tongue Beorkenlau : The place I heere describe is the Burgh, Burrowe or Market towne of Berkeley, and the Castle adioyninge therto, holden of the kinge by knight
                    service

service in Capite; And as it were The head or principall place of the Barony of Berkeley, the p̄sent inheritance of George lord Berkeley.

Of this Towne the booke of Domesdei hath only thus: Ibi vnum forum in quo manent 17. homines, et reddunt censum in firma; wherof read more in the description of Hame. fol: 209.

Markett.
In this towne a market is holden each Tuesday, by the grant of kinge Henry the second made in the first yeare of his raigne to Robert the sonne of Hardinge and his heires, wherby the kinge granted to him to have in his Manor of Berkeley, liberum marcheium cum omnibus libertatibus quæ ad marcheium[1] pertinent, quacunque die septimanæ voluerit, et monetam cum proprio monetario suo; vz, A free market with all liberties to a market belonginge, what day of the weeke him best liked, and money there of his owne stampinge or Coynage: Whervpon Tuesday was chosen, which so continueth to this day: yet it is apparant by the said booke of Domesdei that here was a market in the time of William the Conqueror, and before in the time of Edward the Confessor, if forum, signify there a market.

ffaire.
But I finde not that the lords of this market towne had any faire heere before that Thomas lord Berkeley the fourth of that name did in the 18th yeare of kinge Richard the second, obtaine of that kinge to have one there holden, on the Vigill and day of the invention of holy Crosse, called Holy Rood day, in May with all liberties and free customes to such a faire apptaininge, which soe also continueth to this day; contentinge themselves with the faires formerly obtained in their townships of Wotton, Dursley, Newport, and Cambridge, within their hundred of Berkeley, (not mentioninge the market and faire granted to the Abbot and Covent of S! Augustines in their manor of Almondesbury, wherof I have formerly written,) as in the description of those places is to bee read: The reason wherof seemes in part to have beene, for that in times soe active and stirringe as all those former ages were, the lords of this towne would not drawe such a concourse of people of all sorts, as then when the way to London was scarce frequented, accustomably resorted to Cuntry faires, foe' neere to their Castle gates, wherby soe important a peece might by their opposites sodainly and easily have been surprised. Which name also

Burgh. 78
of Burgh or Burrowe, notes vnto vs from the Saxon, that the place very anciently was fortified, the prints wherof in | some places not yet digged downe and washed out; The name also of Lockfast-bridge yet remaininge, leadinge to the towne from Hame over the further ewe or water, seemeth to imply as much.

from

---

[1] See Ante, Note B, Vol. I., page 62.

From which lord Robert this Burrowe and market towne by his death in 17. H. 2. difcended and came to the lord Maurice his fonne and heire; And by his death in 1. R. 1. to the lord Robert his fonne and heire; And by his death without iffue in 4. H. 3. to the lord Thomas his brother and heire; And by his death in 28. H. 3. to the lord Maurice his fonne and heire; And by his death in 8. E. 1. to the lord Thomas his fonne and heire; And by his death in 14. E. 2. to the lord Maurice his fonne and heire; And by his death in 20. E. 2. to the lord Thomas his fonne and heire; who, A die pafche in vnū menfem in 23. E. 3. by ffine, (as alfo by Deeds,) entayled this (amongſt other manors and lands) with a render to himfelfe for life, The remainder to Maurice his fonne and heire apparant and the heires males of his body, the remainder to the faid lord Thomas and the heires males of his body, the remainder to the right heires of him the faid lord Thomas: By whofe death 12. yeares after in 35. E. 3, it came to the poffeffion of the faid lord Maurice; And by his death in 42. E. 3. to the lord Thomas his fonne and heire; And by his death in 5. H. 5. without iffue male of his body, to the lord James his nephew and heire male, as beinge fonne a nd heire of Sir James, who dyed 6. H. 4. brother of the faid lord Thomas: And by the death of the faid lord James in 3. E. 4. to the lord William his fonne and heire; who in 21. E. 4. was created Vifcont Berkeley, And in 1. R. 3. Earle of Nottingham, And in 3. H. 7. **Marques Berkeley**, with the Offices of Earle Marfhall and great Marfhall of England; Which William in 4. H. 7. entayled this manor (amongſt many others) with a render to himfelfe and the heires of his body, The remainder to that kinge H. 7. and to the heires males of his body, the Remainder to the right heires of him the faid William; By whofe death the 14th of ffebr: in the 7th yeare of that kings raigne, without any iffue of his body, This of Berkeley and many others, by that and other ffines and conveyances, came to that kinge and the heires males of his body, And from him to his fonne kinge Henry the 8th and the heires males of his body, And from him to his fonne kinge Edward the fixth, who dyed without iffue male or female; wherby after 61. yeares, 4. monthes, and 20. daies, this Berkeley Towne with many other manors, entailed upon kinge H. 7. as aforefaid, reverted to Henry lord Berkeley as right heire to the faid William lord Marques Berkeley, then | of the age of Nyneteene yeares; As beinge fonne and heire of Thomas lord Berkeley, who dyed in 26. H. 8, fonne and heire of Thomas lord Berkeley who died in 24 H. 8, brother and heire of Maurice lord Berkeley who died without iffue in 15. H. 8, fonnes of Maurice lord Berkeley who died in 22. H. 7, brother and heire of the faid William lord Marques Berkeley. And by the death of the faid Henry lord Berkeley in 11. R^c. Jacobi, the fame difcended to

his

his grandchilde and heire George lord Berkeley aforesaid, sonne of Sir Thomas Berkeley knight, only sonne of the said lord Henry, who dyed in 9. Jacobi p̃rt.; which is somwhat the more pticulerly heere set downe, because I intend to this place to referre other Manors of like discent and conveyances: As also I may my reader to theis Exchequer records, vz, Mich: Rec̃. 1. Mar̃. Rot. 50. Pasch: 1. Eliz. Rot. 36. Originat: 1. et. 2. Ph: & Mar̃. 2. ps. Rot. 68. Originat 2. ps. 2. et 3. Ph: & Mar̃. Rot. 73. And inrolled with the Auditors, Mich term̃, 4. et 5. Ph: & Mar̃. bis.

This towne of Berkeley is seated on an hill and hill side though not of the greatest, consistinge of theis streets, vz, High street, Salter street, Marybroke street als Madbrook street, Redcum street, Canonbury als Spurryers street, and S! Michaells lane: with some others, whose houses are longe since decayed: ffrom hence it beholds Cottswald hills, the fforrest of Deane, the river of Severne, and the city of Gloucester, fower remarkeable eminencies.

The Towne it selfe was so much demolished in the raignes of kinge Henry the sixt and of kinge Edward the sowerth, through the incursions sutes and seidges laid about it, and the Castle adioyninge, by Richard Beauchamp earle of Warwicke and his wives coheires, That the street called S! Michaell street, and some others, are not now to bee found, other then in old Rentalls and evidences before that time, which declare that such there were; And that thirty pounds of old rent which before those devastations it yealded to the lord is nowe as ever since come downe to Ten pounds per ann: consistinge only of 80. housholds at this day: And in many old Deeds is called 𝖓𝖔𝖛𝖆 𝖛𝖎𝖑𝖑𝖆, but where or how neere to it 𝖛𝖊𝖙𝖚𝖘 𝖛𝖎𝖑𝖑𝖆, the old towne, was seated, or whether in part of this that nowe is, I cañot affirme.

The Towne vnderlyeth the government of a Maior and his brethren, such as have byn maiors; But was never any other incorporacõn but by prescription, nor ever had any Burgesse for the parliament, which I have much sought after: yet divers grants have very anciently byn made to them by the name of the Burgesses and marchants of Berkeley their heires and assignes; By which words Maurice lord Berkeley in 46. H. 3. released to them all exaction and clayme of Toll, and all kinds of Thallage or Toll which hee had or might demaund of them. And Thomas lord Berkeley, father of the said lord Maurice, about 20. H. 3. granted to the Burgesses of Berkeley to have comon of pasture without the Towne of Berkeley, as they were wont to have, And that none of them should bee chosen Reeve against his will, And that no Attachments should bee made in the Burrow of
Berkeley

Berkeley

Berkeley but by the Reeve or bayly of the burrowe: But however affaires have gone of old the inhabitants may bee said to have at this day, *nomen sine re*; and may better boast of their market Townes antiquity, then the towne of their abillity or government amongst themselves.

The little ryver that ariseth in Nibley a village three miles from Berkeley, hath its course by the side of this towne, and thence into the river of Severne about a myle belowe the towne; which when it meeteth with salt water somwhat above Berkeley, it looseth its name of Doverley, And then againſt the towne of Berkeley a little beneath the towne mill, als the Castle mill, maketh a pretty safe haven close by the towne side, whither barkes of 40. tunnes and more doe come and safely ride at springe tides: ffrom whence in times past great profits came to the lords of this burrowe towne, as appeares by many of their evidences which I have read for warfage and Toll, which may seeme to have caused the purchasinge of those charters in the time of kinge Henry the third formerly mentioned; noe other memoriall therof, in effect, now remaininge, save of two pence for wheelage, taken by the Maior for every wayne load of coale, wyne, oyle, salt, and the like, there vnladen and caryed through the towne.

A race of ancient ffreeholders (wherof Robert Avery who lived in the time of kinge Edward the second, sonne and heire of Richard Avery, was the last of that sirname,) have by their longe possession and seisin of divers lands and tenements neere adioyninge to this haven and place of landinge and vnladinge of marchandize, given not only the name of Averies stocke to this place, But to his old mantion house also adioyninge called Averyes place, to this day; though the stocke called Averyes and the landinge place of wares bee parcell of the wast ground of the manor; which messuage and lands by the heire generall of Robert Avery came to John Payne, who in 26. H. 6. conveyed part of these lands to John Dirlinge and Isable his wife, daughter and heire of William Skott, and to the heires of their bodies, The remainder to John Thorpe of Wainſwell and Margaret his wife, and to the heires of their bodies, with divers remainders over; The estate tayle of ! Dirlinge and his wife was soone spent; wherby the same came to John Thorpe and Margaret his wife, who had issue Richard Thorpe father of Thomas Thorpe, father of Thomas, father of Nicholas, father of George, who in 15. Regis Jacobi sold the same to Thomas Machin and his heires; who since sold the same to Walter Abevan.

The other part of theis Averies lands and Averyes place, the said Isable wife of John Dirlinge, in her widowhood, in the first yeare of kinge E. 4. granted to
Willm

Averys stocke and Averys land.

81

Wiłłm Ruſſell, als Gwiłłam and to Margery his wife her daughter, and to their heires; which after came to the foreſaid family of the Thorps of Waniſwell, and ſold by the ſaid George Thorpe to the ſaid Thomas Machin by the ſame conveyance.

Alſo I have ſeene a Deed dated 11. Julij. 3. E. 4. wherby Richard Clavile and Agnes his wife, granted to John Thorpe and to Margaret his wife, and to the heires of the ſaid John, one houſe and 4. ſhops infra le Averyes, cum vna porta ibm et pcella terræ iuxta eandem terram, ac vnā paſturā vocaī Averyes greene iuxta curſum aquæ Sabrinæ, et vnū Croſtū ibm et vnū aliud croſtū, boundinge them pticulerly, which the ſaid Richard Clavile and Agnes had, (ſaith this deed,) ex feoffamento Wiłłi Ruſſell ałs Gwiłłam Ruſſell et Margeriæ vxori eius; which nowe Thomas Machin hath as aforeſaid.

And ſuch of ancient daies ſeemes to have byn the concourſe of people to this market towne, And therby the vent or vtterance of drinke, That the Tolceſters or brewings of ale, for ſoe I engliſh the latine word (tolceſtrum,) at the Innes and Alehouſes, yealded yearly to the lord therof—7^{li} and 8^{li} after the rate of 4^d and 6^d for every brewinge, which intimates a vaſt proportion; which now is not one penny and yet a maſſe of ale and beere drowned in the gutts of drunkards. And vſually, till the end of kinge Edward the third, were 4. Leets or Lawdaies, viewes of franke pledge, yearly held in this towne, wherat ſuch preſentments were, which ſince have byn reduced to two.

Pariſh Church.

The pariſh church ſeated in this towne anſwereth in greatnes to the large extent of the pariſh, built at firſt as it ſeemeth with aptnes and relation to the greatnes of the lords demeſne lands, and his numbers of Tenancies within the limitts therof; which from the place called ffillimores bridge by Hurſt, which parteth it from Slimbridge pariſh, to the further end of Hille ałs Hull, next Oldbury, which parteth it from Thornbury pariſh, is eight longe miles in a rich and fruitfull ſoile; And from the midſt of Severne (acroſſe the former length) to Marten and Swynburne bridges in Nibley, which parteth it from | the pariſh of Wotton, (to which Church Nibley is a Chaple,) neere as many miles more; wherby it may ſeeme there was good cauſe for the Abbotts of Sṭ Auguſtine by Briſtoll for their buildinge of eight tythe Barnes of noe meane greatnes for the Inninge of the tyth corne therof, which yet there continue; As the Tyth barne of Canonbury, of Hame, of Wike, of Stone, of Bliſbury, of Hill, of Oldminſter, and of Bradſton; within the lymit of which Tyth barne of Hame, a cuſtome hath anciently prevailed to pay three

three pence in money for the tith hay of every acre mowed, and not in kinde; which received a refolucon accordingly in a fuite betweene Hooper and Mallet in 38. Eliz. wherin my felfe was a Comiffioner for examinacon of Witneffes.

In this parifh are two Chaples of eafe, as they are comonly called, Stone, and Hill als Hull, wherof more in their alphabeticall courfes. fol : 225. 355.

The Church and Advowfon of this parifh with its Chapples was by Robert the fonne of Hardinge, the firft lord Berkeley in the time of kinge Henry the fecond, given (amongft others) to the Monaftery of St Auguftines aforefaid at his firft foundacon therof; which the Abbot and Covent fhortly after found meanes, with the Bifhop of Worcefter and an incumbent of their owne prefentinge, to appropriate with others. The guift is in theis words.

Robertus filius Hardingi Omnibus hominibus et amicis fuis, et vniūfis fanctæ ecclefiæ fidelibus, ad quos hæc carta pveñit, falutem : Sciatis quòd cùm Dñs Rex Henr̃ Maner̃ de Berchat et totam Berchalei hneffe mihi in feodum et hereditatem dediffet, et carta fua confirmavit, cum omnibus libertatibus et rebus ad Berchalei hneffe pertinentibus, in ecclefiis, in nemoribus, in pratis et pafturis, et in omnibus alijs rebus, ficut fuerant tempore H : regis avi fui ; ego confenfu et affenfu ipius dñi mei regis, Eccleias de Berchalei herneffe, fcilt eccleiam de Berchat, et eccleiñ de Wotton, et eccleiam de Beverfton, et ecctiam de Effelleswrd et ecctiam de Almondefbur̃, fingulas cum capellis et terris et libertatibus ad ipas ecctias ptineñ, pro falute animæ m[e]æ et Dñi mei regis et anteceffo₃ meo₃, et vxoris meæ et libero₃ meo₃, Dedi et conceffi ecctie fancti Auguftini de Briftoll, et Canonicis regularibus ibm deo fervientibus, in perpetuam et liberam eleemofinam, nullo iure retento mihi vel heredibus meis in predictis ecctijs cùm eas vacare contigerit. Similiter et omnes ecclefias de Berchale₃ herneffe vbicunq̃ fuerint, cum capellis et omnibus omniũ pertinentijs, dedi et conceffi predictis canonicis in perpetuam elemofinam, et hac mea carta confirmavi. Hijs teftibus, Henrico decano Moreton et Mauricio fratre eius, Cerino perfona ecctie de Wotton, Galfrido Capellano, Nigello filio Arturi, Reginaldo perfona ecctie de Cama, Wil̃o de Saltemar̃, et Adam fratre eius, Helie filio Hardingi, Rico fcriptore, et Alano de Bedmeniftra.

As for the other churches of Berkelei herneffe not heere mentioned (with the former) in perticuler, as Cromhall, Came, Horfeild, Slimbridge, Durfley, Vley, Cowley, Kingfwefton, Arlingham, and fome others, I conceive that they formerly were
given

given, either by the said lord Robert or by kinge Henry or by Mawd the Empresse his mother or by kinge Henry 1, to the Monasteries of St Peter of Glouc̃, and of Readinge, and of others: And the Abbot of Redinge, (of the foundac̃on of the said Empresse Mawd,) pretended soe stronge a title to this of Berkeley and some others, That this Monastery of St Augustines paid to the said Monastery of Readinge for the same a pention of—13^li. 6.^s 8.^d from this time till the Dissoluc̃on of both those Monasteries in 31. H. 8. As in the history and life of the said lord Robert I have elswhere written. And wherof also more (heere to have byn inserted) may bee formerly read in Almondesbury fol: 47. And in Arlingham. fol: 55. And in Ashelworth fol: 66. And in Cromhall fol. 165.

The Abbot of St Augustines beinge thus seazed of theis Churches and Advowsons by the grant of the lord Robert sonne of Hardinge, as aforesaid, They found meanes in the time of the lord Maurice his sonne to appropriate and convert to their owne vses and for the better feedinge of themselves, theis fower churches formerly mentioned; as by the Deed of the Bishop of Worcester appeareth, wherof the effect and substance followeth, as breifly as I could abstract the same: who (saith the Bishop) takinge considerac̃on of the honest conversac̃on of the Abbotts of this monastery and Cannons there, and of the poverty of their house, and of their diligent care as well in receivinge of strangers as in nourishinge of poore people, doth take their whole monastery churches and ecclesiasticall goods into his protection: And to the end the benefits which from the first foundac̃on of their house have byn bestowed on them might more abundantly to Gods honour bee dilated, doth by his episcopall authority grant vnto them that they may convert to their proper vse the fruits of the Churches of Berkeley Wotton Almondesbury and Ashelworth, for the sustentac̃on of the said Channons receivinge of guests and reliefe of poore people: Savinge alwaies this dignity of his Church of Worcester, and honest sustentac̃on of the Vicar servinge in the said churches. But howe or in what other certainty the Vicaridges were nowe or after endowed, I have not yet seene. But howe faire soever the glosse bee, **Appropriac̃ons** are at this day censured by divines to bee one of those monstrous births of Covetousnes begotten in the darke night of superstition and yet suffered to live in this day light of the gospell, to the great hindrance of learninge, the impoverishment of the ministery, decay of hospitallity, and infamy of our religion and profession. |

84   **This** Church or Appropriac̃on of Berkeley in the hands of the farmors therof is accompted worth—350^li. by the yeare, in tith graine and hay: And the vicaridge worth in lesser tythes—150^li. by the yeare.   The

Berkeley

The appropriacōn of the Church, as alſo the Vicaridge, which is preſentative, belonge to the Deane and Chapiter of Briſtoll, of newe erected in 34. H. 8. beinge then made one of the ten Deanaries, then by that kinge founded and endowed of newe: Of which Church the bleſſed virgin Mary was the tutelarly ſainte, to whom the ſame was dedicated: and vnder whoſe protection it remained, as divers Deeds doe ſhewe.

And if compariſons were as lawfull in the makinge, as cōmonly they proove offenſive in the matchinge, I would reckon this pariſh of Berkeley in all valuable reſpects before any other in this County.

I have, from the viccar of this pariſh, and eſpecially from John Hall for many yeares tenant and farmer to Edward Greene vicar, byn informed, that they have had 110. yea 130. tythe calves, nay more, in one yeare, yet hee that hath ſix or vnder in a year, paies none; wherby the greatnes of the breed of Rother cattle may bee conceived, which by reaſon of the yearly decay of tillage, and convertinge arrable ground into paſture, cañot but increaſe, makinge the vicaridge better, and the rectory worſe. Vicaridge

Of able men in this pariſh ſitt for warre betweene 20. and 60. yeares old, at a generall muſter taken by Henry lord Berkeley then Lieutenant of the county, which appeared before him, whoſe names ages and abillities of body were then taken, and after by my ſelfe and Clarkes entered into a booke, were—483. vz, in this burrow towne—97. In Hame manor. 187, In Alkington. 106, In Hinton—46, In Bradſton—11, And in Hill—37. Able men in the Pariſh

In payment of the fifteene or kingeſilver when it is granted by parliament, The onus or Charge of this Burrow or market towne is in the exchequer—3ˡⁱ 11ˢ 8ᵈ q. The deduction for the decay therof is—20ˢ The Remanet paid into the Exchequer is 51ˢ 8ᵈ q, by the Collector. fifteene.

In the laſt Subſedy in the 5ᵗʰ yeare of kinge Charles were in this towne 9. ſubſedy men, who paid—3ˡⁱ 2ˢ 8ᵈ Subſedy.

And of trayned Souldiers now are vnder Wiłłm Thorpe Eſq, their Captaine—8. wherof 1. Corſlet and 7. muſketts. Trayned ſouldiers.

And

| Rates. | And if the whole Division called Berkeley division (esteemed a 4th part of the whole county,) bee rated to pay in any taxe for Kinge or Comon wealth—100ˡⁱ. This hundred of Berkeley therof paies—33ˡⁱ 3ˢ. And this towne of Berkeley—4ˢ.

| Tyth barne. | In the northeast end of this towne, standeth one of the 8. tith barnes called Can-bury als Canonbury barne, worth by the yeare—[blank.] |

| 85 Chantryes. | The lady Katherine Berkeley, the widow of that Thomas lord Berkeley the third lord of that name, who dyed in 35. E. 3. did in the dayes of her husbands grandchilde and heire in 8. R. 2.[1] found a Chantry in the said parish church of Berkeley, for a Chaplen and his successors perpetually to pray at the Alter of S! Andrewe in that church, for the good estate of her selfe, and of Thomas then lord Berkeley, and of the lady Margaret his wife; endowinge the same with divers lands and tenem⁽ˢ⁾ in Berkeley, Alkington, and Hame manors; ffor which, after an Inquisicōn found vpon a writt of **Ad quod damnum** remaininge in the Tower of London in 7. R. 2. shee obtained the kings licence for that alienacōn in Mortmaine. And thervpon also a confirmacōn from the Bishop of Worcester; And from that Alter was called S! Andrewes Chantry vntill the dissolucōn therof in 1. E. 6. ; Out of which George lord Berkeley that now is receiveth from the kings receiver an yearly cheife rent of—5ˢ. As likewise his Ancestors have done since the foundinge therof.

| Of our Lady. | In this church also, Thomas lord Berkeley in [ ] E. 3. founded an other Chantry, which was called S! Maries Chantry or our Ladies chantry, endowinge the same with divers lands and tenements in   , Out of which the said George lord Berkeley that now is receiveth of the kings receiver an yearly cheife rent of—14ˢ 10ᵈ, as likewise his ancestors ever did since the foundinge therof, though the inheritance of the said lands bee longe since sold away by the Crowne, as after followeth. Of the Advowsons of which two Chantries Thomas lord Berkeley is, by an Inquisicōn after his death in 5. H. 5. found to dye seised.

| Of S. Maurice. | In this Church also was another Chantry called the Chantry of S! Maurice founded in   E. 3. with divers lands and tenements therto given, by   , for maintenance of the preist celebratinge at that Alter : which likewise cominge to kinge E. 6. in the first yeare of his raigne by Act of parliaments, were by him granted in fee, As also part of the lands belonginge to our ladies Chantry, to   Burchier, who sold part of them to Hall, and

[1] It was founded 7 Rich. II. See Rot. Pat. of that year, pars 2. membr. 1. [ED.]

and hee to Edward Hall and William Hall in fee, which William dyed in 11. Regis Caroli. In which grant the kinge reserved a tenure of his Castle of Berkeley by fealty only, wherof that kinge was then seised, to him and the heires males of his body. And the chantry lands belonginge to the chantry in the said Church called Berkeleys Chantry, with some others, were by kinge E. 6. in the second of his raigne granted in fee to Sir John Thin and Lawrence Hide, As by the grant inrolled in the Chancery, And after in 3. pte original in sc̄c̄io. in 2 : E. 6. Rot. 26. cum Remen̄ Thesaur̄, appeares. |

A part of theis chantry lands remained in the crowne from the dissolucōn in 1. E. 6. till 5. Jacobi, when that kinge by his tres patents dated 1. Junij aº 5ᵗᵒ p̄d, granted the same (amongst many others) to Sir William Herricke and Sir Arthur Ingram and their heires, To hold of East greenwich in free and com̄on soccage, paying the ancient rent of, 41ˢ 4ᵈ, paid to this day by the heires and assignes of Arnold Oldisworth and George Thorpe Esq͕ᵗ. To whom the said patentees by their Deed inrolled in Chancery, dated 25. Junij. Anno sexto Rᵉ Jacobi p̄d, sold the same, payinge the rent aforesaid ; shortly after scattered by them to other men vpon their severall sales, who amongst them pay the said rent of—41ˢ 4ᵈ to this day aº 1639. **86**

The Lords of this Manor anciently vsed to pay to the bishop of Worcester yearly—16ˢ 11ᵈ in the name of Peter pence, And hee the same (with others) to the bishop of Rome : which beinge vnpaid for certaine yeares by reason their lands came into the hands of kinge Edward the second, by the rebellion of Maurice lord Berkeley, qui propter inimicitiam et rebellionem sibi impositas voluntati regis se reddidit, The bishop was now restored to have them againe paid vnto him as anciently hee had ; As theis Records in the tower of London doe shewe ; Rot. Clauss de terr̄ forisfact. 15. E. 2. ps. 2. membr. 2. And Rot. clauss. 16. E. 2. membr. 26. And Rot. clauss. 15. et 16. E. 2. ps. 2. membr. 8. when restitucōn was awarded to the bishop of the said Peter pence, and all the former matters recited. *Peter pence.*

In the southest end of this towne is seated the Castle of Berkeley, a great part wherof was built out of the ruines of the Nunnery which stood in the same place, which was demolished by the practice of Earle Goodwyn in the time of kinge Edward the Confessor, as formerly hath byn written fol : 1. et 2. The buildinge of this Castle was by kinge Henry the second in the time of kinge Stephen, whilst the said Henry was Duke of Normandy, as plainly appeares by a Deed of the said Duke Henries made to Robert the sonne of Harding, wherin the Duke doth *Berkeley Castle.*

doth acknowledge to have covenanted with the said Robert to build for him there a Castle, accordinge to the will of him the said Robert, and then gave his oath to performe the same, As also did nyne other noble men with the Duke; The words
Roberto Berkeley. wherof in the originall deed, are Et pepigi et firmare ibi castellum secundum voluntatem ipsius Roberti, Et ego per fidem meam affidavi ei pactiones supradictas tenere illi atque heredibus suis; Et hoc idem affidavit Reginaldus Comes Cornubiæ &c. And I have covenanted with the said Robert to build him a castle at Berkeley
87 accordinge to his owne desire, And have | also sworne to him by my faith to performe the same agreement with him and his heires, And the same with mee is sworne by Reginald Earle of Cornwall, and eight others (named in this deed.)

And to see this buildinge the better yet performed, the said Duke Henry, not longe before the death of kinge Stephen, came in person to Berkeley: howbeit it is certaine that at this first buildinge the Castle contained noe more then the Inmost of the three gates and the buildings within the same; ffor the two vnmost gates and all the buildings belonginge vnto them (save the Keepe,) were the additions of the lord Maurice eldest sonne of the lord Robert, in the later end of kinge H. 2. and of the lord Thomas the second of that name, in 6. E. 2. and of the lord Thomas the third of that name, in 18. E. 3. And as for the great kitchen, (great indeed,) standing without but adioyninge to the keepe of the castle, it was the worke of kinge Henry the seaventh at his first entrance into the possession therof, about the Nynth yeare of his raigne, shortly after the death of William Marques Berkeley, who had conveyed the same (amongst others) to that kinge, as before appeareth fol: 78. 79.

Chaples. In this Castle were of late yeares, (not yet wholly ruined or deformed,) two beautifull Chapples or oratories, indowed with divers priviledges from the Bishops of Rome, The one of them in that part of the Castle called the Keepe, with a goodly well of water vnder it, The other at the vpper end of the great hall staires leadinge to the great dyninge chamber; And for the devout keepinge of the ornaments therto belonginge, divers allowances were by the Lords yearly made, As by divers deeds and accounts in the evidence house in this castle appeares.

Maurice lord Berkeley the fourth lord of that name, in 38. E. 3. obtained of Pope Vrbane the second by his papall Bull and power, That to the end his two chaples, the one of our lady the blessed virgin and the other of St John Baptist, founded in the Castle of Berkeley, might bee renued and frequented with due honors,

honors, forty dayes of pardon and releafe of the penance enioyned to every one that fhould in the faid Chapells in the feftivall daies of the yeare, heare maffes or fay kneelinge three ave-maries, or fhould give any veftments ornaments gold filver bookes chalices or any other aides of charity to the faid Chaples : And that whofoever fhall there pray for him that obtained theis prefents, And for the life and good eftate of the noble lord Maurice de Berkeley and of the noble Lady Elizabeth his wife, and of their children, and for the foules of the lord Thomas his father, And[1] beinge in purgatory, fhall bee alfo releafed of forty dayes of the penance enioyned them : And this | faculty grace or inftrument, for the infalliblenes, is alfo vnder the feales of eleaven of that Popes Cardinalls : perhaps alfo fomwhat the rather procured by this lords wifdome through the great fchifme of three Popes at once that then raigned in the church.

In this Caftle and in this place called the **Keepe** it was where kinge Edward the fecond in the dungeon chamber there was foe barbaroufly murdered, wherof I have at large already written in the life of the lord Thomas Berkeley the third of that name, in my hiftory of that family.

Out of which dungeon, in the likenes of a deepe broad well goinge fteepely downe in the midft of the dungeon chamber in the faid Keepe, was (as tradition tells) drawne forth a Toad in the time of kinge Henry the feventh, of an incredible bignes, which in the deepe dry duft in the bottome therof had doubtleffe lived there divers hundreds of yeares ; whofe portraicture in iuft dimention, as it was then to mee affirmed by divers aged perfons, I fawe about 48. yeares agone drawne in colours vpon the doore of the great hall, and of the vtter fide of the ftone porch leadinge into that hall, fince by pargettors or pointers of that wall wafhed out or outworne with time ; which in bredth was more then a foot, neere 16. inches, and in length more : Of which monftrous and outgrown beaft the inhabitants of this towne and in the neighbour villages round about fable many ftrange and incredible wonders, makinge the greatnes of this toad more then would fill a pecke, yea I have heard fome who looked to have beleife fay from the report of their fathers and grandfathers that it would have filled a bufhell or ftrike, and to have byn many yeares fed with flefh and garbage from the butchers ; but this is all the trueth I knowe, or dare beleeve.

Acinulph

---

[1] There would appear to be fomething omitted here, as is alfo in the Life of the Lord Maurice IV. (Vol. II., p. 372,) where this Charter is cited. Perhaps it was the name of the founder's mother, wife of the Lord Thomas. [ED.]

Witch in Berkeley.

Acinulph of Chester in his Polichronicon hath thus of a witch that lived in this towne of Berkeley in the beginninge of the raigne of kinge Edward the Confessor, libro. 5. cap : 25. de aº 1046. which alſo I have read in an old manuſcript booke called **Chronicon de Abington**, more ancient then the hiſtory of **Acinulph**, remaininge with Sir Robert Cotton, fol : 53. That about that time a certaine woman in Berkeley accuſtomed to evill arts, when as vpon a certaine day ſhee kept a feaſt, A Chough which ſhee vſed delicately to feede cackled more loud and diſtinctly then ſhee was wont to doe ; which when ſhee heard the knife fell out of her hand, her countenance waxed pale, and havinge fetched a deepe groane with a ſigh ſaid, now this day is the plowe come to my laſt furrowe ; which beinge ſaid, A meſſenger cominge in declared to her the death of her ſonne, and of all her family expoſed to preſent ruine : The woman preſently lay downe and called to her ſuch of her other children as were monkes and a nunne, who cominge ſhee thus ſpake vnto them ; I a wicked follower of an evill art and worſe life, vainely thought to have beene | defended by your praiers ; nowe I deſire to be eaſed by you of my torments becauſe Judgement is given againſt my foule ; but peradventure you may keepe my body if it bee faſt ſewed in a ſtags ſkin ; make yee for mee a cheſt of ſtone faſt bound and cemented with iron and lead, ſettinge the ſame vpright, and alſo bound about with three iron chaines ; vſe ſingers of pſalmes for forty nights, and pay for ſoe many maſſes by daies ; And if I ſhall ſoe lye for three nights, on the fourth day bury my body in the ground ; But all was in vaine ; for in the two firſt nights which the pſalmes were in foundinge, the divells havinge eaſily broken the doores as lightly brake the two vtmoſt iron chaines ; And on the third night about cocke crowinge, the place ſhakinge, one with a terrible countenance and of a mighty tall ſtature, havinge broken open the cover of the cheſt commanded the dead body to ariſe, who anſweringe that ſhee could not by reaſon of the bonds, bee thou looſed quoth hee, but to thy woe ; And preſently all the barres beinge broken, hee draweth her out of the church and fetteth her vpon a blacke horſe neighinge before the doore, and ſoe went away with loud ſoundinge cries heard foure miles of ; Theis things, ſay mine authors, although very wonderfull yet are not to bee held incredible by any that read the fourth booke of Gregories dialogues, where the devills caſt out a wicked man buried in the church.

Thus theis two old authors and ſome others : Every mans beleife is left to him ſelfe, and I knowe what my ſelfe thinketh therof and of the like : but, Hæc erat in toto notiſſima fabula mundo ; bee it a lye or a trueth it was generally beleived.

Learned

Berkeley

Learned Campden in his Britañia hath thus ; **Berkeley** is famous for a most stronge Castle ; A Maior who is the head magistrate, and especially for the lords thereof discended from Robert fitz Harding, to whom kinge Henry the second gave this place and Berkeley herneffe ; Out of this house are branched many knights and gent of signall note ; And in the raigne of kinge Henry the seaventh flourished William lord Berkeley who was honoured by kinge Edward the fourth with the stile of Viscont Berkeley, by kinge Richard the third with the honor of Earle of Nottingham, (in regard of his mother daughter of Thomas Mowbray Duke of Norfolke and Earle of Nottingham,) and by kinge Henry the seventh with the office of Marshall of England and dignity of Marques Berkeley ; But for that hee dyed iffueleffe, theis his titles dyed togeather with him.

Campden of Berkeley.

¶ If you bee willinge (faith Campden in the fame place) to knowe by what a crafty fetch Goodwin Earle of Kent, a man most deepely pregnant in devifinge howe to doe iniury, got the poffeffion of this place, you may read a fewe lynes out of Walter Mapeus who flourifhed 430. yeares agone, and worth the readinge, beleeve mee, they are. Thus Campden. To which words before by mee mentioned in fol : 2. et 3. I referre my reader. |

Mape in bibliotheca Oxoñ.

Venerable Trevifa, fomtimes Vicar of this Church of Berkeley, in his polichronicon. lib : 2. ca : 1. fol : 58. tells, that in the time of kinge Edward the third (what time hee writt) fome in Ireland had but one bone, all whole in one fide in ftead of all his ribbs, as was to him affirmed ; But that Thomas Heyward (then of Berkeley) had in the mould of his head, poll and forehead, but one bone, all whole, which hee knoweth : and therfore (faith hee) might well fuffer great ftroakes above on his head without hurt.

90

The Name of this Towne I conceive to bee compounded of two Saxon words : vz, Berk, which is Birch : And lei, which fomtimes is place, and fomtimes water : And fo from the place of birch trees, (wherof the great old outworne ftumps of many of that kinde, heere only found, are yet remaininge ;) Or, from lei which is water, a fcituañon moft agreeable to the name, for three fourth parts in the groves of thofe trees compaffed with water ; wherto I enclyne, becaufe all the neighbouringe townes of that terminañon, as Nybley, Bradley, Cowley, Durfley, Vley, Wortley, Alderley, Hillefley, Stanley, and others, have rivers great or fmall either runninge through or clofe by them, or both.

Name.

The

The old booke of Knights fees in the Exchequer taken by Inquisicon before Richard de Rowell and his fellowes, faith, Thomas de Berkeley holds the Burrowe of Berkeley of the kinge in Capite: And that the Abbot of S.t Auguftines by Briftoll holds the fixt part of the faid towne of the faid Thomas in franke Almes, And hee in Capite.

And the booke called Domina villarum in the same Court, taken also by Inquisicon in 9. E. 2. faith, That in the hundred of Berkeley are two burrow townes, vz, Berkeley wherof Thomas de Berkeley is lord; And Durfeley wherof John the fonne of Will'm Berkeley is lord.

ffreeholds within this burrowe or Market towne of Berkeley.

In this towne are fundry freehold lands the inheritance of feverall men, as followeth; wherof in the high-ftreet, is a meffuage with an orchard and garden called the Hall, and divers other burgage houfes and lands in this towne, Alkington, and Hineton tithings, fomtimes the lands of Robert Pointz, and after of Phillip Waterton of Waterton in Wales; To whom Thomas lord Berkeley the fourth of that name, firft in 1. H. 4. gave the fame for his life, and after in 1. H. 5. gave the fame to him in taile; And after of Thomas Berkeley Efquire yongeft fonne of James lord Berkeley, which Thomas by Margaret his wife daughter and heire of Richard Guy of Mynfterworth, heire in tayle to the faid Phillip Waterton, had iffue John Berkeley and fix other fonnes and daughters, of whom are difcended the Berkelies of Worceftershire, Shropfhire, and other places; which lands the faid Thomas and Margaret by their Deed in 20. E. 4. fetled vpon the faid John their eldeft fonne in tayle, with div's remainders over; And after, the faid Thomas dyed at Berkeley in 2. R. 3. buried in the chancell of that church as his marble tombeftone theweth; The faid John Berkeley died in 28. H. 8. leavinge iffue John and Thomas, which John fonne of John dyed in his yonger yeares without iffue in 31. H. 8. wherby theis lands difcended to the faid Thomas his brother and heire, which Thomas Berkeley by his deed dated 1. Dec. 4. et 5. Ph: & Mar: aliened a meffuage with the appurtenants in Berkeley to Thomas Atwood of Hinton and his heires, called Brewarne houfe in highftreet, next the land of the heires of Richard Berkeley on the north part, which is nowe the inheritance of

And the faid Thomas Berkeley afterwards by his other deeds in 6. et 7. Eliz: fold his lands in Hinton to Anthony Hurne, father of John and Anthony, wherof read

more

Berkeleis lands als Watertons.

91

more in Hinton. fol: 231. And dyed at Berkeley in 20. Eliz: leavinge iffue Jone and ffrances: Jone was firft maryed to Morgan Griffith of Berkeley, to whom the faid Thomas Berkeley about the time of their marriage in 14. Eliz: conveyed part of his lands in Berkeley, and one clofe containinge about three acres in the place called the further Actrees, to hold to them in fpeciall tayle, the remainder in fee to Jone: And in Eafter terme aº 14. Eliz. pit, levied a fine therof: which Morgan and Jone had iffue one fonne and two daughters, of whom is iffue: After the death of Morgan, the faid Jone was remaryed to Richard Oldland of Berkeley, by whom alfo fhee had iffue. And the faid ffrances Berkeley fifter of the faid Jone was maryed to John Smyth of Midleton, in Hinton, and had iffue John Smyth that yet liveth and 8. other fonnes and daughters: The pofterities of which Jone and ffrances have fo fcattered theis lands by their feverall fales, That very little if any remaineth in difcent at this day: And wheras the meffuages and lands in this burrowe or market towne were (amongft other fervices) holden by the cheefe rent of 22ˢ the fame is at this day paid by theis owners of feverall parts therof. viz', Edward Huntley paies —11ˢ James Baily—3ˢ Robert Atkins,—20ᵈ Richard Laverance—20ᵈ Wiłłm Harvey—20ᵈ for one Tenement, And 12ᵈ for another: And fome others purchafors hold other parts, who pay no part of the faid rent, | as   , But whether the fame bee holden by knight fervice, or in Soccage, I certainly know not. See the Court rolls of Berkeley— 31 H. 8. And

Alfo in this market towne is an ancient Inne or wine Taverne, the figne of the Ivy bufh only, now in the tenure of Charles Jaye gen̄, which havinge byn my rendevous for 48. yeares or more, I may not without ingratitude to the Bufh which fo long agone firft beckened mee thither, paffe by, and not declare that it was an ancient part of the poffeffions of the great Monaftery of Sᵗ Johns Jerufalem in England, whofe principall Houfe was in or neere the Parifh of Clerkenwell, without Smythfeild barres by London: And that by the diffolucōn of that Monaftery in the 31. H. 8. it came (with all other the Pryors poffeffions) to that kinge, who in the yeare of his raigne (amongft other things,) granted the fame to Maurice Butcher als Burchier, who was father of William father of Thomas, who maryed with ffortune the daughter of Thomas Cole, after her hufbands death remaryed to Arthur Came, by whom fhee had iffue Thomas Came that now is: Which Thomas Butcher dyinge without iffue, this Inne difcended to his fower fifters and heires, vz. Elizabeth maryed to Edward Wallington, who had iffue Wiłłm Wallington of Wotton that nowe is, (1638.) Jone maryed to Thomas Bayly of Hame, who had iffue

Berkeley Taverne.

issue Jone, maryed to William Laverance of Berkeley that nowe are: Sarah, maryed to Richard Hickes of Bevington, who had issue   Hickes: And Martha maryed to John Smyth of Painthurst, after of Berkeley, who was the eldest sister, and had issue William Smyth and others: And at this day three parts of this Taverne are the inheritance of the said William Wallington, and the 4th part of the said William Laverance, in right of his said wife. Out of which and other lands in this towne sometimes the said Burchiers, George lord Berkeley lord of this manor receiveth an yearly cheese rent of—8^s but I rather conceive that the rent is issuinge out of the other lands and noe part out of this; concerninge which rent question hath byn twice moved before mee as Steward there, yet vndetermined. |

93
Hickes land.

Also in this Burrowe towne are two messuages orchards and gardens which saith an Inquisiĉon in the Chancery in 38. H. 8. found after the death of John Hickes of Tortworth, are holden of the Castle of Berkeley by the yearly rent of five shillings fower pence and sute of Court. And of another messuage and curtelage in Berkeley holden of the Manor of Canonbury late parcell of the possessions of the Monastery of St Augustines by Bristoll, by the yearly rent of—16^d. And that John Hickes was sonne and heire of the said John, then 4. yeares old, who dyed in Eliz: leavinge issue Thomas Hicks, who dyed in 42. Eliz: leavinge issue Wiłłm Hickes then 6. yeares old, As the Inquisiĉon after his death that yeare found, doth shewe. Which William hath lately sold theis messuages and lands by severall Conveyances to Charles Jaye gen̄, and to George Carpenter, and their heires: And the first menĉoned John who dyed in 38. H. 8. was sonne of Richard sonne of John Hickes, who dyed 23. H. 7. Of which name and family see more in Bevington in Hame fol: [103]

Berkeley church.

Concerninge the Church of Berkeley and the Presentaĉons to the vicarage therof, and of presentaĉons in divers kings times to the Chantryes in that Church, at the Alters of our lady St Mary the Virgin, and of St Andrewe, and of St Maurice: And to the Chantry in Newport: and to the Chantry at the Alter of our blessed Lady in the Chaple of Stone founded by John Sergeant. And the manner of payment of Peter pence in this parish of Berkeley, more is to bee read in the Registers office with the Bishop of Worcester, but not much inlarginge nor any thinge differinge from what is before written. Only I will somwhat more fully then before heere shewe, That kinge H. 8. by his tres patents dated 18. Novembr: 34. regni sui, granted (inter alia) Decano et Capitulo ecclix̄ cathedralis s̄ce et individue Trinitatis Bristoll, Omnes illas rectorias, capellas, et ecclesias de Berkeley Herons, &c.

Ac

Ac omnia maneria, meſs, terras, decimas, &c. in Wike, Stone, Bevington, Bradſton, Canbury, als Canonbury, Oldminſter, Hame, Hill, Berkeley Herons, et Wapley in Coin Glouč. Hēnđ ſibi et corū ſucceſſoribus. &c. Tenenđ de nobis heređ et ſucceſſoribus n̄ris in purā et ppetuā eleemoſynā, Reddendo p Anñ ad feſtū Sc̄i Michis in Scc̄io pro oībus in tris pateñ contentis—85ˡⁱ 10ˢ, William Snowe then the firſt Deane And then had a large rentall of each pticuler contained in the tres patents delivered to them. All which I had the advantage, to take theis notes out of, as they were given in Evidence at Lent Aſſiſes Anno 14. Regis Caroli in this county, before Judge Jones, then holden at Cirenceſter, betweene Doctor Chetwinde then Dean, Vicar of Berkeley, plē, and Edward ffuſt Eſq, lord of Hill, | and Davis, clerke, Defᵗˢ, wherin the queſtions were Whether the ſaid townſhip of Hill was within the pariſh of Berkeley or not, And whether the Church of Hill was a Donative, appertaininge to the ſaid Edward ffuſt to preſent, or as parcell of the Vicarage of Berkeley, and the ſmall tithes there belonginge therto: Which paſſed againſt the ſaid Doctor Chetwind the plt ; but vniuſtly, as I and others then conceived : And not vnlikely therefore to come about heereafter, if Doctor Chetwind live a yeare about, which in his owne opinion hee is not like to doe. |

Beverſtone.

Beverſtone: In the booke of Domeſdei written Beureſtane ; A name derived (as may bee conceived,) from the great blewe ſtones wherwith the place aboundeth more then in any other townſhip or place of this hundred or County : wherin the Conqueror and before him kinge Edward the Conſeſſor had in Demeſne ten hides of land, as that booke ſheweth :

This townſhip beinge a member and parcell of the great manor of Berkeley, was by kinge Henry the ſecond, (as formerly I have written in Berkeley fol : 78,) given amongſt many other inferior Manors to Robert the ſonne of Hardinge and his heires, when alſo by that grant hee firſt created him a Baron and peere of the Realme, to hold by knight ſervice in Capite, as the tenure is to this day ; Which lord Robert not longe after conveyed this Beverſton (and Weſton als Kingſweſton with Elberton, as is afterwards mentioned,) to Robert his third ſonne and his heires, com̄only in old Deeds written Robertus filius Roberti filij Hardingi, And Robertus Dn̄s de Were, becauſe his habitac̄on was vſually at Were in the County of Som̄ſet;

By

By whofe death in the time of kinge John this manor difcended to Maurice de Gant his fonne and heire, By whofe death without iffue in 14. H. 3. the fame difcended to Robert de Gurnay, fonne and heire of Eve, fifter of him the faid Maurice de Gant; who dyinge in 53. H. 3. the fame difcended to Anfelme de Gurnay his fonne and heire, who dyed in 14. E. 1. levinge iffue John de Gurnay,[1] which John dyed within 5. yeares after his father in 19. E. 1. leavinge his manor and all other his poffeffions to difcend vpon the faid Elizabeth his daughter and heire; who was maryed to Sir John ap Adam who dyed in 5. E. 2. leavinge iffue by his faid wife Sir Thomas ap Adam; who by fine and other affurances in the 4. E. 3. fold this manor (amongft others) to Thomas then lord Berkeley called Thomas the third, and his heires, wherby after 170. yeares continuance in the iffue of this third fonne of the faid lord Robert the fonne of Hardinge, it came againe into the poffeffion of the heire of the faid lord Robert at the comon lawe. Not longe after, the fame lord Thomas Berkeley in 28. E. 3. by a fine then levyed and by other affurances entailed the fame vpon himfelfe and Katherine then his fecond wife, and the heires males which hee fhould beget on the body of the faid Katherine, The remainder to his right heires; who had iffue betweene them Sir John Berkeley knight, who by Elizabeth his wife daughter and heire of Sir John Bettifhorne, had iffue Sir Maurice Berkeley knight; The faid Thomas lord Berkeley dyed feifed of this manor (and Caftle therin much by him reedifyed,) in 35. E. 3. And the faid Katherine him furvivinge held the fame till her death in 9. R. 2. whervpon the fame came to Sir John Berkeley aforefaid, and the heires males of his body, by force of the faid entaile; By whofe death in 6. H. 6. the fame came to the faid Sir Maurice his fonne and heire, who died in 38. H. 6. leavinge iffue by Lora his wife daughter of Henry lord ffitz hugh, Sir Maurice and Sir Edward; The faid Sir Maurice fonne of Maurice, died in 14. E. 4. And by Anne his wife daughter of Reginald Weft lord de la ware, left iffue Sir Willm Berkeley knight and Katherine; Which Sir Willm dyed in the firft yeare of kinge H. 7. without iffue male; wherby this manor of Beverfton, with the Caftle (a part therof,) by vertue of the faid entaile of 28. E. 3. came to the faid Sir Edward, vncle of this Sir William; which Sir Edward dyed in 21. H. 7. leavinge iffue male by Alice his fecond wife, three fonnes, Thomas, Maurice, and William: The faid Thomas by Elizabeth his wife daughter of George Nevill lord Abergavenny, had iffue John Berkeley and fower daughters, and dyed in 15. H. 7. in the life of his father: Which John dyed the kings

---

[1] The ftatement made, Ante Vol. I. p. 53, that John de Gurnay, fon and heir of Anfelm, who was 20 years old on the death of his father, married a certain Oliva, leaving Elizabeth his only daughter and heir, is here omitted. [ED.]

kings ward, without issue male: Maurice Second brother of the said Thomas, dyed in 5. H. 8. before his nephewe John, without issue: William the third sonne of the said Sir Edward was also a knight, and by Margaret his wife daughter of William Pawlett Marques of Winchester, had issue Sir John Berkeley, and dyed in 5. E. 6. And the said Sir John Berkeley who dyed in 24. Eliz. left issue John Berkeley; who after in 39. Eliz: aliened the said Manor and Castle to Sir John Pointz knight, whose sister[1] ffrances hee had maryed, and by whome hee hath issue: Till which time this manor had continued and gone with the heires males as aforesaid without any alienacōn or discontinuance; The owners wherof were distinguished from all others of their name by beinge called Berkeleis of Beverston. It was not longe after the purchase soe made by Sir John Pointz before hee againe sold it to Henry ffleetwood of Graies Inne: And hee shortly after sold the same to Sir Thomas Earsffield, and hee againe to Henry ffleetwood; And from him it came to Sir Michael Hickes. And by his death in [1612] to his sonne Sir William Hickes Baronet, nowe owner therof Anno, 1639.

In this village standeth an ancient castle called Beverston Castle, which doubtles is a pile of as ancient buildinge as any is at this day standinge in this hundred; many yeares yea many ages more ancient then that of Berkeley, which is still kept in good repaire And oftentimes the dwellinge house of the lord therof: ffrom this Castle it was, as all histories of that time and since treatinge of, That that famous Earle Goodwyn earle of Kent (formerly mentioned in the description of Berkeley,) set forth with his army, what time hee made shewe | (if peace by moderation had not followed) to have given battell to kinge Edward the Confessor, who had likewise with an army drawne himselfe to Gloucester for the same purpose; the cause of the quarrell I leave to the relation of our English comōn Chronicles; Which castle and townshipp I conceive to have lately before come to the hands of the said Earle by the suppression of the monastery of the Nunnes at Berkeley, as also forīily is there mentioned.

Castle of Beverston.

The Records of Rot. claus. 11. H. 3. membr. 14. and of Rot. pateñ. 13. H. 3. declare how Maurice de Gant aforesaid was questioned for buildinge (or rather repairinge) his castle of Beverstone without the kings licence, and also fortifyinge of it; who confesseth and submitteth, And in the second yeare after hath the kings writt directed to the Sheriffe of this county That the castle which hee had built at his manor of Beverston should for ever remaine to him and his heires, and then it was, turrited; (the latin word is firmatum;) whose death followed the next yeare after

---

[1] For *Sister*, read *Aunt*. [ED.]

after, as is aforesaid. ffrom whom by his heires at comon lawe, it came after divers difcents with the manor (inter alia) to Sir Thomas ap Adam who in 4. E. 3. fold the fame to Thomas lord Berkeley and his heires, who in the next fix yeares much repaired and beautified the fame, with the parke adioyninge, as formerly is touched, as by divers Accompts of the Reeves of that manor in the caftle of Berkeley appeares.

Church

The Church of Beverfton is a mother Church with the Chapple of Kingefcote therto belonginge, And was with the other Churches of Berkeley Herneffe given by Robert the fonne of Hardinge to the Monaftery of St Auguftines by briftoll, as before is written. fol: 81, 82. But by what meanes in fhort time after it came to the family of the Gurnays aforefaid lords of this manor of Beverfton, I have not found; But the faid Anfelme de Gurnay, the yeare of his death in 14. E. 1. gave this Church of Beverftane to the Abbot of St Peters of Glouc. and his Covent and their fucceffors: ffor confirmacōn wherof John de Gurnay fonne and heire of the faid Anfelme (after fome quarrellinge,) levies a fine therof and of five fhillings rent of land, to the faid Abbot and Covent, vpon a licence obtained from the kinge to alien in mortmaine; ffor which fee thefe records. vz—Inq: 14. E. 1. poft mortē Anfelmi de Gurnay. Rot. patēn. 14. E. 1. membr. 17. in arce London. Plita et Jurat apud Glocefter. 15. E. 1. Rot. 29. in dorfo. in recepta Scaccarij.

In 4. E. 1. before the Juftices itinerant then fittinge at Glouc, it was by the Jury (amongft other things) prefented, That Maurice then lord Berkeley claymed to have returne of writts throughout his hundred of Berkeley, The ratinge of the Affize of bread and Ale, Gallowes for execucōn of theeves, and the like; And that hee had diftrayned Anfelme de Gurnay afwell in the Kings highwaies as without, in his manors of Beverfton, Ailberton, and Kingfwefton, which are holden of the kinge in Capite by knight fervice, becaufe hee would not take his meafures of Affife from his ftanderd, wheras hee ought to receive them from the kings marfhall, As by Rot. Ragemañ in 4. E. 1. in Recepta fcaccarij appeareth. But why the faid lord Maurice fhould clayme to have **Returna brevium et executiones eorundem** within this hundred, which was not granted to any his progenitors vntill to his great grandchilde Thomas lord Berkeley in 4. E. 3, as before is faid, I have not found, vnles you can picke it out of the firft charter made by kinge H. 2. to Robert fonne of Hardinge. fol: 81. 82. 86. 87.

100

Market

In 21. E. 1. that kinge granted to John ap Adam and Elizabeth his wife and to their heires, to have within their manor of Beyerftane A market on Munday weekely,

weekely, And a faire for three daies on the vigill day and morrowe of the affump-   Faire
tion of our lady : And to have free warren in all their demefne lands there. Dated   Free warren
10. Junij. a° ƥct. As by Rot. Cartarum in 21. E. 1. membr. 3. appeares ; where this
towne is written Berucſtan.

 Belonginge to this ancient Caſtle was a Coneſtabulary or the office of a
Coneſtable belonginge : And by a Deed dated 28. Julij. 4. E. 3. Robert Praterd
then Coneſtable releaſed to Thomas lord Berkeley Totum jus et clameum de et in
officio Coneſtabulariæ caſtri de Beverſtan, &c. which hee held for terme of his life
by the grant of Sir Thomas ap Adam. And this was imediately after the faid
lords purchaſe, And perhaps a part of the agreement with the faid Sir Thomas ap
Adam vpon his ſale therof, for the lord Berkeley to ſettle in that office one of his
owne ſervants of whoſe fidelity hee might be more aſſured.

 To the Leet or lawday holden yearly at Berkeley for the hundred of Berkeley
at Michas and Eaſter, amongſt the Tithingmen and Coneſtables of . 28. townſhips
which there perſonally appeare, cometh the Conſtable of this townſhip of Beverſton
alone, without any other inhabitant with him, choſen and ſworne at the Leet of that
townſhip, where they have a Leet amongſt themſelves ; And vpon his apparance at
the barre in the court houſe called the guild hall before the Steward and grand
Jury acknowledgeth the ſoveraignty of that Court and Leete, And faith That | with   101
them Omnia benè, That all things with them in their Leet at Beverſton, are well :
wiſheth proſperity to the lord of the Leete of that hundred, and ſoe departeth, beinge neither ſworne nor preſenteth any things preſentable in a Leete. And for
negleƈt of this ſervice or rather of the ſonnes duty and acknowledgemᵗ to his father
for his liberality in giveinge the Caſtle manor and Leet to his ſonne, as before is ſet
downe, I have impoſed a fine of ten ſhillings and more ; And twice or thrice, ſince
I was Steward of the Hundred Leet cauſed the ſame to bee levyed by diſtres :
Howbeit I have heard ſome of thoſe coneſtables affirme That that ſervice, as they
have heard, ought to bee done by the Coneſtable of the Caſtle, and not of their
townſhip of Beverſton, as willinge perhaps to eaſe themſelves of a Journey of 9. or
10. myles.

 A record in Hill: terme. 5. H. 4. Rot. 3. in the Exchequer in the office of the
Remembrancer to the lord Treſorer, doth ſhewe That Sir John Berkeley knight,
ſonne and heire in tayle to that entayle before mentioned created by Thomas lord
Berkeley father of him the ſaid Sir John in the 28. E. 3. was drawne into that
                                      Court

Court to shewe by how many knights fees he held of the kinge his manor of Beverston in Capite, vpon a demand which the kinge made of him for Ayde towards the marriage of Blanch his eldest daughter; Who thervpon pleaded to the kinge, That hee held his said Manor of Beverston in the hundred of Berkeley imediately of Thomas lord Berkeley, by the third part of one knights fee, And not of the kinge; Which vpon that issue was by a Jury found for him against the kinge, And to bee of the said lord Berkeley as hee had pleaded, whervpon he had Judgm! and was dismissed.

And to strengthen the said record in point of tenure might also bee produced the office in 6. H. 6. after the death of the said Sir John Berkeley; And also the office in 38. H. 6. after the death of Sir Maurice Berkeley; And also the office in 14. E. 4. after the death of another Sir Maurice Berkeley; And also the office in 2. H. 7. after the death of Sir William Berkeley; wherin the originall estate taile to the heires males in 28. E. 3. is pleaded and found (wherby the daughter and heire of the said Sir William was put by, but how iustly, in regard of a Comon recovery suffered of his manor in Easter Terme 18. H. 6. Rot. 312. in the Comon pleas I may not determine:) As also might some others bee produced to avoid a tenure of the kinge by knight service in Capite: But when I looke on the other side I see an army of Records and proofes provinge the kings tenure, which seeme vnanswerable; As a booke of knights fees in the Exchequer temp: H. 3. and E. 1. And the Escuage roll in the tower of London in 5. E. 1. And the office 28. H. 3. after the death of Thomas lord | Berkeley: And the plea in the Exchequer of the said Thomas lord Berkeley, himselfe the Conusor: And the two pleas in the Exchequer in Michas Terme, 7. H. 7. Rot. 34. And in Easter terme 16. H. 7. rot: 9. confessed to bee in Capite by the lords themselves, And more then 40. more the like to this day; I doe conclude, that the tenure of this Manor is of the Crowne by knight service in Capite.

By an Inq: 6. H. 6. John Berkeley knight dyed seized of the Castle and Manor of Beverson, with the Advowson of the parish church of Cernecote in the county of Wiltes, belonginge to the said Castle and Manor.

Fifteene

In payment of ffifteene or tenth, or kinge silver, when it is granted in parliament, the Onus or charge in the Exchequer is—5^{li} 2^s 9^d The deduction is—50^s The remainder paid into the Exchequer by the Collector is—52^s 9^d Of which payment read more in fol: 4. 5. 37.

In

Bevington

In the laſt Subſedy in aº 5ᵗº Rᵗ Caroli were 7. ſubſedy men in the townſhip, who paid—40ˢ.   *Subſedy*

Of able men for the warres betweene 20. and 60. yeares old were in aº 6ᵗº Jacobi which at a general muſter then appeared—41.   *Able men.*

And now of trayned Souldiers vnder Edward Stephens Eſqʳ their Captaine, are—   *Soldiers.*

And if the wholl diviſion of Berkeley accounted a 4ᵗʰ part of the county, called Berkeley Diviſion, bee rated in any tax or payment to pay—100ˡⁱ to Kinge or Comon wealth. Then this hundred of Berkeley paies therof—33ˡⁱ 3ˢ. And the townſhip of Beverſton—15ˢ.

Bevington.

Bevington: vſually pronounced Bamton: Is an hamblet of   houſes within the pariſh of Berkeley, parcell of the manor or lordſhip of Hame, the inheritance of George lord Berkeley, holden by knight ſervice in Capite.

ffor certaine parcells of land in this hamblet wherof one was called Grombals hay, was a ſute in 40. Eliz. betweene one Phelps leſſee to John Harvy of Bradſton, and one Danfeild, tenant at will to Huntley a copiholder for life vnder the lord Berkeley, which was tried at the Aſſiſes at Glouc̃, 9. mcij, aº 40. Eliz. pd. As formerly had another tryall beene in 31. Eliz. pd. And after another ſute by Engliſh bill before the Preſident and Counſell in the Marches of Wales, from whence the lord Berkeleys tenant was diſmiſſed with coſts, which John Harvy paid; ffor more wherof ſee the Records of Michas terme 31. & 32. Eliz. Rot. 524. And of Hill: terme, 39. Eliz. in Banco.

In this hamblet John Mallet holdeth in fee by ſeverall purchaſes of late made A meſſuage with a yard land therto belonging comonly called Hickes land, which was late the land of Richard Hickes, who dyed in—12. Jacobi, ſecond ſonne of Richard Hickes who dyed 10. Eliz., ſonne of John Hicks who died at Wickwarre in 38. H. 8., ſonne of Richard Hickes who died   H. 8., ſonne of John Hickes, who   *Hickes land now Malletts.*

who dyed in 23. H. 7.; holden of George lord Berkeley as of his manor of Hame by fute to his hundred court of Berkeley from 3. weekes to 3. weekes, the yearly rent of—23ˢ And by

Of which lands fee in two Inq: the one in 38. H. 8. after the death of John Hickes, and the other in 12. Jac. after the death of Richard Hickes. Of which name of Hickes fee alfo in Berkeley fol: 93. To which Richard William Hickes was fonne and heire, who fold part of this land to Maurice Mallet, By whofe death in 19. Jac. it difcended to Thomas Mallet his fonne, by whofe death that yeare without iffue, it difcended to the faid John Mallet beinge his vncle and heire; vide Co: roll of Hame. 19. Jac. And by the death of the faid John Mallet to Alice his daughter and heire marryed to Walter Kirle Efq,.

Hurnes land.

Deere alfo is a meffuage and halfe a yard land therto belonginge the inheritance of Mary and Elizabeth the two daughters and Coheires of Thomas Hurne, who dyed in Aᵒ 4ᵒ Regis Caroli; fonne of John Hurne who died in 44. Eliz., fonne of Wiłłm Hurne who died 3 & 4. Ph: & Mar̃, fonne of Richard Hurne; holden of George lord Berkeley as of his manor of Hame by fute of | Court from 3. weekes to 3. weekes, the yearly rent of—10ˢ and by knight fervice: And alfo of a parcell of land adioyninge holden by like fervice and the yearly rent of—5ˢ All which have for diūs generations byn occupied togeather; ffor which meffuage and premiffes the faid Mary and Elizabeth are now in Ward to the faid lord Berkeley, As alfo was the faid Thomas Hurne to Henry lord Berkeley grandfather to the faid George: By the death of which Thomas Hurne without iffue male faileth the name of Hurne, which had continued in a lineall difcent, fince the firſt and originall grants made of the premifes by two deeds, to William the fonne of Robert of Bevington and his heires, about 10. H. 3. by Thomas lord Berkeley the firſt of that name, and which was after in the fame kings time confirmed by Maurice lord Berkeley fonne and heire of the faid Thomas, To hold as aforefaid: Who tooke that firname of Hurne from the little thicket or grove of thornes fmall fhrubs or the like called an Hurne, adioyninge: As others in Hinton and other places in this hundred have done; wherof more may bee read in an Inq: found in 44. Eliz. after the death of the faid John Hurne: And in a parchment booke fol: 6. et 28. containinge fuch wardfhips as have fallen to the faid lord George or his Anceſtors in theis laſt hundred yeares.

Withers land: Abbot of Kingfwoods: now Edward Ifuſts.

It appeares vpon a Writ called Ad quod damnum, and vpon the Inquifiĉõn thervpon taken (remaininge in the tower of London) in 2. E. 2. nᵒ 112., And by the

the Deeds that followed thervpon, And by a fine in Trinity terme A⁰ 3. E. 2. in Berkeley caſtle ; That Robert Wither aliened to the Abbot and Covent of Kingſ-wood and to their ſucceſſors A meſſuage and yard land, and alſo 29. acres of land, and 13ˢ 6ᵈ yearly rent, in Hull, Berkeley, Pockhampton in (Hinton,) and Bevington; And that the ſaid meſſuage and yard land in Hulle are holden of Nicholas the ſonne of Raphe (lord of the Manor of Hull) by 2ᵈ yearly rent ; which Nicholas holds the Manor of Hulle by knights ſervice in Capite of the Kinge, by halfe a knights fee, in which manor the ſaid meſſuage and yard land doe lye : And that 3. acres, parcell of the 29. acres, and the tenements wherout the 13ˢ 6ᵈ is goeinge in Bevington, Berkeley, and Pockhampton, are holden of Thomas lord Berkeley by 1ᵈ yearly rent, which hee holds over of the kinge in Capite, with other lands, **per Baroniam.** And that ſtill remaines to the ſaid Robert Wither a Meſſuage and 8. oxgangs of land, (8. bovatas terræ,) in Bevington, wherof hee hath the fee ſimple, holden of the ſaid Thomas lord Berkeley in Capite, by the rent of a Roſe. Which meſſuage and 8. bovatas terræ laſt mentioned, I conceive to bee nowe the inheritance of Edward ffuſt Eſq, and in the tenure of Richard Archer, leſſee to Mʳ ffuſt. | This was ſomtimes in the occupaćōn of William Tilladam ſonne of William, by leaſe, aſwell as the farme of Bliſbury. fol: 106 | 105

Blisbury. 106

Blisbury als Blisberrie : A farme houſe within the hamblet of Bevington, in the pariſh of Berkeley, the inheritance of William Baſſet Eſq, contayninge about 100. acres, holden of the Crowne by knight ſervice in Capite, ſomtime parcell of the poſſeſſions of the Abby of Kingſwood neere Wotton Vnderedge ; which com̄-inge to the Crowne by the diſſolućōn of that Monaſtery in the 31ᵗʰ of kinge H. 8. was granted in

This was of late the freehold of Wiłłm Tilladam, ſonne of Wiłłm for his life. |

Bradley. 107

Bradley, als Bradleigh : In an hamblet within the tithinge of Synwell in the pariſh of Wotton Vnderedge, and parcell of the ſervices of the Manor of Wotton
 fforren,

P 2

fforren, holden of that Manor by knights fervice and fute of Court to that manor, and to the hundred Court of Berkeley from three weekes to three weekes ; Or rather, as many records doe fpeake, held of the manor of Berkeley by knight fervice, and fute to that hundred Court as aforefaid.

It was of it felfe a manor at leaft in reputacōn, and extendeth it felfe into the villages adioyninge, of Bradley, Nybley, Synwell, Swyney, Woodford, Combe, and Wotton towne, vntill by pticuler fales of the parts therof in 3. 4. 5. 6. et 7th yeares of the raigne of kinge James it was deftroied, as after perticulerly followeth.

The principall and moft remarkeable houfe ; efteemed as the Seite or Capitall meffuage with a Carucate of land and 50^s rent of tenants that held for lives of this manor, was in the times of kinge R. 1. and of kinge John his brother the lands of Hugo de Bradeleia and of William his brother ; And after of
who left iffue Alienora his daughter and heire maried to Thomas de Luida, or de Lude, who aliened as after followeth to Thomas lord Berkeley the fecond of that name and his heires, as after followeth.

S^t. Auguftines land. modo Decō. et Capit͠ Briftoll.

IN this hamblet of Bradley the Abbot and Covent of the monaftery of St Auguftines by Briftoll had an ancient meffuage with divers lands therto belonginge, by feverall guifts and purchafes by them made and to them given at feverall times, as after followeth : which at laft came to bee called Canon-Court efteemed by them as the feite of a manor, longe time held by Copy of Court roll by the family and name of the Dangervills their tenants for many generations at the old yearly rent of—lxvj^s viij^d granted at their Manor houfe in Berkeley called Canon bury, whither thefe tenants did their futes : which by the diffolucōn of that monaftery in 31. H. 8. cominge to kinge H. 8. hee erected the fame into a Cathedrall church in the 34th of his raigne, And as part of the poffeffions of the Deane and Chapter there, gave this meffuage and lands (amongft others) to them and their fucceffors: And is nowe in leafe to Mr Willm Leigh an Atturney of the kings bench, whofe father John Leigh of late yeares bought the eftate for lives which the Dangervils then had therin ; And fince have twice renewed the fame with the Deane and Chapiter aforefaid : An houfe of late new built and much reedified by the faid Willm Leigh : And this meffuage before of old was the land of John de Bradeleia fonne and heire of Reginald Buchard ; | And in the time of H. 3. given to this Monaftery of St Auguftines by Thomas lord Berkeley and Jone his widowe.

To

Bradley

To this messuage and land (now the said Deane and Chapters,) is an ancient Deed without date to bee referred, wherby Willm de Braglega confirmed to the Abbot and Covent aforesaid the grant which Reginald de Camma made to them of halfe a yard land in Wotton, which Juliana de Berkeley gave to the said Reginald; which land also Hugh de Bradley brother of him the said Willm, sold to the said Julian for 7. markes and an horse. Redd. 1. libr̃ cumini for all services, salvo regali servicio, &c.

As also in one other Deed dated 1273. a⁰ 1. E. 1. wherby John sonne of Reginald de Ssaftebury gave to the said Abbot and Covent, Totam terram suam de Bradeleia illam scilt quod tenuit de Johanna de Berkeley apud Bradley extra Wotton, et totam terram suam de Wotton, quam pater eius de dictis Abbate et conventu tenuit in villa de Wotton.

But the 4. Deeds and fyne followinge are to bee referred to the manor of Bradley, aliened to divers freeholders, as followeth, the tenure whereof is formerly said to bee by knight service; One, without date wherby **Domina Johanna de Berkeley** relicta quondam Dñi Thomæ de Berkelee, gave to William Berkeley her sonne and to the heires of his body, All the land which shee bought of Ralph de Wiplet in Bradley in the manor of Wotton, vizt, one Messuage and one yard land which Adam de Bradley somtimes held, And also 7. acres of land which Thomas de Jacelyne holds in the said Manor of Wittune. Rendringe to the cheife lord—18^d yearly, and regale servicium: And to her, tres clavos cariophit ad natale dni. Agreeinge to this is the Inquisic̃on 33. E. 1. n⁰ 242. pro Thoma de Luida et Alienora vxor[e] eius.

2. An other deed dated [die] Jovis post festũ conũnionis s̃cti Pauli. a⁰ 18. E. 1. wherby Amicia le Ercedekene, somtime the wife dni Odonis le Ercedekene, in her widowhood, granted and released All her right in toto tenemento et terra in sicco et humido apud le Hame infra manerium de Wotton iuxta Abbathiam de Kingswood in coñ Glouc̃, to Thomas de Luida and his heires, To hold of the cheife lord of the ffee by the services due and accustomed.

3. An other deed without date wherby Maurice of Came sonne of William de Berkeley knight, granted all his lands in Bradley which hee had from the said William his father vnto Odo le Archidiakedeno and his heires.

                          4. Another

4. Another Deed in 18. E. 1. wherby Amicia fomtime the wife of Odo le Ercedekene reciteth That whereas Jone lady Berkeley deceafed enfeoffed Sir Wiłłm de Berkeley her fonne and the heires of his body of certaine lands called la hame and of others called Bradley, vpon condicon that if hee dyed without iffue then the faid land fhould revert to the faid lady Jone and her heires: Which Sir Wiłłm Berkeley fold the fame to John Sethvile | and his heires, who enfeoffed her the faid Amicia and her heires; which Sir William dyed without iffue of his body, wher- vpon Thomas lord Berkeley grandchild and heire to the faid lady Jone impleaded her the faid Amicia and her faid hufband for the faid land in the kings court; which dependinge, her faid hufband Odo beinge her fecond hufband, dyed; Nowe fhee the faid Amicia releafeth all her right in the faid lands to the faid Thomas lord Berkeley and his heires.

5. By a fine in the court of Comon pleas in a° 33. H. 3. Roger de Berkeley de Durfley and Conftance his wife gave a yard land in Bradley to Reginald de Jetefbury and to Ifable his wife, in frankmarriage, and to the heires of her body: Againft which fine Maurice then lord Berkeley apponit clameum fuum; As by the indorfement on the backe of that fyne appeares.

The forefaid Thomas lord Berkeley beinge afwell by his purchafe from the faid Thomas de Luida and Alienor his wife as otherwife feized in fee of theis Bradley lands (foe to call them,) dieth in 14. E. 2. wherby the fame difcended to the lord Maurice his fonne and heire, the third lord of that name; who beinge foe feized, (or others rather in truft to his vfe,) The fame by his direction were (as by divers deeds with Richard Berkeley Efq, late of Stoke Gifford, and in the Caftle of Berke- ley, appeares,) conveyed to Maurice Berkeley knight fecond fonne of the faid lord Maurice, and to the heires males of his body, leavinge the revertion in himfelfe; Which Maurice the fonne dyed in 21. E. 3. at the feidge of Calais, After whofe death, in the fame yeare, the tenure of his manor of Bradley was by Inquificon found to bee holden of Thomas lord Berkeley eldeft fonne of the faid lord Maurice by the fervice of one rofe for all fervices, And that Thomas was fonne and heire of the faid Sir Maurice, then 13. yeares old and in ward to the kinge for other lands holden by knight fervice in Capite; By the death of which Thomas Berkeley in 35. E. 3. then a knight alfo, this Manor difcended to Sir Maurice Berkeley knight fonne and heire of the faid Sir Thomas; By whofe death in 2. H. 4. the fame came to Sir Maurice Berkeley his fonne, who was borne after the death of his father; And by his death in 4. E. 4. it difcended to Sir William Berkeley his fonne, Which
Sir

Bradley

Sir William dyinge in 16. H. 7. left iffue Richard, and John ; Of both which as followeth.

1. The faid Richard dyed in 5. H. 8. levinge iffue Sir John, who dyed in 37. H. 8. leavinge iffue Sir Richard, who dyed in 2º Jacobi, levinge iffue Henry, father of Richard Berkeley that now is, who aliened as afore and after is mentioned.

2. The faid John Berkeley yonger brother of the faid Richard, fonnes of Sir Willm, dyed in the life of his father, leavinge iffue James Berkeley called of Bradley, becaufe this manor of Bradley was by the faid Sir Willm conveyed vpon his maryage to him the faid John ; | which faid James dyed in 38. H. 8. leavinge iffue 2. fonnes, vz, John, who dyed in 4. & 5. Ph : & Mar : without iffue, and Brice Berkeley who dyed in 21. Eliz : leavinge this manor to difcend to Elizabeth his only daughter and heire, who was firft maryed to Edward Berkeley Efquire, and fecondly to Sir Edward Berkeley knight, And thirdly to Nicholas Strangwaies Efq, yet had noe iffue by any of them ; And in the time of her laft widowhood, (havinge formerly given an eftate in remainder in taile after her owne life to the faid Richard Berkeley that nowe is, fonne of Henry,) ioyned with him in divers fales of parts of this manor to fundry perfons in 3. 4. 5. 6. et 7º. Rº Jacobi, wherby the wholl was aliened ; And is now Aº. 14. Regis Caroli, the feverall inheritances of my felfe, Chriftopher Purnell fecond fonne of Thomas ; Thomas Purnell, brother of Robert, fonnes of   Purnell ; Brice Weekes cozen and heire of Brice Weekes ; Anthony Hungerford geñ, Willm Marten, Richard Marten fonne of the faid William, John Jobbins fonne of Willm Jobbins, Richard Tindall fonne of   , John Leigh and Willm his fonne ; Thomas Peirs, late by him purchafed of   ; Henry Hayward, late by him purchafed of Patricke Dunninge ; John Nelme of Wotton fonne of Henry ; Thomas Perry the elder als Hunter : William Beale of Nibley and Edward his fonne, John, eldeft fonne of John Graile clerke, yonger fonne of Thomas Graile of Huntingford ; John Cooke, John Howe, Thomas White, Thomas Denny, Willm Streat, Willm fonne of William Bird, fonne of Peter ;   fonne of Willm Trotman, fonne of   ; And   and   , two other yonger fonnes of the faid Willm fonne of   Trotman ; And   of   fonne of James Plomer, Thomas May of Nibley ; And of Robert fonne of Edward Oldifworth eldeft fonne of Arnold Oldifworth Efq, late Clarke of the Hanaper, owner of the faid Capitall meffuage and lands called Bradleys houfe, who added to thofe buildings which Edward Berkeley Efquire firft hufband

husband of the said Elizabeth had erected in 10. Eliz: Which Arnold, (to vse a short digression,) was the sonne of Edward Oldisworth and of Tacy his wife daughter of Sir Arthur Porter, sonne of Roger and of Margaret his wife daughter of John Arthur, sonne of Richard and of Alice his wife daughter of James lord Berkeley and of the lady Isable his wife, daughter of Thomas Mowbray Duke of Norfolke.

Oldisworths land.

III

Which Arnold, (before his departure into Virginia where hee dyed much indebted,) by Deed dated 20. Julij, A° 9° Jacobi, purchased of Henry lord Berkeley to him and to Edward his sonne and heire apparant and to their heires, (makinge the same as an addition to their said capitall messuage or manor house,) one Close of six acres called Bradly mead, (with a Dovehouse vpon | the same,) And three quarters of an acre in Beckhams mead, and one other close of two acres adioyninge to his other lands, And one close of three acres called Tanners close on the backside of his stable, And three quarters of an acre called silken acre, next the former: To hold to them and their heires vnder the yearly rent of 39^s. 2^d. sute of Court twice by the yeare to the said lord Berkeleys manor of Wotton fforren, or 4^d. for every default, And—26^s. 8^d. in name of an heriott after their deathes, and of every one dyinge tenant to the premisses or of any part therof: Howbeit, the tenure of theis 5. parcells thus lastly purchased is of the kinge by knight service in Capite, beinge before this grant parcell of the said Lords manor of Wotton fforren in demesne, Which is soe holden of the kinge.

By fine in Michas terme 11. H. 4. Robert Stanshawe and Isable his wife purchased to them, and his heires of William Parker and Alice his wife, a messuage and 14. acres of land in Bradley, Wotton, and Wortley: which the said Robert the same yeare sold to Thomas lord Berkeley and his heires.

More of this manor of Bradley is to bee read out of theis Records, vizt:
ffinis in banco Ternī Michis. 20. E. 1. inter Thomā Dn̄u Berkeley q^r et Thomā de Lude et vxor̄ imped, de 1. mess et 1. carucat̄ terræ, et 50^s. r̄. in Wotton et Bradley. The deed also in Berkeley Castle.
Inq: 33. E. 1. vpon an Ad quod damnū p^t mortē Thomē de Luida. n°[204]
Inq: 15. E. 2. pro terris Mauricij Berkeley et alijs rebellis.
Inq: 21. E. 3. p^t mortem Mauricij filij Mauricij de Berkele.
Inq: 29. E. 3. p^t mortem Thome Berkeley miltis.
Pasch: Records. 44. E. 3. Rot. 8. cū Rr̄ni Thesaur̄ in Scc̄io.

Inq:

Bradston

Inq : 2. H. 4. p̃ morte Mauricij Berkeley.
Inq : 10. H. 5. p̃ morte p̃l Mauricij ; Melius Inquirend.
Inq : 4. E. 4. p̃ morte Mauricij Berkeley.
Inq : 4. Jacobi p̃ morte Nichi Strangwaies ar———p ſervie mil.
Inq : 4. et 5. Ph : & Mar : p̃ morte Johis Berkeley.
ffinis in banco termi Michis : 4. Jacobi, Inter Hale et Webb, qr̃, et Berkeley et al def.
Inq : 20. Jac : p̃ mortem Thome Purnell.—per ſervic militare.
Inq : 17. Caroli, p̃ morte Johis Smyth ar̃. authoris huius libri.—p ſerv : mit.
Inq : 15. Car̃. p̃ morte Henrici Nelme (virtute officij) in Soccagio.
Inq : 16. Car̃. p̃ morte Johis Grayle Clici.—in focagio. |

Bradston.

Bradston: Anciently written Bradeſtane, Bratheſtan, Bretheſtan, and Brodeſtane ; is an hamblet or Tithinge within the pariſh of Berkeley, wherin ſtandeth one of the eight Tythe barnes belonginge to the Rectory of that pariſh.

The name I ſuppoſe was originally taken of the great broad ſtones wherwith the ſuperficies of the earth round about the Manor houſe is covered, more then is to bee obſerved in any other part of this hundred.

It hath anciently byn at leaſt reputed a manor ; And in the time of kinge Richard the firſt was the inheritance of Bernardus de Bratheſtan ; After in the times of kinge John kinge H. 3. and of kinge . E. 1. of Andreas de Bradeſtan, of Gilbert de Bradeſtan, of John de Bradeſton, and of Robert de Bradeſton ; Which Robert held the ſame almoſt all the raigne of kinge Edward the firſt, and dyed in the fowerth yeare of kinge Edward the ſecond, leavinge the ſame to diſcend to Thomas his ſonne ; Of whom after : A ſucceſſion of remarkeable gentlemen, homagers and ſervants to the family of the lord Berkeleis of Berkeley Caſtle, as a world of deeds and other evidences, which I have ſeene doe teſtify ; though the time when or by what lord Berkeley the ſame was firſt given, I have not yet found : But (as by many records and evidences appeareth,) the ſame is holden of their Manor of Alkington by the fourth part of a knights fee, ſute to their hundred Court of Berkeley from three weekes to three weekes, and by the yearly rent of—1ᵈ

The

Q VOL. III

The said Thomas de Bradſton ſonne of Robert dyed in the 34ᵗʰ of kinge E. 3., who for his great warlike ſervices vnder that kinge was firſt made a Banneret, And after a Baron and Peere of the Realme ; And amongſt many other great guiſts from that kinge, had 500. markes by the yeare given to him and his heires out of the kings Exchequer, which his heires at comõn lawe receive to this day : ffor which ſee Rot. clauſ. 16. E. 3. in dorſo : and Rot. clauſ. 15. E. 4. membr. 11. and many others ; In honor of whoſe memory and great deſervings both towards his country and to the family of the lord Berkeleis wherin hee was bred and longe ſerved, I have ſome yeares ſince written a ſpeciall tract, in the ſecond volume of my hiſtory of that family.[1]

This noble Thomas de Bradſton by Agnes his ſecond wife had iſſue Robert de Bradſton, who dyed in the life of his father leavinge iſſue Sir Thomas de Bradſton, and John de Bradſton ; Of which John (to whom the manor of Winterborne not farre from Briſtoll was given,) more ſhall anon bee ſaid, and of his male poſterity which yet continues. But the ſaid Sir Thomas elder brother of the ſaid John by Ela his wife daughter and coheire of John de Pauely had iſſue Elizabeth his only daughter and heire ; | which Sir Thomas dyed in 48. E. 3. And Ela his wife ſurvivinge dyed in 11. H. 4. havinge byn remarried to Richard de Sancto Mauro, als Seymore, who dyed alſo before her in 2. H. 4. As by Rot. finiũ. 49. E. 3. membr. 12. And Rot. clauſ. 2. H. 4. ps. 1, mem : 8. appeares. The ſaid Elizabeth was maried to Walter de la poole who dyed 12. H. 6. And ſhee dyed   ; betweene whom was iſſue only Margaret ſole daughter and heire, maryed to Thomas the ſonne of Sir John Ingaldeſthorpe, which Thomas dyed   , And the ſaid Margaret dyed   ; betweene whom was iſſue Sir Thomas Ingaldeſthorpe knight, who dyed 35. H. 6. and by Jone his wife, daughter and heire of John Lord Tiptofte, had iſſue Iſable their only daughter and heire ; The ſaid Joan died in 9. H. 7. The ſaid Iſable was firſt maryed to John Nevill Marques Mountague, who died 11. E. 4. by whom ſhee had iſſue as followeth ; And ſecondly was maryed to Sir William Norris, and dyed 22. H. 7. by whom alſo ſhee had iſſue as after followeth. And the ſaid Iſable dyed 16. E. 4. And this pedegree for the laſt eight diſcents thereof is proved by Rot. Clauſ. 15. E. 4. membr. 11. and by Rot. Clauſ. 17. E. 4. membr. 7. in the tower of London.

The iſſue which the ſaid Iſable had by Norris her ſecond huſband, which were Willm Norrys knight, Alice and Jone, are needles heere to bee mentioned, becauſe this

---

[1] See Ante, Vol. I., p.p. 282—286. [ED.]

this manor of Bradſton went alonge with her iſſue by her firſt huſband Nevill the Marques Mountague. Betweene whom was iſſue one ſonne and five daughters, viz: George Nevill, who was created Duke of Bedford, and dyed without iſſue in 1. E. 5. A° 1482. And 5. daughters, Anne, Elizabeth, Margaret, Lucy and Iſable. Anne the eldeſt was married to Sir William Stoner knight, to whom this manor was allotted in partition, of whoſe iſſue I heere only write: And betweene them was iſſue John Stoner, who died in 2. H. 7. without iſſue; And Anne maryed to Sir Adrian ffortefcue, who was attainted and beheaded in 30. H. 8. wherby his owne lands eſcheated, not his wives, who was dead longe before in 10. H. 8. And by him ſhee had iſſue Margaret her only daughter and heire maryed to Thomas lord Wentworth lord Chamberlen, who dyed in 5. E. 6. And the ſaid Margaret dyed in 1. E. 6. leavinge iſſue Thomas lord Wentworth, who by his Deed inrolled in the Court of Comon pleas in Michas terme, 3. et 4. Eliz. Rot. 14. dated the firſt day of September laſt before, aliened divers parcells of this manor of Bradſton, and of his other manor of Stinchcombe adioyninge thereto, (and which had all the diſcents in this pedegree of the Bradſtons and their diſcendants ever gone to-geather;) to Trotman, Burchier and Nelme, three of the tenants to parts therof, who forthwith after (according to agreement formerly made) granted divers parcells therof to other men, that thoſe Manors ſeemed in effect to bee deſtroyed. And after, the ſaid lord Wentworth, by his other Deed inrolled in the Chancery dated the laſt day of Auguſt in the eighth yeare of Qu: Eliz. granted the | Manors of Bradſton and Stinchcombe, (ſuch as then they were,) to Richard Pate Eſq, and his heires, which (as before is ſaid) in the lyne before laid downe had continued in diſcent without alienaĉon from the time of kinge R. 1. (if not longer.) And vpon his ſales delivered accordinge to a Covenant in his ſaid Indenture more then 300. peeces of Evidence which are to this day kept in a cheſt in the tower of Stinch-combe Church, which I have not yet ſeene; ſome wherof would perhaps manifeſt, when and by what lord Berkeley the ſame was firſt granted and ſevered from their great Manor of Berkeley, wherof at firſt I ſuppoſe them to have byn parcells; And this Manor of Bradſton is nowe A° 1639. A° 15. Regis Caroli, the ſeverall inherit-ances of theis 11. perſons; vz, Wiłłm Harvey in his minority, ſonne of Edward, brother and heire of Nicholas, ſonnes of John Harvey of Bradſton geñ; Tobias Paine ſonne of William, Thomas Walter ſonne of John Walter gent and of Martha his wife daughter of William Payne; Thomas Smyth of Waniſwell, in right of Sarah his wife daughter of Samuel Trotman, ſonne of Wiłłm Trotman of Stan-combe, ſonne of John Trotman of Came; Thomas Andrewes of Bradſton, ſonne of Thomas, ſonne of Richard, who dyed 38. Eliz; Richard Organ ſonne of Richard;

Samuell,

Samuell, brother and heire of John Trotman, sonnes of Maurice lately deceased, yonger sonne of Wiłłm Trotman, a yonger sonne of John Trotman of Came, who dyed 19. Eliz: and of William Lawrance in right of Jone his wife daughter of Thomas Baily late of Hame and of Jone his wife, sister and one of the fower coheires of Wiłłm Butcher alˢ Burchier, sonne of Thomas, for one fourth part of the farme or capitall messuage; Thomas Came of Nuport sonne of ffortune Came of Wike lately deceased, for another 4ᵗʰ part of the said farme, which shee by Deed 1. April. 11. Jacobi. for 300ˡⁱ purchased of Wiłłm Smyth sonne of John Smyth and of Martha his wife, second sister and coheire of the said Wiłłm Butcher alˢ Burchier, sonne of Thomas; John Trotman of Stinchcombe, who purchased another 4ᵗʰ part of the said ffarme, of Wiłłm Hickes, sonne of Richard and of Sarah his wife, an other sister and coheire of the said Wiłłm Butcher alˢ Burchier, sonne of Thomas; And of William Wallington of Wotton, sonne of Edward Wallington and of Elizabeth his wife, (yet livinge) the 4ᵗʰ sister and coheire of the said William Butcher alˢ Burchier, sonne of Thomas; who holds another fourth part of the said ffarme.

Chapell of Bradston.

In this Hamblet or tithinge the aforementioned excellent souldier Sir Thomas de Bradston Banneret, did in 18. E. 3. found a Chaple, (often called Bradston Colledge,) and gave 3. messuages 4. yard land, 12. acres of meadowe 6 acres of wood and 5ˢ rent p Anñ. reserved vpon divers leases of other lands, lyinge within the Lordships of Hame, Alkington and Came, Capellano | custodi Capellæ Sc̃i Michis de Bradston, et duobus alijs Capellanis ad divina singulis diebus in capella prædicta celebratura, pro animâ suâ, et Isabellæ nuper vxoris eius; Which Thomas lord Berkeley the 24ᵗʰ of May the same 18ᵗʰ yeare of kinge Edward the third, confirmed, Salvis sibi prædicto Thomæ Dño Berkeley et heredibus suis servicijs et dnio quæ prius habuit de tenementis predictis: which foundacõn was by other charitable benefactors much enlarged: All which by the Act of Parliamᵗ in 1. E. 6 which dissolved Chantries and the like guilds and fraternities, was given to that kinge; who by his Lres patents inrolled in Chancery dated the 9ᵗʰ of May in the third yeare of that kings raigne, granted the same to Sir John Thinne knight and Thomas Throkmerton Esq, and their heires; To hold of the Manor of Bulford in the county of Wiltes in free and comõn soccage, by fealty only; Who forthwith after sold the same to Henry Ligon and Thomas ffransam, and their heires; And they by severall sales scattered the same amongst many purchasers, with whose posterities theis lands still doe remaine, The nowe lord Berkeley havinge only a rent of   paid him yearly by the kings Receiver, as parcell of the some of

Bradston

of—lxiiij: vj! paid for theis and other the Chantry rents in Berkeley, Newport, &c.

Of theis Chantry lands Chriſtopher Purnell of Nibley hath divers tenements and parcells in Stancombe, in the pariſh of Came, which his father Thomas Purnell purchaſed of Jonn Adye, ſonne of John Adye of fframpton, who purchaſed the ſame of the ſaid Thomas ffrantham.

And Samuell Trotman, brother and heire of John, ſonne and heire of Maurice Trotman, ſecond ſonne of Willm Trotman, holdeth the meſſuage called the Chaple houſe and the Scite of the Chantry of Bradſton, with the cloſe of paſture called the Wardens hall, containing two acres, with divers other parcells, pticulerly in an Inquiſicōn found after the death of the ſaid John Trotman, the 9th day of Aprill, A? 16. R̄ Caroli, mentioned.

Alſo in this Tithinge of Bradſton is one ancient meſſuage with divers lands therto belonginge the inheritance of William Harvy, ſonne of Edward, brother and heire of Nicholas Harvy, who was in ward to Henry lord Berkeley, ſonne of John Harvey, and of Julian his wife, daughter and coheire of John Atwood of Hinton, ſonne of Edward Harvy, ſonne of John   ſonne of   , ſonne of   Harvey, ſonne of Robert, ſonne of Robert Harvey, who lived in | the 35th yeare of kinge E. 3. ; ſonne of   Harvey, ſonne of   Harvey, to whom   de Bradſton gave the ſame, To hold (amongſt other ſervices) in focage, by payment of two heriotts after every of their deaths. An ancient family reputed as gentlemen, and as may bee ſaid, gentlemen by preſcripcōn in all their foreſaid generations, yet never of coate Armor, for any thinge I could ever obſerve; And, as tradition goes had this land given by the Bradſtons for their ſervice vnder them in the Warres of ffrance, as I have been informed their evidences doe ſpeake, which I have not ſeene.

Harvie's lands.

117

Owners alſo they have beene of divers other faire lands in Berkeley burrowe, Hinton, Alkington, Hame, Cambridge, Woodford, Slimbridge, Wanifwell, Stone, Newport, and Bevington, in the Manors of the lord Berkeleys in this hundred; and holden by knight ſervice, ſute of Court of their hundred of Berkeley from three weekes to three weekes, And by ſeverall yearly Cheife rents ; As   to Hame manor, And   to Hinton manor, And   to Alkington manor, And   to Berkeley burrowe, And   to Slimbridge manor ; As alſo they have byn (as the yonger branches of this family ſtill are,) copiholders

for

for lives and tenants by Indenture to the lorde of thofe manors; Which their ancient poffeffions were of late much inlarged by the maryage of John Harvy with the faid Julian daughter and coheire of John Atwood late of Hinton, fonne of Thomas Atwood; As alfo by a purchafe which the faid John Harvey made in 26° Eliz. of Phillip Jones of Thornbury and Cicely his wife, the other daughter and coheire of the faid John Atwood, fonne and heire of the faid Thomas Atwood; As alfo owners of a fifth part of a manor in the parifh of Hawkefbury called Cawkley, by the mariage of   Harvey aforefaid with   , holden of that manor by

And for further proofe of thefe Harvies landf are theis Records viz'. An Inquificon in 2. Jacobi, poſt mortem Joħis Harvey geñ. Inq :

Bradſton of Winterborne.

The forementioned John de Bradſton yonger brother of the faid Sir Thomas de Bradſton Banneret, (of whom I promifed fomwhat further to write,) had as I have faid for his portion the manor of Winterburne, 12. miles from this hamblet towards Briſtoll, from whom it difcended to Edmond his fonne, who was father of Thomas, father of John, father of Thomas, father of Anthony, father of Robert and Henry; | which Robert had iſſue Elizabeth only, who died without iſſue; and the faid Henry had iſſue Robert, lately dead; heere noted by mee for the honors fake of the name and difcent.

fifteenths.

In payment of Tenths and fifteenes with other like regall duties It is included and runneth with Came, whereof fee more in Came.

Subfedy.

In the 5ᵗʰ yeare of kinge Charles were only 4. fubfedy men inhabitants there, who paid—38ˢ.

Able men.

In 6ᵗᵒ Jacobi heere were of able men for the warres, betweene 20. and 60. yeares old, which appeared at a generall muſter then taken,—11.

Rates.

If Berkeley Divifion bee rated at—100ˡⁱ This hundred of Berkeley paies— 33ˡⁱ 3ˢ therof, And this hamblet of Bradſton—8ˢ.

Souldiers.

Of Trayned fouldiers vnder Wiłłm Thorpe Efq, their captaine, it hath—4. vz. 2 corfletts and 2 mufketts.

Bradston

By an Inquisitõn in the tower of London in 1. E. 1. Willm Mauduit is found to hold 8. acres of land in Bradeneston of the lord of Bradeston, and to have byn hanged for felony; which then had byn a yeare and a day in the kings hands.

More of this Bradston is to bee read in theis, Records, viz:

Rot. pateñ, 8. E. 3. ps. 1. in dorso.
Rot. Clauš. 16. E. 3. in dorso.
Inq: 34. E. 3. p^t morte Thome de Bradeston.—in capite de Dño Berkeley.
Rot. pateñt. 34. E. 3. ps. 3. membr. 7.
Extract subsed in 1. E. 3. Bradston eft hameletĩ de Came in Sectio.
Inq: 37. E. 3. de feodis Baroniæ de Berkeley in Sectio.—per dimid feod.]
Rot. clauš. 43. E. 3. membr. 6.
Rot. finiũ 43. E. 3. membr. 19.
Inq: 48. E. 3. p^t morte Thome de Bradston.
Rot. clauš. 48. E. 3. membr. 21.
Rot. finiũ. 48. E. 3. membr. 6. 19. 21.
Rot. finiũ. 49. E. 3. membr. 12.
Rot. clauš. 13. R. 2. ps. 1. membr. 26.
Inq: 2. H. 4. p̃t mortem Ricĩ de sĩo Mauro.
Inq: 11. H. 4. p̃t morte Elæ vxoris Thome Bradston. in capite de Dño Berkeley.
Inq: 12. H. 6. p^t mortem Walteri de la Poole.—Ignoramus.
Inq: 35. H. 6. p̃t morte Edm: Ingaldesthorpe.—per 4. p̃t feod miltis.
Triñ Recĩ. in Sectio. 22. H. 6. rot. 17.
Rot. clauš. 15. E. 4. membr. 11. The wholl pedegree
Rot. clauš. 17. E. 4. membr. 7.
Inq: 16. E. 4. as in Stincheombe.
Inq: 2. H. 7. p̃t morte   Middlesex.—for ye whole pedigree.
Rot. pateñt. 3. E. 6. p Thin et Throgmton.
Inq: 44. Eliz. p̃t morte Ricĩ Andrewes —per serviciũ mil.
Inq: 44. Eliz. p̃t morte Willi Payne.—per serviciũ mil.
Carta irrotulat in Cancell in Octobr̃. 8. Eliz. inter Wentworth et Pate.

See more in Stincheombe. fol: 343.

Inq: 14. Caroli, p̃t morte ffortunæ Came vid—per serviciũ mil.
Inq: 2. Jacobi p̃t morte Johis Harvey geñ.—per servic̃ militare.

Liber

Liber Wardoȝ et Relevioȝ. fol : 9. 24. et 25.—per serviciũ mil.
Inq : 16. Caroli, p̃t mortē Johis Trotman filij et heredis Mauricij Trotman. —per servicium militare. |

120 blank

Caldecote.

Caldecote ; often written Cawcote, and Coldcote ; deservedly soe to bee written and called from the cold scituaõn, from whence (doubtles) is the name : It is a faire farme house with 450 acres of ground therto belonginge, anciently parcell of the possessions of the Abby of Kingswood by Wotton Vnderedge ; A Monastery, seated and in the county of Wiltes, (of the foundation of that ancient Saxon family of the Berkeleys of Durseley,) though compassed round about with the parts of Gloucester-shire ; And hath byn taken as part of that manor of Kingswood anciently of old called Acholt, wherin the Abby house was seated ; though now severed by the grant of   in the   yeare of his raigne made to

This Calcote is nowe generally conceived to lye within the parish of Bagpath before mentioned ; And is nowe the inheritance of Thomas Estcourt Esq, sonne of Edmond Estcourt, brother and heire apparant whilest hee lived, of Sir Thomas Estcourt of Lasseborrowe knight, who dyed in 22º Jacobi. Concerninge which Sir Thomas and the setlinge of his estate to freinds in trust what time hee lay vpon his death bed, see a large Decree of more then 100. sheetes of paper inrolled in the Chancery by consent of parties, in Aprill in the 13th yeare of kinge Charles, betweene the lady Mary Estcourt the widowe of the said Sir Thomas, And the said Thomas Estcourt Esq, sonne of Edmond and theis trustees ; which is also a reasonable good survey not only of this farme and of the manor of Dursley, but of all other the possessions of the said Sir Thomas Estcourt wherof hee dyed seized.

The word (cote) the last sillable of this farme, anciently signified an habitation mantion or abidinge house, though of the meanest reputaõn : Of which were divers others in this hundred, as Woodmancote in the parish of Dursley : Westmancote in the parish of Arlingham : Hulmancote in the parish of Cowley : Kingescote in the parish of Beverston ; and Hasilcote an hamblet in Kingescote ; And Pitcote in Nybley, (now called Pitcourt,) of all which see more in their alphabeticall places.

As

Came

An Inquisicōn in the tower of London vpon an Ad quod damnum in 12. H. 4. findeth That the granges called Hafelden and Culkertone in Hafelden, And the granges of Owfelworth, Tettebury, Bagefton, Hull, and Caldcote, doe belong to the Abbot of Kingfwood, which are all that the Abbot hath in the county of Glouc̄. And the Roll of patents a° 22. E. 1. membr. 6. et 7. fheweth of what Order each monaftery in England was of; And that this of Kingefwood was de Ciftercienfibus: See alfo Simondfall. fol :—323.

And kinge Henry the third in the xith of his raigne confirmed to the Abbot of Kingfwood and his Covent the manor of Acholt, | which Roger de Berkeley (of Durfeley) gave to that monaftery, and all other their lands, as freely as kinge Henry the fecond his grandfather confirmed them to them: In which are alfo divers liberties, recited, And to bee free ab omni feculari exactione et fervicio ; As by Rot. Cartaş. 11. H. 3. ps. 1. mem : 12. appeares. ffor which Charter of Confirmacōn the Abbot gave to the kinge 10. m̄ks. as by Rot. finiñ. 11. H. 3. appeares, where of the premiffes is alfo a pticuler expreffion.

The impropriate Rectory of Kingfwood (if I may fo call it,) as the 7^h p anñ of ancient cuftome paid by the inhabitants there, or rather 6^{li}. 13^s. 4^d, were by the Lr̄es patents of Queene Eliz. dated 21. Julij. a° 5to Eliz : granted (inter alia) to Humphrey Shelton and Edmund Hunt and their heires, from whom the fame forthwith came, accordinge to the truft in them repofed, to Thomas Hanbury one of the Auditors, And from him to ffrancis his fonne, who aliened the fame to Roger Tulfe.

The laft Abbot of this monaftery before the diffolucōn therof was Wiłłm Bewdeleye, as a leafe fhewes made by him 20. December. 28. H. 8. And the Monaftery was diffolved by furrender. |

Came.

Came: In Domefdei booke. **Camma**: wherin Wiłłm the Conqueror had fix hides of land in demefne, and eleaven other hides of land there which were (as I conceive) in tenants hands, fuch as copiholders for lives there at this day are ; And fuch lands as fince that time have byn enfeoffed to divers men and given in tayle by the Lords of this manor, wherof many are after mentioned.

Hundred of Berkeley

It is a large and goodly parish divided by a pretty little sweete river runninge through the midst of it into two parts; vpper Came or Vpthorpe; and lower Came, or the neyther towne; Vpper Came comprehendeth in it Ashmead and Churchend; and Lower Came comprehendeth Dreicote, Cleihunger, comonly pronounced Clinger; wherto may bee added Stinchcombe and Snitend and halmer. A manor of 100^{li} p añ of old rents, or neere therabouts, the inheritance of George lord Berkeley and parcell of his Barony of Berkeley, holden by knight service in Capite, containinge in the intire compasse of it selfe at least five myles, besides the village of Stinchcombe and Snytend.

A Township foe evenly pertakinge of hill and vale, with an wholsome aire to both, And so equally furnished of timber and wood for buildinge fire and all Bootes vsefull in husbandry, with arrable meadowe and pasture grounds for the feed and breed of all sorts of Cattell, with store of all kindes of graine vsefull for man, with fish foule fruite for pery and cyder and the like; That it would abundantly suffice for the maintenance and well beinge of its owne inhabitants, without supply from any other of her neighbors in any needfull thinge which the hart of man wuld moderately desire.

This manor and parish of Came was (amongst others) granted by kinge H. 2. in the first yeare of his raigne to Robert the sonne of Hardinge and his heires, wherby also hee was created Lord Berkeley, a peere of the Realme, and Baron of Parliament: ffor I hold the opinion as orthodox That vntill the time of king Richarde the first or of his brother and heire kinge John, each subiect to whom the Crowne gave land to hold by knight service in Capite was therby made a Peere of the Realme and had voice in Parliament; And that all those mentioned in the red booke in the office of the kings Remembrancer in the Exchequer to have accordingly certified their tenures to kinge Henry the second about the 14th yeare of his raigne, were the peeres and Barons of that time; As elsewhere in the life of the said lord Robert sonne of Hardinge and of James lord Berkeley the first of that name I have written more at large:[1] But towards the latter end of kinge John and after Barons by a more speciall creation were by patent and lastly by Writt. |

ffrom which lord Robert sonne of Harding this manor came to the lord Maurice his sonne and heire, who was father of Robert and Thomas; Robert dyed without issue, And Thomas his brother and heire had issue Maurice, father of
Thomas

---

[1] See Ante, Vol. I., p. 30, and Vol. II., p. 50. [Ed.]

Thomas, father of Maurice, father of Thomas, father of Maurice, father of Thomas and James ; Which Thomas dyed without iſſue male, And James (who died in the life of his elder brother,) had iſſue James, heire to this manor after his vncle Thomas death : Which James, ſonne of James, had iſſue William and Maurice ; Which William was created Earle of Nottingham and Marques Berkeley, and dyed without iſſue ; And Maurice had iſſue Maurice and Thomas ; Which Maurice dyed without iſſue ; and Thomas had iſſue Thomas, father of Henry, father of Thomas, father of George now lord Berkeley, owner of this manor as aforeſaid. A⁰ 1639. And for the times when each of the ſaid lords dyed and for the Entayles which any of them made, or other Conveyances of this manor, I referre my reader to fol : 6. et. 7. and fol : 78. And to my deſcripc͠on of Berkeley towne fol : 77. 78, heere omitted in avoydinge double repetitions ; As alſo I ſhall in ſome other pariſhes and manors following, doe the like.

The Church, with the Chapell of Stinchcombe, was anciently given by to the Abbot of S.t Peters Monaſtery in Glouc͠, in the time of [1] ; who vpon each death and avoydance preſented till the time of kinge E. 3. when it was impropriated to that Monaſtery, in A⁰ 1360. in 34. E. 3. And thereby (as by the Regiſter booke of the Biſhop of Worceſter appeareth,) became a poore ſtipendiary Cure, with the pention of—13.ˢ 6.ˢ 8.ᵈ to the Curate ſervinge the Alter : And cominge to the Crowne by the diſſoluc͠on of that Monaſtery in 31. H. 8. was, vpon that kings erection of the Biſhoppricke of Glouc͠, in the 34.th yeare of his raigne, given (amongſt other poſſeſſions,) to the Biſhop and his Succeſſors ; vnder whoſe demiſe Walter Woodward Chriſtopher Woodward and Richard Woodward nowe hold the ſame at 41.ˡⁱ rent by the yeare, and pay alſo the ſaid 20. marks to Vicar or Curate there, whom they preſent, at leaſt are tyed by their leaſe to provide ; Howbeit I have byn informed that the ſtipend to the Curate is a little increaſed within 2. yeares laſt, vpon the late renewinge of their leaſe with Biſhop Goodman that now is, A⁰ 1639. At leaſt promiſed or hoped for to bee ſoe ; but the leſſor, it is ſaid, departed from his promiſe.]

Church

The ancient dedication of this Church of Came was to S.t George, accompted the tutelary Saint therof, whoſe great picture artificially cut in wood and ſtandinge at

---

[1] The Church of Came with its appurtenances was granted *inter alia* by Robert de Berkeley, ſon of Maurice, by Alice, daughter of Roger Berkeley of Durſley, to the Monaſtery of St. Peter, at Gloucester, in 1156, which grant was confirmed by King Henry III., and John, (Paynam,) Biſhop of Worceſter. (Hiſt. et Cart. Monaſterii Sancti Petri, Glouceſtriæ, Vol. I., p. 114.) [ED.]

at the porch of the Church was from thence in the raigne of kinge Edward the sixt, caryed to Colbrooke in a Clothiers waine, 15. myles from London, in his travell with his cloth thither towards Blackwell hall; whose settlement at Coldbrook begate the great Comon Inne called the George in Colbrooke to this day, 1639; ffor which tutelary Saint, see the Will of William Hardinge in 37. H. 8. And the Inquisition after his death the same yeare, in this County.

ffifteenes. The payment of the ffifteene or Kingsilver in this parish of Came, when it is granted by parliament, is ioyned with Bradston as there hath byn said: The onus or charge both togeather is in the kings Excheq̄r—11^{li} 9^s 11^d. The deduction is —3^{li} 3^s 4^d. The remainder paid into the Excheq̄r to the kinge, wherwith the Collector therof is charged, is 8^{li} 6^s 7^d.

Subsedy. In the last Subsedy, taxed in A^o 5to R^s $Car̄$, there were in this Manor of Came, (not accomptinge Stichcombe nor the hamblets therof) 23. subsedy men who paid— 11^{li} 6^d 8^d.

Able men. And of able men for the warres betweene 20. and 60. yeares old were in A^o 6to R^s Jacobi, which then shewed themselves before Henry lord Berkeley then lord Leiutenant of the County,—121.

Soldiers. And now are of trayned soldiers vnder William Thorpe Esq, their captaine, 22. vz. 12. corsletts and 10. muskets.

Rates. And if the wholl division of Berkeley accompted a 4th part of the county of Glouc̄, bee rated in any tax for kinge or comon wealth to pay—100^{li}, then this hundred of Berkeley paies therof—33^{li} 3^s And this manor of Came (besides Stinchcombe)—53^s 4^d And soe after that rate, bee the tax more or lesse.

freeholders within this manor or Lo⁺ of Came.

Draicote. One of the most ancient and remarkeable freeholds is called Draycotes, or the manor of Draycote; And was by Roger Berkeley of Dursley sonne of Robert Berkeley, in the time of kinge Henry the first, given (by the name of all the land of Draycote with the appurtenants,) to John the sonne of Ewstace of Came and his heires, To hold by the fourth part of one knights fee, and the yearly rent of—3^s 9^d. As by the originall deed, which I have seene, appeareth: And this manor or land of Draycote extendeth into the villages or hamblets of Came, Dursley, Nybley, and Cowley. | And is nowe the severall inheritances of my selfe, Richard Bower, John

Came

John Browninge, William Sage, John Trotman, John Stinchcombe, Wittm [over Edward] Hill, John Parflowe, John Walkeley in minority, and John Hardinge, which hee purchafed of Thomas Pope; And Ifaack Smyth of Durfley, who hath the greateft part therof, worth—100^h per ann; which in A^o R^e Caroli hee purchafed of Jofeph Hardinge fonne of George, fecond fonne of Richard Hardinge, the purchafer thereof from

The forefaid Roger Berkeley of Durfley is hee who then held the great manor of Berkeley, wherof the manor of Came is a member and parcell, of that kinge H. 1. 1. in feefarme; whofe daughter Alice (accordinge to an agreem^t made at Briftoll in the houfe of Robert the fonne of Harding often before mentioned, in the prefence of kinge Stephen, and of Henry then Duke of Normandy after kinge of England by the name of Henry the fecond,) was fhortly after maryed to Maurice fonne of the faid Robert fonne of Hardinge; vpon which agreement the faid Roger Berkeley of Durfeley releafed all his title and claime in this manor of Came and in the faid manor and Barony of Berkeley, to the faid Robert fonne of Harding and his heires, To whom Henry the fecond then Duke had lately before given the fame, As in the life of the faid Robert fonne of Hardinge I have at large written, in the hiftory of his family: And this Deed of the land of Draicote, thus made by the faid Roger Berkeley of Durfley, was afterwards in the time of kinge Henry the third recited and confirmed by Thomas then lord Berkeley, fonne and heire of the faid Maurice and Alice, fonne and heire of the faid Robert fonne of Harding, To hold by the forefaid rent and fervices; which Deed alfo I have feene: To the pofterity of which John fonne of Euftace of Came, and alfo to other families who came by difcent or purchafe to bee owners of this land of Draicote. The remarkeablenes and feizin therof gave them the Sirname of Draicote, or de Draicote, fo longe as it continued entire in one mans poffeffion; Such were, Radus de Draicote who lived in the time of kinge H. 2., Johes de Draicote who lived in the 20. and 32. of kinge H. 3., Robtus de Draicote who lived in the time of kinge E. 1., Stephus de Draicote who lived in the 35. of the faid kinge E. 1., and in the time of kinge E. 2. and leaft iffue John Draicote, who lived in the time of kinge Edward the third; whofe daughter and heire called Jone Draicote was maried to from whom iffued (after one or two difcents betweene) Robert Draicote als Tanner, father of John Draicote als Tanner, written alfo John Dreicote als dictus John Gilman of Durfley gent, who dyed in the third yeare of kinge Henry the feaventh. leavinge this land to difcend to his two daughters and heires, vz, Jone and Ifable, often written Elizabeth: Of whom

1. The

1. The said Jone was firſt maryed to Thomas Stanton, by whom ſhee had noe iſſue; and ſecondly maryed to Henry Beale, by whom ſhee had iſſue three daughters; vz. 1 Alice (written alſo Aliva in ſome records) firſt maried to Robert ffeylond, and after to Richard Goffe: 2 Jone, maried to John Moody, And 3 Anne: which Jone and Anne dyed without iſſue, and the said Alice the eldeſt ſiſter dyed in 4. H. 8. which yeare alſo dyed the ſaid Jone.

2. The said Iſable (written ſomtimes Elizabeth,) ſiſter alſo of the ſaid Jone Dreicote, was maried to Richard Catſon als Plowmaker and dyed in 7. H. 8. leavinge iſſue Margery, maried to Henry Baynam, who died in 12. H. 8. without iſſue, wherby the ſaid Alice her cozen germane became her heire; And theis are thoſe woemen and their huſbands who in the times of kinge H. 8. and of Queene Eliz: have aliened this ancient freehold and parcell of land in ſuch ſort, by their ſeverall ſales at ſeverall times, that it is become the inheritance of thoſe 10. ſeverall perſons before named, wherof my ſelfe am one; but noe one acre therof is in the poſterity or iſſue of the ſaid John ſonne of Euſtace of Came, the firſt feoffee, though many remaine at this day.

And for proofe of the greateſt part if not of all before written of this Draicote, conſult with theis records, vizᵗ.

Finis in banco, 32. H. 3. Inter Came et Draicote.
Inq: 2. H. 8. p̄t mortem Joḣis Dreicote als Tanner.
Inq: 20. H. 8. p̄t mortem Margeř Baynham.—per ſerviĉ militare.
Triñ Reč in Sčĉio. 21. H. 8. Rot. 20. c̄m Reñi Theſauř.—p ſerviĉ mil.
ffinis in banco. 35. H. 8. p Riĉo Hardinge.
ffinis in banco. 35. H. 8. p Joḣe Hardinge
ffinis in banco. 37. H. 8. p Joḣe Tomlins als Minor.
Miĉhas Reč. 16. H. 8. rot. 9. in ſcĉio c̄m Reñi theſauř.—p ſerviĉ mil.
Reč. in banco. 4. & 5. Ph: & Mař. Rot. 836.
ffinis in banco. Triñ 5. Eliz. Inter Joḣem Cowley et Riĉm Gough als Goffe, de medietate maiḣij de Draicote, et teñ in Nibley.
Triñ Reč. 5. Eliz. Rot. 41. in ſcĉio c̄m Reñi Theſauř.—per ſerviĉ mit., beſt. |
Reč. in banco. 10. Eliz. de partitione, inter Hardinge, et al.
ffinis in banco. 30. Eliz. pro Browninge.
Inq: 4. Caroli, p̄t mortem Joḣis Browninge.—very good:—p ſerviĉ mit.
Inq: 15. Caroli. p̄t morte Riĉi Walkeley—p ſerviĉ mit.—found by himſelfe.
Rot.

Came

Rot. pateñ. 2. E. 2. ps. 1. in dorso. in arce London. Stephus de Draicote arr assisam versus Riĉm Astmead etiam de teñ in Came.
And after in Draycote fol: 173.
Inq: 37. E. 3. de feodis de Berkeley in seĉio.—p serviciũ mil.
Co: roll, in a paper booke, 4. H. 8. p̃t morte Johe Beale.—p serviĉ mil. et her.
Court roll in pchm̃ of Came 20. H. 8. p̃t morte Margeriæ Baynam—p herioẗ. good.
Co: rolls of Cowley. 1. et 3. Eliz. p̃t morte Johis Parslowe. r̃ 34ˢ 4ᵈ et p serviciũ militare.
Co: roll of Came. 7. H. 8. p̃t morte Isabellæ vxoꝛ Riĉi Plowmaker. r̃. 44ˢ p homaḡ et herieẗ.
Co: roll of Cowley.

Heere also in Came is one other ancient freehold called the Hall place, which as eminent above others gave the name to some of the owners (inhabitants in the messuage,) to bee anciently written John At Hall, Thomas At Hall, &c. And was by William Hopton the elder in the 7ᵗʰ yeare of kinge Charles, purchased (in the names of his five feoffees,) who after conveyed the same to William Hopton, sonne and heire of the said William,) of William Harding sonne of John Hardinge, sonne of Thomas Hardinge, sonne of Richard Hardinge, sonne of William Hardinge, who died in 37. H. 8: As by two Inquisicõns remaininge of Record, found after his death, appeareth: Hee beinge sonne of Thomas Hardinge and of Margaret his wife daughter and coheire of Willm Heyward, sonne of John Heyward and of Lucia his wife daughter and heire of Roger de Came, sonne of Henry de Came, sonne of Raphe de Came, who dyed in 16. E. 1. as by Rot. siniũ. 16. E. 1. membr. 11. in the tower of London appeares: Before which Raphe, it was the land of Maurice de Came, and of Roger de Came, And in the raigne of kinge R. 1. of Hugh de Came: much the greater part of which messuage and lands is holden of the manor of Dursley by knight service, and the residue of the lord Berkeley as of his manor of Came, as in the foresaid Inquisicõns is perticulerly specifyed: ffor which messuage and land see also the will of the said William Hardinge sonne of Thomas and Margaret, dated 2. ffebr: 36. H. 8. wherby hee did severally convey theis and other his lands amongst his sonnes, mentioned also in the said Inquisicõns of 37. H. 8. whose posterities hold part of them in Cowley and Slimbridge to this day Aᵒ 1639. And this messuage and most of the land is within the Leete of the manor of Dursley and not of the Leet of Berkeley: And one Cotage orchard and garden

Hall place. late Hardings now Hoptons.

garden ground the said last mentioned Wiłłm Hardinge sonne of John sold in fee to Samuell Trotman, and hee to ffrancis Webbe of London, And hee in the yeare, 1638. to Edward Hall of Came, to whose other freehold there it adioyneth. And for this land see alsoe an Inquisicōn in 19. E. 2. after the death of Wiłłm Coriet, which also findeth Wiłłm Hoptons cheife rent of—12^s 4^d lately questioned against him: See also fol: 159.

Planches, nowe Soũmers.

Heere also in this parish is another ancient freehold messuage and land, called Planches, or la planca, of old esteemed halfe an hide of land, called the ffarme of Planches in many evidences, now the inheritance of John Somers, sonne of Lawrance Somers who dyed in 19. Jacobi, having in 18. Eliz. purchased the same of William Berkeley of Cressage in the parish of Cond in the County of Salop, who was brother and heire of Edward Berkeley, sonne of John Berkeley, sonne of Edmond, sonne of John, sonne of Edmond, sonne of John Berkeley called also Planch, sonne of John de Planches, sonne of John Berkeley, third sonne of Maurice lord Berkeley the third lord of that name, who by his Deed dated on wednesday the feast day of the Epiphany, the 6th of January in 15. E. 2, conveyed the same to the said John Berkeley, his sonne, and to the heires males of his body, by the name of all his lands and tenements at planches in Came, with the services of those his tenants there, which Thomas lord Berkeley father of him the said lord Maurice had purchased of Thomas Monmouth, lord of the said lands called planches; Rendringe to him the said lord Maurice vnam capellam rosarum, (one chaplet or garland of roses,) on midsoffier day, for all services; As by the two duplicates of the originall Deed, the one in Berkeley castle the other with the said John Somers., appeareth: ffor which roses the said John Somers payeth a penny of yearly rent to this manor of Came at this day; A° 1639. Howbeit the ancient tenure of this farme or halfe hide of land was of the manor of Dursley, within the Leet wherof it still is and not of Berkeley: wherof see more in the description of Dursley fol: 175.

130 And in the time of kinge Henry the second this halfe hide of land was the | inheritance of Hugo de planca, And in the time of kinge Richard the first of Rogerus de planca; And in 3. E. 2. of John Monmouth, sonne and heire of Walter de Monmouth, who then dyed seized therof, And Thomas was his brother and heire then 16. yeares old, sonne also of the said Walter de Monmouth.

By an Inquisicōn in the tower of London in 45. H. 3. William Lesseborrowe held one carucate of land in la planch in Came of Thomas de la planch, by the rent of halfe a marke and sute to the court of Dursele, And that Agatha the wife of Henry de Deane was his daughter and heire, 20. yeares old.   **By**

Came

By Inq: 50. H. 3. Willm Mauduit was found to hold one yard land in la planch, and to have byn againſt the kinge in the ſeidge of Marlebge and in the battell of Lewes.

By Inq: 3. E. 2, John Monmouth ſonne and heir of Walter, and Thomas ſonne and heire of John Monmouth, are found to hold 10. acres at la planch of Thomas lord Berkeley: And alſo to hold 87. acres of the heire of William Berkeley of Durſeley, in ward to the kinge.

In 6. E. 3. Katherine the widowe of Thomas Monmouth did arraigne an aſſiſe for theis lands of planches againſt John Berkeley aforeſaid, by the name of John ſonne of Maurice lord Berkeley. Rot. pateñ. A: 6d. in dorſo.

Deere alſo in another ſmall freehold of a quarter of a yard land the inheritance of William Seliman, holden of George lord Berkeley as of his manor of Came by knight ſervice ſute of Court heriot ſervice and the yearly rent of—10: 6:ᵈ Which Thomas lord Berkeley the ſecond lord of that name by his Deed dated in aº 29. E. 1. gave, by the name of totum illud ferdellum terræ cum ptinen̄ in Came, to Walter Seliman and Maud his wife, and to the heires of their bodies, To hold vnder the yearly rent of—10: 6ᵈ and heriot accordinge to the cuſtome of that manor for all ſervices, ſavinge the regall ſervice (regali ſervicio) which as the Deed proveth, is by knights ſervice: An eſtate taile that I ſuppoſe yet continueth vndiſcontinued; which Walter and Maud the donees had iſſue John Seliman, father of John, father of John, father of John, father of Auguſtine and John, which Auguſtine dyed without iſſue in 1º. Mař. leavinge John his brother and heire, who died 13º Eliz: and had iſſue William Selman that yet liveth, 1639. And ſurely the honeſt ſimplicity of this William Selman, (and of all his forefathers as credible tradition delivers,) is agreeable to the name, beinge plaine ſilly ſimple men, livinge of this little in all their generations, without diminucõn or increaſe of further | eſtate then this quarter of an yard land: And ſome little more they have in Stancombe, which came

Selimans lands als Selmans.

Which originall deed vnder ſeale in Berkeley caſtle for the rarity it ſhall not greive mee to have copied out in thies words, vz,

Omnibus xp̄i fidelibus hoc prefens ſcriptum inſpecturis, Thomas Dn̄s de Berkeley ſaltm in dno: Noveritis me dediſſe conceſſiſſe et hoc preſenti ſcripto confirmaſſe

Waltero

Waltero Selyman de Came et Matildæ vxori suæ, Totum illud ferdellum terræ cum ptineñ quod priùs de me tenuerunt ad terminum vitæ in Came: Hēnđ et teneñd totm p̄dēm ferdellum cū ōibus ptineñ fuis, de me et heređ meis, p̄dc̄is Waltero et Matildæ vxori fuæ et heređ fuis de corpore eo₷ legittime procreatis, liberè, quietè bene et in pace, Reddendo anuatim mihi et heređ meis p̄dc̄i Walterus et Matilda vxor eius ad terminū vitæ eorundem, dimidiam marcam argenti ad quatuor anni terminos principales equali porc̄one. Et fex denarios pro vna acra et dimiđ claudend iuxta la holewell ad terminos p̄ī dum in claufo durauerit; Et poft deceſſum p̄dic̄torū Walteri et Matildæ, heredes eo₷ legittime de corporibus fuis procreati reddent anuatim decem folidos et fex denarios, ad terminos fupradic̄tos, pro eođ tenemento et claufo, pro omnibus fervicijs et fecularibus demandis ad me vel heredes meos ptinentibus, Salvo regali [fervicio] quantum pertinet ad tantm tenm in cođ feodo, et denariis beati Petri et herieto cùm acciderit fcđm confuetudinē Maīīij. Et falvis duobus adventibus apud Berket p anñ ad vifum francij pledgij. Et fi contingat q̄d p̄dc̄us Walterus et Matilda proximo herede eorū infra ætatem exiftente obierint, volo q̄d dc̄us heres, non obftante minoritate, feifinam dc̄i teñti ftatim heat per recīm et debitum releviū fcđm vfū maīīij fine contradic̄tione. Et ego p̄dc̄us Thomas et heredes mei totum p̄dc̄um ferdellum terræ c̄m ptineñ p̄dc̄is Waltero et Matildæ et heređ eo₷ de corporibus fuis legittime procreatis in forma p̄dc̄a contra omnes mortales warrantizabimus imppetuū. In cuius rei teftimoniū huic fcripto bipertito figillum meū appofuimus. Datū apud Berket die fc̄i marci evangeliftæ, anno regni regis Edwardi, vicefimo nono. Hijs teftibus, Roḃto de Berkel, Thoma de Swonhungre, Henrico de Came, Waltero Hathemere, et alijs.

But quære, whether this deed difchargeth the wardfhip of the body, as it doth of the land.

<small>Naffe Court, nowe Trotmans.</small> Heere alfo is another ancient meſſuage and two yard land called Naffe Court, the inheritance of John Trotman comonly called of the knapp, accordinge to the feituac̄on of the faid Meſſuage; Which John is fonne of Nicholas Trotman who died in 19° Eliz., fonne of John Trotman who dyed about 20. houres before the faid Nicholas, fonne of Thomas Trotman, who in 1. et 2. Ph: et Mar̄, purchafed the | faid meſſuage and lands of John Berkeley of Beverfton Caftle, then efquire, after knight, therby feveringe it from his manor of Woodmancote in the parifh of Durfley wherof it was parcell, And till then held by Copy of Court roll accordinge to the cuftome of that manor, as by the copy therof amongft the evidences of the faid   which I have feene, appeareth: And the faid Thomas Trotman

Came

Trotman the purchaſer of this land dyed in A̅o̅ 5. et 6. Ph: & Mar̃. And was ſonne of Henry Trotman who died in 18. H. 8. ſonne of John Trotman who dyed in ____, ſonne of Elias Trotman who died in ____, ſonne of Robert Trotman who died in 5. H. 5. brother and heire of Walter, ſonnes of John Trotman, ſonne of Richard, who lived in the time of kinge E. 2. ffor which purchaſe made by the ſaid Thomas Trotman of John Berkeley ſee a fine in banco in Triñ terme. 5. Mar̃ de teñ in Came et Slimbridge. And for the diſcent of the ſaid John Berkeley, whoſe anceſtors had for many diſcents held this meſſuage and land, ſee in Beverſton. fol: 97. And Woodmancote fol: 389. And is holden of George lord Berkeley by knight ſervice, ſute to his hundred court of Berkeley from 3. weekes to 3. weekes, and by the yearly rent of—10ˢ. And of—6ᵈ more paid for other lands which longe have beene occupied therwith: Some part of which lands, viz. a meſſuage and one acre and a quarter of ground, are nowe the inheritance of Nicholas Trotman, ſonne of Edward Trotman of Came, called of the Stepps, As by an Inquiſicōn found the laſt yeare A̅o̅ 14. R̃c̃ Car̃ 1638, after the death of the ſaid Edward, appeareth; And which hee the ſaid Edward by Deed dated 20. Junij Anno 12. R̃c̃ Jacobi purchaſed of John Trotman his eldeſt brother, as the ſaid Inquiſicōn ſheweth: And for which the ſaid John hath 40ˢ p Añ paid to him as a rent charge out of the ſame.

And by Deed 20. E. 3. Walter de Naſſe Dñs de Naſſe, granted to Thomas lord Berkeley the third lord of that name A meſſuage and 2. yard land, by the name of all his lands and teñts in Came which were Henry de Naſſe his fathers: To hold to the ſaid lord Thomas for his life, And after his death to Maurice his ſonne (poſtnatus) and to the heires males of his body, the remainder to the heires males of the body of the ſaid lord Thomas and of Katherine his ſecond wife, the Rem̃ to the right heires of the ſaid lord Thomas; To bee held of the cheife lord by the rents and ſervices accuſtomed: (but the ſaid deed though made that yeare yet is not dated:) And the ſaid John Berkeley who aliened this land to Thomas Trotman, was the heire male of the body of the ſaid lord Thomas and Katherine, As in Woodmancote fol: 389 appeareth: And from the ancient ſeiſin of this Walter de Naſſe and his anceſtors continueth the name of Naſſe court to this day, 1639, to this meſſuage and land. |

This Naſſe court with other lands the ſaid John Trotman hath by his deed dated 6. mcij. A̅o̅ 14. R̃c̃ Jacobi, ſetled after the death of himſelfe, vpon Henry his eldeſt ſonne and the heires males of his body with Remainder over, the Remainder to the heires of the ſaid John.

Heere

Hundred of Berkeley

Baffetts lands.

Heere are about 25. acres with an houfe vpon part therof alfo, called Baffetts lands, late the inheritance of William Baffet Efq, which lineally had difcended vpon him from the time of kinge Henry the third, holden of this manor of Came by knight fervice, fute of Court, and the yearly rent of 12^d; wherof (efpetially for the difcent) read more in Ewley, fol: [188]. And are nowe the feverall inheritances of Thomas Mors, fonne of John, who holdeth 10. acres therof and paies—7^d cheife rent, part of the faid—12^d And of Thomas Cliffe who holds 15. acres therof, and paies—4^d parcell of the faid 12^d And of John Hutchens who holds the faid Cotage cm ptiñ and paies—1^d the refidue of the faid 12^d All which theis Records (befides many other evidences) doe fully fhewe, viz!;

See after in this page.

p: if Cliffe have all yt Giles Hitchins p'cha: of Baffet.

Inq: pt mortē Edmondi Baffet.
Rot. patent. 11. E. 3. in arcē Lond:
Inq: 24. H. 7. pt mortē Robti Baffet.
Inq: 35. H. 8. pt mortē Egidij Baffet.
Inq: 16. Eliz. pt mortē Robti Baffet.
Diverfæ Cartæ cum Willimo Baffett pr̄t, quas perlegi.
See more in the defcription of Ewley.

And a Deed in Berkeley Caftle without date, wherby Richard Berkeley granted to Anfelme Baffet and Margaret his wife, and to the heires of Anfelme, 30. acres and an halfe, in the townes of Came and Chofley, wherof 16. acres and an halfe in Came, To hold of him and his heires, Rendringe and doeinge to the cheife lords the fervices and rents due and accuftomed. This Richard was fonne to the lord Maurice the firft, and great vncle to the faid Margaret.

Came Co: roll: 8. Jac. for the alienacōns and apportionment of the 12^d rent.
Co: roll of Came. 38. Eliz. Willm Baffet obijt. 7. 12^d.

And in this manor of Came is a meffuage garden and 60. acres of land, and 3. acres of meadowe, holden of the lord Berkeley by knight fervice, wherof Edmund Baffet in 4. E. 2. dyed feifed, as his office fheweth; which in partition amongft his three fifters and heires were allotted to Margaret maried to Nicholas de Valers, who | fhortly after fold them or the greater part to Thomas lord Berkeley, as by Deeds in Berkeley caftle doth appeare.

By Deed 30. April. A° 8. Jac, Willm Baffet aliened in fee to John Morfe a clofe of pafture called Shortworthy cont̄. 6. acres, And an acre of mead in Brightenmead, in 2. places therof; And 3. acres of arrable land in Downfeild.

By

Came

By deed, 1. Maij. A° 8. Jac. Willm Baffet aliened to John Hutchens in fee, A meffuage garden and a peell of pafture ground adioyninge containing one rood.

And by Deed dated 1. Maij. A° 8. Jac. aliened to Giles Hutchens in fee, A meffuage garden orchard and a clofe called the homeclofe cont halfe an acre, A clofe called hangingly cont 2. acres, A clofe called Credins brooke cont 2. acres, And 3. acres and an halfe of arrable land in fouthfeild, in 4. places, And a clofe of pafture in hidefeild called Bufhinge grove cont. 3. acres, and 2. ac̄ of arr̄ land in hidefeild called Bankefland; And other two acres of arrable in the faid hidefeild abutt on the kings highway on the north end.

Heere alfo neere vnto the church is an ancient meffuage with 60 acres of land meadowe and pafture therto belonginge, cōmonly called Oulpens, holden of this manor of Came by knight fervice, fute of Court, and the yearly rent of—7ᵈ ob. nowe the inheritance of Willm Hardinge, who paies—6ᵈ ob. therof; And of Thomas Mors, who paies—1ᵈ. Thomas Cliffe, alfo Thomas Daunt, Somers, and Willm Plomer, hold fome other parts of this land, but pay noe part of the rent: See the Court roll of Came. 2°. et 10° Jacobi.   *Daunts lands. olim, Olpens.*

By an Inq: in 24 Eliz. Edward Woolworth als Webb is found to dye feifed of 34. acres of land in Came, holden by fute of Court and the yearly rent of—2ᵈ ob.; And to bee conveyed in taile to Chriftopher Woolworth and Willm Woolworth, the remainder to his owne right heires. And that Margery the wife of Thomas Rawlyns als Compton, daughter of John Woolworth, is his grandchilde and heire, of full age: This land fhortly after came by purchafe to Edward Trotman of Came, who with Edward his fonne and heire after aliened the fame to Willm Hardinge and others.

And for further proofe, fee an Inq: 13. H. 8. 2. bundle, after the death of Margery Daunt daughter and heire of Robert de Oulpen, from whofe feifin and of many of his anceftors theis lands receiued their name of Oulpens, which holds to this day. And fee alfo an Inq: in 35. H. 8. after the death of Chriftopher Daunt fonne and heire of the faid Margery. And more fully in my defcription of Oulpen fol: 309. which I heere omit, in avoidinge double repetitions. |

Heere alfo in another ancient meffuage called Woodends houfe, with two yard land therto belonginge, now the inheritance of Edward Hill gent, which this prefent yeare, 1638. hee purchafed of ffrancis Webb of London as after followeth; holden   *135 Woodend-houfe. late Trotmans nowe Hills.*

of

of the lord Berkeley as of his manor of Came, by knight service sute of Court and the yearly rent of 24ᵈ as after more pticulerly followeth: who also for some other small parcell of land longe occupied therwith and togeather paieth—2ᵈ more. Which lands have removed as nowe followeth.

By Deed without date, (which I have seene,) Robert lord Berkeley (the second of that name) who died in 4. H. 3, as formerly in Berkeley and other places appeares; granted to **Roger de Woodend** (the true scituacōn of this house and lands,) vnam dimidiam virgatam terræ in Came, scilt, illā dimidiā virgata terræ cum messuagio et ōibus alijs ptincñ suis, que Raďus de Boleia tenuit, Tenendum sibi et hereď suis, de me et hereď meis, liberè honorifice et quietè, Reddenď mihi et hereď meis pro omni servicio, consuetudine et exactione, octo solidos, vz, Ad sestm Michis—4ˢ et sestm beatæ Mariæ in ñicio 4ˢ Salvo Dñi regis servicio, vz, quantum ptinet ad dimiď virgatā terre in eaď. villa.

And by another Deed without date also, (which I have likewise seene,) Thomas lord Berkeley brother and heire of the said lord Robert (the first of that name,) who died in 28. H. 3, as formerly also in Berkeley and other places appeares, Remisit Ricō filio Rogeri de la Wudende de Came pro homagio et servicio suo, in liberū maritagiū cum Sibilla filia Petri Sammelis, quatuor solidos redditus de viginti octo solidis, quos dictus Rogerus mihi singulis annis reddere consuevit, pro vna virgata terræ et dimiď quam bone memoriè Robtus de Berket frater meus dicto Rogero et hereď suis, dedit et cartis suis confirmavit; (A deed I have not yet seene;) Et insuper dictus Thomas remisit dicto Ricardo in liberˉ maritagiū eˉm pdicta Sibilla et hereď suis, sectā hundredi mei nisi tantùm quod tèr in anno ad hundredum meum rationabilitèr vocatus accedat, vz, ad prox hundreď post sestm sci Michis, et ad prox hundreduˉ pt sestm sci Hillarij, et ad hundredum de Hockday; with a confirmacōn of the said yard land and an halfe: Rendringe yearly—24ˢ at the fower feast daies, of xˉmas, Easter, Sᵗ John Baptist, and Michas, for all services exactions and worldly demands, Salvo tantū regali servicio quantūm ptinebit ad vnā virgatā terræ et dimidiā in eadem; As by the Deed, with a seale of red wax with the George mounted, circumscribed **Sigillum Thome de Berkelei**, appeares.

In the 17ᵗʰ of E. 2. it was the land of Thomas at Woodend.

By a Deed in Berkeley castle in 4. H. 5. Willm Kedon, cozen and heire of Richard Wodeende of Came, released to Willm Longford of Came and to John Cowley

Cowley of Stinchcombe and their heires, All his right and estate in all those lands and tenements, which to him discended after the death of Richard Wodeende his cozen in Came. [And by another Deed, there also, in 6. H. 5. John Cowley aforesaid released to the said William Longford and his heires, All his estate right title &c. in all those lands tenements revertions &c. in Came, which hee had of the guift and grant of Willm Kedon cozen and heire of Richard Wodeend of Came. And thus moved this land from the family and name of Woodend, to the name and family of Longford.

In the 9. H. 5., 1. H. 6., 21. H. 6., 26. H. 6., it was the land of Willm Longford aforesaid, who in that 26th yeare gave the same by the name of a messuage and one yard land and an halfe called Woodends, to John his sonne in taile, the remainder to his owne right heires ; In which name of Longford (wherby the lands are to this day called Longfords lands,) it continued vntill the time of kinge Henry the seaventh.

In the 13th of kinge Henry the seaventh, John Longford, a marchant in Bristoll, conveyed the same to Mathew Catchmay and his heires, by the name of all his lands in Came or elsewhere within the hundred of Berkeley.

In 21. H. 8. Willm Catchmay conveyed to Richard Brayne and his heires, A messuage in Came and all his lands there which discended to him after the death of Agnes Catchmay his grandmother.

In 35. H. 8. the said Richard Brayne conveyed to Thomas Trotman and his heires, All those two messuages with their appurtenants called Longfords ; And one other messuage and halfe a yard land in Whetenhurst, Which (with a Releafe also,) is inrolled with the clarke of the peace of this county ; And in 1. E. 6. A fine was levied of theis lands betweene Thomas Trotman q̃. and Richard Brayne and Eliz. Ashby widowe, def⸍ by the names of 3. mess and 180. acres, &c. in Came and Whetenhurst.

ffrom which Thomas Trotman this land came to Richard his second sonne and his heires, Against whom, a title to theis lands was pretended by George Goffe in right of Mary his wife, Jone ap Roberts, widowe, and Thomas James, as coheires to Mary Catchmay after wife of William Warren, which beinge ended by Arbitrement, A fine (amongst other assurances) was levied in Trinity terme, 20. Eliz. betweene Richard Trotman plt, and George Goffe and Mary his wife, Thomas James

James, and Jone ap Roberts, widowe, coheires of Mary Catchmay dec.ᵈ by the names of 3. meſſ. and 180. acres, &c. in Came ; The Indenture leadinge the vſe to the ſaid Richard Trotman and his heires, And the Arbitrement, That the queſtion was for Woodends houſe in Came, and one yard land and an halfe therto belonginge : And for another houſe and halfe a yard land therto belonginge in Came alſo, called Lampland. Touchinge which Lampland, all I have found is That 24º Auguſti. 3. E. 6. the kinge granted 2ˢ rent p Anñ to Wiłłm Saule and Wiłłm Bridges and their heires, who 18. Octobr̃. the ſame yeare granted the ſame to Thomas Trotman and his heires, goeinge out of a certaine tenement in Came called Longfords houſe, Ad ſuſtentandum vnū lampadem in Eccleſia de Came.

The ſaid Thomas Trotman dyed (as hath byn ſaid) in 5. et 6. Ph : & Mar̃, leavinge this land in Came to Richard his ſecond ſonne aforeſaid, who built a faire houſe thervpon And after died in 35. Eliz. wherby it diſcended to Edward his eldeſt ſonne, who vpon maryage of Edward his eldeſt ſonne with the widowe of John Aylway, conveyed the reverſion after his owne life in fee or fee tayle to the ſaid Edward his ſonne, ſince a Reader in Court and bencher in the Inner Temple, yet livinge. Who after ſundry mortgages therof and of other lands to Henry Prat of London, made by him and Edward his ſonne and heire apparant, And to Wiłłm Hill of Tuexbury and John Wakeman, Samuell Trotman, and Throgmorton Trotman, his brothers and kinſmen, vpon loanes of monies and for their indemnities from debts as ſuerties for him the ſaid Edward, They all by ffine Recovery and Deeds in 10. Regis Caroli, conveyed the ſame to the vſe of ffrancis Webb aforeſaid and his heires ; Who by Deed and fine in 14. R̃ Caroli, conveyed the ſame to Edward Hill aforeſaid and his heires, to whom Elizabeth my third daughter is wife. The Epitaph of which Edward Trotman the father is in Came church in theis words : Heere lyeth the body of Mr. Edward Trotman the elder, late of Eſtwood, ſonne of Mr. Richard Trotman of Poole court in Worceſterſhire, by Katherine his wife daughter of Edward Tindall Eſquire : Hee was borne the 5ᵗʰ day of October, aº Dñi. 1545. and comfortably departed this life the 6ᵗʰ of June. 1633. Thus his Tombe.

Aſtmead in Came.

In this pariſh of Came, in the hamblet called Aſtmead als Aſhmead which confiſteth of 4. ancient dwellinge houſes, is one meſſuage called Miles place at White croſſe greene with halfe a yard land therto belonginge, of old parcell of the foreſaid manor of Draicote, nowe of late the inheritance of John Stinchcombe, ſonne of John ſonne of Robert and Welthian his wife, daughter of John Tomlins
als

Came

als Minard, to whom the said John by his Will devised the same in generall tayle, haveinge in the 37ᵗʰ. H. 8. purchased the same (inter alia) of John Nelme, sonne of Richard sonne of John sonne of William Nelme, and of Tibote his wife, daughter of Jone Dreycote, daughter and coheire of John Dreycote, sonne of Stephen de Dreycote, wherof see more in Dreycote fol: 125. 126. And is holden as the rest of that farme or manor of Draycote, by knight service, and suite of Court, as before is written fol: p̃dc̃o. |

Deere also, is a messuage watermill and lands com̃only called Mabsons lands, now or late the inheritance of John Trotman, holden of this manor of Came by knight service sute of Court and the yearly rent of—13ˢ. 4ᵈ, which John is sonne of Nicholas who dyed 19. Eliz., sonne of John who dyed also 19. Eliz., sonne of Thomas who dyed 5. et 6. Ph: et Mar̃, sonne of Henry Trotman who dyed 18. H. 8, haveinge by deed dated 17. Aprit aº 3. H. S. purchased the same of Henry Mabson, and which before were the lands of William Mabson, who was in ward for the same; ffrom whose seisin and other of their Ancestors the name of Mabsons land still continueth; Nowe the inheritance of Henry Trotman sonne of John.

138
Mabsons lands. nowe Trotmans.

Of this land also, theis have part, viz:ᵗ,

Deere also is an ancient messuage with 90. acres of ground, anciently esteemed a Carucate of land, with a grist mill and two fullinge mills com̃only called and knowne by the name of Coriets, als Coriets place; now the inheritance of Samuell Hardinge, sonne of William lately dead who purchased the same of Arnold Oldisworth Esq̃, in 10. Jacobi, And hee by deed dated 20º. Julij Aº 9º. Jacobi p̃d, of Henry lord Berkeley, whose grandchild and heire George lord Berkeley now is, wherin the said Lord reserved the feefarme rent of—3ˢ. p añ, anciently paid, paiable halfe yearly, And 39ˢ. rent to bee paid to John Hardinge, (now Willm Hoptons) and to Thomas Taylor, and their heires yearely, and sute of court to his manor of Came, or 4ᵈ for every default.

Corietts.

These of old were the lands of Walter Coriet and other of that Sirname, very ancient freeholders there, which com̃inge by purchase (as I conceive) to the hands of the Lords of the manor of Came, were for many yeares, yea ages, granted by copy of court roll according to the custome of that their manor, for 3. lives successively, the last copihold wherof was John Somers; Howbeit, vpon an Informac̃on of of Intrusion, exhibited in the Exchequer by Queene Eliz. in the 22:th of her raigne againſt the ſaid Henry lord Berkeley, grounded vpon the Attainder of John Dudley Duke of Northumberland, hee was by Jury found guilty, and hee and his ſaid tenant John Somers, then an old man above 80. yeares, turned out of poſſeſſion, by a Decree in the Court of Wards in Eaſter terme in the 42:th yeare of her raigne; haveinge till that time continued a quiet poſſeſſion notwithſtandinge the ſaid Recovery vpon the ſaid Informacõn, as beinge noe true ancient parcell of this manor of Came but ſomtime the freehold land of the ſaid Walter Coriet, wherof much more is to bee read in the ſaid Decree, and in the Bill Anſweres and Depoſitions of witneſſes taken in that cauſe, wheron that Decree was grounded, whither I ſend him that deſireth more.

See an Inq: for that land in Januar̃. 15. R̃ Caroli. 1639. p̃ morte

Trotmans of the Stepps.

Heere alſo is a meſſuage and 36. acres of land, late the inheritance of Edward Trotman, called of the Stepps from the greeſings or ſtaires of ſtone leadinge out of the ſtreet vp into the ſaid meſſuage; And alſo 7. acres of land late James Kings, And alſo one cloſe called Sparkhill cont 8. acres, which hee by deed dated the firſt of July a:o 9:o Jacobi, purchaſed in fee farme of Henry lord Berkeley, then copihold lands held accordinge to the cuſtome of that manor by Willm Bendall and others, Reſervinge the yearly rent of thirty ſhillings and ſix pence payable quarterly, And —3:li 6: 8:d for an heriot after the death of each tenant of the ſame, or of any part therof, And like ſute to the Halimot court of this manor of Came as other cuſtomary tenants there doe, or 4:d in money for every default: Howbeit the tenure is of the kinge by knight ſervice in Capite, beinge part of the ſaid Lord Berkeleys manor of Came before the ſaid grant, which is ſoe holden: Which Edward dyed 9:o Maij. a:o 14:o Car̃ regis, As an Inquiſicõn after his death; a:o 14. R̃ Caroli ſã, ſheweth; And the ſaid lands remained in fee tayle generall to Nicholas his ſonne by a ſecond wife; And not to Richard ſonne of William, eldeſt ſonne of the ſaid Edward Trotman by his firſt wife.

Eſtcourts land. Mileſmore.

Heere alſo is a paſture ground called Myleſmore containinge 7. acres, the inheritance of Thomas Eſtcourt Eſq, ſonne of Edmond Eſtcourt late of Tetbury, brother and heire of Thomas Eſtcourt of Laſſeborrowe knight, which Thomas his father purchaſed of Richard Bridges, And before the land of Edmond Woolworth ats Webbe, wherof read more in the deſcription of Durſley: Holden of this manor of Came by ſealty, and the yearly rent of—5:s Inq: 1. R. 2. Niclius Berkeley tenuit Mileſmore

Milefmore iuxta Durſley de Dño de Berkeley p 2ˢ 6ᵈ redd p ōibz ſerviē. Et tenuit vnā paſturā vocāt Tannerſcroſt iuxta Durſley de Joħe de Berkeley milite, (de Beverſton) | per redd--5ˢ p anñ pro ōibus ſervicijs.

See alſo the Co: roll of Came 3. Eliz. when Agnes the wife of George Jones died, who held this Milefmore for her life, viz! vnū clauſum vocāt Milefmoore in Durſley, ptiñ manerio de Came, per redd—5ˢ Rob: Wikes eſt proximus heres: Which Agnes was before the wife of John Wikes ſonne and heire of Wikes of Dodington.

Deere alſo in Came, and likewiſe in Cowley, are divers lands and tenements comonly called Taylors lands, now the ſeverall inheritances of John Trotman of Came called of the knapp, John Browninge of Cowley, Edward Hill, Wiłłm Effington, Nicholas ſonne of Edward Trotman of the ſtepps, which the ſaid Edward purchaſed of Griffith Trotman ; which, for thoſe in Cowley were the lands of John Tailor, ſonne of Thomas, called Beeſlies, and were by William Browninge, father of John who died 5 Mař., father of Richard who died 37. Eliz., father of John who died 4. Caroli, father of the ſaid John Browninge of Cowley that now is, 1639. purchaſed of the ſaid John Taylor ſonne of Thomas, And are holden of that manor of Cowley by the yearly rent of—34ˢ as there appeares.

Tailors lands in Came and Cowley.

And the lands in this manor of Came were by Wiłłm Taylor and by his father Thomas, who was ſonne of John, ſonne of Thomas, aliened to the perſons aforenamed and their anceſtors, and to thoſe whoſe eſtates they have. In which family of the Tailors the ſame had continued for many diſcents ſince the time of kinge H. 4.; ffor more wherof and for the tenure ſee a Decree in the Court of Wards and liveries, formerly mentioned vnder the name of Hoptons lands late Hardings: And alſo for theis Tailors lands, And the 39ˢ goeinge out of Coriets lands ſaid to bee paid to Wiłłm Hopton and to the heires and aſſignes of Taylor ; See alſo a fine in banco 10. H. 4. inter Henricum Tailor plť And Walter Knight and Elizabeth his wife defť?

See alſo an Inq: 14. Caroli, for part of theis lands found after the death of the ſaid Edward Trotman father of Nicholas.

And an Inq: 4. Caroli. pt morte Joħis Browninge, Co: roll of Came, 38. Eliz. Ricus Browninge aᵒ preced. rent—40ˢ p terř in Came. |

Deere

Hundred of Berkeley

141
Vpthord, in Came. now Henry Trotmans.

Heere alfo in the little hamblet of this parifh of Came called Vpthorpe, that is the vpper or higher part of the towneſhipp, is a meſſuage and 46. acres of ground therto belonginge, the inheritance of Henry Trotman an Atturny at the Counſell in the Marches of Wales, which hee had with ſome other lands by conveyance from John Trotman his father, yet livinge, dated 6. m̃cij, 14. R℥ Jacobi; And hee the ſaid John as heire to Nicholas his father, eldeſt ſonne of John Trotman, whoſe third brother (called alſo John Trotman) purchaſed this meſſuage and land of
And left it for life to Katherine his wife daughter of William Trotman of Wotton; And by the death of the ſaid John Trotman (called of Vpthorp) without iſſue, the ſame diſcended to the ſaid John Trotman as his next heire, who conveyed it to the ſaid Henry his ſonne vpon his maryage as aforeſaid.

q: if Daunts.   And was before the land of   See for this the Co: rolls
of Came, 44. Eliz. when the ſaid Katherine died.   And

By Deed without date Thomas lord Berkeley the firſt of that name granted to Willm de Berkeley his ſonne in fee, one yard land in Came which William le Bell held of him, To hold by 4ᵈ rent for all ſervices, Salvo regali ſervicio. And by another deed granted to the ſaid Willm in fee one other yard land and an halfe in Came, To hold by 2ᵈ rent for all ſervices, Salvo regali ſervicio, which (doubtles) is knights ſervice. But whoſe theis lands nowe are I knowe not.

Bourtſley. nowe Hoptons.

By deed in 29. E. 1. Thomas lord Berkeley gave to Henry de Came and to his heires, Totam illam culturam terræ que vocatur Bouresley continent 27. acras et dimiđ in Came, In exchange for 24: 6ᵈ rent to bee yearly received of John de Hulmancote of Cowley and his heires. By what meanes and how many diſcents this ground is come from the ſaid Henry de Came to Willm Hopton, whoſe nowe it is, reputed as parcell of the meſſuage in Came called the Hall place, See before in fol: 128.

142   By the record of Extract donacon̄, in 11. E. 3. membr. 12. et 36. Rex conceſſit Simoni Baſſet et hered ſuis, duas mercatas añui redditus in Came in Com̄ Glouc̄ quæ fuerunt Johis de ffoules ſcoti, et ad manus patris regis devenerunt ratione inimicitiæ p̄dicti Johis.

See in Slimbridge fol: 332. for the freehold of Robert Davis which hee purchaſed of Thomas Veel, Rentinge to Came manor—17ˢ 4ᵈ p ann̄.

And

And in Hurſt fol: 248. for the freeholders of Selewins land, nowe the inheritance of Beniamin Bridger Robert Davis and others, Rentinge to Came manor—10ˢ p anñ. |

Cambridge.

Cambridge: An hamblet or ſmall village within the manor and pariſh of Slimbridge, holden by George lord Berkeley by knight ſervice in Capite; Through which lyeth the great Road way leadinge betweene the Cities of Glouc̃ and Briſtoll.

In this Village on Sᵗ Katherines day, the 25ᵗʰ of November, is kept a faire if I may ſoe call it; but for any grant of ſuch to have byn made by the Crowne I could never find, nor thinke that any ſuch hath byn.

Heere alſo was a Chaple wherof Thomas lord Berkeley had the advowtion, as by an Inquiſic̃on found after his death in 5. H. 5. appeares; founded to the honor and worſhip of Sᵗ Katherine and of Sᵗ John Baptiſt, and endowed with competent maintenance for the preiſt, by Thomas lord Berkeley in 17. E. 3. with ſuch ſtatutes and ordinances, appointinge what kindes of Maſſe collects and praiers ſhould bee ſaid and ſonge by him, vpon vſuall daies ordinary holidaies and vpon ſpeciall feſtivall daies, in ſoe decent and holy a manner That they may ſeeme to walke hand in hand with the doctrine of theis our times in the reformed church of England: And for manners and honor of his profeſſion forbiddeth this his preiſt to take any money of any, or to bee ſervant or Chaplen to any perſon but to God only in ſpiritualities, and to himſelfe in honeſt and neceſſary temporalities: And that hee ſhould live chaſtly and honeſtly, and not goe to any markets alehouſes or tavernes, neither ſhould frequent playes or vnlawfull games, with other like ſtatutes and ordinances: ffor which foundac̃on endowment and ordinances hee obtained both the licence of that kinge and the Biſhop of Worceſters confirmac̃on.

Of this hamblet ſee more in Slimbridge fol: 325, and after. |

144 blank.

Canon bury.

Canon bury: als the manor of Canonbury: A compounded lordſhip or manor made of divers peices at ſeverall times put togeather, as after followeth: Heretofore it was by ſuch additions as it received a faire manor of remarkeable value, but nowe
ſoe

foe pared by perticuler purchafes made of feverall parcells therof, That not the 40th part therof remaineth to George lord Berkeley, who hath the Leet or lawe day of all the old refiants, and manor or Court baron, which yealdeth him yearly—5ˢ. 9ᵈ. 2ᵈ. only, the moſt wherof is in cheife rents; Which manor hee holdeth by knight fervice in Capite. And out of the fame paieth alfo for a tenth to the Crowne—2ˢ. 6ᵈ parcell of 47: 5ᵈ referved vpon the Lr̃es patents of king Edward the fixt, as more largely followeth.

It was parcell of the poffeffions of the Abby of Sᵗ. Auguſtines by Briſtoll, and came to the Crowne by the diffolucõn of that Monaſtery in 31. H. 8. The firſt creation or compoundinge togeather of this manor was thus;

Robert the fonne of Hardinge, the firſt lord of Berkeley, not longe after his foundinge of the faid Monaſtery, which hee dedicated to God and to Sᵗ. Auguſtine, the Engliſhmens Apoſtle, neere Briſtoll, in the time of kinge Stephen, did (amongſt divers other manors and lands) endowe the faid Monaſtery with divers lands and tenements in Arlingham, and with halfe of his fifhings there, and the tithe of the other halfe, And with the church and Advowfon of Berkeley, with the two Chaples of Hill and Stone therto belonginge, as before in the defcripcõn of Arlingham and Berkeley, I have written.

Afterwards the lord Maurice his fonne and heire, havinge in the time of kinge H. 2. confirmed to the Abbot and Covent of the faid monaſtery, the foundation and guifts of the faid lord Robert his father, gave more to them (amongſt other lands,) one hide of land at Hinton in the faid parifh of Berkeley, And one meſſuage and a yard land at Alkington in the faid parifh, And alfo one other meſſuage and a yard land at Oldminſter in Hinton aforefaid.

Afterwards the lord Robert his fonne and heire, havinge confirmed (amongſt other things) the aforefaid grants made by his father and grandfather; Hee alfo further gave to the faid Abbot and Covent divers lands and tenements in Hame in the faid parifh of Berkley, And his great wood in Nybley in the parifh of Wotton, called Ewcombe, And alfo a meſſuage and a yard land in Cowley, And alfo his watermill by Berkeley neere Lockfaſt-bridge, after called Sextons mill, and alfo a meſſuage and yard land neere to the faid mill: and a meſſuage and yard land at Hulmancote in Cowley. And a meſſuage and one yard land in Pockampton in Hinton aforefaid; And alfo gave to the Abbot and Covent of Kingſwood (which

after

after came to this Abbot and covent of S.ᵗ | Auguſtine by purchaſe,) 4. yard land at Arlingham and divers other fiſhings there, And alſo halfe a yard land at Ryam in Alkington aforeſaid; And divers houſes in Berkeley towne, And two yard more land in Arlingham, which this lord gave to the Chanons of Hereford, from whom this Abbot and covent of S.ᵗ Auguſtines after purchaſed the ſame.

Afterwards Thomas lord Berkeley brother and heire to the foreſaid lord Robert, gave to the ſaid Abbot and Covent of S.ᵗ Auguſtines other meſſuages and lands in Cowley Berkeley and Hincton, And diſchargeth all other their lands within the hundred of Berkeley (from whomſoever obtained or purchaſed,) from all manner of ſervices and earthly demaunds.

Afterwards, Maurice lord Berkeley ſonne of the ſaid lord Thomas, in 53. H. 3. confirmed to the ſaid Abbot and Covent, All thoſe former grants of his Anceſtors, and of all others, which any freeholders within his fee and ſeignory had made vnto them, Releaſinge therewithall all his free rents and ſervices which they owed to him for any their lands; And further gave more to them divers lands and tenements in Berkeley Bevington and Walmegaſton in the pariſh of Berkeley, And in Erlingham. And now had the Abbot a fixt part of Berkeley towne, at the end wherof the Capitall Meſſuage of Canonbury is ſeated, as the old Exchequer booke of Knights fees ſpeaketh, whither to his Courts hee drewe all other his tenants.

Afterwards in 35. E. 1. Thomas then lord Berkeley ſonne of Maurice lord Berkeley, ſonne of the laſt mentioned Thomas lord Berkeley, and Maurice his ſonne and heire apparant, granted to the ſaid Abbot and Covent to have a viewe of franke pledge (behold the riſinge) of all their owne tenants in all his manors and lands within the hundred of Berkeley, and in all their Loᵗ⁽ˢ⁾ in the county of Glouc̃; And to have Stockes, Cage, tumbrill, pillory, Cucking ſtooll and other Judicialls, Colliſtrigia, et trebuchets,[1] &c. All which Thomas lord Berkeley ſonne of the ſaid Maurice in 4. E. 3. recitinge the ſaid wholl deed, confirmed to the ſaid Abbot and Covent.

And afterwards the ſaid laſt mentioned Lord Thomas, ſonne of Maurice, ſonne of Thomas, ſonne of Maurice, ſonne of Thomas, brother and heire of the ſaid lord Robert, in 11. E. 3. granted to the then Abbot and Covent of this monaſtery of S.ᵗ Auguſtines, omnia animalia et alia, vt Cumeling et extrahura inventa et per ballivos

---

[1] Pillory and Cucking-ſtool or Tumbrell. [ED.]

ballivos fuos capta et arreftata in ōibus dnicis fuis infra hundredum fuum de Berkeley; And thus was this manor of Canonbury hatched and framed, with the liberties thereof, out of the devotion of 7. Lords in their fucceffive generations. |

147   **Thus** continued this manor, but much more enlarged with the appropriate Rectory of Berkeley, till by the diffolution of the monaftery it came to the Crowne in 31. H. 8. and was in the beginninge of E. 6. his raigne granted to Sir Thomas Seymour knight lord Seymor of Sudely Caftle, by whofe attainder of high treafon fhortly after it came to the Crowne: And fhortly after, the faid kinge Edward the 10th of September in the 4th of his raigne, granted the fame to John Dudley Earle of Warr̃, (not longe after created Duke of Northumberland) and his heires. And the 16th of the fame September the faid Earle of Warr̃, conveyed the faid Manor to Sir Richard Sackvile knight, Chancellor of the court of Augmentations, and to Winifride his wife and to the heires of the faid Sir Richard; As by the Deed inrolled in the Chancery doth appeare, To hold by the 4th part of a knights fee. Which Sir Richard by his deed dated 1. October 5. et 6. Ph: & Mar̃, vpon the maryage of Thomas his eldeft fonne with the daughter of Sir John Baker of the privy Counfell to Queene Mary, fetled the fame vpon his faid fonne and the heires of his body, with remainder to his owne heires: which Thomas created Lord Buckhurft after the death of his father, And after Earle of Dorfet by kinge James, did in Hillary Terme a^o 13. Eliz. by his deed dated 3. ffebr̃. and by fine then levied, fell the faid manor of Canonbury to Nicholas Thorpe Efq$_r$, Wittm Laverence gent̃, Wittm Beconfawe, Thomas Cole, Thomas Pleydell, Richard Tilladam, and Nicholas Webbe, and their heires, who alfo therby agreed amongft themfelves how much and what parts of the faid Manor each of them fhould have in feveralty, And the vfe of the faid ffine, for fuch parts as each of them was to have, declared by Indentures to bee to them and their feverall heires in perticulers by deed 3° ffebr̃. fid. And by another deed feptempartite the 16th of the faid ffebr̃ the forefaid feaven purchafors agreed how much of the tenth or rent of—47^s 5^d referved to the Crowne vpon the faid Lr̃es patents, fhould bee paid by each of them and their heires, at Michas only, vz. Nicholas Thorpe to pay therof—4^s Wittm Laverence–16^s Richard Beconfawe–12^s 5^d Thomas Pleydell–12^d Richard Tilladam—4^s Nicholas Webb—6^s 6^d and Thomas Cole—4^s to bee paid at the houfe of the faid Wittm Laverence in Berkeley called Canbury; who was alwaies after to fee the fame paid to the Crowne at his perill and charges. Towards which they all further agreed, That Nicholas Thorpe fhould pay—6^d Richard Beconfawe —6^d Richard Tilladam—6^d Nicholas Webb—6^d And Thomas Cole—6^d With a diftres

Canon burp

a diſtres by Wiłłm Laverence and his heires if not paid: And with a Covenant from Wiłłm Laverence to pay the ſaid tenth, and to ſave each of them harmles therfrom: And the ſaid Richard Beconſawe, afterwards, by his deed dated   ſold his parts, vz. Sextons mills to Wiłłm Machin father of John, father of Thomas ſtill owner therof; And a meſſuage and 40. acres therto belonginge neere therunto to Giles Harvey, whoſe ſonne   ſold the ſame to Lawrance Bridger clerke, father by his third wife to Joſeph Bridger, that nowe holdeth the ſame. And to the lord Henry Berkeley ſold the Leet and Court baron with certaine cheife rents &c. as before. And in the joynt deed made to them three | by Richard Beconſawe agreed, That Wiłłm Machin ſhould of his 12ˢ 5ᵈ pay–vjˢ Giles Harvey–4ˢ 1ᵈ and the lord Berkeley—2ˢ 4ᵈ. Accordinge Beconſawe levied a fine to them three And they three releaſed mutually each to other.

148

Howbeit, accordinge to the ſhuſtings of thoſe times, the 23ᵗʰ of Auguſt aⁿ 4. E. 6. aforeſaid, An exchange of this manor (inter alia) was made betweene the ſaid Earle and the kinge, wherby the kinge had this manor from the ſaid Earle; And the Earle and Jone his wife had againe this manor to them and the heires of the ſaid Earle, To hold as is aforeſaid: Whervpon, for inequality or other miſtake in this exchange, A title by the proſecucōn of one Tipper (a great factor in concealments) was pretended by Queene Elizabeth, and thervpon for quietinge therof in conſideracōn of—188ˡⁱ 9ˢ 8ᵈ A new łres patents obtained from her vnder the great ſeale dated 21ᵒ ffebř. aᵒ 45ᵗᵒ regni ſui, to George Thorpe ſonne of the ſaid Nicholas, John Denys Eſqꝫ named by the lord Henry Berkeley, Thomas Cole aforeſaid, Richard Webbe ſonne of the ſaid Nicholas, John Machin, Lawrance Wilſhire, and Robert Webb, and their heires, Rendringe per ann̄–47ˢ 5ᵈ beinge the aforementioned tenth; Who ſhortly after accordinge to the truſt in them repoſed granted to each freeholder and leſſee the like eſtates which they formerly had, raiſinge the ſaid money by an equall proportion vpon the ſaid land and eſtates, wherwith I was well acquainted.

More is to bee read in theis Records;

Originalls. 4. E. 6. ps. 5ᵗᵃ Rot. 46. Glouc̄. in Sc̃c̃io. Rex alienavit Manerium de Canonbury Ric̃o Sackvile et Wineſride vxori eius et hered ipꝰus Ric̃i. Trin̄ Records, 13. Eliz. in Sc̃c̃io c̃m Rc̄n̄i Theſauř. Rot 44. et 47. are large pleadings for this manor of Canonbury, wherin many of the former alienacōns doe appeare.

And

And for the ffreeholders holdinge of this manor, I have rather chosen to mention them in the description of the townships wherin the lands they hold doe lye. As in Alkington. fol : 41. 43. And in Cowley. fol : 160. 161. |

149
Clinger.

Clinger : Anciently written Cleihunger : Is an hamblet within the Chaplery of Stincheombe and parish of Came ; whereof read more before in Beoly fol : 75. And in Stinchcombe . fol : 343. et 345.

By Inq : 1. E. 1. it is found, That halfe a yard land which Wittm Mauduit (who was hanged for felony) held in Cheihunger, had byn a yeare and a day in the kings hands, And was held of the Abbot of S! Peter of Glouc̃. |

150 blank

151
Combe.

Combe ats Wottons Combe, ats Combe iuxta Wotton ; Is an hamblet or village within the parish of Wotton, And one of those five wherof the manor of Wotton fforren is compounded, wherof read more at large in Wotton ats Wotton vnder edge.

This hamblet by a kinde of excelleney hath its name from the scituation therof in a bottome betweene two remarkeable Combes or hills almost inclosing it : ffor though the words **Combe** and **Compe** in the Saxon tongue signify a feild or Campe for an Army to abide or foiourne in, as somwhat declyned from the latine **Campus**, yet this Combe wherof I heere write is not from thence but from the Hills declininge as abovesaid.

freeholds within the hamblet of Combe.

Birds land, late Bridges.

Heere is one most ancient and remarkeable freehold which doubtles foe was before the time of William the Conqueror, as by a Deed remaininge in the possession of that ancient genf Anthony Kingscote of Kingscote, which I have read, appeares ; of later time (not nowe) reputed a manor ; The most part wherof is nowe the inheritance of Giles Bird genĩ, which hee the last yeare, a⁰ 1638. purchased chafed of John Bridges fonne of Richard, and of Henry fonne and heire of John; wherof the lord Robert fonne of Hardinge (often before mentioned) in the beginninge of the raigne of kinge Henry the fecond enfeoffed Elias his brother and his heires, by the name of vnam hidam terræ de Combe, illam quam ego emi de Mahihele filio Anfgeri de Combe, vz, one hide of land which I purchafed of Mahihell the fonne of Anfger of Combe; To hold of the faid Robert and his heires by the fifth part of one knights fee: To which deed remaininge in the caftle of Berkeley theis are witneffes, vz, The lady Eva wife of the faid lord Robert, and Maurice, Nicholas, and Robert his three fonnes, Otho filius Willi, Nigellus filius Arthuri, Rogerus et Hardingus de Stintefcombe, Willus filius Bernardi, Ricus filius Hardingi de Covely, Ractus de Draycote, &c.

ffrom which Elias the feoffee the faid land difcended to Willm his fonne, who had iffue Willm, whofe wardfhip was in the 17th yeare of kinge H. 3. controverted betweene Thomas then lord Berkeley, fonne of Maurice, fonne of the faid Robert, And the Abbot of Kingfwood; which William fonne of William, called Willus Camerarius, or Willm the Chamberlaine, afterwards granted the fame to another William fonne of another Elias, Refervinge a rent to the cheife Lord of—13^s 4^d yearly, which is paid to this day. 1639.

By a Deed without date, Willus Camerarius dedit Abbati de Kingefwood &c. affenfu et voluntate et petitione Willi filij Eliæ liberi hominis fui, annuũ redditũ vnius marci argenti, et omnia fervicia eiufdem Willi filij Eliæ et heredum fuorum, quæ fibi vel heredibus eius facere debebant, de feodo quod de fe tenuerunt in villa de Coombe, et totam dominationem fuã et totum ius fuũ, quod in ipfo Willo et hered̄ fuis et feudo fuo habuit. | whervpon the faid Willus fit Eliæ did his homage to the faid Abbot, faith this Deed, wherto 21 are witneffes: which feemes to have occafioned the former fuite: But howe the faid 13^s 4^d came backe to bee paid (as this day it is and longe hath byn,) to the heire of the lord Robert the firft feoffer, I knowe not yet. A deed in the box of Kingfwood fent mee by M^r. Hale from London.

In the beginninge of the raigne of kinge Edward the third it was the land of Walter de Combe, and towards the middle of that kings time it fell vpon Jone de Combe daughter and heire (as I conceive) of the faid Walter, who was maried to Berley, who in 2. R. 2. fold the fame to Lawrance Jewet, who in 12. H. 4. granted the fame to Robert Longe and Margaret his wife, daughter of him the faid
Lawrance

Lawrance Jewet, and to the heires of their two bodies, who had iffue Henry Longe who dyed in 6. H. 7. without iffue, And Thomas Longe fonne of John Longe brother of the faid Henry was his heire : which Thomas Longe, then knight, died in 24. H. 7. leavinge Sir Henry Longe of Draycote in Wiltfhire, who in 17. H. 8. fold the fame to ffrancis Butler Efq.; which ffrancis in 32. H. 8. fold the fame to Thomas Davis of Michelhampton, who died in 37. H. 8. levinge iffue Giles Davis who died in   and ffrancis Davis, who died in 5. et 6. Ph : et Mar. And two daughters, Elizabeth maried to John Poole, and Mary maried to Willm Weltden : The faid Giles and ffrancis died without iffue, And the faid Willm Weltden and Mary his wife, in the third yeare of Queene Elizabeth fold their moity to John Bridges and his heires ; And the faid William Poole and Elizabeth his wife had iffue John Poole, which John in 7. Eliz. fold his other moity to the faid John Bridges and his heires, who died in the   yeare of the faid Queene, leavinge iffue Richard Bridges, who died in 18. Jacobi, havinge fetled the fame vpon the faid John his fonne for life, and the inheritance in tayle vpon the faid Henry fonne and heire apparant of the faid John : Who aliened to Giles Bird, as is firft above mentioned. Michaell Bridges brother of the faid Henry holdeth in fee by his grant, A Cotage and garden ground, parcell of this hide, lately burned to the ground, nowe newly built againe. Alfo divers other parcells therof by way of Exchanges are holden by

<small>Dangervills meffuage and lands.</small> Maurice Lord Berkeley the third of that name by his deed in   E. 2. (which the lord Thomas his fonne and heire after in 3. E. 3. confirmed,) granted divers lands and tenements in Bradley and Combe, with the reverfion of thofe other lands and tenem^{ts} which Alienor de Bradley holds for her life within the manor of Wotton, to Maurice Berkeley his fecond fonne and the heires males of his body, as before

153 is written in the defcription of Bradley:| which meffuage and yard land in Combe is now the inheritance of Robert Webb of Sinwell by purchafe from John Bridges and Henry his fonne aforefaid ; whofe father Richard Bridges purchafed the fame of Thomas Graile of Huntingford, and hee of the lady Eliz : Berkeley of Bradley and Richard Berkeley of Stoke Efq.; and is called Dangerfeilds, holden of the manor of Wotton fforren by a Red rofe payable on Midfomer day : And is (as tradition tells) to bee on that morninge fet vpon a poft at a gate there : But the Deed is with falvo regali fervicio, which is knight fervice, et fectam ad Curiā Hundredi de Berkeley de tribus in tres feptimañ.

Co :

Cowley

Co : roll of Wotton fforren 19. Eliz. Edward Berkeley Esq, died seised of a messuage and a yard land in Combe, holden per vnā rosā rubeam, solvend ante exortū solis die natalis sci Johis baptistæ, Et pro defctu solucōis tunc diſtringere pro—ij^d.

More of this hamblet of Combe is to bee read in theis Records : vz,

Terñi Michis. 4. H. 3. Rot. 26. in banco. Niclius de la mare et Grecia vxor eius demaund againſt Robert Cotele two carucates of land in Combe, in a longe plea in dower; which Grecia was the widowe of Cotele, now remaryed to de la mare.

Plita in banco. Terñi Michis. 17. H. 3. Rot. 1.

ffinis in banco, Terñi Michis. 8. H. 5. Inter Johem Priorem de Bath, de 16. mesſ et al̃ terr̃ in Combe et Wotton vnderedge.

Inq : 6. H. 7. p̃t mortē Henrici Longe.

Carta irrotulaī in banco, Terñi Michis. 33. H. 8. Rot. 2.

Inq : 38. H. 8. p̃t mortē Thome Davis.

Inq : 4. et 5. Ph : & Mar̃. p̃t mortē ffr̃ Davis. ps. 1.

Original c̄m reñi Thesaur̃ in sc̃cio. 4. et 5. Ph : & Mar̃. ps. 1. Rot. 28.

ffinis in banco terñi pasch : 3. Eliz. Inter Johem Bridges et Willm Weltden et al̃.

Rot. finiū Terñi Triñ 4. Eliz. Rot. 4. Glouc ; in sc̃cio c̄m Reñi Thesaur̃.

Inq : 19 Jac : p̃t mortē Rici Bridges.

Rot. patent. 34. E. 1. in dorso, Willus filius Willi de Combe arrainavit assisā versus Walterū de Combe et al̃ de vno mesſ vno molend 26. acr̃ terre et prati in Hillesly, Alderly, Wotton, et Berkeley.

See also in Simondsfall. fol : 323.

Inq : 15. Regis Caroli, p̃t mortē Egidij Bird.

Of Trayned soldiers vnder Thomas Veel Esq, their Captaine this hamblet of Combe with Symondsfall, furnisheth | Souldiers.

154 blank

Cowley.

Cowley : In Domesdei booke Couelege. A parish and Manor wherof George Lord Berkeley is Lord, part of his Barony of Berkeley, and holden by knight service in Capite : The Demesnes wherof consisted of fower hides of land as Domesdei booke sheweth.

In

In this parish are theis hamblets, wherby the habitacons of the inhabitants are more readily diftinguifhed, vz, Churchend, Pinelfend, Hulmancote, and

This manor was (amongft others) given by kinge Henry the fecond in the firft yeare of his raigne to Robert the fonne of Hardinge and his heires, vnder the words Berkelai et totam Berkelei herneffe manerium cum omnibus appendicijs fuis; which Robert by that grant was alfo created a Baron and peere of the Realme, and had iffue Maurice, who had iffue Robert and Thomas ; Robert dyed without iffue, and Thomas had iffue Maurice, father of Thomas, father of Maurice, father of Thomas, father of Maurice, father of Thomas and of James ; which Thomas dyed without iffue male of his body ; And the faid James had iffue James, to whom this manor with the refidue of the Barony (formerly entayled vpon the heires males) difcended after the death of the lord Thomas his vncle ; which James the nephewe had iffue William created Marques Berkeley, Maurice and others ; William entayled this manor (amongft others) vpon kinge Henry the feaventh and the heires males of his body, and after dyed without iffue ; And the faid Maurice had iffue Maurice, and Thomas ; Maurice dyed without iffue, And the faid Thomas his brother had iffue Thomas, father of Henry, who in the firft of Queene Mary, entred vpon this manor, the iffue male of Henry the 7th beinge fpent in the death of kinge Edward the fixt ; and the faid Lord Henry had iffue Thomas, who dyed in the life of his father, leavinge iffue the faid George Lord Berkeley who is owner of this manor, a^o. 1639. as abovefaid. ffor more pticularity of which difcent, times of each lords death, &c. fee before in fol : 7. et 78, and other places in this booke.

To this parifh of Cowley adioyneth the parifh of ffroucefter, an ancient parcell of the poffeffions of the Abbot of St Peters in Glouc, whofe corne there growing was by ancient cuftome vfed to bee cut mowed and reaped by the lords tenants of this manor of Cowley, and of his other manor of Came, next alfo adioyninge ; ffor which fervice the faid Abbot by like cuftome was at his priory of Stanley (a Cell to this monaftery and neere adioyninge,) to feaft the baylies and tenants of the faid manors of Cowley and Came in Harveft time : The faid Abbot complaines to Thomas lord Berkeley the fecond of that name then lord of thofe manors, That to his great wronge and greife many came to that feaft fayninge themfelves tenants to that lord, fervants and Bailies of thofe his manors, when they were not : whervpon in 32. E. 1. it was agreed, That in lieu of the faid feaft, every Reeve and bayly of the faid manors fhould thenceforth have—4^d, And every reaper—3^d, and every gather and binder—2^d, And every raker of the faid corne—1^d ob, in lieu

of

of their feaft, which order held till the | diffolucōn of that Monaftery in the time of **156**
kinge H. 8. or neere therto.

In 6. E. 2. was an agreement by deed indented betweene the forefaid Thomas lord Berkeley and the faid Abbot of S: Peters, for intercomīnge betweene their tenants of Cowley and ffrouceſter, and for inclofinge part of the feilds of thofe manors : which holds to this day.

The kinge is patron of the Vicarage and prefenteth : The Rectory and appropriacōn is the inheritance of John Browninge, by a purchafe therof made by John his father in November, 7: Jacobi, from Morris and Phillips, who had the fame (inter alia) from the faid kinge by his Lr̃es patents dated the 7th. of September before, in ffee farme, at 15th. yearly rent ; which rent alfo in the 18th. yeare of the faid kinge, hee granted away by like lr̃es patents to Whittacre and Price and their heires, who fhortly after fold the fame to the faid John Browninge the father ; which rectory or appropriacōn was after the diffolucōn of the monaftery of S: Peters in Glouc̃ (to which it anciently belonged,) granted to Sir Anthony Kingſton and his heires. And from him it came againe to the Crowne ; It is holden nowe of the kinge as of the manor of Eaſt Greenwich in free and comon foccage by fealty only.

Church.

The which Church was dedicated to S: Bartholomew the tutelary faint therof, On whofe feaſt day yet continueth fuch concourfe and refort of people That it hath the name of Cowley ffaire day, wheron moſt kindes of country wares are brought and fold in boothes and ſtandings purpofely fet vp : But by noe grant or Charter from the Crowne or otherwife then the intertainment of the faid John Browninge and his Anceſtors, and fome other of the inhabitants, both on that day, and on the Sunday after called Cowley ffeaſt or Wake day ; which even now begins, both in faire and hofpitallity, to diminifh and growe fickely.

Of this parifh it may bee faid, as before I have written of Came, That if it were inclofed round from all other fociety and comerce of men, it would abundantly fuffice for the fuſtentacōn and well beinge of the inhabitants, without fupply from other places that the minde of man could neceffarily defire.

The durty ſtreetes wherof feeme recompenced in part with the hills encompaſſinge the Eaſterne part of this parifh : The moſt eminent wherof is called Cowley pike ; where to behold younge men and maids afcendinge and difcendinge and
boies

boies tumblinge downe, especially on Comunion daies in the afternoones what times the resort is greatest, bringeth noe small delight to many of the elder sort also delightinge therin.

Marle poole

Remarkeable is a marle poole in the feild of this parish called South worthy, by the naturall contract of the inhabitants Suckerdy ; A durable remembrancer of the old husbandry heere vsed (as in all the parishes adioyninge,) for betteringe of their arrable lands, wholly neglected since the times of kinge Henry the sixt] and kinge Edward the fourth, when not only the civill warres betweene the two houses of Yorke and Lancaster, but the daily inroades and incursions of the two cozen germane families of Berkeley and Lisle, the one residinge at Berkeley Castle the other at Wotton vnderedge, which they made by night and day the one vpon the other and their poore tenants, almost to the destruction of this and other manors wherto their mutuall titles were pretended, wherof this of Cowley was one ; And not yet neither in this nor any of the rest of the parishes or manors within this hundred brought into vse againe : One mayne cause also why soe much is nowe inclosed and converted from tillage into pasture ; Of which marle and marlinge of grounds read before in Alkington. fol. 34. A poole nowe only vsefull for the infinite numbers of horseleeches it yearly produceth ; phisitions for the wholl country to evacuate over aboundinge repletions, from hence fetched in great abundance.

Springs.

Through this Towne and parish runne two pleasant streames arising from the foote of the former hills, first shewinge themselves not many yards asunder ; The one holdinge it's race through the hart of the Towne, close to the church yard and by the threshold of each good huswife, keepinge therby her pultry from the pipp ; The other watringe most of their old and newe inclosures and pasture grounds ; wherin after such time as it hath met with the like streame from Came, or draweth neere thereto, are often found certaine stones resemblinge cockles periwinkles, oysters and the like, of much curiosity and delight to looke vpon and to consider of ; which I rather thinke to bee the gamesull sports of nature, then with ffracastorius the great philosopher of this age to have byn somtimes livinge creatures ingendred in the Sea, and by the waters cast vp in this and the like places, and soe to bee shell fishes stonified.

ffisteene.

The payment of the ffisteene or kingesilver when it is granted by parliament, is. in the Onus or charge in the Exchequer in this parish—5ˡⁱ 14ˢ 6ᵈ The deduction is—22ˢ The remainder paid into the Exchequer by the Collector thereof, is— 4ˡⁱ 2ˢ 6ᵈ [sic.]

In

Cowley

In the laſt Subſedy in aᵒ 5ᵗᵒ Caroli were 18. ſubſedy men, who paid—9ˡⁱ 4ˢ   *Subſedy.*

Of able men for the warres betweene 20. and 60. yeares of age, in 6ᵗᵒ Regis Jacobi, which appeared at a generall muſter then taken, were—102. And now of trayned Souldiers vnder Captaine Willm Thorpe, are—22. vz, 2 corſlets and 13. muſketts.   *Able men. Soldiers.*

And if the wholl Diviſion of Berkeley, accompted a 4ᵗʰ part of the county of Glouc̄, bee rated in any taxe for the kinge or com̄on wealth at—100ˡⁱ, then this hundred of Berkeley paies therof—33ˡⁱ 3ˢ, And this pariſh or manor of Cowley—50ˢ, And ſoe after that rate. |

Freeholders within this pariſh and Manor of Cowley. vz.   *Cowleis land of old, late Warres*

Heere is one very ancient freehold more remarkeable then the reſt, heertofore reputed a manor, holden of the manor of Berkeley by the ffifth part of one knights fee, ſute to the hundred Court of Berkeley from three weekes to three weekes, and by the yearly rent of 20ᵈ; which in the time of kinge Henry the ſecond was the land of Dn̄s Ric̄us de Cowley filius Hardingi, whoſe ſonne Simon and himſelfe are witneſſes to that Deed which the lord Robert the ſonne of Hardinge in the time of kinge Henry the ſecond made to Elias his brother, of the hide of land in Combe formerly mentioned fol: 151. And in the time of R. 1. the land of another Richard de Cowley, and ſoe alſo in the time of H. 3. of Richard de Cowley and of Mawd his wife; And in 18. E. 1. of Robert de Cowley of Cowley, father of John Cowley of Cowley, who by Ellena his wife daughter and heire of   had iſſue Robert; which John died in 19. E. 1. as an Inquiſic̄on after his death ſheweth, Which Robert ſonne of John, had iſſue John who died in 7. H. 5, leavinge iſſue John who had iſſue 3. daughters, Elizabeth, Alice, and   maried to Baſſet whoſe iſſue I have not obſerved; And the ſaid Alice was maryed to Walter Woodward who died without iſſue; And the ſaid Elizabeth was maried to John Davis, who had iſſue John Davis, who died in 27. H. 8. as his office or Inquiſition found after his death ſheweth; And by Jone his ſecond wife left iſſue Nicholas who after dyed without iſſue, And Auguſtine Davis who died in 3. E. 6, beinge father of Anne borne after the death of her father, who died in 2ᵒ Jacobi, havinge byn firſt maryed to Thomas Saintbarbe of Lacocke in Wiltſhire, who died in 33. Eliz: and after remaried to Thomas Baynard who died in 1ᵒ Jacobi, by whom ſhee had noe iſſue; But by her firſt huſband Thomas Saintbarbe, ſhee had iſſue Elizabeth maryed to Richard Warre; And after ſhee died in the 14ᵗʰ of kinge James, leavinge iſſue Roger

Warre,

Warre, who with his said father Richard Warre in the 6. and 7th yeares of kinge Charles aliened in fee such of theis lands to John Browninge, Richard Yerworth, Richard Walkeley, John Hardinge, and William Pegler, and their heires, as remained till that time vnsold: Of which lands also Thomas ffrench of Ewley hath

Essington. And also of theis lands Thomas Essington of Cowley, sonne of Thomas sonne of John, hath a messuage and 34. acres in Cowley, which the said John purchased of Thomas Davis second sonne of that John Davis who is before mentioned to dye in 27. H. 8, to whom his said father gave the same, as his said office of that yeare sheweth. And also (as by a fine in the comon pleas in 25. H. 3. appeares,) the Prior and covent of Lanthony by Glouc̄, purchased of the forementioned Richard de Cowley, and of Mawd his wife, two carucates of this land in Cowley in lieu of Covent ale bread money and clothes for their lives; which againe the successors of the pryor and Covent in 25. E. 3. sold to Thomas then lord 159 Berkeley for the Rectory of Awre | which they had from him; Which land is nowe at this day held by Copy of Court roll accordinge to the custome of the manor of Cowley by John Browninge and Richard Partridge, retaininge still the name of Canons Court or Can-court.

Of which little manor somethinge more may bee observed out of theis records; vz,

Inq: 19. E. 2. p̃ morte Johis de Cowley.—p serviciū militare.
Inq: 37. E. 3. de feodis Mañij de Berkeley in terñi Michis in ligula brevium in 38. E. 3.—per servicium militare.
Inq: 27. H. 8. p̃ mortem Johis Davis.
Inq: 33. Eliz: Regine, p̃ morte Thome Saint barbe in Coñi Wilt.
Inq: 14. Jacobi, p̃ morte Eliz. Warre in coñi Wilt.
Compus Johis Hampton Escaetor. 19. E. 2. ām Reñi Rc̄, in baga,—per servicium militare.
Hal de Cowley 33. Eliz. et 14. Jac. p̃t morte Saint barbe et —per serviciū mit.
Inq: 16 Caroli p̃ morte Rici Walkeley p̃d.—per serviciū mit.

Hardings land, als Wariners. Here also is one other ancient messuage with two yard land and an halfe therto belonginge, of old accompted half an hide of land, now the inheritance of John Hardinge, sonne of Maurice who died   , sonne of John who died in 9. Eliz., sonne of Willm Hardinge who died in 36. H. 8., havinge in purchased the same of John Wariner als Warner, sonne of Willm who died

sonne

sonne of Thomas who died   , sonne of Robert Wariner who died in 23.
E. 4, who was sonne of   Wariner, sonne of John Wariner, sonne of William
Wariner, sonne of Robert Wariner, (who in 6. E. 2. purchased other lands in Cowley
of Thomas lord Berkeley vnder the yearly rent of—2ˢ); Which messuage and 2. yard
land and an halfe are holden of this manor of Cowley by knight service, sute to the
hundred court of Berkeley from three weekes to three weekes, heriot service, And
by the yearly rent of—22ˢ. and a pound of comyn.

And for theis lands and for the further pedegree of this John Hardinge, See
before in Came fol: 128.

See also the Will of Willm Hardinge, And 2. Inquisitions after his death in
36. et 37. H. 8.

See also the Co: roll of Cowley in 4. H. 8. pˢ mortē Alienoræ nup vxoŕ Johis
Madocke, et quondam vxoŕ Thome Warner.—good.

See also the Co: roll of Cowley, 2. R. 3. And, 9. Eliz: very good; per servicium
militare, et herieť. |

Here also is one other ffreehold now the inheritance of Richard Davis and of **160**
Richard Partridge, comonly called Muddensall, containing 18. acres or therabouts,   Maddensall,
holden of this manor of Cowley by knight service, sute to the hundred court of   lands.
Berkeley from 3. weekeſ to 3. weekeſ, and by the yearly rent of—10ˢ; which Maurice
lord Berkeley the second of that name, in the later end of the raigne of kinge H. 3.
gave to William Atte wood and to Mabill his wife and to the heires of their bodies,
To hold as aforesaid; which after many discents in that name of Atte wood, and
Atwood (a name agreeable to the scite of the land,) came to the two daughters
and coheires of Thomas Atwood, vz. Julian maried to John Davis, who had issue
betweene them George Davis who died in 7ᵉ Eliz:, father of John Davis who died
44. Eliz: father of the said Richard Davis that nowe is, holding one moity in
severalty, and as I suppose the estate taile therof not discontinued; The other
daughter and coheire of Thomas Atwood, was maried to John Selewine, who had
issue Richard Selewine who died 16. Eliz:, father of John who died 17ᵒ Eliz: from
whom it came to Richard by   , who in 29ᵒ Eliz: sold the same to
Thomas Trotman of Duresly who died in 4. Jaĉ. and leaft it to Nicholas Trotman
his second sonne, who in   Caroli Rˢ sold the same to Richard Partridge
aforesaid

aforefaid and his heires, who betweene them pay the faid rent of—10ˢ. And doe the other fervices. And alfo the faid Thomas Trotman left to the faid Nicholas his fonne a meffuage and 11. acres of land in Cowley which hee in 3. Jacobi purchafed of Richard Bridges.—Rent—2ᵈ

Twinens land nowe Effingtons. late ffourds olim Piftors als Bakers.

Heere alfo is one meffuage with a yard land therto belonginge containinge about 40. acres, the inheritance of Roger Effington of Cowley, and others as followeth, holden of George lord Berkeley as of his manor of Canonbury, by knight fervice, fute of Court, heriot fervice, and the yearly rent of—20ˢ; Which Thomas lord Berkeley the firft of that name, in the time of kinge H. 3. gave to Hugh Piftor (his baker) and his heires, vnder the faid rent of—20ˢ for all fervices, Salvo regali fervicio quantùm ptinet ad vnam virgatam terræ in villa de Cowley, as by the originall Deed which I have read appeares: The pofterity of which Hugh the Baker held the fame in lineall difcent till about 38. E. 3. when this land came into the Sirname of Atte fourde, foe called accordinge to the manner of thofe times, from the fourd or paffage over the water runninge by the faid meffuage, continuinge in that lyne and name till Richard fonne and heire of John ffourd in 21. Eliz: left it by difcent to Edithe his only daughter and heire maried to John Twinen, whofe fonne and heire Robert Twinen, by deed dated 20. Augufti. A⁰ 14⁰ Rᵉ Jacobi, fold the faid meffuage and 17. acres therof to the faid Roger Effington, who paieth—11ˢ of the faid—20ˢ foe apportioned in the faid Deed of purchafe; And William Effington, brother and heire of John, fonnes of Robert Effington for another part thereof payeth—viijˢ. of the faid—20ˢ And Giles Browne for another part therof payeth—xijᵈ which is the full 20ˢ. ffor this land fee the Co : roll 19. et 20. E. 3. when an oxe price—12ˢ was paid for an heriot. To which effect alfo are 2. court rolls in 23. E. 3. et 6. et 29. H. 6. and others, as fpetially the Court Roll of Canonbury 22 Eliz. when the old deeds were produced by the faid Edith. Soe a cleere tenure as abovefaid.

Wilkens land late Macies and others.

Heere alfo is one meffuage and one yard land therto belonginge lyinge in the hamblet called Hulmancote, which the faid Thomas lord Berkeley the firft of that name in the time of kinge H. 3. granted alfo to the faid Hugh Piftor als Baker and his heires, nowe the inheritance of John Browninge and others as after followeth; holden of George Lord Berkeley as of his manor of Canonbury by knight fervice, fute of Court, heriot fervice, and the yearly rent of—20ˢ wherof 10ˢ is paid for two quarters of wheat, as the originall deed which I have read fheweth. This meffuage and land had like continuance in the pofterity of the faid Hugh the Baker, till about the

Cowley

the said 38. yeare of kinge E. 3. when it came (I thinke by mariage of one of Hughes heires, as the other yard land also I suppose did,) into the Sirname of Wilkens, continuinge in that name till the end of the raigne of kinge E. 4. when Thomas Wilkens sonne and heire of John Wilkens, sonne and heire of Wiłtm Wilkens, who died in 11. H. 6. leaft it to Jone his daughter and heire, after maryed to Richard Millard, who had issue Thomas Millard who died   , leavinge issue William Millard who in the beginninge of kinge James sold part therof to Ewd. Trotman th'elder of Came who died in 9. R͡e Caroli, which, Edward Trotman of the Inner temple his sonne and heire, not longe after sold to William Effington of Cowley that nowe is, who payeth of the said rent of 20ˢ the soñe of—5ˢ 4ᵈ And another part was by the said William Millard sold to John Browninge th'elder of Cowley who died in 4. R͡e Caroli, and John is his sonne and heire that nowe holdeth the same, and paieth—20ᵈ of the said rent of, 20ˢ An other part is the inheritance of Thomas Came of Cowley, who payeth—2ˢ pcell of the said rent of—20ˢ An other part is the inheritance of Richard Andrewes, which hee lately purchased of Richard sonne and heire of James Elland of ffrocester, and hee of William Millard aforesaid, who payeth—12ᵈ parcell of the said rent of—20ˢ Another part is nowe the inheritance of John Browninge, sonne of the said John Browninge th'elder aforesaid, which hee purchased of Vrsula wife of Wiłtm Tyndall, Anne wife of John Waftseild, and of Debora wife of Restall, the three sisters and Coheires of John Macy, sonne and heire of James Macy who purchased the same of the said William Millard, and payeth 10ˢ rent, the residue of the said—20ˢ And Edward ffrape hath   of this land, but payeth noe part of the cheife rent.

ffor this land see the Co : rolls in 11. et 14. H. 6. and 18. et 24. et 26, H. 6. And 41. et 38. E. 3. And 23. E. 4. And a Rentall 14. E. 4. which are most full and pregnant, with others, and make a cleere tenure, as abovesaid. See also the Inq : 4. R͡e Caroli found after the death of the abovenamed John Browninge. |

Deere also is a messuage and a yard land containinge about 30. acres of land therto belonginge, wherof William Docket sonne of Richard sonne of John, died seized in fee simple in the third yeare of kinge James, whose sisters and heires to whom the said land then discended were, Alice maried to Robert Coxe, Elizabeth maried to Richard Carswell, Jone maried to John Warner, Margery maried to Henry Bowen, Edith maried to Henry Bicke, Katherine maried to Richard Millard, Agnes maried to John Culverhouse, and Margaret maried to John ffreame, who dyinge before her brother William Docket, left two daughters, Katherine ffreame

162 Docketts land.

ffreame and Vrfula ffreame, then maried to Thomas Bicke; And vpon partition betweene them by Deed indented of nyne parts, dated 22. Maij. A⁰ 7. Regis Jacobi (drawne by my felfe,) Theis lands in Cowley were allotted to the faid Robert Coxe and to Alice his wife, and to John Warner and Jone his wife, and to Henry Bowen and Margery his wife, and to Henry Bicke and Edith his wife; And other lands in Teinton in the fforreft of Deane were allotted to the other co-heires and their hufbands by the fame Deed indented, in lieu of theis; Since which time the faid Alice by the faid Robert Cox her hufband had iffue Rofe, maried to a fonne of the faid Robert Cox by a former wife, who hath had her part; Jone wife of John Warner ftill keepeth her part; Margery wife of Henry Bowen is dead without iffue, And her part is difcended in Coparcinery; And Henry Bicke and Edith his wife have fold her part to fflower of Stonehoufe. A⁰ 1636.

This land was parcell of the poffeffions of the Monaftery of S:t Peter in Glouc̄, and cominge to kinge Henry the 8th by the diffolution therof in the 31th of his raigne, was by him granted in the   of his raigne to Sir Anthony Kingfton knight and his heires, who in 3. E. 6. granted the fame to John Sanford and his heires, who in the firft of Qu: Mary granted the fame to the faid Richard Docket abovementioned and his heires; By whofe death in 28. Eliz: the fame difcended to the faid Wittm his fonne, And from him to his faid fifters, and heires, who made pticon as abovefaid; And is holden of the Crowne by knight fervice in Capite, by the 100th part of a knights fee: See Pafch: fines 29. Eliz: Rot. 8. in Scc̄io.

Effingtons land and others late Redings. **Heere** alfo in this parifh of Cowley, and in Came, are a meffuage, a mill, and divers lands therto belonginge, fomtime parcell of the poffeffions of the monaftery of S:t Peter in Glouc̄, holden of the kinge by knight fervice in Capite, late the inheritance of Roger Redinge of Halmer in Came, from whom, by his death in 31. Eliz. they difcended to his three daughters and coheires, viz:t Elizabeth maried to John Effington, Margery maried to Thomas Effington, who have left iffue Thomas Effington, And Katherine maried to George Pegler; Which Margery was fomtimes the wife of Anthony Watkins; And nowe a⁰ 1639. the inheritance of Thomas Effington called of Halmers mill, which hee had from John Effington

163 his kinfman; Which Roger Redinge about 1. Mariæ reginæ new built the | fullinge mill, and grift mill. Of which lands fee more in Triñ Rec̄ 31. Eliz: Rot. 69. in fcc̄io c̄m Reñi Thefaur̄. And in Memorand̄ fc̄ij in Termino Pafch: 27. Eliz: Regine. And with the Auditor eifdē terñii et a⁰ And in 4. libr̄ feedut̄ fol: 319. in Cur̄ wardoȝ. And was by kinge H. 8. the 11th day of June in the 37th of his raigne granted in fee

to Willm Romefden and Edward Hoppy, And which they the daye after by their deed dated 12. Junij. 37. H. 8. p̃d granted to John Effington in fee, by the name of a watermill in Cowley in the parifh of ffrocefter: Inrolled coram Willo Berners; Auditoī Dñi Regis cuī Augñi. 37. H. 8.

Also in this parifh of Cowley is an ancient meffuage with divers lands therto belonginge, called Hulmancote, (quafi Hill-mans-cote,) agreeable to the fcituacõn, now the inheritance of Richard Millard fonne and heire of John Millard who purchafed the fame of the patentees of Qu: Eliz: a° 33° r̃ni fui, and after died in 5. Jac̃: And was anciently belonginge to the Chantry of S.t Katherine in Cambridge in the parifh of Slimbridge; Out of which meffuage and lands is paid to George lord Berkeley the yearly rent of—8.s And—2.s more, for liberty to inclofe a moore containinge 4. acres, neere to the land of the faid Chantry of Cambridge. *Hulmancote. Millards land.*

Also in this parifh of Cowley are divers lands and tenements containing about 16. acres, now the inheritance of Richard Partridge, who in a° 2° R̃ Caroli, purchafed the fame of Nicholas Trotman, a yonger fonne of Thomas Trotman, to whom the faid Thomas at his death in   Jacobi left the fame in fee, who did in 43. Eliz. purchafe the fame of Richard Bridges and Richard Rawlyns als Compton; which Richard Bridges was brother and heire of Alice the wife of Edward Cottington; And the faid Richard Rawlyns als Compton was fonne and heire of Margery wife of Thomas Cooke, and before the wife of Thomas Rawlyns als Compton, daughter and heire of John Woolworth als Webbe, brother and heire of Chriftopher Woolworth als Webbe, and were purchafed by   Woolworth als Webbe of Robert Hurd and Alice his wife, fifter and heire of Thomas Woodward fonne of John. *Partridge lands: late Woodwards olim Hurds.*

By an Inquificõn in 24. Eliz. Edward Woolworth als Webbe is found to dye feifed (inter alia) of a meffuage and 16. acres of land in Cowley, holden of William Clavild as of his manor of Ewley in Soccage, limitted in taile to Chriftopher and Willm Woolworth als Webbe, the Remainder to his owne right heires; And that Margery the wife of Thomas Rawlyns als Compton, is his grandchilde and heire, vz, daughter of John Woolworth fonne of the faid Edward. This land re verâ, is holden of George lord Berkeley as of his manor of Cowley, by 2.d cheife rent, whither the faid Richard Partridge doth his fervice, And out of the fame, as a rent focke, payeth—10.s p ann̄ to Thomas Pointz in right of Eliz: his wife the widowe of the faid William Clavild: whereof read more in my defcription of Benecombe. fol: 73. |

In

164
Bramwich land, late Codringtons. olim Tefte.

In this parifh alfo is a Cottage and an orchard, and 24. acres of land meadowe and pafture in the tenure of Roger Effington for many yeares to come, the inheritance of Ifaack Bromwich Efq, holden of George lord Berkeley as of his hundred or manor of Berkeley by fuite to the faid hundred Court from three weekes to 3. weekes, And by the yearly rent of—27ˢ.

This was fomtime the land of John Clifford, father of Alice maried to William Tefte, who lived in the time of kinge Henry the fixth, father of Lawrence Tefte who died in 23. H. 7. father of John Tefte who died the fame yeare without iffue, And of Giles Tefte clerke, who died in 34. H. 8. without iffue alfo; And of Grace, Margaret, and Mary Tefte, which Grace and Margaret had noe part of this land, But it wholly came to the faid Mary, who was maryed to ffrancis Codrington Efq, who died in 4. Mar̄; And they had iffue Giles Codrington who died in 23. Eliz., levinge iffue ffrancis Codrington who died in 24. Eliz., leavinge iffue Margaret his fole daughter and heire maryed to Edward Bromwich of fframpton vpon Severne Efq, who had iffue the faid Ifaack that nowe is, 1639. See in Slimbridge. fol: 329. 330.

See more heerof in theis records, vz,
    Inq: in 34. H. 8. p̄t mortē Egidij Tefte.
    Inq: 2. H. 8. p̄t mortē Laurencij Tefte.
    Inq: 4. & 5. Ph: & Mar̄. p̄t mortē ffranc̄ Codrington.
    Inq: 23. Eliz. p̄t mortē Egidij Codrington.
    Inq: 24. Eliz. p̄t mortē ffrancifci Codrington.
    Rot. pardoñ. 11. E. 4. p Lawrenc̄ Tefte.

Coriett's land of old; nowe Lord Berkeleys.

By an Inq: 19. E. 2. Willm Coriet is found to dye feized of a meffuage and 41. acres of land in Cowley, holden of the Caftle of Berkeley in Capite, by homage, and by the yearly rent of—7ˢ viijᵈ. And to Henry de Came—12ˢ 4ᵈ, And that Walter was his fonne and heire 30. yeares old: which 12ˢ 4ᵈ is at this day paid by Roger Effington out of a copihold hee holdeth of the lord Berkeley in this manor; which fhewes either that this land efcheated, or that it was purchafed by the Lord of the manor with that charge on it.

ffor other lands in this parifh of Cowley which were heertofore peell of the manor of Dreycote, nowe in the tenure of John Browninge, William Sage, and others; See after in Dreycote fol: 173. |

                                                                Cromhall.

Cromhall.

Cromhall: als Cromhale; In Domefdei booke in the Exchequer written Cromale. A Manor and parifh longe fince parted into two; The one called Cromhall Abbots from the longe poffeffion of the Abbot of St Auguftines by Briftoll, To whom the lord Robert fonne of Hardinge vpon the firft foundinge therof (amongft many other manor^s and lands,) gave the fame, As before is written fol: 47. 64. 65. which I will not againe repeate: And to this day is part of the poffeffions of the Bifhopricke of Briftoll, of new erected by kinge H. 8. in the 34th of his raigne, out of the ruines of part of that monaftery, and endowed with part of the poffeffions, wherof this Cromhall was part, and is now leafed by the Bifhop for life at 17^{li} rent p añ; which in the 31th yeare of that kinge vpon the Act of parliament that diffolved that and other monafteries, was given to the Crowne: And this part of the parifh of Cromhall (called alfo Abbots fide,) in all payments wherwith the wholl parifh is charged, payeth an intire third parte, and confifteth of 12 inhabitants, payers and office bearers; And hath a Leete for it felfe and a Tithingman afwell as Cromhall Ligon; And is holden of the kinge by [the rent of £33. 6. 8 p añ for all the lands and manors granted] as in the tres patents of 34. H. 8. [pt. 10. m. 4] is contained.

The other part of this parifh is called Cromhall Ligon, becaufe the family of the Ligons were longe owners therof, as after followeth; And is nowe the inheritance of Sir Richard Ducy Baronet, fonne and heire of Sir Robert Ducy late Alderman of London who died in 10. Caroli R^{is}, haveinge in a^o.   before purchafed the fame of Sir Horatio Vere, Lord of Tylbury, and the Lady his wife, who in a^o.   Jac. R^{is}, purchafed the fame of Sir Willm Throgmerton Baronet, fonne of Sir Thomas Throgmerton who died in 6. Jac Regis, haveinge in the 38th yeare of Queene Elizabeth purchafed the fame of William Ligon, as after followeth.

This parifh is part of the Hernelfe, nookes or corners of Berkeley, not adioyninge on any fide or part to any other part of the manor or hundred of Berkeley; And wherin William the Conqueror had two hides of land in demefne, as the booke of Domefdei in the Exchequer fheweth.

It was (amongft many others) given by kinge Henry the fecond to Robert the fonne of Harding and his heires, To hold of the kinge by five knights fees, I meane, all the manors and lands that paffed to him by that grant; But when or what yeare or to whom the faid Robert the fonne of Harding, who dyed in 17. H. 2.

as

as the great pipe Roll in the Exchequer sheweth, did grant away the same I have not observed: But I finde that toward the end of that kings raigne and in the times of kinge Richard the first and of kinge John, This part (which in all rates beareth two parts of three,) wherof I nowe write, (and to which the advowson of the church is appendant,) was the land of Bernard de Cromhall, and of Wiłłm the sonne of Bernard, And after of Phillip and Walter de Cromhall, and after of Peter de Cromhale, (perhaps some of them brothers;) And in the time of kinge H. 3. of Richard de Cromhale and of Dionisia his wife, which Richard was slaine in Scotland about 39. H. 3. leavinge issue three daughters and co-heires, vz, Dionisia maried to John de Wawton, Margaret maried to Nicholas de Limesi, And fflorence, who I suppose, was either not maried or died without issue. All which appeareth | by the pipe Rolls aº 14. Johis and 43. H. 3. in the Exchequer: And by Rot. Clauš. 39. H. 3. pars. 1. membr. 4. in the tower of London.

ffrom which John de Wawton and Dionisia his wife issued Wiłłm de Wawton, to whom kinge E. 2. in the 4th yeare of his raigne granted licence, quod ipse Cameram suam infra mansum suum de Cromhale in Coñ Glouč. Kernellare possit, et sic Kernellatam tenere sibi et heredibus suis: which is now the inheritance of Thomas Hicks, and soe still in part as yet it remaineth, though his late buildings and his fathers, since their purchase therof of Sir Wiłłm Throgm̃ton, have somwhat altered part therof: where, by the way, I will note, from the words Kernellare mansum suum, that the word [Kernellare] seemes to bee made latine out of the old french word, Charneaux, which signifieth that indented part or forme of the top of a wall, which hath vent and crest, comonly called Embattelinge.

The foresaid Sir William de Wawton died in 15. E. 2. seised of this manor, now at this day called Cromhall Ligon, leavinge issue Sir William de Wawton who died without issue, and Thomas de Wawton his brother and heire who by his Deed in 26. E. 3. inrolled in the Chancery released all his interest and estate in this manor and advowson to Elias Daubeny and Agnes his wife and their heires; and therby the wholl united; Which Elias was the sonne of John de Albiniaco als Daubeny and of Cicely his wife, And had issue Richard who died without issue in 38. E. 3. And Elizabeth maryed to Sir Gilbert Gifford who died in 48. E. 3. After which Sir Gilbert and Elizabeth this manor came to Sir John Gifford his cozen and heire who died in 10. R. 2. without issue, and William Gifford was his brother and heire; ffor which later proofes See the patent Rolls. 33. E. 3. ps. 3. mem: 3. And patent 38. E. 3. And Close rolls. 48. E. 3. m. 19. And Close roll. 8. R. 2. m: 5. title Southton. And Inq: 47. E. 3. pro Kinsholme in coñ Glouč.

Which

Cromhall

Which William Gifford, brother and heire of Sir John, is hee who in 23. H. 6, then lord of this manor, enfeoffed John Dorney and others of the Church houfe and other lands in Cromhale, to the vfe of the church, Rendringe to him and his heires —15ᵈ p anñ, paid at this day; And after died in 30. H. 6. levinge iffue Nicholas Gifford, who by Margery his wife had iffue Anne maried to Thomas Ligon, To whom and to the heires of their two bodies the remainder to the right heires of Anne, the faid Nicholas by his Deed 15. November Aº 6. E. 4. conveyed this manor; fhewed to mee by Sir Wittm Throgmton in his Clofet at Tortworth the 17ᵗʰ day of March, 1607. the better to rectify this difcent and pedegree.

But by what difcent or meanes John Gifford who lived in 8. H. 4. And Sir John Gifford knight, who died in 25. H. 6. without iffue, who were in feverall deeds which I have read ftiled Lords of the manors of Cromhale and Legamton and feifed therof, I have not found.

The faid Thomas Ligon died in 22. H. 7. leavinge iffue by the faid Anne Gifford his wife, Richard Ligon who died in 4. H. 8, leavinge iffue Richard Ligon who died in 4ᵗᵒ Mar., levinge iffue Wittm Ligon who died in 10. Eliz., leavinge iffue Richard Ligon who died in 27. Eliz, leavinge iffue William Ligon who in 38. Eliz. aliened this manor and advowfon to Sir Thomas Throgmerton and his heires as aforefaid; By whofe death in 6ᵗᵒ Jač. the fame came to his only fonne Sir William, who havinge made many leafes for lives of moft part of the manor, fhortly after granted the reverfion to the fame men for 21. yeares, to begin vpon the expiration of their former eftates for lives; And fhortly after that in Aº 14 Jacobi, granted divers other parts therof to feverall men in ffee fimple, referving the old rent or more; wherby this ancient manor which by the feifin of fix remarkeable gentlemen of the Sirname of Ligon is called Cromhall Ligon, is nowe Aº 1639. the feverall inheritances of 23. men, vz. of Sir Richard Ducy aforefaid, who hath a manor yet kept on foote with the faid rents foe referved, Robert Webb fonne and heire of Robert Webbe, Nicholas Webbe fonne and heire of Nicholas, Thomas Hickes fonne and heire of Arthur Hickes, Morgan Hickes, brother of the faid Thomas, Arthur Hickes another brother of the faid Thomas, John Hoale Clerke, John Atwell, Thomas fonne of Thomas Dimery, Richard Arnold, Robert fonne and heire of [Thomas?] Arnold, William Nelme in right of Agnes his wife daughter of John Mafon, Robert Griffith fonne and heire of Thomas Griffith, Thomas Griffith brother of the faid Robert, Sarah Blanch one of the daughters and coheires of Jeremy Blanch, and John Knight in right of   his wife the other daughter and coheire

heire of the said Jeremy Blanch, Thomas Stinchcombe, Willm Venery als Pike, Thomas Wheeler in right of Susan his wife daughter of Edward Crome, Walkeley sonne and heire of Henry Walkeley, John Packer sonne and heire of Henry, Thomas Jopson sonne of Thomas, who is said to have aliened lately to John Knight, And Nicholas Hickes who is said to have lately aliened to
And Arthur Hickes aforesaid brother of the said Thomas, sonnes of Arthur Hickes, for lands late of Jone Lawrence widowe and Henry Allens, and John Bakers, and Henry Haywardens.
And for proofe of the Tenure to bee by knight service, See after fol: 169. 170.

<small>Cromale faire.</small>   Upon the feast day of St Andrewe the Apostle, the last of November, hath for the space of 90. yeares past byn held a kinde of ffayre, by resort of pedlars pearmongers and the like petty Chapmen, by like authority as that of Cowley before mentioned fol: 156. And vpon like ground; ffor doubtles Charter or grant from the Crowne at any time there hath byn none: which beinge laid vpon soe incertaine a foundation beginneth at this day to melt away, and shortly the place therof will not bee found, as that of Cowley.

<small>Rates.</small>   In all rates for payments to Church poore or kinge, this of Cromhal Ligon beareth two third parts, And that of Cromhall Abbotts the other third part; And
<small>Advowson.</small>   to this manor of Cromhale Ligon is the Advowson of the Church belonginge, wherof Sir Richard Ducy by the purchase of his father is patron, and accompted as appendant to this manor; yet was it given to the said Abbot of St Augustines by the said Robert the sonne of Hardinge, vpon his first foundinge of that monastery, as in the originall grant therof, which I have read, appeares; But howe or when it came back to the Lords of this manor, or from whom, I have not found.

The wholl parish is within the Deanary of Haukesbury, as the Roll of Taxations in 20. E. 1. sheweth, in the tower of London. |

<small>168
Wake day.</small>   The tutelary Saint of this Church, to whose protection in the daies of our great grandfathers it was committed, was St Andrewe the Apostle, when on the sunday followinge the wake or sfeast day is holden; which in the age of hospitality might give the first rise of the ffaire above mentioned.

<small>Free warren.</small>   The Abbot of St Augustines often before mentioned had free warren in this his third part of this parish called Cromale Abbots, by the grant of kinge E. 1. in the
13th of

13.th of his raigne, as before I have written in the defcription of Almondefbury, fol: 49. which is likely to bee in generall words (at leaft) derived downe to the Bifhop of Briftoll and his fucceffors from H. 8. as amply as the Act of parliament in 31. H. 8. gave it to him.

The payment of the ffifteenth or Kinḡ filver, when it is granted by parliament, is, in the Onus or charge for this wholl parifh,—3^li. 10^s. 5^d. ob. q. The deduction is—18^s. 1^d. ob. q. The remainder paid into the Exchq^r by the Collector, is—52^s. 4^d. — Fifteene.

In the laft Subfedy, A° 5° R̄ Caroli, were of Subfedy men in this parifh—16. who paid—6^li. 15^s. 4^d. — Subfedy.

Of able men for the warres betweene 20. and 60. yeares old, which at a generall mufter appeared before Henry Lord Berkeley, then Lord Lieutenant of the County, were—80. wherof in Cromhale Abbots, or Abbots fide—20. — Able men.

Of trayned Souldiers vnder Thomas Veel Efq their Captaine are   , wherof Corfletts   , mufketts—   . — Souldiers.

And if the wholl Divifion of Berkeley accompted a 4th part of the County of Glouc̄, bee affeffed in any taxe for kinge or Com̄onwelth at—100^li. Then this hundred of Berkeley paies—33^li. 3^s. And this parifh of Cromhale—20^s. And foe after that rate. — Rates.

Freeholds within this parifh, befides thofe 23. formerly mentioned to have lately beene parcell of Cromhale Ligon.

Here is a meffuage with divers Cotages and lands therto belonginḡ containinge about 44. acres, late the inheritance of Robert Dorny and nowe of Robert Webbe, fonne of Robert Webb, who purchafed the fame in 11. Jac̄ R̄, of the faid Robert Dorney, fonne of John Dorney; holden of George Lord Berkeley as of his caftle of Berkeley by knight fervice, and fute to his Hundred court of Berkeley from 3 weekes to 3 weekes; which John Gifford aforenamed, then lord of the manor of Cromhale, by deed dated 6. Maij, A° 8. H. 4. granted to Richard Shevely and his heires, which I have read; wherin, though hee referved to himfelfe and his heires the old rent of—21^s 8^d and the other fervices of old due and payable to his manor of Cromhale for the fame, yet the tenure is, as aforefaid, by force of the Statute of Quia — Dorneys land, nowe Webbs.

Quia emptores terrarum, made in 18. E. 1. Which Richard Shevely left issue Jone his only daughter and heire, maried to John Dorney, who had issue John Dorney who died in 21. E. 4, father of Richard Dorney who died in H. 7., father of Richard who died in H. 8. father of Robert Dorney who died in   Eliz : father of John

169 Dorney, who by his first wife had issue | Alexander and John : And by Christian his second wife, had issue Robert Dorney, to whom by the restles importunity of his mother, hee the said John by a fine levied in 32. Eliz., the vse whereof was by Indenture 10. yeares after leade to bee to himself for life, the Remainder to the said Christian for her life, the remainder to the said Robert his eldest sonne by the said Christian and to the heires males of his body, the remainder to John Dorney his second sonne by his first wife and to the heires males of his body, the remainder to the right heires of him the said John Dorney the father, who after died on St Stephens day Aº 3º Jaĉ, Rç : leavinge the said Robert then 18. yeares old, who after sold the same in 11º Jacobi, to Robert Webb father of the said Robert, as is aforesaid.

ffor further proofe, see

Inq : 7. Jaĉ. p̃t mortē Johis Dorney.—p serviĉ militare.

Inq : 14. Rç Caroli, p̃t mortē Robti Webbe, who died 17. yeares before, aº 6to Caroli Rç.

ffinis in banco in Michas Term̃. 11. Jaĉ. wherby Nicħus Webb (who died aº 6to Caroli,) purchased 8. acres of this land of the said Robert Dorney, sonne of John, which Nicholas sonne of the said Nicholas Web nowe holdeth, 1639.

<small>Cromes land late Berkeleys of Beverston.</small>

Also in this parish of Cromhale, Richard Crome sonne of John Crome sonne of Richard Crome, holds a messuage and about 80. acres of land meadowe and pasture therto belonginge, in the tenure of himselfe and of his lessees for life, knowne by the name of Talebrockes ; which the said Richard his grandfather did in the first of Qu : Mary purchase of John Berkeley of Beverston, after knight, and was of old in the time of kinge Richard the first, the land of Phillip de Cromhale, who granted the same to Talebrocke and his heires, To hold of him in Soccage, from whose seizin it is called Talebrockes to this day. The originall deed is with the said Richard Crome, which I have read.

In Easter Terme, aº 16to Caroli Rç, the said Richard Crome levied a fine of this land, And in Michas Terme after suffered (by warrant of Atturny,) a Com̃on recovery

recovery to cut of an Entaile with divers remainders over created by John his father; And by an Indenture leadinge the vſe therof, the ſaid Richard diſinherited his iſſue male which hee had by his firſt wife, and ſetled the ſame vpon his ſonnes by Suzan his ſecond wife ; Such power have younge wives over old huſbands, as in divers places of this deſcription of this hundred appeareth, which through the ill reliſh never have my approbation.

Though the tenure of this manor of Cromhale Ligon is undoubtedly by knight ſervice of the lord Berkeley, as formerly I have written ; yet becauſe the Inquiſic͠ons found after the death of the ſaid Ligons import otherwiſe, I will, for clearinge the truth therin, And alſo of the diſcents of the manor formerly mentioned, ſet downe togeather ſum̄arily the ſubſtance of ſuch records as I have met withall, omittinge ſuch accompts court rolls and deeds as are in the evidence houſe in the Caſtle of Berkeley, vz ; |

The great Chartulary in Berkeley Caſtle hath 3. diſcents of Richard de Cromhale, fol : 164. which alſo is in the great roll of the Pipe, 1. R. 1. et annis, 11, 12, 13, 14, 15.

 R͡c Joh̄is. glouc̄. et 14. Joh̄is in Com̄ Wiltes̄.
 Rot. Clauſ. 39. H. 3. ps. 1. membr. 4. in arce London.
 Quia Joh̄es Wawton qui duxit in vxor̄ primogenitam filiam et heredem
  Rc̄i de Cromhale, &c. Rot. pipæ. 43. H. 3. to the ſame effect. Rot.
  finiū, 44. H. 3. pars 1. to that effect.

Liber feod̄ milı̄m in ſc̄io c̄m Rem̄ theſaur̄. fol : 337. Willm de Wawton (ſonne of John) holdeth the fourth part of Cromhale of Thomas de Berkeley : And Chriſtiana de Mariſcijs holdeth another fourth part, vt antea. Which (being a booke of knights fees,) is foe to bee taken and expounded.

Inq: 15. E. 2. pro terris rebelliū in Com̄ Glouc̄, findes, That William de Wawton held the moity of the manor of Cromhale to him and his heires in fee ſimple.

Inq : 37. E. 3. of knights fees belonginge to the Caſtle and manor of Berkeley. Hurſt. Galfridus de Blunt tenet vnum feodum in Cromhale.

Rot. Patent̄, 3. E. 3. in dorſo, Will̄us de Wawton arr̄ aſſiſa verſus Abb̄em de Briſtoll, de quodam ſtagno in Cromhale ; Rot. patent̄. 4. E. 3. ps. 1. in dorſo. et ps 2. a᷎ 4᷎ idem. See alſo Patent̄ 10. et 11. E. 3. dorſo.

By deed 28. H. 3. Maurice lord Berkeley (inter alia) endowed his mother Jone de toto servicio Riĉi de Cromhale. In Berkeley Castle. This implyeth a tenure by knights service.

Rot. pateñ, 38. E. 3. ps. 1. The marriage of Elizabeth, sister and heire of Richard sonne of Elias Dawbeny, is granted to Gilbert Gifford by the kinge. See Rot. Clauŝ. 8. R. 2. membr. 50. pro Elia Daubeny &c.

Inq: aᵒ. 6ᵗᵒ Jacobi Rᵉ post mortem Thome Throkmrton miltis.—p serviciũ mil.

Inq: aᵒ. 10ᵒ. Regis Caroli, post mortem Robti Ducy miltis et Baronetĩ.— p serv: mil.

Theis with those other formerly mentioned in the description of this manor of Cromhale, with the seisin of the services expressed in my booke of wardships and Releeses, happened to the lord Berkeley, may seeme to suffice. Vide etiam.

Hillar Termi in banco, aᵒ. 10. Rᵉ Johis. Rot. 5. Amicius de Woodstocke opponit se versus Riĉm Cromhale et Dionisiã vxorem suam, Willm de Laurd et filoram vxorẽ suam, et Niĉim de Limesi et Margaretã vxor̃ suam, et Robtum de Corbet et Sibillam vxorẽ suã, de ptito conventionis invadiaĩ

Termĩ Hillar̃, 38. H. 6. A fine inter Riĉm Choke de Mañio de Cromhale, &c, the fee to Nicholas Gifford.

See also Rot. patenĩ. 4. E. 2. ps. 2. membr. 12. And Rot. clauŝ. 24. E. 2. ps. 1. membr. 3. And Rot. clauŝ. 26. E. 3. membr. 7. in dorso. And Inq: 48. E. 3. pᵗ morte Gilberti Gifford miltis.—p. serviciũ militare.

Co: roll of Wotton fforren, 36. H. 6. Willm Gifford died seized of the manor of Cromeale, holden by one knights fee; But nothinge happeneth for a mountuary, quia vxor ejus habuit statum coniunctim in dicto manerio, et sic mountuar̃ et releviũ (faith the Roll).

Draicote.

Draicote: An hamblet or petty manor within the parish of Came, whereof I have formerly written in the description of Came, fol: 125, 126, 127, as the most eminent freehold within that parish.

Of

Draicote

Of this manor which I faid extendeth into the villages of Durfley, Cowley, Nibley, and Came, Richard Browninge of Durfley hath a mill and certaine grounds therto belonginge, parcell of the manor of Draicote, wherof hee in 38. Eliz: purchafed three fourth parts of John Browninge of Cowley his elder brother. And by the conveyance they agreed that either of them fhould pay five fhillings the peece of the cheefe rent of—10^s. And the other fourth part hee purchafed alfo of his faid brother, and hee of Richard Hardinge in a^o 7. R^e Jacobi, for which fourth part—3^s. 4^d, the refidue of—13^s. 4^d the cheefe rent goinge anciently out of the faid mill, is paid; As amongft other evidences an ancient Accompt of the manor of Came in 18. E. 2. doth fhewe; which mill in divers writings is called Buftorpe als Tanhoufmill, and lyeth in Durfley.

In the parifh of Cowley is an ancient meffuage and 55. acres of land therto belonginge, late parcell of this manor or land called Draicote, nowe in a^o 1639 the feverall inheritances of Willm Sage of Briftoll and of Thomas Pope of Came parifh, who purchafed the fame of George Parflowe, fonne of William Parfloe who died in 18. R^e Jacobi, fonne of John Parfloe who died in 1° Eliz: and did purchafe the fame of John Moody and Jone his wife, one of the two daughters and coheires of John Draicote als Tanner, who died in 3° H. 7.; which faid meffuage and lands were excepted out of a fine levyed of the manor of Draycote in 35. H. 8. wherof read more in Came. And this meffuage and land is holden of George lord Berkeley by the third part of a knights fee, fute to the hundred court of Berkeley from three weekes to 3. weekes, and by the yearly rent of—34^s. 4^d; whereof alfo fee more in the booke of Wardfhips and releefes, fol: 3. et 22. See alfo the court Roll of Cowley 1°. Eliz. p^t mort$\bar{e}$ Johis Parfloe. F. 34^s. 4^d p fervici$\bar{u}$ militare.

Parfloes land nowe Sage, and Pope

In Cowley alfo are two other meffuages with divers lands to them feverally belonginge, now the inheritance of John Browninge, fonne of John who died a^o 4. R^e Caroli, fonne of Richard who died 37. Eliz. fonne of John who died in 5°. et 6° Ph: & Ma$\bar{r}$: fomtime parcell of this manor of Draicote, which were excepted out of the fine levied of that manor in 35. H. 8. And which were by the laft mentioned John Browninge purchafed of Alice Goffe and Jone Moody, the two daughters and coheires of Jone fomtime the wife of Henry Beale, one of the two daughters and coheires of John Draycote als Tanner; holden of George lord Berkeley by knight fervice.

ffor this and other peells of Draicotes, See the office after the death of the faid Browninge in 4° R^e Caroli,—per fervici$\bar{u}$ militare. |

Durfclep. 174 blank

Durseley.

Durseley: In Domesdei booke written Derfilege, and soone after Dureslega, wherin Wittm the Conqueror had three hides of land in demesne, as that booke sheweth, which with one other hide of land the old inheritance of the Berkeleis, were late the inheritance of Sir Thomas Estcourt knight, who died without issue in 22. Jaĉ Rĉ, and now of Thomas Estcourt Esq̃, sonne of Edmond brother of the said Sir Thomas, all holden of the kinge by knight service in Capite.

Name. — The name of this ancient towne I conceive to come from the British word **Dour**, which signifieth water, which plentifully both ariseth and runneth by and through the same; And the Saxon word **lega, lege** or **lei** which beinge all one doe somtimes signify water and somtimes place; In either very agreeable to the scituation, whereof see before in the description of Berkeley fol: 77. And the water runninge through this towne, is at this day called Ewelme.

Deanry — The towne gives the name to one of the Deaneries of this county called the Deanary of Dursley, wherin are the churches of Berkeley, of Slimbridge, of Cowley, of Came, of fframpton, of Durseley, of Iweley, of Newenton, of Beverston, and of Wotton; As by the ancient roll of taxation in 20. E. 1. in the tower of London appeareth.

Survey in Canĉ: — Upon a Bill exhibited in Chancery by the Lady Mary Estcourt the widowe of Sir Thomas, in ffebr. 1637. Aº 13. Caȓ. against the said Thomas Estcourt, it is set out That Sir Thomas her husband was seized in fee of this manor of Dursley, and of the Manors of Shipton, Lasseburrowe, and of the ffarmes of Coldnewenton, and Calcote, And of divers lands in Newenton Bagpath; And by two Indentures of 20. Junij. 22. Jaĉ, and of 26. Junij p̃d, did settle the same on certaine ffeoffees to divers vses, therin perticulerly laid downe: nowe since that time, vpon controversies arisinge, they are agreed, for the quietinge thereof, That a Decree shall bee had by consent, which was done the 19ᵗʰ of Aprill followinge, aº 14. Rĉ Caroli, containinge 133. leaves of paper in the drawinge vp; And indeed is a good and comendable survey of all the said manors and lands, and of each tenants estate that held any part of any of them; And by which the inheritance was setled in fee vpon the defendant.

Rectory — The Rectory or Personage of Dursley is accompted the corps or body of the Archdeaconry of this county of Glouĉ, And is of Custome and right the incumbency

of

of him that is for the time oculus episcopi, the Archdeacon, which at this time is Hugh Robinson Doctor of Divinity.

The aforesaid hide of land was the old habitation of the ancient family of the Berkeleis called of Durſley, in a Caſtle by them built before the Conqueſt, (the ruines whereof are fruitfull with barley and oade there growinge,) And they afterwards alſo held from Edward the Confeſſor and from Willm the Conqueror and from his 2. ſonnes, Willm Rufus and H. 1. and alſo halfe the raigne of kinge Stephen, the firſt mentioned three hides in Domeſdei booke, with the wholl manor of Berkeley (in effect) and all Berkeley herneſſe, (wherof Durſley was an hamblet or parcell of thoſe kings,) in fee farme, at the yearly rent of—500^{li} 17^s 2^d as the great roll of the pipe in the firſt yeare of kinge Henry the ſecond doth ſhewe. |

Durſeleis Caſtle.

The firſt of which family whoſe name I can certainly faſten vpon, is Roger Berkeley mentioned in the ſaid booke of Domeſdei, who alſo lived in the time of kinge Edward the Confeſſor, who was father of William Berkeley, who in the time of kinge Henry the firſt founded the Abby of Kingſwood by Wotton Vnderedge, in that time and after called the manor of Acholt, as amongſt many other prooſes the confirmacōn of kinge Henry the ſecond in the 11th yeare of his raigne, made to the Abbot of that monaſtery for 10. marks fine, ſpeaketh, ſpecified in the great pipe Roll of that yeare in the Exchequer; which Willm Berkeley was father of Roger Berkeley, who lived in the time of kinge Stephen, who by Haviſia his wife, was father of Robert,[1] who by Helena his wife daughter of the Lord Robert ſonne of Harding, firſt lord of Berkeley, had from her fathers guift, this manor of Durſley in fee ſimple for her mariage portion: Betweene whom was iſſue Roger, who by Hawiſia his firſt wife had iſſue Henry: which Henry by Agnes his wife had iſſue John;

176 Berkeleis pedegree of Durſley.

---

[1] Smyth is in error here. Sir Henry Barkly in an able Memoir *On the Earlier Houſe of Berkeley*, ("Trans: Briſtol and Glouceſterſhire Archæol: Society, Vol. VIII.") has ſhewn that William Berkeley was not the father of Roger, but that there were five Rogers in ſucceſſion, extending from the time of the Domeſday Inqueſt (1086) to 1221. William Berkeley, who was Cuſtos of the Honour of Berkeley in 1131, is ſuppoſed to have been the ſon of Euſtace, brother of Roger II. He it was who founded Kingſwood Abbey in 1139, and ſurrendered the founderſhip to his nephew Roger III., in 1148. In the previous year he was enfeoffed in Eldreſfield by Robert Earl of Glouceſter, in which he was ſucceeded by his ſon William and grandſon Robert who, as appears from *Teſter de Nevil*, held it in 1216. According to Sir Henry Barkly, he is miſtaken here, as he is in his Life of Robert Fitz Harding (Ante Vol. I., p. 55.) in ſtating that Helena, Fitz Harding's eldeſt daughter, married *Robert* ſon and heir of Roger de Berkeley. Her huſband, he ſhews, was Roger (IV.) ſon and heir of the above-named Roger III. It is remarkable that neither the name of Roger Berkeley's eldeſt ſon nor of either of the ladies occur in the agreement made between the parents, which will be printed poſt under Slimbridge. [ED.]

John; which John by Sibill his wife had issue Henry; which Henry by Jone his wife had issue William, John and Henry; which William and John died without issue, leavinge this manor to difcend vpon the said Henry their brother and heire: which Henry had issue John, who died in [23rd Edw. III?] And by Hawisia his wife left issue Nicholas and Maud: which Nicholas maryed Cicely sifter and heire of Sir John de la more of Bitton, but died without issue in 6. R. 2. A° 1382. wherby this manor discended to the said Maud his sifter, who was maried to Robert de Cantelo, and died in the 4th of H. 4. by whom shee left issue Robert who died in leavinge issue Elizabeth his only daughter and heire maried to Richard Chedder, which Richard and Elizabeth his wife were they who in 13. H. 4. sold by a fine then levied the Advowson of the said Abby of Kingswood to Thomas then lord Berkeley the 4th of that name, wherof the said William Berkeley in the time of kinge H. 1. was founder; After the death of which Richard Chedder and Elizabeth in the time of kinge Henry the sixth, this manor of Dursley came by discent to Thomas Wike, als Wikes, who died in 13. E. 4. leavinge issue John Wikes who died in 1. H. 7, and was father of Edmond Wikes who died in 6. H. 8, father of Nicholas Wikes who died in 4. & 5. Ph: & Mar, whose sonne John Wikes died in the life time of his father, leavinge issue Robert Wikes who in 9. Eliz. sold this manor of Dursley to Richard Bird and his heires, And hee shortly after to Edmond Woolworth als Webbe, who died in   Eliz: leavinge issue Willm, who in Eliz. sold the same to Richard Bridges, who sold the same in   Eliz. to Thomas Eftcourt Esq., who died in   Eliz. leavinge issue Sir Thomas Eftcourt knight, who dyinge in 22. Jac. without issue, left the same to Thomas Eftcourt his brother Edmonds sonne, as is aforesaid; Howbeit, Richard Webb als Woolworth sonne and heire of the said Willm, to this day receiveth 20^s p Ann̄ out of this manor for his life, from the heire of the said Richard Bridges.

It cañot bee vnpleasinge to you, delightinge in such reverend Antiquities, to read out of that venerable booke called the Red booke in the office of the kings **Remembrancer** in the Excheq^r, the Certificate of the said Roger Berkeley made to kinge Henry the second in the thirteenth yeare of his raigne, in the originall | words, thus; Gloūc: Carta Rogeri de Berkeley. Sciant dn̄s Rex, q̄d ego Rogerus de Berkeley habeo duos milites et dimid sesatos de veteri scoffomento, vnde Hugo de planca tenet dimidiam hidam; Et de istis integrum militem habetis ad dimidium faciend, tenet, vz, Rad̄us de Yweley dimidiam hidam; ffemina Rad̄i Cantileue dimidia hidam; Rogerus de Alba mara vnam virgatam; Simon de Coveleḡ vnā virgatā; ffemina Riči Ganseli tres virgatas; Prior de Stanlega vnam virgatā; Et

sic

fic habetis dimid militem. Ad alterum militem faciend, Walterus de holecombe tenet tres hidas et dimid ; Reginaldus de Alba mara tres hidas ; Et ita tenent ifti tres decem hidas, vnde nolunt mihi facere ferviciū nifi de tribus virgatis, fz, vnufquifq de vna virgata : Et ita habetis duos milites et dimidiū feodatos, nullumq feffatum habeo de novo de meo tempore. Si vobis in antea de dominio meo placet audire, In manerio meo de Coburly habeo feoda duorum militum ; Apud Stanley feodum vnius militis, cum vna hida de Chedrington ; In Newenton habeo vnum feodum militis; In Durfeley vnā hidam ; In Efflewrda dimidiā hidam ; In Duddington tres hidas et dimidiam ; In Slimbridg tres hidas, quas ego veftro affenfu dedi Mauricio filio Roberti, vnde nullum habeo fervicium. Kingefwedam tenent albi monachi ex dono Willi de Berkeley, vnde vobis integrum militem facio, quam ipfi mihi nullum fervicium facere volunt. — **Thus that Certificate.** And vpon this hide of land in Durfley doubtles was his dwelling place, in his Caftle anciently built theron, which was an old freehold of it felfe and not parcell of the manors either of Berkeley or of Durfeley.

An ancient booke of knights fees of the time of kinge E. 1. in the Excheq', with the Remembrancer to the lord Treaforer, thus ; Henricus Berkele tenet Durfeley et Newenton de Rege in capite per ferviciū duorum militum.

An Inquifition in the Tower in 15. E. 1. numero 18. findeth, that Henry Berkely (inter alia) died feized of the manor of Stanley S[t] Leonard, qd ptinet ad Baroniam de Durfeley, and that Willm was his fonne and heire, 15. years old.

The patent roll, 38. H. 3. membr. 2. et 6. fhewes, that the kinge granted liberty to Willm Berkeley of Durfeley,[1] for terme of his life, with his hounds to hunt the fox, wolfe, hare, wild catt, badger, &c. And that hee fhould not bee returned upon any Jury, nor bee made Sheriffe, Coroner, &c. againft his will.

And

[1] Smyth has here improperly introduced the words "of Durfley" after the name of the grantee. No fuch words occur in either of the records he cites, (Charter Roll 37.[b] and 38th Henry III., Roll 50, &c.) We are at prefent unable to fay who was this William de Berkeley that ftood fo high in the kings favour. It is clear he was not William, 5th fon of Thomas I., Lord Berkeley, who was conftrained to quit the realm in 56th Henry III., (1272) "never to returne," (Ante Vol. I., p. 120,) whereas the William who married Avicia Blakeford, is ftated in the Inquifition, taken after her death, for Devon (Inq. p. m. 56th Henry III., No. 21,) fhews that her hufband William Berkeley was then (1270) deceafed.

The Patent Rolls cited by Smyth belonged to the Vafcon or Gafcon feries. They contain grants made by the King during his Expedition into Gafcony in 1253 and 1254. They have been by fome overfight feparated from the Patent Rolls, and are now placed with the Charter Rolls, but have not been Calendared. [ED.]

And by the patent roll, 39. H. 3. ps. 2. This Wiłłm Berkeley was valettus regis, one that waites on the kinge in his bedchamber: And by Patent. 40. H. 3. membr. 9. hee ftood greatly in his favour; And foe intimates Liberał. 41. H. 3.; And had to wife Avicia, in whofe right hee had the manor of Brampton in the county of Devon. Clauſ. 45. H. 3. membr. 9. et 22. And Clauſ. 46. H. 3. in dorfo, to like effect.

And by the patent roll, 53. H. 3. ps. 1. mem: vltimâ. This William de Berkeley was pardoned by the kinge his partakinge with Roger de Clifford in his rebellion and ftirres raifed againft the kinge becaufe hee would not keepe the ftatutes and provifions of the parliament made at Oxford.

This Henry de Berkeley lord of Durfley had in 9. E. 1. a tryall with Thomas lord Berkeley, the fecond lord of that name, for the liberties of |

And in the faid 9ᵗʰ and 13ᵗʰ yeares of the fame, hee, (as it feemes) put forward two writs of **Quo warranto** againft the faid Thomas lord Berkeley, which cominge to triall at Glouſ, the Jury found That the Anceftors of the lord Thomas in the times of Kinge H. 2. and of kinge John vfed That if any theeves were taken either in the Court or in the towne of Durfeley, to bringe them the fame day to the caftle of Berkeley, if the day fufficed, and there they were accuftomed to receive their Judgment, and to have Juftice executed vpon them; But if that day of their takinge fufficed not, then to be brought to the faid Caftle the morrowe after.

The booke in the Exchequer called **Nomina villarum**, remaininge in the office of the Remembrancer to the lord Treaforer, compiled in 9. E. 2. faith, That in the hundred of Berkeley are two burrowe townes, vz. Berkeley wherof Thomas lord Berkeley is lord, And Durfley wherof John fonne of William Berkeley is lord.

The faid John fonne of William Berkeley, in 4. E. 3. takinge the advantage of the time whileft Thomas lord Berkeley grandchilde and heire of the laft mentioned lord Thomas was in tryall by parliament for his life and fortunes about the murder of kinge E. 2. in his Caftle of Berkeley, exhibites his petition in that parliament, fettinge forth Howe himfelfe holds the manors of Durfeley and Newenton in the county of Glouſ of the kinge by knight fervice in Capite, And that the faid Thomas Lord Berkeley beinge one of the gardians of the peace there, hath by his Seigniory and office often wrongfully diftrayned him by his plowe cattle, And that noe
deliverance

deliverance would bee made of them by the Sheriffe nor by his bayly or other Minifters, for that they are all of his fee and Livery and of his houfhold fervants; And foe by his Seigniory, and by Dures, and by colour of a new purchafe which of late hee hath made, and by the aid of Sir Roger de Mortimer late one of the kinges Councellors to have returne of Writts and all other royall ffranchifes within his hundred of Berkeley, which before was guildable, would encroach to him the attendance and Seigniory of him the faid John, to his difinherifon and to the damage of the kinge; wherof hee nowe praies remedy in this high Court of parliament; Whereto the anfwere was, That the Rolles of the Chancery fhould bee viewed; And more, I thinke, followeth not heervpon. Howbeit if you defire to read other futes betweene thefe parties of as angry a nature, let the hiftory booke of the life of this lord Thomas, vnder the title of his fuites in Lawe, bee confulted withall, which heere I purpofely omitt.

In this Towne is a Market each Thurfday, and two fayre daies yearly, The one on the 25th day of Aprill called St Marks day, And the other on the 23th day of November, called St Clements day; But when or by what kinge firft granted to the Lord heereof, I have not obferved. Marketts. ffaires.

The Government of this towne is by a Magiftrate called the Bailiffe, yearly chofen by the Lords Steward and the Jury at the Leete or Lawday holden within a month after Michaelmas day.

In this towne is a rocke of a ftrange ftone called a Puffe ftone or as fome pronounce A tough ftone, wherin is noe chinke, cracke, chopp or Lifne at all; like a fpunge; of an incredible durance, as the walles of Berkeley caftle made of the ruines of the old nunrye there demolifhed neere 700. yeares agone may witnes; very eafy to bee cut, and foft; through which rocke divers vaults houfes cellers mills and water courfes in the towne, are cut, and runne. The like is faid not to bee elfwhere found; and by it and through part of it runneth the ftreame from the faire fountaine there called Ewelme, | anciently in the time of H. 3. and before written Hewelme in divers deeds. Puffe ftone.
179
Ewelme water.

To have vifited an ancient hermitage feated in the midft of the defert woods hanginge over this towne, may feeme in daies of fuch beleife to have byn an expiatory or meritorious worke, through the paines taken in the vneafy and dangerous clyminge and acceffe to the hermites cell, vp and downe the fteepe and craggy hills leadinge Hermitage.

leadinge therto: The laſt time I finde mention of Heremite or Heremitage, is in the Court roll of the Manor of Ham, in 8. H. 8. when hee was awarded at that court (bina manu) with two hands, to proove that the horſe which had thither ſtrayed and there taken vp was not theiſe-ſtollen by him, but his owne proper goods But though hee had reſtitution, yet doubtleſſe moſt of them were hypocriticall knaves.

Nunnery.   Heere alſo is a place which to this day is called the Nunnery.

ffifteene.   The payment of the fifteen or Kingſilver when it is granted to the kinge by parliament, is in the onus or charge in the Excheq^r, 6^{li}· 15^s· 5^d· The deduction is—13^s· 4^d· The Remanet paid into the Exchequer by the Collector is—6^{li}· 2^s· 1^d·

Subſedy.   In the laſt Subſedy in 5to Caroli were in this pariſh 9. ſubſedy men, who paid—3^{li}· 8^s·

Able Men. Soldiers.   And of able men for the warres betweene 20. and 60. yeares old, in a^o· 6to Jacobi, were—101. And now of trayned fouldiers vnder Thomas Veel Eſq_r their Captaine are   , wherof   corſletts, and   muſketts.

Rates.   And if the whole Diviſion of Berkeley, accompted a 4th part of the county of Glouc̃ bee rated in any tax for kinge or com̃on wealth to pay—100^{li}· Then this hundred of Berkeley paies therof—33^{li}· 3^s· And this towne of Durſley—8^s· And ſoe after that rate. |

180 blank

181

Egeton.

Egeton: written alſo Eckcton, and Ecton, and Ecton Halmer, and Eckton: Is one of the 11. hamblets within the pariſh of Berkeley wherof the ſpacious manor of Hame confiſteth, wherof ſee more in that manor. fol: 239.

This hamblet alſo is called Halmer, and included in the bounds thereof doth for the moſt part confiſt of freehold lands heertofore in the times of R. 1. and kinge John, and of H. 3. granted by the lords of Berkeley caſtle in fee, not only heere but throughout their wholl hundred of Berkeley, as in each leaſe almoſt in this deſcription is to bee read: A great part of which land in this hamblet was in the time of kinge John and of his ſonne kinge H. 3. the land of John de Egeton, and after

Elberton

after of Walter and Wiłłm de Egeton, and in the time of kinge E. 3. of John de Egeton; from whom it came into the name and family of Vſher, who alſo was called Donell als Danyell; As a pardon in Rot. pdonū. 30. H. 6. membr. 31. made to William Donell nup de Berkeley yeoman, als Wiłłm Vſher of Biſely yeoman; And as an other pardon in Rot. perdonū. 36. H. 6. made to Wiłłm Donell als Wiłłm Vſher, als Wiłłm Danyell of Berkeley geñ, doe plainly ſhewe. And from them it came to the family and name of Reme als Reom als ſfreme (as at this day wee pronounce it,) of Lipiat, with whom the moſt of thoſe lands remaine, wherof part in Hame, Hinton, Hahner, Alkington, and Berkeley Burrowe, as in the deſcription of all thoſe places or moſt of them ſhall appeare, in the freeholds there. fol: 211. and for 5. leaves after. And in Hinton fol: 230. And fol: 220. 221. |

Elberton.

Elberton: als Ailberton, als Hailberton, als Elbrighton, als Eldberton, quaſi The old Barton or farme place; In Domeſdei booke it is written Eldbertone, wherin Wiłłm the Conqueror had 5. hides of land in demeſne.

The manor is nowe the inheritance of Humphrey Hooke a marchant of Briſtoll, who purchaſed the fame of Sir Arthur Smythes, ſonne of George Smythes a goldſmith in London, who purchaſed the fame of Walter Walſh of Sodbury Eſquire, to whom Henry Walſh his cozen (after ſlaine in ſingle combate by Sir Edward Wintour,) conveyed this and other manors: Which Henry was the ſonne of Nicholas Walſh, ſonne of Maurice Walſh who died in 4. Mar̃, ſonne of Sir John Walſh, ſonne of John Walſh of Oldeſton and of Elizabeth his wife, daughter of Richard fforriſter als ffoſter of Sodbury: And is holden by knights ſervice in Capite of the Crowne.

This manor was parcell of the Herneſſe, viz Nookes or corners of the great manor of Berkeley; And by kinge Henry the ſecond in the firſt yeare of his raigne, granted (inter alia) to Robert ſonne of Harding and his heires, who afterwards about the 12th of the ſaid kinge gave the ſame (inter alia) to Robert his third ſonne and his heires, and died five yeares after; and by the death of the ſaid Robert ſonne of Robert in the time of kinge John, it diſcended to Maurice de Gant his ſonne and heire, By whoſe death without iſſue in 14. H. 3. this manor diſcended and came to Robert de Gurnay, ſonne and heire of Eve ſiſter and heire

of

of the said Maurice: which Robert dyinge in 53. H. 3. left it by discent to Anselme de Gurnay his sonne, and by his death in 14. E. 1. it discended to John de Gurney his sonne, who dyinge without issue five yeares after his father, leaft the same to Elizabeth his sister and heire, who was maried to Sir John ap Adam, who died in 5. E. 2. leavinge issue by his said wife, Thomas ap Adam; who by a fine and other assurances in 4. E. 3. sold this manor (with Kingeswerston) to Maurice Berkeley knight and his heires, second sonne of Maurice lord Berkeley the third of that name, who had issue Sir Thomas Berkeley, called of Ewley, and died in 21. E. 3. And the said Sir Thomas died in 35. E. 3. leavinge issue Maurice Berkeley knight, who died in 2. H. 4. leavinge issue Sir Maurice Berkeley borne after the death of his father, who died in 4. E. 4. leavinge issue Sir William Berkeley knight, to whom this manor (inter alia) discended. As the Inquisicōn found that yeare after his death sheweth; the said Sir Willm then 28. yeares old, who after died in 16. H. 7. leavinge issue Sir Richard Berkeley.

But forasmuch as the said Sir Willm Berkeley was in 1. H. 7. attainted of high Treason, by parliament, for pertakinge with kinge R. 3. slaine in battell at Bosworth feild: and this manor granted by kinge H. 7. with his other possessions to Jasper Earle of Pembroke in taile, Though the said Sir Willm was restored to most of his lands after composicōn made with the said Earle; And his sonne Sir Richard after his fathers death to all the rest, yet sith neither of them are found to dye seized of this manor, nor to sue Livery therof, nor any of their posterity after them, I cañot but conceive that one of them sold away the same; But when or to whom I have not observed: But since come downe to Humphrey Hooke, as is first before said. |

183
Champneis land.

In this parish of Ailberton is one ancient freehold created by the aforesaid Anselme de Gurnay by a grant therof made to Thomas Norris and his heires, who after sold the same to Thomas Trepyn and his heires; And hee to John Champneis and his heires; All which severall Alienations are laid down in a pardon dated 18. Julij A° 10° E. 3. beinge made without licence; yet that record saith That theis lands are holden of John Lidiard in Capite; And are nowe, Anno 1639, the inheritance of Thomas Herynge and of James Segar, worth one hundred pounds per Añ; And had in the name and posterity of the said John Champneis continued in lineall discent, till Edm: Champneis that yet is and his father sold the same of late yeares. ffor somwhat more of theis lands see an Inquisicōn in 11. E. 2. after the death of John Trepin. And an Inq: vpon an Ad quod damnum in 10. E. 3. aforesaid faid, which layeth downe what is before written: And in the fecond volume of my hiftory of the family of the Berkeleis, in the title of the iffue of the lord Maurice the third.

The Church of Eldberton is within the Deanry of Briftoll, and in fome Deeds faid, (as alfo ffilton,) to belonge to the mother church of Almondefbury, as Chaples therof.   *Church.*

The payment of the ffifteenth or Kingefilver when it is granted by parliament, goeth with Kingfwefton vnder one fome; The onus or charge of both places togeather is—10^{li}. 14^s. ob. q. The deduction is 26^s. 8^d. The Remanet paid into the Exchequer for both Townfhips by the Collector is—9^{li}. 7. 4^d. ob. q.   *ffifteene.*

In the laft Subfedy in a° 5to. Caroli R^s were 13. fubfedy men in this parifh of Elberton, who paid—4^{li}. 16^s.   *Subfedy.*

Of able men for the Warres betweene 20. and 60. yeares old in a° 6to Jacobi R^s, which fhewed themfelves before Henry lord Berkeley then Leiutenant of the County at a generall mufter, were—41.   *Able men.*

Of trained Souldiers vnder their captaine Thomas Veel Efq, now are   *Soldiers.*

And if the wholl Divifion of Berkeley, accompted a 4th part of the county, bee rated in any tax for the kinge or comon wealth at—100^{li}. Then this hundred of Berkeley paies thereof 33^{li}. 3^s. And this towne of Elberton 20^s.   *Rates.*

    Somwhat more of this Elberton is to bee read in theis records, vizt,
       Inq: 53. H. 3. p^t mortem Roberti de Gurnay.
       Inq: 14. E. 1. p^t morte Anfelmi de Gurnay.
       Inq: 21. E. 3. p^t morte Mauricij filij Mauricij de Berkeley.
       Inq: 29. E. 3. p^t morte Thomæ Berkeley de Vle chr. |
                                                                              184 blank

Eweley.

Eweley: In Domefdei booke written Eunelege, Soe called of the faire or beautifull water there; wherin William the Conqueror had two hides of land in demefne, as that booke fheweth; nowe at this day holden by feverall lords by feverall tenures, as after followeth;

                                                                                   I have

I have not in all my tumblings over of Records and Deeds obferved any one place to be foe diverfly written and fpelled as this townfhip, as theis 20. diverfities fince the booke of Domefdei will declare: As Eweley, Vley, Ewly, Euwely, Euweley, Ewelye, Heuweley, Iweley, Iwely, Iowley, Iveley, Yweley, Yweleigh, Youlay, Yevele, Vly, Vle, Vlee, Vleygh, Vwely, and Eweleḡ.

Baffetts manor. **In** this parifh are two manors, and both ancient, The one called Baffetts manor, The other White court: ffirft of the firft, as after.

But becaufe I cañot well in certainty diftinguifh to which of the faid two manors divers old deeds which I have read and noted doe belonge, I will in this defcription of this parifh firft fet them downe, leavinge it to you in the ripenes of See fol: 1. your further knowledges and obfervations to apply them to both manors, or either, or to ffreeholds within the parifh, as after alfo will followe.

To begin with Domefdei booke, it hath only two hides of land, which is 8. yard land in comon acceptation at this day; And this doubtleffe was by kinge H. 2, afwell when he was but Duke of Normandy as when hee was after kinge of England, granted in the firft of his raigne to Robert the fonne of Harding firft Lord of Berkeley and to his heires, which Robert died in 17. H. 2. and Maurice his fonne and heire in 1. R. 1. and Robert fonne and heire of the faid Maurice in 4. H. 3. without iffue, And Thomas was his brother and heire, who died 28. H. 3. Nowe in the time of kinge Henry the fecond it was the land of Walter de Iwele, and in the time of kinge R. 1. and of kinge John the land of Peter de Iweleia, and of Peter yweleye his fonne, who doubtles had not the fame from the faid Robert, Maurice, nor Robert; and therfore I am in mine owne opinion compelled to fay, That the fame was given to them by the family of the Berkeleys of Durfley, betweene the makinge of Domefdei booke and the agreement made at Briftoll in the 7th of kinge Stephen, betweene the faid Roger Berkeley of Durfley and the faid Robert the fonne of Hardinge, by the mediation of kinge Stephen and of Henry Duke of Normandy, after kinge, as before appeares: that hee did the like in Draycote and as after in Wainfwell and divers others, as the deeds themfelves of thofe lands which I have feene, doe witneffe; All which time that family of the Berkeleis of Durfeley held the whole Manor of Berkeley and all Berkeley herneffe in fee farme of the Crowne, as before I have written, fol: 175. 176. 177. And after that peace thofe grants foe made were confirmed by the faid Robert the fonne of Harding and his heires, to the feoffees and their heires, by feverall deeds,

Many

Ewley

Many of which I have alfo feene. And thus doubtles I may fay of divers other old freeholds, fuch as Pitcourt in Nybley, and Cromhale, and Bradſton, and Stintefcumbe, and Peers court and Melkeſham court in Stintefcumbe, and

Whofe originall grants (wherby they were firſt derived out of the great manor of Berkeley) I have not mett withall, nor perhaps will you, as beinge in the length of foe many ages periſhed from amongſt the writings of men: Alfo the Certificate of Roger de Berkeley of Durſley formerly | mentioned in Durſley. fol: 177. which hee made to Henry the fecond in the 13ᵗʰ yeare of his raigne, what time hee maryed his daughter Matilda (Maude) to the Duke of Saxony, much confirmes the fame, with theis and others in Yweleiġ als Ewley: which Certificates then made by all the great men of moſt counties that held of the kinge by knight fervice, beinge after collected into one body by Alexander Archdeacon of Salop̄, is that remarkeable booke in the Excheq' called the Red booke at this day.

Also Raphe de Iuley was one of the 8. pledges for the faid Roger de Berkeley in the time of king Stephen, that hee ſhould keepe the faid Agreement then made with Robert the fonne of Harding, who is mentioned after in the faid certificate of the faid Roger, made to kinge H. 2.

By Deed without date (but temp: R. 1.) Peter de Iweleia granted to Robert de Berkeleia, totam terram fuam de Weſtcote, in fee: And if the faid Peter could not warrant the faid land, then to give him of his land in Iweley to the value thereof.

By Deed without date, in the time of kinge John, or H. 3. Peter de Yweleye granted to Sir Willm Berkeley knight, All his land in ywet, nomine hereditatis, To hold of him and his heires, faciendo capitalibus dnis feodi fervicia p̄dc̄æ terræ debita et confueta.

By Deed in aº 1262. in 47. H. 3. Peter de Ewley granted to Willm Berkeley knight and to his heires, all his lands in Ewley, expſſinge therein the names of divers furlonge and places, Rendringe to the Cheife Lords the fervices accuſtomed, et regale ferviciū cùm acciderit.

By Deed without date, John fonne and heire of the faid Peter of yweley granted and confirmed to the faid Sir Willm Berkeley and his heires, All the forefaid lands and teñts which hee had in Cowley, To hold to the faid Willm and his heires; Which came after to Anfelme Baſſett, as followeth in fol: 188.

The

Carta.   The forefaid Thomas lord Berkeley (brother and heire of Robert who died in 4. H. 3. without iffue,) by his Deed in hec verba.   Sciant p̄ntes et futuri quod ego Thomas de Berkel dedi conceffi et hâc carta meâ confirmavi Margaretæ filiæ meæ pro homagio et fervicio fuo, Totam medietatem man̄ij mei de Eweleg̃, et medietatem molendini q̃d habui in eod̄ main̄o, cum ōibus libtatibus et liberis confuetudinibus ad medietatem d̄ei manerij ptinentib͡9 et cū ōibus alijs ptinentijs fuis In wainagijs, bofcis et planis, in pratis et pafturis, in fervicijs liberoꝝ hominum et confuetudinarioꝝ, in vijs et femitis, in Stagnis et molendinis, in aquis et aquaꝝ curfibus, et in omnibus alijs rebus ad medietatem d̄ei manerij ptinentib͡: in omnibus locis.   Et p̄terea dedi et conceffi d̄ce Margaretæ de incremento ad Curiam fibi edificandam in d̄co manerio, vnam virgatam terræ cum omnibus ptinentijs fuis, feł, illam virgatam terræ quā Idonea de Eftgate vidua aliquando de me tenuit ;   Quare volo quod d̄ca Margareta habeat et teneat totam medietatem d̄ei manerij et medietatem d̄ei molendini, et virgatā terre p̄dcā cū ōibus libertatibus et liberis confuetudinibus ad medietatē d̄ei Main̄ij ptinentib͡9, et cū ōibus alijs ptinen̄ fuis in omnibus locis, de me et de heredibus meis fibi et heredibus fuis de corpore fuo procreatis, liberè et quietè bene et in

187   pace iure | hereditario imperpetuū ;   faciendo mihi et heredibus meis d̄ca Margareta et heredes fui de corpore fuo procreati, quartam partem fervicij vnius militis, et duas fectas ad hundredum meum de Berkel p añ p̃ fe vel per Attornatū ad rationabilem fumonic̄oem, feł, ad proximū hundredū poſt feſtum ſc̄i Michis vnā fectā, et ad prox hundredū poſt Hokeday aliam fectam pro ōibus fervicijs fecularibus, exactionibus et demandis.   Et ego Thomas de Berkel et heredes mei d̄ce Margareī et heredibus fuis de corpore fuo procreatis totā medietatē d̄ei main̄ij et medietatē molendini et virgatā terre prenominatā cum ōibus libtatibꝫ et al̄ ptinen̄ fuis contra omnes gentes warrantizabim͡9, acquietabim͡9 et defendem͡9 impetuum.   Et ut hæc mea donatio, conceffio et cartæ huius confirmatio rata fit et ſtabilis, figillū meum huic cartæ appofui.   Hijs teſtibus.   D̄no Wiłło Graffo primogenito, D̄nis Ottone filio Wiłti, Henrīc de Berkel, Petro de Stintefcumba, Simon̄ de Ollepenna, Waltero de Burgo, Johe de Durefleg̃, Thoma Maudutt, Nicho Ruffo, Rogero de Camma, Johe de Draicote, et alijs.

2 Carta.   And by another Deed, in hæc verba.   Sciant p̄fentes et futuri, quod ego Thomas de Berkele dedi conceffi et hac p̃nti carta mea confirmavi Margarete filie mee pro homagio et fervicio fuo, totam medietatem totius manerij mei de Eweleg̃ cum ōibus ptinen̄ fuis, feł, totam medietatem totius dnici, tam in gainagijs[1] quam in
                                                                                                                             bofcis

---

[1] Gainagium—Gainage—Lands held in villanage, alfo the gainage or profit arifing from fuch lands. Wainagium, (above) is the fame word in a different form, having the fame fignification.   [ED.]

boscis et pratis, sc̃dm rationabilem divitionem, Et totum serviciũ totaꝜ terrarũ cum ōibus suis ptinen̄, quas Walterus de sc̃o Jacobo, Adam Stut, Joh̃es de Ekinton et Walterus de cimiterio de me tenuerunt in feodo, In homagijs, in redditibus, Relevijs. gardis, et eskeitis, c̃m ōibus alijs servicijs, quæ de p̃dc̃is terris exeunt, vel exire poterunt. Et preterea totam illam terram cum suis ptinen̄ quam Ric̃us le Bele de me tenuit, in villanagio, et dc̃um Ric̃um c̃m tota sequela ip̃ius. Item totam illam terram cũ suis ptinen̄ quam Rob̃tus West de me tenuit in villanagio, et dc̃m Rob̃tum cũ tota sequela ip̃ius. Item totam illã terrã cũ suis ptinen̄ quam Adam de la Hulle de me tenuit in villanagio, et dc̃m Adam cũ tota sequela ip̃ius. Item totam illã terrã cum suis ptinen̄ quam Walterus Edritch de me tenuit in villanagio et dc̃m Walterum cum tota sequela ip̃ius. Item totam illã terrã cũ suis ptinen̄ quam Rogerus le Weite de me tenuit in villanagio, et dc̃m Rogerum c̃m tota sequela ip̃ius. Item totam illã terram cũ suis ptinen̄ quã Tomus porcarius de me tenuit in villanagio, et dc̃m Tomum cum tota sequela ip̃ius. Item totã illã terrã cum suis ptinen̄ quam Margeria Mortimer de me tenuit in villanagio, et dc̃ã Margeriam cum tota sequela ip̃ius. Item totam illam terram cum suis pertinen̄ quam Spilemannus faber de me tenuit in villanagio, et dc̃ũ Spilemannũ cum tota sequela ip̃ius. Et preterea tota illa virgatã terræ cũ suis ptinen̄ quam Idonia de Estgate de me tenuit ad curiam p̃dc̃æ Margaretæ edificandam. Et preterea totam medietatem molendini quod habeo in eod̃ manerio. **Quare** volo q̃d dc̃a Margareta filia mea heat et teneat totã medietate dc̃i mañij in ōibus p̃dc̃is cum ōibus libtatibus et liberis consuetudinibus ad medietatem dc̃i mañij ptinentib9 et cum ōibus alijs pertinentijs suis, in boscis et planis, in pratis et pasturis, in vijs et semitis, in aquis, et in aquarũ cursibus, in stagnis et molendinis et in omnibus alijs locis et rebus ad medietatem dc̃i mañij ptinentib9, de me et de heredibus meis in feodo et hereditate sibi et heredibus suis de corpore suo procreatis, libere et quiete, bene et in pace, integre et honorifice imppetuum. ffaciendo mihi et heredib9 meis dc̃a Margareta et heredes sui de corpore suo procreati quartam partem servicij vnius militis, et duas sectas ad hundredum meum de **Berkel** p añu, sc̃t, ad proximum hundredum post festum Sc̃i Michis vnã sectã, et ad proximũ hundredũ post Hockday aliã sectã pro ōibus servicijs et secularibus demandis. Et ego Thomas de Berkel et heredes mei, p̃dc̃æ Margaretæ et heredibus suis de | corpore suo procreatis totam medietatem dc̃i manerij et medietatem molendini et virgatam terræ prenominatam ad Curiã sibi edificandam, cum ōibus libertatibus et liberis consuetudinibus ad medietatem dc̃i mañij ptinentib9, et cum ōibus alijs ptinentijs suis in ōibus locis contra omnes gentes warrantizabim9 acquietabim9 et defendem9 imppetuum. Et vt hæc mea donatio concessio et cartæ huius confirmatio rata sit et stabilis, huic cartæ sigillum meum apposui. Hijs testibus, Dñis Witlo Graffo

Hundred of Berkeley

Graffo primogenito, Ottone filio Wⁱ, Riĉo de Cromhale, Petro de Stintefcumba, Henriĉ de Berkel, Simoñ de Oillipeñā, Riĉo de Brunelhā, Philippo de Cromhale. Nicho Ruffo, Johē, de Draicote, Rogero de Camma et pluribus alijs.

Theis two deeds (written both with one hand,) thus made, fhortly after one the other, the faid Thomas lord Berkeley in 28. H. 3. died ; About which time as I conceive the faid Margaret was maried to Sir Anfelme Baffet knight, who fhortly after purchafed to himfelfe and to the faid Margaret his wife and their heires of the before mentioned Sir William Berkeley, All his lands in Vleigh which himfelfe had formerly bought of the faid Peter de Ewley, Which Maurice Berkeley fonne of Sir William after confirmed, as by the Deed it felfe remaininge with William Baffet that nowe is, A^o 1639. which I have read, appeares. And by this purchafe was the moity of this manor much enlarged.

The faid Sir Anfelme Baffett died in 8. E. 1. as by Rot. pateñ, in 13. E. 1. membr. 25. in arce Londini, appeares ; And by his faid wife left iffue John and Edmond, both of them knights : John died without iffue, and the faid Edmond was his brother and heire ; who by Ifable his wife, fifter and one of the three coheires of one other Edmond Baffet, remaried to   Puncherdon, had iffue Symon Baffet knight, and died   E. 2. which Sir Simon by Maud his fecond wife, (for by Elizabeth his firft wife hee had noe iffue.) daughter and coheire of John de Button, had iffue John, Maurice, and Edmond Baffet, and died in 37. E. 3 ; whom the faid Maud furvived and died in 12. R. 2. Which John was a knight, and the yeare before his father died without iffue, As alfo did Maurice : And Edmond their brother had iffue John Baffet, who died in 12. H. 6. leavinge iffue Robert Baffet, who died in 4. H. 7. leavinge iffue Giles Baffet who died in 35. H. 8. leavinge iffue Robert Baffet who died in 16. Eliz. and left iffue Wiłłm Baffet, who by Jone his wife daughter and coheire of John Afhe of Tykenham, had iffue Edward Baffet, and died in 38. Eliz. Which Edward Baffet by Ifable his wife daughter of Henry Ligon, had iffue Wiłłm Baffet, and died in 44. Eliz. which Wiłłm fonne of Edward died in   Jacobi R^c, leavinge iffue Wiłłm Baffet that nowe is, a^o 1639. who in Decembr 1632. for theis lands in Vleigh paid to George lord Berkele a Releefe of —25^s accordinge to the firft refervaĉon of the tenure by the 4th part of a knights fee ; Howbeit, that fome parts of theis lands by feverall exchanges and fales are nowe the inheritances of theis that followe, vizt

1. Richard Browninge of Durfley by deed dated 20 April. 8. Jaĉ. R^s p'chafed in fee of William Baffet, fonne of Edward, fonne of William, one clofe called
Spratts

Spratts contaninge 4. acres, next the comon river on the South side: and one close in west feild contaninge 2. acres, shootinge on the said close called Spratts on the Southend, in Ewley.

2. Giles Dancey sonne of Thomas, by Deed dated 4. Junij 8. Jac. R$\bar{e}$, purchased in fee to himselfe and the said Thomas his father, and to the heires of him the | said Giles, one cottage or tenem^t called Tetpens contaninge halfe an acre, in Owlpen or Bagpath or one of them. One close called Cowleazes con$\bar{t}$. 4. acres, Overmead, con$\bar{t}$. 4. acres., 14 acres of arrable land in the Downefeild and other places there. One close called Tetpens con$\bar{t}$ 3. acres next the said Cowleazes. And also one other close called Tetpens con$\bar{t}$ also 3. acres, at the lower end of the former.

Of this moity and land somwhat more may bee found in theis Records, viz,
Rot. fini$\bar{u}$ in arce Lond. 4. E. 2. membr. 8. wherby Isable Punchardun one of the sisters and heires of Edmund Baffett, Nichus Valers and Margaret his wife another sister and heire, and Katherine Bifet the third sister and heire, did their sealties for their purparts of a messuage and carucate of land in Ewley, which the said Edmond held of the heire of William Berkeley of Dursley the kings ward, by the 16th part of a knights fee. Agreeable to the Inquific$\bar{o}$n. 4. E. 2.
Inq : 4. H. 7. p^t mortem Rob^{ti} Baffet.
Inq : 24. H. 7. p^t mort$\bar{e}$ p$\bar{d}$ei Rob^{ti} vpon a Qu$\ae$ plura.—per serv : mil :
Inq : 35. H. 8. p^t mortem Egidij Baffet.—per servici$\bar{u}$ militare.
Inq : 16. Eliz. p^t morte Rob^{ti} Baffett.—p servi$\bar{c}$ mil.
Com$\bar{p}$us libertat$\bar{i}$ de Wotton. 12. H. 6, et de manerio de Wotton 14. H. 6. —per servi$\bar{c}$ mil : et in warda D$\bar{n}$o.
Originat 4. E. 2. Rot 32. cum Rem$\bar{i}$ thesaur$\bar{i}$ in Sc$\bar{c}$io.
Liber Relevio$\bar{r}$ loco p$\bar{d}$eo, in Term$\bar{i}$ Trin 6. et 7. E. 2.
Court Roll of Wotton 17. April : 16. H. 6. very full.—per servi$\bar{c}$ mil.
A Deed in 1. E. 4. and divers other excellent evidences to proove both the tenure of this land and the discents, are in the custody of the nowe William Baffet, which his father shewed mee in a^o. 1606.—per servi$\bar{c}$ militare.

John Trye of Inwoods receiveth (wth he in 7° Caroli purchased with certaine grounds called Inwoods of Will$\bar{m}$ Trye of Hardwicke his elder brothers sonne,) a rent charge of—40^s per Ann, issuinge out of theis lands or part thereof, created. |

The

190   **The** other manor in this parish of Ewley was from the ancient buildinge of the Capitall messuage or manor house, called White Court ; And had two parkes stored with deere belonginge vnto it, called the great parke and little parke, And was the other moity or halfe of the entire manor, which the said Thomas lord Berkeley reserved to himselfe when hee made the former guift in taile, to his daughter Margaret as aforesaid ; And is holden of George lord Berkeley as of his Castle of Berkeley by halfe a knights fee, and suite to his hundred court of Berkeley from three weekes to three weekes : And vnder the severall alienations of Sir Richard Berkeley in 8° Eliz. is nowe the freehold of almost 40. men.

This moity also or manor called White Court came with the other to the said Lord Robert the sonne of Hardinge by the foresaid grant of kinge H. 2. who had issue Maurice, father of Robert who died in 4. H. 3. without issue, leavinge Thomas his brother and heire, who I suppose aliened this moity also, because, in the inquest of office found after his death in 28. H. 3. of all the lands hee had at the time of his death, it is not mentioned ; nor after the death of Maurice his sonne and heire, who died in 8. E. 1. nor of any of their heires ; But what yeare, by whom, or to whom, I have not certainly found, or further then the Deeds or Records heereafter followinge doe declare ; but thinke it was by the said Thomas in the time of kinge Henry the third.

A booke of knights fees with the Remembrancer to the lord Tresr in the Exchequer in the time of kinge E. 1. compiled of divers Inquisiĉons taken by Richard de Rowell and others, saith ; **Robart de Brampton** and Willm de Bett hold severally of Thomas lord Berkeley two halfe knights fees in Ewley.

A Deed without date, which I have read, with Richard Berkeley of Rancombe late of Stoke Gifford, shewes that Walter Brampton, whose wife Jone held Vley manor in dower, didd Covenant with Bryan Brampton not to alien the said Manor to any other then to him.

By an Inquisiĉon in 5. E. 2. after the death of Walter de Glouĉ, it is found that hee and Hawisia his wife were seized in fee simple of the manor of Ewley holden of Thomas lord Berkeley, but by what service the Jury knowe not, And that Walter was his sonne and heire 17. yeares old.

And Rot. Clauś. in 5. E. 2. membr. 23. in arce London, shewes, that the said Hawisia the widowe of Walter de Glouĉ had assigned for her dower (inter alia) the

moity

moity of all his lands and tenements in Iveley in the county of Glouc̄, valued at—7ˡⁱ· 15ˢ· 9ᵈ· p Ann̄.

And the Rot. paten̄ 5. E. 2. pars. 1. membr. 4. in arce London, shewes that the kinge owed Gilbert de Clare Earle of Glouc̄—3500. m̄ks, for his expenses in the warre against Scotland. And nowe for payment therof assignes to him divers wardships as they fall: And (amongst others) assignes him the custody of the body lands and maryage of Walter sonne and heire of Walter de Glouc̄, who held the moity of divers lands and tenements in Iveleigh, extended at—77ˢ· 10ᵈ· p ann̄.

By Rot. paten̄, 7. E. 2. pars. 2. The said Hawisia was remaried to Walter de Bello campo, who held in her right theis lands and ten̄ts in Iveleigh. Rot. paten̄ 15. E. 2. ps. 1. in dorso.

And Rot. paten̄, 9. E. 2. ps. . dorso. Alienor the widowe of Mathewe the sonne of John, arraignes an assise against Walter de Bello campo and Hawisia his wife for divers lands and ten̄ts in Vleighe.

By a booke of tenures composed by divers Inquisic̄o͞ns in the time of kinge E. 1. in the office of the Remembrancer to the lord Tres̄r in the Exchequer, Thomas de Berkeley tenet de rege in Capite, Berkeley, Hame, Alkington, Arlingham, Cowley, Slimbridge, Came, Ewley, Kingston, Wotton, Cromhall, Ashelworth, Almondesbury, et Horesfeild, per servic̄iu trium militum.

And in the same booke, Robtus de Brampton tenet dimidium feodum in Iveley; Willus de Bett, dimid̄ feodum ibm:

In Rot. Claus̄. A° 6. E. 3. in dorso, is a Deed inrolled dated 26. m̄cij aᵒ p̄d, wherby Hawisia late the wife of Walter de Glouc̄ released to the Abbot of Evesham, All rents actions and demaunds saving her right and clayme to the manor of Iveleigh in the county of Glouc̄, The Abbot prayinge for the soules of the said Walter and of Walter his sonne.

And the same 6. E. 3. John the sonne of Walter de Glouc̄ arraigned an assise against John Inge for divers lands and ten̄ts in Iveleigh. Rot. paten̄. 6. E. 3. dorso.

By an Inq: vpon a Writ of Ad quod damnum in 16. E. 2. it is found, That Hawisia somtime the wife of Walter de Glouc̄ did give to the Abbot of Evesham divers lands in the counties of Glouc̄ and Worcester: And that over and besides the

the said guift, shee had remaininge to her selfe the manor of yweley in the said county of Glouc̃, holden of the lord of the castle of Berkeley, but by what services the Jury knowe not.

By another Inq: vpon the like writ of Ad quod damnum in 17. E. 2. in the county of Surrey, it is found that the said Hawisia somtime the wife of Walter de Glouc̃ gave lands in Surrey to the Abbot of Certesey in the said county, and that besides the lands soe given shee still had remaininge to her the manor of Vweley in the county of Glouc̃, holden of the lord Berkeley by halfe a knights fee, And were worth by the yeare—40ˡⁱ.

Thus stood this moity or halfe of Vley when the said Hawisia about the end of kinge E. 2. dyed; Howe the revertion in fee moved or came from the heire of the said Walter de Glouc̃, by discent or purchase, to Margery, maried about 8. E. 3. to Maurice Berkeley Bannerett, then of Stoke Gifford, second sonne to that Maurice lord Berkeley the third of that name, who dyed in the last of that kinge prisoner in the castle of Wallingford, I have not found: but wife to the said Maurice Berkeley bannerett shee was in 8. E. 3. as the patent roll of that yeare ps. 2. membr. 38. sheweth: wherof hee died seised in fee the 12ᵗʰ of ffebruary in 21. E. 3. holden (saith the Inq: found the same yeare after his death,) of Thomas lord Berkeley by knight service; whom the said Margery his wife surviveth, and dieth about 3. yeares after in 25. E. 3. leavinge this manor to bee inherited by Thomas lord Berkeley, sonne and heire of the said Maurice and Margery, then about 16. years old, as by Rot. clauś. 25. E. 3. membr. 21. And by Rot. siniũ. 25. E. 3. membr. 22. in the Tower of London appeares.

The said Thomas Berkeley was vsually written of Vley, and by Katherine his wife one of the sisters and coheires of John Bottetort had issue Maurice Berkeley, and died in 35. E. 3. As by the Inq: found after his death that yeare, and by Rot. clauś. 35. E. 3. mem: 2. 3. 7. And by Rot. siniũ. 35. E. 3. mem: 4. et 5. appeares, seised of this manor of Vle, holden of Maurice lord Berkeley by knight service, leavinge the said Maurice his sonne and heire then 3. yeares old: whom the said Katherine his wife survived, after remaried to Sir John de Thorpe; which Katherine died in 11. R. 2. As by Inq: in 11. R. 2. found after her death; And by Rot. siniũ. 11. R. 2. mem: 12. And 12. R. 2. membr. 19. and 37. E. 3. mem: 8. appeares.

The said Maurice Berkeley, was also written of Vley, and died in 2. H. 4. leavinge Johane his wife grossemͭ enseint, who is shortly after delivered of a sonne called

called Maurice, whom, for diſtinction ſake, I will call Poſthumus Maurice; which Jone dyed in 13. H. 4. As by two Inquiſicōns in 9. et 10. H. 5. after her death, appeares.

The ſaid poſthumus Maurice Berkeley by Ellen his wife had iſſue William, and dies in 4. E. 4. ſeized of this manor of Vley holden of William Lord Berkeley in Capite, as by Inq: after his death appeares, whom the ſaid Ellen ſurvives.

The ſaid William Berkeley ſonne of Poſthumus Maurice, maried Anne, and was attainted of Treaſon in 1. H. 7. then ſeized of this Manor of Ewley, touchinge whom A record in the Exchequer in the office of the Remembrancer to the lord Treaſorer in Michas terme 27. Eliz. Rot. 108. pleaded by the purchaſers of that manor of Sir Richard Berkeley, in diſcharge of a tenure by knight ſervice in Capite of the Queene, preſſed againſt them, vz, Thomas Dorney, Chriſtopher Dorney, Thomas Payne, Rich: Payne, Thomas Pegler, Giles ffrench, Giles Browninge, Chriſtopher Sparke, Chriſtopher Dancey, John Dauncey, John Parflowe, Thomas Jocham, and John Hill, ſhall thus informe; That the ſaid William Berkeley beinge ſeized in fee of this manor of Vley, was in 1. H. 7. | attainted of treaſon, and after by an other act of parliamᵗ in 11. H. 7. that act of 1. H. 7. was made void, except for the Lṝes patents and grant made by the kinge of this and other manors, to his vnckle Jeſper Earle of Pembroke, after Duke of Bedford, and the heires males of his body: And that after the ſaid Dukes death without iſſue male, the kinge ſhould have the ſaid lands for his life, And that a former grant made by the kinge in the 4ᵗʰ yeare of his raigne to the ſaid William Berkeley of certaine of his lands for his maintenance, ſhould bee void; That the ſaid Duke dyed ſhortly after without iſſue male of his body, And that the ſaid William alſo dyed in 16. H. 7. And that Richard Berkeley was his ſonne and heire, whom that kinge by his Lṝes patents the ſame yeare reſtored to this and all other his manors and lands, To hold as before and of old hee held them; which for this Manor (ſaith this record) was of the lord Berkeley by knight ſervice, As by an Inq: in 21. E. 3. found after the death of Maurice Berkeley Banneret, appeareth: And that the ſaid Richard Berkeley died in 5. H. 8. And John was his ſonne and heire who died 37. H. 8. leavinge iſſue Richard Berkeley his ſonne and heire, Who all held this manor of the lord Berkeley by knight ſervice as is aforeſaid: And that the ſaid Richard afterwards, by good aſſurance in the lawe, conveyed this manor to the vſe of them and their ſeverall heires. Vpon which plea a confeſſion of the Atturney generall and Judgement of the Court is had, and they diſmiſſed.

Which

Which conveyance of the said Richard Berkeley (needfull to bee knowne) is to this effect; That by his severall Deeds indented dated in or about the first of Aprill a⁰ 8⁰ Eliz. hee granted to each of the said purchasors all their lands in perticuler, boundinge each parcell; And to each of them such comon as they were to enioy, And to each in comon by vndivided parts part of the streets lanes highwaies and wast grounds; And to each of them part of the cheife rents and services which six or more freeholders paid for lands they held of this manor lyinge in Vley, Bagpath, and Oldpen; Togeather with all such liberties and franchises as himselfe had in those townships or places: And in his said Conveyances reserved the some of fforty pounds payable yearely to him and his heires from the said purchasers, which was somwhat more then before hee received for the rent of his wholl manor: wherin also provision is made for a Reeve or officer to gather vp and pay to him the said —40ˡⁱ which—40ˡⁱ his grandchilde Richard Berkeley that nowe is after sold to John Purnell of Woodmancote, who havinge sold—15ˢ p ann therof to Thomas Dancey a freeholder there, left the residue to William Purnell his yonger sonne, who of late hath sold it to Thomas Daunt of Oldpen aforesaid, a village adioyninge, and to his heires.

ffrom which 13. originall purchasers this manor soe sold by Sir Richard Berkeley is nowe the inheritance of theis—

Thomas Dorney the yonger, sonne of John Dorney, who died— |

194   Thomas Dorney th'elder sonne of Richard holds, which by Deed dated 30⁰. Augusti. 11. Jacobi hee purchased of John Webb als Wilkens and of Martha his wife, One messuage in Vley with a close of pasture called Bradley containinge one acre, and 3. acres of arrable land in Nether feild, West feild and Hidefeild, each one acre; which Thomas Payne father of the said Martha, by his will dated 12. April 4. Jac. pd, bequeathed to her in fee, servinge a rent charge of 5ˢ p ann out of the same.

Michaell Payne sonne of

John Manninge

Thomas Dorney sonne of Michaell holdeth a messuage and halfe a yard land, containinge about 40. acres, for which hee was in ward to George lord Berkeley, who

who by his Deed dated 3. mcij 20. Jacobi, granted his wardſhip to Thomas Pointz then huſband to the ſiſter of the wards mother, as by the Deed thereof appeareth; which Michaell Dorney was the fourth ſonne of Thomas Dorney the elder by his ſecond wife, and had the ſame by conveyance from his ſaid father, And hee from his brother Chriſtopher Dorney, who was one of the purchaſers of Sr Richard Berkeley as aforeſaid fol: 192.

John Parſloe ſonne of

Willm Smyth

Willm Dancey

Richard Dancey

Anthony Hill, ſonne of

Thomas Peglar ſonne of Thomas Peglar the purchaſer mentioned in the foreſaid exchequer Record before in fol: 192. 193. to have byn one of the purchaſers of Sir Richard Berkeley, And who died in 14. R^e Jacobi, holdeth three meſſuages and 100. acres of land in Vley.

John Wood

Thomas ffrench, ſonne of Thomas, who died in 6. Jac̄. R^e, holdeth about 62. acres of land, which Gyles his father purchaſed of Sir Richard Berkeley as aforeſaid fol: 192. mentioned in the Exchequer pleadings there expreſſed.

William Payne

Richard Whittard, by deed dated 2° Decembr̄. 39. Eliz. purchaſed of Thomas Dangerfeild a meadowe ground called Roxford, 4. acres of arrable called Lay knap; 3. acres and an halfe of wood called the Ley wood, with a houſe and garden in Vley; To hold for 1000 yeares vnder the yearly rent of—12^d

Thomas

Thomas Points

John Browninge, fonne of John Browninge of Cowley who dyed in 4ᵗᵒ Caroli, fonne of Richard, holdeth 4. acres of meadowe in whitney and a meadowe in Cowley called Moore mead containinge 4. acres, parcell of the manor or capitall meſſuage called Whitecourt in Vley, of the caſtle of Berkeley by knight ſervice: Soe found by Inquiſiċon in aº. 4ᵗᵒ Regis Caroli p̄d.

John Purnell |

196   Richard Browninge

William Baſſet Eſq

Thomas Daunt genṫ

John Pegler of ffroceſter.

Henry Dancey th'elder.

William Harper

Walter Woodward

Iſaac Smyth |

197
Name.   The name of this towne feemes not vnprobably to bee compounded, (as divers other in this hundred are,) of Ewe, which in french is water, and lei or lega wᶜʰ in the Saxon tongue is water or place; ffor ſweeter ſprings and a ſweeter ſtreame both riſinge and running through the wholl towne is rarely to bee found.

Ewelep

Campe. In the promontary of a steep hill or mount at the vtter edge thereof in this parish is an ancient fortresse or campe, doubly trenched, very large, which as tradition heere goeth (true or false I knowe not,) was cast vp by Earle Goodwyn as hee marched from Beverstan with his army towards Glouc̄, where kinge Edward called the Confessor then abode with a like Army; betweene whom at that time battell was feared, but composed by the mediation of the great Lords and prelates then adheringe to either party.

Great tooth. It hath byn often credibly affirmed to mee by divers credible men, That heere was digged vp or found a mans tooth three inches square, which vntill within 40. yeares last was kept by the family of the Bassetts in the parlor windowe of their mansion house heere, as a wonder of mankinde; which my incredulity is as vnapt to beleive as the Legend of Lyes.

Church. Of the Rectory or Church the kinge is patron, which came to the Crowne by the suppression of the Monastery of St Peter in Glouc̄, in 31. H. 8. James Dalton is Incumbent; valued in the office of the first fruits at 12^{li} p ann̄.

In the com̄on pleas at Westm̄ in Trin̄ terme 6. H. 3. Rot. 1. in dorso rotuli, is entred an assise brought by Peter of Euleigh against the Abbot of Glouc̄ for the advowson of this church of Ewleigh, wherin the said Peter de Ewleigh makes his clayme as heire to his father, who last presented: The Abbot makes his title from the grant of kinge Henry the Second to his priory of Stanley, who had only a pention of a marke out of it. Peter replies That kinge Henry the second had not any thinge in the church, nor in the land where the church is: Sue resteth the Record.

ffifteene. The payment of the ffifteene or kingsilver when it is granted by pliam^t, goeth with Woodmancote vnder one and the same som̄e. The onus or charge of both townships togeather, is—3^{li} 14^s 7^d The deduction is 10^s 8^d The Remanet paid into the Exchequer for both, is—3^{li} 3^s 11^d

Subsedy. In the last Subsedy in 5to Caroli were in this parish of Ewley 15 subsedy men who then paid—4^{li} 16^s

Able men. Of able men for the warres betweene 20. and 60. yeares old, in 6to Jacobi, which appeared before Henry lord Berkeley Lord Leiutenant of this county, were—56

Of

Hundred of Berkeley

Souldiers. Of trayned Souldiers vnder Edw: Stephens Esq, their captaine are , wherof musketteers, and pikes.

Rates. And if the Division of Berkeley accompted a fourth part of the shire bee rated in any tax for kinge or commonwealth at—100ˡⁱ then this hundred of Berkeley paies thereof 33ˡⁱ 3ˢ. And this towne of Ewley—20ˢ. And soe after that rate, bee the taxe more or lesse. |

198 **Freeholds** within this parish of Ewley, not formerly mentioned ; viz'.

Dancies land. The noble family of the **Berkeleis of Duresley** had faire lands both in demesne and in service in this parish of Ewley, anciently in time of the Conqueror and longe after holden of them, As before in the description of Came and Duresley fol: 123. 175. hath appeared : The greatest part wherof came to Edmond Baffett, whose office after his death in 4. E. 2. shewes his dyinge seised (inter alia) of a Messuage and a carucate of land in Ewley, holden of the heire of William Berkeley of Duresley by the sixteenth part of a knights fee : And that Isable Punchardoun, Margaret the wife of Nicholas de Valers, and Katherine Bifet, are his sisters and heires : With which office agreeth the record of Original aᵒ 4. E. 2. Rot. 32. in sctio cum Reñi thesaur : and also the booke of Releefes inter fines Terñi Triñ. 6. E. 2. And the same booke in aᵒ 7. E. 2. in the said Office in the Exchequer.

See fol. 231. Part of this land is nowe the inheritance of William Dancey of Ewley, sonne of Thomas, sonne of John, sonne of Giles Dancey, whose ancestor maried the daughter and heire of Arras, who was heire to   Attekins, who purchased them of the said Isable Punchardoun, as the deeds in the custody of the said Willm Dancey which I have read doe shewe. Another part of this land which fell to Margaret the wife of Nicholas de Valers, in Came and Cowley, was in her widowhood sold to Thomas lord Berkeley the third of that name in 11. 13. et 14. E. 2. as the deeds of the purchase thereof in Berkeley castle doe shewe ; As also doth the Accompt of the Manor of Came then made by the Reeve therof, at that time. And the third part which fell to Katherine Bifet in this parish of Ewley, is nowe the inheritance of

Stoutshill place now Giles Aullens. **Also** in this parish of Ewley is one other ancient ffreehold called Stowteshill als Stoutshill place, with about 46. acres of land therto belonginge ; A name taken from the family of the Stuts, or Stouthills, ancient owners therof ; Of whom Adam Stut

Stut is mentioned in the second deed made by Thomas lord Berkeley to Margaret his daughter, wherin (inter alia) hee granted to her the services of the said Adam; In which name it continued till towards the end of kinge Henry the sixth; The next I finde owner of this land was John Davis of Dursley, whose office is after his death in 27 H. 8. who entayled the same vpon his daughter Anne maried to Edward Baffett, who had issue John Baffet, who sold the same to Willm Augustine als Austen, father of Benedict als Bennet, who died in 37. Eliz. father of Giles Austen that nowe is, holden by him, as himselfe saith, of George lord Berkeley as of his | Manor of Came, by the yearly rent of—4ᵈ paid to his Reeve of that manor, and by sute to his hundred court of Berkeley from three weekes to three weekes, but whether in Socage or by knights service, I knowe not. Of this land see a fine levied in Hillary terme 18. R. 2. by John Stouteshill.

Heere also is another ancient ffreehold the inheritance of Willm Selewin sonne of Jesper Selewine Esq, now in the occupacōn of James ffourds als Harper, sonne of John, sonne of Willm, sonne of James ffourds als Harper, ancient lessees therof; somtime the land of Edward Twisell, who by his will devised this land to Jone his daughter in fee, maried to Atkinson, As an office found after her death in 1º Eliz. sheweth; wherby the tenure is said to bee of Mr. Willm Baffetts manor in Socage: Howbeit, hee doth sute for this land to the Court of the lord Berkeleys hundred of Berkeley from 3. weekes to 3. weekes, And by payment of—1ᵈ cheife rent to his reeve of his manor of Came: And payeth also   as a rent secke to the said William Baffett: ffor which see an Inq: in   Caroli, found after the death of the said Jesper Selewine.¹

Selwins land als Twisells.

Co: roll of Came, 43. Eliz. Willm Selwyn de Stanley died seised of a messuage and divers lands in Vley late Twyffells²: Rent—1ᵈ Rich: Selwin is sonne and heire, but the lands come by conveyance to Jesper a younger sonne of the said Willm Selwin.

Also in this parish are two messuages called nether house and Whitings, with divers lands to them belonginge, now the inheritance of Thomas Dorney thelder, sonne

Dorneis land

---

¹ Jasper Selwyn, of Matson, died 1634, and was buried there. Will proved at Gloucester.

² William Selwyn, of Stanley St Leonards, mar. Elizabeth, daughter of John Twyfell, of Kingstanley, (son of John and grandson of Hugh Twyfell?) and had issue Richard, father of another William Selwyn, father of Jasper above mentioned.—See Pedigree of Selwyn, Trans: Bristol and Gloucestershire Archæol. Society, Vol. II., pp. 278, 280. [ED.]

sonne of Richard; holden of the kinge by knight service in Capite, which by the dissolucon of the monastery of Brodstocke in the County of Wilts, came to kinge H. 8. And by   aliened to
About which, through the difficulty of distinguishinge them from other freehold lands holden of the castle of Berkeley by knights service, sutes in lawe longe continued betweene the Dornies brothers of the halfe bloud, till 5ᵗ Jacobi, when by my mediation they were ended. And theis lands were given to that monastery by Thomas lord Berkeley the first of that name, as in the history of his life I have elswhere written; ffor which also see Rot. cartaȝ. 16. H. 3. membr. 6. And also for theis lands see an Inq: 20. Eliz. after the death of Thomas Dorney th'elder; And Michas ffines, 26. Eliz: Rot. 52. in sccio, pro Relevio p̄dci Thome Dorny.

Ellonds land nowe Brownings.   Also in this parish is one other ancient freehold, the inheritance of Richard Browninge of Dursley, purchased by him of John Browninge of Cowley, elder brother of the said Richard, sonnes of Richard Browninge, who purchased the same of   Ellond, holden of the manor of Ewley in socage by the yearly rent of—10ˢ |

200   Somwhat more touchinge the manor of Ewley and the lands therin, not formerly mentioned, is to bee read in theis Records, viz'.

Inq: 5. H. 8. p̃ morte Rici de Berkeley.
Inq: 37. H. 8. p̃ morte Johis de Berkeley.
Michas Rec. 22. E. 3. Rot. 23. in Sccio.
Inq: 2. H. 4. p̃ mortem Mauricij de Berkeley.
Pasch: rec. 14. E. 4. Rot. 5. in Sccio.
Original. 16. H. 7. Rot. 48. c̃m Reñi thesaur̃ in sccio.
Record. 23. H. 7. Rot. 17. in sccio ibm.
Michas rec. 8. H. 8. Rot. 40. ibm.
Original, 22. H. 8. Rot. 39. ibm.
Original, 6. E. 6. Rot. 44. ibm.
Inq: 2. Jacobi, p̃ morte Johis Dorny.
Inq: 3. Jac. p̃ morte p̄dei Johis Dorny sup̃ Melius inquirend.
Inq: 4. Regis Caroli p̃t morte Johis Browninge.—per servic militare.
Diversi fines in banco, in Terñi Michis. 9. et. 10. Eliz. |

Filton

ffilton.

ffilton, als ffilton et hay: written alſo ffelton : A townſhip not mentioned in the booke of Domeſdei, but went vnder the name of Horfeld, wherof ſee fol : 233.

In this village are ſix meſſuages, parcell at this day of the poſſeſſions of the Biſhoppricke of Briſtoll erected in 34. H. 8, whereof read before in Cromhale, and were parcell of the lands belonginge to the Monaſtery of St Auguſtine by Briſtoll where the Biſhops feate is ; And were (amongſt other lands) given by Robert the ſonne of Harding when in the time of kinge Stephen hee founded that monaſtery, as formerly, in Almondſbury Cromhale and other places hath byn written. But in what pariſh theis 6 meſſuages doe lye, queſtion of late yeares hath byn moved amongſt the inhabitants themſelves, which I determine not.

The Biſhop beinge Lord alſo of Horfeild, adioyninge, draweth theſe ſix houſholds to his Leet or Lawday of Horfeild, who are reputed a little manor of themſelves.

The other part of this village is at this day the inheritance of Wm Baldwine of London, draper: whoſe father Wm Baldwyn was by Inq : in 19° Jacobi, found to dye ſeiſed of the manor of ffilton, holden of the kinge by knight ſervice, but not in Capite, And the ſaid W^m to bee his ſonne and heire.

This little manor conſiſteth of 8 houſholds, who are within the great Leet or Lawday of the hundred of Berkeley, wherat at Berkeley they appeare twice in the yeare and preſent all thoſe things which to a Leet appertaineth ; wherin the comon pound ſtandeth, and wherto the waſt grounds doe belonge ; And the orders and Bilawes and preſentments of theis 8. or of this little manor, rule and order the other ſix, who are bound by what theis doe, as all the 45. yeares of my beinge Steward hath byn accuſtomed ; And appeare therat by the name of the Tithingman and Tithinge of ffilton and Hay ; As for that part called Hay only one houſe is nowe ſtandinge theron, (the reſt decayed,) the inheritance of   Mallet Eſq. of   in Somſetſhire.

The ſaid Wm Baldwyne the father of W^m, purchaſed this manor of John Younge, and hee of Richard Revill ſonne of   Revill.

The

Hundred of Berkeley

Church. The Chaple of ffilton is within the Deanry of Briftoll, and the mother church therto is——   ; But of this fee more in Horfeild fol : 233.

ffifteene. The paym^t. of the ffifteene or Kingfilver when it is granted by parliam^t goeth with Horfeild, in one fome, which is—3^{li} 10^s 6^d q, paid into the Exchequer by the Collector thereof.

Subfedy In the laft Subfedy in 5to Caroli were in this wholl village 11. fubfedy men, who paid the kinge—3^{li} 4^s

Able men. Of able men for the warres betweene 20. and 60. yeares old, were in a^o. 6. R^r Jacobi, which then appeared at a generall mufter before the lord Leiuten^t of this county,—18.

Souldiers. Of trayned fouldiers vnder Thomas Chefter Efq, their captaine now are

Rates. And if the wholl Divifion of Berkeley, accompted a 4th part of the Sheire bee rated in any tax for kinge or comon wealth at 100^{li}. Then this hundred of Berkeley paies thereof—33^{li} 3^s. And this townfhip of ffilton—15^s

Take the reft that concerneth this village, as I have obferved the Records mentioninge it. |

202 By patent roll in the Tower of London, 27. E. 1. in dorfo, Elias de ffilton arraigned an affife againft the Abbot of St Auguftine neere Briftoll, for comon of pafture there ; And by the fame roll feemes to bee either Lord or a freeholder in Horfeild.

By Inq : in^t 4. R. 2. after the death of Edmund Blunt, it is found That hee held the day that hee died ioyntly with Margaret his wife, who furvived, the moity of the manor of ffilton (inter alia) by the guift of Thomas fitz-Nicholl and Margery his wife, holden of Reginald de Cobham in right of Alienor his wife, by knight fervice, And that Wm Blunt is his fonne and heire.

By Rot. clauſ. in the tower in 7. R. 2. mem : 22. vpon a Non intromittendo to the kings efcheator, it is recited, That wheras Edmund Blunt deceafed held ioyntly with Margaret his wife the moity of the manor of ffilton, by the guift of Sir

Thomas

Thomas fitz nichol and of Margery his wife, which is not holden of the kinge, Therfore the faid Efcheator fhould deliver the faid moity (inter alia) to the faid Margarett.

By Inq: the fame 7. R. 2. vpon a writ of Ad quod damnum, it was found, That befides other manors entailed by Sir Thomas fitz nichol there remained to him the moity of the manors of ffilton and Harry ftoke, holden of Reginald Cobham by knight fervice, as in right of Alienor his wife.

In Berkeley caftle is a Court roll A° 11. H. 4. which fhewes that Elias de ffilton, fonne of Ralph de ffilton, was then lord therof.

Inq: 6. H. 5. after the death of Sir Thomas fitz nichol, fhewes that hee held the manors of ffilton and Stokehenry of the lord of Berkeley, but by what fervice the Jury knew not: And that Katherine the wife of Robert Pointz, and John fonne of John Browninge and of Alienor his wife, are afwell heires to the faid Sir Thomas as to Margery his wife, vz, the faid Katherine and Margery, daughters and co-heires to them both.

Inq: 8. H. 5. after the death of John fonne and heire of John Browning findes that hee dyed feifed of the manors of ffilton and Harry Stoke holden of the lord Berkeley, but by what fervice the Jury knew not, And that Wittm was his brother and heire, 20. yeares old.

Inq: 32. H. 6. findes, That Willelma fomtime the wife of John Blunt held for her life the manor of ffilton, (inter alia) of the heire of Alienor Seryvet deceafed, but by what fervice the Jury knewe not: And that Edmund Blunt was her fonne and heire.

See alfo the record of Michas terme, 20. H. 6. Rot. 41. in fĉio, ẽm Remem̃ Thefaur̃.|

Gosington.

Gosington als Gossinton: In Domefdei booke written Gofintune, wherin William called the Conqueror had 4. hides of land in demefne, lyinge within the parifh of Slimbridge, the inheritance of George lord Berkeley and efteemed as parcell of his Barony of Berkeley, holden of the Crowne by knight fervice in capite.

Hundred of Berkeley

This hamblet or village of Gofington is at this day reputed parcell of the manor of Slimbridge, but of old was not foe: ffor this of Gofington was part of the great manor of Berkeley, as the booke of Domefday apparantly fheweth; And then was the land of William the Conqueror, And before him of kinge Edward called the Confeffor, and of kinge Harold, and before them of the Abbeffe and Nunnes of Berkeley: And that of Slimbridge was the land of the family of the Berkeleis of Durfley from longe before the Conqueft, vntill the agreement made at Briftoll in the time of kinge Stephen betweene Roger Berkeley of Durfley and Robert the fonne of Harding, and the double mariage of their children that followed therevpon, wherby this of Slimbridge was granted in fee to Maurice fonne and heire of the faid Robert, and to Alice his wife, daughter of the faid Roger Berkeley of Durfley, wherof fee before in Durfley, fol: 175. And in Slimbridge, fol: 325. But this of Gofington and that of Slimbridge havinge almoft ever fince gone togeather, this hath byn and is reputed parcell of that other, And was of larger extent then nowe by moft it is reputed to bee; which Agreement fee after verbatim, in Slimbridge. fol. 325 p̱d.

ffrom which Robert the fonne of Hardinge, (who had this hamblet amongft many others by the grant of kinge H. 2. in the firft of his raigne,) and dyed in the 17th of the fame kinge, this hamblet difcended to the faid Maurice his fonne and heire, who by the confent of Robert his fonne and heire, as the deed fpeaketh, towards the end of the faid kings raigne, gave the fame by the name of the moity of all his land of Goffington to Willm his 4th fonne and his heires, To hold by the 4th part of a knights fee. And afterwards by a fine levied in 7. R. 1. had from the faid Robert his eldeft brother, the other moity of this Goffington, in exchange for his land in Portbury in the county of Somfet, wherby the faid William became feifed of this wholl hamblet or village; The deed wherof remaininge in the caftle of Berkeley, is in theis words;

Mau$\bar{r}$ de Berkel, omnibus hominibus fuis et amicis, faltm. Sciatis quòd ego dedi et conceffi, et hâc meâ cartâ confirmavi, Willo filio meo pro fervicio fuo, medie- tatem totius terre mee de Gofinton, Tenendam et habendam fibi et heredibus fuis de me et heredibus meis in feodo et hereditate, cum omnibus ptinentijs fuis, in pratis et pafturis, et omnibus alijs libertatibus et liberis confuetudinib^{9} ad terrā illā ptinentib^{9}, libere et quiete integre et honorificè per ferviciū quartæ ptis vnius militis mihi et heredibus meis faciend; Et hoc feci confenfu et affenfu Roberti filij mei, et heredis mei; Et vt hæc mea donatio et conceffio firma fit et ftabilis, Eam p̄fenti fcripto

Goſington

ſcripto et ſigillo meo confirmavi ; T. hijs, Willm Laud Epo, Johe Abbate Sčī Auguſtini, Galfr Priore Lanthoñ, Willo Comite Sarreburr, Magro Maur, Magro Petro de Par, Reginald capellañ, Walter Capellañ, Adam de Santuñ, Henriē Eia frib⁰ ſuis, Johe de Cogan, Bernardo de Stañ, Rico de Cohull, Willo de Morevill, Maur fil Nigelli.

The ſaid Maurice died in 1. R. 1. as by the great Roll in the pipe office 2. 3. et 4. R. 1. And by the confirmaćon of R. 1. in the firſt of his raigne, made to Robert his ſonne and heire, appeareth. |

Which fyne alſo betweene the ſaid Robert and Willm his brother levyed in a⁰ 7⁰ R. 1. is in theis words, Glouč et Somerſet : Inter Willm de Berkelai petentem, et Robertum de Berkelai tenentem, frem ſuum, de feodo dimidij militis in Portberi, et de quartá parte feodi vnius militis in Goſington, &č. ſelt, q̃d idem Willus quietum clamavit totm ius ſuum p̃ſato Roberto et heredibus ſuis, q̃d habuit in illa terra de Portberi, tali modo, quod ſi idem Robtus de Berkelai ſine herede deceſſerit de vxore ſibi diſponſata, rediet p̃dča terra de Portberi prenōiato Willo et heredibus ſuis, ſi ſupervixerit ; Et pro hac, &c. idem Robertus de Berkelai reddidit eid Willo et heredibus ſuis medietatem de Goſington, quam Mauricius pater eorum tenuit in dominio (dominico) die quá fuit vivus et mortuus, pro quartá parte feodi vnius militis in Goſington, de quá parte idem Willus facit prenominato Roberto homagium Preterea convenit inter eos, q̃d ſi idem Willus ſine herede de vxore ſibi diſponſata deceſſerit, ipſa terra de Goſington redijt prefato Roberto et heredibus ſuis imperpetuum. Which fine is the firſt that I have mett withall of any land in this hundred, And by miſtakinge is filed in the bundle of Comitat Dorſett, in the Treaſury, in the Abby church at Weſtm̃.

And this fine ſeemes well explained by the great Roll in the pipe office in 9. R. 1. where this Willm de Berkelai paid the kinge—4ˡⁱ 18ˢ for this 4ᵗʰ part of this knights fee in Goſington.

This Willm, who was a knight, had iſſue (as by ſome Deeds which I have ſeene, if not counterfeit, appeared,) Ida maried to John de Cave, who had iſſue Iſarda maried to Robert Brail, father of Robert, father of Iſable maried to Richard Stapleton, who had iſſue Helena maried to Roger de Goſington ; which thus farre of the ſaid Willms diſcent, I ſuſpect ; But certaine it is which nowe followeth ; That the ſaid Roger de Goſington had iſſue Roger who died about 12. E. 2. leavinge

inge John his sonne and heire within age, whose wardship for body and lands Thomas lord Berkeley the second of that name by Deed in Berkeley castle in 14. E. 2. granted to Roger Archer, which grant also is proved by one other deed in 9. E. 3. in the said castle of Berkeley vnder 2. seales, which saith That Gosington is within the manor of Came.

The said John de Gosington died without issue, and Reginald was his brother and heire; who leaft issue Henry, father of Thomas Gosington, which Thomas and Jone his wife about 17. H. 6, aliened the same to James Venables and his heires; ffrom Venables the same came to fforister and his co-feoffees about 11. E. 4. And from fforister and his co-feoffees to John Tame of ffairford about 11. H. 7. And from Thomas Tame and Jone his wife by deed in 29. H. 8. to John Bridgman and Willm his sonne, And by a fine the yeare after levied in Michas terme 30. H. 8. by the said Thomas Tame and Jone his wife, and Edmond Horne, and Elizabeth his wife to John Bridgman and Willm his sonne and their heires, by the name of the manor of Gosington and of divers lands in Gosington, Slimbridge, Arlingham, Came, Cowley, Hurst, and Hame, in the county of Glouc; wherof see more before in Arlingham, fol: 60. in Hedges land, late Bridgmans.

And the said Willm Bridgman sonne of John, in 3. E. 6. sold the same to ffrancis Codrington, By whose death in 4. et 5. Ph: & Mar the same discended to Gyles Codrington his sonne and heire, who dyinge in 23. Eliz. left it to ffrancis Codrington his sonne and heire, who dyed | the yeare after his father without issue male, wherby it came to Richard Codrington his brother and heire male, which Richard in 40. Eliz: sold the same to Willm Tracy and his heires; which Willm Tracy in 43. Eliz. sold the same to Godfrey Goldisborrowe then bishop of Glouc, with whom, for the better satisfaction of the said Bishop, the said Richard Codrington ioyned in the assurance; The Bishop died at Glouc the 26th of May in the second yeare of the raigne of kinge James, leavinge John Goldisborrowe his sonne and heire, then 19. yeares and 5. monthes old; whose education and goverment the Bishop by his will dated 24° Augusti, 1°. Jacobi, (proved in the Arches at London,) comitted to Robert Hill, Clerke, then parson of Tredington and after Archdeacon of this county, and to others, vntill his said sonne John should attaine his age of 21. yeares; Against which Robert Hill who only medled in the education and with the estate of the said John, Henry lord Berkeley in a° 3° Jacobi, brought his acton of Ravishment del gard, And vpon a longe and well defended tryall at the Assises holden at Glouc the 22th of July A° 3^{tio} Jacobi, before Yelverton and Williams Judges,

Judges, recovered four hundred marks damages, wherat my felfe was prefent : Againſt which triall in the terme followinge as much was faid by the def.ᵗˢ counfell in arreſt of Judgement as lay in the power of Art or learninge, but prevailed not : which is entred in the Court of Coṁon pleas in Eaſter terme aᵒ 3ᵗⁱᵒ Jacobi, Rot. 745. Shortly after, the faid Henry lord Berkeley brought another acc̃on againſt Wiłłm Clutterbooke the Biſhops and Archdeacons leſſee for years for the meane profitts of the land, and had Judgement to recover ; And vpon a writt to enquire of damages the Jury gave—60ˡⁱ. As by the record therof in the kings bench in Hillary Terme 3ᵒ Jacobi p̃d Rot. 171. appeareth : The writ alfo to enquire of damages is filed of Trinity terme followinge, Aᵒ 4ᵗᵒ Jacobi. Soe that I hold my felfe fully warranted to fay that this manor land or farme of Gofington is holden of George lord Berkeley as of his manor of Berkeley by the 4ᵗʰ part of a knights fee, fute to his hundred court of Berkeley from 3. weeks to 3. weekes, and by the yearly rent of—6ˢ 6ᵈ though neither the fute of Court nor the faid rent bee mentioned in the originall Deed nor fine.

Afterwards in 15ᵒ Jacobi, I purchafed this land of Gofington of the faid John Goldiſborrowe and Rebecca his wife, wherin I vfed the name of Anthony Gulſton my halfe brother by the mothers fide ; And in the 4. yeares next followinge, annis 15. 16. 17. et 18. Jacobi, I againe fold the fame by 11. feverall Deeds to foe many feverall purchafors of parts thereof, wherof the capitall meſſuage or farme houfe called Gofington hall, was by mee fold to Lawrence Bridger, clerke, parfon of Slimbridge, with 60. acres of land adioyninge ; And delivered therwith all the Evidences, which manifeſted all or moſt part of what is before written, from the faid Reginald de Gofington downwards ; Who by his death in aᵒ 7ᵒ Caroli, left the fame to Jofeph his eldeſt fonne by a fecond wife, who ſtill holds the fame, 1639. And in my conveyances apportioned the faid cheife rent of Six ſhillings fix pence to each purchafor by a ratable part, now paid to the faid Lord Berkeleis Reeves of his manors of Hurſt and flimbridge, lyinge alfo within the faid pariſh of Slimbridge.

The names of thofe who now doe fute to the faid hundred Court and pay the faid 6ˢ 6ᵈ rent are—

1. The faid Jofeph Bridger, who by his fathers conveyance from mee dated 12ᵒ April. 17ᵒ Jacobi is to pay 3ˢ to the faid manor of Hurſt, and 6ᵈ to the faid manor of Slimbridge : The perticulers of whofe p̃chafe, with divers cheife rents amountinge to 33ˢ 9ᵈ, are expreſſed in the deed of purchafe thereof.

2. Samuell

2. Samuell Bridger of Woodmancote in the parifh of Durfley, eldeft fonne of the faid Lawrance by his firft wife, by his deed from mee dated 12° Maij a° 16° Jacobi, purchafed a clofe of pafture containinge 10. acres called Clinger als Cley-hunger, lyinge in Came. And of the faid 6ˢ 6ᵈ paieth—4ᵈ which his faid father afterwards gave to the faid Samuell.

3. Robert Davis of Hurft, fonne and heire of Thomas Davis to whom by deed dated 12. ñcij, 15ᵗᵒ Jacobi I fold my clofe called Reignolds mead cont. 7 acres, and 3. acres and an halfe of arrable land in Southworthy feild, and paies 4ᵈ of the faid cheife rent of 6ˢ 6ᵈ.

4. Richard Spicer of London, Doctor of phificke, who purchafed of Edw: Trotman of the Inner Temple London Efq., and hee of mee by deed dated 30. April a° 16. Jac. inrolled in Chancery, and after by my other deed dated 12° Maij, followinge, granted, releafed and confirmed to him and his truftees, one clofe called Olden cont. 8. acres, one parcell of arrable cont. 20. acres, and one clofe therto adioyninge called Newe leyes cont. 12. acr̃, and 4. peells of pafture cont. 18. acres, then in the tenure of Richard Trotman for 3. lives, wheron hee after built an houfe, and paies 12ᵈ pcell of the faid—6ˢ 6ᵈ cheife rent.

5. Edward Trotman of the Stepps in Came, to whom by deed dated 12. ñcij 15° Jacobi I fold one clofe of pafture called Grovelands cont 8. acres, in the parifh of Slimbridge. And paies 3ᵈ of the faid cheife rent of 6ˢ 6ᵈ. nowe in a° 1639. the inheritance of Nicholas Trotman his eldeft fonne by a fecond wife. As his office after his death in a° 14. Caroli fheweth; wherin the tenure by knight fervice and the other fervices are found. And more, one quarter of an acre of arrable in Cams lower feild, by my deed 2° Novembr̃: 11. Caroli.

6. William Tailor, to whom by Deed dated 12. ñcij a° 15° Regis Jacobi I fold one clofe of pafture called the Old hay cont 1. acre, and 3. acres and an halfe in 3. places in the feild called Southworthy in Slimbridge, and payeth—2ᵈ pcell of the faid cheife rent of 6ˢ 6ᵈ.

7. Robert ffrape, to whom by deed dated 12. ñtij, 15° Jacobi, I fold 2. acres in the great more in Hurft, and one acre of pafture in a clofe of his next Hawthurne feild, and one acre of arrable in Linchfeild, and paies—1ᵈ pcell of the faid 6ˢ 6ᵈ; whereof hee fince hath aliened to Anthony Williams the forefaid acre in

And

Cosington

And alſo to John Taylor the foreſaid acre in [Linchfeild,] And alſo to Arthur Bridger, another ſonne of the ſaid Lawrence, the foreſaid two acres of meadowe in the great moore. |

8. Henry Staples, to whom by Deed dated 12º. Maij. 16º Jacobi. I ſold 5. acres of arrable land in the feild called Hinworthy in Slimbridge, and alſo two roomes of houſinge neere adioyninge to the old warth; And paies 2ᵈ. peell of the ſaid cheife rent of 6ˢ 6ᵈ By whoſe death in   Caroli the ſame diſcended to his two daughters and coheires, viz, Mary nowe the wife of Thomas ffreeman, the widow of Purnell, And to Elizabeth late wife of Richard Hugman, who died this yeare: And the ſaid Elizabeth forthwith after ſold her moity to the ſaid Thomas ffreeman.

9. John Thayer of Stinchcombe to whom by deed dated 30º. April. 17 Jac̄. I ſold one cloſe of paſture called Hengaſton cont one acre, in Came or Stinchcombe or one of them; And paies—1ᵈ parcell of the ſaid cheiſe rent of 6ˢ 6ᵈ By whoſe death in   Caroli, the ſaid land diſcended to John his ſonne and heire, who nowe holdeth the ſame. Aº 1639.

10. John Smyth of ffrogpit in Hinton, to whom by my deed dated 20º. Aug̃. 17º Jacobi, I releaſed and confirmed the Terme of—1000. yeares which hee then had to come by the demiſe of John Goldiſborrowe two yeares before, in one acre and an halfe of mead in Broadmead, To hold to him and his heires; lyinge not farre from Cheſilhunger towards Slimbridge, vnder—1ᵈ rent to the cheife lord, peell of the ſaid—6ˢ 6ᵈ Which John, in 16. Caroli, gave the ſame to Joſeph his younger ſonne and to his heires.

11. John Nelme of Stinchcombe to whom by Deed dated 30º April 17º Jac̄. I ſold one acre of paſture in Cleihunger als Clinger; And paies—1ᵈ peell of 6ˢ 6ᵈ aforeſaid; which hee after aliened to   Bridger.

12. Samuell Bridger aforeſaid holdeth by the grant of the ſaid Lawrance Bridger clerke, his father, wᶜʰ by my deed dated 3. Octobr̄ 18. Jac̄, I ſold to him in fee, one meſſuage in Hurſt neere Reignolds leaze, And one cloſe called Hawthurne cont 4. acres, and 2. cloſes of paſt cont 5. acres in Lyfeild, and 2. acres of arrable in the ſaid Lyfeild in Slimbridge; and one cloſe of paſture called Brodnam in Slimbridge, cont 3. acres, and 2. cloſes cont 3. acres in Came, late in the tenure of Thomas Shell; And for theis paies—5ᵈ peell of the ſaid cheiſe rent of—6ˢ 6ᵈ

Other

Other ffreeholders of the Sirname of Gofington or de Gofington lived very anciently in this village, of much remarkeablenes in their times, not formerly mentioned; As Engewald de Gofington who lived in the time of kinge Stephen, and was one of the 8 noble vndertakers, that the faid Roger Berkeley of Durfley fhould performe his Agreement with Robert the fonne of Harding; which fee in fol : 175, et fol : 325.

Thomas lord Berkeley by his deed dated 23. Junij aº 35. E. 1. granted licence to Roger de Gofington his cozen to enclofe his feild called Oldland lying neere to his court of Gofington, and fo to hold it inclofed all times of the yeare for ever; wherto amongft others Walter de Gofington was a witnes; which Roger is formerly mentioned to dye about 12. E. 2.

Reginald de Gofington in the time of H. 2. and R. 1.

Willm de Gofington, in the beginninge of H. 3.

Reginald de Gofington towards the later end of H. 3. and in the time of kinge E. 1.

Walter de Gofington in the time of kinge E. 2. |

208
Cartæ cum
Roberto Davis
de Hurft.

And by a Deed without date, Robert de Gofington fonne of Robert fonne of Richard had lands heere; But whether of this Hall place or of other fmaller parcells, which I rather beleive, I determine not.

Reginald de Gofington by deed without date gave to Willm his fonne and his heires, halfe a yard land in the towne of Gofington, To hold of him and his heires by 12^d rent for all fervices, excepto regali fervicio, &c. which is knight fervice.

And by one other Deed without date, the faid Reginald de Gofington, gave to Walter fonne of Roger de Gofington and to his heires, a meffuage in Gofington and 11. acres of land therto belonginge, which Roger father of Walter gave to him. And theis two laft mentioned parcells are nowe the lands of the faid Robert Davis of Hurft, which hee in 11º Caroli. aº 1635. purchafed of Simon Mundy als Munden, who lately before had the fame by the laft Will of Simon Ludby, whofe lands and his anceftors they had longe byn, And whofe widowe, is nowe wife of the faid Robert Davis.

To each of which purchafors from mee, Rowland Goldifborrowe fonne and heire of the faid John, for their better affurance, by his feverall deeds in 7º Caroli. releafed, with warranty.

Somewhat

Hame

Somewhat more of this Gofington, is to bee read in theis Records, vizᵗ,
 Inq : de feodis miltum de Berkeley. 37. E. 3.—per fervicium mil.
 ffinis in banco. 17. H. 6. Teriii Hill : pro Venables.
 Inq : 4. & 5. Ph : & Maȓ pᵗ morte ffrancifci Codrington.
 Inq : 23. Eliz : p̄t morte Egidij Codrington.
 Inq : 24. Eliz : p̄t morte ffrancifci Codrington.
 ffinis in banco, pro Odone de Acton et Ifabella vxoȓ eius. 13. E.
 Inq : 14. Regis Caroli, p̄t morte Edw: Trotman de les fteps in Came.—per fervie militare.
 Inq : 9. Caroli, p̄t morte Thome Davis. p fervie militare.
 Court Rolls of Hurft and Slimbridge. 2⁰ Jaē. pᵗ morte Godfriū Goldifborī.
 Teriii Pafch : 3. Jaē. Rot. 745 in c̄ōi banco.—per ferviciū mil.
 Term : Hill : 3. Jaē. Rot. 171. in banco Regis.—per fervicū militare. |

Hame.

Hame, quasi Home : vz. the Home manor. Alfo Ham, in the old Saxon tongue properly fignified a Coveringe; And by a Metaphore An houfe that covereth vs.

This manor of Hame hath noe fpetiall name in the booke of Domefdai, compiled in the 14ᵗʰ yeare of Wiltm the Conqueror, as the other **Berew** members villages or parifhes have within that hundred of Berkeley, which are therin faid to belonge to Berkeley : But indeed this manor of Hame (as longe it hath byn called) is the homefted of the manor of Berkeley, efpecially before the buildinge of the caftle of Berkeley; And the ancient houfe within this manor of Hame nowe called the Grange, was the fcite-place or capitall meffuage thereof; And of this Hame are theis words in the faid Domefdai booke meant. viz; Terra Regis : In Berchelai habuit E. Rex 5. hidas, et in dominico 5. carucaī. et 20. villani, et 5. bordaȓ, cum 11. carucaī, et 9. fervi, et 11. molini de 12. folid. Ibi 10. racheniftres habentes 7. hidas et 7. carucaī; Ibi vnum forum (the market or burrowe towne) in quo manent 17. homines, et reddunt cenfum in firma. And then in that booke doe followe particulerly the villages and members belonginge therto. And the firft time that I doe remember to have obferved the name (Hame) is in 6. R. 1. in the great pipe roll of that yeare in the Exchequer.

Hundred of Berkeley

This manor of Hame is at least 10. miles about in a fruitfull foile, and for the better government therof by Coneſtables, Tithingmen, Heiwards and the like rurall officers, is divided into two parts, Hame and Hamesfallowe, parted by the river runninge into the haven on the weſterne ſide of Berkeley towne; and confiſteth of the Hamblets of Bevington ats Bainton, Clapton ats Clopton, Pedington, Apleridge, Wickſtowe, Stone, divided into vpper Stone and lower Stone: And the ſaid hamblet of Hame, which for the old capitall meſſuage ſake giveth the name of the manor of Hame to both parts of this manor. And the other part or halfe of this manor of Hame called Hamsfallowe confiſteth of the hambletts of Wike ats Wikes-elme, Wanefwell, Swonhunger ats Saniger, Halmer ats Ecton, and Egeton: All of them within the pariſh of Berkeley, the inheritance of George lo. Berkeley, and parcell of his Barony and Honour of Berkeley, and by him holden by knight ſervice in Capite.

This Manor of Hame, (which I conceive to bee of it ſelfe without addition by patches at any time bought in or laid vnto it, the faireſt of the wholl county of Glouc̃,) was amongſt many others granted by kinge H. 2. in the firſt of his raigne to Robert the ſonne of Hardinge and his heires; By which deed alſo, hee was, accordinge to the manner of thoſe ancient times, created a Baron and a peere of the Realme, as before I have written fol: 6. 7. et 77

From which lord Robert this manor of Hame diſcended to Maurice his ſonne and heire, who was father of Robert and Thomas; which Robert died without iſſue in 4. H. 3. and the ſaid Thomas was his brother and heire, who had iſſue Maurice, father of Thomas, father of Maurice, father of Thomas; who by ffine and Deed in 24. E. 3. entailed this manor (amongſt others) to the heires males of his body, and dyed 11. yeares after, leavinge iſſue Maurice, who had iſſue Thomas and James; which Thomas dyed in 5. H. 5. without iſſue male, But the ſaid James who dyed in the life time of his elder brother, had iſſue James, who was heire in taile to the ſaid Thomas his vnkle, which James had iſſue Wiłłm, created Earle of Nottingham and Marques Berkeley, and Maurice: Wiłłm the Marques dyed without iſſue, and Maurice his brother and heire had iſſue Maurice and Thomas; Maurice died in 15. H. 8. without iſſue, and Thomas his brother and heire had iſſue Thomas, father of Henry, father of Thomas, who dyed in his fathers life time, leavinge iſſue George who nowe holdeth this manor as aforeſaid, A⁰. 1639. Hereof and of this Diſcent ſee more perticulerly fol: 6. 7. et 77.

In this manor of Hame rather then in the burrowe towne of Berkeley I conceive the caſtle of Berkeley to bee feated, wherof I have before written in fol: 77.

In

Hame

In this Manor alſo is the parke called Whitcliffe parke, ſtored with fallowe deere and a fewe red deere; anciently written, Witheley, firſt incloſed and made a parke by Maurice lord Berkeley the ſecond of that name in the end of the raigne of kinge H. 3. and after enlarged by Henry lord Berkeley by caſtinge the farme and lands called Comly into it; wherof ſee more largely in my hiſtory bookes of thoſe two Lords lives. — *Whitcliffe parke.*

In this Manor alſo is the parke called New parke, becauſe newer and more lately by about 56. yeares, made a parke and encloſed by Thomas lord Berkeley in the firſt and ſecond yeares of kinge Edward the third, beinge the third lord of that name, and great grandchilde of the foreſaid Maurice, then the former parke called Whitcliffe; At what time alſo hee built that faire ſtone worke lodge, which there yet ſtandeth; then ſtoringe it both with red and fallowe deere; After alſo much enlarged by layinge of the ground called Catgrove and other lands into it, wherof alſo read more in my ſaid hiſtory bookes of that family in the ſecond volume. — *New parke.*

In this Manor alſo is the one halfe of the parke called the Worthy or Caſtle parke, which was encloſed and made a parke by Thomas lord Berkeley the 4th lord of that name, grandchilde of the former lord Thomas, in the time of kinge H. 4.; which afterwards was much inlarged by kinge Henry the 8th in the 13th yeare of his raigne, by layinge into it the Capitall meſſuage or Scite of the manor of Alkington, with the grounds called Hamſtalls, Culverhayes, the Twichen, Manmead, and a parcell of Oakley parke called the Ragge. — *Worthy parke.*

In this Manor alſo is the parke called the little parke, adioyninge to the wall of the Churchyard of Berkeley, incloſed and made a parke when the Worthy was and by the ſame Lord. It ſeemes that Maurice lord Berkeley the ſecond of that name, did in 35. H. 3. intend this into a parke, as a Deed ſheweth in Berkeley caſtle: vpon which fancy to that purpoſe hee drewe much of it togeather by divers exchanges. — *Little parke.*

In this manor in the hamblet called Hame is one of the 8. tyth barnes belonginge to the rectory or pariſh of Berkeley; Of one other called Bliſbury I ſhall write in fol: 106 et   ; And of one other called | Stone-barne, I ſhall write 211 in Stone; All of them within this manor of Hame.

In payment of the ffifteene or Kingſilver when it is granted by parliament, the onus or charge in the Exchequer, is,—9ˡⁱ 10ˢ 1ᵈ. The deduction therout for decayes is — *ffifteene.*

is—20ˢ 8ᵈ The Remanet paid by the Collector therof into the Exchequer, vpon his Accompt, is 8ˡⁱ 3ˢ 5ᵈ

Subſedy. Jn the laſt Subſedy in Aº 5º Regis Caroli were 43. Subſedy men within this manor, who in both parts therof paid—16ˡⁱ 14ˢ 8ᵈ

Able men. Of able men for the warres betweene 20. and 60. yeares old, in 6ᵗᵒ Jač., that appeared in perſon and were inrolled before Henry lord Berkeley, then Leiutenant of this County, were—186.

Souldiers. And now Aº 15º Regis Caroli, 1639. of Trained Souldiers, vnder Willm Thorpe of Waniſwell their Captaine, are—29, viz. 13. corſletts and 16. muſketts.

Rates. Jf the whole diviſion of Berkeley, accompted a 4ᵗʰ part of the Shire, bee rated in any taxe for kinge or comon wealth at—100ˡⁱ, then this Hundred of Berkeley paies thereof—33ˡⁱ 3ˢ And this manor of Hame, with that part therof called Hamſ-fallowe,—4ˡⁱ; And ſoe after that proportion bee the taxe more or leſſe.

Many are the ffreeholds within this manor of Hame in both the parts therof, wherof ſome in each of their hambletts nowe followe; But often ſine ordine, becauſe ſome one mans ffreehold extends into 2. or 3. or more of the ſaid hamblets.

The ffreeholds in Bevington hamblet have already found an alphabeticall place by themſelves, fol : 103

Soe alſo ſhall the ffreeholds within the ſaid hamblet of Pedington, fol : [313]

Soe alſo ſhall the ffreeholds within the hamblets of Waniſwell, Swonhunger, and Halmer.

The reſt of the ffreeholds in either part of this Manor of Hame (which are neere one halfe therof) nowe followe, vz.

Vele ham als Ham veel. Jn this Manor, in Hame, is a farme or little Manor in reputation called Ham-vele, als Veleham ; which in the time of kinge H. 3. was the inheritance of Robert Veel, father of Sir Robert, father of Peter Veel, father of Sʳ Peter le veel knight, who dyed in 17. E. 3. And in his life time conveyed the ſame (inter alia) to Katherine

Katherine his wife, daughter of Sir John Clyvedon, for her life, after remaried to Thomas lord Berkeley the third of that name, who in her right, till hee died, held this little manor; And after to Jone daughter of him the faid Sir Peter de Veel, and her heires, maryed to John Moigne, who had iffue betweene them Sir John Moigne knight; who dyinge in 8. H. 6. left 2. daughters and heires, vz, Ewftatia his yongeft daughter maried to   Bonvile, And Elizabeth his eldeft daughter | maried to Wiłłm then fonne and heire of Sir John Stourton knight, to whom this little manor (inter alia) was allotted in partition; who had iffue betweene them Sir John Stourton of Stourton knight, created Lord Stourton; By whofe death in 2. E. 4. the fame difcended to Wiłłm lord Stourton his fonne, who dyinge in 17. E. 4. leaft iffue three fonnes all Barons in their life times; vz, John lord Stourton the eldeft fonne, who dyed in 1. H. 7. leavinge iffue ffrancis, who 2. yeares after dyed without iffue. Wiłłm fecond fonne of the lord Stourton, was alfo Lord Stourton after the death of his nephewe ffrancis, and dyed in 16. H. 8. without iffue; To whom fucceeded Edward lord Stourton, the third fonne of the aforefaid Wiłłm lord Stourton, and yonger brother of the laft mentioned Wiłłm lord Stourton; Which Edward died in 32. H. 8. leavinge iffue Wiłłm Lord Stourton, who by his Indenture quadripartite dated 3ᵗʰ Julij. 33ᵗʰ H. 8. made betweene himfelfe of the firft part, Richard Hickes on the fecond part, Thomas Griffith of the third part, and Robert Saniger of the fourth part, then inrolled in the Chancery, ioyntly fold the fame to them the faid Richard Hickes, Thomas Griffith and Robert Saniger, By the name of All that the Manor of Fricſham, &c; And from them is nowe, aᵗ 1639. the feverall inheritances of Thomas Machin, Robert Baily, George Watkins, Thomas Tyndall, and lately of John Smyth; Which Thomas Machin r̄.vᵗ is fonne and heire of Margaret late wife of John Machin, daughter and heire of Wiłłm Hickes, fonne of Richard Hicks, one of the faid purchafors. And the faid Robert Bayly, r̄. xvᵗ iiijᵈ is fonne and heire of Thomas Baily who dyed 13° Car̄., cozen and heire of Margaret daughter and heire of Robert Griffith who died in 13° Eliz., fonne of Thomas Griffith one of the faid purchafors. And the faid Robert Saniger fold his part to Wiłłm Laverance als Lawrance, and hee to Richard Hicks aforefaid, father of Wiłłm, father of Margaret wife of John Machin, father of the faid Thomas Machin r̄. iiijˢ 1. lib: cumini that nowe is; vnder whom, by a late releafe of part therof, the faid George Watkins is lately intereffed in fee. And the faid Thomas Tindall is now the kings ward, (for other lands,) fonne of Thomas Tindall and of Katherine his wife daughter and heire of John Harris, by whofe death in 7° Jacobi, his lands difcended to his faid daughter and heire, maryed to Thomas Tindall aforefaid. See the Court Roll of Hame. 40. Eliz.

Which

Which Robert Baily by his deed dated 1º. Aug. 1640. aº 16. Caroli, and by his fine in Michas terme after, aliened to Walter A-Bevan in fee about 17. acres of this manor of Velcham, And therby charged that part with the payment of—vs parcell of his said cheife rent of—15ˢ. 4ᵈ.

Which pedegree of Thomas Griffith one of the said purchasors (though true) is more fully thus explained. ffor Thomas Bayly father of the said Robert that nowe is, was sonne and heire of Willm Baily and of Parnell his wife daughter of the said Thomas Griffith, and sister of Robert Griffith, father of Margaret maried to John Smyth, and of Jone, by whose deathes without issue Thomas Baily sonne of the said Parnell was their cozen and heire, and had this land. Wherin see my booke of Wardships and Releifes. fol: 36. See also fol: 216. |

213 And which ffarme or little manor is holden of George lord Berkeley as of his manor of Hame by knight service, sute to his hundred court of Berkeley from 3. weekes to 3. weekes, and by the yearly rent of 24ˢ and a pound of comin seed : Of which rent—10ˢ. 4ᵈ is paid by Robert Baily, and 5ˢ is paid by Machin, And 4ˢ and a pound of comin by Machin also, And 5ˢ by Walter a Bevan.

And it was 4. April. Aº 5. Rᶜ Caroli, before that Machin and Baily by their mutuall release severed the estate they held either ioyntly or in Comon, a great part of the lands which their ancestors purchased ioyntly of the lord Stourton as aforesaid.

And it cañot otherwise bee conceived, but that this little pettite reputed manor did take its name of Ham-veel or Veel-ham, from the ancient seisin of the ancient family of the Veeles ; And of the greater manor of Hame, wherin in severall of her hamblets it lyeth (as it were) in both parts therof compounded and mixt togeather.

Somwhat more of this little Manor of Veelhame will bee found in theis records and proofes ; viz,
 Inq : 37. E. 3. in Scio de feudis de Berkeley in Michas terñi in ligula brevium. aº 38. E. 3.—per serviciũ militare.
 Inq : 2. E. 4. pᵗ mortē Johis Dñi Stourton.
 Inq : 17. E. 4. pᵗ mortem Willimi Dñi Stourton.
 Inq : 1. H. 7. pᵗ mortem Johis Dñi Stourton.
 Michas terñi Rec : in banco. 7. H. 7. Rot. 441. et 442. in a Quare impedit, for the pedegree.

Inq :

Hame

Inq: 10. H. 7. p.^t mortem Katherinæ Stourton, vid.

Michas termi. 21. H. 7. Rot. 520. A recoũy againſt Wiłtm lord Stourton of the Manor of Vealhame.

Finis in banco. 15. Triñ. 33. H. 8. from the lord Stourton, to Hickes, Griffith, and Saniger.

Inq: 13. Regis Caroli p.^t mortem Thomæ Baily.—per ſerviē militare.

Beſides divers ancient accompts of the Manor of Hame in temp: E. 3. And divers court rolls ſince, &c: with the ſaid booke of Wardſhips and Releeſes fol: 3. et 36. |

Wickſtowe.
It is by Inquiſitiōn in a° 49. E. 3. pars. 1. after the death of John fitz Nichot, found, That Julian Allein held of the ſaid John one meſſuage and one carucate of land at Wickſtowe in Hame, by knight ſervice and ij.^d rent, which the ſaid John fitz Nichot held over of Thomas lord Berkeley by the ſame ſervice and rent.

And by Inq: in a° 5. H. 5. after the death of the ſaid Thomas lord Berkeley; And by another Inq: in a° 17. H. 6. after the death of Richard Beauchampe Earle of Warwicke, (who maryed Elizabeth daughter and heire of the ſaid lord Berkeley,) It is found, That 20. acres of wood incloſed into Newparke purchaſed of William fitz warren, is called Wickſtowe, nowe Catgrove.

And by Deed in 14. R. 2. in Berkeley caſtle, Wiłłm fitz Warren granted to Thomas lord Berkeley in fee, All his lands tenements and ſervices in Hame or elſwhere within the Hundred of Berkeley, which were Wiłtm ffitz Warren his fathers. And then by an other deed Henry Moigne and others, (Waryns feoffees,) releaſed to the ſaid Lord All their lands and tents in Wixſtowe iuxta Wodende de Hull in hundredo de Berkeley.

Willoughbies
In this Manor of Hame, in divers places ſcatteredly, are certaine lands knowne by the name of Willoughbies lands, the inheritance of ſeverall men, as after followeth; holden of the lord Berkeley as of his manor of Ham by knights ſervice, ſute to his Hundred Court of Berkeley, from three weekes to three weekes, and by the yearly rent of 18.^s 4.^d

Theis lands in the time of kinge H. 7 were the lands of Edw. Willoughby Eſq. who left iſſue John and Vincent; which Vincent by his deed dated 10 Julii a° 7. H. 8. releaſed to the ſaid John his brother not only all his Eſtate and right in theis lands, but alſo in his lands in Durſley and in Wickwarre, called Barbaſter, as by a Deed

Deed with Robert Fowler of Alderley appeareth, who hath the said Lands in Durſley. The ſaid John Willoughby, then of Denver, in Norfolke, by his Deed dated 14 Junii, 37 H. 8, granted all theis lands to Yelverton and other Feoffees, to ſuch uſes as are mentioned in a Deed made between himſelfe and Hugh Willoughby his Kinſman, which I have not yet ſeene, (all others herein mentioned I have,) and after dyed in 5 et 6 Ph, & Maȓ. George Willoughby, (then of Bexwell in the ſaid County of Norfolke,) and Eliz. his wife, by their Deed dated 11 Febry. aᵒ 4 Eliz. Regine, enrolled in the Chancery, aliened all his lands and tenemᵗˢ in Berkeley, Newport, Durſeley, and Wickwarre, or elſewhere in the County of Glouceſter, to John Bowſer of Tortworth, Clothier, and his heires ; and in Trinity terme followinge, not only the ſaid George and Elizabeth, but Thomas Gawſell and Mary his Wife, levied a Fine thereof to the ſaid John Bowſer and his heires, with warranty againſt themſelves, and againſt John Willoughby aforeſaid and his heires, and againſt Henry Lord Berkeley and his heires ; which Mary was the former Wife of the ſaid John Willoughby, ſonne of the ſaid Edward Willoughby, | brother and heire to Richard Willoughby, ſonnes of Sir William Willoughby, knight, by Jone his Wife, after remarryed to William Marques Berkeley ; Which Richard and Edward are often mentioned in the vaſt alienations made by the ſaid Marques in the raignes of kinge E. 4. R. 3. and H. 7. ffor which diſcents alſo ſee an excellent plea vpon a warrantia cartæ, brought by Sir John Peter againſt Henry lord Berkeley, entred in Miclias terme in banco in 40. et 41. Eliz. Rot. 3127. And of Trinity terme after, ibm, when the ſaid Mary lived and recoũed alſo in Dower againſt the ſaid lord Berkeley.

Moſt part of theis lands the ſaid John Bowſer by ſeverall deeds in and about the 17ᵗʰ of Queene Eliz. aliened to ſeverall perſons, as after followeth ; And by one of his deeds dated 10. m̃cij. aᵒ 17. Eliz. p̃d, in his ſale of moſt of them to John Richards of Woollaſton, (called of the Bay in waneſwell,) hath an exception of the ſaid—18ˢ 4ᵈ payable to the cheife lord : And are nowe aᵒ 1639. the inheritance of theſe 5 perſons ; vz,

1. **William Thorpe** of Waniſwell holdeth one cloſe of paſture cont about 7. acres, neere Berkeley Towne, called Boddicraft als Berricraft ; which George Thorpe his father, in the life of Nicholas his father, by an Indenture Tripartite dated 3. octobȓ aᵒ 40. Eliz. purchaſed of John Clutterbooke of Hinton and of Jane his wife, of her inheritance, daughter of the ſaid John Richards of the bay, wherof, as alſo in a deed dated 30. Sept. aᵒ p̃d, is a covenant to ſave harmleſſe the ſaid George Thorpe from the ſaid Cheife rent. 2. **George**

Hame

2. **George Clutterbooke** holdeth certaine grounds called Hookſtreet and Howmead with 2. acres of arrable land, in all about 18. acres, which hee had from John his father and the ſaid Jane his wife, daughter of the ſaid John Richards, to whom her ſaid father by his will deviſed the ſame in fee; Of which fee a fine in truſt levied by the ſaid John Clutterbooke and Jane, to Wiłłm Tylladam and Wiłłm Everod. 8^{bo} Michis, a° 39° Eliz.

3. **William Atwood** holds about 10. acres of arrable meadowe and paſture, which John Atwood his father purchaſed of Richard Webbe, brother and heire of Wiłłm Webbe, to whome his father Thomas Webbe gave the ſame in fee. ffor which (inter alia) fee an Inq : 27. Eliz. after the death of the ſaid Thomas Webbe.

4. **Thomas Tyndall**, ſonne of Thomas Tyndall and of Katherine his wife, daughter and heire of John Harris, holds an houſe and 4. acres of land in Waniſwell, which the ſaid John Harris purchaſed of the ſaid John Atwood.

5. **William Hurne** holds one ground called Dalliſcroft containinge about 5. acres, which William ffoſter his grandfather-in-lawe by his will deviſed vnto him, who purchaſed the ſame of—

Of which lands, now called Willoughbies lands, part of them as I conceive were of old Dolyes lands ; And another part of them the lands of— |

Heere alſo in Hame is an ancient meſſunge called Harford, with 40. acres of land therto belonginge, lyinge in Hame and Stone in the pariſh of Berkeley, late parcell of the poſſeſſions of the Abby of Kingſwood in the county of Wilts ; which by the diſſolucōn of that Monaſtery in 31. H. 8. came to that kinge, and continued in the Crowne till Queene Eliz : in the 41th of her raigne granted the ſame (inter alia) to Vtley and Cartwright and their heires ; ffrom whom it came to Hugh Saxey late one of the Auditors to kinge James ; And by his conveyance to Sir Lawrance Hide, Robert Biſſe, and other their Cofeoffees, to charitable vſes accordinge to the direction of the ſaid Hugh Saxey ; who forthwith after the death of the ſaid Saxey, for the better performance of the truſt in them repoſed, granted the ſame to John Crabbe and his heires, by their deed dated 27. Novembr : a° 6to R^c Caroli, 1630. And by their ſaid Deed increaſed the rent of 31: 4^d, (which Crabbe an ancient leſſee therto of old formerly paid,) vnto five pounds p ann̄, payable by Crabbe and his heires at the Towne hall in Brewton in the county of Somerſet : Which John Crabbe

Crabbs land.

Crabbe died in August a° 13° Caroli, as by an Inq: found after his death by the Escheator, virtute officij sui, appeareth, leavinge Jone his only daughter and heire maried to Robert Smith, who dwell vpon the same; And is holden in free Soccage of the kinge, as by the said Lres patents of Queene Eliz: appeareth.

Graftons land nowe Winstons In Halmer.

Of the same condition with the former of John Crabbs, is a messuage with 40. acres of land therto belonginge lyinge in Halmer in this manor of Hame, which also was part of the possessions of the said Monastery of Kingswood, and granted by Queene Eliz: as aforesaid; And was by John Winston at the same time purchased of the said Sir Lawrence Hyde and his said Cofeoffees; And his rent thervpon increased from—30ˢ to—5ˡⁱ, limited to the releefe of the said hospitall founded in Brewton aforesaid by the said Hugh Saxey: holden of the kinge in free soccage, as John Crabbs last mentioned; And this messuage and land was first demised by Hugh Sexey to Thomas Grafton, whose widowe the said John Winston married, and therby came into the purchase of this messuage and lands.

Bailies land of old ffitz Robards.

In that part of this manor of Hame which is called Hamsfallowe are certaine lands containinge by estimacõn   acres, nowe the inheritance of Robert Baily, sonne and heire of Thomas Bayly, cozen and heire of Margaret somtime wife of John Smyth, daughter and heire of Robert Griffith, sonne and heire of Thomas Griffith, And which the said Thomas in 36. H. 8. purchased of Richard James of Woodford, sonne of Willm James, sonne of Richard James and of Jone his wife. And hee sonne and heire of Jone Clifford, daughter and heire of Richard fitz Roberts of Berkeley, sonne and heire of Richard fitz Roberts who lived in the time of kinge Richard the second.   And before the lands of

Of which lands the said Richard James by his deed dated 15. Octobr̃ a° 16. E. 4. enfeoffed John Twyniho, then high Steward of the hundred of Berkeley, which, saith his said Deed, hee had by the grant of Jone Clifford his mother, daughter and heire of Richard ffitz Robards of Berkeley: And a regrant from the said John Twyniho the next day after to the said Richard James and to Jone his wife, and to their heires. | And by another Deed dated 19° mẽij. a° 14.° H. 7. the said Jone in her widowhood granted the same lands to her sonne Willm and his heires; whose sonne Richard James sold the same in 36. H. 8. to Thomas Griffith as aforesaid.   Thus much the Deeds of the said Robert Baily doe declare.   ffor which also see an Inq: in 13. Regis Caroli after the death of Thomas Baily, found by the Escheator virtute officij sui, wherin the tenure of theis lands is found to bee of George lord Berkeley by fute of Court, and the yearly rent of—iij^d late purchafed of Edward Hall.

The formoft part of this pedegree of Robert Bayly is alfo before in fol: [212.]

218 blank

Halmer. 219

Halmer: written alfo **Hal mere**, **Hathemere**, and **Eckton**, and **Elicton**, and **Egeton**; Is an hamblet within the parifh of Berkeley, parcell of the fame manor of Hame, and confifteth of   dwellinge houfes, lyinge in the vtmoft bounds of that manor northwards, moft of them the lands of ffreeholders; wherof fee more in Hame fol: [216], and in Hinton fol: [229.]

In this hamblet of Halmer is one fmall parcell of ground called Herts grove containinge about 2. acres, which Thomas lo: Berkeley in 4. E. 2. gave to Willm Heort and to Mabill his wife and to the heires of their two bodies, by the name of halfe an acre and 4. perches of land lyinge by the kings highway, in Hame, Rendringe 9^d. rent by the yeare et 4. termes, for all fervices favinge the knight fervice, (called fervicium regale,) which is nowe a^o 1639. the inheritance of James fonne of John Heort, fonne of John who died   , fonne of Thomas who died   , fonne of John who died—20. H. 8, fonne of   , The faid eftate taile havinge to this day continued lineally in the iffue male of the faid William and Mabill, not difcontinued; and the faid rent of—9^d accordingly paid at this day: ffor which alfo Walter Heort fonne and heire of the faid Donees, was in 20. E. 3. in ward to the grandchilde and heire of the donor.

Herts grove.

Deere alfo in this hamblet of Halmer als Ecton is a meffuage and about 18, acres of land therto anciently belonginge, holden of the lord Berkeley as of his faid manor of Hame, by knights fervice and fute to his hundred court of Berkeley from 3. weekes to 3. weekes, late in the tenure of John Smyth of Panthurft, And nowe the inheritance of Thomas Smyth fecond fonne of the faid John; which Thomas lord Berkeley the firft of that name about 20. H. 3. gave to Willm Brugg and his heires, To whome Hilde Brugge was daughter and heire, maried to John atte Boure, who had iffue betweene them Robert de la Boure, father of John de la boure, father of John Boure, father of Willm Boure, father of Richard Boure, father of Robert, father of Willm Boure who died 1. E. 6, father of Willm Bower,

Smythes late Bowers.

fomtimes

somtimes high Baily of this hundred vnder Henry lord Berkeley, who died in 5ᵗᵒ Jac̃, who with Wiłłm Boure his sonne and heire in 4. Jac̃, and his said sonne after his fathers death in 6. Jac̃, aliened theis lands to John Smyth of Panthurst, who left them to Thomas his second sonne aforesaid, and his heires. I have the rather noted this discent in a direct succession taken out of the deeds themselves, what time the land was Wiłłm Bowers.

Somwhat more heerof is in theis Records, vz,
Inq : 37. E. 3. de feodis de Berkeley in Sc̃cio, in Term̃ Michis. 38. E. 3. in ligula br̃ium.—per servic̃ militare.
Michas Record in banco. 9. E. 4. Rot. 300.
ffinis in banco. 6. Jacobi, inter Smith et Bower. |

220
Fremes Lands.

Heere also in this hamblet of Halmer, and in Hinton, are those lands which by the old possession of their ancient owner have given to it the name of Ecton, Eketon, and Egeton ; nowe for the most part the inheritance of Thomas ffreame of Lipiat, who havinge also divers lands and tenements in Berkeley towne, and in the manors of Alkington and Canonbury, I will in this place write all I knowe of them all heere togeather.

The said Thomas ffreame, (whose firname I have seene in the times of kinge H. 7. and   to bee written fleme and flrom ats ffreme,) is sonne of Thomas who died in   , sonne of Robert who died in 42. Eliz., sonne of Thomas who died 14. Eliz., sonne of Wiłłm who died in 17. H. 8, sonne of Thomas who died in   . And are holden of George lord Berkeley as of his severall manoʳˢ wherin they lye, by knight service, sute to his hundred court of Berkeley from 3. weekes to 3. weekes, heriot service, and by severall yearly rents, as after shall appeare ; viz, 20. horshoes and their nailes for his lands in Berkeley, somtime the land of   , and 6ᵈ for his lands in Halmer somtime
and 2ˢ 6ᵈ for his lands in Hinton called Barry court als the manor of Barrers late John Vshers, rent. 12ᵈ ; And the 4ᵗʰ part of ffreemans lands in Hinton, rent. 4ᵈ ob.

By a deed without date, but temp : Rẽ Johis. Wiłłus filius Eliæ de falso marisco, assensu Matildis vxoris suæ, concessit Dño Roberto de Berkelei, Totam terram illam et boscum quam Isilia filia Alexandri de Egeton ava sua, de cuius hereditate ipdic̃ta terra fuit, dedit in excambiũ ei Roberto de Berkelai, pro duabus virgatis terræ in Egeton, quæ pertinebant ad Manerium suum de Hineton.

By

Halmer

By another Deed without date, temp: R̄ Joh̄is, Robertus de Berkelai dedit Yſillie filiæ Alexandri de Egeton, duas virgatas terræ in Hineton, and boundeth it perticulerly. Habend̄ ſibi et hered̄ in Excambio for the former lands, &c. And this ſeemes the firſt guift of M! ffreames lands heere.

And 18ˢ 8ᵈ for his lands within the manor of Alkington, vz, for a Meſſuage an orchard and a meadowe ſomtimes John Bakers, in Newport, rent 9ˢ 4ᵈ : And for a paſture called Coles Elme, ſomtime Thomas Coles of Durſley, rent 5ˢ ; And for a paſture in Wikes fallowe neere Nybly grove in Alkington, rent   ; wherof George ffreeman of Newport payeth—9ˢ 8ᵈ for the mead called Coniger meadowe, conī. 2. acres, and an orchard conī. 1. acre, which hee by deed 19. Aug̃. aº 6. Jacobi p'chaſed in fee of Thomas ffreame : And which the ſaid George hath this yeare 14. Caroli ſetled vpon his grandchilde George ffreeman, ſonne of Thomas, ſonne of him the ſaid George.

With Thomas ffreame (as hee faith) is the originall deed made by Thomas lord Berkeley for this purchaſe made by George ffreeman of Thomas ffreame. See the Court roll of Alkington in 13. Jac̃. r̃. 9ˢ 4ᵈ

And 7ˢ for his lands in the manor of Canonbury, vz, a meſſuage and 2. yard land at Egeton als Eekton in Hame, F̃. 2ˢ And two meſſuages and the moity of a yard land, one acre of meadowe, and 3. acres of wood at Egeton in Hame. F̃. 5ˢ As the court Rolls of Canonbury manor in 1. E. 3. and in 3. E. 3. when John de Egeton did his homage and recognized his tenure, expreſſely are. And as the court rolls of 6. et 9. H. 4. and of 24. et 25. et 26. H. 6, And a court roll 17. H. 8. of Hinton, And a Rentall of Canonbury in 14. E. 4. And an Inq : in 31. H. 8. after the death of Katherine Walſh the widowe of Will͞m ffreme Eſq. doe ſhewe, ſome of them before pertition of John de Eketons co-heires, and ſome after.

The firſt of theis of the Sirname of ffreame I have met withall in this hundred of this family, was   , who maried the daughter and heire of John Vſher who died in 2. R. 3. as by the court roll of Hinton of that yeare appeares. And was ſonne of Sir Will͞m Vſher knight, who maried   daughter and heire of   , And was deſcended from John de Eketon als Egeton who died in 6. H. 4. leavinge two daughters and co-heires, vz, Jone maried to John fframilode, of whoſe iſſue ſee in fol: [330] And Iſable his younger daughter then but 2. yeares old, and in 24. H. 6. maried to Will͞m Donell, as the court roll of Canonbury in 24. 25. et 26. H. 6. doe ſhewe.

And

And from Willm Donell and Isable his wife theis lands came to Sir Willm Vsher knight aforesaid, And soe by maryage into this family of the Reoms, now called (euphoniæ gratia) ffremes, gent of a faire race.

The pdon roll, 30. H. 6. m : 31. A pardon to Willm Donell nup de Berkeley yeoman, als Willm Vsher de Bisley yeoman, And the pardon roll of, 36. H. 6. a pardon to Willm Donell als Wm Vsher, als Willm Daniell of Berkeley gent. in arce Londini.

The 6th of July, 1494. aº 10º H. 7. was an Award made which setled peace betweene Richard Thorpe of Wanifwell Esq, on the one part, And Willm Reme als ffreme then a Justice of peace on th'other pte, wherby the controverted tenement in the high streete in Berkeley was awarded to the said Richard Thorpe and his heires, where yet it is, with Willm Thorpe, sonne of George, sonne of Nicholas, sonne of Thomas, sonne of Thomas, sonne of the said Richard. Which Willm ffreme in Triñ terme 13. H. 7. levied a fine of that and other his lands in Berkeley, Wanifwell, Hinton, Sanyger, als Swonhunger, &c.

By an Inq : in 31. H. 8. after the death of Katherine Walsh, late the wife of Richard Walsh, and before the wife of Willm ffreme Esq, (the same Willm mentioned in the foresaid award & fine,) it is found That shee held the said lands in Hinton called the Manor of Barrers or Barry Court, for her life, And also 25. acres of land, 8. acres of pasture, and 120. acres, in the townes of Berkeley, Wike, and Newport, wherof shee was by the deed of the said Willm ffreme her husband, dated 20. ñcij, Aº 8. H. 8. enfeoffed for her life, holden of the Castle or manor of Berkeley by fealty, sute of court to the manor of Berkeley twice by the yeare, and the yearly rent of— 18s 6d for all services : And that Thomas ffreme was sonne and heire of the said William and Katherine, then 23. yeares old. | Though the Tombe stone of the said Willm in the parish church of Berkeley sheweth that hee died in 18. H. 8. yet his death at the Halimot Courts of Hinton and Alkington manors was presented to bee in the 17th yeare of that kinge.

Theis lands in the time of H. 3. were the lands of Walter de Egeton, After of John de Egeton, and Willm de Egeton, And of an other John de Egeton, cozen and heire of Henry de Egeton, when the name by a shorter and smoother pronunciaĉon began, towards the end of kinge E. 3. to bee written Ecton, and Eketon : See fol : 181. in Egeton als Ecton.

A Deed

Dalmer

A Deed in Berkeley castle in theis words ;— Conu seit q̃ ioe Thomas de Berkelee seignour de Berk, ay done et grant et p ce p̃sent escrit confirme al Abbe de S.t Austin de Brist e a Covent de meme le lu en eyde de lour esglise ser, tote les tres et les teñt in Egetone que me eschequeront per la morte Johan de Egetone tant q̃ a plein age Johan sitz et heire le avantdit Johan de Egetone ; En tesmoiaunce de q̃l chose a cest present escrit ay mis mon seale ; Done a Berkelee le iour de Seint George en l'an du regne le roy Edward sitz le roy Henriē trentime quarte. Referre also this, to fol : 181.

Also in this hamblet of **Dalmer** als Ecton als Egeton, is another ancient messuage with divers lands therto belonginge, late the lands of Willm Gough als Gosse, sonne of Willm, sonne of Richard, sonne of John Gough, havinge in that Sirname for many discents without any alienation continued since the later end of the raigne of kinge Henry the third, what time the same (amongst other lands) was parted betweene Hildeburgh then wife of Thomas Mathias and Isable her sister, daughters and coheires of   ; Which Willm Gough hath in the 12.th of kinge Charles. A.o 1636, aliened in fee to Richard Hatheway lessee therto for divers yeares then to come, who by his last will shortly after devised the greater part therof to Richard his younger sonne. in fee ; And are holden of the lord Berkeleis said Manor of Hame by knight service, sute to his hundred Court of Berkeley from 3. weekes to 3. weekes, and by the yearly rent of—9.d And as more plainly appeare in an Inquisic̃on or office found after the death of the said Richard Hatheway, in the 14.th yeare of the said kinge Charles.

Gosses land nowe Hathewaies Palls, and others.

And of late Nicholas Pall of Berkeley clerke hath purchased about 30. acres of this ancient messuage, of the said Richard Hatheway the father, not longe before his death, who payeth 3.d of the said cheife rent of—9.d

And another part therof is conveyed to Edward Hatheway, another yonger sonne of the said Richard the father, cont about 5. acres, by the last will of the said Richard : vz, an house, orchard and close cont 4. acres, called Roberts close.

By a fine levied in 39. H. 3. Philip de Leicester and Isable his wife aliened 54. acres of wood and 12. acres of land in Egeton, to Thomas Mathias and Hildeburgh his wife aforesaid and to her heires, which was an addition to her former part ; And was in his life time the land of the said Richard Hatheway ; who also for one acre of land in Hynamsfeild of Goughes old land, payeth a cheife rent of–2.d ; vide fol : 369. |

223
Oldlands place.

Heere alſo in this hamblet of Halmer and in Waniſwell is an ancient meſſuage called Oldlands place, longe continued in the name and family of the Oldlands, holden of the Manor of Berkeley by knight ſervice, and by ſute to the hundred court of Berkeley from 3. weekes to 3. weekes; nowe the inheritance of John Oldland, ſonne of John, as an Inquiſicōn found after his death, (I thinke virtute officij Eſcaetoris,) in 12º Rº Caroli, doth ſhewe. And as a Deed inrolled in Chancery in 1. E. 4. membr. 23. in dorſo rotuli declareth, was then the inheritance of John. ſonne and heire of John Oldland, who was father of Thomas, father of John Oldland. In the time of kinge Edward the third it was the land of Walter Oldland, who had them in tayle from Thomas Sericant of Stone in 37. E. 3, wherof ſee in Waniſwell fol : 380.

Of the lands belonginge to that meſſuage called Oldlands place, Thomas Butler bought in 14. H. 8. certaine ſcattered parcells of John Oldland, ſonne of Thomas, ſonne of John Oldland who died in aº 1. R. 3. which after, from the heires of Butler, were p'chaſed by Nicholas Thorpe Eſq, as in Waniſwell appeares, fol. 380. with the reſt of all Butlers lands.

Walters land late Harvies.

Heere alſo **Thomas Walter** ſonne of John holdeth a Meſſuage and certaine lands in the tenure of Thomas Huet, containinge about   acres ; which yeald to the lord Berkeley a Cheiſe rent of—vijˢ p anñ. And another meſſuage in the tenure of Wiłłm Tought, with about 12. acres therto belonginge, which yeald to the ſaid lord Berkeley a cheiſe rent of 4ˢ 3ᵈ p anñ, which the ſaid John Walter in aº   purchaſed of Edward Harvy, brother and heire of Nicholas, who died in 20º. Jacobi ; ſonnes of John Harvey who died in 45. Eliz. as by an Inq : after his death in 2º Jacobi appeareth, which perticulerly mentioneth all his lands in this hundred, And in Haukeſbury. See alſo the Court roll of Hame. 20º Jacobi,

Hickes lands.

Alſo in Halmer John Hickes of Tortworth in 38. H. 8. died ſeiſed of a Meſſuage and 70. acres of land therto belonginge, holden of the manor of Wanes- well by yᵗ yearly rent of—3ˢ 4ᵈ. And John was his ſonne and heire then 4. yeares old, as an Inq : found that yeare after the death of the ſaid John Hickes doth ſhewe, who was father of Thomas, father of William Hickes that nowe is.

q : whoſe now.

ffor theis lands alſo ſee another Inq : 42 Eliz. pᵗ mortem Hickes. |

ffor

Hill

ffor other ffreeholds of this hamblet, See in Swonhunger fol: 365. And in 224 Wanifwell. fol: 367. |

Hill.

Hill: In Domefdei booke foe written. But fince and of late yeares, Hill als Hull: An ancient manor within the parifh of Berkeley, holden of the kinge by knight fervice in capite; wherin Wittm the Conqueror and before him kinge Edward called the Confeffor had foure hides of land, as the faid Domefdei booke fhewes.

And in this manor in the time of kinge E. 2. John ffitz Nichoɫɫ then Lord therof had two parkes, as by Deeds with Sir Robert Poyntz, whofe fathers this manor late was, which I have feene, appeares.

This Manor was (amongft many others) given by kinge H. 2. in the firft yeare of his raigne to Robert the fonne of Hardinge and his heires, To hold of him by knight fervice. By which grant alfo hee was created a peere and Baron of the Realme.

This Manor the faid lord Robert not longe after in the faid kings time gave to Nicholas his fecond fonne and his heires, by his Deed in theis words; Sciatis me dediffe et conceffiffe Nicho filio meo, Hullam et Nimdesfeld cum oibus ptinentijs fuas, quas Dñs Rex mihi dedit pro fervicio meo in feodo et hereditate, fibi et heredibus fuis, faciendo illi m̃i fervicium dimidij militis, liberas et quietas ab omni alio fervicio. Tefte Rico Abbate Sci Auguftini, &c. As by the deed remaininge with Sir Edward Coke late Cheife Juftice of the kings Bench, which I copied out, appeareth. And after the faid lord Robert died in 17. H. 2. As by the great pipe Roll of that yeare appeares.

This Nicholas was a Baron and Peere of the Realme, and paid feverall Efcuages to the faid kinge Henry the fecond, in the 7th 8th 32th and 33th yeares of that kinge; And alfo Aid for marriage of Maud his daughter to the Duke of Saxony. And died in the fixth yeare of kinge R. 1. leavinge iffue Roger, who was written Rogerus filius Nicholai, filij Roberti, filij Hardingi, and died in 15. H. 3. leavinge iffue Nicholas: Betweene which Nicholas and Maurice lord Berkeley the
fecond

second of that name arose suites in lawe, for services which that Lord required of him for this manor of Hill and for that of Nimdesfelde, to his Lawe daies at Berkeley, And after those sutes ended by composition, the said Nicholas sonne of Roger died in 46. H. 3. leavinge issue Raph, vsually written Raph sonne of Nicholas, sonne of Roger: which Raph died in 19. E. 1. leavinge issue Nicholas; Betweene which Nicholas sonne of Raph and Thomas lord Berkeley the second of that name arose sutes also about the same services, for theis manors of Hill and Nimsfeilde; And after the said Nicholas [died] in 6. E. 2. leavinge issue John : Betweene which John and the said Thomas lord Berkeley were also sutes in lawe about the same services for the said Manors, As by severall compositions therevpon made which I have read in Berkeley castle and elswhere appeareth; And afterwards the said John died in 49. E. 3. leavinge Thomas sonne of Reginald sonne of him the said John, his grand-childe and heire.

The said Thomas vsually written Thomas fitz Nichol knight, had only two daughters, vz. Katherine, who in the time of kinge Richard the second was maried to Robert Pointz, and Alienor maried to John Browninge, whose discent read in the description of Nimpsfeild. fol : 299.

The said Sir Thomas fitz Nicholl, by a fine in the court of comon pleas levied in 12. H. 4. entayled this manor of Hill to himselfe and to Agnes his second wife, and to the heires males of his body ; The remainder to the said Robert Pointz and Katherine his wife, daughter of him the said Sir Thomas, for the terme of their lives, the Remainder to Nicholas Pointz sonne of them the said Robert and Katherine, and to the heires males of his body, with six other remainders over: which Agnes second wife of the said Sir Thomas fitz Nichol died without issue in the life time of her husband ; And after the said Sir Thomas died in 5. H. 5. without issue male of his body, wherby this manor of Hill, remained and came to the said Robert Pointz and Katherine, and after their deathes, (after some deviations by conveyances amongst their children and Nephewes,) as theis records will shewe: vz, paten, 10. H. 6. ps. 2. m. 15. Rot. pardon, 15. H. 6. m. 27. Claus. 34. H. 6. m : 10. in dorso. Claus. 35. H. 6. m. 1. dorso. ffines 37. H. 6. m. 1. ffines. 39. H. 6. m. 1. et 4. ffines. 49. H. 6. m. 4. wch was, 10. E. 4..) This manor setled in Sir Robert Pointz heire at comon lawe to the said Robert and Katherine, who was a learned and remarkeable gent bredd an vtter barrister in Graies Inne, knight for the body to kinge H. 7, A Councellor and Chancellor to Queene Katherine first wife to kinge H. 8, and high Steward of the Lordship and hundred of Berkeley,

and

and died in 12. H. 8. and leaft iffue Anthony Pointz knight, who was by kinge H. 8. oft imployed in very honorable fervices at home and abroad, in times of warre and peace, by fea and land, in important fervices, and died in [26] H. 8. leavinge iffue Sir Nicholas, who died 3. et 4. Ph: et Mar̃. who leaft iffue Sir Nicholas, who died 28. Eliz. who leaft iffue Sir John Pointz, who in Eliz. aliened this manor of Hill to Nicholas Dimery and his heires,[1] who fhortly after fold the fame to Henry ffleetwood, and hee foone after to Richard ffuift; By whofe death in 13. Jacobi R̃., it difcended to Edward his fonne, an vnderftandinge gent, who nowe holdeth the fame aº. 1639.

Which firft Sir Nicholas Pointz was in 35. H. 8. vice Admirall of the weft Seas, And then delivered over his charge to John Wintour Efq., who was bred vnder Sir Anthony Pointz his father, and directed his often tres, To the right honorable and woll Mr. Sir Anthony Pointz knight; Subfcribed, Your Mafterfhips fervant, John Wintour; Which John Wintour was father of Sir Wiłłm Wintour, Vice Admiral in the fatall yeare 1588 againft the Spaniard, father of Sir Edward, father of Sir John that nowe is, Aº. 1639. A race of 4. eminent and remarkeable gent.

Of this village, through the lowe fcituation and bad water it is faid to bee, Hieme mala æftate molefta, nunquam bona; evill in winter, greivous in Somer, and never good for habitation; wherin the moft remarkeable places are called Brighampton, Bibury, woodend, Redland, Wickftowe, Shepwardend als Sheperdline, and In which Shepherdline, where a paffage is over Seaverne, was a Chaple built, whereof Thomas lord Berkeley was founder, wherunto his heires prefented as to a Chantry till the diffolucõn thereof by act of parliament; And wherto in 25. E. 3. hee gave competent lands to maintaine a preift to finge there. |

Inter ptita coram rege apud Glouc̃. in 37. E. 3. Rot. 29. thus; Johes fitz Nichoł Dñs de Hull non poteft dedicere, quin tenetur folus mundare quandam gurgitem apud Hull, per quam aqua folebat currere ad Severne, quæ obftructa fuit tempore prefentationis, fed nunc mundatur.

The

---

[1] Sir John Poyntz had not fold the Manor of Hill or Hull at the end of the reign of Queen Elizab., for in 1604 he, with others, fuffered a Fine in this Manor to George Huntley and others. This was probably by way of Mortgage. Perhaps it formed a portion of the lands including the lands of Tockington, the Manor of Iron Acton, &c., which he fold to Nicholas Dymeric foon afterwards. (See "Memoir of the Poyntz Family,") pp. 83, 84. [Ed.]

The Copihold rents of this Manor of Hill were in a° 40. Eliz. about 51ˡⁱ per anñ, now leſſened, accuſtomed to bee granted for one mans life, and for foe longe as his wife furvivinge him ſhall continue fole and chaſt; And fo the poſſeſſion by the death of every copihold tenant revertinge to the lord, to bee againe granted to whom it pleafeth him; Alfo the Copiholders eſtate is forfeited by cõmittinge of waſt, as fellinge of Timber without licence, &c. And by beinge not refident vpon his Copihold tenement and lands; By not performance of his fervice at Courts, by demifing for more then one yeare, and other the like; as by an old furvey which I have feene appeareth.

ffifteene. The payment of the ffifteene or Kingfilver when it is granted by parliament goeth with Nimpsfeild in one fome, which in the onus or charge therof in the Exchequer Court, is,—8ˡⁱ 7ˢ 2ᵈ q. The deduction is—36ˢ 8ᵈ. The Remanet paid into the Exchequer by the Collector therof is—6ˡⁱ 10ˢ 6ᵈ q.; wherof this Townſhip of Hill paies—4ˡⁱ 10ˢ 10ᵈ q. And that of Nimsfeild—39ˢ 8ᵈ

Subfedy. In the laſt Subfedy in Anno 5ᵗᵒ Caroli were 10. fubfedy men within this Manor, who paid—56ˢ

Able men. And of able men fit for the warres betweene 20. and 60. yeares old, who appeared in a° 6ᵗᵒ Jacobi at a generall muſter before Henry Lord Berkeley, then Lord Leiutenant of the county, were in this Townſhip—37.

Souldiers. And now in a° 1639. are of trayned fouldiers vnder Willm Thorpe Efq, their Captaine,—15, wherof—7 corfletts and 8 mulketts.

Rates. And if the wholl divifion of Berkeley accompted a 4ᵗʰ part of the county bee in any tax or rate for the kinge or comõn wealth rated at—100ˡⁱ Then this hundred of Berkeley paies thereof—33ˡⁱ 3ˢ And the townſhip of Hill—15ˢ And foe after that proportion bee the tax more or leſſe.

Freeholds within this townſhip of Hill, which I thought fitteſt to remember, are, vz:

Scotlands in Hill. An ancient meſſuage with 30 acres of land therto belonginge called Scotlands, the inheritance of Thomas Mallet of Rockhampton, and by him purchafed of Thomas Veel Efq, late before the lands of Richard Bridges, and fomtime the land of Willm Holfred, And before Clarkes, And before, the land of Richard Moore of Hill;

Hill; And are holden of George lord Berkeley as of his manor of Hame by the yearly rent of—12ᵈ, fute to his hundred Court of Berkeley from 3. weekes to 3. weekes, And by |

In this Townſhip, in a place called Woodends leies, are about 7. acŕ of land, late the lands of James Purlyn, ſonne of Thomas, the inheritance wherof is in the 3. ſiſters and coheires of the ſaid James; vz, Alice maryed to Richard Adams of Oldbury, who had a third part; Thomas Kitch of Cleverton in Wiltſhire, ſonne of another ſiſter, another third part; And the third third part is parted betweene the 2. daughters and coheires of Dimery, ſonne of a third ſiſter of the ſaid James Purlyn; vz, Alice maried to Edward Knight of Yate, and Mary maried to Henry Baynham of Yate, aforeſaid: And are holden of George lord Berkeley as of his Manor of Hame by the yearly rent of—2ˢ and fute of Court to the ſaid Manor.

228 Purlins lands.

And by Inq: in 44. Eliz. after the death of Maurice Tovy of Thornbury, it is found That hee died ſeiſed of a meſſuage, orchard, garden, one curtelage, one cloſe of arrable and paſture ground called Hiſefeild als Hewiſh feild cont̃. 12. acres, in Pedington, Hame, Hill, and within the pariſh of Berkeley; holden of Henry lord Berkeley as of his Manor of Canonbury, but by what ſervice the Jury knewe not: And that Mary the wife of John Babor, Jone the wife of Nicholas Baker, and ffrances the wife of Thomas Taylor, are his daughters and heires, of full age.

Purlins

This land Maurice Tovy aforeſaid, by deed dated in Jan. aᵒ. 27ᵒ. Eliz. purchaſed of Robert Tilladam, And are part of the lands called Purlyns.

See for Wickſtowe fol: 214. in Hame, et Hill.

Somwhat more of this Townſhip of Hill is to bee read in theis Records not formerly mentioned, vz,
    Inq: 33. E. 1. pro Adamo le Walſh, et Nicholao filio Radulphi.
    Inq: 6. E. 2. p̃ morte Nichi filij Radĩ p̃t.
    Inq: 2. E. 2. An Ad quod damnum pro Roberto Wither.
    Inq: 9. E. 2. An Ad quod damnum pro Ada le Waleis.
    Inq: 14. E. 2. An Ad quod damnum pro Wiħo Martell.
    Inq: 15. E. 2. An Ad quod damnum pro Johe filio Nichol.
    Inq: 16. E. 3. An Ad quod damnum pro eod̃ Johe fitz Nichol.
    Inq: 29. E. 3. An Ad quod damnum pro eod̃ Johe fitz Nichol, et Eva vxore eius, pur faire entayle de Hull, &c.

                                                                                            Inq:

Inq: 7. R. 2. An Ad quod damnum pro Thoma fitʒ Nichot.
Inq: 6. H. 5. p̃ morte Thome fitʒ Nichot chīr.
Michas record in Sc̃c̃io, 20. H. 6. rot. 41. cum Rememĩ Thefaur̃.
Inq: 12. H. 8. p̃t mortem Roberti Pointz miltis.
Inq: 3. & 4. Ph: & Mar̃, p̃ mortē Nichi Pointz miltis.
Inq: 28. Eliz. p̃t mortē Nichi Poyntz militis.
Hillar̃ Rec̃. in Sc̃c̃io, 29. Eliz. Rot. 50. et 51. c̃m Reñi Thefaur̃.
Inq: 12. Jacobi, p̃ mortem Rici ffuſt. |

Hinton.

Hinton: als Hineton; In Domefdei booke written Hinetune; An ancient manor lyinge by Severne fide within the parifh of Berkeley extendinge on that fide vfq, ad filum aquæ Sabrinæ, to the middle of the chanell of that removinge river where for the time the Char.nell runneth deepeſt. In which manor Wiħm the Conqueror had (as that booke fheweth,) and before him kinge Edward the Confeſſor had, fower hides of land in Demefne.

This Manor is parcell of the Barony of Berkeley the inheritance of George Lord Berkeley, holden of the Crowne by knights fervice in Capite; And was by kinge H. 2. given to Robert the fonne of Harding and his heires, amongſt many other manors, from whom it hath difcended to the lord Berkeley as heire male to the faid Robert, as before I have written. fol: 7. 78. etc. .

This Manor of Hinton confiſteth of theis fmall hamblets or remarkeable places, vz, Midleton, ffifhringe, Pockhampton, Ridlesford, Hinamfeild, Oldminſter, Kingſ-hill, ffrogpit, Brokend, part of Swonhunger, als Saniger, Shobenaffe and Metrefden.

Jn this Manor is one of the 8 tith barnes within the parifh of Berkeley, called Oldminſter barne. About the leafe whereof made by Burton then Abbot of S.t Auguſtines not longe before the diſſolucõn of that Monaſtery, to Anne lady Berkeley mother of the late lord Henry, a longe and bitter contention was betweene the faid lord Henry and Sir Thomas Throgm̃ton of Tortworth in 22.o Eliz. and divers yeares after; Whereof in the life of that Lord in the third booke of the hiſtory of his family I have at large written.

Heere

Hinton

Here also the said Abbot of S.t Augustines had an ancient halfe hide of land, which Maurice lord Berkeley the first of that name, in the time of kinge H. 2, gave to the said Abbot, wherof see before in fol. 64. 65. in the confirmacōn of Thomas lord Berkeley his sonne: And is nowe the inheritance of

The payment of the ffifteene or Kingsilver, when it is granted by parliament, goeth with Alkington in one some togeather; Wherof the onus or charge in the Exchequer is—9.li 10.s 6.d The deduction 3.li 3.s 4.d The Remanet paid into the Exchequer by the collector, is—6.li 7.s 2.d, wherof this of Hinton paies—3.li 3.s 7.d And Alkington foe much more. *ffifteene.*

In the last Subsedy in a.o 5.to Caroli were in this village 21 subsedy men, who paid—8.li 10.s 8.d   *Subsedy.*

Of able men for the warres betweene 20. and 60. yeares old in 6.to Jac, that then appeared before the Lieutenant of the County at a generall Muster, were—46.   *Able men.*

And of Trayned souldiers vnder Wi.llm Thorpe Esq,r their Captaine, are 19. vz, 8. Corsletts, and 11. musketts.   *Souldiers.*

And if the wholl Division of Berkeley, accompted a 4.th part of the county, bee rated in any taxe for the kinge or comōn wealth at—100.li This hundred of Berkeley paies thereof—33.li 3.s And this manor of Hineton—20.s And foe after that proportion, bee the taxe more or lesse.   *Rates.*

Shobenash, Shepnesh, Shepnesse, and Shepnash, is accompted one of the little hambletts of this manor: And wherin the Lords therof very aunciently, (in the time of kinge R. 1. at least,) had a parke, which parcell of ground to this day retaineth the name of Shepnash parke, though since disparked: A name wherof the latter sillable seemes to bee taken from the Saxon word Nesse, which seemes also to bee derived from the latine word Nasus, and signifieth a nebbe or nose of the land extended into the sea, as this place is into the river of Severne; In like sort as other places of like position neere adioyninge, As Nesse point on the other side this river, and others, have their derivations and names.   *230 Shepnash parke; or Shepnash point*

Freeholders lands within this Manor of Hineton, and the small hamblets thereof.

In the said hamblet called Pockhampton is an ancient messuage and about 40. acres of land therto belonginge, the inheritance of John Hurne, who dwelleth thervpon,   *Hurnes land.*

thervpon, holden of George lord Berkeley by the 16th part of a knights fee, And by fute to his hundred Court of Berkeley from 3. weekes to 3 weekes, and by the yearly rent of—10ˢ. As by an Inquifitiõn found after the death of John Hurne his father in aº. 4. Rº Jacobi appeareth, hee the fonne then about 18. yeares of age, whofe wardfhip the faid Lord thervpon had ; which John the father of John died in 39. Eliz., and was fonne of Robert Hurne who died in aº 1º Mariæ, and paid an heriott ; fonne of Thomas Hurne who died in 36. H. 8, fonne of Willm Hurne who died in   , fonne of Robert Hurne who died in 21. H. 7, fonne of   Hurne, fonne of Walter at Hurne, fonne of   Hurne, fonne of Alexander in la hurne ; To whom and to Agnes his wife and to their heires Maurice lord Berkeley the fecond of that name, in the end of kinge Henry the Third his raigne, gave the fame, To hold as aforefaid : which hath ever fince continued in a lineall difcent in their iffue male, drawinge their Sirname from the place ; for a Hurne is a little thicket of thornes fhrubbs or the like fmall wood, as there then was, and yet is : Which originall deed remaininge with the firft named John, I have read, made to Alexander de Pockhampton and to Agnes his wife, as aforefaid, by the name of halfe a yard land in Hineton in pockhampton, late before held in villenage ; Rendringe-10ˢ p Ann̄ at 4. termes, &c. for all fervices and demaunds, Salvo regali fervicio, quantum pertinet ad dimidiam virgatam terræ de coī feodo, which is knight fervice.

And alfo with him refteth one other Deed made by the faid lord to the faid Alexander, by the name of Alexander in la hurne, of 3. acr̄ of land and of the revertion of two little meffuages, &c. To hold in fee, Rendringe per Ann̄—12ᵈ And to hold as aforefaid.

ffor which fee alfo an Inq : in 37. E. 3. of knights fees belonginge to the caftle of Berkeley, which findeth, That the heire of Walter at Hurne then held in Hinton, the 16th part of a knights fee, which Record is in the Office of the Remembrancer to the lord Treaforer in the Exchequer. |

231
Hurnes land late Berkeleis nowe Malletts

Heere alfo in Hinton is a meffuage with about 40. acres of land therto belonginge, the inheritance of Nathaniell Mallett, in right of Sara his wife, daughter and heire of John Hurne, fonne of Anthony Hurne, who by fine in Michas terme Aº 6. et 7. Eliz: and by other affurances, purchafed the fame of Thomas Berkeley of Berkeley gen̄, brother and heire of John Berkeley, fonnes of John Berkeley, fonne and heire of Thomas Berkeley, yongeft brother of Willm Marques Berkeley, fonnes

of

of James lord Berkeley, nephewe and heire male of Thomas lord Berkeley the 4th of that name; ffor which see more in Berkeley fol: 90. And is holden of George lord Berkeley as of this manor of Hinton by knight service, sute to the hundred court of Berkeley from three weekes to three weekes, And by the yearly rent of—11ˢ 2ᵈ ffor which, see an Inq: after the death of the said John Hurne in aᵒ 11ᵒ Caroli; Which services are also mentioned in the deed of 1. H. 5. wherby Thomas lord Berkeley aforesaid gave the same (inter alia) to Phillip Waterton, als Chamberlyn (becaufe his Chamberlaine,) and to Cicely his wife, and to the heires of his body begotten on her; To hold by—10ˢ rent, and other services of old due: which Anthony Hurne died in 39. Eliz. and was a branch derived out of the family of John Hurne of Pockhampton, aforesaid, ancient lessees heervnto; ffor John Hurne in 15. H. 6. held the same vnder the foresaid Phillip Waterton.

Also in **Hinton**, in the hamblet called Midleton (quasi Midletowne,) is an ancient messuage and about 40. acres of land therto belonginge, the inheritance of Willm Dancey of Ewley, sonne of Thomas who died   , sonne of John who died   , sonne of Giles who died   ; which is called Midletons messuage, which hath continued in the sirname of Dancey from the time of kinge Henry the ffifth; And was before the land of Arras, and before the land of Atkins als Attekins, To whom Thomas lord Berkeley the first of that name about 12. H. 3. gave the same in fee, To hold of him by knight service, sute to his hundred Court at Berkeley from three weekes to three weekes, and the yearly rent of—3ˢ paid at this day; See in Ewley. fol: 198.   *Dauncies land.*

Also John ffryar of Halmer, sonne of William ffryar who died in   , brother and heire of Maurice who died 1ᵒ Jacobi, sonnes of Thomas ffryar who died   , sonne of Thomas who died in   , nephew and heire of Richard ffryar who died 15. Eliz., sonnes of John ffryar who died in 5. Eliz. holdeth two messuages with divers lands to them severally belonginge, wherof the one lyinge in Halmer in Hinton and Hame was sometime the land of John ffrigg; And the other lyinge in Halmer Hame and Hinton also was somtime the land of John Attemead, By   service, sute to the hundred Court of Berkeley from three weekes to three weekes, And by the yearly rent of—3ˢ 4ᵈ for a pound of comyn. | *ffryars land.*

Here also are divers lands and tenements nowe the severall inheritances of Richard Laurence and George Lewes, which they by severall deeds in 13. 14. 15. and 16. yeares of the raigne of kinge James purchased in fee of George Thorpe Esq., sonne   *Thorps land:*

sonne of Nicholas, sonne of Thomas, sonne of Thomas, sonne of Richard, sonne of John, sonne of John Thorpe and Isable his wife, sister and heire of John Swonhunger ats Sanyger, sonne and heire of Elias Swonhunger; holden of George lord Berkeley by knight service, sute to his hundred Court of Berkeley from 3. weekes to 3. week͡s, And by the yearly rent of—2ˢ 6ᵈ to this Manor of Hinton; whereof the said George Lewes paies—2ˢ And the said Richard Laurence—6ᵈ; who also paid—9ᵈ rent for some part of the said lands lyinge within the manor of Hame. The severall yeares wherin each of the severall owners of these lands died, see after in Wanifwell, fol: 367. 368.

By Rot. paten̄ 2. E. 2. ps. 1. in dorso, Adam Eliott arraigned an assise against Maurice sonne of Thomas lord Berkeley sen̄, et alios, de ten̄tis in pockampton et Hineton neere to Berkeley.

Within this manor of Hinton are severall peells of land now the inheritance of Thomas Perry, sonne of Thomas Perry of Wotton gen̄, and of Samuell Perry sonne of the said Thomas by Margery his second wife; heertofore peell of the possessions belonginge to the Chantry of Sᵗ Andrew in the church of Berkeley, and were by Queene Eliz. 1° Junij. aᵒ 34° r̄ni sui, granted vnto Henry Best and John Wells, Scriveners in London, and their heires, to hold of Eastgreenwich in Soccage: who by their Deed inrolled dated 20ᵒ Julij. 32ᵒ Eliz. & inrolled 24ᵒ Julij next followinge, granted the same to Thomas Perry and his heires: who by his last will devised them to Samuell his eldest sonne by his second wife aforesaid, but in regard that he died seized of severall lands held in Capite, the said Thomas, sonne of Thomas, claymed a third part to discend vnto him, wᶜʰ was ended by arbitrament, and peell of theis lands given vnto him, and hee to release the rest vnto Samuell his halfe brother. |

Horfeild.

Horefeild: In Domesdei booke **Horefelle**; A township within two miles of the Citie of Bristoll, wherin Wittm the Conqueror, (which also Edward the Confessor had, as that booke telleth vs,) eight hides of land in demesne, nowe parcell of the possessions of the Bishoppricke of Bristoll; And hath for its neighbour borderers the fower Stokes, of great Stoke, Little Stoke, Stoke Gifford, and Harry Stoke.

This

Horfeild

This Manor and townſhip was part of the ancient poſſeſſions of the Abbot and Covent of the Monaſtery of Sᵗ Auguſtines by Briſtoll, And one of the Manors given by Robert ſonne of Harding, when in the time of kinge Stephen hee firſt founded the ſame, whereof ſee before in Almondeſbury fol: 47, And in Aſhelworth fol: 66, And in Berkeley fol: 82, And in Cromhall fol: 165, And in ffilton fol: 201; And continued in the hands of thoſe Abbotts till the diſſolucõn of that Monaſtery in 31. H. 8. And vpon that kings erectinge of the Biſhopprick of Briſtoll in the 34ᵗʰ yeare of his Raigne, became by his grant parcell of the poſſeſſions of the Biſhoppricke, As more largely in the fol: vouched doth appeare. See alſo a confirmacõn of this manor to the Abbot. fol: 64. 65.

ffor ffreewarren and other liberties granted by kinge E. 1, and after recited and confirmed by kinge E. 4, See before in Almondſbury, fol: [49]

A booke of knights fees in the Exchequer, with the Remembrancer to the lord Treaſorer, faith; John Gifford holds halfe a knights fee in Horefeild of Thomas de Berkeley, which is nowe the land of   *Regiſtrum Epĩ Wigorñ.*

In the yeare 1472, Aº. 12. E. 4, A compoſition was made betweene Walter Newbury then Abbot of the monaſtery of Sᵗ Auguſtines by Briſtoll, And Wittm Meredith then Rector of the pariſh church of ffilton in the Dioces of Worceſter, concerninge certaine tythes, Reall mixt and perſonall, out of lands in the limitts and borders of the Chaple of Horefeild, called Breweſhold; wherby the Abbot was to have the Tithes, and to pay the Rector of the Church of ffilton—6ˢ 8ᵈ p annñ at Micħas; which was confirmed by John then Biſhop of Worcᵗ, And is to this day paid by the Biſhop of Briſtoll, within which Deanry of Briſtoll this Chaple or Church is.   *Chapell*

The paymᵗ of the ffifteene or Kingeſilver when it is granted by parliament, goeth in one foñe with ffilton, And pay into the Receipt of this Exchequer 3ˡⁱ 10ˢ 6ᵈ qᵥ.   *ffifteene.*

In the laſt Subſedy in aº 5ᵗᵒ Caroli Rᵉ. were 4 Subſedy men in Horfeild, who paid—42ˢ   *Subſedy.*

In 6ᵗᵒ Jacobi, vpon a generall view of able men betweene 20. and 60. years old, were inrolled, ſerviceable for the warres,—16.   *Able men.*

And

Hundred of Berkeley

Soldiers. And now in aº 1639. are of trayned Souldiers vnder Thomas Chester Esq, their Captaine.

Rates. And if the wholl Divifion of Berkeley accompted a 4ᵗʰ part of the County bee taxed at—100ˡⁱ vpon any rate for Kinge or Comon-wealth, The Hundred of Berkeley paieth thereof—33ˡⁱ 3ˢ And this townſhip of Horfeild—15ˢ |

234 blank

Huntingford.

Huntingford: not mentioned in the booke of Domefdei; Aunciently written Hunteneford, and

Of old noe manor; After, a manor; nowe only a manor in reputation, within the parifh of Wotton vnderedge, and Leet of the hundred of Berkeley; where at Berkeley the Inhabitants appeare and ferve vnder the name of a Tithingman and his tithinge; And is holden of George lord Berkeley as of his Manor of Wotton Vnderedge by the 4ᵗʰ part of a Knights fee, and fute to his hundred Court of Berkeley from 3. weekes to 3. weekes.

This ffarme of Huntingford, (for foe it is nowe fitteft to bee called,) was given by kinge Henry the fecond in the firft yeare of his raigne to Robert the fonne of Harding and his heires, amongft much other land; And paffed vnder the name of Wotton as parcell of that manor and lyinge in the vttermoft fkirt therof, South-weft ward; Wherof fee more in Wotton, fol: 403.

Of this land ffarme or Manor, the faid Robert the fonne of Harding about 10. H. 2. enfeoffed Elias his brother in fee, by the name of one hide of land, to hold of him by the 4ᵗʰ pte of a knights fee: which Elias had iffue Hardinge, who from the place of his abode was vfually written **Harding of Huntingford**, and by Dionifia his wife had iffue one daughter called Matilda, als Maud, who was maried to Galfridus vitulus, als Geffry le Veel, a gentleman of a remarkeable family, much favoured by kinge John, and of fpeciall acceptation with many great Lords of that time. As by divers Records in the Tower of London in thofe daies appeareth. To wᶜʰ Geffrey Veel alfo Robert Lord Berkeley, grandchilde of the forefaid Robert fonne of Harding, did in the time of the faid kinge John give in ffrankmaryage

with

with the said Matilda or Maud his cozen, diūs other parcells of land in Hunteneford, and in the skirts of his chase (or fforrest as in that Deed it is called,) of Mukelwood, wherby the aforesaid hide of land was much enlarged.

Which Geffry and Maud had issue Robert Veel who died in   H. 3. leavinge issue Robert Veel knight, who by Hawisia his wife had issue Peter Veel, and died in   E. 1. The said Peter Veel died in the life time of his father, but by Cicely his wife left issue Peter Veel who died in 17. E. 3. leavinge issue by Cicely his wife another Peter Veel knight, who died in   , And by Elizabeth his wife left issue Sir Thomas Veel knight, who died in   , and by Hawisia his wife left issue John Veel who died in 36. H. 6. And by Alice his wife who died in 3. H. 7. leaft issue Robert Veel, 2 Wittm, and 3 John; The said Robert Veel died in 13. E. 4. and by Elizabeth his wife leaft issue Alice his only childe maried to Sir David Mathew knight, which Alice died in   , whom her said husband survived and died in 19. H. 7. Betweene which Sir David and Alice were 4. daughters and coheires; viz, Elizabeth maried to   Hurd, of whom is issue at this day; Anne second daughter maried to John Baynham of Westbury, father of Wittm Baynham, father of Joseph Bainham, father of Alexander Bainham, who by Elizabeth his wife, daughter of Arnold Oldifworth late of Bradley, have issue [Joseph] Bainham, and others, that nowe are aº 1639. And also the said Anne was maried to Thomas Morgan Esq: Katherine the third daughter of the said Sir David and Alice was maried to Henry Ogan, who died in 10. H. 8. And the said Katherine died in 24. H. 7. before her husband. Betweene whom was issue Jone their only childe, maried to Richard Cornewall Esq, who died in 11. Eliz. And the said Jone died in 36. H. 8. before her husband; betweene whom was issue Edmond Cornwall, called Baron of Burford in Shropshire, who aliened this manor or farme of Huntingford, as after followeth. And Margaret, the fourth daughter of the said Sir David Mathew and Alice, was married to Wittm Throckm̄ton, sonne of Christopher; which Wittm died in 28. H. 8. And the said Margaret died in   ; and had issue betweene them Sir Thomas Throkm̄ton knight, who died in 10. Eliz. And by Margaret his wife daughter and coheire of Thomas Whittington Esq, who survived her husband, and died in 21. Eliz. had issue betweene them Sir Tho: Throkmerton knight, who died in aº 5º Jacobi, who purchased in aº   Eliz. this manor or farme of the said Edmond Cornwall, Baron of Burford, to whose grandmother Katherine maried to Ogan, and to his mother Jone, a great part therof was allotted in ptition, wherby the said Sir Thomas Throkmerton, addinge to what hee before had from his grandmother (Margaret,) became sole seised therof; and

and foe dyed feized, leavinge Sir William Throkmton knight, created Baronet, his only fonne and heire ; who by his deed inrolled in Chancery dated 1º Novembr. aº 6. Jacobi, aliened the fame to Thomas Tracy, who with the faid Sir William by their Deed inrolled in the court of Comon pleas, wherin they ioyned, dated 18. April. 13. Jacobi, fold the fame to Sir Henry Bainton knight ; And from him the fame came to Elizabeth his daughter, and her heires, by his will the yeare after, aº 14. Jacobi, who was maried to John Dutton of Shirborne, who had this land (inter alia) in fee conveyed vnto him as her mariage portion, who lately hath fold the fame to Thomas Graile, fonne of Edmond, whofe the fame nowe is, aº 1639.

The faid Willm Veel fecond brother of Robert Veel died in 9. H. 7. leavinge iffue Willm Veel who died 23. H. 7. and was father of Edward Veel of Over, and of Willm Veel of Acton ; Which Edward had iffue Edward Veel and others, of whom is iffue at this day, 1639. And the faid Willm Veel of Acton had iffue Nicholas Veel of Allefton, who had iffue Thomas Veel of Allefton that nowe is, aº 1639, Captaine of a trayned band of 150. fouldiers in this hundred of Berkeley, often before mentioned ; A prudent gent of much remarkeablenes in his countrey ; The ancient word or mottoe of whofe family is, face aut tace. Betweene which William Veel, who died in 9. H. 7. and Willm his fonne and heire who died in 23. H. 7, who claymed this land (with others) as heire male to the faid Robert, by an old entaile, And the faid David Mathew and Alice his wife as in her right, who claymed as heire generall to the faid Robert Veel her father, were great and longe contentions in the times of kinge H. 7. and H. 8 ; in the fecond yeare of whofe raigne thofe fuites tooke endinge, when the heire generall caryed this land.

Mathewes land.   **Also** of this old ffarme or manor John Mathewe, fonne of John Mathewe Clerke, holds about 32. acres with a mill in Huntingford, which the faid John the father in   Jacobi, purchafed of Elianor Meffenger, who in 3ºio Jacobi purchafed the fame of Jerome Vizar, And hee by deed dated 1º mcij, aº 41º Eliz : of John Bridges ; And hee by deed dated 20. Maij, Aº 22º Eliz. of the faid Edmond Cornewall, fonne of Richard and Jone his wife, as aforefaid. |

237
Hickes land.   **Also** another part of this old ffarme or Manor containinge about 40. acres is the inheritance of Willm Hickes fonne of Thomas Hickes who died in 42º Eliz. fonne of John Hicks who by deed dated 9º Maij 10 Eliz. and by a feoffment in Aprill aº 14. Eliz. purchafed the fame of the faid Edmond Cornwall, one of the coheires of the faid Robert Veel, defcendinge to him as is aforefaid ; which faid John Hickes the purchafer died in 31. Eliz.

                                                          Also

Huntingford

Also another part of this ffarme or manor containinge about 18. acres, in two closes lyinge togeather called Veelfraydings in Nybley adioyninge to Michaelwood, is the inheritance of you John Smyth my sonne, conveyed by mee vnto you vpon your mariage; And which I purchased of the said Sir William Throkm̃ton, and which had difcended to him as aforefaid. *Smythes land.*

Also the said Willm Hickes sonne of Thomas holdeth a meſſuage in Hunting-ford and a ſmall parcell of land therto belonginge, which Thomas ap Morgan and Anne his wife, ſecond daughter and coheire of the said David Mathewe and Alice his wife, daughter and heire of Robert Veel aforeſaid, by deed dated 17º Martij. 36. H. 8, sold to John Hickes clothier; which Deed is in the cuſtody of Morgan Hicks of Cromhale, who hath divers lands which were the said Willm Hickeſ's in the piſh of Tortworth, which paſſed in the said Deed; And which alſo is inrolled before Richard Braine then Juſtice of Peace and Willm Shotteſſore then clarke of the peace of this county: Which John Hickes the purchaſer was father of John Hickſ, father of the said Thomas Hickſ, father of the said Willm; Of which difcent fee more in fol: 93. 103. *Hickes land*

By deed without date Dñs Robertus le Veel granted vnto Ade de Durſewelle tres acras terræ arrabilis in angulo campi mei qui vocatur Camelham iuxta Mucle-wood, infra villam meam de Hunteneforde. To hold vnto the said Ade and his heires, vnder the yearely rent of—18ᵈ payable at Midsom̃er and at Michas. pro õibus fectis fervicijs et demandis fecularibus: Which peece lyeth vnder the fouth hill of Michaelwood above Damery bridge, (and is reputed within the tythinge of Alkington;) ffrom which Ade de Durſewelle for a courſe of above 400. yeares, (vz, from the beginninge of H. 3. when this Sir Robᵗ le Veel lived,) this land with a ſmall tenem̃t in Tortworth of about 40ˢ p anñ, is difcended in the male line vnto George Duſwell fonne of   Duſwell, the prefent owner thereof, 1641. *Durfewells land.*

Kinge H. 3. in the 12ᵗʰ yeare of his raigne did difafforreſt his forreſt of Hor-wood, not farre from Sodbury, for 500. markes, paid by the men dwellinge about the fame (faith the Record,) And the fame yeare for 200. markes more paid by the men of Glouceſterſhire hee difafforreſted all the woods lands and townes inter boſcum de furcis prope Briſtoll et Hunteneford; et inter aquam de Severne, &c., tàm de venatione, quàm de õibus alijs quæ ad foreſtam et foreſtarios pertinent. So that the bounds of huntinge and of the kings game of deere and his progenitors' on the | further fide, And the confines of the Lord Berkeleys manor and hundred *The name.*

of

of Berkeley, of their free warren and huntings on this side that river and sourd, (both heere at this manor houfe meetinge and bounded with a mutuall ne plus vltrà on either fide,) may probably feeme to have given the name, from that fourd, to the ffarme or hide of land adioyninge therto. Rot. finiũ. 12. H. 3. ps. 1. mem : 5. et Rot. cartaʒ. 12. H. 3. membr. 5. Et 13. H. 3. ps. 1. membr. 18.

By a Deed in Berkeley caftle without date but in the time of kinge John, Maud la Veel daughter and heire of Harding and of Dionife of Huntenford, (wᶜʰ Maud was wife of Geffry le Veel,) gave a mill and certaine lands in Kingfwood to the Abbot of Kingfwood, in pure Almes ; To which deed are 36 witneffes ; And this lies next about the Monaftery.

Kinge John, in the 7ᵗʰ yeare of his raigne, confirmed to Geffry Veel (amongſt many other things) the land hee had of the guift of Robert lord Berkeley with Maud the daughter of Hardinge of Hunteneford in frankmariage, All the land which came to her from her father in Hunteneford, And all the land which came to her from Dionifia her mother in the fame towne, with many other parcells in this record perticulerly rehearfed ; And alfo confirmed to him All other lands which hee fhould afterwards purchafe of any perfon. Rot. Cartaʒ. 7. Johis. nº 80. membr. 9.

See before, fol. 31, 32.

By a deed without date, which was fhewed mee by Sir Thomas Throkmurton in 20. Rſ. Jacobi, wherout I then tooke theis notes, That Robert de Berkel gave to Geffry Veel and his heires, divers &c. the faid Deed is in latin to this effect ; Robtus de Berkel dedit Galfrido vitulo et heredibus fuis diverfas parvas parcellas terre in Huntenford, Et totum affartum illud in orientali parte bofci fui de Muclewood, quod Radulphus feai affartavit, Reddendo p̄dc̄o Roberto et heredibus fuis quindecim folidos per Anũ ad feftm Sc̄i Michis et feftm Pafche, pro ōibus fervicijs et demandis, Salvo regali fervicio quantùm ad vnam virgatam terræ pertinet. Et etiam conceffit viginti porcos, quietos de pannagio in bofco fuo de Muclewood p̄dc̄o, five claufus fuerit five non ; Habend et tenend p̄dc̄o Galfrido vitulo et heredibus fuis, &c.

And alfo in this deed is another parcell of land affarted out of the faid wood called Muclewood, granted to the faid Geffery Veel and his heires, lyinge next Woodyates on the north part, and the meadowe ground called Wingefmore on the eaſt part, and the ground of the faid John Mathew called Huntall on the South part ; And is divided from the other grounds of the faid Thomas Graile by a little brooke

Huntingford

brooke on the east and south parts called Camilham, which ground foe assarted containes about 8 acres, and is called Woodleies; And for this ground is paid—6ᵈ towards the kings ffifteene or tenth when it is granted by parliament, with the tythinge or manor of Alkington.

By Inq: in 6ᵗᵒ Jaĉ. after the death of the said Sir Thomas Throkmorton, it is found that hee died seized in fee of the manor of Huntingford, holden of the lord Berkeley as of his manor of Berkeley by knight service: And also of divers small parcells of land in Huntingford, And of a certaine assart in the east part of Michael-wood wood containinge 8. acres, other then the manor of Huntingford aforesaid, holden of the heire of Robert de Berkeley by—15ˢ yearly rent, but by what other services the Jury knewe not; And that hee died 31 Januar̃. 5ᵗᵒ Jacobi, And that Wittm was his sonne and heire, 28. yeares old.

Rot. Clauŝ, in arce Londoñ. 18. E. 3. ps. 1. in dorso, containes a procedendo in the sute betweene Katherine the widowe of Sir Peter le Veel, and Jone the widowe of Henry le Veel. for the third part of the manor of Huntingford and of Oldbury iuxta Thornbury. |

The payment of the ffifteenth and Tenth goeth with   **239** ffifteene.

In the last Subsedy in 5ᵗᵒ Regis Caroli, were only two Subsedy men in this hamblet, who paid—14ˢ 8ᵈ   Subsedy.

In aº. 6ᵗᵒ Jacobi, vpon a generall Muster, were 4. able men betweene 20. and 60 yeares old, serviceable for warre.   Able men.

And nowe, 1639, hath of Trayned souldiers   , vnder Thomas Veel Esq̃, their Captaine, wherof   Souldiers.

And if the whole Division of Berkeley bee taxed at—100ˡⁱ then this hundred paies therof—33ˡⁱ 3ˢ. And this hamblet of Huntingford—5ˢ wherof the ffarme paies the one halfe, and the rest of the inhabitants the other.   Rates.

The whole hamblet or Tithinge consists but of 5 tenements besides the farme, In all which at this day are 27 soules. See after in Wotton fol: 415.   People.

More

More of this farme or manor or tythinge of Huntingford may bee read in theis Records, none of which are formerly mentioned ; vz

Liber feod miltum in Sċċio. in temp : E. 1.
Inq : 19. H. 7. p! mortem David Mathew miltis.—per serviċ mil.
Inq : 20. H. 7. p! mortem Willi Veel.—per serviċ militare.
Trinity Records 20. H. 7. Rot. 3. in Sċċio, ēm Reñi Thesauŕ.—per serv : mil.
Inq : 23. H. 7. p! mortem Willi Veel.
Originall : 2. H. 8. Rot. 54. in Sċċio, ēm Reñi Thesauŕ.—per serviċ mil.
Original. 3. H. 8. Rot. 42. in Sċċio ēm Reñi Thesauŕ.
Inq : 3. H 8. p! mortem Katherinæ Ogan in Sċċio.
Originall. 7. H. 8. et 8. H. 8. Rot. 35. in Sċio preď.
Inq : 10. H. 8. p! mortem Henrici Ogan.—per serviċ mil.
Hill : records. 11. H. 8. Rot. 7. in Sċio p̄d.
Mich : Records 12. H. 8. Rot. 28. in Sċio p̄d.—per serviċ mil.
Inq ; 36. H. 6. p! mortem Johis Veel : with a good court roll the same yeare ;—per servicium militare.
Michas reċ. 13. H. 8. Rot. 11. in Sċċio.
Pasch : reċ. 2. E. 6. Rot. 32. in Sċċio p̄d.
Inq : 10. Eliz. p! mortem Thomæ Throkmilton miltis.
Inq : 12. p! mortem Johannæ Cornwall.—per serviċ mil.
Inq : 42. Eliz. ps. 2. post mortem Thomæ Hickes.
Carta irrotulať in Cancellaŕ, 6. Jaċ. inter Throkmilton et Tracy.
ffinis in banco, 13. Jac : Terñi pasche, Inter Bainton Tracy et Throkmilton.
Carta irroť in banco, Pasch : 13. Jac : Rot. 33. inter Bainton et Tracy.
Vltima voluntas Edŕi Bainton p̄d, about aᵒ 14ᵉ Jacobi.
Inqu : 6. Jac : p! mortem Thomæ Throkmilton miltis.—per serviċ mil.
Court roll of Wotton fforren, 36. H. 6. Johes le Veel Aŕ obijt seitus de manerio de Huntingford, tenť per medietatem feodi miltis.—Reddť—15! et Secť de 3. septimañ in tres septiñi, et mountuaŕ, vñ equs et vna cella et freno cum alia armatura, et Robtus est filius et heres 26. annoṛ. |

240 blank

Hurst.

Hurst: anciently written **Herst** and **Hirst** ; wherof George Lord Berkeley is Lord ; A manor lyinge within the parish of Slimbridge, consistinge of the small hamblets of Gosington, of which I have before written in fol : 203, and of Kingston,

Morend

Hurst

Morend, Woodwards greene, and Hurst it felfe, which giveth name to the wholl manor and tithinge.

It feems the name is derived from the fcituaçõn of the Capitall meffuage or manor houfe called Hurst or Hirst farme, at this day rented at—211ˡⁱ p ann, feated vpon the vppermoft rifinge or topp of a fmall hill in a plaine, In old Saxon Englifh called an Hirst; or in thother old fenfe of Herst which in the fame tongue is a wood, it well agreeth with this manor houfe, feated in and by the woods of Chifelhungre, Priors wood, Redwood, Brandwood and others, for moft part converted nowe into pafture and arrable grounds.

By an Inq: in 42. E. 3. after the death of Maurice Lord Berkeley the 4ᵗʰ Lord of that name, this manor is found to bee holden of the Lord Clifford of the North, wherwith alfo agreeth the Certiorare of that record in 16. H. 6. But more truly, I take this manor to bee an ancient parcell of the manor and Barony of Berkeley, and holden of the kinge by knight fervice in Capite, though it bee not mentioned in the booke of Domefdei, nor in any record that I have obferved before the raigne of kinge H. 3; and paffed to Robert the fonne of Hardinge by the grant of kinge H. 2. vnder the name of Came, with all the reft of the Berewic or members appertaininge then to Berkeley, which fee before in fol: 7. et 8. Otherwife Came neither had nor hath foe many hides of land as are mentioned in Domefdei booke.

Freeholds within this manor and tithinge of Hurst and the hambletts therof, of moft remarkeablenes, vz,

Ryvers lands als Archers.

In the hamblet of Kingfton principally, but fcatteredly throughout the whole manor of Hurst and parifh of Slimbridge, are certaine freehold lands comonly and of old called Rivers lands, but from a later owner often alfo called Archers land, as after followeth; holden of George lord Berkeley as of his manor of Hurst aforefaid, by knight fervice, heriot fervice, and fute to his hundred court of Berkeley from 3. weekſ to 3 weekes, and by the yearly rent of   paid to this manor of Hurst, and   paid to the manor of Slimbridge.

The originall creation of the tenure of this land is found by verdict of a Jury at Gloue vpon an Affife tryed before William de Saham and his fellowe Juftices itinerant, entred in the comom pleas records in Eafter terme, 15. E. 1. Rotulo 3. in dorfo; which fhewes that Thomas Lord Berkeley (the firft of that name) in the time of kinge H. 3. therof enfeoffed one Alured de Kingfton in fee, who had iffue
Richard

Richard de Kingſton, who had iſſue Robert de Kingſton knight, who for theis lands, was in ward to Thomas lord Berkeley (the ſecond of that name) grandchilde of the ſaid lord Thomas the ffeoffor; which Sir Robert died without iſſue, And that Alice was his fiſter and heire, maried to Madreſdon, who (ſurvivinge her huſband) did by the name of Agnes de Madreſdon in 5. E. 2. gave the ſame to Richard de riparijs and to Sara de Hagle her neece in marriage, and to his heires, by the name of a Meſſuage and a carucate of land in Kingſton and Goſington, ſomtimes the lands of Robert de Kingſton. To which Richard de Riparijs (als Ryvers) and the ſaid Sara his wife, and to the heires of the ſaid Richard, Thomas lord Berkeley the third of that name by his deed in 4. E. 3. granted comon of paſture vpon the warth called Slimbridge warth, for all his tenants of his ſaid lands and tenements in Kingſton, Goſington, Slimbridge, and Hurſt, at all times of the yeare, without any thinge payinge or doinge for the ſaid comon in the name of Agiſtment: which deed, copied lately by mee out of the originall vnder ſeale remaininge with Joſeph Bridger of Goſington hall, is in theis words.—Universis Chriſti fidelibus preſens ſcriptum viſuris vel audituris, Thomas de Berkeley Dñs de Berkeley ſalutem in Dño. Noveritis me conceſſiſſe et preſenti ſcripto confirmaſſe, dno Richardo de Rivers et Saræ vxori eius, cõiam paſturæ in quadam placea paſture vocata le Warth, quæ quidem placea iacet inter aquam Sabriñ ex vna parte, et villatas de Kingſton et Slimbrugg ex altera parte, vz, comunicant in paſtura p̄dca cum ōibus ſuis tenentibus in terris et tēntis ſuis de Kingeſton, Goſington, Slimbrugg, et Hurſt, quocunq, tempore anni. Habend et tenend cōiam paſtur̄ p̄dc̄am cum ōibus ſuis pertineñ p̄ſat Ric̄o et Saræ et heredebus p̄dc̄i Ric̄i, liberè, quietè, bene et in pace, abſque aliquo mihi vel heredibus meis dando vel faciendo pro cōia p̄dc̄a nomine agiſtiamenti vel aliquo alio modo imperpetuum. In cuius rei teſtimonium huic ſcripto preſenti ſigillum meum appoſui, Hijs teſtibus, Roħto de Aſton, Witħmo de Chiltenham. Johanne Sergeant, Ric̄o Billinge, Johe Colines et alijs. Datū apud Berkeley in feſto circumciſionis Dñi, Anno regni regis Edwardi tertij a conqueſtu quarto. A priviledge continued to this day, 1639. ffrom the poſſeſſion of which Richard Rivers theis lands have the name of Rivers lands frequently in the ſpeach of each inhabitant there.

The ſaid Richard Rivers, afterwards a knight, ſonne of Robert de riparijs, had to his ſecond ſonne to whom hee gave theis lands, Richard Rivers, who alſo had iſſue Richard Rivers, who left iſſue Iſable and Jone, his two daughters and coheires. Iſable the eldeſt daughter was maried to   Clavild, who had iſſue Richard Clavild a marchant of Briſtoll, who died in 1. E. 5. leaving iſſue Richard Clavild, who

who died in 2. R. 3. without iffue ; wherby his lands reforted to feeke an heire in the iffues of Jone his grandmothers fifter ; which Jone was married to John Archer fonne of Thomas Archer, who had iffue betweene them John Archer ; And the faid Jone died in 8. H. 5. In whofe raigne died alfo the faid John Archer her fonne, leavinge iffue John Archer who died in   , leaving iffue Thomas Archer who died in 23. H. 7. leaving iffue two daughters and coheires, vz. Jone firft maried to Richard Hanis, and fecondly to Robert Taylor, by both whom fhee had iffue as followeth ; And Ifable her fifter was maried to Richard Spratton.

The faid Jone by Richard Hanis her firft hufband who died in 25. H. 8. had iffue Thomas Hanis, who died in 2º. Eliz. leavinge iffue Thomas Hanis, who died in 36. Eliz. leaving iffue Willm Hanis, who with his eldeft fonne have aliened all the purpart that belonged to them foe that nothinge remaineth. And the faid Jone by the faid Robert Taylor her fecond hufband had iffue Willm Taylor, who died   leavinge iffue John Taylor, father of John Taylor yet livinge, who and his fonne Humphrey Taylor have in 21. Jacobi, and in 2º Rº Caroli, aliened all their lands which their anceftor had from the faid Jone, to Ambrofe Huntley als Simonds and his heires, except one houfe and orchard called Dukes place, wheron the faid John Taylor now dwelleth, 1639. and one clofe cont 3. acres neere the fame, which alfo were parcell of theis lands called Rivers lands : And by the death of the faid Ambrofe Huntley als Simonds in Sº. Caroli, | his fonne Stephen then of the age of 13. yeares became in ward to the Lord Berkeley, and foe yet is.

And the faid Richard Spratton and Ifable his wife, fecond daughter and coheire of the faid Thomas Archer, aliened in 21. H. 7. their part of theis Rivers lands to Thomas Cooke of Salifbury, who died in 15. H. 8. leavinge iffue Willm Cooke, who died in   leavinge iffue Thomas Cooke, who in   Eliz. fold the fame to Richard Trotman, who died in   Jacobi, and was father of Edward Trotman, by whofe death in 16. Jac. his fonne Richard Trotman, who yet liveth, became in ward for the fame to the Lady Eliz. Berkeley widowe, who then had the manors of Hurft and Slimbridge in Joincture : ffor more wherof fee my booke of Wardfhips and Releifes, fol : 17. 18. And by the death of the faid Richard fonne of Edward in 15. Car. Richard his fonne was in ward, As his office in 16º Car. fheweth : And how hee difpofed of part of his lands to 4. of his yonger fonnes ; See after fol : 244, 248, 249, 250.

The faid Ifable the elder of the two daughters and coheires of Richard Rivers, maried to Clavild, vpon the death of their grandchilde Richard Clavild in 2. R. 3.
leaft

Hundred of Berkeley

leaſt ſuch an entaile of part of their ſaid lands called Rivers lands as brought a good portion of them to Richard Tindall, who died in   leavinge iſſue John Tindall who died in 6. H. 8. leavinge iſſue Richard Tindall iun of Southend in Stincheombe; By whoſe death in 15. Eliz. the ſame diſcended to his 2 daughters and coheires, vz, Katherine maried to Robert Aſhton, and to Alice maried to Thomas Aſhton, two brothers to two ſiſters, who betweene them have likewiſe ſold all away as after in part ſhall appeare; The evidences which make good what is before written touchinge theis Rivers lands, have beene lent mee to peruſe by the ſaid Willm Hanis, and John Taylor; The reſidue are either in Berkeley caſtle, or in theis Records followinge not formerly mentioned; vz,

  Inq : 23. H. 7. p! mortem Thome Archer, virtute officij: but filed in the bundle of 3. H. 7. by a miſtake of the clarkes.

  Recuperatio in terñi Michis, 21. H. 7. Rot. 453. per Cooke, verſus Ricum Sprotton et Iſabellā vxorē eius.

  Inq : 15. H. 8. p! morte Thomæ Cooke.

  ffinis in banco in Michas terme. 22. et 30. Eliz. pro Pleadall.

  Inq : 30. Eliz. p! morte Rici Tindall.

  Inq : 33. Eliz p! morte p.dci Rici Tindall, Melius Inquirend.

  Inq : 15. Caroli p! morte Mathei Smyth,—per ſerviciu militare.

  Inq : 7. Car. virtute officij, p! morte Simonis Ludby,—per ſervie mil et heriet

  Inq : 8. Car. p! morte Ambroſij Huntley als Simonds,—per ſervie mil.

  Inq : 37. E. 3. in ſcēio pro feod ſpectañ ad Mañiu de Berkeley.

  Inq : 2. Caroli, p! morte Rici Bower,—per ſervie mil et heriet.

  Inq : 6. Jacobi, p! morte Willi Huntley,—per ſervie mil.—a wardſhip.

  Inq : 2. Caroli, p! morte Willi Teele :—per ſervie mil.—et heriet.

  Grant of Willm Effingtons wardſhip 2° Caroli, to Laur Bridger,—for part of Rivers land,—per ſervie mil et heriet.

  Inq : 9. Caroli, p! morte Thome Davis,—per ſervie mil et heriet.

  Grant of Richard Trotmans wardſhip and heriots, 2° Jac, vt antea.

  Grant of the wardſhip of Anne daughter of Willm Huntley in 6. Jac. to mee, And my aſſignement to her mother; wch Anne died in 8. Jacobi.

  Court Roll of Hurſt 6. H. 8, John Tindall died &c; cap: meſſ called Rivers, &c: p ſervie militare, et heriet. wardſhip. And 1. E. 3. when Richard Clayſeild died,—per ſervie mil. et heriet.

  Inq : 16. Re Caroli, p! morte Johis Trotman, filij Mauricij, fil jun. Willi Trotman blij jun. Johis Trotman.—per ſervie militare. |

                         Inq : 16.

Hurst

Inq: 16. Regis Caroli, p' morte Riči Trotman apud Tetbury: Wardſhip and two heriotts, vt antea.

Alicia de Kingſton aforeſaid, by her deed without date about the end of kinge H. 3, granted to Maurice lord Berkeley and his heires All the ſervices of Robert de Dounton her nephewe and of his heires, of thoſe lands and tenements which ſometimes were Robert de Kingſton's her brother, which are by knight ſervice: ffor which the ſaid lord Maurice paid—5^{li}.

Rot. pateñ 25. E. 1. ps. 2. in dorſo rotuli; Thomas de Kingſton arř aſſiſā verſus Thomā Dñū de Berkeley et al, de 50. acř terre in Slimbridge.

Theis lands called Rivers lands have afforded 10 ſeverall wardſhips to the Lords of the Seignoury ſince I was Steward of this manor of Hurſt; As appeareth in a velam booke in quarto carefully kept by mee: And nowe are the ſeverall inheritances of theis 36. perſons; vz,

Richard Trotman, now in ward, 1640, ſonne of Richard, ſonne of Edward, ſonne of Richard, (of whom, ſee before, fol: 243.) holdeth a meſſuage in Kingſton in the pariſh of Slimbř, with 40. acres of land therto belonginge, mentioned in an office after the death of Richard Trotman the father, found virtute officij in 16. Rē Caroli; ſhewinge alſo how hee bequeathed pte of his lands to 4. of his yonger ſonnes, as followes, fol: 248.

Joſeph Bridger, ſonne of Lawrance Bridger, clarke.

Richard Bower, ſonne of Richard who died in 18° Jacobi, as an Inq: in 2° Caroli ſhewes, ſeiſed of 3. Cottages and 10 acres of land, holden by knight ſervice and heriott, and 8^d ob. rent: which Richard, at the death of his ſaid father, was vnder the age of 9. yeares.

Giles Parke. |

William Eſſington.

Robert ffrape.

John

John Taylor,

Vrian Wife, gen̅.

The heires of Humphrey Taylor,

John Thaier, fonne of John,

Thomas Smyth, fonne of Mathewe, holdeth 2. meſſuages and 2. acres and a quarter in Slimbridge and Came, therto belonginge, peell of theis Rivers lands; holden of the lord Berkeley as of his manor of Hurſt by ſute to his hundred Court of Berkeley from 3. weekes to 3 weekes, and by knight ſervice: ffor which fee a very perticuler and exact office in 15. Caroli, found by himſelfe.

John Lewis,

Edward Bower, |

Arthur Bridger,

Robert Davis holdeth one cloſe of meadowe called Tacheroft containinge 6. acres, and 3. acres of arrable land in the feilds called the Linch and Southworthy, which hee purchaſed of Simon Munden and Richard Munden, to whom Simon Ludby deviſed the fame in fee in 7. R͡e Caroli, havinge formerly purchaſed the fame of John Taylor and Humphrey his fonne, As by office found in 7. Caroli, after the death of the ſaid Simon Ludby appeareth.

William Sheppard in right of Margaret Bromwich his wife, the reverc͠on to

Maurice Edwards,

Guy

Guy Heathfeild tenant by the curtefy after the death of Elizabeth his wife, daughter and

John Ward in right of Edith Davis his wife,

Andrew Pegler,

John Wood,

Thomas Powell, |

Elizabeth, one of the 3. daughters and coheires of Thomas Lucas,

Mathea, one other of the 3. daughters and coheires of Thomas Lucas,

Agnes, one other of the 3. daughters and coheires of Thomas Lucas,

Nathaniell Cowley,

Richard Smyth, clerke, in right of Mary his wife one of the three fifters and coheires of Wiłłm Hardinge, fonne of Richard

Elizabeth, one other of the 3 fifters and coheires of the faid William Hardinge, fonne of Richard,

Sara, one other of the 3 fifters and coheires of the faid Wiłłm Harding fonne of Richard,

Richard

Richard Peglar,

Richard Andrewes,

Thomas ffreame, in right of Alice his wife, daughter and heire of |

Stephen Huntley ats Simonds, fonne of Ambrofe, for

Simon Ludby,

John Ludby, in right of   his wife, daughter

Elizabeth Bower, daughter of

Samuell Trotman, brother and heire of John, fonnes of Maurice Trotman of Bradfton, holdeth one Clofe of meadowe called the breach, containinge 4 acres in Slimbridge, which the faid Maurice by Deed dated 6. Julij. a° 17° R° Jacobi purchafed of the faid Willm Hanis and Thomas his fonne ; ffor which fee an Inq : virtute officij found after the death of the faid Maurice, 9. Aprill. a° 16? R° Jacobi.

William Trotman.   See after, fol : 249, for the 4 fonnes of Richard before mentioned, fol : 244.

Selewins lands in Hurft, pcell of Came, olim Brayfords.

Deere alfo in this Tithinge of Hurft are certaine lands containinge about acres, called Selewins lands, holden of George lord Berkeley as of his manor of Came by knight fervice, heriot fervice, fute of Court, and the yearly rent of—10ˢ yearly paid to that manoʳ of Came, which had from the time of kinge Edward the firft, (if not longe before,) continued by a lineall difcent in the firname of Selewine; whofe longe feizin hath faftened vpon them the comon name of Selwins lands; And were in   Jacobi, aliened by Thomas Selewine, fonne of Richard who died

in

Durst

in   , sonne of Thomas who died in 5ᵗᵉ Eliz., sonne of Richard who died in 25. H. 8, sonne of   who died in   ; And are nowe in aº 1639. the severall inheritances of divers ffreeholders, wherof Edward Trotman of the Middle Temple, a Reader in Court, late held a messuage and 18. acres of the said land in Hurst. And of the said rent of—10ˢ was apportioned to pay—6ˢ 3ᵈ; nowe the inheritance of Beniamin | Bridger, with whom such ancient deeds of this land remaine, as when I once expostulated with the said Thomas Selwine why hee would sell away his lands which soe many ages had continued with his forefathers, Hee replyed Why, what should I keepe such land, when noe man could read my deeds they were growne soe old: And of William Cowley who holdeth a messuage and one acre late by him purchased of John strape, And of the said rent payeth by like apportionment—xᵈ. And of Wiłłm Buddinge who holdeth 3. acres in Cams seild and in Southworthy, And of the said—10ˢ rent paieth—1ᵈ. And of Robert Davis sonne of Thomas Davis, who holdeth 3. acres in Hinworthy seild, and one acre in the Linchseild, and one acre in Cams seild, and of the said rent paieth—4ᵈ. And of Richard Smyth, clerke, in right of Mary his wife, Elizabeth, and Sara, the 3. sisters and coheires of Wiłłm Hardinge, who hold 4. acres of pasture called Hurst leis, and 6. acres in   , and pay—2ˢ 6ᵈ rent soe apportioned; who makes vp the foresaid—10ˢ.

Also one acre of this land was aliened by Richard Selewine to John Trotman *Gylmins land* of Vpthorp in Came, lyinge by Halmers lane in Came; late the land of Wiłłm sonne of Wiłłm Trotman of Wotton by the last Will of Katherine his sister, to whom her husband the said John Trotman by his will devised the same in fee; now the land of

Inq: 9. Caroli, pᵗ morte Thome Davis p̄d. tent p serviᵗ militare, et heriot. See the Court rolls of Came, 25. H. 8., 5. Eliz.

Deere also are certaine lands in Kingston containinge about   acres, nowe the inheritance of   ; lyinge in Kingston, late in the tenure of John Gilmin als Gilman, sonne of John, who died   , sonne of Wiłłm who died   sonne of James who died   , sonne of John who by deed dated 16 Maij, Anno 20. H. 7. purchased the same of John Davis of Dursley, and hee of Wiłłm ffreame, And—

I conceive it to bee truly said by the Inhabitants, That they have two Comons *Woodwards-* within their tythinge, of different conditions; one called the Eylands, reputed as *greene.*
part

part of Slimbridge warth, which will cure rotten sheepe, at leaft make them fat for the butcher : The other called Woodwards greene, that fodainly will rott a found sheepe, at leaft bringe him from a noble to nine pence.

More of ſilvers Lands.

Willm Trotman, fecond fonne of Richard, fonne of Edward, holdeth by the laſt will and Teſtament of the faid Richard his father, dated 7° Julij. 16!º R̃ Caroli. 1640, one meſſuage, cottage, and an orchard adioyninge, called Berrymeads houſe, and two cloſes called berrymeads leies, conī about 6. acres, in Slimbridge, in the tenure of Richard Pegler ; which was deviſed to him in fee ; ffor which fee an Inquiſicōn taken by the Eſcheator at Tetbury, virtute officij fui, 22. die Sept. a° p̃dc̃ō.

John Trotman, third fonne of the faid Richard, fonne of Edward, holdeth by the faid laſt will and teſtament of his faid father, deviſed to him in fee, one tenement or Cottage with an orchard and parcell of paſture ground adioyninge, called Dekins houfe, in Slimbridge aforefaid, nowe in the tenure of John Naſon : ffor which alſo fee the faid Inquiſicōn in Sepī Aº 16. R̃ Caroli, aforefaid. |

Thomas Trotman, 4th fonne of the faid Richard, fonne of Edward, holdeth by the faid laſt will and Teſtament of his faid father, deviſed to him in fee, one tenement or cottage with an orchard adioyninge called Adens houſe, and a fellion or rudge of paſture ground, and one fellion or rudge of arrable land, in Slimbridge aforeſaid, nowe in the tenure of Simon Longe.

And alſo one acre of meadowe ground called Squire acre in Little moore in Slimbridge aforefaid, in the tenure of Stephen Symonds ; ffor which alſo fee the faid Inqu : taken at Tetbury, Aº. 16. R̃ Caroli aforefaid.

Samuell Trotman 5th fonne of the faid Richard, fonne of Edward, holdeth by the faid laſt will and Teſtament of his faid father, which hee deviſed to him in fee ſimple, One parcell of meadowe or paſture ground called Throughbridge, conī about an acre, in Slimbridge aforefaid ; ffor wᶜʰ fee alſo the faid Inquiſicōn taken at Tetbury Aº 16. R̃ Caroli p̃d. ; ffor all which laſt 4 deviſees lands, and for the meſſuage and 40 acres difcended to Richard Trotman, eldeſt fonne of the faid Richard, is paid alſo to the manor of Hurſt the yearly rent of—6ˢ 9ᵈ And to the Manor of Slimbridge the yearly rent of—iijᵈ |

Kingeſcote :

Kingescote.

Kingescote: In Domesdai booke written Chingefcote; wherin Wiłłm the Conqueror had, as that booke fpeaketh, fower hides of land in Demefne; holden of George lord Berkeley as of his manor of Berkeley by halfe a knights fee, and fute to his hundred court of Berkeley from 3. weekes to 3. weekes.

A manor wherof Anthony Kingefcote Efq, is lord, confiftinge of 30 families, In reputačōn a parifh, but re vera a Chaple within the parifh and belonginge to the mother Church of Beverfton; yet vfeth all Eccficall rites there which belonge to a parifh, as to chriften infants, bury the dead, marry, receive the Sacrament, &c. In like fort as at Nibley a Chaple to Wotton; Stincheombe a Chaple to Came; Stone and Hill, Chaples to Berkeley; and fome others in this hundred, without any relation in outward obfervance to thofe their mother churches.

Chaple.

This manor and tithinge of Kingfcote was by kinge H. 2. in the firft yeare of his raigne, given to Robert the fonne of Hardinge and his heires, with many others, then parcell of his Barony of Berkeley; whereof the faid Robert was then by that grant created a Baron of parliament and peere of the Realme, accordinge to the manner of thofe times: wherof I have formerly written in fo. 7. et 78. And in my hiftory bookes of his family in the lives of the faid lord Robert, fol: 60 in my firft daught [draft?]; and in the lives of the lord Robert the fecond, And of the lord Thomas the firft.

Shortly after which grant, the Lord Robert gave this Kingefcote to Nigell the fonne of Arthur, in mariage with Aldena his daughter, To hold of him by halfe a knights fee, which guift the faid kinge Henry the fecond by his deed confirmed; both which I have feene vnder feale with Mr. Anthony Kingefcote: Which Nigell made Combe the Joincture of the faid Aldena, as witneffeth another deed with him.

The faid Nigell and Aldena had iffue betweene them, Adam and Robert: Adam had iffue Richard, who after his fathers death and his owne full age died without iffue, leavinge the faid Robert his vncle to bee his heire; which Robert had iffue Nigell and Richard, To which Nigell and his heires Robert lord Berkeley, the fecond of that name, in the time of kinge R. 1. by the name of Robert de Berkeley, fonne of Maurice, fonne of Robert fonne of Hardinge, confirmed this manor of Kingefcote; which, faith the deed, (which I have feene,) Robert his grandfather

grandfather gave to Nigell his grandfather in mariage with Aldena his daughter: which Nigell afterwards died without iffue, leavinge the faid Richard his brother and heire; Which Richard had iffue Nigell, who died in 12. E. 2. and was father of Willm, father of Nicholas, father of [William] Henry, father of John who died in the life time of his father, leavinge iffue Willm who was ward to William Lord Berkeley, father of William who died in 16. H. 8, and was father of Willm who died in 32. H. 8, and was father of William who died in 25. Eliz., father of Chriftopher who died in 5to Jacobi and was father of the faid Anthony that nowe holdeth the fame, A^o 1639.

q : of this Henry, if any fuch.

I have alfo feene a Deed wherby Maurice de Berkeley, the firft of that name, in the latter end of the raigne of kinge H. 2. confirmed to Adam his nephewe, fonne of Nigell, fonne of Arthur, the Manor of Kingefcote, which Robert the fonne of Hardinge his father, gave to the father of the faid Adam, and to Aldena fifter of him the faid Maurice, To hold of him by halfe a knights fee for all fervices.

Vpon Exchanges of late time made by Chriftopher Kingefcote, fome fmall parts of this manor are nowe the feverall inheritances of Willm Workeman, Richard Heaven, John Waight and |

252 It may be faid of this ancient gentleman and of his family, as doubtles of noe other in this county nor I thinke of many others in this kingdome, That hee and his lineall anceftors have continued in this little manor nowe about 500. yeares, never attainted nor dwellinge out of it elfe where; nor hath the tide of his Eftate higher or lower flowed or ebbed in better or worfe condition; But like a fixed ftarre in his firmament, to have remained without motion in this his little orbe, without any remarkeable change; And as the name of his firft anceftor that is not perifhed, —**Ansgerus**, importeth, is hereditarily a Saxon.

By patent roll 37. H. 3. Barthol de Owlepen ar̄ aſſiſam ve[r]ſus Nigellum de Kingefcote de cõmunia pafture in Kingefcote.

An ancient booke of knights fees with the lord Treaforers Remembrancer in the Exchequer, fol: 337. hath thus; Ricardus de Kingefcote tenet dimidiũ feodum in Kingefcote de Thoma de Berkeley.

By Inquifitõn in 14. E. 1. after the death of Anfelme de Gurney lord of Beverfton it is found, that he died feifed of a yard land and of one wood pertain-inge to Kingefcote, holden of Richard de Kingefcote by the yearly rent of—12^d

The

Kingescote

The payment of the ffifteenth or Kingſilver, goeth togeather in one ſome with Owlpen: The onus or burden of both is—4ˡⁱ 2ˢ ob. The deduction is—18ˢ The Remaine paid into the Exchequer by the Collector is—3ˡⁱ 4ˢ ob. wherof Kingeſcote payeth— . *fifteene*

In the laſt Subſedy in aᵒ 5ᵗᵒ Caroli were 9. ſubſedy men who paid—3ˡⁱ 5ˢ 4ᵈ to the kinge in this tithinge. *Subſedy*

In aᵒ 6ᵗᵒ Regis Jacobi vpon a generall muſter were—33. able men ſerviceable for the warres betweene 20. and 60. yeares old, wᶜʰ ſhewed themſelves before the Lord Leiutenant. *Able men.*

And nowe hath of trayned ſouldiers vnder Edward Stephens Eſq, their captaine, . *Souldiers.*

And if the whole diviſion of Berkeley bee taxed at 100ˡⁱ this hundred of Berkeley payeth thereof—33ˡⁱ 3ˢ And this Tithinge or manor of Kingeſcote—20ˢ. And ſoe after that rate. *Rates.*

Freeholds in the tythinge of Kingeſcote.

Peere is one meſſuage called Bares court, with 12. acres of land therto belonginge, holden of the kinge by knight ſervice in capite, which Henry lord Berkeley by deed dated 10. Junij aᵒ 9ᵗ Rᵗ Jacobi, granted to Willm Shipton and his heires; And was till that time reputed parcell of the ſaid Lords Manor of Wotton fforren: And is nowe, 1639. the inheritance of — *Shiptons land called Barres Court.*

Peere alſo are certaine lands called Redecrofts, lyinge betweene the old Icies and the Larder, containinge acres, now the inheritance of purchaſed of Thorpe by deed in aᵒ ; which had continued in his anceſtors poſſeſſion from the time of E. 1. if not longe before, wherof reade more in Waniſwell: And then were the lands of Thomas de Stone. And by Alice his daughter and coheire came to | John Swonhunger, and ſoe to the name of Thorpe, as there appeares fol: 368. 369. 370. And by 4. other Deeds, which I have ſeene, all without date, Nigell of Kingſcote gave totam illam dimidiam virgatam terræ in territorio de Haſilcote, to Alice his daughter and her heires, Rendringe a roſe for all ſervices, Salvo regali ſervicio, &c. which is knight ſervice. One of which 4. deeds is to her in taile, and are nowe in Berkeley caſtle. *Thorps land nowe*

Lokiers land

By an Inquisicōn in 5º Jacobi, Leonard Lockier is found to dye seized in fee, in aº 3ᵗⁱᵒ Rᵉ Jacobi p̃d, of a messuage and 15. acres of land and 7. acres of pasture in Kingescote, holden of Christopher Kingescote of Kingescote Esq, by the 40ᵗʰ part of a knights fee; And that John Lockier was his sonne and heire 4. yeares old, whose wardship the said Christopher had: And after his full age sold his said lands to Anthony Kingescote aforesaid, sonne and heire of the said Christopher, wherby, the menalty¹ beinge destroied, the said messuage and lands came to bee holden imediately of the said George lord Berkeley, as the rest of that manor is.

Willms dn̄s de Kingescote, by deed in 5. E. 3, released for that yeare to the Abbot of Kingswood vnam saldam ducentas ovium, quas tenebatur invenire super terras p̃dc̃i Willi in campo de Kingescote.

More of this Tithinge or Manor of Kingescote is to bee read in theis Deeds and Records not formerly mentioned.

Diũsæ Cartæ cum Anthonio Kingescote p̃d, a me bis perlectæ.
Diũsæ Cartæ cum Dño Berkeley in castro suo de Berkeley.
Rot. pipæ. 3. R. 1. in scio.
Inq: 15. E. 2. de terris inimicorū d̃ni Regis in com̃ Glouc̃.—p servic̃ militare.
Inq: 19. E. 2. p! mortem Nigelli de Kingescote.—p servic̃ mil.
Inq: 16. H. 8. p! mortem Willi Kingescote.—p servic̃ mil.
Inq: 32. H. 8. p! mortē Willi Kingescote. p servic̃ mil.
Rot. finiū. 23. H. 8. Terñi pasche. Rot. 2. Glouc̃ c̃m Reñi Thesaur̃ in scio.—p dimid feodi militis.
Michas Rec̃. 7. Eliz. Rot. 66. c̃m Reñi Thesaur̃ in scio., which is instar omnia for the tenure:—p servic̃ militare.
Triñ Records. 33. Eliz. Rot. 105. in scio, c̃m Reñi Thesaur̃.
Inq: 37. E. 3. in scio de feodis ptinen̄ ad mansium de Berkeley.—p quartā pte feodi militis.
Hillar̃ Record. 28. H. 8. in scio, cñi Reñi Thesaur̃—p servic̃ mil.

Liber

¹ Halliwell gives as the meaning of *Menaltie*: "the middle classes of people," and cites the following passage from Hall's Chronicle in illustration: "Which was called the Evyll Parliamente for the nobilitie, the worse for the *menaltie*, but worste of all for the commonaltie."

Du Cange, however, explains *Menalgium* as "military service with a horse." It must be used in this sense by Smyth. By the sale of the land by John Lockier to the Lord of Kingscote the service of the 40ᵗʰ part of a knight's fee, by which it was held ceased, or, in Smyth's words, was "destroied," for the Lord of Kingston would render no greater service to the Chief Lord than he did before. Smyth should have written *mesualty*. [ED.]

Liber feodo$ in Sĉcio c̃m Reñi Thefaur̃ temp: E. 1. fol: 337. ibm. p dimid feodi mittis.

Carta in caſtro de Berkeley, 13. E. 4. A wardſhip had and granted to Nicholas Bay clerke. |

254 blank

Kingesweston.

Kingesweston: In the booke of Domefdei written **Westone**, wherin Willm the Conqueror had (as that booke faith) 7 hides and one yard land; holden of the Crowne by knight fervice in Capite, And now the inheritance of Sir John Wintour of Lidney, knight, fonne of Sir Edward Wintour, fonne of Sir Willm Wintour vice-Admirall of England, who in the 12ᵗʰ yeare of Queene Eliz. purchafed the fame of Sir Richard Berkeley of Stoke Gifford knight; And lyeth within the parifh of Henbury: Of which family of the Wintours, See before in fol: 226.

This manor of Wefton nowe altogether called Kingefwefton was by kinge H. 2. in the firſt yeare of his raigne granted (amongſt others,) to Robert the fonne of Harding and his heires, then parcell of the great manor of Berkeley, and paffed vnder the words in that kings grant of **Berkelei herneſſe**, as beinge one of the nookes or corners thereof, neere to the vtter bounds of this county of Glouc̈. not farre from the paffage over the river of Hungrode called Crock and pill, leadinge into Somerfetfhire.

Shortly after which grant of kinge H. 2. to the faid Robert the fonne of Harding, hee conveyed the fame with the manor of Beverſtone to Robert his third fonne and his heires, who was comonly written Robertus filius Roberti filij Hardingi, and fomtimes Robert lord of Were, because his dwellinge was for moſt part at Were neere Axbridge in the county of Somerfet; which Robert de Were had iffue Maurice and Eve, and died in temp: Johis. The faid Maurice was comonly called Maurice de Gant, and died without iffue in 14. H. 3. leavinge this manor with many others to difcend to the fonne of the faid Eve his fifter, who was maried to

Gurnay and died in temp: H. 3. before her brother; Between whom was iffue Robert de Gurnay who died in 53. H. 3. leavinge iffue Anfelme de Gurnay who died in 14. E. 1. leavinge iffue John de Gurnay who died in 19. E. 1. leavinge iffue Elizabeth his only daughter and heire, maried to Sir John ap Adam knight, betweene whom was iffue Sir Thomas ap Adam; In what yeare the faid Elizabeth

died

died I have not obferved, but the faid Sir John her hufband died in 5. E. 2. to both whom the faid Sir Thomas ap Adam was fonne and heire, who in 4. E. 3. fold this manor of Kingefwefton, with the other of Elberton (whereof I have already written in fol: 182.) to Sir Maurice Berkeley knight; who leaft iffue Sir Thomas Berkeley called of Ewley, who had iffue Sir Maurice, father of Sir Maurice, father of Sir Wiłłm, father of Richard, father of Sir John, father of Sir Richard Berkeley who in 12º Eliz. fold this manor to Sir Wiłłm Wintour as aforefaid ; Of which difcent fee before alfo in Beverfton fol: 97. and in Ewley, fol: 185. 192. which againe to expreffe (as there) in pticuler is needles.

Rot. pateñ. 4. E. 3. pars. 1. membr. 7. fhewes that kings Licence granted to Sir Maurice Berkeley to demife his lands in Kingefwefton and Ailberton, to his tenants, for yeares or lives.

Placita in banco. Hill: Terñi 10. H. 3. Rot. 7. Johes Cordwainer et Wiłłus filius Adami, appo: fe verfus Johem de Sautemerfh filium Simonis, pro manerio de Weftun: which I take to bee this.

By Inq: after the death of Katherine lady Berkeley in 9. R. 2. it is found, That fhee died feifed for life of a meffuage and a carucate of land in Kingefwefton, holden of Sir John Thorpe knight, as of his manor of Kingefwefton, by knight fervice; which Sir John Thorpe was fecond hufband to | Katherine Berkeley of Stoke Gifford, widowe of Sir Thomas Berkeley, who held in Joincture the faid manor of Kingfwefton. Which Katherine died in 11. R. 2. and John Berkeley knight was her fonne and heire; which is foe likewife found to bee holden after the death of the faid Sir John Berkeley by Inq: in 6. H. 6. But in 38. H. 6. after the death of Sir Maurice Berkeley fonne of the faid Sir John, And in 14. E. 4. after the death of Sir Maurice his fonne and heire, And in 2. H. 7. after the death of Sir Wiłłm Berkeley his fonne and heire, the faid meffuage and carucate of land is found to bee holden in Soccage; which nowe is the freehold of   Hort and others, lyinge in Lawrence Wefton.

fifteene.   The payment of the ffifteenth or Kingefilver in this manor goeth with Elberton in all Exchequer Accompts, in one fome togeather ; The onus of both is—10ˡⁱ. 14ˢ. ob. q. The deduction is—26ˢ. 8ᵈ. The remaine paid by the Collector into the Exchequer is—9ˡⁱ 7. 4ᵈ. ob. q.

Subfedy.   In the laft Subfedy in aº 5ᵗᵒ Regis Caroli were in this townfhip 13. fubfedy men, who paid to the kinge—5ˡⁱ 5ˢ 4ᵈ

In

Kingeswood—Lorrenge

In aᵒ 6ᵗᵒ Jacobi regis vpon a generall muster were of able men, which out of this townshipp appeared before the Lord Lieutenant, fitt for warres betweene 20 and 60 yeares old,—24. — Able men.

And now hath of trayned Souldiers vnder Thomas Chester Esq, their captaine,— Souldiers.

And if the wholl Divition of Berkeley bee taxed towards any rate at —100ˡⁱ. This Hundred paies thereof—33ˡⁱ 3ˢ. And this Kingfweston—20ˢ, and foe after that rate. — Rates.

More of this Township and Manor of Weston, als Kingsweston, is to bee read in Beverston, and in theis records, viz⁴,

Inq : 53. H. 3. p̄ mortē Robti de Gurnay.
Inq : 14. E. 1. p̄ mortē Anselmi de Gurnay.
Inq : 21. E. 3. p̄ mortē Mauriē filij Mauricij de Berkeley.
Inq : 29. E. 3. p̄ mortē Thomæ Berkeley de Ewley.
Inq : 35. E. 3. p̄ mortē Thome Berkeley de Ewley.
Inq : 35. E. 3. p̄ mortē Thomæ Dñi Berkeley.
Inq : 9. R. 2. p̄ mortē Katherine Berkeley vid de Beverston.
Inq : 11. R. 2. p̄ mortē Katherine Berkeley de Stoke.
Inq : 2. H. 4. p̄ mortē Mauricij Berkeley.
Inq : 9. H. 5. p̄ mortē Johannæ Berkeley.
Inq : 6. H. 6. p̄ mortē Johannis Berkeley.
Inq : 4. E. 4. p̄ mortē Mauricij Berkeley.
Inq : 5. H. 8. p̄ mortē Riči Berkeley.
Inq : 37. H. 8. p̄ mortē Johis Berkeley.

Kingeswood.

See in Caldecote. fol : 121. 122. |

Lorrenge.

Lorrenge, als Lorwinch ; Is a farme house neere Berkeley heath of 120ˡⁱ value p ann, nowe the inheritance of Thomas Hodges, sonne of Thomas, holden of the kinge by knight service in Capite ; which paies to Leonard Stanley all rates and dues

dues taxed for the vfe or benefit of the Church or poore there, And all other payments to Came and Bradſton, in which two tithings the grounds belonginge to this farme doe lye.

Anciently this farme was parcell of the Manor of Berkeley, and vnder the name of Came paſſed by the grant of kinge H. 2. to Robert the ſonne of Hardinge and his heires, in the beginninge of that kings raigne; By the death of Robert in 17. H. 2. it diſcended to the lord Maurice his ſonne and heire, By whom it was converted into an hofpitall, called the maſter and brethren of Lorwinge: In whoſe deed of foundation hee expreſſed that hee did the fame for the profperity and foules health of his two younger ſonnes, Thomas and Maurice; Which Thomas, by the death of Robert eldeſt ſonne of the ſaid Lord Maurice without iſſue, cominge to bee Lord Berkeley, hee about 9. H. 3. five yeares after the death of the ſaid Lord Robert, gave the ſaid hofpitall or ffarme of Lorwenge to God and to the Abbot of S! Peter of Gloũ, as beinge pryor of the church of S! Leonard of Stanley, and to the monkes of Gloũ. there ſervinge God: In which condition it continued till the diſſoluc̃on of that monaſtery in 31. H. 8. when cominge to the Crowne, that kinge, ſhortly after granted the fame (inter alia) to Sir Anthony Kingſton and his heires: ffrom him it came to Willm Stumpe father of Sir James Stumpe; And from him to Elizabeth his daughter and heire, maried to Sir Henry Knevet, And from them to M! Wikes, and from him to John Windoe th'elder, father of John Windowe; and from him to Sir John Pointz of Acton, who fold the fame to Sir John Spenſer[1] an Alderman of London, whoſe daughter and heire [Elizabeth] was maryed to [Sir William Compton] Lord Compton, created Earle of Northampton, who fold the fame to Sir George Snygge one of the Barons of the Exchequer, who gave the fame to Anne his daughter, who dyinge without iſſue gave it to her fiſter, maried to Thomas Hodges, And from her, to Thomas Hodges her ſonne and heire aforeſaid.

Out of which, or rather out of a ground containinge 10. acres and an halfe called Manland, of old occupied therwith, the lord Berkeley hath a cheife rent of— 12ᵈ. reſerved by a Deed without date made by Thomas lord Berkeley the firſt of that name to the Abbot and Covent of S! Peter of Gloũ, Pryor of Stanley, with a clauſe of Diſtres (if vnpaid) in any of the lands belonginge to this farme of Lorwinge; Which by negligence hath not byn received for 50. yeares laſt paſt.

By

---

[1] Sir John Spenſer was Lord Mayor of London in the 36ᵗʰ of Elizabeth and was emphatically ſtiled *the rich Spenſer*. [Ed.]

By an Inq: in 6. E. 6. after the death of Willm Stumpe, this farme is found to bee holden by knight service in Capite, And James Stumpe knight to bee his sonne and heire, 33. yeares old.

By an Inquisiçõn in 5ᵗᵒ Eliz: pars. 1. after the death of the said Sir James Stumpe knight, this farme and divers lands in Clinger als Cleihunger, wherof hee dyed seized, are found to bee holden by knight service in Capite ; And that Elizabeth the wife of Sir Henry Knevett is his daughter and heire, 20. yeares old.|

By an Inq: in 30ᵒ Eliz: John Windowe th'elder is found to dye seized of this farme of Lawrenge, and of those lands in Clinger which hee purchased of Mr Wikes ; And that John was his sonne and heire, 7. yeares old. See in Wanisfwell. fol: 382. |

Longbridge.

Longbridge ; is a Chaple and pryory at the north end of Berkeley towne, but without the fame, from which that part of Berkeley called to this day Longbridge streete, tooke name ; founded by Maurice lord Berkeley the first of that name in the later end of the raigne of kinge Henry the second, and seemes to have taken that name from a longe wooden bridge which bounded the ground wherin this little Chapple and Priory stood, towards the west : In place whereof is a large causway nowe cast vp pitched with Stone : And the place it selfe where the Chaple and pryory stood, (whereof I have neere 46. yeares since seene some part standinge,) is nowe plaine and fruitfull meadowe ground ; whereof havinge written at large in the life of that Lord Maurice in my manuscript history of the family of the Berkeleis,[1] I will heere confine my selfe with this abstract ; That it beinge suppressed by the Statute of 1. E. 6. it was by the Lres Patents of Queene Elizabeth dated 31. Decembr. aᵒ r̄ni sui 4ᵗᵒ granted to Sir Edward Warner knight and his heires ; wherin it is recited how the said Queene by her former Lres patents dated 15. Sept. aᵗ 3ᵗⁱᵒ had granted the same to Ralph Sheldon and the said Sir Edward Warner and their heires. By the name of all that pryory free chappell or hospitall of Longbridge., in Longbridge. Slimbridge, Dursley, Nibley, Came, Arlingham, and Berkeley, in the county of Glouc̃, To hold of the Manor of Eastgreenwich in free and comon Soccage : All which the said Sir Edward Warner by his deed inrolled in the Chancery

---

[1] See "Lives of the Berkeleys," Vol. I., pp. 69 et seq. [ED.]

Chancery dated 10. Januarij aº 4ᵗʰ Eliz: ſd, fold to Nicholas Purſloe and Willm Buckbert and their heires; And they by like deed inrolled, dated the 23ᵗʰ day of the fame month, fold to Richard Denys Eſqʳ, and his heires, who after aliened the fame to the feverall leſſees and occupiers thereof, and their heires; And is nowe the land of 14 feverall perſons, wherof my ſelfe, for a wood called Ewcombs hill or veombs wood in Nibley, am one; Richard Browninge for the large paſture grounds in or neere Halmer called Pryors wood, is another; And John Atwood, for the Scite place of the hoſpitall or Pryory, is an other. And what remained of the ſtones of this Chaple and hoſpitall (of any worth,) vncaried away by others, Henry lord Berkeley about the 20ᵗʰ yeare of Queene Eliz: bought, wherwith hee built the arched ſtone bridge leadinge into the firſt gate of Berkeley caſtle, where a wooden drawbridge was before.

title **The** Stile of the Warden or Cuſtos of this pryory, in their deeds and leaſes, were ffrater A. cuſtos et prior hoſpitalis ſc̃æ Trinitatis de Longbridge extra Berkeleiam, et eiuſdem loci fratres et ſorores, ſalutem.

And heere the place invites mee, once for all, to ſhewe That in theis ancient daies the greateſt perſonages held Monkes, fryars, and Nunnes, in ſuch veneration and likinge for their holynes, That they thought noe Citie in caſe to flouriſh, noe houſe likely to have longe continuance, nor Caſtle ſufficiently defenſed, where was not an Abby, priory, or Nunnery, either placed within the walles, or planted at hand and neere adioyninge; As this lord Maurice in this place, as ſoone as at firſt hee came to dwell at Berkeley caſtle; And his father the lord Robert, at Sᵗ Auguſtines by Briſtoll, where hee then dwelt, founded that Monaſtery cloſe therto; And others of their poſterity (with others) abundantly doe witneſſe, wherof in their lives I have more largely written: But nowe, Tempora mutantur et nos mutamur in illis. |

260 blank

Nibley.

Nibley, als **Northnibley,** diſtinguiſhed by the Northerly ſituatiõn therof from a little hamblet or village of the ſame name in the pariſh of Weſterley, lyinge ſouth from this.

Not to deſcribe this village, And withall not to ſpeake of the ſituation of the Chaple heere, not more pleaſantly ſeated on a comely hill then healthfull, then wᵗʰ
none

Nibley

none in the county or scarce in the kingdome standeth in a sweeter aire, insomuch as some of the most expert inhabitants sticke not to affirme their knowledge of divers persons which have byn longe visited with sicknes, not curable with phisicke, to have repaired their health by that sweete salutary aire; vpon which the hope of Sir Thomas Berkeley, then sonne and heire of Henry lord Berkeley, by the advice of his learned phisitions, fetched from Bath, and other remote places, was founded, when in the nynth yeare of kinge James hee removed from Berkeley castle to my house not farre from this Chaple church of Nibley: I say, not to describe this Chaple village and mother church of Wotton somwhat more perticulerly then others, were ingratefully to passe by the place where by the blessed providence of the guider of all men I have byn more then 40. yeares seated, and am nowe drawinge on the last scene of my life in the 72th yeare of my age; And not to acknowledge the great mercies which the Almighty hath in this place powred vpon mee, with a posterity of 21. derived from mee, would bee the neglect of an ingratefull and evill man.

Nibley, therfore, anciently written Nubbelei, Nubbeleigh, Nubeleḡ, and Nibeleigh, quasi (if descant vpon the name may bee allowed,) Cloudwater, or obscure place; An etymology (if one) agreeable to the springes and water heere and their covert scituation; Is a village or hamblet of 162 houses, wherin are livinge about—1000. soules; A member and parcell of the manor of Wotton als Wotton sorren, or Wotton sorinseca, And the principall of those five hamblets which make that manor: the inheritance of George Lord Berkeley, and parcell of his Barony and manor of Berkeley, holden of the Crowne by knight service in Capite.

Nibley, in comon country reputation is a parish, vsually called the pish of Nibley; But, re verá, it is a Chapple belonginge to the mother church of Wotton, and within that parish; though soe free a Chaple in practice and vse, that in it are vsed all ecclieall rites, in christnings maryages, receivinge the Comunion burialls and the like, without any relation to Wotton at all in outward semblance; wherof see more in sol: 294.

The Tyth of this village, and whatsoever of what kinde soever that hath byn or is accompted divine or spirituall, (as also that of Wotton,) belongeth to Christ church colledge in Oxford, who in their Indentures of demise accustome to take a Covenant from the lessee for the time beinge, to provide for the cure heere, And to

pay

pay him $8^{li.}$ p ann; Which poore falary or wages was about 26. yeares laft paft, by the peticōn of the inhabitants heere, vpon the tenants next renewing of his Leafe, made—10^{li}; And within 7. yeares nowe paft, by the like peticōn, or clamor rather, of the inhabitants heere, (feconded alfo with the lres of the Lord bifhop of the Dioceffe,) was vpon another renewinge of the tenants leafe, made,—13^{li} 6^{s} 8^{d}; both which had my beft furtherance, but not—j^{d} from the colledge; and hope to fee it further increafed.

And for this poore daughters fake, the Chaple of Nibley, I will in this place (though more proper to have come in in Wotton) inlarge my felfe to write of her mother, the Rectory or mother church of Wotton her felfe, how fhee hath walked in the world, and in what families made her abodes; As firft, and of old, till the raigne of kinge Edward the Confeffor, with the Abbeffe and Nunnes of Berkeley, Next with Earle Goodwin and his fonne kinge Harrold, from the | fuppreffion of that Nunnery, by the wily practice of that Earle (wherof I have formerly written, fol: 2. et 3,) vntill kinge Harold was flaine in battell by William Duke of Normandy called the Conqueror: ffrom which time it abode in the Crowne, and with the family of the Berkeleis of Durfley, who held the fame with many other Rectories, Churches, and Manors in fee farme at—500^{li} rent by the yeare, vnder the two Williams, Henry the firft, and part of the raigne of kinge Stephen; At what time, and efpetially in the firft yeare of kinge Henry the fecond, it fetled by that kings grant, with the whoíl Manor and hundred of Berkeley, in Robert the fonne of Harding and his heires; Vpon whofe foundinge of the monaftery of St Auguftines by Briftoll, it came to the Abbot and covent therof by the guift of the faid Lord Robert, with all other the churches and chaples of that manor and hundred.

In the age next after, this church of Wotton by the death of the Incumbent becometh void; The Abbot thervpon prefents one William Clarke to the Bifhop of Worcefter, (at that time in the Dioces of Worc^r.,) whom the Bifhop admits to this church and to the chaples of Nibley and Symondfall belonging therto, vpon condicōn that hee fhould duringe his incumbency pay an yearly pention of three markes out of the fame to the faid Abbot and covent his patrons.

Not longe after, the faid bifhop of Worcefter (to vfe the words of his owne deed) takinge into his confideracōn the honeft converfation of the faid Abbot and his covent, and of the poverty of their monaftery, and of their diligent care, afwell in receivinge of ftrangers as in nourifhinge of poore people, doth take their wholl houfe house churches, and ecclesiasticall goods into his protection; And to the end that the benefits of Charity which from the firft foundation of their houfe have byn beftowed on them, might more abundantly to Gods honour bee dilated, (as hee in this his deed faith,) doth by his Epifcopall authority grant vnto them, that they may convert to their owne proper vfe the fruits of the churches of Berkeley Wotton Almondefbury and Afhelworth, for the fuftentation of the faid Abbot and Covent, receivinge of guefts, and releife of poore people; Savinge alwaies the dignity of his church of Worcefter, and honeft fuftention of the Vicars fervinge in the faid churches: And foe it feemes in that condition to have continued till 35. E. 1, what time Edmond the Abbot of that monaftery, by two deeds, granted and releafed to Thomas then lord Berkeley and to Maurice his fonne and heire apparant, and to their heires, the Advowfon of this Church of Wotton with the rights and appurtenants therof; wherby it became again prefentable in the hands of this Berkeleian family; but by what art or devife in the lawes I knowe not, neither doe I knowe what effect followed vpon the licence of kinge E. 2. which in the 5th yeare of his raigne hee granted to the Abbot of this Monaftery to appropriate this church of Wotton, As by the Patent roll of that yeare, pars. 1. membr. 22, appeareth: Nor what followed vpon the Inquifiçõn of Ad quod damnum in 3. E. 2. numero. 16. when the Jury vpon that writ prefented, That it would not bee to the kings damage if hee granted Licence to this Abbot and Covent to appropriate to their owne vfe the Church of Wotton, which is de advocatione fuâ propriâ, And foe appropriated, To hold to them and their fucceffors, And that it valueth p anñ— 20. mks: Neither can I handfomly | reconcile theis Deeds and Records, feeminge thus to quarrell one at another: And alfo the fine roll, A° 5. E. 2. fhewes, That the Abbot then made ffine with the kinge for 50. mks paid to him for his licence to appropriate this church of Wotton: It feemes nothinge; ffor, from that Maurice who furvived his father this Advowfon with the Chaples therto belonginge difcended to Thomas his fonne, father of Maurice, father of Thomas, who in 5. H. 5. was with the lady Margaret his wife, buried in that church: ffrom which Thomas it came to James lord Berkeley, his brothers fonne and heire male, by vertue of a ffine levied in 23. E. 3. Which James had iffue Wittm and Maurice: (of his other 2. fonnes I have noe need to fpeake;) which William was created Marques Berkeley, and died without iffue in 7. H. 7. havinge in the third yeare of that kings raigne, by a fyne then levied, conveyed the manor of Wotton with this advowfon, for want of iffue of his owne body, to that kinge and to the heires males of his body, with remainder to his owne right heires; At what time and for divers years after one Robert Logge was Incumbent and parfon there.

Thus

Thus stood this Advowson in the time of kinge H. 7. for 12. yeares after the death of the said Marques Berkeley, till the 19th yeare of the said kinge. The 17th of March in which 19th yeare of H. 7. Maurice Lord Berkeley brother and heire of the said Marques Berkeley exhibites his petition of right to that kinge, prayinge therin that Justice and right may bee done vnto him, and hee restored to this Advowson: And for his title therto layeth downe the said ffyne levied therof (inter alia) in 23. E. 3. by his ancestor the lord Thomas Berkeley aforesaid, deductinge downe that estate tayle to his brother the Marques and himselfe, shewinge howe vpon the death of his said brother, hee was remitted to his eigne[1] estate taile, to him and to the heires males of his body; Wherupon, after all theis conveyances had by Inquisicōn by Jury in this County of Glouc̄ beene found, hee was by Judgement in June followinge, restored to this Advowson; And the same by act of parliament the same yeare confirmed with other manors to him accordingly.

And nowe beinge thus seized of this Advowson, and consequently of her two Chaples aforesaid, Hee the said Lord Maurice Berkeley, accordinge to Covenants which the 16th day of March before had byn made betweene him and his 2. sonnes Maurice and Thomas on the one part, And the Abbot and Convent of the Monastery of Tuexbury on the other part, for the assuringe of this church of Wotton to that Monastery before the 13th of July then next followinge, They imediately vpon this restitution assure the same accordingly: And noe sooner was the Monastery of Tuexbury thus seised therof, but they forthwith found meanes to incorporate the same and appropriate it to the feedinge of themselves, as the composition for endowinge of the vicaridge declares; what time—20. m̃ks p ann̄ therby appointed was thought a competent maintenance and livinge for the Vicar, to bee paid in fruits and not in money, as nowe it is and hath ever since beene: Howbeit I nowe vnderstand as I am in reviewe heerof, That John Ackson Vicar of Wotton hath by questioninge of his patrons the Colledge of Christchurch, and Margaret Bodle widowe their tenant, obtained vpon an agreement in the end of those sutes to have his 20. marks per Ann̄ increased to neere—35[li], with the addition of an house also, which before hee and his predecessors vicars wanted.

Note by the way, that the plea of Maurice lord Berkeley for this advowson is entred in Termi Michis, 20. H. 7. Rot. 532. and the recovery of the | Advowson is entred of Trinity terme, 20. H. 7. Rot. 525. in banco c̄oi.

The Abbot and Covent of Tuexbury, havinge thus appropriated this faire advowson (at this day worth—400[li] p ann̄, with her Chaples,) did for the first 25. yeares

Eigne=Eldest. [ED.]

yeares after lett to the vicar whom they had placed both the appropriate rectory and vicarage, at 33ˡⁱ rent p annū de claro, to bee paid to their Monastery; And after by their Indenture dated, 10ᵒ Decembr̃. 23ᵗⁱᵒ H. 8. demised the same to Thomas Matson and Thomas Hollister for 30. yeares, at the said yearly rent of—33ˡⁱ. And to pay to the vicar there—13ˡⁱ 6ˢ 8ᵈ by the yeare, (which then was one — Gunne,) and not in fructibus, in fruites, as the composition at first was; And to pay also to the Chaplein ministringe in the Church of this Nybley his stipend; And to two deacons ministringe in the Church of Wotton and of Nibley their stipends.

Thus stood this Church of Wotton with her Chaples, 8. yeares after the makinge of the said Lease to Matson and Hollister, vntill in 31. H. 8. that Monastery was dissolved and by Act of parliament given to the Crowne, As the Accompts of the Court of Augmentation doe shewe; And then the 11ᵗʰ day of December 38. H. 8. that kinge by his Lr̃es patents of that date, (but 6. weekes before his death,) gave the same to the Deane and Chapter of the Cathedrall church of Christ in Oxford, of the said kings foundation, By the name of all that Rectory and church of Wotton subedge, with all the rights and appurtenants therof to the late monastery of Tuexbury in the county of Glouc̃ late belonginge and appertaininge; And all messuages, lands, tenements, Rents, services, &c. in Wotton, Nibley, wortley, Symondsfall, Synwell and Combe, in the said county, aswell spirituall as temporall, to the said Rectory vicarage and manor belonginge, or as member part or parcell of the same, before knowne, accepted, reputed, demised or letten beinge.

In the yeare 1554. in 1ᵒ et 2ᵒ Ph: & Mar̃. James, Bishop of Glouc̃, admitted Robert Knight to the Rectory of Wotton vpon the p̃sentacõn of Henry lord Berkeley, patron thereof.

In 3ᵒ Eliz. two yeares before the lease ended made to the said Matson and Hollister, (till when the question about this church had continued,) Henry lord Berkeley impleaded the said Deane and Chapter for that Rectory, who in the yeare followinge came to a composition, wherby the Deane and Chapter granted to the said Lord Henry and his heires the Advowson of the vicaridge of Tetbury, somtime belonginge to the monastery of Eyntham in the county of Oxford, vpon condicõn that they might quietly hold this rectory of Wotton; whervpon the said Lord made to them further assurance, And acknowledged netitheles that they had good right to this of Wotton by the grant of the said Lord Maurice his ancestor made to the Abbot of Tuexbury as aforesaid, and himselfe to have noe right at all. Vpon

the

the expiraĉon of Matson and Hollisters lease, the deane and chapter parted the same into two leases, one made to George Dunnynge of Nybley, of the Chaple and tythes of Nibley for 60. yeares, dated 5º Decembř. aº 5º Eliz., and the other lease to Bedle, of the Rectory of Wotton and tythes within the residue of that parish: In which condition by other severall leases since made the same continue to this day 1639.

Pĺita coram rege apud Glouĉ, Triñ. 21. R. 2. Ecclesia de Wotton vnderegge vel vnderhegge, cognoscitur per vtrumq̨ nomen per veredicĩ Jurado₂. And the parliamᵗ roll, in 1. H. 4. numero. 91. containeth a notable processe which seemes to pursue the foresaid verdict, betweene Wiłłm Seward als Chedder parson of Wotton vnderedge, and John Dantree clerke, wherin | appeares that Seward after five yeares possession lost his parsonage and incumbency, vpon difference of the word (vnderhegg) for Wotton vnderegge, and Dantree was admitted: But nowe by Judgement in parliament, Seward was restored againe and Dantree put out.

<small>Nybley greene.</small>

The Greene called Nybley greene, a Comõn or parcell of wast ground containinge about 100. acres, is famous to this day for the incounter that was in 10. E. 4. betweene Thomas Talbot viscont Lisley and Wiłłm Lord Berkeley and their fellowships: The ground of their quarrell thus arose;

Thomas Lord Berkeley the 4ᵗʰ of that name died in 5. H. 5. leavinge issue one only daughter called Elizabeth, maried to Richard Beauchamp Earle of Warwicke, by whom hee had issue three daughters, Margaret Eleanor and Elizabeth, who pretended title (amongst other lands) to the Manor of Wotton, with the Advowson; And which in partition amongst [them] in 6. E. 4. was allotted to the said Margaret, who was maried to John Talbot Earle of Shrewsbury, beinge his second wife, by whom hee had issue John Talbot viscont Lisle, who had issue the said Thomas Talbot viscont Lisle: Against whom the said Wiłłm lord Berkeley made title as heire male to the said Thomas lord Berkeley, as sonne of James lord Berkeley, sonne of Sir James Berkeley brother of the said lord Thomas, by vertue of an entayle created by his grandfathers fine levied in 23. E. 3.

The said Thomas Talbott viscont Lisle at this time lived at Wotton, at the manor house by the Church there, And Wiłłm lord Berkeley in his castle of Berkeley five miles of; Betweene whom and their servants were often quarrellings, which in the end drewe from the said viscont Lisle a Letter of Challenge, written to the said Lord Berkeley, in theis words, vz;

William,

William, called **Lord Berkeley**, I marveile yee come not fourth with all your carts of gunnes, bowes, with oder ordinance, that yee fet forward to my manor of Wotton to beate it doune vpon my head: I lett you witt ye fhall not nede to come foe nye, for I truft to God to mete yee neere home with Englifhmen of my one nation and neighbors; wheras yee by fubtile craft have blowen about in divers places of England that I fhould intend to bringe in Welfhmen for to deftroy and hurt my one nation and country; I lete the wite I was never foe difpofed nere never will bee; And to the proofe heerof I require the of knighthode and of manhode to appoint a day to mete halfe way, there to try between God and our two hands all our quarrell and title of right, for to efchewe the fhedding of chriften mens bludd, or elfe at the fame day bringe the vttermoft of thy power and I fhall mete thee: An anfwere of this by writinge, as yee will abide by, accordinge to the honour and order of knighthood.

Thomas Talbot, ye vifcont Lifle.

To which Lfe fent the 19th day of March in the Tenth yeare of kinge Edward the fourth, A^o Dñi. 1469, the Lord Berkeley the fame day returned this Anfwere; |

Thomas Talbot otherwife called Vifcont Lifle, not longe continued in that name but a newe found thinge brought out of ftrange cuntries; I marveile greatly of thy ftrange and leude writinge, made I fuppofe by thy falfe vntrue counfell that thou haft with thee, Hugh Mull, and Holt: As for Hugh Mull, it is not vnknowne to all the worfhipfull learned men of this Realme, how hee is attaint of falfenes and rafinge of the kings records; and as for the falfe mifchevous Holt, what his rule hath bee [?been] to the deftruction of the kings lege people in my Lordfhip of Berkeley, afwell to the hurt of their bodies as the loffe of their goods, againft Goddis lawe confcience and all reafon, it is openly knowne; Soe that every worfhipfull man fhould refufe to have them in his feloufhip; And alfo of his owne free will, vndefired of mee, before worfhipfull and fufficient witnes, was fworne on a maffe booke that hee fhould never bee againft mee in noe matter that I had a doe; And efpetially in that vntrue title that you claime, which ye hold my livelihood with wronge. And where thou requireft mee of knighthood that I fhould appoint a day and meete thee in the midway betweene my manor of Wotton and my caftle of Berkeley, there to try betwixt God and our two hands all our quarrell and title of right, for to efchewe the fcheddinge of chriften mens bludd, or elfe the fame day to bringe the vttermoft of my power and thou wouldft mete mee: As for the determininge betwixt our two hands of thy vntrue clayme and my title and right of my land and true inheritance,

heritance, thou wotteſt right well that there is noe ſuch determinaçõn of land in this realme vſed: And I aſcertaine thee that my lyvelode, as well my manor of Wotton as my caſtle of Berkeley, bee intayled to mee by fyne of record in the kings courts, by the adviſe of all the Judges of this land in that daies beinge; And if it were ſoe That the matter might bee determined by thy hands and mine, the kinge our ſoveraine Lord and his lawes not offended, thou ſhouldeſt not ſoe ſoone deſire but I would aſſoone anſwere thee in every point that belongeth a knight; ffor thou art, God I take to record, in a falſe quarrell, and I in a true defence and title; And where thou deſireſt and requireſt mee of knighthood and of manhood to appoint a day and that I ſhould bee there with all the power I could make, and that thou wouldeſt meete mee halfe way, I will thou underſtand I will not bringe the tenth part that I can make, and I will appoint a ſhort day to eaſe thy malitious heart and thy falſe counſaile that is with thee: ffaile not too morrowe to bee at Nybbeleis greene at 8. or 9. of the clocke, and I will not ſaile with Goddis might and grace to mete thee at the ſame place, the which ſtandeth in the borders of the livelode that thou keepeſt vntruly from mee, ready to anſwere thee in all things, that I truſt to God it ſhall bee ſhewed on thee and thine to thy great ſhame and diſworſhip: And remember thy ſelfe and thy falſe counſaile have refuſed to abide the rule of the great Lordis of this lond, which by my will ſhould have determined this matter by thy evidence and mine: And therefore I vouch God to record, and all the company of heaven, that this fact and the ſcheddinge of chriſten mens bludd wch ſhall bee atwixt vs two and our ſelouſhips, if any hap to bee, doth growe of thy quarrell and not of mee, but in my defence and in eſchuinge of reproach, onely through thy malitious and miſcheivous purpoſe, and of thy falſe counſell, and of thy owne ſimple diſcretion: And keepe thy day, And there the trueth ſhall bee ſhewed by the mercy of God.

William Lord Berkeley. |

267 Both parties keepe their day and place, where the vicont Liſle was ſlaine; Of which incounter and of the numbers of men that either Lord brought that day into the feild, the cuntry people dwellinge therabout, (beinge the children and grandchildren of the groſſe of both Armies on either ſide, with more then 20. of whom fifty yeares agone I have talked heerof,) deliver in wonders: wherof I have more largely written in the hiſtory of this Berkeleian family, treatinge of the life of this Lord William Berkeley, which heere againe to repeate, ſith copies of my three bookes therof are in your hands, ſeemes needleſſe.[1]

In

---

[1] See "Lives of the Berkeleys," Vol. II. p. 111. et ſeq. [Ed.]

Nibley

Springs. In the easterne part of this village of Nybley arise divers springs of excellent sweete water, which vnited and brought into one streame, make a pretty river; wheron are seated seaven tuck mills and grift mills, most of them double mills, before the said streame bee passed through this village; The like wherto I knowe not within this County.

This village is divided into theis parcells or knotts of houses, as beinge remarkeable distinct places; vz ffourd end, Mylend, Horend, fforthay, Southend, Churcend, Woodallend, Swyney, Snytend, Birchley, and the Greene, or Nybley greene men, wherof I have made former mention, besides others of note, which followe.

ffifteene. The payment of the ffifteene or king silver, when it is granted by parliament, goeth with the rest of the manor of Wotton forren, which in the wholl is—13^{li} 12^s 2^d wherof the hamblet of Huntingford payeth—10^s, Bradley 10^s, Simondsall with its hamletts—24^s, Combe—40^s, Synwell—32^s 4^d, Wortley—52^s, Pitcourt alone—10^s, And this Nybley—4^{li} 13^s 10^d. In all—13^{li} 12^s 2^d as aforesaid.

Subsedy. In the last Subsedy in a^o 5to Caroli were 18 Subsedy men in this village, who paid—7^{li} 6^s; wherof my selfe was rated at—12^{li} land, then a Comissioner for the taxinge therof.

Able men. In a^o 6to Jacobi, vpon a generall viewe of able men fitt for the warres betweene 20. and 60. yeares old, were in this village, which then shewed themselves before Henry lord Berkeley, then Lieutenant of the county,—126.

Souldiers. And now of trayned souldiers vnder Thomas Veel Esq. their captaine—20. wherof—10. are corsletts, and—10. are musketts, furnished by the inhabitants therof. And with one light horse called a Curasseire, found and furnished by the author of this description.

And if the whole division of Berkeley, accompted a 4th part of the county, bee taxed at—100^{li} vpon any rate for kinge or Comonwealth, The hundred of Berkeley paieth therof—33^{li} 3^s. And this of Nybley—25^s.

The

Pitcourt.

The ffreeholds in this village are many, and those ancient, wherof 7. carry alonge with them the names of Courts, and were Capitall messuages or manor houses; vz, Pitcourt, Burrowes court, Warrens court, Small combes court, Bassetts court, Huntscourt, and Bellamies place: Of each of which in their order; And after of others.

Pitcourt, (written somtimes Pitcote,) continueth a Manor with a Court baron yearly holden to this day, the inheritance of Anthony Hungerford Esq, extendinge into Nybley, Stinchcombe, Stancombe, Alkington, Huntingford, Symondsale, and the Ridge, wherin yet are three copiholds for lives with widowes estates after their husbands death; but now soe pared that | by his severall sales hee hath made severall freeholders more then himselfe, And in likelihood will not dye seized of the residue that yet remaineth; vz, my selfe, and you my sonne John, Willm Curnocke and John his sonne, Willm Purnell of the little greene, John Purnell of Wike, Thomas Evered of Bradley, Samuell Trotman, Henry Hayward, Gilbert ffreeman of Wike, Christopher Purnell, Thomas May, Thomas Peers, Willm Gibbins of Wotton, Willm Longe, James brother and heire of John Baker of Snytend, Tobias Hatheway for halfe an acre in Westfeild purchased of Willm Purnell, Robert Oldisworth sonne of Edward sonne of Arnold Oldisworth, for a ground called Burrowhill: Willm Trotman of Stancombe for 1. acre and an halfe in Ruckombe close, late peells of Burrowes court, James Gibbes for a cotage and an acre in Wike, And— And is holden of George lord Berkeley as of his Manor of Wotton forren by the third part of a knights fee, sute to his hundred court of Berkeley from three weekes to three weekes, heriot service called a Mountuary, And by the yearly rent of—30ˢ.

This little manor extendinge as aforesaid, was the old inheritance of the ancient family of the Schais, wherof Roger de Schai was one of the 8. noble pledges who in the time of kinge Stephen vndertooke that Roger lord and Baron of Dursley should performe the agreement and Covenants then made at Bristoll, by mediation of the said kinge Stephen and of Henry then Duke of Normandy, after kinge of England by the name of Henry the second, betweene the said Roger and Robert the sonne of Hardinge, wherby the manor and Barony of Berkeley was established vpon the said Robert and his heires; Of whom, and of his discent deduced downe to the nowe lord Berkeley, I have before written fol: 7. et 78. et 209. And the said Agreement see before also fol: 176, and after, 325, in Slimbridge: After which Roger de Schai, it came to the names of Mathew le Schay, and

and of John le Schay, sonne and heire of John Schay, and of Walter his sonne; And after of Thomas Schay, sonne and heire of John Schai, and of others of that name, (though I cañot in a perfect difcent range them,) in which name this manor continued till the time of kinge Edward the fourth, when Walter Schay als Skey leaft iffue one only daughter and heire, called Agnes, maried to Thomas Joachim, and died in 9. H. 8. five yeares after her hufband, leavinge iffue betweene them John Joachim, who died in 22. H. 8. leavinge iffue Elizabeth his only daughter and heire, maryed to Anthony Strange, who died 12. yeares before her hufband in aº   leavinge iffue two daughters, Anne, and Edith; Of whom, Anne was maried to Edmond Wefton and died in 22. Eliz. leavinge iffue Anne, firft maryed to Leonard Ivye and after to John Danvers, by neither of whom fhee had any iffue, and died in   Eliz: The faid Edith the other daughter and coheire of the faid Anthony Strange and of Elizabeth his wife, was maried to Thomas Hungerford who had iffue the faid Anthony that nowe is, 1639. travailinge in the 85th yeare of his age: who alfo by the death of the faid Anne his cozen germane inherited the wholl.

Somewhat more of this little Manor of Pitcourt is to bee read in theis records, which alfo prove the tenure; vz,

  ffinis in banco in Terñi Michis. 27. H. 6. Inter Ricm Tefant et al de mañio de Pitcote, in Nybley, &c. Et al, in 18. E. 4.
  Pafch: Rec̃: 9. H. 7. Rot. 293. in cõi banco.
  Inq: 9. H. 8. p! mortẽ Agnetis vxoris Thome Joachim—Juratores ignoř.
  Hillař Rec̃. 13. H. 8. Rot. 5. c̃m Reñi Thefauř in Sc̃io.
  Inq: 22. H. 8. p! mortem Johis Joachim.—in Soccage.
  Hillař Rec̃. 22. H. 8. Rot. 8. in fc̃io. c̃m Reñi Thefauř.
  Inq: 34. H. 8. p! morte Eliz. Strange.—in Soccage.
  Inq: 34. H. 8 p! morte Anthonij Strange. |
  Pafch: Rec̃. 29. H. 8. Rot. 26. in Sc̃c̃io c̃m Reñi Thefauř.
  Triñ Rec̃. 36. H. 8. Rot. 38. in fc̃io p̃d.
  Pafch: Rec̃: 4. & 5. Ph: & Mař: Rot. 3. in Sc̃c̃io p̃d.—per ferviĉ militare.
  Accompt of Wotton. 23. E. 3. in Berkeley Caftle.—per ferviĉ mil.
  Accompt of Wotton. 10. H. 6. ibm.—per ferviĉ militare.
  Co: Roll of Wotton. 36. H. 6. iba:—per ferviĉ mil. et mountuař, very pfect.
  Co: Roll of Wotton. 4. H. 8. Thomas Skey obijt, good.
  Inq: 16. Caroli, p! mortem Wilti Curnocke.—per ferviĉ mil.
                   Inq: 17.

Inq : 17. Caroli, p̃ mortẽ Joħis Smyth authoris huius libri.—per serviẽ mil.
Inq : 17. Caroli, p̃ mortem.
Inq : 17. Caroli, super Melius Inquirend p̃ mortẽ Joħis Purnell.—per serviẽ mil.

Note, that the occupiers of this manor of Pitcourt have anciently paid to the Abbot of Kingswood, And since the dissolucõn of that monastery to the Crowne, and still doe, the some of—7ˢ conceived by the Kings receivor and Baylies to bee a cheife rent issuinge out of this manor, but is not, but goeth only out of such their lands as lye in Swinhey in Nybley which are nowe the inheritance of Thomas May, Thomas Peirs, John Wilkens, George Longe, Henry Hayward, and others, aº 1640. which they have purchased of the said Anthony Hungerford and Thomas his eldest sonne, and their feoffees, As by the originall Deed with my selfe, wherin the said—7ˢ is reserved, appeareth.

Of which aforesaid purchasers of severall parts of this manor of Pitcourt;
My selfe, and my sonne John, doe hold

Wiłłm Curnocke and John his sonne doe hold, as after in fol : 271, 272, 273, and as after in fol : 270, in Henry Hayward. And for this land fee an office in 16. Rẽ Caroli, after the death of the said William.

William Purnell of the Little greene holdeth a messuage at the bottome of the little greene called Nybley greene, with a grist mill and fullinge mill vnder one roofe neere the same, with   closes of meadowe and pasture containinge about   acres, neere the said messuage, called
which hee purchased of the said Anthony Hungerford and Thomas his sonne in 20º Jacobi, and in his deed of purchase agreed to pay—3ˢ peell of their cheife rent of—30ˢ ; of which hee after vpon his sale of
to John Purnell put over—   of his said rent.

John Purnell of Wike holdeth one close in Clayfeild mead 2. acres., 5. acres of arrable in Redfeild and Baynam feild, A close called Howcroft conĩ. 3. acres, a close called Cresway ground conĩ 2. acres ; A close called Newland conĩ. 1. acre & an halfe, and 1. acre of meade in Clayfeild ; All which hee purchased of the said Anthony Hungerford in fee, in Annis   Regis Caroli, And of the said Cheife rent of—30ˢ paieth—2ˢ |

Thomas

Nibley

Thomas Everod of Bradley holdeth 270

Samuell Trotman of Stancombe holdeth

    Henry Hayward holdeth one clofe of meadowe and pafture ground called great Tidnams, lyinge in Swiney, cont about 6. acres, which hee by deed in 22. Jac purchafed of the faid Willm Curnocke and John his fonne; And they (inter alia) of the faid Anthony Hungerford and Thomas his fonne as aforefaid; and of the cheife rent of—5ˢ which the faid Willm and John by their deed of purchafe from the faid Anthony Hungerford and Thomas his fonne agreed to pay as parcell of their—30ˢ the faid Henry therof by his faid Deed agreed to pay—4ᵈ.

    Gilbert ffreeman of Wike holdeth   acres in Matford mead in the tithinge of Alkington, which hee in Rᵉ   purchafed of the faid Anthony Hungerford, but paieth noe part of the faid cheife rent of—30ˢ.

    Chriftopher Purnell holdeth a Meffuage orchard and garden at ffordend in Nybley, with divers clofes and grounds therto belonginge, called the Penynge, the Combe, a ground by Combe gate, Birchley, greenhincheombe, Harley, Ruydings, Burrowes mead; and of arrable land, vz, 2. acres in Tetcombe, 4. acres in Willefley, 2. acres in Aldercombe, 8. acres in Wincheombe, and 2. acres in Ruydings, which hee with mee   Apr. 10. Caroli purchafed of Anthony Hungerford, And the faid Chriftopher Purnell of mee by releafe in   Caroli; And of the faid cheife rent of—30ˢ payeth—18ᵈ.

    Thomas May of Howley in Nybley holdeth one clofe of pafture called the grove cont 6. acres., a meadowe called Wickley cont one acre and an halfe., and a ground called the Penynge cont 5. acres, all lyinge in Swiney; And which in aᵒ Caroli Rᵉ hee purchafed of the faid Anthony Hungerford; And of the faid cheife rent of—30ˢ payeth—6ᵈ.

    Thomas Peirs holdeth halfe an acre in Slades next the hedge, and 5. acres late arrable in the Deane feild, and 3. clofes called Buttefcrofts in Swyney; And an houfe orchard and garden, and a clofe adioyninge in ffortʰay cont 2. acres; And one acre more in the faid Deane feild, and 2. acres more of arr in Slades; All   which

which hee purchased of the said Anthony Hungerford in a°   Regis Caroli ; And of the said cheife rent of—30ˢ paieth 12ᵈ.

William Gibbens of Wotton holdeth one acre and an halfe in Bournfeild of arr̄ land, which hee in A° Rꝫ Caroli purchased of the said Anthony Hungerford, And of the said Cheife rent of—30ˢ payeth 6ᵈ.

William Longe, sonne of George, holdeth one close of pasture in Tetcombe feild cont̄ 1. acre, which hee purchased of the said Anthony Hungerford, And of the said cheife rent of—30ˢ paieth—   ; wᶜʰ was purchased in A°   Caroli Rꝫ.|

271   ffrancis Baker, brother and heire of John Baker of Snitend in Nybley, holdeth one acre in Rackcombe iuxta Stancombe, which the said John purchased of the said Anthony Hungerford: And of the said cheife rent of—30ˢ paieth—   ; purchased in   Caroli Rꝫ.

Tobias Hatheway of Snitend holdeth halfe an acre of land in west feild which hee purchased of Wiłłm Purnell aforesaid, and hee of Anthony Hungerford in a° Rꝫ Caroli ; And of the said cheife rent of—30ˢ paieth—   .

Robert Oldisworth sonne of Edward, sonne of Arnold, holdeth a pasture ground called Burrough hill cont̄ 5. acres, which the said Arnold in a°   Rꝫ Jacobi purchased of the said Anthony Hungerford, And of the said cheife rent of—30ˢ paieth—

William Trotman of Stancombe, holdeth one acre and an halfe in Ruckcombe close, which hee in a° Rꝫ   purchased of the said Anthony Hung'ford, And of the said cheife rent of 30ˢ paieth—

James Gibbs holdeth one Cotage and an acre of ground enclosed therto adioyninge, in Wike, which hee purchased of Thomas Mundy, and hee of my selfe, and I of the said Anthony Hungerford in a°   Rꝫ   , And of the said cheife rent of—30ˢ paies—

Isaack Smyth of Dursley holdeth a messuage and divers lands therto belonginge lyinge in Charfeild, which hee by a Deed inrolled in the court of Comon pleas in Michas terme a° 9° Rꝫ Caroli, and by fine and other assurances some wherof beare

date

date the 21th of November aº 9º. ḃd, purchased of the said Anthony Hungerford, and were parcell of this manor of Pitcourt, as those his conveyances and many of the former doe shewe.

William Curnocke of Burrowes court, holdeth, &c. wherof read in the next page: And vpon his purchase, beinge to pay 5ˢ of Anthony Hungersfords cheife rent, Set over—4ᵈ therof to Henry Hayward vpon his sale of Tydnams, as formerly appeares fol: 269. |

Burrowes Court: A Messuage at the lower end of the little greene neere vnto Marten bridge, which in processe of time tooke the name of Burghes or Burrowes court from William de Burgo, to whom and his heires Thomas Lord Berkeley the first of that name, about 10. H. 3, granted the same by the name of halfe a yard land, (containinge about 43. acres,) which Richard le Butt somtimes held of him in villinage. To hold by the yearly rent of 20ˢ and by knight service, as by the deed it selfe, which followeth, appeares.

272
Burrowes Court.

Sciant p̃sentes et futuri quod ego Thomas de Berket dedi concessi et hac p̃nti carta mea confirmavi Willo de Burgo de Nubbeleye pro homagio et servicio suo, Dimidiam virgatam terræ cum ōibus suis pertinentijs, Illam videlicet quam Ričus le But aliquando tenuit in villinagio in villa de Nubbeleye: Tenend̃ et habend̃ de me et heredibus meis sibi et heredibus suis liberè, quietè, et integrè, iure hereditario imperpetuum: Reddendo inde anuatim mihi et heredibus meis ipse et heredes sui, viginti solidos argenti ad quatuor anni terminos, videlt ad natale Dñi quinq̃ solidos, Ad Paschā quinq̃ solidos, ad nativitatem beati Johis Baptistæ quinq̃ solidos, et ad fesťm sči Michis quinq̃ solidos, pro omnibus servicijs et secularibus demandis, Salvo regali servicio quantum ptinet ad tantum teñtum in eod feodo; Ad quem redditum terminis p̃dčis solvend̃, Idem Willus concedit pro se et heredibus suis, quod ego dčus Thomas de Berket et heredes mei possimus eundem Willimum et heredes suos quotiescunq̃ necesse fuerit distringere, libere et quiete super quibuscunq̃ tenementis quæ tenent vel tenere contingant apud Nubbeleye et alibi infra libertatem de Berket. Ego vero dčus Thomas de Berket et heredes mei p̃dčam virgatam terræ c̃m ōibus suis ptinentijs p̃dčo Willimo et heredibus suis contra omnes mortales per p̃dčtum servicium imperpetuum warrantizabimus. In cuius rei testimonium, huic p̃senti cartæ ad modum cirographi confectæ sigilla ñra alternatim sunt apposita. Hijs testibus, Dño Robto de Berket, Petro de Stintescumbe, Elia de Cumbe, Willo de Cumbe, Warino filio Willi, et alijs.

The

The said William de Burgo the feoffee had iffue Walter de Burgo, who was father of William de Burgo, who in 6. et 7. E. 2. was in ward to Thomas lord Berkeley the fecond of that name, grandchilde of the forefaid Thomas the feoffor, for this land; As the Accompts of thofe yeares made by the Reeve of the Manor of Wotton doe fhewe, which are in Berkeley Caftle.

Shortly after this land came to the family of Schay, lord of Pitcoᵘ, but whether by purchafe or by mariage of the heire of de Burgo it is the private evidences of the faid Anthony Hungerford only that muft tell, for I, as yet, cañot: But therby (as I conceive) the cheife rent of Pitcourt, before but—10ˢ, was increafed to—30ˢ. p anñ. And fo this land of William de Burgo continued in the fame lyne of Schai with Pitcourt before mentioned, vntill the faid Anthony Hungerford in the 20ᵗʰ of kinge James fold this Burrowes court with the lands therto belonginge to Wiłłm Curnocke and John his eldeſt fonne ioyntly in fee: By reafon of which longe poffeſ- fion in one and the fame lyne this Burrowes court was reputed generally to bee part of that manor of Pitcourt: And vpon feverance thereof by fale in 20. Jacobi, the cheife rent of—5ˢ pcell of the faid—30ˢ was agreed betweene the purchafors and feller to bee thenceforth paid, and foe mentioned in their deed of bargaine and fale: And the faid John Curnocke died before his father in 14º Caroli, and by Jane Burbage his wife had iffue Margaret only childe, vpon whom this yeare. 1639. 15ᵗᵒ Caroli, the faid William hath fetled moft of this land, The pcells of all fee after in this page.

Plita affifaз. aº 32. H. 3. Walterus de Burgo et Alicia vxor eius petunt verſus Nigellum filium Roberti de Kingefcote, vnam carucatam terræ in Nybley: Which Nigell had iffue Maurice, who maried Eve, and dyed without iffue before his father; And the faid Alice was daughter of the faid Robert, who was to have the land by conveyance after the death of Eve, who was nowe dead: Heerin they drewe to iffue vpon the grant, and compounded.

Rot. pateñ. 4. E. 3. in dorfo rotuli: Wiłłus fit Wiłłi de Burgo arř affifam verſ Thomã fit Mauricij de Berkeley chr et ał, de teñtis in Nubbeley iuxta Berkeley.

Co: Roll of Wotton fforren. 36. H. 6. Johes Skey obijt (inter alia) de vno meffuagio voĉ Burrowes, ĉm diuſis terris eid fpcĉlañ in Nybbeley. Redd.— heriet duæ vaccæ. Walter eft frater et heres, 40. añoэ.

The parcells anciently belonginge to Burrowes Court fold by Anthony Hunger- ford aforefaid to Wiłłm and John Curnocke in fee, are theis; viz, The dwellinge houfe house called Burrowes Court, orchard and garden adioyninge. 8. acres of arrable land in the west feild, 2. acres in Stretly, one acre in Bowry, one acre in ruckombe, halfe an acre in Chesley, a meadowe called Burrowes mead conť 1. acre and an halfe, Burrowes moore conť 2. acres, a meadowe in West feild called Overly conť 2. acres, a close of pasture in Clay feild called Hufwifes acre, conť 1. acre, A pasture ground called the grove conť 3. acres, A pasture ground called the Ley conť 8. acres; A pasture in West feild conť 3. acres; A pasture called Swineburne conť 5. acres; A pasture called great Tidnam in Swiney conť 6. acres, and a ridge called the Racke ridge in Winley feild:—wherof theis persons have purchased theis parcells since vz,

Henry Heyward purchased the said pasture called great Tidnam in Swyney conť 6. acres of the said William and John Curnocke, of whom see before in fol: 269, amongst the purchasers of the manor of Pitcourt. |

Warrens Court: This was the Capitall messuage and ancient habitacōn of Sir Peter the sonne of Warren knight; After, of Warren sonne of William; After of Warren sonne of Warren; After of Willm fitz Warren, And lastly of Thomas fitz Warren; In which name and family of the Warrens it continued vntill about 40. E. 3, when by the purchase of the lady Katherine Berkeley, the second wife and widowe of Thomas Lord Berkeley the third of that name, in the names of Milkesham and Oldland, preists, her feoffees in trust, And vpon her foundinge of the free grammer schoole in Wotton-vnderedge in 9. R. 2, it became parcell of the possessions therof; In which condicōn it still remaineth, and my selfe tenant therto for more then 40. yeares past; Wherof read more in the description of Wotton vnderedge fol: 407. And out of theis Records; vz, 274 Warrens Court.

    Rot. finiū. 9. E. 1. membr. 16.
    Rot. finiū. 15. E. 3. membr. 2.
    Rot. pateñ: 16. E. 3. ps. 1. in dorso.
    Rot. clauš. 23. E. 3. ps. 1. membr. 24. in dorso.
    Michas Reč. in banco regis. 28. et 29. Eliz. Rot. 308. et 310.

And from the ancient seisin and possession of the generous Sirname of **Warren**, it retaines the name of Warrens court to this day; 1639.

Smalcombe Court: The name is ancient and seemes to have byn taken, from the first buildinge of the house, from the standinge and scituacōn of the mansion or manor Smalcombe Court.

manor house vpon a small combe hanginge or declininge of an hill, by which it standeth.

Anciently this messuage was in the name and family of Thomas de Ecclesia, and Thomas de la church de Nubbeley, who lived in the time of kinge H. 3. and before; And seemes to drawe that name from the scituaçon of the house and grounds, neerest to the Church or Chapple there of any other: Which Thomas was father of Robert de Ecclesia, father of John de Nubbeley, who lived in the time of kinge E. 1. and of E. 2. And imediately after of the Smalcombes, the place I suppose changinge the name, and not the family, as Willm de Smalcombe, Thomas de Smalcombe, John de Smalcombe. and some others; somtimes omittinge the french particle, (de) denotinge the genetive case, as the englisħ (of) doth.

After it came into the name of Harsfeld by marriage of the heire of Smalcombe, and soe continued till Thomas Harsfeild, sonne and heire of Thomas, in 37º. Eliz. sold the same to Willm Tracy Esq, who afterwards aliened the same to my selfe and others, as after followeth: ffor which Alienaçons and rent, see the Court rolls of Wotton fforren, 39. Eliz. And

By the guift of part of this land to a Chantry preist, it proved, after the statute of 1. E. 6. that gave them to the Crowne, a land of much contention; and contrary verdicts were given vpon severall issues one against another, aswell at the Exchequer barre as at Assises in the countrey, not reconciled till the titles of all contrariant parties were brought in and a Recovery had in a writt of right, after issue ioyned: As after fol: 287. |

In this place, because of your seisin heerof, my sonne, to whom I have vpon your mariage given the same, I will borrowe leave to declare once for all, and the rather through the often changes or variations of the Sirnames of the owners of this messuage, That wheras before the Norman conquest most part of places had their names, either of their scituaçon or of some notable accident or noble man, wherof this hundred presenteth some of each kinde: That imediately after the arrivall of the Normans who obtained those lands, and who first brought into this Realme of England the names of Thomas, John, Nicholas, ffrancis, Stephen, Henry, and the like, nowe most vsuall; Men began to bee knowne and sirnamed of their dwellings and possessions, as heere of the little or small combe wheron the ancient capitall messuage is scituate, as hath byn said. And certaine also it is, That the

Normans

Normans at their first entry after their victory obtained laboured by all meanes to supplant the English tongue, and to plant their owne language amongst vs: And for that purpose both gave vs the lawes and all manner of pastimes, games, and sports, in the french tongue, as hee that will peruse the lawes of the Conqueror, and consider the termes of hawking, huntinge, tennis play, dice, card plaies and other disports, shall easily perceive: And which seemeth most of all reiected the Saxons characters and their wonted manner of writinge, bringinge in their owne alphabet and frame of letters.

The tenure of this Smalcombe Court and of the   acres of land of old therto belonginge, is of George Lord Berkeley as of his manor of Wotton fforren, in socage, by 12^d. rent, and suite to his hundred Court of Berkeley from three weekes to three weekes: Of which 12^d you my sonne by an apportionment therof made in the Court of the said Manor pay—9^d. And—1^d by Willm Curnocke is paid for a ground called Burrowes mead containinge 6. acres, And—1^d by Willm Marten is paid for 3. acres of meadowe in Swynehey, called Swyneis mead. And—1^d by Joseph Jobbins for an house and   acres of land called Shabhill, which hee lately aliened to ffrancis Heyward als Peers a carrier, which Joseph was a younger sonne of ffrancis Jobbins deceased, who gave it vnto him; And the said William Curnocke hath also two acres of meadowe in Winley, and one acre of meadowe in westfeild.

Bassetts Court. An ancient capitall messuage and manor house of old called Bassetts Court. Sherncliffe court, from a clesse or hill of that name affronting on the east, nowe the inheritance of James Gibbs and others as after followeth, holden of George lord Berkeley by knight service, sute to the hundred Court of Berkeley from 3. weekes to 3. weekes, and by the yearly rent of—26^s. 8^d. But whether of the lord's Manor of Wotton fforren, to which the cheife rent is paid, and wherto I encline, or of his manor of Alkington, sith question hath byn moved by a sute at lawe, I will not absolutely determine.

The originall grant of this land was by Thomas lord Berkeley the second of that name, by a deed without date, but neere about the 16. E. 1. in theis words; vz, |

Omnibus xp̄i fidelibus ad quos presens scriptum pervenerit, Thomas de Berkel 276 dn̄s de Berket salm in dno. Noveritis me dedisse et hoc p̄senti scripto meo confirmasse Ricō dicto de camera, pro homagio et servicio suo, totam illam terram cum ptinentijs

ptinentijs, quam Robtus de Wike quondam tenuit apud Nubbeley: Dedi etiam et
concessi eid Ricō totam illam terram cum pertinentijs quam Radulphus Mareschallus
quondam tenuit in Swynheye; Dedi etiam et concessi eid Ricō totā illā terrā cum
pertinentijs quam Walterus Rolse quondam tenuit apud Wyneley, quam quidem
terram Nichus saber quondam tenuit: Hend̄ et tenend̄ ōia p̄dc̄a terras et teñta im
ōibus suis ptineñ dc̄o Ricō et heredibus de corpore suo sittime procreatis, de me et
heredibus meis, libere et quietè, integrè bene et in pace, cum libero introitu et exitu
vt in domibus, edificijs, gardinis, curtilagijs, pratis, pascuis et pasturis, cōibus, et
ōibus alijs libtatibus et liberis consuetudinibus ad p̄dc̄a terras et teñta quoquo modo
spectantib9, iure hereditario imppetuum. Reddendo inde anuatim mihi et heredib9
meis dc̄us Ric̄ et heredes sui de corpore suo legittimè procreati, duas mareas argenti
ad quatuor anni terminos principales, equali portione: vz, ad natalē Dn̄i sex solidos
et octo denarios, Ad paschā sex solidos et octo denarios, Ad sestm nativitatis beati
Johis Baptistæ sex solidos et octo denarios, et ad sestm sc̄i Michis sex solidos et octo
denarios, pro ōibus servicijs et secularibus demandis: Salvo regali servicio, vz, tantum
quantm pertinet ad tantm teñtum in coñ seodo: Et salvis mihi et heredibus meis
sectis ad hundredū meū de Berkel de tribus septimanis in tres septimanas Et ego
p̄dc̄us Thomas et heredes mei totā p̄dc̄a terrā c̄m ōibus suis vbiq, pertinentijs p̄dc̄o
Ricō et heredibus suis de corpore suo legittime procreatis, in forma p̄dc̄a contra ōes
mortales warrantizabimus imperpetuum. Et si contingat dc̄m Ric̄um sine herede de
corpore suo legittime procreato in sata discedere, ex tunc omnia p̄dc̄a terræ et teñta
c̄m ōibus suis vbiq, ptinentijs mihi et heredibus meis sine contradictione alicuius
plenarie et integre revertantur. In cuius rei testimonium huic p̄senti scripto ad
modum Cirograph confecto, sigillum meum et sigillum dc̄i Ric̄i alternatim sunt
apposita. Hijs testibus, Robto de Stone, Robto de Bradeston, Waltero de Chalde-
seild, Willo de Combe, Willo de Burgo, Robto de Draicote, Thoma de Swonhungre,
et alijs.—Which deed is in my custody from William Bassett who gave it mee.

There is another Deed in theis words; vizt.—Sciant p̄ntes et futuri, q̄d ego
Thomas Dn̄s de Berkeley dedi concessi et hac p̄nti carta mea confirmavi Ricō de la
Chamber, pro homagio et servicio suo, et Dionisiæ vxori eius et Thome filio eorundem, Totm illud tentm et terrā c̄m ōibus eoȝ ptineñ, quod Robtus de Wike quondam
tenuit in villa de Nybbely, q̄d quidem tentm Barthot de Olepen tenet ad terminū
vitæ suæ: Preterea dedi et concessu p̄dc̄is Ricō, Dionisiæ et Thome, totm illud tentm
et terram c̄m ōibus vbiq, eoȝ ptineñ, q̄d Nichus molend aliquando tenuit apud
la Swinchey; q̄d quidem tentm Radus Mareschall tenet ad terminū vitæ suæ:
Hend̄ et tenend̄ ōia et singula antedicta c̄m ōibus eoȝ vbiq, ptineñ de me et
heredibus

heredibus meis, p̱dc̄is Ric̄o Dionisiæ et Thomæ, et hered̄ suis, libere, quiete, integre, bene, et in pace, cum o͠ibus libtatibus et liberis confuetudinib9, in pratis, boscis, pascuis, et pasturis, in o͠ibus rebus et locis c̄m o͠ibus eoꝝ vbiꝗ ptinc̄n ad p̱dc̄a tent̄a aliquo modo ptinc̄n, iure hereditario fine vllo retenemento imppetuum; Reddendo inde anuatim mihi dc̄o Thomæ toto tempore vitæ meæ tant̄m, et post deceffu͠ vitæ meæ Jacobo de Berkeley filio meo et heredibus suis de corpore suo legittime procreatis, sex solidos argenti ad quatuor anni terminos vsuales, equis portionibus pro tent̄o apud le Swynchey; Et etia͠ | pro tent̄o quonda͠ Roberti de Wike post **277** deceffum vitæ dc̄i Barthot de Olepen p̱dc̄o Jacobo et hered̄ suis de corpore suo legittime procreat̄—20ˢ argenti ad quatuor anni terminos vsual, equis portionibus. Post deceffum vero vitæ p̱dc̄oꝝ Ric̄i Dionisiæ et Thomæ, heredes sui solvere tenentur pro p̱dc̄is duobus tent̄is p̱dc̄o Jacobo de Berkeley filio meo, et hered̄ suis de corpore suo procreat̄, 30ˢ argenti ad 4. anni terminos vsuales equis portionibus pro omnibus servic̄ et secular̄ demandis quocunꝙ modo contingen̄; Salvo regali servicio quantum ad tant̄u tent̄u de eod̄ feodo in ead̄ villa ptinebit, Et salvis sec̄tis ad hundredum meum de Berkel de 3. septiman̄ in 3. septiman̄ raconabit sumonic̄ prius habita. Et ego dc̄us Thomas et heredes mei o͠ia et singula antedic̄ta c̄m o͠ibus eoꝝ vbiꝗ ptinc̄n vt p̱dc̄m est p̱dc̄is Ric̄o Dionisiæ et Thomæ et hered̄ suis, in forma p̱dc̄a contra o͠es mortales warrantizabim9 acquietabim9 et imppetuum defendebimus. In cuius rei testimonium huic p̱nti cartæ in modum Cirographi indentat̄ sigilla sua alternatim sunt appensa. Hijs testib9, Dn̄o Rob̄to de Berkel, Rob̄to de Stan̄, Rob̄to de Brad̄ston, Petro de Stintescumbe, Wº de Burgo, Waltero de Chaldsfeild, Wº de Combe et alijs.

And by a Deed dated 1 Maij. aº 34. E. 1. Joh̄es de Berkelee, filius Dn̄i Thome de Berkelee, remisit dc̄o d̄no Thome tot̄m ius et clameum quod fuit in duobus mc̄is annui redditus et o͠ibus alijs servicijs Ric̄i de Wike apud Sharnclive in Nebbele. Howe this John Berkeley had this, I have not observed.

From the issue of which Richard de Camera, (groome of the said Lords Chamber,) called afterwards Richard de Wike, (where also hee had more land then this,) this messuage and land came about 10. E. 3, by p'chase as I conceive, to bee the inheritance of Sir Simon Bassett knight, a gent fitted tam Marti quàm Mercurio, a great comaunder in the Battell of Poitiers, many yeares Escheator and Sheriffe of this County: And from him by divers lineall discents it came to Wittm Bassett, (whose discents, with the times of their severall deathes see before in Ewley, fol. 188. et 31,) which Wittm Basset sonne of Edward, in 4º Jacobi, sold the same to Wittm Gibbs and to Henry Hatheway ioyntly and to their heires: And vpon partition,

partition, after their ioynt fales of fome remote parts of the grounds by them made, This wholl meſſuage and almoſt all the grounds and cloſes adioyninge, were allotted to the faid Wiℳ Gibbs and his heires; And from him afwell by deed in his life time, as by his laſt will dated   was conveyed to James Gibbs his yongeſt fonne and his heires, now dwellinge vpon the fame: But fuch and foe many have byn the morfells pared from this meſſuage, that 18. feverall freeholders at this day have feverall parts therof; fome from the ioynt fale of Wiℳ Gibbs and Henry Hatheway before their partition as aforefaid, which was in
fome by Henry Hatheway alone after partition, And fome by the faid Wiℳ Gibbs, as followeth;

My ſelfe and you my fonne hold therof, 2. acres in Sharncliffe hill, Turnors croft 3. acres, one acre in lower Stretly, 3 acres in Eweombs, 1. acre inclofed in church feild, 3 acres in clayfeild, inclofed; a meadowe called Marſhalls, and a ground called the lower pennynge.

John Grayle fonne of John Graile clarke, holds one clofe of paſture containinge 4. acres in |

278   William Trotman of Stancombe, in right of his wife the widowe of Robert Purnell, the revertion in fee to Robert Purnell fonne of the faid Robert, holds one clofe in Elfoulds containinge   acres.

Jefper Eſtcourt genſ holdeth 6. acres of meadowe ground in Edgeborne, and one acre called Hockmead, and 4. acres in Broadcroft, and halfe the ground called Longmead.

John Smyth of Southend holdeth one acre of paſture in Ridings.

John Purnell of Wike holdeth a meadowe and paſture clofe called Percy furlonge containinge   acres. And one clofe called ffoules grove adioyninge to the vpper end of Buſh ſtreete, conī about 7. acres, whereof read after fol:

William Curnocke of Burrowes Court aforefaid holdeth three little grounds called the Stockes, Rodes, and Brookfurlonge, containinge about   acres.

Samuell Trotman holdeth one clofe called Goofmead, and 4. acres of land in Weſtfeild.

John

Nibley

John Hale of Nybley holdeth one acre.

William Purnell of the greene holdeth a meadowe ground called Worth hayes, and another called the hurne.

William Gibbens holdeth a Messuage and a close adioyninge cont 2. acres, parcell of the ancient messuage called ffrendsplace.

Humphrey Spicer holdeth an house and backside called Cobbs house.

John Selman sonne of John, holdeth 3. acres of arrable land in Giftingthorne.

John Wilkens holdeth one close of pasture called Hawgrove cont 7. acres, which hee in a°.   purchased of

Nicholas Gibbs, eldest sonne of Willm Gibbs aforesaid, holdeth, one close of meadowe and pasture called Beane close cont 8. acres, adioyninge to Baffets court.

James Gibbs, youngest sonne of Willm Gibbs, holdeth the said capitall messuage called Baffetts court with divers closes of meadowe and pasture ground therto adioyninge cont about 60. acres.

ffrancis Purnell holdeth one close called Yongcrofts cont acres in

Maria Taylor holdeth one acre which her father Robert Tailor als Evans purchased of |

By an Inq: 35. H. 8. after the death of Giles Baffett, hee is found to dye seized (inter al) of the manor of Sharneliffe in Nybley, holden of the kinge as of his Castle or manor of Berkeley by fealty and 34ˢ rent for all services, joyninge the same vnder the same tenure with his lands in Came, as there appeares, fol : [133]

See the Co: roll of Wotton fforren 39. Eliz, for the alienacōn to Edward Baffet ; rent 33ˢ 4ᵈ Releife vpon the alienacōn.

By Inq : found at Berkeley 10ᵉ Augusti. 17. Rᵉ Caroli, after the death of the said Willm Curnocke, it was found that hee died in

              Huntscourt :

Huntſcourt.

Huntſcourt: is an ancient capitall meſſuage with 58. acres of land therto belonginge, havinge taken the name from the feizin of the ancient owners therof, who (though they poſſeſſed other lands in other places) heere made their abode for many generations; holden of George lord Berkeley as of his manor of Wotton fforren by knight ſervice, vz, the xth part of a knights fee, ſute to his hundred court of Berkeley from three weekes to 3 weekes, and by the yearly rent of—15^d.

In the beginninge of the raigne of kinge Edward the firſt, it was the land of Robert le Venor; after of Michaell Venator ats Hunt, who dyed in 9. E. 2, leavinge John Hunt his ſonne and heire within age, therby in ward to Thomas lord Berkeley the ſecond of that name: After him it came to two other of the ſame name of John Hunt; And laſtly, another John Hunt towards the end of kinge E. 4. left iſſue a daughter, maryed to Hugh Tyndall ats Hutchins, who died in   , father of John Tyndall ats Hutchins who died in   , and was father of Thomas who dyed in   , father of Richard Tyndall who died in 19º. Eliz, father of Richard who died in 18. Jacobi, father of Thomas Tyndall who dyed   , father of Thomas Tyndall that nowe is, aº 1639, ward to the kinge for other land, holden by knight ſervice in Capite, As the office or Inquiſiĉon found vpon his death in Rᵉ Caroli ſheweth. |

280
Bellamies in Bircheley.

Bellamies, in Bircheley, in Nybley, is a meſſuage longe ſince decaied in the north eaſt end of Nibley containinge about 30. acres, now the inheritance of Chriſtopher Purnell, holden of George Lord Berkeley as of his manor of Wotton fforren by knight ſervice, ſute to his hundred court of Berkeley from 3 weekes to 3. weekes, and by the yearly rent of—xᵈ.

Anciently this was the land of Nicholas de la grove, ſomtime written Grover, and after of Belamy, And in 36. H. 6. of Thomas Skey ſonne of John Schay, And in the time of   of Elizabeth Audely, who by her will in   deviſed the ſame to Nicholas Rogers and Katherine his wife, and to the heires of the ſaid Katherine: which Nicholas dyed in 1 Eliz: and Katherine ſurvived and died in 2. Eliz. leavinge iſſue John Rogers, who died in 13. Eliz. leavinge iſſue David Rogers and Thomas Rogers: David died without iſſue in   , And Thomas Rogers was his brother and heire, who in 35. Eliz: aliened the ſame to Jenkin Rees, and hee to Willm Hopkins of Briſtoll, who in   aliened the ſame to Thomas Purnell, who by his will in 20. Jacobi deviſed the ſame to his ſecond ſonne the ſaid Chriſtopher Purnell, and his heires, nowe owner therof. Aº 1639.

In

Dibley

In Berkeley castle are the Accompts of the Reeves of the said Manor of Wotton fforren, in 6. et 7. E. 2. which shewe this to bee then the land of Nicholas de la grove als Grover, whose sonne and heire Richard was in ward for the same to Thomas then Lord Berkeley; which Richard by a fyne levyed in 7. E. 2. aliened the same to Walter Belamy and his heires, ffrom whose seisin it keepes the name of Bellamies to this day, 1639. Of which Belamy more next is to bee said.

See for this the Court Roll of Wotton fforren. 25. Eliz. And 13. Eliz.

Co: roll of Wotton fforren, 36. H. 6. Johes Skey obijt seitus de vno mess c̃m diversis terris eid spectañ, vocat Bellamies in Birchley, herẽ. redd. Walter est frater et heres, 40. añog.

Bellamies place in the southend of this village of Nybbeley, is an ancient messuage with divers lands therto belonginge contayninge about   acres, a myle from the former Bellamies, some parts wherof extended into Bradley and Huntenford, And had also its name from the possession of the foresaid Walter Bellamy, a very remarkeable ffreeholder in his time, which continues to this day: And is holden of George Lord Berkeley as of his manor of Wotton fforren by the xvjth part of a knights fee, sute to his hundred Court of Berkeley from 3. weekes to 3. weekes, and by the yearly rent of—vj^d.

Bellamies place, in Southend.

This Bellamies place was anciently in the beginninge of the raigne of kinge Henry the third, and before, the land of Robert de Stone, father of Robert de Stone, father of Thomas de Stone, who in the beginninge of the raigne of kinge Edward the second was in ward for the same to Thomas then lord Berkeley, And lett by him to the said Walter Bellamy for 40^s p añ, as the Reeves Accompts of that manor of Wotton fforren from 6. E. 2. to 1. E. 3. doe shewe, which are in Berkeley Castle. |

The said Thomas de Stone dyed in 9. E. 2. leavinge 2. daughters and coheires, wherof the yonger called Alice was within age, whose wardship also the lord Berkeley had, as the said Accompts doe also shewe.

The other daughter called Jone, then of full age, was maried to John Sergeant an ancient freeholder in Stone: And in a particōn by Deed in 21. E. 3. made betweene Jone daughter and heire of the said Jone, then wife of Walter Hurst,

And

And Willm Swonhunger fonne of the faid Alice, either of them had one halfe part allotted in feveralty of theis lands, and foe continued for divers generations; wherof fee more in Stone, fol: 356, 357, And in Wanifwell, fol: 368, 369; And fee the pticōn verbatim. fol: 282.

The foresaid Jone maried to John Sericant had iffue Jone aforementioned. firft maryed to Walter Hurft, fecondly to Walter Brokenburrowe, and thirdly to Edmond fford; By her two later hufbands fhee had noe iffue, but by Walter Hurft fhee had iffue Ifable maryed to Sir John Bitton knight, who had iffue Katherine maryed to Thomas Rugge, who had iffue Jone firft maryed to Sir Robert Grendore knight who dyed in 22. H. 6, as his office found after his death fheweth, And fecondly to Sir John Barre knight who died in 21. E. 4, as the office or Inquificōn found after his death fheweth: And laft of all the faid Jone dyed without iffue in 1. H. 7, Shee and her hufband Sir Rob: Grendore, havinge in 16. H. 6. entayled all her lands in Stone, Hame, Alkington, Wanifwell, ffafeild, and Nybley, with the advowfon of our ladies chantry in the Chaple of Stone, for default of iffue of her body, vpon Thomas Sergeant of Monmouth towne, and the heires males of his body, with remainder to her right heires, which I conceive either to have byn himfelfe, as next of the whole bloud to that John Sergeant and Jone his wife, daughter and coheire of Thomas de Stone formerly mentioned, or next collaterally:- The iffue male of which Thomas (nowe by her death in 1. H. 7. the laft of this her lyne,) became to bee feized firft of theis lands, which after his death difcended to John Sergeant his fonne, who was father of   Sergeant, father of Thomas Sergeant, father of Thomas Sergeant, who in 6. E. 6. fold theis lands in Nybley to one John Smyth. who after conveyed the fame to James Hadlowe, fonne of James Hadlowe clerke, who in aº fexto Rº Jacobi, fold the fame to Henry Hatheway, who alfo by purchafe had the part of Alice the other daughter and coheire of Thomas de Stone, as after followeth: And the faid Thomas Sergeant, fonne of Thomas, after dyed in 8º Eliz. leavinge iffue Thomas Sergeant the yonger (as hee was comonly called,) who in 14º and 16º Eliz. Rñe aliened all the reft of his before mentioned lands to Hugh Smyth and others, As in the defcription of Stone fhall appeare fol: 355, and after

See a fyne of all theis lands levied in Octabis purificacōis, aº 15. R. 2. inter Norton et Shawe capellañ, et Edñi fford et Johā vforē eius, which is inrolled in Rot. claus. aº 1. H. 4. in arce Londini.

See the Court roll of Wotton fforren, 42. Eliz. after the death of the faid John Smyth, and his conveyance of this land, &c.]

The

The aforesaid Alice yongeſt daughter of the ſaid Thomas de Stone, was maryed to John Swonhunger, ſonne and heire of John Swonhunger, who had iſſue betweene them Thomas Swonhunger, who after his father died without iſſue, And Willm Swonhunger who was father of Elias, father of Elias, who left iſſue John Swonhunger, who died without iſſue in 3. H. 4. and 2. daughters, viz, Elizabeth maryed to James Gayner, who alſo dyed without iſſue, and Iſable maried to John Thorpe of Briſtoll, who had iſſue betweene them John Thorpe who died in 9. E. 4. leavinge iſſue Richard who dyed in 6. H. 8, and was father of Thomas who dyed in 17. H. 8, and was father of Thomas Thorpe who dyed in 34. H. 8, father of Nicholas Thorpe who dyed in 42. Eliz, leavinge iſſue George Thorpe who the next yeare after his fathers death, by the deed dated 16º Aprilt aº 43. Eliz, ſold the ſame to John Birton and his heires, by the name of his meſſuage called Bellamies, &c: which John Birton the ſame yeare of 43º Eliz. (the yeare hee dyed,) by his will deviſed the ſame to Thomas Oakes of Wotton and his heires, who in aº 3º Rº Jacobi, ſold the ſame to the foreſaid Henry Hatheway, (then huſband to Katherine ſiſter of the ſaid John Birton, and to his heires: wherby in him theis two ſiſters parts, Joane and Alice, were after 287. yeares ſeverance againe vnited; which lands in all the ſeverall parcells of them in all places did lye ſoe equally together, That the lands themſelves would have declared to him that had noe further knowledge, that they were the equall parted parts of two ſiſters: Of whoſe diſcents, ſince H. 3. to the ſale of George Thorpe in 43. Eliz, ſee after in Waniſwell and Swonhunger als Saniger, fol: 365. 367. 368.

But ſince the vnitinge purchaſes of the ſaid Henry Hatheway, hee and his eldeſt ſonne John have aliened one cloſe called Ruydings containinge about 7. acres thereof, to John Smyth of Southend; And the ſaid meſſuage called Bellamies place with almoſt all the reſt of the lands, to you William Archard and your heires, as your ſelfe by deare purchaſes and by newe buildings and beautifyinge of the ſame, this and the laſt two yeares, beſt knowe by your accompts, which like a wiſe man I preſume you have kept.

As for the toſte and 71. acres of land in Nybley called Grovers, which Thomas lord Berkeley purchaſed of Walter Bellamy mentioned in the Inquiſiçõn found after the ſaid lords death in 5. H. 5, it is the land of John Wilkens of Nybley which hee purchaſed of Henry lord Berkeley in fee farme, wherof ſee after in fol: 290.

ffor more of this **Bellamies place** ſee the Court Roll of Wotton fforren 44. Eliz. pt mortẽ Johis Birton; redd 3ᵈ

The

The aforementioned partition made betweene the coheires of Thomas de Stone, remaininge in Berkeley caftle, is in theis words; vz,

Cest endenture fait a Berkele le Luinday prochein apres la fefte faint michel larchangell lan du regne le roy Edward tiers puis le conqueft vint et vtime, perentre Wiłłm Swonhungre cofyn et vn des heires Thomas de Stone de vn part, et Water Hurft et Johanne fa feme cofin et coheire le dit Thomas de Stone d'altre pte, Teftmoine, q̃ les dits Wiłłm Water et Johanne ount fait la purperty et la feũaunce de vn mees vn virge de terre ove les appurtennences in Nibbeleye les q̃x mees et terre remiftrent adevant en coñiune enter les heires le dit Thomas nynt departe; Ceftaffavoir, q̃ de mees le dit Wiłłm avera et tenera a luy et fes heires a toutz iours, la fale et la haute chambre devers le haut chimin ove la moity du gardin deuers cele part, forfpris treffe | arbres pomers: Et les dits Water et Johanne auerount et tendrount a eux et a fes heires a toutz iours dit mees la graunge et la perftrine et la mafon apele wainhoufe, et la moitie du gardin devers cele part, et les [blank] et treffe arbres, ou la purpartie le dit [Wiłłm] entres de yceł. Et de terre pre et bois accord eft enter eux q̃ le dit Wiłłm aũa le moitie devers le Eift, Et les dits Water et Johanne averont le moity devers le weift, felom les metes et les bounds de ceo enter eux fait; Et les dits Water et Johanne releffent a le dit Wiłłm et fes heires tout lour droit q̃ ils ont en cele moity ove les appertunants. Et le dit Wiłłm releffe et quite clayme pur luy et pur fes heires a toutz iours as dit Water et Johanne et lour heires tout fon droit q̃ il ad en cele moite a eux alote et oblige luy et fes heires a garaunter cele moite a eux et lour heires a toutz iours. En teftmoiance de quel chofe a ceftes indentures les parties avantdits entrechangeablement ount mis lour feales.

Jobbins land. olim Chawfies.

Heere alfo in Nybbeley is one ancient freehold late the inheritance of ffrancis Jobbins fonne of Robert, fonne of John Jobbins, and nowe of John Smyth of Southend and others, as after followeth; confiftinge of a meffuage and one yard land called Chaufies als Chalfters in Southend in Nybley, holden of George Lord Berkeley as of his manor of Wotton fforren by knight fervice, fute of Court, heriot fervice, and the yearly rent of—6ᵈ paid as followeth.

Thomas lord Berkeley the firft of that name, who dyed in 28. E. 3. as the Inquificõn after his death in that yeare fheweth, by his deed without date, graunted the fame to John de Egeton in theis words, vz, |

ffrom

Nibley

ffrom the said John de Egeton it shortly after came to William de Chaufey, but whether by difcent or purchafe I have not obferved; By the death of which William in 27. E. 1. his heire then in minority was granted with his wardſhip to Richard de Wike, by Thomas lord Berkeley grandchilde of the faid lord Thomas, by his deed in theis words; viz¹,

Omnibus xp̄i fidelibus ad quos hoc fcriptum pveñit, Thomas de Berkeley Dn̄s de Berkeley falt̄m in Dn̄o. Noüitis me dediſſe et conceſſiſſe Rico de Wike cuſtodiam terraȝ et teñtoȝ quondam Willi de Chaufy de Nubbeley, que vel quas idem Willus de me tenuit in capite die quo obijt, vnacum maritagis heredis five heredum dc̄i Willi, Habend et tenend d̄ca cuſtodiam et maritagium ſibi Rico et aſſignatis ſuis vſq̨ ad legittimam ætatem heredis five heredum dc̄i Willi, falva rationabili dote Luciæ quondam vxoris dc̄i Willi de dictis terris et teñtis ſibi de iure contingent; Ita tamen quòd heres five heredes dc̄i Willi per ip̄m Ricm vel aſſignatos ſuos non ſint diſparagati. Ego vero deus Thomas heredes et aſſignati mei d̄ca cuſtodiam et maritagium p̄fato Rico et aſſignatis ſuis in forma p̄dca contra ōes mortales warrantizabimus. In cuius rei teſtimonium huic p̄nti fcripto ſigillum meum appoſui. Hijs teſtibus, Miloñ de Redeburne, Johe Champenyes, Roberto de Bradeſton, Thoma de Beoleye, Thoma de Swonhungre, et alijs· Datū apud Berket die Jovis in feſto ſc̄i Michis, Anno r̄ni regis Edwardi filij regis Henrici vicefimo octavo. A deed in my cuſtody borrowed longe fince of the heire of the grantee.

After fome difcents in the firname of Chaufye it came to John de Chaufye, vpon whofe death in 36. H. 6. a bullocke prized at 2ˢ was paid for a mountary, as the court roll of the manor of Wotton fforren of that yeare ſheweth : when alfo the deeds were produced.

After it was the land of Nicholas Chaufye who dyed in   , leavinge iſſue Elizabeth his daughter and heire maried to   , who had iſſue Margaret maried to Robert Stanſhawe, (then lord of Stanſhawe by Sodbury and of Alderley by Wotton vnderedge,) who died in 12. E. 4. havinge in his life time (as the Inquiſicōn after his death ſheweth,) purchafed the meſſuage and land of John Chaufye, and had enfeoffed the fame to the vfe of his laſt will, (which I have not feene,) leavinge Thomas his fonne and heire who was father of John Stanſhawe who dyed in 8. H. 8, leavinge iſſue Margery his only daughter and heire maryed to   Walſh, who had iſſue Sir John Walſh knight, who in 38. H. 8. fold this meſſuage and land to John Jobbins who died in   , leavinge iſſue Robert

Robert Jobbins who died in   , leaving iſſue ffrancis Jobbins aforefaid, who in   Jacobi R̃ aliened about 20. acres therof to William Marten, And hee about 17. acres therof to Richard Marten his eldeſt ſonne and his heires, with whom the originall Deed made as aforeſaid to John de Egeton remaines, and all other the aforementioned conveyances ; And of the ſaid—6ᵈ. cheife rent, paies—1ᵈ. And alſo aliened more to the ſaid Willm Marten about 16. acres, which hee againe ſold to one Willm Jobbins and his heires, brother of the halfe bloud to the ſaid ffrancis Jobbins, whoſe ſonne John Jobbins now holds the ſame and paies another penny of the cheife rent of vjᵈ. And the ſaid ffrancis Jobbins ſold the ſaid meſſuage and the greater part of the ſaid yard land to Henry Hatheway and his heires, And hee to Tobias Hatheway his youngeſt ſonne, And hee in aᵒ.   Caroli to John Smyth of Southend and his heires, who dwelleth vpon them ſame ; And of the ſaid cheife rent of—6ᵈ. paieth—4ᵈ: Howbeit ffrancis Purnell a yonger ſonne of Robert Purnell deceaſed holds one cloſe called Younge crofts containinge about 8. acres, lyinge neere to Schoolmaſters grove, which the ſaid Robert Purnell purchaſed of the ſaid William Jobbins, but paies noe part of the ſaid cheefe rent : And alſo Willm Beale the elder of Nibley holds of this land in fee, two acres of arrable land in Tetcombe feild, and halfe a quarter of an acre of arrable land in Bournſeild, next the kings highway, in the vpper part of his other land there, which hee purchaſed of the ſaid Willm Marten, and hee (inter alia) of the ſaid ffrancis Jobbins, but paies noe part of the ſaid cheife rent. 1639.

More of this land may bee read in theis Records, vz, ffinis in banco. 19. R. 2. Inter Johem Thornbury Clicum de maño de Alderley, talliato Roberto filio Johis de Stanſhawe et Margaretæ vxori eius, filie Elizabethe, filie Nicholai Chauſey, et poſtea eiſ Margaretæ vxori p̄dc̄i Robti. ffeodũ eiſ Johi de Stanſhawe : which I heere note for the pedegree.

ffinis in banco. 11. H. 4. Inter Robtum Stanſhawe, de teñtis in Bradley, Wotton, et Wortley, feoð eiſ Roberto. Inq : 12. E. 4. pᵗ mortem Robti Stanſhawe ař ; Wherin (inter alia) is found That hee dyed ſeized of one meſſuage and one yard land, 10. acres of meadowe, and 5. acres of paſture, in Northnybbeley, purchaſed of John Chawſey.

Rot. clauſ. 18. E. 4. membr. 17. in dorſo. in arce Londini, for the pedegree ; Thomas Stanſhawe ſonne and heire of Robert Stanſhaw ſeñ, lord of Alderley and other manors.

Inqu :

Nibley

Inqu : 8. H. S. p̄ mortem Johis Stanſhawe.

Court roll of Wotton fforren. 36. H. 6. John Chauſey dyed ſeized of a meſſuage and one yard land in Nybbley, Rent—6ᵈ Mountuary paid : And Robert Stanſhawe is next heire by purchaſe ; At this Court the deeds of the lands were ſhewed.

William Warren by deed dated 3. ffebr̄. 15. Jacobi, aliened to Wiłłm Jobbins 286 and his heires of this Chauſies land, a cloſe called Middle leies cont̄ 4. acres, and a cloſe called Youngcrofts perrocke cont̄ 1. acre : which John Jobbins ſonne of the ſaid William hath aliened in fee to Thomas Dawe of Wotten, who nowe holdeth the ſame. 1639.

And alſo by the ſaid deed hee aliened more to the ſaid William Jobbins in fee, one cloſe called Wickley cont̄ 5. acres, which the ſaid John Jobbins ſonne of the ſaid William hath this yeare aliened to Thomas May and his heires. Rendringe— 1ᵈ for all, parcell of the ſaid—6ᵈ.

And the ſaid John Jobbins ſonne of the ſaid Wiłłm holdeth about one quarter of an acre, taken by him out of the ſaid cloſe called Wickley and incloſed into the garden and orchard of the ſaid John, for the inlarginge therof. Soe this land called Chauſies is nowe aº 1639. 15. Rᵗ Caroli, the feuall inheritances of John Smyth of Southend 4ᵈ, Richard Marten, jᵈ, Thomas May, Thomas Dawe, and John Jobbins, who pay the ſaid—6ᵈ. cheife rent as aforeſaid : And alſo of ffrancis Purnell and of Wiłłm Beale, who have other parts of this land as aforeſaid. Aº 1639.

In Nybley alſo is an ancient meſſuage with one yard land of late therto belonginge, containinge about 76. acres, called **Draistes** als **Drapsides** lands ; The capitall meſſuage wherof is nowe the faire mantion ſeate of Chriſtopher Purnell younger ſonne of Thomas Purnell of Wike, who in 8ᵒ Jacobi purchaſed the ſame with part of the ſaid land therto belonging of Wiłłm Tracy Eſq., And hee in 4ᵗᵒ Jacobi of Thomas Duninge, ſonne of Richard, ſonne of Thomas, ſonne of James Duñinge and of Alice his wife daughter and coheire of John Draiſie, ſonne of Wiłłm Draiſye, brother and heire of Walter Dreyſey, ſonnes of John Dreyſey, ſonne of Thomas Dreyſey and of Matilda als Maud his wife ; and before of Richard Drayſide ; And in 1. E. 3. of Nicholas Draiſide, And before of Reginald Drayſide, and of former Anceſtors of that ſirname ; from whoſe longe ſeiſin theis lands are vſually called Draiſies lands to this day, wherof my ſelfe and you my ſonne have

Draiſies land, late Dunnings

have about 40. acres: And as an old deed sheweth, with Mr Willm Baffet (which I
have seene,) was the land of | Otho sonne of William, lord of the manor of Wood-
mancote, who enfeoffed therof William the sonne of Edwyn; and was somtime
the land of Robert, the sonne of Brightwin, who lived neere, if not at or before,
the Norman Conqueft; And was holden of the manor of Woodmancote by knight
service, sute of Court, and the yearly rent of—20ˢ; nowe the land of 5. or 6. men,
All of vs havinge bought out all our services of late yeares, save fealty only: wherof read more in Woodmancote fol: 389. And out of theis Records, vz,

Triñ Records in Banco, 2: H. 4. Rot. 314. And Micñas Record 3. H. 4. in
banco Rot. 125, for a fine levied in 35. E. 3 betweene Roger Chaufey of Nybley
pl̃t, And Thomas Drayfide and Jone his wife, defᵗˢ: of 2 messuages and 23 acres
of land, then parcell of theis.

Rot. Rediffeifiñ in arce Londini in aᵒ. 4. H. 4. which shewes, That Thomas
Drayfide recovered seifin of a messuage and 12. acres of land in Nybbeley againft
Richard Elliat of Nybbeley, who againe diffeifed Drayfide.

A Comon Recovery of this messuage and land is in banco cōi in Eafter terme,
16. H. 7. Rot. 299, againft John Drayfey the elder.

The Inquificōn in 6. H. 6. after the death of Sir John Berkeley of Beverfton
knight findeth, That hee dyed seized of the manor of Woodmancote, with the
hamblet of Nybbeley to the faid manor appertaininge, And that Maurice was his
sonne and heire: And in truth hee had in Nybbeley in demefne and service neere
a sixt part of Nybbeley, nowe wholly sold away, as in Woodmancote appeareth,
fol: 389.

Chantry of Nybley.

In this Nybley was a Chantry called Schaies chantry, als our Ladies Chantry,
wherof a Record in the Exchequer Court in Eafter Terme, Aᵒ 4ᵗᵒ Eliz: Reginæ,
Rot. 19. setteth downe the perticuler lands therto belonginge, And in whose tenure
the same then were, with the possession of kinge E. 6. for two yeares; And a Leafe
therof made to Willm Shellitoe, by that Court. And that 16 acres of that land was
heertofore given to that Chantry by one Thomas Munday; And the other 62 acres
by one Schay, All of them then in the tenure of George Dunninge.

This land after grewe very contentious, with much tumblinge thereof, through
diversity of verdicts, one againft another on either side; At laft by purchafe from

all

all titles and competitors it came to Willm Tracy Esq, and others in fee, And from them, to my selfe and others : About which land at last a Recovery was had in a writt of right, after issue ioyned. As before is said, fol : 274. |

The Chantry house wherin the Chantry preist lived, is next to the vicaridge house, both of them adioyninge to the Churchyard : And was by Lres patents dated 2° Decembr̃. a⁰ 2° E. 6. granted by that kinge, to Anthony Burcher and his heires, (inter alia,) And by divers meane conveyances is nowe the inheritance of my selfe, a⁰ 1639. **288**

Here also in Nybbeley are certaine lands and tenements comonly called Vincents lands, the inheritance of 12. severall men, as after followeth, holden of George lord Berkeley as of his manor of Wotton fforren, by sute to his hundred court of Berkeley from 3. weekes to 3. weekes, and by the yearly rent of—10ˢ paid by ffrancis Baker, brother and heire of John Baker lately dead ; But whether in Socage or by knight service, iudge you, out of the Evidences followinge. *Vincents lands.*

In the time of kinge Henry the Third theis were the lands of Burwe or Burgo, After of Walter Burwe ; Betweene whose coheires, vz, Katherine Woht and Richard Cliveden, partition was made by Deed in 48. E. 3. ; And after they were the lands of Richard Wooth her sonne, And after of Robert Wooth, And after of Vincent their cozen and heire, whose seisin gave and still preserves the name of Vincents lands, continuinge in that name of Vincent from the time of kinge H. 6. vnto the 30. H. 8. as appeareth by the Deeds and other Evidences, wherof part doe remaine with the said ffrancis Baker, and some with my selfe, wherin the names of the owners of theis lands are spelled and written as before I have written them.

In which 30. H. 8. Willm Vincent sold theis lands to Sir Nicholas Pointz the elder, knight ; And after in the same yeare, the said Sir Nicholas sold to John Baker and his heires the messuage in Snitend in Nybley, (which is inrolled with the Clerke of the peace,) with the lands therto belonginge ; Which John Baker had also a fyne from the said Willm Vincent in Michas terme a⁰ 4. et 5. Ph : & Mar̃., who was sonne of Edward and of Emott his wife ; which fyne is of—104. acres of land in Northnybley, Stone, and Berkeley, which I conceive was of all the lands that at any time were the said Vincents, wherof John Baker had but a small part, wherof hee dyed seized in 18. Eliz. leaving the same to James Baker his sonne and heire, who dyed in 37. Eliz. leavinge issue Robert and Thomas ; Robert dyed with-

out

Hundred of Berkeley

out issue in   , And Thomas was his brother and heire who dyed in   Jacobi, leavinge issue John Baker and ffrancis Baker; which John dyed in September last, 1639. without issue, And the said ffrancis inheriteth his said house and lands as his brother and heire; Howbeit Elizabeth widowe of the said John holdeth the said house and the lands therto belonginge in Jointure by the conveyance of the said John and Thomas his father, who in this month of June 1639. remaryed to Edward Hopkins of Wortley in the parish of Wotton: And by the tenant | of this messuage and land is paid the said—10ˢ cheese rent.

By Deed also inrolled with the Clerke of the peace the said Sir Nicholas Pointz in the same 30. H. 8. sold to Thomas Rogers and his heires nyne acres and an halfe of this land, which hee the same yeare had purchased of the said Willm Vincent; The said Thomas Rogers and his heires payinge yearly to him and his heires one red rose at Midsomer for all services; which (however the reservacõn bee,) is paid to the said Lord Berkeley at this day, and other services done.

The said cheife rent and services were anciently paid and done to the Manor of Cowley, vntill Henry lord Berkeley grandfather of the said lord George, for the ease of his Reeves of that manor of Cowley and of the ffreeholders of theis Vincents lands, (then growne to bee many,) did in Sᵒ Rᵗ Jacobi at their request appoint them and two copiholders more David and Richard Rogers to pay those rents and doe their services at Wotton fforren, wherin the lands doe lye and themselves dwell, and not at Cowley, 3. miles of.   See fol: 292.

In Berkeley Castle is an accompt of the manor of Wotton fforren in 16. H. 6, which shewes That Willm the sonne and heire of Richard Othe als Ethe was in ward to Richard Beauchampe Earle of Warwicke for his lands in Nibley, let for 20ˢ 10ᵈ p ann: At which time the said Earl held the said Manors of Wotton and Cowley by an award made betweene him and James lord Berkeley, for his life.

Their lands called Vincents are the severall inheritances of my selfe and of you my sonne John, John Purnell of Wike sonne and heire of Thomas, Editha Marten of Bristoll daughter of Richard, John Cole of Bush streete, late Thomas Rogers who died 22ᵒ Jacobi, sonne of Richard Rogers who died 32. Eliz, sonne of Richard who died in   , sonne of that Thomas Rogers who as aforesaid purchased his part of theis lands of Sir Nicholas Pointz in 30. H. 8. Richard Browninge of Dursley, ffrancis Baker aforesaid, Willm Rudiford sonne of Thomas, John Cole of
Bush

Bush streete aforesaid, for the house and backside wherin the said Thomas Rogers lived; Samuell Trotman of Stancombe, Willm Curnocke, Willm Marten of Nibley, Willm Reece of the Rodegreene neere Holts, and John Rogers sonne of John Rogers a younger brother of the said Thomas.

More of this hamlet of Snitend, (wherin this land of Bakers is,) is to bee read in Stinchcombe, in fol: 351. |

Heere also in Nibley and in Sinwell is a messuage at the place called Wood-all-ends well, with halfe a yard land anciently therto belonginge, and a meadowe called Grovers mead containinge about 6. acres in Northnibley. And also one Toft and close of pasture and one farundell of land in Sinwell, and two acres and an halfe of arrable land in the feild in Nibley called Slades; which Henry lord Berkeley by his deed dated 10. Augusti a° nono Regis Jacobi granted to John Wilkens and his heires, reservinge the old rents of—3ˡⁱ· 12ᵈ payable quarterly, And—3ˡⁱ· 6ˢ· 8ᵈ· for an heriot after the deceafe of every tenant of the same or of any part therof, And such sute to the Halimot Courts as the customary tenants there doe performe, and—4ᵈ· in money for every default. Howbeit the tenure is of the kinge by knight service in capite, beinge part of the said Lords manor of Wotton fforren, soe holden before the said grant: which John Wilkins still holdeth the same, 1639. See fol: 282.

Wilkins land in Nybley & Sinwell. 290

And I suppose this to bee that land or the greatest part therof wch Robert lord Berkeley in the time of kinge John for 10. markes granted to Adam de Grava and his heires by the name of Totam illam virgatam terræ in villa de Nibbeleia versus Swunhaiam, Rendringe one pound of Cumin at Michas, Salvo regali servicio. And which Richard-atte-grove sonne and heire of Nicholas-atte-grove, great grandchilde of the said Adam, in 19. E. 2. aliened to Walter Bellamy and his heires; and in 3. E. 3. levyed therof a fyne for his further assurance: Which Walter Belamy had also divers other lands in Nubbeley Wotton and Alkington, containinge 30. acres, somtime the land of the said Richard le grover, which hee in 13. E. 3. sold to Thomas lord Berkeley and his heires; And which the said Lord forthwith after his purchase demised to the said Walter Belamy and to Gonneld his wife and to John their sonne, for their lives, at the yearly rent of—20ˢ·

Heere also in Southend in Nibley, is a messuage and 40. acres of land therto belonginge: And also one Toft and halfe a yard land containinge 30. acres in Swyney in Nibley aforesaid, And also three acres and an halfe of arrable land

Martens land in Nibley.

in

in Nibley aforesaid; All which Henry lord Berkeley by his Deed dated 13°. Novembr̃. A°. 8. R̃ Jacobi granted to Wm̃ Marten and his heires, reservinge the old yearly rent of—33ˢ. 8ᵈ. payable quarterly, And sute to the halimot court of Wotton fforren as other customary tenants doe performe, or 4ᵈ for every default. Howbeit the tenure is of the kinge by knight service in Capite, beinge part of the said lords manor of Wotton fforren, soe holden before the said grant, And which the said William Marten then held by Copy of Court Roll accordinge to the custome of the said Manor: Which Wm̃ Marten hath aliened these parcells therof, vz,

William Curnocke holds one close called Pilwell containinge 8. acres, and paieth of the said—33ˢ. 8ᵈ. rent—4ᵈ. |

291 John Carpenter in right of Margaret his wife daughter of Henry Hayward, holds one close of pasture called Wickley cont. about 10. acres, And paieth of the said—33ˢ. 8ᵈ. rent 4ᵈ.; which the said Henry purchased of the said—

Gyles Clarke holdeth 7. acres of arrable land in Bournfeild vnder the Cockshoot, and an heystall there containinge about 2. acres, and of the said—33ˢ. 8ᵈ. rent paieth 2ᵈ which hee purchased of John Jones, And hee of the said Wm̃ Marten.

Richard Marten sonne of the said William, which his father conveyed to him vpon his mariage, vpon good consideracõn, holdeth

And I my selfe doe hold

Trotmans land, and mine, in Fee-farme. **Also Henry lord Berkeley** by his deed dated 13° Novembr̃. a° 8° R̃ Jacobi, granted to Thomas Trotman of Nybley and his heires, Three messuages with 101. acres of land to them severally belonginge, in Nybley, reservinge the yearly rent of—3ˡⁱ. 3ˢ. 4ᵈ. payable quarterly, and sute of Court as other customary tenants doe performe, or 4ᵈ in money for every default; And 40ˢ. the peece in name of Heriotts for every of the said three messuages, after the decease of every one dyinge tenant to the premisses or any part therof; One only of which Messuages in fforthey in Nibley

Nibley

Nibley with 42. acres of land therto belonginge, fomtime in the tenure of Robert Richards, remaineth at this day to the faid Thomas Trotman and John his eldeft fonne, vnder the yearly rent of—33ˢ 4ᵈ And the refidue is by feverall grants from him the inheritance of my felfe, and others, as followeth, who pay the refidue of the faid rent, beinge—30ᵒ Aᵒ 1639. That meffuage in ffortheỵ wherein the faid Thomas Trotman nowe dwelleth beinge holden by knight fervice in capite, and was before held by copy of court roll accordinge to the cuftome of the faid Lords manor of Wotton fforren.

ffor the refidue of the faid meffuages and lands my felfe at that time of purchafe contracted with the faid Lord and his Comiſſioñs, and put the fame into the conveyances made to Thomas Trotman, ffor then, and for neere 2. yeares after, the inheritance was in Wiłłm Dutton of Shirborne Efq, and my felfe, wherby beinge a grantor with the faid Lord and Mʳ Dutton, (as wee were in more then 100. feefarme leafes to tenants and abfolute fales,) I could not, (till Mʳ Dutton and my felfe had difcharged the truft,) take the fame in mine owne name, and till after our regrant to the faid lord and his heires by ffyne ; ffor this manor of Wotton and divers others were alfo fecurities to him and my felfe for above—6000ˡⁱ which wee vpon our owne fecurities borrowed for the faid lord to pay to Robert Lord Lifle Earle of Leieʳ, vpon the | compofiçõn at that time in 7ᵒ Jacobi, made with him.

One of which meffuages which I contracted for lyeth in Snytend and was then in the tenure of Richard Nelme, and is holden in Socage, and was fomtime the land of Peter fonne of Thomas de Stintefcombe, of whom the anceftor of the faid lord Henry purchafed the fame, for which I pay the old yearly rent of 18ˢ

The other two meffuages (nowe but one, in the tenure of Wiłłm Payne the younger,) lye togeather at the great greene called Nibleis greene, and were fomtime in the feverall tenures of David Rogers and Richard Rogers vnder the feverall rents of—12ˢ and 10ˢ which I ftill pay ; And were by them held by copy of Court roll accordinge to the cuftome of the manor of Cowley, yet holden in Socage alfo, and were in the time of kinge E. 3. purchafed by Thomas lord Berkeley of the Prior of Lanthony with other lands in Cowley called Can-court, or Cannons-court, nowe there held by copies alfo by John Browninge and Richard Partridge, as the Deeds with my felfe doe fhewe : And theis rents were by Henry lord Berkeley turned over to bee thenceforth paid to his manor of Wotton fforren, As I before have written in Vincents lands, fol : 289.

Ralph

Ralph Willet of Wotton an Atturney at lawe, holdeth certaine inclosed grounds wheron an house is of late built called Binley, cont 7. acres, which hee purchased of John Trotman eldest sonne of the said Thomas Trotman, to whom, vpon his mariage with the sister of the said Ralph Willet, hee conveyed the same, and were peell of his messuage at fforthay aforesaid, but paieth noe part of his rent.

You also my sonne John hold 3 small closes in Swyney, nowe in the tenure of Thomas Hughes, which I purchased of the said Thos: Trotman and John his sonne and gave to you, cont 4. acres; And more, which I purchased of them, viz, two closes called Broadmead and Cherry mead cont 3. acres, in Swyney aforesaid, nowe in the tenure of ffrancis Purnell, but pay noe part of his rent of—33^s 4^d.

Patricke Dunninge, mason, holds one acre and an halfe at Bournstream, wheron hee hath lately built an house, which hee purchased of the said Thomas Trotman, and of his said ffee-farme rent payeth—2^d to the said Thomas Trotman.

John Smyth of Southend Clothier holdeth 3. acres of arr and pasture ground in Rodleis Deane, neere the house of Willm Archard, which hee purchased of Tobias Hathaway younger sonne of Henry Hathaway, who purchased the same of the said Thomas Trotman, And of his said ffee-farme rent paieth—8^d.

And the said Patricke Dunninge holds also the quarre by Bournstreame neere his said house, which hee purchased of the said Thomas Trotman, And hee of the lord Berkeley by his deed aforesaid ; And was part of the copihold land of George May of Southend, and paies to the lord Berkeley per ann—4^d holden in capite.

Anthony Hungerford Esq, holdeth |

ffor other purchasers of ffee-farme lands, see in Wotton, fol : [409] and after.

Mandaies lands.
Moores mill.

Also in Nibley is an ancient messuage, with divers lands and a fullinge mill and grift mill under one roofe, of old therto belonginge, comonly called **Mundaies** land ; which messuage is scituate at the bottom of the great greene called Nibleis greene, which I conceive to bee holden of the manor of Woodmancote by fealty only. Theis in the time of kinge H. 5. were the lands of John Munday, who had issue Thomas
Munday

Munday, who had iſſue Willm Munday and Walter Munday, which Willm left iſſue Thomas, who had 4. daughters his coheires, vz. Jone maryed to John Rugge, Alice als Agnes firſt maried to Humphry Hadley, and after his death remaried to David Bendall, Eliz: and Jane, who dyed without iſſue, though maryed alſo; Of the two firſt iſſue remaineth at this day, As may bee ſeene in a ſute proſecuted by Engliſh bill in the Chancery in 42º Eliz: by Thomas Rugge ſonne of the ſaid Jone, and John Rugge, againſt Nicholas Munday ſonne of Thomas Munday, ſonne of the foreſaid Walter brother of Willm, who claymed as heires males of the body of Thomas ſonne of the firſt John Munday, which eſtate tayle hee created by a Deed, (nowe with mee,) and prevailed therby in that ſuite: Which Nicholas dyed the yeare after that ſuite ended in 43º Eliz: then very old: leavinge iſſue Willm Munday who dyed in 16º Jacobi, leavinge iſſue 3. ſonnes, viz, Nicholas who died without iſſue in 2º Rᵉ Caroli, after hee had aliened ſome part of this land; And Willm Munday yet livinge, who hath alſo aliened part, and ſtill holds ſome part, And Thomas Munday, to whom his brother Nicholas deviſed the ſaid meſſuage and greateſt part of theis lands in fee, Of whom in 3º Rᵉ Caroli I purchaſed them.

As for the ſaid Griſt and fullinge mills, ſomtimes in ancient deeds called Mundaies mills, the foreſaid Rugge and Hadley and their ſaid wives aliened them to John Moore in fee, (from whom they retaine the name of Moores Mills, at this day moſt comonly vſed,) who in temp: Mariæ Reginæ aliened them to Hampden: And hee about 3. Eliz: to Hilpe, And hee in 9º Jacobi Rᵉ, to Jones; whoſe daughter and heire | called Jone is nowe wife of Richard Triſtram of Briſtoll, who offer them to ſale at this day, 1639.

Alſo in Southend in Nibley is an ancient meſſuage with divers lands therto belonginge, nowe the inheritance of Chriſtopher Purnell aforeſaid, yonger ſonne of Thomas Purnell, to whom and his heires his ſaid father deviſed the ſame by his will, and which hee had purchaſed of Willm Curnocke of Southend, ſonne of Thomas Curnocke, who purchaſed the ſame of Hanbury, one of the Auditors to Queene Eliz: And hee of the ſaid Queene; holden in comon Socage, and was parcell of the poſſeſſions of the monaſtery or Abby of Kingſwood, and came to the Crowne in 29. H. 8. by the diſſolucōn of that Monaſtery; An houſe lately by caſuall fire burned to the ground, yet vnbuilt.

Purnells land in Southend late Curnockes.

I have ſeene a faire Deed in 4. E. 4. wherby the yearly rent of—8ᵈ was given ad inveniendam vnam lampadem ardentem coram imagine beatæ Mariæ virginis in Eccleſia

Nybley church. antea, fol: 261.

Ecclesia Sči Martini de Nybley: Soe that it seemes the Church was dedicated to S! Martin (the bishop,) whose festivall was the 11.th of November, (the sixt returne day of Michas Terme,) and hee the tutelary Saint therof; wherof see before fol: 261. Howbeit the south Isle of this church was of newe added since that deed to the rest of the old church; As in the office of the Register to the Bishop of Worcester at Worcester, (as I am informed) appeareth.

Nybley an hamblett to Woodmancote.   Soe great a part of this Township of Nibley was belonginge in demesne and service to the manor of Woodmancote, As that by Inquisicōn in 6. H. 6. after the death of Sir John Berkeley, the Jury found that Nibley is an hamblett belonginge to the manor of Woodmancote. Wherof see in Woodmancote, fol: 389.

295
296
297
298 } blank

299

Nimesfeild.

Nimesfeild: In Domesday booke written **Nimdesselle**, wherin William the Conqueror had, as that booke saith, three hides of land in demesne, nowe the inheritance of George Bridgeman, sonne and heire of Sir John Bridgeman knight late cheife Justice of Chester, who dyed this last yeare, a° 1638. Holden by knight service in Capite.

As I have formerly written of the discent of the Lo.p or manor of Hill, fol: 225. In like manner is to bee written of this of Nimesfeild; which beinge granted by kinge H. 2. (amongst many others) to Robert the sonne of Hardinge and his heires, was shortly after, within the first 17. yeares of that kings raigne, conveyed by him to Nicholas his second sonne and his heires, As by the deed mentioned in the description of Hill appeares: Both which Manors kept togeather in the possession of the said Nicholas and his issue male, without severance, vntill the death of Sir Thomas fitz-Nichol knight in 5. H. 5. and then this of Nimesfeild discended in coparcinery to Katherine and Alice[1] his two daughters and heires; Katherine was maried to Robert Pointz, and Alice was maried to John Browninge, whose posterities and names continue at Acton and Cowley at this day, 1639, as in Hill hath byn declared, though neither of their families hath any of theis manors.

John Browninge and Alienor his wife died in the life time of the said Sir Thomas fitz Nichol her father, leavinge issue two sonnes, vz, John Browninge then 20. yeares

---

[1] Called Alienor in the description of Hill, and below.

20. yeares old, who after dyed without iſſue, and Wiłłm Browninge: which William in 10. H. 6. (before partition was made for ought I finde,) aliened his moity of this manor of Nimesfeilde to Thomas Pointz and Jone his wife in tayle, with the remainder in fee to Robert Pointz his father; To which Thomas and Jone the ſame Robert and Katherine his wife had the ſame yeare in like manner conveyed their other moity of this manor: And ſoe this Loᵖ of Nimesfeild again became vnited. Nimesfeild thus in one, the ſaid Thomas and Jone had iſſue—

And the ſaid Sir Edmond Tame dyinge without iſſue in   , this manor of Nimesfeild deſcended to his 3. ſiſters and heires; vz. Margaret maried to Sir Humphrey Stafford knight, who in pertition had land in Tetbury and other places: Alice. maried to   Verney, to whom this manor of Nimesfeild with others was allotted; and Anne, maried to   Watkins of Herefordſhire. And for the perticularities of the ptitions amongſt theis 3. coheires and their huſbands, ſee a Deed inrolled in the Comon pleas in Michas Terme Aᵒ 2. E. 6. and another in the ſame Court in Michas terme, annis, 13ᵒ et 14ᵒ Eliz. Reginæ. |

Which ſaid   Verney and Alice his wife had iſſue—   , father of Sir Richard Verney knight, who in   Jacobi Rᶜ, ſold this manoʳ to the ſaid Sir John Bridgeman, who by his death as aforeſaid left it to his ſaid ſonne George, as aforeſaid.

A Manour neither great nor good, but worſe and leſſe, without the old and rich Chantry of Kinley wherwith it is nowe beautified: Vnhappy it ſeemed to bee in the controverſies that aroſe betweene Sir Thomas Throkmerton of Tortworth knight and Sir Henry Winſton of Standiſh knight, and their abbettors; The cauſe wherof An Inquiſicōn in 28. Eliz: taken after the death of Wiłłm Smyth ſhall let you in to knowe; who is therby found to dye ſeized of the Manor of Kinley (for ſoe is the Chantry often written) with the appurtenances in Kinley, Nimesfeild, ffairford, and Hampton, holden of Henry lord Berkeley, as of his Caſtle of Berkeley hernes, in free ſocage by fealty only, for all ſervices; And of two acres in Nimesfeild called the Greenes, holden by knight ſervice in Capite: And that the ſaid Wiłłm Smyth died 9. yeares before, in 19ᵒ Eliz; And that William was his ſonne and heire, 10. yeares old at his fathers death.

This

This land the said Willm Smyth in 31º. Eliz: sold to one Wheler, and hee to Hanbury a goldsmith in London, and hee to Sr. Henry Winston aforesaid: And for a lease that the said William Smyth in the same 31. Eliz: but three daies before hee sealed his conveyance to Wheler, for 1000. yeares at the rent of a pepper corne, to one Bretland, who in 39. Eliz: assigned the same over to Richard Messenger, (trusted for Sir Thomas Throkmerton,) have all those fatall bills and sutes both in the Starchamber and other courts sprange vp, like Hidraes heads, betweene those two knights and their partakers, wherof one was heard in the Starchamber in Michas terme 43. et 44. Eliz: what time my selfe was present, then intendinge this description.

Of which Willm Browninge who aliened to Thomas Pointz as aforesaid, it may be said perijsset nisi periisset, for by a wastfull youth hee became thrifty in elder yeares, ffarmer and tenant to the Abbot of St. Peters in Glouc̄ for his impropriate personage or Rectory of Cowley, a parish next adioyninge to this of Nimesfeild, where hee dyed in the   yeare of kinge   , leavinge issue John Browninge, noe lesse watchfull over his estate then his fathers elder yeares, as the pardon of kinge E. 4. in the 16th. yeare of his raigne may witnes; who dyed in   , leavinge issue John and Willm: John was a preist and dyed without issue, and Willm had issue John and died in   ; The said John sonne of Willm died in 5. Mar̄. leavinge issue Richard who dyed in 37º. Eliz:, leavinge issue John Browninge who dyed in 14º. Caroli regis, and left issue John, Mary, and Vrsula, that nowe are, 1639. By which Mary the author of this description hath issue five sonnes and 4. daughters nowe livinge, And the 4. eldest of them 13. more; Of whom you my eldest sonne by Anne the eldest daughter of Sir Edward Bromfeild knight have six for your part, & likely to have more; Thus hath the Almighty multiplied mee, farre beyond hope, for which blessed bee his holy name evermore. And the said Rectory of Cowley hath ever since continued in the posterity of the said first named Willm Browninge, and still doth; Each of them in their severall discents havinge added to the former possessions of his ancestor, And this John that nowe lives, the best husband of them all. |

301
Common Inne.

A common Inne in this village addes fame therto, by the constant customary baytes of the Ryppiers and their horses, each thursday in the yeare, at fower of the clocke in the afternoone, for one houre only; bringinge South sea fish in their passage to the Cities of Glouc̄ and Worcester, what time many neighbors are furnished.

Nimesfeild

Sir George Huntley late of ffrocefter knight about 20. yeares paft, found **The Parke.** meanes by purchafes exchanges and otherwife, to enclofe a very great proportion of ground with a ftone wall, and therof made a Parke, wherin at his death within 3. or 4. yeares after, (occafioned by a fall from his horfe, wherof hee fodainely dyed, as hee was in openinge of a gate,) hee leaft deere, Conyes, hoggs, fheepe, horfes, rudder beafts, fifh, wood, water, ftones, and quid non! wherof 300. acres or more were taken out of this manor of Nimesfeild; And the inhabitants out of a rurall reluctaçon againft fuch enclofures, afcribe to the iniuftice of that act not only his fuddaine death forthwith after at the place, But the fale of that and all the reft of his land made by his fonne Wiłłm Huntley in a fhort time after, to Sir Robert Ducy an Alderman of London, whofe fonne Sir Richard Ducy now dwelleth there- vpon, 1639.

By an Inqu: in 17. E. 2. in the Tower of London, John Gifford of Nimsfeild is found to dye feized of a meffuage and 60. acres of land in Nimsfeild, holden of the Kinge in Capite by two pound of pepper: And alfo of 12 acres of land in Nimsfeild holden of John de Oulpen by 2^d rent; And that John is his fonne and heire, 21. yeares old. And by Rot. finiū: 17. E. 2. membr. 7. the faid John did fealty to the kinge for the meffuage and 60. acres holden as aforefaid.

By Rot. claus: 8. E. 1. membr. 8, In a longe proces about the Chaple of **Kinley.** Kinley in Nimesfeild, the inheritance of Nicholas fitz Raph, then within age, and the kings ward, the bifhop is forbidden to vifite it.

By Inqu: in 6. E. 6. in the Chaple of the Rolls, Wiłłm Stumpe Efq, is found to dye feized of the manor of Kinley with the appurteñnts, in Kinley, Nimpsfeild, ffairford, and Hampton, holden of the manor of Berkeley hernes by fealty only for all fervices. And that Sir James Stumpe knight was his fonne and heire, 33. yeares old: But that this manor of Kinley was fetled vpon Wiłłm Stumpe his yonger fonne by a fecond wife, then but 3 yeares old.

By a deed dated on Eafter day, a° 32. E. 1. It was agreed betweene Thomas de Swonhunger of the one part, and dominum Walterum capellanum cuftodem de Kinley, et focios fuos ibidem deo et beatæ Mariæ fervientes, of the other part, That they fhould hold all the arrable land of the faid Thomas without the enclofure in Nemedesfelde, Yweley, et Olepen, for 9. yeares, &c. |

The

Hundred of Berkeley

302
Fifteene. The payment of the ffifteene or Kingfilver, when it is granted by parliament, goeth with the village of Hill, vnder the some of 8ˡⁱ 7ˢ 2ᵈ q, in the onus or charge in the Exchequer; The deduction there, is—36ˢ 8ᵈ for decaies: The Remanet paid by the Collector into the Receipt is—6ˡⁱ 10ˢ 6ᵈ q,; whereof this parish of Nimesfeild paies—39ˢ 8ᵈ

Subfedy. In the laſt Subfedy in aᵗ 5ᵗᵒ Rᵉ Caroli were 5. ſubſedy men within this parish, who paid—28ˢ Beſides Sir John Bridgeman then lord therof, beinge at that time Cheife Juſtice of Cheſter, rated by himſelfe.

Able men. Of able men for the warres betweene 20. and 60. yeares old, in 6ᵗᵒ Jacobi Rᵉ at a generall muſter that appeared before Henry lord Berkeley then Lieutenant of the county, were—26.

Souldiers. And nowe, 1639, of trayned Souldiers vnder Edward Stephens Eſq, their captaine, are

Rates. And if the wholl Diviſion of Berkeley (accompted a 4ᵗʰ part of the county) bee in any taxe for kinge or commonwealth rated at—100ˡⁱ, Then this hundred of Berkeley paies therof—33ˡⁱ 3ˢ And this parish of Nimesfeild—15ˢ And ſoe after that proportion bee the taxe more or leſſe.

If what is already written ſuffice not, read more of this township and Manor of Nimesfeild out of theis Records; vz,

Inq: 33. E: 1. pro Adam le Walſh, et Nicho fit Radulphi.
Inq: 6. E. 2: pᵗ mortē pdči Nichi filij Radi.
Inq: 15. E. 3. Ad quod damnum, pro Johe fitz Nichoł.
Inq: 29. E. 3. pro Johe fitz Nichoł et Eva vxore ſuā.
Michas Records. 20. H. 6. Rot. 41. in Sčcio, c̄m Reñi Theſaur̄:
Inq: 9. H. 5. pᵗ mortē Thome fitz Nichoł miltis.
ffinis in banco, 3. R. 2. by Thomas fitz Nichoł aforeſaid, de Mañijs de Nimesfelde et ffilton.
Triñ Record in Sčcio. 17. E. 4. Rot. 4. c̄m Remeñi Theſaur̄.

The Deed triptite in the c̄omon pleas inrolled in Michas terme 2. E. 6. betweene Humphrey Stafford and other the coheires of Edmond Tame, for a partition amongſt them, is already mentioned, with another that followed in Michas Terme, 13ᵒ et 14ᵒ Eliz. |

Oakeley

Oakeley Parke.

Oakeley Parke: wherof see before in Alkington, fol: 30. et 64. In the time of kinge H. 3. written Acle.

Vpon this parke or parcell of pasture ground called at this day Oakely or Oakeley parke, but anciently Oeley and Hockley, doe hange, (as also vpon Hackmill in Wotton and some other lands,) In-supers with the kings Auditors and Receivors of this county; Arrearages of ten times a greater value then the fee simple of the same are worth: Occasioned in those tumblinge times of kinge E. 6. by a purchase made by Sir Edward Seymour, (brother to the Duke of Somset, Protector to kinge E. 6.,) of the said kinge in the   of his raigne, whilest the Manor of Alkington (wherof this parke is parcell) was in the Crowne, togeather with the residue of the Barony of Berkeley called **Berkeleys lands** in all the said Accompts, entayled by William Marques Berkeley vpon kinge H. 7. and the heires males of his body in the 4th yeare of his raigne, wherof see before, fol: [7] Which againe were by the said Sir Edward Seymour given backe to the said kinge E. 6. in the   yeare of his raigne, by way of Exchange for other lands, after Sir Edward had disparked and improoved them; But into theis Henry lord Berkeley as right heire to the said Marques Berkeley entered in 1° Mariæ, imediately after the death of kinge E. 6, And soe held them till hee dyed in 11° Jacobi, as his grandchilde and heire the lord George Berkeley ever since hath, and still doth.

Likewise vpon this parke and other lands doe hange other arrearages, which yearly increase before the kings aforesaid Officers, occasioned by grants and re-grants made after the death of Sir Edward Seimour and his attainder, betweene the said kinge E. 6. and Sir John Thyn; which I heere the rather remember, because ever since (once in 7. yeares at the least,) proces cometh forth for the levellinge of theis arreares and somes of money out of the Exchequer, directed to base and meane persons whom nothinge will satisfy or keepe from distraininge save bribery & some money; which the lord Berkeley may avoid (as is well knowne to the Exchequer officers,) by his remainder in fee, for want of issue male of the body of kinge Henry the seaventh.

The said Sir John Thyn died in 22° Eliz. as the office then found after his death sheweth: And by Christian his first wife had issue Sir John Thyn, father of Sir Thomas Thyn that nowe is, 1639. And by Dorothy his second wife (after remaried

remaried to Sir Carewe Raleigh,) had iſſue Sir Henry Thyn, Charles, Edward, William, Egremond a Sergeant at lawe, Katherine, and Greſſam. |

304 blank

305

Owſelworth.

Owſelworth: In the booke of Domeſday in the kings Exchequer is written **Osleuuorde**; wherin kinge Edward the Conſeſſor had, as alſo William the Conqueror had, as that booke faith, halfe an hide of land in demeſne, nowe the inheritance of Sir Gabriell Lowe knight, holden of the kinge by knight ſervice in capite.

A pariſh and manor conſiſtinge of 14. dwellinge houſes, wherof I accompt the mantion or dwellinge houſe of the ſaid Sir Gabriell Lowe, called Newe worke, to bee one: The rectory none.

Roger Berkeley of Durſeley was ſeiſed of this manor in the times of the ſaid Conſeſſor, and of the Conqueror, as the ſaid booke of Domeſdai ſheweth, who leaft iſſue Willm Berkeley, who in the time of kinge Henry the firſt, the Conquerors ſonne, founded the Abby of St. Mary of Kingſwood by Wotton, endowinge it with faire poſſeſſions, wherof read before in Durſeley, fol: 176. And if the ancient Redd booke in the Exchequer had not expreſſed the certificate of Roger Berkeley ſonne and heire of the ſaid Willm, (which ſee before in fol: 177.) wherby hee gives kinge Henry the ſecond to vnderſtand, That in Eſſlewrd (foe therin written) hee then had in his demeſne halfe an hide of land, I would have ſaid That the ſame had byn given by the ſaid Willm Berkeley to that monaſtery at his firſt foundinge therof; But a great farme or grange was which the Abbot had, which continued with an increaſe as after followeth till the diſſolution of that monaſtery in 29. et 31. H. 8; wherof reade before in Caldecote fol: [211]. And was by them called a manor or the manor of Owſelworth; which foe cominge to the Crowne was by—

it came to Thomas Rivet an Alderman of London, To whom Henry lord Berkeley by his deed dated 20. Maij. 14º Eliz; at the requeſt of Sir Nicholas Pointz, (as the deed ſpeakes,) releaſed all his right and intereſt in the capitall meſſuage called Owſelworth houſe als the Newe buildinge, and in the lands therto belonginge,
And

And in all thofe lands in Wortley late parcell of the Chantry of S! John Baptift in Wortley. And in divers lands in Wortley called the lampe lands; The counterpart of which Deed is in Berkeley caftle.

ffrom which Sir Thomas Rivet by fale it came to S! Thomas Lowe, als Loe, another Alderman of London, and from him to the faid Sir Gabriell his fonne and heire nowe owner therof, as aforefaid, Captaine of the 50. trayned horfe in the Divifion of Berkeley; whofe forefaid dwellinge houfe called New-worke was in the time of kinge E. 6. built by Sir Nicholas Pointz the elder, father of the forefaid Sir Nicholas, partly with the ftones and timber of the forefaid demolifhed monaftery of Kingfwood, fearce two miles diftant, And partly with the ftones pulled from the Croffes in the parifhes therabouts.

An houfe whofe fcituaçòn may feeme (with fmall helpe from the figure Hyperbole,) to overlooke the North pole: from whence may bee feene the Church and village of Owfelworth feated in the depth of a deepe valley, where the inhabitants may (if vfually they doe not) cut make and caft their billet wood and fagots in at their chimney pots, to fave other cariage. |

A place the parifh is, where for a great part each bufh hath its burrowe, and each burrowe a litter of foxes, (delicias humani generis,) ffrom whence the yearly rent to the furrier is ten dozen of cafes; And as George Huntley of Boxwell Efq. who dwelled hard by fearce 40. paces from the borders of this manor, and Giles Daunt gent his fellowe huntfman, dwellinge in the faid houfe called New-worke, (gent of ancient families,) have 30 yeares fince informed mee, their flaughter of foxes (vnles you will call them a quarry) have byn 231. in one yeare, if they miftooke not their Arithmeticke, which I beleive they did not. Parturiunt ifti montes, ready by the next earthquake to cover towne houfes chimnies wood and foxes, Sed non nafcitur ridiculus mus, as the proverbe in Erafmus is; But nafcuntur feptem fancti fontes, feaven excellent fountaines, fprings of admirable water and holy vertue, (as fpeake the inhabitants) iffue forth in reftles abundance, at the feete therof: Theis feaven holy fprings once affembled into one channell, make Hellmill, the inheritance of   , And thence followinge their valley and channell downe and downe, confine this hundred of Berkeley from that of Grombaldfafh, vntill they fall into the river of

In this manor is that little fort called the **Broome**, famous for the duell about 30. yeares paft betweene Sir Willm Throkmton Baronet and Walter Walfh, then of

little

little Sodbury, Esq.; both of them since devoured by riot and improvidence, with their patrimonies in Tortworth and Sodbury.

By a writt called an old Ad quod damnum, dated 10. April. 35. E. 1, and by an Inquisition thervpon in the same yeare, it appeares That this Abbot of Kingswood purchased of the Abbot of Glouc̃ one acre of land in Bagpath with the Advowsons of the churches of Owselworth and of west newenton, by way of Exchange. In lieu of ten pound rent in Hasenden and Culkerton given by the Abbot of Kingswood to the Abbot of St Peters of Glouc̃; And that the said Churches are holden of John sonne of Willm de Berkeley, in ward to the kinge, in puram eleemosynam; And that the said 10^{li} rent is holden of Peter de Breowsa, in puram eleemosynam, also.

An ancient booke of knights fees in the Exchequer with the Remembrancer to the Lord Treasorer, in the time of kinge E. 1. saith, The Abbot of Kingswood holds Owselworth of Henry de Berkeley of Dursley, And hee of the kinge.

By a deed without date, Robert de Rochford granted to the Abbot of Kingswood, Totam donationem Willimi de Bretun de vna cotelda terræ in villa de Osewrde, quam Alicia Toki eid Willelmo vendidit. And also by his other Deed without date, granted to the said Abbot, Donacõem Galfridi filij Galfridi de Chauci de alia cotselda terre in eadem villa de Owselworth. To which Robert de Rochford Cecilia was wife, and survived him, in a° 1241, 27. H. 3. As 3 deeds in Berkeley castle doe shewe.

By a deed without date, Lucia filia Roberti de Rochford, soror et heres Willi de Rochford, released to the Abbot of Kingswood All her right and interest in the Manor of Owselworth. |

By deed without date, John sonne of Robert the nephew, of Owselworth, gave to Thomas de Rochford All the land which Roger de Berkeley of Dursley gave to Thomas his brother in Owselworth.

By deed without date, John the Nevou of Owselworth, gave halfe his mill in Owselworth to Robert de Rochford, in fee.

By deed without date, Katherine de Rochford gave to Agnes her daughter 8. acres of land in the manor of Owselworth, which shee had of the guist of Robert de Rochford her father in franke marriage.

All

Owselworth

All theis Deeds in Berkeley castle.

The Records of Michas terme in 4. H. 3. Rot. 11. in coi banco shewe, That Robert de Rochford granted to Andrew de Bere and Alice his wife in taile, the manor of Owselworth, To hold of him by halfe a knights fee.

By the said Record of Michas terme in aº 4. H. 3. aforesaid, Andreas de la Bere et Alicia vxor eius veniunt et cognoscunt quod tenent de Roberto Rochford manerium de Owselworth per serviciū dimidij feodi militis, et inde cepit homagium suum.

Triñ Recc. in banco, 27. H. 3. Johes de Berkeley de Durlley impleades Thomas de Rochford for his lands in Owselworth, except the advowson of the church there. Plita Assisaȝ. 32. H. 3. shewes That Richard de la Bere and Thomas de Rochford were vncle and nephewe, and heere tryed their severall titles; (my notes therin taken were too short.)

By the Records of Triñ terme in banco. 34. H. 3. Rot. 6, Sibill the widowe of Walter de Owselworth recovered dower of a third part of 4. hides of land in Owselworth and Newenton, againſt the Arch-bishop of Yorke.

By Rot. pateñ, 42. H. 3. ps. 1. Jone the widowe of Thomas lord Berkeley brought a writt of Attaint againſt Henry de Wildby, concerninge certaine lands in Owfelworth.

See also Simondsfall fol: 323. for Owselworth grange.

Saint Nicholas was the tutelary saint and protector of the church of Osle- *Church.* worth, as appeareth by a Deed without date, To whom it was dedicated.

Many other were the perticuler purchases of this Abbot of Kingswood in this pariſh of Owselworth. As the Deeds remaininge with Sir Robert Pointz of Acton, which I have read, doe shewe.

By Deed dated 1272. 56. H. 3. Henricus de Berkeley Dñs de Durſley recepit 80. marcas de Dño Abbate et Conventu de Kingswood pro confirmatione Manij de Owselworth et fine inde facto. |

In

308 ffifteene.	**In** payment of the ffifteenth or Kingſilver when it is granted by parliament, The onus or charge to the collector therof is with Newton als Newenton and Bagpath, which goe togeather in the ſome of—[4ˡⁱ 2ˢ] wherof this of Owſelworth payeth ; The deduction is [10ˢ], And the remainder paid by the Collector into the Exchequer is [3ˡⁱ 12ˢ]
Subſedy	**In** the laſt Subſedy in aⁿ 5ᵗᵒ Rᵉ Caroli, were in Owſelworth and in Newton Bagpath 11. ſubſedy men, who paid—6ˡⁱ 17ˢ 4ᵈ
Able men.	Of able men for the warres betweene 20. and 60. yeares old, were in 6ᵗᵒ Jacobi Rᵉ, which then out of this village appeared before the Leiuteñt of this County at a generall muſter, and in Newton and Bagpath who appeared togeather as alſo, was the officers returne—47.
Souldiers.	**Of** Trayned ſouldiers vnder
Rates.	**And** if the wholl Diviſion of Berkeley accompted a 4ᵗʰ part of the ſhire bee rated in any tax for the kinge or comon wealth at an—100ˡⁱ. This hundred paies therof—33ˡⁱ 3ˢ. And this of Owſelworth with Newton and Bagpath—20ˢ. And ſoe after that proportion bee the tax more or leſſe.

309   **Ouldpen.**

Ouldpen als **Olpen**, als **Owlpen**; A little Manor ſeated according to the name; The ſcituation rather givinge the denomination, vz, old, anciently, Aald; And pen, in the Brittiſh head: So compounded of two Saxon or Brittiſh words: Vnles it better like you, Olde, quaſi holepen, (as ſomtimes anciently I have found it written,) the ſcituačõn beinge in as deepe an hole or bottome as elſewhere is to bee ſeene.

It may perhaps like ſome to derive the Etimology from **Owlepen**, quaſi a **penne** or Cage for owles; ſith noe fforreſt made vp of Ivy buſhes can exceed the fitnes for breed and harbour of owles; which derivačõn alſo the coate or bearinge of the Owlpens (owners therof before the time of kinge H. 2.) ſeemeth to countenance, vz, Argent a Cheuron ſable betweene three owles heads pper: which is alſo their ancient, and moderne bearinge to this day.

Ouldpen

In the time of kinge H. 2. it was the land of Barthol de Olepen; After in the times of kinge Richard the first and of kinge John of Simon de Holepen, written also in those times, Simon de Ollepenne : After in the time of kinge H. 3. and of E. 1. of Bartholomewe de Olepen ; After in the same time of E. 1. his raigne and of kinge E. 2. of John de Owlepen, (two at least of that name succeedinge one another,) And after was the land of another John de Owlepenne, whose wardship for body and lands Thomas lord Berkeley the third of that name granted in 3. E. 3. to Wiłłm de Cheltenham then his steward, by his deed in theis words in french vnder the seale of the said lord.

A touts ceux q̃ c̃e tre verrunt ou orrunt, Thomas Seigneur de Berkel salutz in dieux. Sachetz nous avoir done et grant a Wiłłm de Cheltynh'm et a ses heires et ses assignees, la gard de touts les t̃res et tenements John le fitȝ Robert de Oulepenne neueu et heir John de Oulepene ; enseement avouis done et grant au dit Wiłłm, le mariage del dit John fitȝ Robert, issuit q̃ il ne soit disparage ; A avoir et tenir la dit gard des dits t̃res et teñts au dit Wiłłm et a ses heires et a ses assignes, de nous et de nous heires, durant le nonage le dit John fitȝ Robert ; Et si il avigne q̃ le dit John fitȝ Robert devy avant son leal age, grantom9 au dit Wiłłm en la manere susdite la gard des dits t̃res et teñts et la mariage de son prochein h̃re s'il soit deins age, et ensi de heir en heir, tanq, al age de prochein heir ; En testmoigniance de q̃ chose a cestes tres auom9 mis ñre seale, Don a Berkel le pmer iour de Novembr̃ l'an de ragne le Roy Edward tierz apres le conquest, tiertz. (In Berkeley Castle.)

After the death of this John the ward the sonne of Robert, was another Robert de Oulpen who lived in the time of kinge H. 6. and had issue Margery his only daughter and heire, who in the time of kinge E. 4. was maried to John Daunt sonne of Nicholas Daunt : And the said John and Margery dyed togeather in 13. H. 8. As by an Inqu: that yeare virtute officij, after the death of the said Margery appeareth : And left issue Christopher Daunt who died in 35. H. 8. leavinge issue Thomas Daunt who died in 16. Eliz:, leavinge issue Henry and Thomas ; Which Henry dyed in 33. Eliz. leavinge issue Gyles and ffrances ; Gyles dyed in 39. Eliz: six yeares after his father, without issue ; And the said ffrances his sister pretended to bee heire to her brother the said Gyles, and about that time was maried to John Bridgeman, then a younge Barrister of the Inner temple, After a Sergeant at lawe and knighted, and Cheife Justice of Chester, lately dead, shee yet livinge, 1639, who pretended title to this land in right of his wife, but was opposed

by

310 by the said Thomas Daunt, brother of Henry, | her vncle, by vertue of a former entayle to the heires males, wherby hee caryed the land, maugre the oppofition of her hufband and of that powerfull and plottinge gent Sir Thomas Throgmton then of Tortworth knight, who both made the maryage, and abetted the title; Againſt whom the faid Thomas Daunt exhibited fuch a Bill in the Starchamber, difcoveringe fuch plots and practices, as forthwith (for a fome of money by way of compoficōn paid to Mr Bridgeman and his wife) drewe on peace, and further affurance to the faid Thomas Daunt from them both: which Thomas after dyed in aᵒ 20. Jacobi, leavinge iffue Thomas Daunt that nowe is, owner of this little manor or rather at this day reputed manor, of Oulpen; which is holden of George lord Berkeley by the fervice of halfe a knights fee, and fute to his hundred Court of Berkeley from 3. weekes to 3. weekes; Some of the Records heerafter mentioned findinge the tenure of the faid Lords caſtle of Berkeley, and others as of his manor of Wotton vnderedge, to which latter a cheife rent of five fhillings is yearly paid: which heere I difcuffe not. The Capitall meffuage or feite of this manor (wheron the faid Thomas refideth when hee is not in Ireland, as for moſt part hee is there dwellinge,) is in Owlpen, but much the greater part of the lands lye in the parifh of Newton Bagpath. The inhabitants of this Townfhip with their Tythingman are within the Leete of the hundred of Berkeley, where at Berkeley they appeare twice in the yeare.

ffifteene.	**The** payment of the ffifteene or Kingfilver when it is granted by parliament, is paid with the Townfhip of Kingfcote, as hath byn faid, fol: 252.
Subfedy.	**In** the laſt Subfedy in aᵒ 5ᵗᵒ Rᵉ Caroli, the faid Thomas Daunt was only a Subfedy man in this tithinge, who was rated at 4ˡⁱ in land, And paid—16ˢ
Able men.	**In** aᵒ 6ᵗᵒ Regis Jacobi, of able men ferviceable for the warres betweene 20. and 60. yeares old, who appeared before Henry lord Berkeley then Leiutenant of the county, taken by fpeciall direction from that kinge, were—17.
Souldiers.	**Of** Trayned Souldiers vnder Edward Stephens Efq their captaine, nowe are— wherof—
Rates.	**If** the wholl Divifion of Berkeley bee in any rate for kinge or comon wealth taxed at—100ˡⁱ, Then this hundred of Berkeley paieth therof—33ˡⁱ 3ˢ, And this village—5ˢ. And foe after that rate, bee the taxe more or leffe.

More

Oulpen

More of this village of Oulpen is to bee read in theis Records, vz,

A booke of Knights fees with the Lord Trèors Remembrancer in the Exchequer in the time of kinge E. 1. faith, That John de Oulpenne holds there halfe a knights fee of Thomas Lord Berkeley.

Inqu: 4. E. 2. p' mortem Edmundi Baffett, holden—

Vetus Rotul manerij de Wotton temp: E. 1. Robtus de Oulpen tenet vnā virgatam terræ, et debet sectam Curiæ de 3. septimañ in 3. Septiñi et servicium (regale wants in the Roll.) |

Rot. ffranc. 22. E. 3. in dorso. John de Oulpen continued many yeares beyond the seas with Maurice de Berkeley, And therefore was not to bee distrayned in his lands.

Rot. finium 22. H. 6. membr: 15. Johes Oulpen dat 6ˢ 8ᵈ solut in hanaperio pro brevi de forma donationis habend. Glouc.

Rot. pardoñ, 24. H. 6. membr 33. A pardon to Nicholas Daunt of Wotton vnderedge g̃. brother of John Daunt late of Bernardes Inne in Holborne in the Suburbs of London genť, sonnes of Nicholas Daunt of Wotton Vnderedge geñ.

And Rot. pdict. in eod. A pardon to John Daunt of Wotton Vnderedge geñ, als dictus John Daunt late of Bernards Inne geñ, sonne of Nicholas Daunt aforesaid.

Triñ Rec̃. 20. H. 6. Rot. 10. in Sec̃io c̃m Reñi Thesaur̃, pro Oulpen croft in Owlpen, parcell of the possessions of Sᵗ Barthol Hospitall in Glouc.

Inqu: 13. H. 8. p' morte Margeriæ Daunt, before mentioned.

Inqu: 13. H. 8. p̃d, p' mortem Johis Daunt: this is misfiled in the bundle of 1. E. 6. in the Rolls chapple.

Hill Rec̃ in Sec̃io c̃m Reñi Thesaur̃, 21. H. 8. Rot. 3.

Pasch: Rec̃. ibm. 23. H. 8. Rot. 7.

Rot. finium ibm. 23. H. 8. Rot. 3.

Inqu: 35. H. 8. p' mortem Christopheri Daunt.

Inqu·

Inqu : 20. Eliz : p̃ mortem Thomæ Daunt.

Inqu : 20. Jacobi ; p̃ mortem Thomæ Daunt.

Paper booke temp : H. 8.—per servicium militare.

Of this Manor Thomas Dorney hath part, vnder an Exchange made with Henry Daunt in 28. Eliz : Reginæ. |

Pedington.

Pedington: Is an hamblett within the Manor of Hame and parish of Berkeley, And for the most part the inheritance of George lord Berkeley.

In this hamblet are two ancient capitall messuages, both of them called by the name of Pedington farme ; the one the inheritance of George lord Berkeley, parcell of his manor of Hame, somtimes also called Somers farme, or Somers house, and late in the tenure of Somers, and holden by the said Lord in Capite by knights service as parcell of his Barony of Berkeley : The other was the late inheritance of ffrancis Dynely als Dingley Esq, and nowe of Walter Kirle Esq in right of Alice his wife daughter and heire of John Mallet late of Bevington deceased, who purchased the same of the said ffrancis, knowne also by the name of Kendalls court : And was in the time of kinge Henry the third the land of Avone, and after of Walton, and after of Trefray, and after of John Kendall; by whose attainder of high Treason by parliament in 1. H. 7. for takinge part with kinge R. 3. slaine at Bosworth feild not farre from Leicester, by that kinge, the same (amongst other lands) escheated to the Crowne, As by an Inquisition found by the Escheator virtute officij sui in 4. H. 7. appeares : And soe rested in the Crowne, till kinge H. 8. in the 4th yeare of his raigne granted this farme (or manor of Pedington as therin it is called,) with Avonscourt (nowe called Baynham farme,) and Wike Court, to John Dingley, To hold at will. And afterwards by tres patents dated 12. ffebr̃. 9° H. 8. againe granted the same to the said John Dingley and to the heires males of his body, To hold in Capite and by payinge two greyhounds as often as the kinge shall come within two miles of this Pedington.

This John Dingley had issue male Henry Dingley and died ; And the said Henry had issue the said ffrancis, and died in 32° Eliz., As an Inqu : after his

Pedington

his death in that yeare sheweth, wherin the said Lres patents and tenure as aforesaid are mentioned ; And these called by the name of three Tents or manors of Pedington, Avonscourt, and Wike : And that ffrancis was his sonne and heire 39. yeares old, who vsed, at one if not at all of these three farme places or manors, once in 5 or 7 yeares, to assemble his tenants or lessees and to hold a Court Baron, whervnto they were in their severall leases made suitors by Covenant.

Thus stood theis lands, till kinge James by his Lres patents dated 8. ffebruaī. A⁰. 13. regni sui Angliæ, et Scotiæ—49, granted vnto Gifford Moigne and to the said ffrancis Dingley, Omnia illa Maneria de Pedington, Avonscourt, et Wike, annui valoris—13ˡⁱ. 6ˢ. 8ᵈ. quondam parcell terrarum Johis Kendall, et nuper Johis Tressray, et postea Johes Dingley et heredum masculorum de corpore suo littime procreaī per tras suas pateñ dated 22. Octobī 10. H. 8. (soe recited if not mistaken, for surely there are tres patents dated 12. ffebī: 9⁰ H. 8. as aforesaid :) To hold to the said Dingley and Moigne and their heires, by such and the like services and rents as before the same were held. And the 16ᵗʰ of May aº 44. Jacobi, after a comon recouy suffered, the said Moigne and Dingley made pertition : And accordingly, (for all this was to enable Dingley to alien,) in 15º et 16º Jacobi, The said ffrancis Dynely als Dingley and Elizabeth his wife, and Henry his sonne and heire and Jone his wife, ioyned in | sale of almost all the said ffarmes and lands, (Baynham starme als Avons Court excepted,) to Mathew Smyth of Wanefwell, Robert Atkins of Newport, and John Saniger of Saniger, and their heires, who according to the trust reposed in them forthwith in the same and the next yeare after granted over to other pticuler lessees therof, that which themselues held not or were not to keepe : vpon which sales made of 370. acres or therabouts, the said Mr. Dingley raised—1130ˡⁱ of about 24. lessees : which before this yeare, 1639. aº 15º Rc Caroli, haue afforded the kinge 7. or 8. wardships, with as much losse almost to the lord **Berkeley**, for that the most of them held lands of the said Lord by knight service, haveinge noe other land held of the Crowne save small parcells of this, nowe thus purchased, wherof they severally (some scarce of one acre,) died seized.

Theis Records will shewe somwhat more touchinge Pedington, with Baynham farme, and Wike Court, then formerly is delivered, vz,

Triñ Recī. 1. et. 2. R. 3. Rot. 138. in banco. Willus Minsterbrooke petiī versus Willimum Berkeley Comitem Nottingham,—59ˢ. reddɫ cū ptiñ in Pedington, Avonscourt, et Wike, cū ptineñ.
Originaɫ in Sc̄cio ēm Reñi Thesaur̄. 4. H. 8. Rot. 139.
                                                             Originaɫ

Original ibm. 10. H. 8. Rot. 13.
Triñ Rec̃, ibm. 7. H. 8. Rot. 27.
Pafch : fines : 33. Eliz : Rot. 6. in Sec̃io p̃d.
Pafch : Rec. 37. Eliz : Rot. 134.

Planches : or la planca.

See before in Came. fol : 129.

Pockhineton ; als : Pockhampton, als Pockington :

See before in Hineton : fol : 229. et 230. |

The Ridge.

The Ridge ; or **Le Edge** ; or **la Egge** ; is an hamblet confiftinge of dwellinge houfes within the parifh of Wotton vnderedge, feated betweene the vpper part of Nybley and Symondfall, reputed at this day to bee parcell of the Manor of Owfelworth the inheritance of Sʳ Gabriell Loe als Lowe, knight, holden by him of the kinge by knight fervice in Capite : Howbeit anciently it was a part of the lord Berkeleis great Manor of Wotton, and fevered as followeth ;

Thomas Lord Berkeley the firft of that name (who dyed in 28. H. 3.) did about 20. H. 3. give to Thomas de Berkeley his fecond fonne and to his heires, amongft others, theis lands at the Edge ; As indeed they lye at the edge or browe of a fteepe hill there defcendinge from Symondfall. Which Thomas dyinge vnmaried and without iffue in 31. H. 3. gave the fame to the Abbot of Kingfwood and the Monkes there, by feverall Deeds which at this day are in Berkeley caftle, wherin hee mentioneth the intents of his guifts to bee for the welfare of his owne foule, and of his fathers and mothers, and of all his anceftors and freinds ; Which
guifts

guifts the lord Maurice Berkeley his eldeſt brother afterwards confirmed to that Monaſtery, As by their Deeds yet in Berkeley caſtle appeareth: In this ſort remained theis lands, till the diſſolucōn of that Monaſtery in 31. H. 8. And then were granted with the manor of Owſelworth as parcell therof, As in the deſcription of that Manor I have formerly mentioned. fol: 305.

An Inquiſicōn in 27. E. 1. findeth, That Walter Paſſelowe gave to the Abbot and Covent of Kingſwood the 4th part of a meſſuage and of one yard land in la Edge, als the Ridge.

And by a Deed in Berkeley Caſtle, in 10. E. 2. A^o. Dñi. 1317. Sir John Berkeley knight a younger ſonne of Thomas Lord Berkeley, and the Lady Havyſia wife of the ſaid Sir John, havinge noe iſſue, made this Abbot of Kingſwood and their Covent their heire, to whom they gave all their lands in this place.—Thus was this hamblett made vp to that Monaſtery.

See more heerof in Symondſfall. fol: 323. |

Severne.

Severne: or the River of Severne is remarkeable in each Engliſh hiſtory: my intention is to touch only ſuch obſervations as I have met withall, not in any of them, as I conceive.

Severne waſheth the ſhoare of this hundred of Berkeley about 18. miles, not accomptinge crookes turnings or meanders; The midſt of wch length I place at the houſe of John Toyte in Hineton, where the paſſage is into the fforreſt of Deane, (even nowe in a^o. 1639. in diſafforreſtinge,) called Pirton als Piriton paſſage, where this River at full ſea is not much leſſe, if leſſe, then two myles broad: In this place it floweth 3. hours and ebbeth 9. twice in each 24.

And for the time of the full ſea at this paſſage, the time of the firſt turne, and the houre of floud, for every natural day, from the full of the moone, or from the change, take this table followinge as I have received it, ſent mee for my direction in paſſage.

The

The first of the seaven columes sheweth the dayes of the moone from the full or change: The second and third columes the houres and minutes of full sea: The 4th and 5th the houres and minutes of the first Turne: The 6th and 7th. The hours and minutes of floud that day.

Moones Age	Full Sea		First Turn		Flood	
	H	M	H	M	H	M
1	8	48	12	8	5	8
2	9	36	1	36	6	36
3	10		2	24	7	24
4	10	30	3	12	8	12
5	11	10	3	36	8	36
6	11	50	4	6	9	9
7	12	20	4	50	9	50
8	1		5		10	
9	1	30	5	30	10	30
10	3		7		12	
11	4		8		1	
12	5		9		2	
13	6		10		3	
14	7		11		4	
15	8		12		5	

Only note, that the beinge of the winde may somwhat further or hinder the time of passage at full sea, but not much: yet if the winde blowe stronge vpon the East, the passage will bee one houre sooner then usuall.

And note also, That if the Moone bee at the full or change in the afternoone, your accompt in this table must begin from the day followinge.

In January in the 4th of kinge James, a° Dñi. 1606, was soe great a Tyde, made greater with a stronge winde, that it overflowed a great part of the lower countrey adioyninge, drowninge divers men and woemen, and cattle of all sorts; The like wherof happened that time 40. yeares before; growne remarkeable in many histories already, which Mr. Camden placeth in January 1607. by beginninge the yeare of our Lord the first of that month, which I followe not, neither heere nor in any part of theis descriptions. |

By often conference with the fishermen inhabitinge this river, and especially at my holdinge Courts for those Manors that doe adioyne to the river, togeather with

with mine owne obfervations, I have found 53. forts of fea fifh in this river within the limits of this hundred, which have byn in the time of my Stewardfhip taken therin, and called as followeth ; viz,

The Sturgeon, Porpoife, Thornpole, Jubertas or a yonge whale, ats the herringe hogge, The Seale, the Swordfifh, the falmon, wheat trout or fuen, The turbut, Lamprey, Lamperne, Shad, tweat, the wray, the houndfifh ats the dogfifh, the fole, the flooke, ats the flounder, the fand flooke, refemblinge the fole, A barne, a Cod, a Card, An eele pout, A mackarell, the Sunfifh, the hake, An haddocke, a Roucote, the fea tad, A plaice, the millet ats mullet, the Lynge, A dabbe, A yearlinge, An horncake, the Lumpfifh, A gurnard, both red and gray, A cuttlefifh, a whitinge, a little crabbe, the Conger ats the conger eele, beinge the hee-fifh, and the Shee fifh is called a quaver, the Dorry, the hufwife, the herringe, the fprat, the pilchard, the prawne, the fhrimpe, the eele, a fauzon, or great fat eele, Elvers, fuppofed by fome to bee the younge eele, the bafe, the fea breame, and the Halibut : In all—53.

Of a fewe of which, experience affures vs That the leffer the Sturgeon is the more wholfome and tender, and the belly to bee preferred before the backe.

The belly of the falmon is tendreft fweeteft and pleafanteft, and his eies wholfomer then of any other fifh : The falmon growes by theis degrees and ages : vz, 1. a pinke ; 2. a botcher ; 3. a falmon trout ; 4. a gillinge ; 5. a falmon ; Soe in perfect and full age at 5. yeares. As an oxe or bucke ; **And** (generally) in this part of the River, the prime feafon for the goodnes of the falmon goes out when the Bucke comes in ; And comes in when the Bucke goes out.

The Sole wee call our Seaverne Capon ; A meate of prime note.

Of the plaice, wee fay quanto grandior eò melior.

Prawnes and **Shrimpes** are held by vs an excellent food for every age and conftitution ; Of excellent temperature and fubftance, and of eafy concoction ; If fifhes may bee reftorative theis wee fay are they.

With the Lamprey, I will conclude my cookifh obfervations ; A fifh of note and eminency, entringe this river with the newe yeare and then of five monthes abode ; whofe ancient and old eftimation conceive by theis Records in the Tower of London.

Rotulus

Rotulus finium. 2. Johis. Homines de Gloucestria dant Dño Regi 40. marcas, pro habenda benevolentia sua, quia eum non refpexerunt, ficut debuerunt, de lampreis fuis.

Rot. Liberačoñ: 10. H. 3. membr. 3. Commandment is given by the kinge to the Sheriffe of Gloucestershire to proclayme in the County that noe Regrators shall buy **Lampreyes** taken in feverne, wherby the kinge or his people should pay the deerer for them.

Rot. Liberačoñ. 14. H. 3. The kinge the 12th of March commaunds the faid Sheriffe to buy for him 24. lampreyes, and to fend them to him to Lurgefall.

Rot. Liberačoñ. 17. H. 3. and other like Rolls shewe that noe yeare paffed, but that the kinge had Lampreys and heryngs from Severne.

Rot. Clauf. 21. H. 3. membr: 16. The 4th of March, the kinge then beinge at Canterbury by his writt commands the Sheriffe of this County to bake for him all the lampreyes hee can gett, and to fend them to him by his Cooke: And when hee should bee neerer Severne, then to fend them vnbaked, as longe as they may come fweete, for him and his Queene to eate. |

Rot. Liber. 24. H. 3. mem: 16. The 27th of ffebr, the faid kinge by his writt commaunds the Sheriffe of this County not to fuffer any man to buy any lampryes, but that hee buy and fend them all to him wherfoever hee bee, for all the lent.

Rot. Liber: 26. H. 3. ps. 1. mem: 4. shewes, That the Sheriffe of this county fent the kinge in Lent this yeare—188. lampries, and 56. fresh heryngs; All which coft the kinge—12^{li} 7^s 3^d

Rot. Clauf. 32. H. 3. The kinge by his writt the 28th of ffebr. commands the Sheriffe of this County to fend two parts of all the Lampreies hee can buy or get, to him to Norwich, And the other third part to his Queene to Windfore Caftle.

And in Berkeley Caftle is an Accompt of the keeper of the Wardrobe in 41. E, 3. which shewes, That Maurice lord Berkeley in December, fent the kinge fix lampries, which coft him—6^{li} 7^s 2^d And the cariage of thofe 6. to the king coft— 6^s 8^d; And in Aprill followinge fent the Abbot of Glaftenbury other 6. lampries, which

which cost him 31s. 6d. But enough of this Lamprey, though of them the fishermen never thinke they have enough: such continueth their estimation to this day, 1639.

¶ In this River, as farre as this Hundred of Berkeley extendeth, the lord Berkeley and his tenants holdinge vnder him, have from Shepardines passage, (which is neere to the Lop. of Hill,) alonge the river by the deepest part of the Channell, a severall and free fishinge, extendinge to the vttermost part of the Lop. of Slimbridge: Howbeit at certaine places and seasons of the tide in lakes or pooles, any stranger may with a Becknet or Ladenet, fish, (but not with any other longe net or draught nett,) and take any other fish (save pisces regales, vz. Royall fishes, as Sturgeon, Seale, Thornpole, or Porpoise, which are solely to the said lord,) And they are the fishermans owne, except the fish soe taken bee salmon, gillinge, Shad, or Lamprey; The custome of which, (called galeable fishes,) is in this manner; The fisherman sets the price of such his fish; The Lord chooseth whether hee will take the fish and pay halfe that price to the fisherman; or refuse the fish and require halfe the price of the fisherman soe set by him; The price or moity taken is called the Gale; The Lords servant or farmer therof, the Galor; And theis foresaid sorts only are called Galeable fishes, or the gale fishinge; Howbeit it is said That if the fisherman, before the lords galor can come cry or call to him, doe escape or gett soe farre as past the full sea marke with his fish to land, and put grasse into the mouth therof, that therby that fish is freed from payment of gale. But noe stranger may fish in the Chañell with Longnett Becknett or Ladenet, nor may shoote any racknett within any of the pooles in this River, vntill the dead lowe water, that is vntill the poole hath left drivinge.

¶ In the 4th yeare of kinge James a troublesome suite in the Court of Chancery arose, betweene Henry lord Berkeley plt and one Willm Dunninge, yet livinge, and others of the fforrest side of Deane, defts, wherin many witnesses were examined: In which suite one mayne question was who should set the price of the galeable fish, whether the fisherman who takes the fish, or the Lords galor: Which was adiudged for the Lord, that the fisherman should set the price; To which sute I referre you if you desire to vnderstand more of the Customes of this noble river; The proceedings wherof are in Berkeley Castle exemplified vnder the great Seale of England.

¶ If a Sturgeon bee taken, in whose severall fishings or putts soever, it is the Lord Berkeleis, And by the taker to bee brought to his Castle of Berkeley: Howbeit

beit the lord of cuftome gives the taker vpon delivery of the Sturgeon halfe a marke in money, and a longe bowe and two arrowes, or halfe a noble in lieu therof:[1] But if a whale bee taken, (as a younge whale or Jubertas of 22. foote longe was, in the 18th yeare of kinge James, A° 1620. whofe picture, rudely drawne, is in the great hall in Berkeley caftle,) that hath noe retribution of right from the Lord : not foe much as for makinge the dray wheron that fifh was drawne, wherat were tyed 35. yoke of oxen ; A fifh which yeilded an oyle then faid and ftill beleived to bee very foveraigne and medicinable for aches, &c.

All fifh that is taken ought of ancient cuftome to bee brought to the Markett Croffe in Berkeley towne, and there to bee pitched one houre, before the fifherman may carry and fell the fifh out of the hundred to any other ; which havinge, through the abfence of the Lord and his cheife officers, for fome yeares byn neglected, was of late yeares, through the livinge and abode of the lady Elizabeth Berkeley, mother and guardian to the nowe lord George, at Berkeley and Whiteliffe parke lodge, fomwhat revived.

In this river is alfo a tyde in each weeke called the Lords tyde, when the lord hath all the fifh in certaine places taken therat : And the next tide, called the parfons tide, for his tithe fifh ; The Lords on the Thurfday, the parfons on the friday the next after ; wherof the faid fute in Chancery againft Dunninge and others, fpeakes more at large : which Roger Kemis, conftable of Berkeley caftle, then in the time of kinge James livinge there, revived and enioyed.

The liberty of the lord of this hundred in this river, beginneth, as hath byn faid, at Sheperdines paffage, extendinge alonge the river by the deepeft part of the channell where for the time it is, to the vttermoft part of the manor of Slimbridge, which is there divided from the liberty of other men by a fmall river or frefh Inlet called fframptons pill : And of foe much of the faid river of Severne as lyeth within the parifh of Arlingham, with the pooles and lakes therin, with liberty and freedom of pitchinge rowes of ftakes overthwart or croffe the faid lakes or pooles.

See more of this River in the Manors of Hill, Hame, Hinton, Slimbridge, and Arlingham, which bound vpon the fame ; The middle of whofe channell is their vtmoft bound on that fide, each of them. |

Simondfale

[1] We learn from Mr. James Herbert Cooke, F.S.A., the prefent Steward of the Berkeley Eftate, that £1 is now paid for every Sturgeon brought to the Caftle. [Ed.]

Simondsale.

Simondsale; In the booke of Domesdai, written, Simondeshale; wherin kinge Edward called the Confeffor had, as that booke faith, one hide of land in demefne; An ancient manor parcell of the Barony of Berkeley, the inheritance of George Lord Berkeley, and holden by knight fervice in Capite.

It is within the parifh of Wotton, and had anciently its Chaple belonging vnto it, Which, with that of Nibley, were all the chaples belonginge to that mother church of Wotton: But this is now decayed, the ruines fcarce appearinge; And the manor it felfe hath altered its effence, reputed at this day but a farme, called Simondfall farme.

Noe place for health and habitation from the midft of Aprill to the middle of October, can bee better feated; The aire foe wholfome and digeftive., That it hath created a comon and conftant proverbe of bringinge to our tables Simondfall fauce, meaninge a good and hungry appetite to eate: And as the aire is pure, foe the farme houfe (well worth—230^{li} per Ann,) ftands in the higheft place of all this hundred, it beinge generally beleived That the little hill or tumpe neere to this houfe, (fuppofed to bee a Danifh or Saxon grave of fome great Lord,) is the higheft earth in the kingdome of England; And yet noe place is or can bee better watered with many delicate and wholfome fprings then this, heerin arifinge: And wee hundredors are perfwaded, That if any Englifh fcituation could bee wholfomnes of aire promife eternity of daies, it were heere to bee expected; So that the inhabitant bee furnifhed with a great wood pile for winter.

Simondfall farme and the hamblet of Combe make but one Tithinge, and are within the Leet or Lawday of Berkeley hundred, And equally pay togeather in all levies and rates.   Rates.

If the Divifion of Berkeley, (often and againe before fpoken of,) bee rated in any levy to the kinge or Comon wealth at 100^{li}, Therof Simondfall and Combe pay —20^{s}, as beinge a iuft hundredth part therof. wherof fee before in Combe, fol: 151.   Rates.

By a Deed without date, the Abbot of Kingfwood granted to Maurice lord Berkeley fonne of Thomas de Berket and his heires, and to all his tenants of Simondfale, to have free ingreffe and egreffe through his land of Egge, (which the
Abbot

Abbot had of the guift of Thomas de Berkeley brother of the said Maurice, whereof fee before fol: 315.) for all manner of their cattle to drive and lead from Simondfall vnto the water called Lodewell, and there to water, foe that the Abbot bee not damnified in his corne or pasture.—In Berkeley castle this Deed.

The 10th. of ffebr: A° 31. E. 1. An award by mediation of freinds therin named, was made betweene Thomas lord Berkeley and Maurice his sonne and heire of the one part, And the Abbot of Kingswood of the other part; That the Abbot and his successors should finde a pound or fold of—240. sheepe at their charges, from the third day of May yearly vntill All Saints day, vpon the said Lords land at Simondsale, except 3. daies for the said Abbots shearinge of his sheepe; But provided, that if the Abbot have noe sheepe vpon his granges of Egge Owselworth and Caldecote, becaufe of Rott or other necessity, (all fraud and malice excluded,) then, duringe that time, not to bee bound to finde that fould: Nor if the said Lord and his tenants (called villanos in this award,) have at any time above 800. sheepe vpon their pasture of Simondsale, then also the Abbot not to bee bound to finde the said fould.

See Caldecote. fol: 121, And Owselworth. fol: 307.

324 blank

Slimbridge.

Slimbridge: Anciently written Slimbrugg, is a remarkeable parish, The Church or Rectory whereof belongeth to Magdalen colledge in Oxford by the guift of Maurice lord Berkeley the 5th. of that name, in 19. H. 7; Howbeit his elder brother whilest hee was Earle of Nottingham had by a defeasible title given the same; who dyinge without issue, it was by the said Maurice his brother and heire of newe granted, of the value of—250li. per Annū; Whose last Incumbent Lawrence Bridger sate Rector there 55. yeares, and dyed very rich and honest, in a° 1632, nowe succeeded by Nicholas Richardson, a learned man, senior fellowe of that Colledge.

The Manor of Slimbridge is the inheritance of George Lord Berkeley, holden of the kinge by knight service in Capite; And is not mentioned in Domesday booke in the Catalogue of those manors which make the great Manor of Berkeley, whereof

fee

Slimbridge

see before fol: 6. 7. et 209. But then was the inheritance of Roger Berkeley of Durfeley, father of William Berkeley founder of the Monaftery of Kingfwood; whofe fonne Roger Berkeley in the time of kinge Stephen gave this Manor of Slimbridge to Alice his daughter in mariage, when fhee vpon the Agreement then made betweene her faid father and Robert the fonne of Harding, became wife to Maurice fonne and heire of the faid Robert fonne of Harding; which agreement copied out of the originall vnder feale, is in theis words, vz;

Iſtæ funt pactiones quæ factæ fuerunt inter Robertum filium Hardingi et Rogerum de Berkeley, in domo Roberti filij Hardingi apud Briſtow, in prefentia Dñi Henrici Ducis Normanniæ, Aquitañ, et Comitis Andegaviæ, eiufdem affenfu, et in prefentia multorum aliorum Clericorum et laicorum: Mauricius filius Roberti filij Hardingi cepit filiam Rogeri de Berkeley in vxorem, Ita quod Rogerus dedit Mauricio cum filia fua in matrimonio Slimbrugg, quæ eſt de hereditate fua, hoc eſt, decem libratas terræ; Et Mauricius affenfu patris fui Roberti filij Hardingi dedit filiæ Rogeri quam cepit in vxorem in dotem virginti libratas terræ de feodo de Berkeley, affenfu Dñi Henrici Ducis, tali convencõne; quod fi Mauricius filius Roberti moreretur antequàm cepiffet filiam Rogeri in vxorem, frater poſt eum primogenitus acciperet eam in vxorem p fupradictas conventiones; Et fi ille alter filius Roberti moreretur ante fponfalia filiæ Rogeri, quifquis de filijs Roberti poſt eum heres remaneret, filiam Rogeri in vxorem acciperet; Similiter fi filia Rogeri antequam defponfaretur Mauricio filio Roberti moreretur, fecunda poſt ipfam Mauricio daretur in vxorem, vel cuicunq, fratrum fuorum qui heres remaneret poſt ipfum Mauricium; Ita et de ceteris filiabus Rogeri fi primogenita morerentur, illa quæ remaneret poſt ipfas daretur illi de filijs Roberti filij Hardingi qui heres eius remaneret, ficut fuperius prelocutum eſt: Preterea filius Rogeri de Berkeley qui heres eius eſt debet accipere in vxorem fuam de filiabus Roberti filij Hardingi, et Rogerus de Berkeley debet illi filio Roberti dare in dotem manerium de Siſton de Briſtoll, quod manerium eſt de hereditate Rogeri. Et Robertus filius Hardingi debet dare in matrimonium cum filia fua filio Rogeri, decem libratas et decem folidatas terræ apud Durfeley, eo pacto; quod fi vna de filiabus Roberti filij Hardingi moreretur, antequam filius Rogeri eam acciperet in vxorem, altera filia daretur illi; Et fi vtraq, filia Roberti ante fponfalia moreretur, filius Rogeri qui eius heres eſt acciperet in vxorem filiam Hugonis de Hafele, neptem Roberti filij Hardingi. Silter fi | primogenitus Rogeri de Berkeley moreretur ante fupradicta fponfalia, ille de tribus fuis qui remanet poſt ipfum primogenitus et heres, acciperet in vxorem vnam de filiabus Roberti filij Hardingi qui domi funt, vel fi vtraq, ante

fponfalia

sponsalia moreretur, filiam Hugonis de Hasele per supradictas pactiones: Has pactiones affidaverunt Robertus filius Hardingi et Rogerus de Berkeley, tenere et servare sine fallacia et dolo, et posuerunt Dñum Henricum Ducem obsidem et Justiĉ inter se de servandis his pactionibus. Hoc etiam affidaverunt probi octo viri ex parte Roberti, et alij octo ex parte Rogeri, quorum nomina sunt hæc; Ex parte Rogeri, Wiłłus filius Henrici, Rogerus de Schai, Ractus de Iweley, Walterus, Engewaldus de Gosinton, Guido de rupe, Guayfarus de planca, Hugo de planca ffer eius. Ex parte Roberti, Hugo de Hasele, Nigellus filius Arthuri, Robertus de Sautmaris, Elias ffer Roberti filij Hardingi, Jordanus frater eius, Jordanus le Faire, Riĉus filius Roberti, David Duncepouche; Et isti viri Robertus et Rogerus in his pactionibus servandis totis viribus tenebunt; Quod si Robertus et Rogerus de his pactionibus vellent exire, Isti cogent eas pactiones tenere quantum poterint; Et si ipsi acquiescere noluerint isti viri de servicio et amore eos reducent. Et propter has supradictas pactiones, Rogerus de Berkeley clamavit quietum totum chalangum suum, et quicquid iuris habebat in firmā de Berkeley.[1]

Theis

[1] The following is a literal copy of this important and interesting Deed, now existing in the muniment room at Berkeley Castle, for the loan of which we are indebted to the courtesy of Mr. James Herbert Cooke, before mentioned.

Iste sunt pactiones quę factę fuerunt inter Rod'tū filiū hardingi 7 Rogerū de Bercket in domo Rodbti filii hardingi apud Bristov in p̃sentia dñi henrici ducis Normannoȝ 7 Aquitanię 7 Comitis And, eiusdē assensu. 7 in p̃sentia multoȝ alioru clericoȝ 7 laicoru̅. Maurici⁹ fili⁹ Rodbti filii hardingi cępiit filiā Rogeri de Berckel in uxorē. Ita qd Rogerus dedit Mauricio cū filia sua in matrimonio. Slimbrugiā quę + de sua hereditate hoc + decē libratas terrę. 7 Maurici⁹ concessu pat'f sui Rodbti filii hardingi dedit filię Rogeri qua ipse cępit uxorē; in dotę . XX . libratas terrę de feudo de berckel assensu dñi Herici ducis. Tali conuentione q⁰d si Maurici⁹ fili⁹ Rodbti moreretur anteq̃m cępisset filiā Rogeri uxorē; frater ei⁹ post eū p̃mogenit⁹ acciperet eam uxorē, p sup̃dictas conuentiones. Et si etiā ille alter filius Rodbti moreret' ante sponsalia filię Rogeri; quicq̃s'f. de filiis Rodbti post illū heres remaneret; filiā Rogeri uxorē accipet. Similiter si filia Rogeri anteq̃m desponsaretur Mauricio filio Rodbti moreret'; scła p⁰ ipsā Mauricio daret' uxorē ut cuilibet c'm suoȝ qui heres remaneret post Mauriciū. Ita 7 de cet'is filiabȝ Rogeri si primogenite moreret' illa que remaneret post ipsas daretur illi de filiis Rodbti filii Hard qui heres ei⁹ remaneret, sic supius plocutū est. Preterea filius Rogeri de Berckel qui heres eius est debet accipe uxorē unā de filiab⁹ Rodbti filii hard, 7 Roger⁹ de berckelai debet illi filię Rodbti dare in dotē maneriū Siftone ṗpe Bristou qd maneriū est de hereditate Rogeri. Et Rodbertus filius hard debet dare in matrimoniū cū filia sua filio Rogeri X . libratas et . X . folidatas terrę apud derselegā. eo pacto qd si una de filiabȝ; Rodbti filii hard moreret' anteq̃m fili⁹ Rogeri eam accipet uxorē; altera filia Rodbti daret' illi. Et si utraq̃ filia Rodbti ante sponfalia moreret'; fili⁹ Rogeri qui heres ei⁹ esset accipet uxorē filiā hugonis de hasele neptim Rodbti filii Hard. Similiter si p̃mogenit⁹ Rogeri de berkel moreret' ante sup̃dicta sponsalia ille de fratribȝ suis qui remaneret post ipsū p̃mogenit⁹ 7 heres accipet uxorē unā de filiab⁹ Rodbti filii hard que domi fūt, ut si utraqȝ ante sponsalia moreret'; filiam hugonis de Hasele p sup̃dictas pactiones. Has pactiones affidaverunt Rodbt⁹ fili⁹ hard, 7 Roger⁹ de berckelai tenere & servare sine fallacia 7 dolo, 7 posuerūt

Slimbridge

Theis mutuall crosse or reciprocall mariages tooke effect, and were blessed with issue on both sides, as none more noble in all the county nor scarce in the West part of England; The said Maurice and Alice, daughter of the said Roger de Berkeley (such was her name), had issue Robert and Thomas; Robert, called Robert de Berkeley dyed in 4. H. 3. without issue, leavinge the said Thomas his brother and heire; which Thomas had issue Maurice, father of Thomas, father of Maurice, father of Thomas, father of Maurice, father of Thomas and James; which James dyed in the life time of his elder brother Thomas, leavinge issue James: And after the said Thomas dyed in 5. H. 5. without issue male, And James sonne of the said James, by force of an Entayle of this manor (inter alia) by fine in 23. E. 3. became heire male thereof; which James sonne of James dyed in 3. E. 4. leavinge issue William and Maurice; which William was created Earle of Nottingham and Marques Berkeley, who in 4. H. 7. (covettinge to disinherite his brother Maurice, out of displeasure that then raged betweene them), conveyed (amongst other manors) this of Slimbridge To the vse of himselfe and the heires of his body, The Remainder to kinge H. 7. and to the heires males of his body, The remainder to his own right heires; and in 7. H. 7. dyed without issue of his body, whervpon kinge H. 7. entred, and had issue male kinge H. 8. who entred, and had issue male kinge E. 6. who entred and dyed without issue male of his body; At whose death Henry lord Berkeley, then about 19. yeares old, entred as right heire to the said William Marques Berkeley, vz, sonne of Thomas, sonne of Thomas, brother and heire of Maurice, sonnes of the said Maurice, brother and heire of the said Marques. Which Henry had issue Thomas who dyed in 9. R^o Jacobi, two yeares before his father, leavinge issue the said George, nowe Lord of this Manor aforesaid.

The Manor of Slimbridge comprehendeth the hamblets of Cambridge, Slimbridge street, Churchend, and the remarkeable places called Slimbridge warth, Roules Court, and Southworthy feild, of which I shall make after mention. And
the

dñm henriev ducē obsidē̃ & justiciā inter se de servandis his pactionibȝ. Hoc etiā affidauerunt . viii . ꝑbi viri ex parte Rodbti, 7 alii . viii . ex parte Rogeri quoȝ nomina hec sunt. Ex parte Rogeri ; Willm⁹. fili⁹ henrici, Roger⁹ desekai, Radulf⁹ de huclega, Walkelin⁹., Engebald⁹ de Gosintuna, Guido de Rupe, Gwalter⁹ de planca, hugo de planca ff ei⁹; De parte Rodbti; Hugo de Hasela, Nigellus fili⁹ Arthuri, Rodbtus de Saltemarif, Helyai ff Rodbti filii hard, Jordan⁹ ff ei.⁹, Jordan⁹ le warre, Nicholaus filius Rodbti, David duncepucke, Et isti viri Rodbtū 7 Rogerū in his pactionibȝ servandis totis uiribȝ tenebūt. Q^{o}d si Rodbt⁹ 7 Rogerus de his pactioibȝ uellen exire: isti cogen eo^s pactiōes teste q^{a}ntū po^{c}int. Et si ipsi adq^{i}esce noluerit ; isti uiri de servicio 7 amore eos recedent. Et pp^e. has sup^{a}dictas pactiones; Roger⁹ de Berkel clamauit q^{i}etū totū ekalangiū suū, 7 q^{i}cq^{i}d juri^s habebat ; i firma de berkelai.

C Y R O G R A P H I V M

the parish alfo comprehendeth more, the Manor of Hurſt formerly mentioned, fol: 241, with all the | hambletts therof, The Manors of Sages and Gofington. A parifh that is great and rich in foile, yet few of the inhabitants wealthy, moſt very poore: The warth and other waſt grounds of this manor and parifh, if inclofed, would yeald above 1500ᴸⁱ per Añ, wherin is verified the obfervation of many wife men, That the more large the waſt grounds of a manor are, the poorer are the inhabitants; fuch coṁon grounds, coṁons, or waſt grounds, vfed as coṁonly they are, and as heere I knowe they are, yeild not the 5ᵗʰ part of their true value, drawe many poore people from other places, burden the townfhip with beggerly Cotages, Inmates, and Alehoufes, and idle people; where the greater part fpend moſt of their daies in a lazy idlenes and petite theeveries, and fewe or none in profitable labour: And I am perfwaded, that amongſt other motives, this hath byn one, and yet is, and none of the leaſt, why kinge James and the kinge that nowe is have reduced into feveralty and into fmaller parcells let to private mens vfes, and farmers therof, foe many of their fforreſts, Chafes, and wild and waſt grounds in moſt fhires of the kingdome, as they have done, to the private benefit of themfelves and the generall good of the Comon wealth, both in the breed of ferviceable men and fubiects, and of afwerable eſtates and abillities; wheras now, not one of theis beggars, lazy and idle people, thus livinge and bred, are any waies vfefull or ferviceable in any kinde: And what you my fonne John doe nowe in this prefent month and yeare of Auguſt 1639. obferve in the forreſt of Deane, nowe in difafforreſtinge and in convertinge to better private profitts, wherin as a Comiſſioner I vnderſtand yow are imployed, in the very houre and day wherin I write this page, your after yeares and riper obfervations will more pregnantly appeare and informe you.

I cañot but remember, in comparinge times paſt with times and practice prefent, That to this Church the bifhop of Worceſter, in whofe dioceſſe the fame then was, did in nono regis Johis Aᵒ 1207. As his Regiſter fhewes, admit to this Church Walter Berton, to hold the fame duringe the minority of Symon de Berkeley Clerke, with the cuſtody of the faid Simon then an infant in the meane time, and then the faid Simon to bee Rector there, who was prefented by Robert lord Berkeley aforementioned, patron therof. Of which church fee the Rot. finium. 17. H. 6. membr. 2. in the tower of London.

The tutelary Saint to whofe honour this Church was built and dedicated, was Sᵗ John the Evangeliſt; As in the Bifhops Regiſter at Worceſter in aᵒ 1425. in 4. H. 6. vpon the admiſſion of John Horton to this Church and Rectory, appeares.

Deere

Slimbridge

Heere alſo was a Chapple and Chantry founded by Thomas lord Berkeley the third of that name, in the hamblet of Cambridge, wherto hee preſented till the diſſolution therof in 1. E. 6: wherof read more in Cambridge, in fol: 143.

Holweber, the tradition of the herbe called Bloudwort, growinge only in the feild called Southworthy, als Succerdy, bee ſayned by the inhabitants, who avowe

yet the hiſtory of that bloud there ſpilt, is true, That in the raigne of
        yeares before the Norman conqueſt.

In this pariſh hath longe continued the family of the Knights, men of meane ranke, of whom 4. lineall generations of well proportioned men are remembred to have had five fingers and a thumbe on each hand; And tradition aſcends to former of their Anceſtors. |

Adiopninge to the north part of this pariſh of Slimbridge, parted by a ſmall river, is the pariſh of fframpton vpon Severne in the hundred of Whitſtane, nowe the inheritance of Humphry Hooke a marchant of Briſtoll, lately by him purchaſed of John Arundle of Lanheron Eſq; the old inheritance of Richard Clifford and of Robert the ſonne of Pagan; which Thomas lord Berkeley the ſecond of that name in 31. and 32. E. 1. purchaſed of them, And after by his deed and a fyne therof levied in 33. E. 1. regranted in fee farme to the ſaid Robert the ſonne of Pagan and to Iſable his wife (one of the two ſiſters and coheires of the ſaid Richard Clifford,) and to the heires of the body of the ſaid Robert; Reſervinge the old yearly rent of two and twenty marks, then beinge the true value of that manor; As by the deeds therof and fyne in Berkeley caſtle appeareth: A rent conſtantly paid to this day, 1639, to George lord Berkeley heire male to the ſaid lord Thomas: which John Arundle who aliened to Humphry Hooke aforeſaid, was ſonne of Sir John Arundle, ſonne of Sir John Arundle, ſonne of Sir John Arundle, ſonne of Sir Thomas Arundle, ſonne of Sir John Arundle and of Katherine his wife, daughter and coheire of Sir John Chideocke, ſonne of Sir John Chideocke, ſonne of Sir John Chideocke and of Iſable his wife, daughter and heire of Robert fitz Paine,
                                                     ſonne

328
Frampton rent
Arundle.

sonne of the aforesaid Robert the sonne of Pagan als fitz Pain and of Isable his wife, the Conuzees[1] in the said fyne levied in 33. E. 1. as is aforesaid.

Betweene which John Arundle that I suppose yet liveth, who aliened to Humphry Hooke, and Henry lord Berkeley, who dyed in 11. Jacobi, And the lord George Berkeley his grandchilde and heire, and their severall tenants of the said Manors of Slimbridge and fframpton, concerninge grounds newe gayned from and leaft by the river of Severne, called the newe warth and the newe gotten grounds, for comon of pasture claymed theron by the inhabitants of Slimbridge and fframpton, divers great and tedious sutes from 7º Jacobi for 10. yeares after, in the Courts of Kings bench, Comon pleas, Chancery, Court of Wards, and Starchamber, have byn multiplied; wherin the lord Berkeleis two farmors, Arnold Oldisworth and George Thorpe Esquires, were somtimes pl^{ts} and somtimes defend^{ts}; And you Willm Archard may remember, That after such time as my selfe had by their assignment a third part from them, who at that time had not so much legall knowledge betweene them both, as I knowe at this time you have, though otherwise two prudent men; I did direct you (out of the confidence I had in the vnion of possession in Thomas lord Berkeley of those two Manors of Slimbridge and fframpton, then in him, simul et semel, therby extinguishinge the Comon of most of fframpton tenants,) to take a distresse vpon the old warth; which accordingly you impounded at Slimbridge, (I havinge not longe before found the said Deeds and fine of 31. et 33. E. 1. and enabled my selfe with the knowledge of the pedegree of the feoffees,) relatinge at that time to you, that if the inhabitants of fframpton had noe right of Comon vpon the old warth, though they had longe vsed the same, much lesse could they vpon those grounds (which wee had then lately inclosed) called the newe warth and new grounds, which had not 40. yeares then before (remembred by many hundreds of men and women then livinge,) byn cast togeather and left by the river of Severne, especially by removinge of her channell, as often times it vseth; it beinge then remembred (even by my selfe) when a great part of those grounds were the body and maine part of the channell it selfe and the deepest part therof: which after longe and curious pleadings (as your selfe knoweth,) sped foe well that you recovered and had Costs; And after did once or twice distraine againe with like successe, as the Records heerafter expressed doe witnesse: Which Acts of yours and mine, (especially your first distresse,) how dislikinge soever at first to my two partners, yet they brought peace, more then either Chancery orders or decrees in the court of Wards; And foe cooled the great heate of fframpton

[1] For meaning, see ante. "Lives of the Berkeleys," Vol. II., p. 52 n.

Slimbridge

ton Inhabitants, that they have permitted those our enclosures to | stand quiet to this day. a⁰. 1639.

To recompence which great troubles and expences that amounted to—1500ᴸ for my part alone, In the last 10 or 12 yeares, are 300 acres at least more of sand heapes cast togeather at the lower end of the said new grounds, and least by another remove of the Channell in that part; which 3. yeares nowe last past began to beare weedes and graffe, And daily (by my Cribs and other fortifications to preserve and better it) foe bettereth it selfe, that it is more then likely to become in fewe yeares a fruitfull pasture; Noe other feare therof nowe left mee, but least Severne in her rage weare it away againe; To prevent which I doe yearly fortify as you knowe: An old courfe which in that part of this parish of Slimbridge this River hath kept, witnes the Record in the Tower of London of Rot. Claus. 18. H. 3. membr. 22, which shewes, that it was found by Jury. That that part of land in Slimbridge called the warth, wᶜʰ was claymed by the Townships of Slimbridge and Aure one against the other, did belonge to Slimbridge and not to Aure; becaufe before the water of Severne did weare away that ground, castinge it to Aure feilds, it was part of Slimbridge arrable and pasture feilds; And nowe beinge worne away from Aure and cast to Slimbridge feilds againe, it ought to bee pasture belonginge to Slimbridge: And thervpon a writt was awarded to the Sheriffe of this County of Glouc̈, to give the lord Berkeley feizin therof accordingly. *The old warth*

As touchinge an Assife tried at Gloucester Assises in 11. H. 4. wherin Thomas lord Berkeley was pli against William Teste John Doppinge the elder and John Cooke, (three of the principall inhabitants of fframpton,) for disseizinge him of 600. acres of land in Slimbridge, beinge his freehold: which vpon Not guilty pleaded was tryed by Jury against them, and they found to have diffeifed him; I have not further informed my felfe therof, Then that the Record (shewinge foe much) was, by James lord Berkeley nephewe and heire male of this manor to the said lord Thomas in 15. H. 6. exemplified vnder Seale, which is in Berkeley Castle; what time I suppose other newe futes were about the soile of this warth, or comon of pasture claymed by fframpton men vpon the fame. *Warth.*

In this parish of Slimbridge are certaine lands and tenements called Testes, containinge about 40 acres, late the inheritance of Edward Bramwich of fframpton aforefaid, in the right of Margaret his wife; by whom hee had issue Isaack Bromwich that nowe is, the said Margaret beinge nowe remaryed to William Sheppard, *Bramwich lands, als Testes.*

Sheppard, who was daughter and heire of ffrancis Codrington Esq; somtime the lands of John Clifford, father of Alice maried to William Teste, (one of the defts in the said assise brought by Thomas lord Berkeley in 11. H. 4. aforesaid;) betweene which Willm and Alice was issue Laurence Teste Esq, who died in 22. H. 7, And by Jone his wife left issue John Teste, who dyed the same yeare of his father without issue, and Giles Teste was his brother and heire, who died also without issue in 34. H. 8. leavinge Grace, Margaret, and Mary, his three sisters and heires; Which Mary was maried to ffrancis Codrington Esq, who died in 4. Mar. To whom all theis lands were conveyed; And left issue Giles Codringtō who dyed in 23. Eliz., and was father of ffrancis Codrington who died in 24. Eliz. the yeare after his father, and leaft issue the said Margaret only; first maried to Edward Bramwich, and secondly to Willm Sheppard, as first aforesaid: And are holden of George lord Berkeley as of this his manor of Slimbridge by sute to his hundred Court of Berkeley from 3. weekes to 3. weekes, and by the yearly rent of—27ˢ. 10ᵈ. but whether in Socage or by knight service I yet knowe not. |

330   The aforesaid pedegree and what is before written is taken out of the Evidences of the said Edward Bramwich, and out of theis Records followinge, with some Court Rolls in Berkeley Castle. See in Cowley. fol: 164.

Rot. pardoñ. 11. E. 4. made to Lawrance Teste, civi et pannario London, als de fframpton sup Sabrinam.

Inq: 2. H. 8. p̃ mortem Laurencij Teste p̃dc̃i.

Inq: 34. H. 8. p̃ mortem Egidij Teste.

Inq: 4. & 5. Ph: & Mar. ps. 1. p̃ mortem ffrancisci Codrington.

Inq: 23. Eliz. p̃ mortem Egidij Codrington.

Inq: 24. Eliz: p̃ morte ffrancisci Codrington.

Barnsdales land, als Smithes als fframilodes lands.

Heere also in this parish of Slimbridge are divers lands and tenements late held in Comon by vndevided moities, of Willm Smyth als Barnsdale, Doctor of phisicke, who died in 6ᵗᵒ Jacobi, sonne of Henry: And by Benedict Tysson, sonne of John: nowe in aº 1639. the inheritance of Anne wife of Sir James Stonehouse knight, daughter and heire of the said Willm Smyth als Barnsdall, And of John Gilman, and of Richard Powell in right of   his wife, And of Richard Nicholas: wherof the one moity was the ancient land of the fframilods, of whom Simon fframilode lived in the time of kinge H. 3. After the lands of Thomas de fframilode, and of Edward de fframilode, sonne of John, and after of John fframilode sonne of Richard; And after of Thomas Lewis; And after of Richard Gilman, who died 31. H. 8.

31. H. 8, the one of whofe two daughters and heires called Alice had the wholl moity conveyed to her from her father, and was maryed to John Tyffon, father of Brian Tyffon who dyed without iffue, wherby that moity difcended to Agnes the other daughter and coheire of the faid Richard Gilman, maryed to the faid Henry Smyth als Barnfdale aforefaid : And is held of George lord Berkeley by knight fervice, heriot fervice, Sute to the hundred Court of Berkeley from 3. weekes to 3. weekes, And by the moity of the yearly rent of—13ˢ 6ᵈ.

The other moity of the faid lands and tenements were parcell of the poffeffions of a Chantry in Cirencefter called **Richards Chantry**, wᶜʰ after the diffolution therof in 1. E. 6. came to John Vaughan, And nowe or late of Benedict Tyffon aforefaid, fonne of John Tyffon, brothers fonne and heire of Brian Tyffon of the fathers fide : And payeth the other moity of the faide cheife rent of—13ˢ 6ᵈ but is holden of the kinge in free focage.

Of theis lands called **fframilodes lands** als **Lewses lands**, fee an Inq : in 31. H. 8. the third bundle, virtute officij, after the death of the faid Richard Gilman, very full for the pedegree.

And an excellent Court Roll in a paper booke, holden for the manor of Hurft in 1. R. 3. after the death of Eliz : late the wife of the forefaid Richard fframilode ; Heriot ; Serviciũ militare ; Wardfhip.

Rot. Pateñ. 7. E. 3. pars. 1. dorfo, in the Tower.

Edwardus de fframilode et Alicia vxor eius arraiñ affifa verfus Richardum Phelips et Katherinam vxorem eius, de teñtis in Slimbridge, Kingfton, Gofington, et Iweley, in two futes.

Carī Roll there, 42. E. 3. Edward de fframilode fonne and heire of John fframilode. |

Court Rolls of Siimbridge and Hurft, 6ᵗᵒ Jacobi pᵗ mortem Willimi Smyth als Barnfdale.—per fervicium militare.

Vpon the death of Sir James Stonehoufe in 15. Regis Caroli, to whofe vfe his wife Anne had conveyed her part of theis lands nowe worth 50ˡⁱ p Anũ ; A releife of—12ˢ 6ᵈ after the rate of the 8ᵗʰ part of a knights fee was paid by Thomas Davis
                                                                                                the

the Reeve of the Manor of Slimbridge, vpon his Accompt for that yeare, Soe proportioned to bee holden for the quantity of the tenure for the time to come; and were then in the occupacon of Eleanor Gilman, Robert ffrape, John Biford, and William Davis; Of which lands a fine was by Sir James levied in Hillary terme 17º Jacobi, for a confirmacon of a leafe of part of theis lands then made to Thomas Davis, father of the said William

Bottillers lands Batts & Knights land.

In this Manor of Slimbridge is alfo one ancient freehold confiftinge of a meffuage and halfe a yard land, which Alice the widowe of Maurice lord Berkeley the firft of that name, daughter of the said Roger Berkeley of Durfeley in the time of kinge R. 1. (then a widowe, for her hufband Maurice died in 1. R. 1.) gave to Elias the fonne of Toki her Nurfe, and his heires, by Deed in theis words, vz,

Common in the warth.

It appeareth by a Decree in Chancery dated 12º Novembr. aº. 32º. H. 8. wherin Thomas Woodward and other the inhabitants of Slimbridge and fframpton were plts, againft Edward Trotman and John Bower Defts, vpon the examinacōn of very many witneffes; That noe man havinge any eftate within thofe Townfhips of Slimbridge and fframpton might put any beaft or fheepe to comon in the warth, vnles hee lived himfelfe within one of thofe townfhips.

Which Cuftome was againe confirmed by another Decree in Chancery had by confent, bearinge date 12º Julij aº 38. Eliz: wherin Thomas Heminge and Willm Hennis with other the Inhabitants of Slimbridge and fframpton were plts, againft Sir Henry Winfton and Sir John Pointz knights, with others, Defts |

332 Davies land late Ludbies. Of old, the Priors of Sᵗ Ofwalds.

Heere alfo in Slimbridge is a meffuage and 10. acres of land meadowe and pafture therto belonginge, nowe the inheritance of Robert Davies, fonne of Thomas Davis of Hurft, which the said Robert about 10º Caroli, purchafed of Simon Munden; to whom Simon Ludby in 7º Caroli by his will devifed the fame in fee; fomtime belonginge to the priory of Sᵗ Ofwalds in Glouc, But of whom or by what fervice the fame are holden, I knowe not; ffor which lands fee an Inquifition found after the death of the said Simon Ludby in 7º Caroli.

Heere

Slimbridge

Heere alſo in Slimbridge is a meſſuage and ſix acres of land, now the inheritance of Robert Davis of Hurſt, called Woodhouſe, which Simon Ludby purchaſed of John Huntley and Margaret his wife, Edmond Monileux and Vrſula his wife, and Pointz Mill and Elizabeth his wife, daughters and coheires of John Sydenham Eſq; And of one acre in the little moore purchaſed of   Andrewes: And which the ſaid Simon Ludby by his will in 7° Caroli deviſed in fee to his kinſman Richard Munden, of whom the ſaid Robert Davis of late purchaſed the ſame: And are holden of George lord Berkeley as of his manor of Hurſt by ſealty and ſute of Court to that manor.

Davies land; late Ludbies late the coheires of Sydenham.

ffor which ſee an Office found in 7. Regis Caroli, after the death of the ſaid Simon Ludby. And of old the land of

Heere alſo in Slimbridge is one other ancient freehold containinge a meſſuage and 32. acres of land, nowe in a° 1639. the inheritance of Robert Davis of Hurſt, which hee in July 1634. a° 10. R(° Caroli, purchaſed of Thomas Veel Eſquire, ſonne and heire of Nicholas Veel Eſq; who in 19° Jacobi, (with other lands) by his deed inrolled with the Cuſtos Rotulorum of this County, purchaſed of Nicholas Bridges, a younger ſonne of Richard Bridges, then of Combe; To which Nicholas the ſaid Richard his father in 17° Jacobi gave the ſame in fee: And which the ſaid Richard Bridges (amongſt other lands) in 26° Eliz: purchaſed of Woolworth als Webbe: And which the ſaid Willm by fyne levied in Eaſter Terme a° 6to Eliz: and other aſſurances in 5. et 6. Eliz: ſd. purchaſed of Robert Hurd and Alice his wife, ſiſter and heire of Thomas Woodward, ſonne and heire of John Woodward.—

Davis land, late Bridges: before Woodwards

And are holden of George Lord Berkeley as of his Manor of Came, by knight ſervice, ſuite to his hundred Court of Berkeley from 3. week(° to 3. weekes. And by the yearely rent of—17ˢ 4ᵈ. To which manor of Came the ſaid Cheife rent is paid |

The ſaid Robert Davis holdeth alſo certaine other lands in this pariſh of Slimbridge in the tithinge of Hurſt, containinge about   acres, which hee in   Caroli regis purchaſed of Simon Munden, who had two parts therof by the will of Simon Ludby in [7°] Caroli, whoſe widowe the ſaid Robert Davis hath ſithence maried; ſonne of David Ludby, ſonne of Simon Ludby, ſonne of
                                                                                    Ludby

333 Ludbies land. nowe Davies.

Ludby, whose ancestors had longe held the same: And also purchased the other third part of John Coxe, sonne and heire of Elizabeth., and of Mawde Ludby, sisters of the said David Ludby and heires at the comon lawe to the said Simon the Devisor, which to them discended after his death by reason of the tenure, which is of George lord Berkeley as of his Manor of   by knight service, and   ; ffor which fee an Inqu: found after the death of the said Simon Ludby in 7º. Caroli, wherin the tenure is found to bee as aforesaid.

Frapes land: somtimes, ffowlers.

Also in this parish Edward ffrape (and others as after followeth,) holdeth a messuage and 10. acres of land, which hee in   Caroli Rº p'chased of Henry ffowlar of Stonehouse, And hee in 43º. Eliz: of Thomas Curnocke and Jone his wife, and of William Richford als Rochford and Alice his wife, daughters and coheires of James Tailer, second sonne of Willm Taylor: which William also left issue John father of William, that dyed in his minority without issue: which said Willm father of John and James purchased the said messuage and land of John Longe of Came in 33º. H. 8. sonne and heire of Richard Longe, sonne and heire of Willm Longe, who in   purchased the same of Richard fframelode and others: And are holden of this Manor of Slimbridge by sute of Court to the hundred of Berkeley from 3. weekes to 3. weekes, the yearly rent of—12ˢ. 10ᵈ. And—

Of which land Richard Pegler holdeth one acre in Cames seild, wᶜʰ hee purchased of the said Robert ffrape, who bought it of John Wilkens, And paieth—10ᵈ. of the said cheife rent of—12ˢ. 10ᵈ.

See for this the Court Rolls of Slimbridge, 44. Eliz: and 43. Eliz. rent 12ˢ. 10ᵈ.

Rowles Court.

Heere also is an ancient messuage called Rolls Court with 100. acres of land of late therto belonginge, the inheritance of George lord Berkeley, reputed as beinge the manor house or Capitall messuage of the said Lords manor of Sages, lyinge within this parish of Slimbridge: By many heertofore conceived to bee the messuage called Sages place, or Sages court, but vndoubtedly is not, for that was in Hurst, nowe wholly decaied, As by a Deed in E. 3. time, in Berkeley castle appeares. This Manor of **Sages**, called also Sages land of Sages livelode, was the old inheritance of the family of the Sages, And was in 18. E. 3. purchased by Thomas then lord Berkeley of John Sage, then of the value of—17ˡⁱ. p anñ: whose ancient possessions foe fastened the name, that it continueth to this day. 1639. |

In

Slimbridge

In payment of the ffifteenth or Tenth when the same is granted by parliament, The onus or charge in the Exchequer is—11ˡⁱ 8ˢ 5ᵈ ob. q. The deduction is— 3ˡⁱ 10ˢ The Remanet paid into the Exchequer is—7ˡⁱ 18ˢ 5ᵈ ob. q. 334 ffifteene

In the last Subsedy in 5ᵗᵒ Caroli were 25. subsedy men, who paid—10ˡⁱ 12ˢ 8ᵈ Subsedy.

In aº 6ᵗᵒ Jacobi, vpon a generall muster, were in this parish—116. able men serviceable for the warres, betweene 20. and 60. yeares old, which appeared before Henry lord Berkeley Leiutenant of this County. Able men.

Of trayned Souldiers vnder William Thorpe Esq, their captaine, are 7. corslets and 12. musketts. Souldiers.

And if the wholl Division of Berkeley bee in any tax to the kinge rated at— 100ˡⁱ, Therof this hundred of Berkeley paies—33ˡⁱ 3ˢ; And this of Slimbridge,—35ˢ Rates.

I will conclude what more I intend of this manor or parish of Slimbridge, with a late Exchequer sute brought in the name of the kinge by Sʳ John Bankes his Matⁱᵉˢ Attorney generall, and prosecuted by Sir Sackvile Crowe Barronet and others, against the said George Lord Berkeley my selfe and others, as followeth; The defence wherof I only vndertooke, though somwhat to the dislike of my fellowe defendants, as yee knowe: And how I endeavoured therin, almost beyond my health, yee both may well remember, havinge therin the assistance of one of you in counsell at the Barre, And of the other in the Court with mee in marshallinge of my evidences, which were more then my life had formerly seene in any other tryall; yet have I beene at tryalls (quarum pars magna fui,) which have in delivery of Evidence lasted more then 8. houres at the barre; The foundation of this suite was thus laid and begun. Exchequer suite New grounds. Dumball

Before the said Sir Sackvile Crowe, Sir Bainham Throkmerton, Barronetts, and ffrancis Smyth, (who made themselves Comissioners, taken out also and sollicited by themselves,) which bare date the 21ᵗʰ of July, Aº 13º Rⁱˢ Caroli, with 6. articles of instructions therto añexed; It was the 6ᵗʰ of September next after, aº 1637, before them and one John Taylor of Bristoll, (one of their fellowe farmers of the kings iron workes in the forrest of Deane,) by a Jury (most ptially by their meanes returned,) at Newenham, presented; That a parcell of ground within the parish of Slimbridge called the Newe inclosed grounds, containinge by estimacõn two hundred

dred acres, adioyninge and abuttinge vpon fframptons pill on the North, And vpon the regall river of Severne on the weſt, &c. within 40. yeares then laſt, was flymy and muddy ground, and parcell of the great and comon regall river of Severne, and covered with the water therof; and wheron the water of the ſaid River had, time out of minde, vſed to flowe and reflowe: Et quod p̄dc̄e ducentæ acre vſq̄ tunc, fuit com̄une navigium, et com̄unis navium, naviculorum et cimbarum tranſitus pro o͞ibus ſubditis regni Anglie, prout in alto mari. And that within the ſaid 40. yeares, the ſaid 200. acres, per derelictionē aquæ ab eiſdem, became dry, And within 30. yeares laſt were incloſed and imbanked from the ſea, And were in the poſſeſſion of my ſelfe, but by what right or title they of the Jury knew not, and were worth by the yeare two hundred markes.

And the ſaid Jury then further preſented, that one other parcell of land lyinge in the ſaid pariſh, called the Dumballs, newe gayned grounds, containinge by eſtimac̄on thirty acres (indeed 300. acres,) lyinge at the end or point of the newe warth, were within twenty yeares laſt flymy and muddy grounds, and parcell of the great and com̄on river and regall water of Severne and covered with the ſame, vntill what time the ſea time out of minde had uſed to flowe and reflowe, &c. as before; and were alſo in the tenure of my ſelfe, but by what right or title they of the Jury knewe not; and that every acre therof was worth—v̓. And the better to lay this their foundation, the Depoſitions of 12. witneſſes (by the ſaid Com̄iſſioners privately taken) were returned with the ſaid com̄iſſion and Inquiſition, into the office of the kings rem̄ibrancer in the Exchequer: Wherto in Eaſter terme followinge, A̓. 14. Regis Caroli, I pleaded, That the firſt of October a̓. vndecimo Jacobi, Henry lord Berkeley was ſeized in fee of the manor of Berkeley, wherof the ſaid 200. acres and the ſaid 30. acres are parcell, And that hee, the 26ᵗʰ of November, Anno vndecimo p̄dc̄o, died therof ſeized, And that the ſaid Manor of Berkeley diſcended to the ſaid George lord Berkeley his grandchilde and heire, who entred, and was ſeized, And the firſt of Auguſt a̓. 10. R̓ Caroli, demiſed to mee, to hold at Will, &c. Abſq̄ hoc, quod. &c.; traverſinge all the materiall points aforeſaid, mentioned in the ſaid Inquiſition: which to this day ſoe reſteth.

But in Hillary terme before, next after the returne of the ſaid Inquiſic̄on, his Matᵉ Atturney generall exhibited an Information of Intruſion againſt the ſaid George Lord Berkeley, Elizabeth Longe widowe, my ſelfe, and John Dryver my tenant to all the ſaid grounds, for intrudinge therinto and keepinge the poſſeſſion therof from the kinge, from the laſt of Aprill A̓ 1̓. R̓ Caroli, to the time of yᵉ

exhibitinge

Slimbridge

exhibitinge of this informačon. I only followed the caufe takinge the fole care therof; And after much ftruglinge, at laſt (as divers orders of Court doe witneſſe and affidavits made,) obtained to plead the generall iſſue—Not guilty: And not fpetially, as was much laboured for vs to have done; which by Mr Hall our Attorney in the faid Eaſter Terme wee did: wherin, and in Trinity terme followinge, many orders vpon motions on either fide were made, cheifely concerninge a tryall to bee by Jury at the barre the fame Trinity terme: which was foe ordered by the Court, with my confent, to bee: The like Information of Intrufion was then alfo for the faid 30. acres called the Dumballs newe gained grounds; And the like plea of—Not guilty, pleaded: which to this day foe refteth; ffor his Maties Atturny generall would only in that Trinity terme trye the faid Iſſue for the 200. acres, as by Order appeareth.

A Jury was in the end of Whitfonweeke in the vacation betweene thofe two termes returned by Sir Robert Pointz high Sheriffe, preſſed for favour therin by fpeciall tres and meſſengers fent to him on purpofe, but hee dealt moſt iuſtly therin: Thofe of the Jury foe by him and Mr Hooper his Vnderſheriffe thus returned, which that Trinity terme appeared, were; Thomas Hickes of Cromhall geñ, Thomas Walter of Horfeild geñ, Thomas Hearinge of Elberton geñ, Willm Kemis of Wickwarr geñ, Thomas Morgan of Lidney Efq, Edward Morfe of Deane magna geñ, John Winiat of Dimocke geñ, Grombald Pancefoote of Newent geñ, Adam Bainham of Yate geñ, Willm Whittington of Coldafton geñ, Edward Thurſton of Thornbury geñ, and Thomas Crifpe of Marſhfeld geñ.; which 12. were fworne for tryall of the iſſue: foure others alfo appeared, vz. Stephen ffowler of Stonehoufe geñ, John Sandford St Leonard geñ, John Howe of Caſhes Compton Efq, and Robert Hall of Arlington geñ, but the Jury filled before, for noe one was challenged on either fide: The plts extraordinary confidence | would not fuffer him, And my knowledge of the great abillity and vnderſtandinge of the whole pannell tooke from mee all thought therof.

ffor the kinge nyne witneſſes were fworne, who depofed all the materiall points in the Informačon and Inquifičon; And were the fame (almoſt all) that were examined at the Comiſſion of Newenham before Sir Sackvile and his fellowe Comiſſioñs, who nowe ſhewed themfelves openly to bee parties and intereſſed: And proved further, That a great part of the 200. acres was the channell of the river in that place at lowe water, which was not further denyed, neither more replyed to them then that they were very poore men, and of leſſe reputation. In the time of their

their depositions Theis thinges were touched by the kings Counsell, who were 7 at the barre, the ablest of the kingdome; wherof my selfe and others for mee tooke notice, viz;

1. That the kinge hath Admiralls Jurisdicčon in the place where the 200. acres doe lye.

2. That the kinge hath royall fishes in Severne, in iure Coronæ.

3. That the kinge hath waives and wreckes in Severne.

4. That Severne is a passage for the kings shipps.

5. That it floweth and refloweth with salt water more then 20 miles beyond the 200 acres in question.

6. That Severne is meta forestæ de Dene, and therfore integrè pertinet dno regi.

7. That all which the sea overfloweth by its ordinary springe tides belongs to the kinge: ffor the Sea is more worthy then the land on wch it lyeth: As by the grant of a wood, the soile doth passe; And though it lye dry when the tide is out, yet it is absurd to say that that should alter the property from the kinge, who cañot bee barred but by matter of Record, or by prescription, which doth presuppose a grant from the kinge.

8. Those things which are flotinge on the sea, or the Armes or branches therof, as wreckes, &c. are the kings; a fortiori, that which is fixed, as the soile.

9. Every thinge in the sea and in the royall Armes and branches therof, are the kings; And theis newe risen grounds is a part of the revenue of the sea, and participates of the nature of the Sea.

10. That all shoares and soiles within any port belonge to the kinge; And that there is noe shore in the kingdome but is within one port or other; Witnes an ancient Exchequer booke.

11. That land gained from the sea, is as land gained from an enemy: And therfore if the kinge should recover Callis, those which had former right have lost it; The like in royall Armes and branches, as of this in Severne.

12. That

12. That the sea is the bounds of the kingdome, and all bounds belonge to the kinge, as the bounds of a fforrest doe.

13. That which noe Subiect can clayme is the kings alone, for the lawe alloweth noe Comunity; And that ground not yet risen forsaken or cast togeather by the sea, is not (as may bee said) as yet to bee in rerum naturâ.

14. If a subiect should have a great sea which is after drayned, hee shall have the soile, And the kinge must not bee in worse case then the subiect.

15. That the subiect hath in all ages taken grants from the kinge of such lands soe gayned, as this in question, Ergo, the Kinges: And that it can bee noe part of any manor borderinge theron, as in the Inquisicõn it is found.

16. The case of Sutton marsh, which a fewe Termes past had received a Judgement in this Court, was not forgotten, with the reasons therof, by my adverse counsell.

Of my counsell were Mr Platt of Cirencester, Mr Lenthall, Mr Tempest, Mr Hall, and you my sonne.

When the kings witnesses had spoken all they could, and more then was true, or they knewe: Mr Platt who was well instructed both at severall Conferences of my Counsell togeather, and at his chamber, and on whom I most relyed, stated the case, to this effect; vz,

1. That the manor of Berkeley was originally granted to the progenitors of the nowe def.^t George Lord Berkeley by the charter of kinge H. 2. in theis words, vz, Berkelei et totam Berkelei Herneffe, manerium selt, cum õibus appendicijs suis, in aquis, in placitis, et in omnibus rebus et eventibus: vnder which and the severall Confirmacõns of divers his Mat.^{ye} progenitors, And by a syne levied in 23. E. 3. by Thomas then lord Berkeley, the same was derived to William Lord Berkeley, created Marques Berkeley, who in 4. H. 7. levied a syne therof, with a Render to himselfe in tayle, the Remainder to kinge H. 7. and the heires males of his body, the Remainder to the right heires of the said Marques Berkeley. That for want of issue of the said Marquesse it remained to kinge H. 7., And for want of issue male of the body of kinge H. 7. it reverted in primo Mariæ to Henry lord Berkeley, whose grandchilde and heire the nowe lord Berkeley is.

2. That

2. That this manor of **Berkeley** is a great Manor and a Barony, extendinge it selfe as large as the hundred of Berkeley; And somtimes included the inferior manors of Hill and Arlingham, and still includes the inferior and reputed manors of Hame, Hinton, and Slimbridge, which five are borderinge vpon Severne for 8. miles in length; And also it includeth 16. other inferior manors, lyinge vpwards in the hundred of Berkeley.

3. That the River of Severne at the 200. acres in question, and all alonge the coasts of the great manor of Berkeley, and the bankes, shoares, sands, rocks, Channell, and soile of the said river of Severne, vnto the middle of the Channell, called filum aquæ, belongeth to the said lord Berkeley, and is parcell of his said great manor of Berkeley, and of the said inferior Manors of Hame, Hinton, Slimbridge, &c. And therfore the 200. acres in question, although somtimes part of the shoare or chanell of Severne, belongeth to the lord Berkeley, and is parcell of his said Manors. And this (quoth hee) is our title.

1. **The** course of our proofe (said hee) shall bee thus; ffirst, That the river of Severne dividinge (by her Channell) the manor of Berkeley from the Manors on the other side the river is such, That the same is capable of private property or ownership, aswell as any other Inland or private river; And foe the first and second charges of the Informacōn falles.

2. That as this river of Severne is capable of private property, Soe, de facto, the said river, the soile, sands, shore, Channell, and rockes, vsq, ad filum aquæ, to the middle of the streame or Chanell, have byn in all ages (as for 500. yeares and more wee shall proove by more then 1000. peeces of Evidence), possessed held and enioyed by the Lords of the great Manor of Berkeley: and the Lords of all other Manors above belowe and over against the same, as parcell of their said Manors.

And for the first generall of our proofe, namely: That the River of Severne where it divides the manors of Berkeley, Hame, Hinton, Slimbridge, &c. from the manors on the other side, and farre belowe the same, is in the nature of a private and inland river, and therfore capable of private property or ownership. And that it is not part of the sea, &c. thus,

1. That this river at the place in question is about 120. miles distant from the sea, havinge on this side the counties of Glouc̄ Monmouth and Glamorgan, through

all

all which the river paſſeth before it venteth itſelfe into the ſea, or loſeth its name of Severne. |

2. That this river at the place in queſtion is above 40. miles by the water above any of the kings Ports, the neereſt wherof is Briſtoll and Kingrode.

3. That this River is not paſſable for any ſhipps of burden betweene Kingrode, lyinge 40. miles belowe, and the place in queſtion ; Neither is this river navigable or paſſable at the higheſt ſpringe tides at the place in queſtion, nor for many miles belowe, other then with flat bottomed barges, as at Henley vpon Thames.

4. That this river at the place in queſtion and for many miles belowe, is not ſoe broad at lowe water, as Thames is at Henley, neither doth it vent halfe ſoe much water : And is paſſable and fordable over in the ſomer times without danger vnder the midd thighes of a man ; yea, this yeare, a wayne with oxen was driven over.

5. That by reaſon of the flatnes and levelnes of the ground, and lightnes of the ſand and ſoile, in and about the place in queſtion, the river doth often by inſenſible degrees remove its channell, and accordingly doth benefit or preiudice the lands adioyninge ; And that the river vſually changeth its courſe once in 20. yeares at leaſt.

6. That the middle of the Chanell at lowe water towards which ſide or ſhoare, on this or the further ſide ſoever it bee, ever hath byn and ſtill is accompted the mete and boundery of the pariſhes, manors, townſhips, and liberties : And alſo the bound of the forreſt of Dene, on this ſide, per medium aquæ Sabrinæ, or per filum aquæ, which are both of one ſenſe.

7. That the perambulations of that fforreſt extend ſoe farre into the river, ad filum aquæ, and noe further : And that the ſeverall Townſhips manors and Pariſhes doe ſoe farre on each ſide make their ſeverall perambulations : And there alſo ſeverall Lords of manors, pariſhes, parſons, and vicars, havinge Tythes, doe extend their ſeverall fiſhings on rockes and with netts, and in digginge of ſtones, takinge of ſand, pitchinge of poles for fiſhinge, and the like.

And for the second generall part, It ſhall bee to proove, by invincible matter of evidence and of record, That the ſhoare river and ſoile therof, the Rockes ſands, &c.

&c. vnto the middle of the Channell at lowe water, hath from the time of kinge Edward the Confeſſor belonged, and ſtill doth belonge, and is part of the great manor of Berkeley and of its members to this day; And ſoe enioyed reputed and held; And that the middle of this river is the comon boundary of the manors pariſhes, &c. on both ſides, in the foreſaid Counties, as farre vpwards and downwards, as this river carrieth the name of Severne. And thus (ſaid hee) will I marſhall my proofes;

1. ffirſt, by 24. witneſſes of the ableſt and prime gent and yeomen, dwelling neere vnto this river, on either ſide ſome.

2. By 86. Copies of Court roll, wherby the ſands, ſhoares, rockes, weares, gurgites, ſtaches, &c. in Severne, are and have byn granted by the Lords of the Manors of Berkeley and the inferior members therof; And widowes eſtates vpon ſuch grants vſually had and enioyed, accordinge to the Cuſtome of thoſe Manors.

3. By 46. Deeds from the Norman Conqueſt downwards to this day, in every kings time ſome, wherby the ſoile ſands rockes ſtaches &c, in Severne, are granted by 20. ſucceſſive lords of this Manor of Berkeley and the members therof.

4. By 21. Rent Rolls, wherof ſome before date, ſome in the times of E. 1., E. 2., R. 2., H. 4., H. 6., and ſoe downwards, wherin 154 freeholders names, Copiholders, and Tenants by Indenture, are named, with the rents they ſeverally paid for the Rockes, weres, Putts,[1] kedellas,[2] gurgites,[2] ſtadia,[3] ſtaches,[4] Borachias,[2] charibdes,[5] pooles in Severne, fiſhings in Severne, and for parcells of the water and ſand of Severne, in this manor of Berkeley and the hambletts therof.

5. By

---

[1] *Putts*, from Putta, Puteus, Foſſa—Engliſh pit or ditch, Saxon pitt or pytt, uſed in this ſenſe in a Charter of Anno 1217 (Du Cange.)

[2] Theſe words ſignify generally weirs—e.g. *Kedellas*—Kiddle, a dam or open weir in a river, with a loop or narrow cut in it accommodated for laying of Engines to catch fiſh (Blount.)

Gurgites—is uſed as a Latin word for weirs—"Tres *Gurgites* in aqua de Monew attachiantur per Homines de Groſſmonte."—Black Book of Hereford, fo. 20.

Borachius—Probably ſhould be Borachias from Boëra, ſignifying a weir.

[3] *Stadia*—Stadium—Anglo-Saxon Stæd or Stad, a ſhore or bank, landing place. This word may be uſed in the ſenſe of its equivalents, ripa—a river bank; or littus, a ſhore.—See above, ſections 2 and 3 (Du Cange.)

[4] *Stache*—from Stachia—in Anglo-Saxon Stace, and means a ſtake or pole. Here it ſignifies a dam of flakes, earth, ſtones, &c., to ſtop a water-courſe.

[5] *Charibdes*—Whirlpool—derived from the famous whirlpool Charybdis.—[Ed.]

Slimbridge

5. By 3. survey bookes in 36. H. 8. in 1º. Mariæ, and 22º. Eliz: wherin more then 40 of the cuftomary or copihold tenants in the Manors of Hincton, Hame, Slimbridge, and Arlingham, members of the great manor of Berkeley, are mentioned and expreffed, to hold, rockes, putts, fifhinge places, and parcells of the river and | fands of Severne, according to the Cuftome of thofe Manors.

6. By 50 Accompts made by Reeves and Bailies of the faid manor of Slimbridge, of the profitts of that manor, before the Auditors of the Lord therof, from the 15. E. 1. till the end of H. 6. The like of Hame and Hinton manors.

7. By 3 grants of Rents charges and Anuities for lives, in 20. and 21. H. 6. out of the warth, &c.

8. By 4. grants to the Monaftery of S^t. Auguftine by Briftoll, before date, by the lords of this Manor of Berkeley.

9. By 2. deeds of Exchanges in fee, in 14. E. 2, and in 35. E. 1.

10. By 2. deeds of partition, in 27. E. 3. and in 6. E. 4. by coperceners.

11. By 15. Inquificōns or offices after the deathes of freeholders wherin in all ages fince H. 3. they are found to dye feized of rockes, putts, fifhings, &c. either on this fide Severne, or on the other fide the Chanell over againft the place in queftion, as belonginge to the feverall manors, &c.

12. By a fine at comōn lawe levied by John Thorpe in 11. H. 4. of two Rockes and fifhinge pl.ces in Severne.

13. By an Action of waft in 18. H. 6. brought by John Thorpe againft Ecton, for 3 fifhinge places or rockes.

14. By one Decree in Chancery in 9. Jacobi; And by 4. decrees in the court of Wards, in 12. 13. 15. et 16. Jacobi R(', wherby the poffeffion of the grounds in queftion (amongft others) was eftablifhed for Oldifworth and Thorpe, vnder whom, three of the nowe def^{ts} doe clayme.

15. By an Army of Witneffes examined in the times of H. 8. Queene Eliz: and kinge James, (all nowe dead,) provinge the Rockes, fifhings, and cuftomes
vfed

vfed in Severne ; And that the midſt of the Channell is the bounds of all mens Manors and pariſhes on both ſides, all alonge the River.

16. **Laſtly,** hee remembred the booke of Domeſday made in the Conquerors time ; And the perambulations of the fforreſt of Dene in tempore R(' Johis, et E. 1.

And then called for my Witneſſes, Of whom when the Court had heard nine, the Barons talked togeather a good ſpace privately, and then called to them the Atturney generall, who after ſome Comunicacõn, returninge to his place, drewe a Juror, never hearinge any one peece of Evidence wᶜʰ there I had before them in 2. trunkes and 3. baggs, beſides plotts of the river, Rockes, and Channell ; And printed mapps both in generall and in perticuler. And foe this fearfull ſute came to nothinge, which had threatned all the grounds on both ſides the river for 140. myles, lyinge betweene the high and lowe water markes, which were more worth then—20000ˡⁱ p anñ ; wherof, for the greateſt part, Inquiſitions were about the former time, found and returned : And doubtleſſe the expectacõn of the ſucceſſe of this ſuite was great, which cauſed many gent and Lords of Manors adioyninge willingly to furniſh mee with very many peeces of their Evidences : And to this hearinge wherof came a number of proiectors, as they ignominiouſly by as many of better condicõn then alſo preſent, were ſtiled ; Of whom I have not ſince heard, nor hope that heerafter I ſhall.

The paper I wrote in Breviats abſtracts and other needfulls (as my ſelfe conceived) came almoſt to a reame of paper, which remaine for moſt part ſtill with mee.

This Tryall fallinge foe ſodainly and vnexpectedly of, prevented mee from deliveringe an Invective ſpeach, which, with ſome bitternes, I had determined to have ſpoken in Court at the end of my Evidence, before the Jury, againſt Sʳ Sacvile Crowe eſpecially ; who not only was the prime proiector of this Severne buſines, but at his owne charges ſet himſelfe at worke, ſueinge out this Comiſſion, makinge himſelfe and his fellowes (intereſſed with him) Comiſſioners ; himſelfe alſo defrayinge all charges in diet and expenſes to Jurors and Witneſſes, but corruptly with a bribe of 3ˡⁱ to the vnderſheriffe to returne ſome of the Jurors by him named, And 20ˢ the peece to 3. or 4. of them to appeare and ſerve his turne : But alſo thruſt out of the chamber at Newenham aforeſaid ſuch of my Lord Berkeleis Counſell and mine, and of Sir John Wintours of Lidney, as came thither ; reiectinge to heare ſuch evidence as was then offered to bee given by them, ffor all which
I had

I had proofe ready in Court: And to have concluded with my with, That his next proiect might bee to keepe that little of his owne land that remained, if any, to pay his owne debts, for which hee was in sute: And to let mee and others rest in quiet with that little which had cost vs deere: And foe his voyage to Constantinople as ffactor for the Turky marchants, whither hee goeth, will prove more prosperous.

That as touchinge Comon of pasture claymed by the Inhabitants of Slimbridge and fframpton vpon Severne, vpon any the newe grounds either nowe in comminge and beginninge to beare graffe, as the Dumballs: Or already come bearinge graffe, as the 200. acres nowe in question; All my Counsell were of opinion, (the Court foe also seeminge to bee,) That none of them could prescribe to have comon for their Catell (though many former sutes had byn for the same by them,) becaufe the same were cast togeather by the Tydes within memory of man; And that the ground and soile therof (ad centrum terræ) was the Lord Berkeleis, as beinge within the bounds of his Manor. | Note

Stincheombe.

Stincheombe; of old and alwaies, till about the time of kinge H. 6, written **Stintescombe**; for there stinteth the Combe or Hill, as after followeth: from whence doubtles the name is.

It is generally by most men reputed to bee a parish, but certainly it is but a chappell of ease within the parish of Came, though free; As before I have written of Nibley.

This Manor or freehold of Stincheombe is holden of George lord Berkeley as of his Manor of Berkeley by the 20th part of a knights fee, sute to his hundred Court of Berkeley from 3. weekes, to 3. weekes, and by the cheife rent of—14ᵈ and a pound of comin, price—4ᵈ collected by the Reeve of his Manor of Came, as a freehold therof.

It consisteth of the inferior or little hambletts called Churchend, Southend, Clinger ats Cleihunger, Inwoods, Stancombe, Snitend, and Overend.

It was the old inheritance of the Bradstons of Bradston, whose discent see before fol: 113. and continued togeather in one and the same owner, vntill Thomas
lord

Hundred of Berkeley

Lord Wentworths Manor.

lord Wentworth by his feverall Deeds inrolled in the Court of Comon pleas in Michas Terme. 3. et 4. Eliz: Rñe, Rot. 13. et 14. bearinge date on or about the firft day of September in the faid third yeare of Queene Eliz: conveyed the fame to Trotman, Burchier, Nelme, Tindall, and others, wherof fee more in Bradfton. fol. 113. pd; which heere againe to repeate I am not willinge: And thofe bargainees accordinge to the Truft in them repofed, to divers others, in fuch fort as in this yeare, 1639. A° 14. R° Caroli, it is the inheritance of 26. ffreeholders, whofe names doe followe; vz, John Hollifter, Thomas Tindall, John Trotman in right of Mary his wife daughter and heire of John Hickes, John Selman fonne of John, John Browninge fonne and heire of Richard, John Thayer fonne of John, Katherine Thayer widowe, John Nelme iun fonne of John, Willm Rees, Willm Selman, Richard Diryat, John Belfher, John Hickes, Thomas Pope, Richard Hiett in right of Jone his wife daughter of   , Willm Tindall, John Diriatt, Samuell Trotman, Richard Atwood, Richard Woodward, John Nelme thelder, Edward Jobbins, Thomas Browninge, my felfe, and you my fonne, and fome others.

And by a Covenant in one of his Indentures of bargaine and fale, delivered all the old evidences and deeds, afwell of this Stinchcombe as of Bradfton, (which are faid to be 300 peeces) to bee kept by them in their church fteeple in a Cheft with three keies, to the equall vfe of himfelfe and of the purchafers, which I could never obtaine to fee. About a falfe purloininge of fome of them, fuppofed by one of them felves, a bill in Chancery was 3. yeares paft exhibited which beinge by the def^t denied vpon oath, proceeded noe further.

And laftly, the faid Lord Wentworth fold the Manor it felfe (fuch as it then was) to Richard Pates Efq, and his heires, by his deed inrolled in Chancery dated 31° Augufti a° 8° Rñe Eliz: wherin hee covenanted with the faid Lord not to impeach any his former fales made to others, well worth the pervfall vpon any occafion heerafter.

The faid Richard Pate dyed in   Eliz: leavinge iffue Margaret maried to Richard Brookes, who betweene them had iffue Suzan, firft maried to Ambrofe Willoughby knight, and after to Sir Robert Lovett, who by their Deed dated 24° Aprit, a° 5° Jacobi R°, (befides other affurances,) fold the fame, by the name of their Manors of Stinchcombe and Bradfton, to John Hollifter and his heires: After whofe death an office was found, 9° Junij a° 7° Jacobi, That hee died feized (inter alia)

Stincheombe

alia) of the Manor of Stinchcombe, holden of the lord Berkeley as of his Manor of Berkeley, by fealty, two shillings rent, suite of Court, and in free socage, for all services; And that Roger Hollister was his sonne and heire, of full age: Of the sonne of which Roger, called John, Samuell Trotman of Stancombe purchased the same in   , nowe owner therof: who also from his fathers purchase and his, had formerly other pts of this Manor. |

It probably seemeth, (as before is touched,) That the name of Stintescombe, (as in very many ancient old deeds it is ever written,) is taken from the great combe or edge of the great Hill, which at this town slinteth and ceaseth, not extendinge it selfe that way any further: And that a parcell or hamblett thereof called Stane-combe, hath its name from the same stony combe also.

344 Name.

Upon this great and eminent Hill or Combe standeth a Beacon, erected in 48 E. 3, as by evidence which I have seen, appears; which for eminency and prospect may compare with any of those in Palestina, Italy, in the Isle of Man, of Hainborrowe in Cornwall, so greatly celebrated with Geographers: For if the day bee cleere, the extent of an ordinary eye discerneth the most objected parts of Seaven Counties, with the Cities of Bristol, Gloucester, Worcester, Hereford, &c.

Beacon.

> Stinchcombe's wide prospect at once both feedes and gluts the eye
> With Berkelei's wholl extent, as it in bredth and length doth lye.

Touchinge the antiquity and name of Beacons, the Saxon word, Beenian, to beckon, gives the name, reduced from Stackes of wood; to Posts and pitch potts, in the time of king E. 3; and were of elder time, for the more speedy spreadinge of the knowledge of the enemies cominge, assisted with nags or hobies called Hobeliers.[1]

Heere in Stinchcombe is a parcel of ground called blu-meade; from whence wee hundredors in theis parts have amongst us the name of Blu-meade Sunday, the second Sunday after the feast of Pentecost: a Place where the younger sort of both sexes accustomed in the afternoon of that day to meete from the Townships adjoininge to dance, leape, wrastle, and disport themselves till eveninge; of late yeares by some severe and rigid Catoes exclaiminge against such recreations, quite discontinued.

Blumeade Sunday.

---

[1] Hobblers were men who by their tenure were obliged to keep little light nags and act as sentinels and give notice of the approach of an enemy. [ED.]

discontinued. My opinion whereof and of other like sociable meetings, Church-ales, Wakes, Saints Feast-daies, &c, I purposed in this place to have left to you, as a plain legacy of my minde thereon: As also I did in the description of Alkington, fol. 30, when I wrote of Riam-meade Sunday, which is the Sunday next before this of Blu-meade: and the rather becaufe I throughout this description have expressed to what Saints each Church was dedicated and the Feast kept; but nowe through the great length whereto this booke is growne, and of what more I will herein save paper and paines, and refer you my sonne (amongst many others,) to M.r Carewe's Survey of Cornwall, fol. 68, 69, and forwards: And to M.r Burton's booke of Melancholy fol. 256, 257, and forwards, in his third edition, with whom I joyne in opinion, and subscribe to the kinge's declaration; and like well, in this my decrepit age, to walke in somer-time, on Sundaies after Eveninge Prayers, with my wife to Hodleys Green betweene our two houses, and there to behold my neighbours children and servants, with yours and mine owne, to runne at Barley-breakes, dance in a ringe, and such like sports as they like best; A laudable recreation, which hath no oppugners save wayward dispositions, and men of too sterne a judgment, as though the text of Solomon were Apochriphall, That,—There is a time for all things. |

345

Inwoods now Trye's.

Freeholds within the Village and Tithinge of Stinchcombe.

Thomas Lord Berkeley the second of that name, sonne of Maurice Lord Berkeley, by his Deed in 27 E. 1, (which shall follow verbatim) gave, or rather but confirmed, to Robert Berkeley his Nephewe, second sonne of the said lord Maurice, and to the heires of his body, All his wood of Inwood in Came, with all the hedges and ditches about the same, To hold by the yearly rent of—40ˢ; which is in theis words; viz,

Anno regni regis Edri vicesimo septimo die sabbi in festo sci Johis Apli et Evangeliste, ita convenit inter Dñum Thomam Dñum de Berkeley tradentem ex vna parte, et Robtum de Berkeley nepotem dci Dñi Thome recipientem ex altera parte, vz, q̃d deus Dñs Thomas de Berkeley tradidit dedit concessit, et hac p̃senti carta sua confirmavit p̃dc̃o, Robto de Berkeley pro homagio et servicio suo, Totum boscum suum de Inwode in Chamme cum oĩbus haieijs et fossatis circumiacentibus, et omnibus alijs pertinen suis, Hendum et tenendum totũ boscũ p̃dẽm p̃fato Robto et hered suis de corpore suo matrimonialiter procreatis, de p̃dc̃o Dño Thoma et hered suis, liberè, quiete, integrè, et in pace, iure hereditario imppetuum. Ita q̃d bene licebit dco Robto et hered suis de corpore suo matrimonialiter procreatis, totm boscm

Stincheombe

boſc̃m p̱dc̃m claudere, et in clauſum tenere, excepta vna via per medium, et p̱dc̃m boſeum toĩm, vel in p̱te pro voluntate ſua aſſartare. Reddendo inde añuatim p̱dco Dño Thomæ et hered ſuis, p̱dc̄us Robtus et heredes ſui, quadraginta ſolidos ſterlingoꝫ ad quatuor anni terminos, vz, Ad Paſcha decem ſolidos, ad feſtm̃ ſc̄i Johis Baptiſtæ decem ſolidos, Ad feſtm̃ ſc̄i Michis decem ſolidos, et ad natale Dñi decem ſolidos, pro ōibus ſervicijs ſecularibus et demandis; Salvo regali cum acciderit, et ſecta hundredi de Berkel de tribus ſeptimañ in tres ſeptimañ ; Et ſi contingat dc̃m Robm̃ in p̱dco redditu terminis p̱texatis in toto vel in p̱te deficere, quod abſit, ſubmiſit ſe et heredes ſuos diſtrictioni dc̄i Dñi Thomæ et heredum ſuorum q̃d poſſint eum diſtringere per toĩm tenm̃ ſuum de ſeodo de Durſeley, adeo bene, ſicut de ſeodo ſuo proprio, et in omnibus licis infra hundred de Berkeley vbi bona ſua poſſunt inveniri, tam in bobus et ovibus, quam in alijs animalibus et ſingulis bonis ſuis mobilibus et imobilibus, quovſq̃ ſup̱ p̱miſſo redditu ſibi et hered ſuis plenarie fuerit ſatisfactum, per p̱dc̃m Robertum et heredes ſuos. Predictus vero Dñs Thomas et heredes ſui toĩm boſc̃m p̱dc̃m cm̃ ōibus ſuis p̱tineñ dc̃o Robto et hered ſuis de corpore ſuo matrimonialiter procreatis, contra omnes mortales warrantizabunt imppetuum. In cuius rei teſtimonium partes p̱dc̄e huic ſcripto in modum Chirographi confecto ſigilla ſua alternatim appoſuerunt. Hijs teſtibus, Dñis Robto de Berkeley, Waltero de Helyn, Johe de Weliton, Robto de Veel, Petro Crok, militibus; Rič̄o de Byſeley, Robto de Bradeſtun, Robto de Stanes, Robto Wither, Rič̄o de Avene, Thoma de Swonhungre, et alijs.

Seaven yeares after came an agreement betweene the ſaid lord Berkeley and the ſaid Robert de Berkeley, in ffrench in Berkeley caſtle ; in theis words, vz ;

Le ſetime iour de Januier l'an du regne le roy Edward fits le roy Henry trent quart, Acovint enter ſire Thomas de Berkel Seigniour de Berkel d'une p̱te, e Robert de Berkel ſon neueuz d'auter p̱te, Iſſeint ceſt aſavoir, q̃ come le dit ſire Thomas vſt ſeoffe le dit Robert du bois de Inwode del aver encloſe et endeſens, come plus pleinment piert p̱ la chartre de ceo ſete ; Si ad le dit Robert grant p̱ luy et pur ſes heires au dit Sire Thomas e a ſes heires a touts iours, e a Water Gilot de Cleihungre peiſant le dit ſire Thomas et a tuz auters q̃ cel tenement tendrunt, le quel il tient, vn chemin p̱ my la wodelane le dit Robert auxi large come e le fuſt le iour de la confeſction de ceſt cart, Et p̱ my le clos memes eely Robert de Inwode un chemin jekes a gate perok de la largeſſe de diz pees en tuz leus de aler e revener od charrs, charettes, chapies e tute maneres des beſtes, ſanz deſturbance le dit Robert ou de ces heires ou de nul auter per mi eux a touts iours. Iſſeint nep'ant

q̃ ſi le

346 q̃ si le dit Water Gilet ou auter q̃ cel tenem'. tendra, nul tems | euenir pur trespas por chacer bestes hors de chemin ou per prendre du bois le Robert ou per pessante del chemin a son damage meintenant per vewe de veisins feit resonablement amend. Pur queus chemins le dit Sire Thomas ad grant q̃ le dit Robt e ses heires receivent du dit Water Gilet e des auters q̃ cel tenement tendre deus chapons de anule rent a la pasch. Et q̃ bien list au dit Robert et a ses heires a distraindre en le dit chemin ver gate prockt' au tant deseth cōe les deus capons serrunt arere, al terme establi. Estre ceo si ad le dit Robt grant pur luy et pur ces heirs au dit sire Thomas et a ces heires q̃ memes celes bonds q̃ fuer̃t nadgeres seces du pre, meme celui Robert en spitnied q̃ git enter le pre le dit monseir Thomas dune pte et de auter e se estent de la tere le dit sire Thomas sus la pasture Robti de Bradston se teignent e estoisont sermes et estables en meme le leu q̃ hore sunt pur toutʒ iours sans disturbance ou remuemēt du dit Robert ou de ses heires a remenant. En testmoiante de queu chose a cest escrit endent, les dits parties ent entrechangeablementes mis lur seals, per ices testmoines. Sires Johan de Button, Johan Bassett, Willame de Walton, chivalers: Robert de Bradston, Thomas de Beoleie, Thomas de Stintescombe, Johan de Olepeñe, Henrico de Came, Warin le fitʒ William, Robert Wither, Water Hathemar̃, et autres. Done a Berkel iour et an de sus ditʒ.

In 4. E. 3. vpon a controversy betweene Thomas lord Berkeley the third of that name, grandchilde of the foresaid Thomas, And the said Robert Berkeley. it was awarded by John Lovell and 4. others, arbitrators betweene them, That the said Robert should pay and doe escuage to the said lord when it happeneth for this land of Inwood, and for his other land at Dangervilfwike in the manor of Alkington, accordinge to the quantity of the said lands, And should also repaire Beoly bridge at Beoly brooke.—which were all the differences controverted betweene them.

ffrom which Robert Berkeley theis grounds of Inwoods, (which before were parcell of the demesnes of the Manor of Came, as by divers Accompts of that manor appeares,) came to Thomas Berkeley second sonne of the said Robert, which Thomas dyed in 6 E. 3. leavinge issue John and Margaret, which John died in 20. E. 3. without issue, then in ward for this land and for Beoly, to Thomas then lord Berkeley: And the said Margaret his sister and heire was first maried to Walter Shoile, by whom shee had noe issue; And after remaried to Raph als Rawlin Trye. by whom shee had issue William Trye and John Trye: which William dyed in the life of his father without issue, And the said John had issue William and John; which William dyed also in the life of his father without issue, And the said
John

Stincheombe

John Try his brother had issue William Trye, who maried Isable daughter of James lord Berkeley, and sister to William created Marques Berkeley: Vpon which maryage betweene the said Willm Trye and Isable Berkeley, a Deed yet remaininge in Berkeley castle, was in theis words; viz,

 Omnibus xpi fidelibus ad quos p̃sens scriptum pvenerit, Willus Berkeley miles Dñs de Berkeley salt̄m in Dño sempiternam. Noveritis me prefat̃m Willm dedisse, concessisse, et hoc p̃nti scripto meo confirmasse Willimo Trye armigero et Isabelle vxori suæ sorori meæ, vnum añualem redditum quadraginta solidoȝ de quoddam scõt redditū, quem idem Willus Try mihi solebat reddere pro certis terris et bosco in Stincheombe in comitat̃ Glouc̃. Habend tenend et peipiend dēm añualem redditum quadraginta solidoȝ p̃fat̃ Witto Try et Isabelle vxori sue in ptem soluc̃onis maioris som̄e, vz, Trescentē marcas leglis monete Anglie. | Et volo quod heredes et executores mei perimplent dēm añualem redditum quadraginta solid eisdem Willo et Isabelle hered et assignatis suis quovsq̃ p̃dca som̃a maior plenaire sit psolut̃ secundum voluntatem Jacobi Berkeley militis Dñi de Berkeley patris mei, vz, pro maritagio p̃dc̄e Isabelle: In cuius rei testimonium, huic p̃senti scripto meo sigillum meum apposui; Dat̃ apud Glouc̃ in domo Johis Pole octodecimo de Augusti, Anno regni Regis Edwardi quarti post conquestum, sexto decimo.

 Which Willm Trye and Isable had issue betweene them John and Willm, which John dyed without issue, and the said William dyed in 14. H. 8. and had issue Edward Trye who dyed in 18. H. 8. and was father of John who dyed 33. H. 8., father of John who dyed in 33. Eliz., father of William who dyed in 8. Jacobi, father of William Try who in the 7th yeare of kinge Charles sold this land to his vncle John Try, who nowe a° 1639. holdeth the same and paieth the said—40^s cheife rent, and the other services.

 Hereof see also before in Beoley fol: 75. where this pedegree is somwhat more particularly, with the time of each mans death, laid downe. And in Stone also, fol: 362.

 Of this land called Inwoods Willm Tyndall purchased of the said William Trye

And also Richard Atwood p'chased 8. acres, nowe the land of Richard Atwood, sonne fonne of Thomas, fonne of the faid Richard, 1639. but pay noe part of the cheefe rent.

More of this Jntwoods is to bee read in theis Records, viz,

 Inq : 15. E. 2. pro terris Mauricij de Berkeley.
 Inq : 37. E. 3. de feodis Baroniæ de Berkeley in Sc̄c̄io c̄m Rem̄ Thefaur̄.
 Inq : 13. H. 7. p! mortem Willi Try.
 Inq : 16. H. 8. p! mortem Willi Try.
 Inq : 18. H. 8. p! mortem Edwardi Trye.
 Inq : 33. Eliz : p! mortem Johis Trye in com̄ Lincoln̄.
 Inq : 8. Jacobi, p! mortem Willi Try.
 Court Rolls of Came, 8. Jac̄.—per fervicium militare.
 Court Roll of Came, 38. Eliz. Johes Try Ar̄ obijt 33.
 Eliz : redd. 40ˢ folvit 40ˢ pro retio.

Peirs Court late Hickes, nowe Trotmans.

Heere in Stinchcombe is an ancient meffuage called Peirs Court, fomtimes written the Manor of Peirs Court, with   acres of land of old therto belonginge, nowe the Inheritance of John Trotman, fonne of Richard, in right of Elizabeth his wife daughter and heire of John Hickes, who died in 20. R̄ȇ Jacobi, fonne of John Hickes who in 3º et 4ᵗᵒ Eliz. R̄ñe purchafed the fame of Thomas lord Wentworth ; As by the Deed inrolled (and other affurances) in Michas terme 3º et 4ᵗᵒ Eliz : appeares : and after died in   Eliz : Which Thomas lord Wentworth was fonne of Thomas lord Wentworth and of Margaret his wife daughter and heire of Anne, wife to Sir Adrian ffortefcue knight, daughter and heire of Anne wife of Sir William Stoner knight, eldeft daughter and coheire of John Nevill Marques Mountague and of Ifable his wife, daughter and heire of Edmond Ingaldefthorpe, knight, fonne and heire of Margaret wife of Thomas Ingaldefthorpe, daughter and heire of Elizabeth wife of Walter de la pole, daughter and heire of Thomas de Bradfton knight, who died in 48. E. 3. and was fonne of Robert de Bradfton who died in the life time of Thomas de Bradfton Banneret his father, who died in 34. E. 3. And for whofe creation, and the guift of 500 m̄ks p anñ to him and his heires out of the kings receipt, See Rot. Clauſ : in arce London. 15. E. 4. membr : 12. where alfo fix difcents of this pedegree are laid downe : And the patent it felfe in 13. E. 3. there alfo, which is paid to this day, 1639. And this Thomas de Bradfton Banneret, was fonne of Robert de Bradfton, Of whofe difcents I have formerly written in the defcription of Bradfton, fol : 113. And this capitall meffuage or farme called Peirs Court is holden of George lord Berkeley as of his Manor

Stinchcombe

Manor of Came, by fute to his hundred Court of Berkeley from 3. weekes to 3. weekes, and by the yearly rent of 4ˢ and a pound of Comin, price 4ᵈ In the time of kinge H. 2. it was the land of Harding de Stintefcombe, Roger and Ralph de Stintefcombe; And in the times of kinge John and of kinge H. 3. and of kinge E. 1. of Piers of Stintefcombe, Peter de Stintefcombe, and of Thomas de Stintefcombe, All ffreeholders of note and eminency, owners of this land and witneffes to more then 300. deeds which I have feene : And their longe and ancient feifin therof and dwellinge vpon the fame gave the name of Piers Court, efpecially 3. or 4. of the name of Peter or Pierfe fucceedinge one another; And from them it came into the family of the Bradftons in the time of kinge E. 3., but whether by purchafe or by maryage of the heire I have not found; Neither doe I thinke any thinge remaineth to informe mee, fave the deeds and evidences formerly mentioned to bee kept in Stinchcombe church : The laft male of that male (as I remember) that I obferved was Thomas de Stintefcombe, who in the extracts of the fubfedy or ayd granted to the kinge is in 1. E. 3. mentioned therin to bee a fubtaxor of that Subfedy : And Stintefcombe and Bradfton to bee hambletts of the manor of Came To which effect alfo is the Quo warranto in 15. E. 1. brought by the kinge againft Thomas lord Berkeley mentioned in fol : 6.

 Somwhat more wherof is to bee read in theis Records ; viz,

  Rec̃ em̃ Rem̃ Thefauŕ in Term̃ Trin̄, 22. H. 6. Rot., 17., very good for the
  pedegree.

  Inqu : 20 Jacobi, pᵗ mortem Johis Hickes.

Heere alfo is another ancient meffuage called Melkefhams Court or the Manor of Melkefham, the inheritance of Thomas Tindall nowe in ward to the kinge aᵒ 1639. for other lands which his father Thomas Tyndall dyed feized of, holden by knight fervice in Capite, who died in   Rᵗ Caroli, fonne of Richard Tyndall who dyed in 18ᵒ Jacobi, and was fonne of Richard who dyed in 19ᵒ Eliz : havinge purchafed the fame by Deed inrolled in   in 3ᵒ Eliz : of Thomas lord Wentworth, fonne and heire of Thomas lord Wentworth and of Margaret his wife, daughter and heire of Anne maryed to Sir | Adrian ffortefcue, daughter and heire of Anne maried to Sir William Stoner, eldeft daughter and coheire of John Nevill Marques Mountacute, and of Ifable his wife daughter and heire of Edmond Ingaldefthorpe, fonne and heire of Margaret, maried to Thomas Ingaldefthorpe, daughter and heire of Elizabeth maried to Walter de la pole, daughter and heire of Thomas de Bradfton : which faid Walter de la pole and Elizabeth his wife (then

Melkefhams Court nowe Tyndalls.

Lords

Lords of the Manor of Stintefcombe) purchafed the fame of Robert Oulpenne, and to whom the faid Robert by his Deed inrolled in Chancery, dated 25° Januař A° 1. H. 5. releafed all his right and eftate in manerio de Stintefcombe als dict Milke-fhams Court, As by the Dorfe of Rot. Clauš 1. H. 5. membr. 6. appeares. And in the times of E. 1., E. 2., and E. 3., and fomwhat after, was the inheritance of the Melkefhams, whofe feifin gave the name of 𝔐elkeſhams Court, which continueth to this day, a° 1639. And is holden of George lord Berkeley as of his manor of Came by a paire of gloves of a penny price, And fute to his hundred Court of Berkeley from 3. weekes to 3. weekes.

Of this ffarme or little Manor of Melkifham, als the Manor of Stintefcombe, fee a fine levied in Eafter Terme 26. H. 6. wherby Edmond Ingaldefthorpe afore-faid feemes to purchafe this manor of Melkefham.

Alfo there are Recoveries therof in Michas Terme 24. H. 6. Rot. 411, And Termi Pafch: 25. H. 6. Rot. 586, and Hillař: 27 H. 6. Rot. 303, in cõi banco, of the Manor of Melkefham in Stintefcombe. This Meffuage, in fome later evidence I have feene written The over Court in Stinchcombe. Rot. Rediffeifiñ. ab anno, 27. to 35. E. 1. membr. 5. And in a° 31. E. 1. p̃d in the Tower of London, fhewes That Richard de melkefham recovered a meffuage and a Carucate of land in Stintefcombe, (which is this,) of Richard Aftmead, who againe diffeifed him, And therfore a writt nowe went out to the Sheriffe of this County to arreft and imprifon the faid Richard Aftmead.

Rot. pateñ. 28. E. 1. in dorfo, Jone Deveroux. Richard Eftmead and John Wither, brought an Attaint againft Richard Melkefham and Cicely his wife for theis lands of Melkfhams Court.

What more might bee written heerof muft bee had from the private Evidences of the faid Thomas Tyndall, and out of the Cheft in the Church there kept as aforefaid ; neither of which I have feene.

See the Court Roll of Came in 18ᵗʰ Jacobi.

<small>Lamports Court. nowe</small> **Heere** alfo is an ancient meffuage with divers lands therto belonging called **Lamports Court**, which was the old inheritance of the Lamports: who nowe holdeth it I knowe not, neither can therof write more then appeares in the Record of Eafter Terme in the Comon pleas, 8. H. 4. Rot. 509., which faith That Adam Lamport

Stintcombe

Lamport dyed without heire of the wholl bloud in the time of kinge E. 3. feized of this meſſuage in Stinteſcombe, ſuppoſed to have then byn holden of Thomas lord Berkeley by 40ˢ yearly rent, heriot, ſute of Court to his Manor of Came from 3. weekes to 3. weekes, and by eſcuage : wherin Ela de Bradſton widowe, pleadeth, That ſhee held the fame of the endowment of Thomas de Bradſton ſomtimes her huſband, the Revertion after her death belonginge | to Elizabeth the wife of Walter de-la-pole daughter and heire of the ſaid Thomas de Bradſton, and wherin iſſue was ioyned, whether the ſaid Adam Lamport dyed tenant to Thomas lord Berkeley grandfather of the ſaid Thomas or not : which appeares not in this Record to have beene tryed. And ſeemes to proceed from the ill pleadings of that Lords pedegree and diſcent : ffor the ſaid Lord Thomas, now demandant, is therin ſaid to bee ſonne of Thomas, ſonne of the ſaid lord Thomas. to whom it ſhould eſcheate ; wheras the demandants father was Maurice who died in 42. E. 3. ſeven yeares after the ſaid Thomas his father. Henſler Prothonotary. See alſo in banco regis eiſdem aᵒ et Terṁi et Rotulo.

By Rot. Clauſ. 1. H. 5. in dorſo membr : 2. William Vrry cozen and one of the heires of Peter de Evercy releaſed to Walter de la pole knight, and to Elizabeth his wife and the heires of the ſaid Elizabeth, All his right title &c. in all rents, lands, tenements, &c. in Stinteſcombe, Stancombe et Meteſdon, called Lamports court, which ſomtimes were Thomas de Evercy knight within the hundred of Berkeley in the county of Glouc̄, dated die Sabbathi poſt feſtum Sēae Luciæ virginis, aᵒ. 1. H. 5.

To this releaſe laſtly mentioned and Lamports Court I will adioyne divers lands and tenements lyinge in Stinchcombe, Stancombe, and other places therabouts, which in the time of R. 1. and kinge John were the lands of Robert de Alba Mara, and in the firſt 20. yeares of kinge H. 3. of John de Alba mara, And after of William de Alba mara, who, as the office found after his death in 40. H. 3. ſheweth, died feiſed of 110. acres of land, 8. acres of meadowe, 3. acres of paſture, one garden, a Watermill, certaine wood, and 5ˡⁱ rent of Aſſiſe paid by tenants in Stinchcombe, holden de dominio Baroniæ de Berkeley per ſervicium—10ˢ et 6ᵈ, p anñ. And held alſo the Manor of Ruardine in the fforreſt of Deane, &c. And that Thomas de Evercy, ſonne of Annora de alba mara, Iſabella de Alba mara, Richardus de Stallinge the ſonne of Katherine de Alba mara, and Matilda de Alba mara, who are of full age, And Wiłłm the ſonne of Wiłłm de Hathewy who is within age, and but 12. yeares old, are his heires.

Alba mara his lands. nowe Selmans and others.

A part

A part of this land lyinge in Stancombe is the inheritance of John Selman, sonne of John, sonne of John, as his evidences doe shewe, who alfo hath a pedegree shewinge his difcent from the said Wiłłm de Alba mara: Which Robert Stallinge in 1. E. 1. aliened to Robert Cantelupe and Margery his wife in franke maryage; which Margery furvivinge her hufband, did in 4. E. 3. with her fecond hufband Wiłłm Wor, give the fame to Walter Selyman with Lucy her daughter in fpeciall taile; fince which time it hath continued in that name of Seliman to this day, a^o 1639.

Rot. pipæ. 17. H. 3. in coñ Glouc̄ faith, Wiłłus de Alba mara; filius et heres Roberti de Alba mara, reddit compūum de decem marcis de fine pro habenda feifina de terra de Rowartin (Ruarden) quam pater eius tenuit de rege per ferientiam.

By a deed without date in the time of kinge H. 3. in Berkeley caftle, John de Alba marł granted to Wiłłm de Metefdon and to Ifable his wife, and their heires, divers lands in Stintefcombe (pticulerly mentioned in the deed) To hold by a peny rent for all fervices; Salvo regali fervicio, &c.

And by another Deed in the faid Caftle without date, the faid John granted to the faid Wiłłm de Matefdon and Ifable his wife and their heires, Totum pratum apud Stintefcombe quod iacet iuxta culturam quæ vocatur Broadruydinge, Redd: p anñ—ob. pro ōibus fervicijs, Salvo regali fervicio, &c. |

351
Snitend.

In the vtmoft fkirt or border of this village of Stintefcombe toward Nibley (where reverà the Combe flinteth by the finall declyninge of the hill, which Stinchcombe is but an hamblet of the manor of Came, and within that parifh.) is a fmall knott of 4. houfes called Snitend, wherof two of them are in Nibley And the other two in Stintefcombe in the parifh of Came: The one of which was lately held of that manor by Richard Nelme by Copy of Court roll; And the other was by John Serieant the younger in 30. E. 3. by the name of a meffuage and 14. acres of land, and one acre of meadowe, and ij^s rent in Came, (the very content at this day,) given to a Chaplein at Stone, to pray in the Chaple there for the foules of himfelfe and of the lord Berkeley and others named in his deed. And was before the land of Wiłłm Snite, ffrom whofe feifin and his anceftors that name arofe in the time of H. 3. and E. 1. By the diffolucōn of which Chantry in 1° E. 6. it came to the Crowne, And was by that kings L̄res patents in the fecond yeare of his raigne, granted (inter alia) to Sir John Thynne and Lawrence Hide, and their heires, who

the

Stinchcombe

the same yeare sold the said messuage and land to Anthony Throgmton and his heires ; who also the same yeare sold the same to Simon Eeles and his heires, from whom it discended to Thomas Eeles his sonne and heire, And from him to John Eeles his sonne and heire, who died in 37. Eliz. as an Inquisicōn found after his death in 12. Jacobi R͡e, sheweth : which also sheweth, That hee by his will in 37. Eliz. p͡d, devised the same to Judith his wife for her life, (after remaried to George Hickes,) And after her death to his three daughters and coheires, Judith, Jone and Elizabeth, and their heires : Of whom the said Elizabeth dyed very yonge, vnder two yeares old. Judith their mother, wife of George Hickes, dyed in July aⁿ 10° Jacobi R͡e ; And the said Judith and Jone sisters of the said Elizabeth, were maried to Nicholas Hickes and Robert Hick͡e, sonnes of the said George by a former wife : who aliened to my selfe and others : Soe two sisters maried two brothers, and their mother to the father of those sonnes ; Which messuage and land is holden of the kinge as of his Manor of Bulford in the County of Wilte͡s, in free and comōn socage, by fealty only for all services. Wherof also read more, fol : [288.]

Heere also is an ancient messuage with certaine lands therto belonginge, con- taininge about 40. acres, in Stinchcombe, the inheritance of John Nelme nowe dwellinge vpon the same ; sonne of Simon Nelme, who died in 6t° Jacobi, brother and heire of Edward, who died in,   Eliz : sonnes of Nicholas Nelme, who in 4. Eliz. purchased the same of John Trotman, Willm Burcher, and Willm Nelme and they of Thomas lord Wentworth, with the rest of the Manor as aforesaid : And as an office found in a° 6t° Jacobi p͡d after the death of the said Simon, sheweth, are holden of the manor of Berkeley by knight service, and sute to his hundred court of Berkeley from three weekes to three weekes ; ffor more whereof See the velam booke of Wardships and Releeses fol : 14 : Which John Nelme hath also other lands in this Township, holden of Estgreenwich in free socage, somtime peell of the Abby of Kingswood, as in the said office is expressed. |

Nelmes land.

Heere also is a Messuage and divers lands therto belonginge, containinge about   acres, nowe in the occupacōn of William Trotman th' elder, lyinge in Stancombe, and wherin the said William nowe dwelleth ; which William Trotman the younger sonne and heire apparant of the foresaid William Trotman the elder, called of Blacke burton, purchased of Anthony Hungerford, lord of Pitcourt in Nibley : which though the same had for many ages and discents in the ancestors of the said Anthony Hungerford byn occupied and gone togeather with Pitcourt, yet I hold not the tenure heerof to bee as that of Pitcourt, (wherof see before in fol : 267. 268,)
But

352
Stancombe late Hungerfords. nowe Trotmans.

But to bee holden in focage of the Manor of Stinchcombe, by

ffifteenes. In payment of the ffifteens or kingſilver, this hamblet or Townſhip of Stinchcombe goeth with

Subſedy. In the laſt ſubſedy in aº 5ᵗº Caroli, were in this village of Stinchcombe 13. ſubſedy men, who paid 5ˡⁱ 12ˢ.

Able men.
Souldiers. In aº 6ᵗº Regis Jacobi, vpon a generall Muſter, were 61. able men heere fit for the warres, betweene 20. and 60. yeares old, who appeared before Henry lord Berkeley then Leiutenant of this County: And nowe hath of Trayned Souldiers vnder Wiɫɫm Thorpe Eſqᵣ their Captaine—8. wherof—5. corſletts, and 3. muſketts.

Rates. And if the whole Diviſion of Berkeley bee in any tax rated at—100ˡⁱ, Then this hundred of Berkeley therof paies—33ˡⁱ 3ˢ, And this village of Stinchcombe—15ˢ; And foe after that rate bee the Tax more or leſſe.

The foreſaid Capitall meſſuage called Melkeſhams Court had ever of old its owner one of the 5. ſubtaxors of the ffifteenes in this hundred, And it ſelfe paid therto—

More of this Hamblet and Village of Stinchcombe is to bee read in theis Records, formerly mentioned, vz,

Rot. Clauſ. in arce Lond: 16. E. 3. in dorſo.
Inqu: 40. H. 3. pˢ mortē Wiɫɫi de Alba mara.
Inī 37. E. 3. de ſeodis Baroniæ de Berkeley in Secio.—per ſerviē militare.
Inqu: 34. E. 3. pˢ mortē Thome de Bradſton,—p ſerviē miɫ:
Inqu: 43. E. 3. pˢ mortē Agnetis vxoris Thome de Bradſton.—p ſerviē miɫ.
Rot. Clauſ. 13. R. 2. ps. 1. membr. 26. Coɱ Somſet.
Inqu: 11. H. 4. pˢ mortē Elæ vxoʳ Thome de Bradſton iuɳ.—p ſerviē miɫ.
Rot. Clauſ. 12. H. 4. membr. 33. in arce Lond.
Inqu: 2. H. 4. pˢ mortē Rici de ſco Mauro.
Triñ Recͤ. 22. H. 6. Rot. 17. in Secio ɱ Remeñ Theſaurͤ.
Inqu: 35. H. 6. pˢ mortē Edm: Ingaldeſthorpe miltis.—p ſerviē miɫ.
Inqu: 12. H. 6. pˢ mortē Walteri de la pole miɫ.

Rot.

Stone

Rot. clauś. 17. E. 4. membr 7. in arce Lond.
Inqu : 16. E. 4. p^t morte Ifabella vxoris Johis Nevill.
Rot. clauś. 15. E. 4. membr: 11 in arce Lond.
Inq : 2. H. 7. p^t morte Ifabelle Nevill. Melius inquirend. Glouc et Heref.
Originał : 2. H. 7. Rot. 8. in Scc̄io.
Originałł : 23. H. 7. Rot. 39. in Scc̄io.
Inqu : 10. H. 7. p^t morte Willi Stoner, Glouc. |
Carta irrotulat̄ in c̄oi banco. Term̄ Hillar̄. 33. H. 8.
Inter Browne et ffranfham, de terris in Stancombe.
Inqu : 5. E. 6. p^t mortem Thome Dn̄i Wentworth, in com̄ Suff.
Inqu : 30. Eliz : p^t mortem Ric̄i Tyndall — per fervic̄iu mił. — exemplified.
Inqu : 33. Eliz : p^t morte p̄dc̄i Ric̄i, met Inquirend̄ :— in Socagio.
Carta irrotulat̄ in c̄oi banco, Term̄ Michis, 3. et 4. Eliz : Rot. 14.
Inqu : 7. Jac : p^t morte Johis Hollifter.
Paf[c]h : fines, 35. H. 8. Rot. c̄m Ren̄i Thefaur̄ in Scc̄io.
Paper booke in fol. temp. H. 8. per fervic̄iu mil.
Booke of wardfhips and Releefes. fol : 2. 14.
Inq : 6. Jac̄, p^t morte Simonis Nelme. — per fervic̄iu. — a wardfhip. |

353

354 blank

Stone.

355

Stone : Anciently written Stan, Stane, and Stanes : And in the old Saxon **Stana** ; now modernly written **Stone** : That is a ftonne, or as Northern men fpeake, a Steane ; Soe called, as is by fome conceived, out of Meerftones very anciently fet vp to divide the three great hundreds or Liberties of **Berkeley**, **Thornbury**, and **Gromboldesash** ; Or rather, as others will, from it felfe, The moft ftony place in that lowe vale wherin it ftands : and from whence the lower country beneath it in the fame hundred are for the moft part furnifhed with fmall ftone for the amendment of their deepe and dirty waies.

It is an hamblet or fmall village diftinguifhed by the inhabitants themfelves into Vpper Stone and Lower Stone, and parcell of the Lord Berkeleis great Manor of Hame, within the parifh of Berkeley, and holden by him, as that Manor is, of the Crowne, by knight fervice in Capite ; To which Manor the waftes as Stones heath and others doe belonge.

Hundred of Berkeley

Chaple.

In this Village ſtands a Chaple, of much eaſe to the inhabitants, belonginge to the mother Church of Berkeley, vnder the Cure and government of the Vicar therof;

Tyth barnes

neere to which Chaple ſtandeth one of the eight tyth barnes belonginge to the pariſh of Berkeley; wherat the inhabitants chriſten their livinge and bury their dead, in ſemblance of a pariſh independant, but is not; in the laſt Age thatched with Broome, now decently covered with lead.

Old freeholders.

In the time of kinge Stephen, Gwidoe de Stone lived, a remarkable ffreeholder, heere, who in that kings daies was one of the 8. pledges or vndertakers for Roger Berkeley of Durſley, that hee ſhould keepe the peace then concluded at Briſtoll betweene the ſaid Roger and Robert the ſonne of Hardinge, concerninge the Barony and manor of Berkeley; wherof read more before in Durſley, fol: 175. And in Slimbridge, fol: 325. where the ſaid Agreement is verbatim. After Gwido, in the time of kinge H. 2. next ſucceſſor to kinge Stephen, lived Bernard de Stana, written alſo in divers deeds Bernardus de Stanes: After him, in the time of kinge H. 3. Maurice de Stane; After him, in the time of kinge H. 3. and E. 1. lived Robert de Stan; who in thoſe times were Witneſſes to many hundreds of deeds, which I have read: And had divers lands in this Townſhip, aſwell by ancient diſcent as by ſpeciall purchaſes from Henry de Waniſwell and others; whereof ſee after in Waneſwell, fol: 367. and as after followeth, fol. 356.

Stone water courſe.

The Manor of Alkington is on the ſouthweſt part divided from this of Stone by a river runninge betweene them, which in the great Rode way called Briſtoll way, and ſomwhat above, beinge turned out of his ancient channell and courſe, begot, ſomwhat more then an hundred yeares agone, the ſettinge vp of newe of a mill there; ffirſt a Blademill, After a corne griſt mill, After a paper mill, nowe at this day both, aᵒ 1639, (ſuch have beene the alterations for profit); ffor which turninge of the watercourſe to the mill The lord Berkeley firſt had a rent of-13ˢ 4ᵈ p anñ: And after Henry lord Berkeley, by a leaſe which hee made dated 22ᵒ Junij. 4. et 5. Ph: & Mař. to Thomas ffranſham, at which time his Receiver for 60. yeares had an yearly rent of 40ˢ, which vpon newe demiſes ſince made, is the rent to this day: The occupiers of which mills beinge alſo to repair that place and part of the Rode bridge, through and vnder which their newe watercourſe from the ſaid Mills falleth, and returneth into its owne chanell againe.

Bridges.

The Record in the Treſory, Pˡita coram rege apud Glouĉ, Terñi Michis. 2. R. 2. Rot. 17. hath thus; Thomas de Berkeley et Peter de Veel de Tortworth

chival

Stone

chivalñ non poffunt dedicere quin ipfi tenentur reparare pontem vocaᵗ Sindleforth inter Tortworth et Stone ratione terrarum et teñtorum fuorum in dᶜis Manerijs. |

The Records of Rot. Pateñ: 30. E. 3. pars. mem: 22., And Rot. finiū, 30. E. 3. mem. 3. And a writt and Inquificōn of Ad quod damnum in 30. E. 3. aforefaid, doe fhewe, That John Sergeant of Stone the yonger founded a Chantry in Stone called our Ladies Chantry, and endowed it with 9. meffuages, 86. acres of land, and 2ˢ rent in Hame, Hull, Alkington, and Came, for a preift there to pray in the Chaple of Stone for the good eftate of himfelfe, and of John Sergeant his father, and of Thomas lord Berkeley, and of Maurice Berkeley his fonne, And of William fonne of Willm Swonhungre, and Alienor his mother, And of Jone late wife of him the faid John Sergeant, and of Margaret late mother of him the faid Maurice. And for the kings licence thus to amortize, hee paid—108ˢ 2ᵈ. as the faid fine Roll fheweth.

356 Chantries in Stone.

And fix yeares after, the faid John Sergeant, vpon an other like writt of Ad quod damnum in 36. E. 3. And by the patent Roll of that yeare, membr. 24: gave 2. meffuages, 20. acres of land, and 1ᵈ rent, in Hame, Berkeley, Hull, and Alkington, to celebrate in like manner in the Chaple of All Saints in Stone.

And the like hee the faid John Sergeant did in 47. E. 3. then givinge more to the Chantry preift there, 5. meffuages, 16. acres of land, and 2. acres of meadowe, in Hame and Alkington, As by a like Inquificōn vpon a like writt of Ad quod damnum in 47. E. 3. And by Rot. finium. 48. E. 3. mem: 3. appeareth: Which Chantries had continuance till the Act of diffolucōn in 1. E. 6. And then fhortly after granted by the Crowne, as after I fhall mention, fol: 363. As alfo I fhall further write of the faid John Sergeant and of his difcent in the next page, And fol: 369.

Likewise the faid Robert de Stane in 13. E. 1. gave 5. m͂ks land and rent in Berkeley for maintenance of a Chaplein to celebrate divine fervice for ever in the Chaple of Stone, ad altare beatæ Mariæ celebrand. in capellà de Stone, which are of the fee of Thomas de Berkeley and holden in Socage faith a writt of Ad q̄d damnum, and the Inquificōn therby taken by Jury: wherof fee more in the patent roll, and Roll of fines of that yeare or the yeare followinge, which I did not. As alfo of the pedegree of the faid Thomas de Stone to this day in the next page; And in Wanifwell fol: 368. And in Nibley fol: 280. 281. at large.

This hamblett of Stone of trayned Souldiers furnifhed 5. corfletts and 1. mufket, vnder William Thorpe Efq, their Captaine.

Trayned Souldiers

Freehold

Freehold lands within this Township or hamblet of Stone; vz,

Old Court in Stone.

Heere in Stone is one very ancient ffreehold, lately reputed a Manor, wherof the Capitall messuage called the Old Court is motted round, over which is a drawe bridge, leadinge into the house; holden of George Lord Berkeley as of his manor of Hame (wherin it lyeth) by knights service, sute to his hundred Court of Berkeley from 3. weekes to 3. weekes, and by the yearly rent of—7^s. 10^d. And is nowe a^o. 1639. the seuall inheritance of 24. men, as more perticulerly shall after bee declared fol: 357. and after.

The owners of this capitall messuage called the Old Court were one of the five ancient subtaxors of the fifteene within this hundred of **Berkeley**, And still, by it selfe, when that manner of payment is to the Crowne, paies—3^s. 4^d.

The old owners of this land were Gwidoe, Bernard, Maurice, and Robert de Stone, formerly mentioned in the page before; And the said Robert de Stone dyed about 10. E. 1, leavinge issue Robert de Stone who dyed in 27. E. 1; And by Agnes his wife left issue Thomas de Stone who dyed in 9. E. 2, And by Alienor his wife, who survived him, left issue two daughters; Jone maried to John Sergeant, sonne of John, And Alice maried to John Swonhunger, sonne of John; Of which Alice and her husband and their issues see before in Nybley fol: 281, And in Swonhunger fol: 365. And in Wanifwell fol: 367. 368. 369.

And the said Jone and John Sergeant her husband (of whom heere only) had issue Jone maried to Walter Hurst, and was mother of Isable, mother of Katherine, mother of Jone, first maried to Sir Robert Greindore, and after to Sir John Barre, And survivinge them both, dyed her selfe in 1. H. 7. without issue, As both in Nibley I have written, fol: [281]; what time theis lands first came to bee the inheritance of the name and family of the Sergeants in their owne right: which pedegree heere againe to have mentioned I held needlesse. Otherwise, or further then that Thomas Sergeant who dyed in S^r. Eliz: by Alice his wife left issue Thomas Sergeant. Who by his severall Deeds inrolled in Chancery in 14°. et 16°. Eliz: The one dated, 24°. Septembr. 14. Eliz: inrolled 21. Apr. after, And by one fyne in Michas Terme, 14°. et 15°. Eliz: And by another deed dated   a^o. 16°. Eliz: aliened to Hugh Smyth Esquire and to his feoffees in trust. vz. Sir Willm Winter, Thomas Carewe, George Winter, and Mathewe Smyth his brother, and their heires, not only all theis which were the said Thomas de Stones, and allotted in three deeds of partition to Jone his eldest daughter maried to John Sergeant, (which deeds I have

have read,) And which came to him as before hath byn faid; But alfo that meffuage and carucate of land in Stone the old paternall inheritance of the Sergeants his Anceftors, mentioned in the forefaid Inquific̃on vpon the faid writt of Ad quod damnum found in the 47. E. 3, there found to remaine to him the faid John Sergeant and his heires, befides what hee gave then to the Chantry preifts of Stone, holden faith that record of Thomas lord Berkeley in Capite by knight fervice: which faid Hugh Smyth and his faid feoffees fhortly after fold and (as it were) retayled the farre greater part to the leffees that then held the fame, and to their heires, as after followeth in perticuler: And then dyed in   Eliz: leavinge what remained vnfold to the faid Mathewe his brother and heire male, who died in 25. Eliz: As the Office found that yeare after his death in the county of Somerfet fheweth, which therby came to Hugh Smyth his fonne and heire, then but 8. yeares old, and in ward to that Queene Eliz: for other lands; who alfo (as after followeth) fold thofe lands that came to him to Henry Parmiter an Atturny at lawe, and to one Thomas Arnold, as after fhall followe; And fo were all againe foe aliened that none remained, noe not the cheefe rents or menalties of fervices to this manor, As nowe followeth, amongft the lift of the ffreeholders, who are the nowe owners, a̅o 1639. 15º R(Caroli.

William Thorpe of Wanifwell Efq, holdeth |

Vrian Wife gent̃   358

Thomas Bowfer

Jofias Graile, fonne of John Graile Clerke,

Thomas Mors

John Mallett

and apportioned vpon the death of the faid John to pay—2ˢ for his releefe, after the fiftieth part of a knights fee; his rent beinge p an̄—5ᵈ

                                                                               Richard

Richard Evered als Everard |

359   William Kirle in right of Alice his wife, daughter and heire of John Mallett late of Bevington.

John Wade

Richard Tippetts

Thomas Atkins

John Clutterbooke

Eddis Wallis, or Woolles,

Richard Cole gent |

360   William Arnold

John Swonhunger, als Saniger, in right of Elizabeth his wife, daughter and heire

Jone ffreeman

John Bradley

Nicholas

Nicholas Morſe by deed inrolled dated 20º Maij. 1642, purchaſed of Samuell Trotman of the Inner Temple Eſq, one meſſuage &c. with a garden, hopyard, and orchard, a cloſe of paſture adioyninge cont̃ 1. acre, and one other cloſe of paſture cont̃ 1 acre, called the pound cloſe, halfe an acre of meadowe ſhootinge vpon the Hame ditch, and halfe an acre of meadowe lyinḡ in Little hame, and 2. rudges of arrable land lyinge in Lobthorne, and a cheeſe rent of—19ᵈ p añ iſſuinge out of the lands of Willm Curnocke; All which (except the rent) the ſaid Samuell by his Indenture dated 30º Sept. 11º Caroli, demiſed to Hugh Street for 99. yeares, if John, Robert, and Daniell, his ſonnes, or any of them, ſhould ſoe longe live, vnder the yearly rent of—24ˢ and 2. capons, and 6ˢ 8ᵈ for an heriott: which lands (inter alia) were heertofore purchaſed by Hugh Smyth of Long aſhton Eſq, and were by him by Indenture bearinge date 18º Sept 34º Eliz: ſold vnto Henry Parmiter of Tockington, who by his Indenture bearinge date 20º Maij. 12º Jacobi ſold the ſame to Richard Trotman of Cliffords Inne gent̃, and hee by his Indenture dat̃ 3º Octobr̃ 19º Jacobi, vnto Edward Trotman the elder gent̃, Edward, and Samuell his ſonnes; Which Edward the father and Edward the ſonne by their deed bearinge date 5º Junij. 9º Caroli, releaſed vnto Samuell, who ſold as before.

The ſaid Nicholas Morſe hath alſo by conveyance from Thomas Morſe his father |

John Oldland   361

John Maſon

John Jenkins in right of   his wife, daughter of John Evered

Thomas Mallett

In this hamblet of Stone is a meſſuage and divers lands therto belonging, 362
containinge about 45. acres, in lower als nether Stone, in the pariſh of Berkeley as Webbs land,
of his manor of Hame by knight ſervice, ſute of Court, and the yearly rents of— late Tryes.
16ˢ and of-12ᵈ farthinge, nowe the inheritance of Nicholas Webbe, ſonne of Nicholas
                                                                                Webbe

Webbe who dyed in 1º R̃ Caroli ; which Maurice lord Berkeley the fecond of that name about the end of the raigne of kinge H. 3. gave to Robert Berkeley his fecond fonne and his heires, who afterwards conveyed the fame to Thomas Berkeley his fecond fonne, who was father of John Berkeley that was in Ward for the fame ; And by his death without iffue the fame difcended to Margaret his fifter and heire maryed to Raph Trye ; betweene whom was iffue John Trye, father of John, father of Willm. father of John and William ; which John dyed without iffue, leavinge the faid Willm his brother and heire ; which William, (who died in 14. H. 8.) had iffue Edward Try who died in 18. H. 8, father of John, father of John, who died 33. Eliz:, father of Willm who died in 8º Jacobi, father of Willm Try that nowe is, who by deed 20º Julij 20º Jacobi, fold the fame to the faid Nicholas Webb, father of the faid Nicholas, lately in ward to the kinge for other lands holden of the lord Stafford, in ward alfo to the kinge, wherby the kinge had gard pur caufe de gard ; late held by Martha Webbe mother of the faid Nicholas for her life, by the will of the faid Nicholas (dated, 1º Januarij, aº 1º Caroli,) her hufband ; Shee lately in this yeare deceafed, 1639.

Of this land fee a fyne 20. Jac̃ in Michas Terme, from Try to Webb. And for this pedegree fee more largely in Beoly fol : 75. And in Inwoods in Stinchcombe fol : 345.

<small>Stones Inne. late Machins. olim Pooles. nowe Gunnes.</small>

Heere alfo in this village is a remarkeable cõmon Inne called Stones Inne, vfefull to travellers betweene the Cities of Glouc̃ and Briftoll, efpecially in the times of the two great marts or faires holden at Briftoll on the daies of Sᵗ Paul and of Sᵗ James, in January and July, with 20. acres of land therto belonginge ; nowe the inheritance of Thomas Gunne, and by him in aº   R̃ Caroli purchafed of Thomas Machin ; And was by John Machin his father in aº   R̃ Jacobi purchafed of Richard Hicks, fecond fonne of Richard Hicks, To whom the faid Richard by his will in   Eliz, R̃ne. devifed the fame in generall taile, havinge before in 2. et 3. Ph : et Mar̃, and by a fine in Michas terme after, purchafed the fame of Mathewe Goffe and Alice his wife, one of the daughters and coheires of Thomas Merfon als Matfon, who alfo not longe before in 36. H. 8. purchafed the other moity of Suzan Merfon als Matfon her fifter, And which the faid Thomas Merfon als Matfon, (then keeper of Whitcliffe parke,) purchafed in 7. H. 8. of Richard Pole of Cotes Efq, and of Leonard his fonne and heire apparant ; which Leonard died in 30. H. 8, and was father of Sir Gyles who dyed in 30. Eliz : and was father of Sir Henry, father of Henry Pole that nowe is, aº 1639. Which Richard

Richard Pole was fecond fonne of John Pole of Chefhire; | And was before the 363
land of

And is holden of George lord Berkeley as of his manor of Hame, by fute to his
hundred Court of Berkeley from 3. weekes to 3. weekes, And

What I formerly faid fol: 356. fhould bee further mentioned of Chantry land, More of Chantries.
take heere; That vpon the diffolucõn of Chantries by the ftatute in 1. E. 6. the
forementioned Chantry of Stone came to that kinge, who in the fecond yeare of his
raigne granted the fame to Sir John Thyn knight and to Lawrence Hide genṫ, and
their heires, by the name of, Totam illam Cantariam beatæ Mariæ in Ecclefiâ de
Stone, And all lands tenem̄ṫ and hereditaments therto belonginge, in the tenure of
Simon Ellis and others, (recitinge them all); Of which Simon Ellis als Eeles fee
before in Snitend in Stinchcombe, as alfo of this Chantry, fol: [351.] The lands of
which Chantry extended into Stone, Woodford, Swanly, Alkington, Hill, Berkeley
and Stinchcombe; To hold in free focage of the kinge, as of his Manor of Bulford
in the County of Wilts, by fealty only; who the fame yeare fold againe the fame
to Anthony Throckmerton and his heires, who alfo fhortly after by feverall fales
retayled the fame, as in thofe townfhips in part appeareth, fol: [44, 90, 98, 116, 356]

Somwhat more of this hamblet of Stone, efpecially for the tenure of parts
therof, may bee read in theis records not formerly mentioned, vz,

  ffinis in banco 15. R. 2. pro Edm: ffourd et Johā vxore eius.
  Rot. Clauſ 1. H. 4. in arce Londini.
  ffinis in banco 16. Eliz: inter Smith, Winter, et al, from Sergeant.
  Inqu: 20. Eliz: pṫ mortē Mauricij Mallett.
  Inqu: 25. Eliz: pṫ mortē Mathei Smyth ar̃, in cõm̄ Som̄ſet.
  Inqu: 9. Eliz: pṫ mortē Thome Sergeant.
  Inqu: 16. H. 8. pṫ mortē Willi Try.
  Inqu: 29. Eliz: pṫ mortē xp̄opheri Wefterdale.—p ferviē miḻ.
  Inqu: 30. Eliz: pṫ mortē Thome Tylladam—p ferviē miḻ.
  Inqu: 42. Eliz: pṫ mortē Rici Evered.—p ferviē miḻ.
  Inqu: 44. Eliz: pṫ mortē Thome Phelps.—p ferviē miḻ.
  Inqu: 42. Eliz: pṫ mortē Nichi Thorpe Ar̃.
  Inqu: 42. Eliz: pṫ mortē Alicie Ward.—p ferviē miḻ.
  Inqu: 12. Jacobi, pṫ mortē Thome Mors.—p ferviē miḻ.
  Inqu: 14. R̄ſ Caroli pṫ mortē Thome Mors. p ferviciū miḻ.

                     A deed

A deed in Berkeley caftle dated on the day of the nativity of our bleffed lady a° 27. E. 1., wherby Agnes the widow of Robert de Stone releafed to Thomas lord Berkeley the fervices of 29. tenants which fhee held in Dower, perticulerly named in the deed: To hold to the faid lord duringe the minority of Thomas de Stone heire of the faid Robert, And then in ward to him.

On the backe of which deed is thus anciently written: Scriptum Agnetis relicte Robti de Stone, fact Dño Tho: de Berkel de diuñs redd et serviç in Berkele, Hame, et Hineton. |

364 blank

Swonhunger.

365

Swonhunger; corruptly called Saniger; wherof before in the defcription of Hame, fol: 209.

This is a fmall hamblet parcell of that Manor of Hame, lyinge within the ffalloe therof, confiftinge of 13. dwellinge houfes; The moft eminent wherof is the inheritance of John Swonhunger als Sanyger, A yonger branch difcended from the ancient old owners of that and many other faire lands, which by the heire female at the comon lawe, came into the name of Thorpe, as next I fhall write in the defcription of Wanifwell, fol: 367, where a good part yet remaine with Willm Thorpe of Wanifwell heire therof; And a great part were aliened by George Thorpe his improvident father, who died in Virginia in 20° Jacobi.

And the faid John Swonhunger als Saniger that nowe is, a° 1639, is fonne of John who died   , fonne of Maurice who died   , fonne of Robert who died   , fonne of William who died   ; holden of the Manor of Hame by knight fervice, fute of Court, and by the yearly rents of vj^d to the faid manor of Hame: And xij^d to the manor of Hinton; which were by divers deeds in 10. 12. et 14. H. 8. purchafed by the faid   of Thomas Lewes als Davis, fonne and heire of John Lewis.

Stantons place.

Heere alfo is another ancient meffuage with 80. acres of land therto belonginge, the inheritance of George Lord Berkeley, which efcheated to his anceftor Willm Marques Berkeley in the time of kinge E. 4. And was after by him in 4. H. 7. conveyed with his Manor of Hame, as parcell therof, to H. 7. and the heires males of of his body, with Remainder to the right heires of him the said Marques Berkeley: By the death of kinge E. 6. the issue male of H. 7. failed, wherby Henry then lord Berkeley entred into that manor of Hame, and consequently into this messuage, as beinge sonne and heire of Thomas lord Berkeley, sonne of Thomas, brother and heire of Maurice, sonnes of Maurice, brother and heire of the said Marques Berkeley: And late was in the tenure of Willm Mallet sonne of Maurice, And of Maurice sonne of the said Willm: And is nowe A° 1639. in the tenure of George Edmonds for life, by the demise of George lord Berkeley, grandchilde and heire to the said lord Henry. When this messuage escheated it was the land of Richard Stanton, who dyed without heire generall or speciall, whose widowe Margaret was after remaried to   Brayne, and was endowed of this land, and died about   H. 8. And was before it escheated holden of the said Manor of Hame by sute to the hundred Court of Berkeley from 3. weekes [to 3. weekes,] and by the yearly rent of   ; And was lett by kinge H. 8. to the said Willm Swonhunger, father of Robert, | father of John; ffor most of what is heerof written see the Court Roll of Hame manor 7. H. 8. till that time. |

Wanswell.

Wanswell: Anciently in the time of kinge H. 2. written **Weneswell**; And in the time of kinge E. 1. it was written **Waynesswelle**; Is an hamblett within the manor of Hame within the parish of **Berkeley**, nowe consistinge of 14. dwellinge houses, but heertofore of greater extent and embracinge the foresaid hamblet of Swonhunger: The greater part wherof lately belonged to the family of the Thorpes, holden of the Lord Berkeley by knight service, by Castle gard, by keepinge and defendinge the fairest and most important tower in the castle of Berkeley against any assault or invasion, called Thorpes tower: And beinge by knight service cañot bee aliened from the Castle but remaines inseperable; As are the booke cases, 1° Assises. Brooke Tenures. 11. 19. E. 2. Assises. fol: 399. Cooke Coñi. fol:

The most eminent messuage of this hamblet is called Wanifwell Court, the ancient habitation of the family of the Thorpes, and nowe a° 1639. of Willm Thorpe Esq, captaine over 150. trayned souldiers dwellinge in the villages round about him: An house defended on each side with a well watered mott, fed with a fresh runninge springe arisinge not farre of nowe called Holy well, held to bee of vertue

Hundred of Berkeley

vertue and medecinable; Anciently called Woden well or Wodenſwell, from the Goddeſſe Woden the Idoll of our old Anceſtors the paynim Saxons, of whom wee have the name of Wedneſday, the third day of our weeke, as Verſtegan faith fol: ; ffrom which goddeſſe and this her well, have byn by our forefathers as tradition tells related ſo many miracles and ſtrange cures there wrought, that from the concurrence and confluence of all ages and ſexes, meetinge at this vn-holy well, The proverbe aroſe, which yet continueth; That all the maids in Wanſwell, may dance in an egſhell : Ovid the wanton poet hath,

Caſta eſt, quam nemo rogavit.
And
Non caret effectu, quod voluere duo.

This faire ſpringe havinge in its courſe, watered the meadowe grounds belowe it, compaſſeth well nigh three fourth parts of Berkeley Towne and Caſtle, and that done, falls into Berkeley haven, where its freſhnes turneth ſalt.

Capella in Waniſwell.

In 40. H. 3. A° 1256. Wiłłm then Abbot of S! Auguſtines Monaſtery by Briſtoll, granted to Phillip de Leiceſter (then huſband to Iſable de Waniſwell, the widowe of Henry de Waniſwell, who held the capitall meſſuage called Waniſwell Court in her right for her life, whom alſo ſhee ſurvived) licentiam erigendi Capellam infra Curium ſuam de Weneſwell, in qua, ſibi, ſuis hoſpitibus, et familiæ ſuæ divina ſumptibus ſuis faciet celebrare, exceptinge in the foure principall feaſts, wherin they muſt come to the mother Church of Berkeley. This Iſable was daughter and heire to |

ffreeholds within this hamblet or village of Waniſwell, and of Swonhunger, which in many places lye intermingled,

The ancienteſt Deed that I have met with, or which I ſuppoſe is extant, naminge this hamblet, is in the time of kinge H. 2. in theis words;

Maielus de Skeneſrid omnibus hominibus et amicis ſuis ſalutem. Sciatis me dediſſe et conceſſiſſe Mauricio filio Nigelli pro ſervicio ſuo et homagio ſuo, terram quam Walterus filius Alwini tenuit de me in Weniſwella, et ſerviciū eiuſdem terræ, et terram Wudewellegrof cū ōibus ptineñ ſuis, ſibi et heredibus ſuis Tenend, de me et heredibus meis, in feodo et hereditate libere et quiete et integre et honorifice, Reddendo

Reddendo inde singulis annis ad festm sei Michis vnam libram piperis vel sex denarios, ad voluntatem Mauricij vel heredum suorum, pro omni servicio, excepto regali servicio, et qñ p̄dcus Mauricius fecit mihi hummagium, dedit mihi de recognitione tres marcas et dimid. Hijs testibus, Dño Mauricio de Berkel, Roberto filio eius, et Riĉo fr̄e eius, Magistro Mauricio, Reg̃ et Thoma Capellañ, Adam seneschallo, Adam filio Nigelli, Riĉo de Cuhulla, Helia de falso marisco, Rogero de Stintescombe, Bernardo de Stanes, Waltero filio Albti, Willo de Paris, Rado de Stintescombe, Robto Gausell, Robto filio Sẽuli, Riĉo puccrũ, Willo Wenri, Waltero de Iwet, Bartholomeo de Olep', Henrico de Stanes, Petro de Haia, Rogero venatore, Riĉo filio Willi, Aluredo Janitore, et multis alijs.

Also another deed shortly after in theis words; Rogerus de Berket ōibus hōibus et amicis suis salm̃. Sciatis me ad petitionem Mahel de Skenefrid concessisse et hac mea carta confirmasse Mauricio filio Nigelli. Terram qua Walterus filius Alwini tenuit de Mahelo apud Wenefwellam, que est de feodo meo, et serviciũ ciusdem terre, et terram Wudewellegrost cũ ōibus p̃tineñ suis, Tenend de eod Mahelo et hered suis libere quiete et integre et honorifice, sicut carta p̄dĉi Maheli testatur. His testibus &c. the same 26. Which shewes that this and the former Deed were sealed at one time, And at the same meetinge, dinner or supper, accordinge to the vse of those times.

This ancient messuage called Wanesfwell Court came after a sewe yeares in the time of kinge H. 3. to bee the inheritance of Henry de Wenefwell, sonne of Henry, of whom read in the page before ; who by his deed without date, for 100. m̃ks sterlinge, sold to Robert de Stanes and his heires, Totam Curiam suam apud Wanesfwell, and all the lands therto belonginge, with the reversion of the lands there which Isable his mother held in Dower, To hold of the cheife Lord by the rents and services accustomed.

And about the same time the said Henry de Wanefwell by his like deed without date, for 112. markes sterlinge, sold All his lands and tenem̃ts in Stone and Woodford to the said Robert de Stanes and his heires, with the Reversion of the lands there which Isable his mother held in Dower : To hold of the cheefe lord by the rents and services accustomed.

By a deed without date, the said Henry de Wenefwell filius et heres magistri Phillippi de Leicester, released to Thomas lord Berkeley a place in Windmilfeild, with the Windmill there built, in fee.

By a deed without date, Robert le Breht conveyed to Phillip of Leicester and his heires divers lands in and about Wanifwell, To hold of him by 6ᵈ rent ; And releafed him the faid Phillip from fute to his Court in Hinton. |

369
By another deed without date, Ifable the widowe of Phillip de Leic! fold to Maurice lord Berkeley and his heires, The wood called Barndewood, (nowe Burnwood,) which the faid lord Maurice had of the grant of the faid Phillip, lyinge in Hinton ; And Hildebrugg fomtime wife of Thomas Mathias, granted the faid wood to the faid Lord Maurice, which fomtime belonged to her freehold, faith this Deed ; See fol : 222.

The faid Robert de Stone als Stanes dyed in 27. E. 1. And by Agnes his wife, who furvived him, leaft iffue Thomas de Stone who died in 9. E. 2. And by Alienor his wife who furvived him, leaft iffue two daughters, vz, Jone and Alice ; Jone was maried to John Sergeant, of whofe iffue and difcent I have formerly written, fol : 356.

The faid Alice was within age at her fathers death, and therby in ward to Thomas lord Berkeley for part of this land, and was maried to John Swonhunger fonne of John Swonhunger : And had iffue betweene them Thomas and Willm : Thomas died fhortly after his mother without iffue, And William was his brother and heire ; And by Ifable his firft wife had iffue Elias Swonhunger Of whom after : And by Jone his fecond wife daughter of John Larrenge had noe iffue that I have found.

Betweene theis fifters Jone and Alice and their hufbands, one partition by a Deed in french was made in 3. E. 3. wherby the lands afwell in Over ftone as in Lower ftone, and alfo the lands in Woodford, were allotted to Jone and her heires : And theis lands in Wanifwell were allotted to Alice and her heires.

And alfo one other partition was after made in 21. E. 3, betweene the faid Willm Swonhunger fonne of the faid Alice, And his cozen Jone wife of Walter Hurft, daughter and heire of Jone maried to John Sergeant, wherby either of them had part of the lands in Nibley, &c. as before fol : 280. 281.

And alfo a third partition was by another deed made in 27. E. 3. betweene the faid Willm Swonhungre brother and heire of Thomas, and John Sericant the
yonger,

yonger, of their faid anceftors lands in Hame, Came, Stincheombe, Kingefcote, and Hafelcote, (except the fifhinge in the river of Severne,) wherby to the faid William were allotted the lands in Kingfcote and Hafilcote, wherof I have formerly written, fol: 252, in Kingefcote: And to the faid John were allotted the lands in Hame, Came, and Stincheombe.

The forefaid Elias Swonhunger, fonne of Willm Swonhunger and of Ifable his wife maried Ifable daughter and coheire of John de Albiniaco als Albeny, who brought with her the third part of a third part of the Manor of Kingelholme by Glouc̄, wherof the Exchequer records in the office of the Remembrancer to the lord Treaforer, in regard the tenure is in Capite by knight fervice, are loaden, and make more then 20. times mention: By which Ifable hee had iffue Elias Swonhunger, who died in   R. 2., havinge had noe iffue by Tibota his fecond wife the widowe of Richard Reeves; And the faid Elias, fonne of Elias and Ifable, died in 13. R. 2. and by Jone his wife daughter of John Bill left iffue John Swonhungre, who was in ward for theis lands to Thomas then lord Berkeley, and died without iffue in 3. H. 4. | And Ifable and Elizabeth were his fifters and heires; Which Elizabeth was maryed to James Gaynor of Kingfholme Efq., and died after without iffue; And the faid Ifable was her fifter and heire then maried to John Thorpe of Briftoll, who furvivinge his wife dyed in 19. H. 6. And John Thorpe called the younger was their fonne and heire, who firft maried Ifable by whom hee had noe iffue and fecondly maried Margaret the daughter of   Toite, by whom hee had iffue Richard Thorpe and Margery; which Margery was in 9. E. 4. maried to Willm Davis of Durfley. Of whom and the land given in mariage with her more followeth, and of her iffue, fol: 379. And dyed in 9. E. 4. Concerning which John Thorpe iun and Margaret his wife, See a fine in the Court of Com̄on pleas, wherby in 34. H. 6. they purchafed of John Bulledon and Alice his wife, one meffuage, one Carucate of land, 15. acres of meadowe and 8. acres of wood, and 7^s 8^d rent in Wike, Lorwinch, Walingafton, Berkeley, Hame, Alkington, and Halmer, in fee.

The forefaid Richard Thorpe in 37. H. 6. maried Margery daughter and heire of Willm Loffe of Monmouth, by whom hee had a faire inheritance there and in the villages adioyninge; And dyed in 6. H. 8, whom the faid Margery furvived and dyed in 10. H. 8. leavinge iffue betweene them Thomas Thorpe, who was Receiver to Maurice Lord Berkeley, and went with him in the Army which in 5. H. 8. was fent into Spaine, and died in 17. H. 8. leavinge iffue Thomas Thorpe by Alice his firft wife, daughter of   Daftin; but by Jone his fecond wife had noe iffue.

The

The said Thomas Thorpe sonne of Thomas and Alice, was in minority at his fathers death and therby in ward to kinge H. 8. for his said land in Kingsholme: And after maried Margaret daughter of William Throgmorton of Tortworth, and dyed in 34. H. 8. leaving issue Nicholas by the said Margaret, who after her said husbands death was remaried to   Welsh, whom also shee survived, and dyed at Berkeley in 9. Eliz. Rñe, 1566. The said Nicholas Thorpe sonne of Thomas and Margaret, was also in ward to the kinge for his said land of Kingsholme, And in 7º. Eliz: maried Mary the daughter of Christopher Wikes als Mason, neece to Sir John Mason a Counsellor of State; by which mariage hee had the manor of Charelton in Middlesex; by whom hee had issue George Thorpe and others; and after her death maried Anne daughter of   Hill, and widowe of Willm Laverence als Laurance of Canonbury by Berkeley, who was till his death in 20. Eliz: Steward to Henry lord Berkeley of his lands in this hundred of Berkeley: By which Anne, who longe survived him, hee also had issue: And the said Nicholas died in 42. Eliz: And the said George the same yeare maried Margaret daughter of Sir Thomas Porter by whom hee had noe issue: And after in 8º. Rº Jacobi, maried Margaret daughter and heire of David Harris of Bristoll, by whom his estate was much inlarged with lands there; And by her had issue William Thorpe aforesaid, John and Margaret; And after shee had 7. yeares survived her husband, died at Wanifwell in 5º Rº Caroli; And the said George Thorpe before his goeinge into Virginia in 18º. Rº Jacobi, where hee dyed | the second yeare after, sold away, (besides his other lands in other Counties formerly mentioned,) theis parcells followinge in the hundred of Berkeley, nowe this yeare, 1639. the severall inheritances of 33. men, as followeth, vz,

William Hopton in right of Agnes his wife, daughter and heire of Thomas Buddinge

Thomas Smyth of Wanifwell sonne and heire of Mathew Smith, (dead this 7th of October, 1639, as I was in holdinge the law day at Berkeley for this hundred. And in reveiwe of this hamblett of Wanifwell,)

John Turner,

John

John Richards,

John Clutterbooke

Giles Hiett |

George Lewes 372

William Jones gent

Thomas Mors

George Clutterbooke

John Winfton

Robert Baily, fonne of Thomas Bayly of Hame |

William Tought 373

Beniamin Pinckett

Jane Howell

Thomas Tyndall, nowe (for other lands) in ward to the kinge, holdeth 3. acres of land in Achinton, in the Tithinge of Alkington.

John

John Smith, of Berkeley heath

James Hart, |

374   George Carpenter

James Clutterbooke,

John Griffith,

Richard Laverence.

John Havard,

Thomas Smyth, cozen and heire of John Smyth, |

375   Thomas Kellinge

James Taught

Richard Dangerfeild

And the said William Thorpe himselfe, |

Wanswell

And for more of this hamblett of Wanefwell and of the tenure of the forefaid lands, And for proofe of the pedegree before laid downe, take theis records, vz.

 Inqu: 16. R. 2. pars 1, p̃ mortẽ Johis Gifford.
 Liber Relevioȝ in Term̃i Hillar̃. 4. H. 4. c̃m Reñi Thefaur̃ in Sc̃c̃io.
 Michas Rec̃. ibm. 17. H. 6.
 Rot. finium. 22. R. 2. membr: 14.—per fervic̃ militare.
 Inqu: 22. R. 2. p̃ mortẽ Johis Swonhunger.—per fervic̃ mil.
 Rot. Clauſ. 22. R. 2. pars. 2. membr. 11.—per fervic̃ mil.
 Inqu: 6. E. 4. p̃ mortem Agnetis Baffett.
 Inqu: 6. H. 8. p̃ mortem Ric̃i Thorpe.—p fervic̃ mil.
 Inqu: 35. H, 8. p̃ mortem Thomæ Thorpe.—per fervic̃ mil.
 Inqu: 9. E. 4. p̃ mortem Johis Thorpe.
 Michas Rec̃. 3. H. 8. Rot. 3. in ſc̃io c̃m Reñi Thefaur̃.
 ffines de Term̃i Trin̂. 7. H. 8. Rot. 1. in Sc̃c̃io ibm.
 ffines de Term̃i Hill: 12. H. 8. Rot. 3. ibm.
 Originall: 6. H. 8. Rot. 7. ibm.
 Michas Rec̃ 9. Eliz: Rot. 168˚ ibm.
 Inqu: 42. Eliz: p̃ mortem Nich̃i Thorpe.—p fervic̃ mil.
 Inqu: 21. Jacobi, p̃ mortem Georgij Thorpe.—p fervic̃ mil.
 A fuite in the Court of wards in Terme, Caroli, George lord Berkeley plt̃, Will̃m Edwards def ̃—very good for all the purchafers names and lands purchafed.—In Berkeley caftle.
 Diuñ Rotuli Curiæ mañij de Hame, 42. Eliz:
 Compi Mañij de Hame, 2˚ Jacobi.

The tenure alfo of part of this land may feeme to bee created by a Deed indented without date, made by Thomas lord Berkeley the fecond of that name, to the forementioned Thomas de Stone fonne of Robert, Of two yard land in Wanifwell, And of a feild called Windmilfeild, and of a pafture ground called Old fifh were, And of 2. acres of land at Stone in Hame, And of 4. acres of land at Woodford in Alkington, To hold to him the faid Thomas de Stone and the heires of his body, vnder the yearly rent of—4ˡⁱ for all fervices, falvo regali fervicio &c, et falva fec̃ta magnæ Curia fuæ de Berkeley de tribus feptimañ in tres feptimañ. Which rent and fervices are to this day paid and done, 1639.|

Heere alfo is an other meffuage (one of the former 14. in Wanifwell), called Smythes place, the inheritance of Thomas Smyth, fonne and heire of Mathew aforenamed

Smythes place

aforenamed, sonne of Thomas who died 1° Eliz: and of his wife daughter of   Eliz:, sonne of William who died in , heire in taile to John Neel of Swonhunger, to whom and to the heires of his body John Sergeant of Stone granted the same by Deed, in theis words;

Omnibus xp̄i fidelibus ad quos presens scriptm̄ indentatum pveñit, Johes Sergeant de Stone salt̄m in Dño; Noveritis me dediffe conceffife et hoc p̄nti scripto meo confirmaffe Johanni Neel de Swonhungre, Omnia terras et teñta quæ quondam Wiłłus de Swonhunger de me tenuit ad terminum vite sue, in Hame: Habend et Tenend ōia p̄dc̄a terras et teñta, cum pratis, pascuis, pasturis, boscis, hāis, foffatis, et ōibus alijs vbiq, suis ptineñ p̄sato Johi Neel et hered de corpore suo legittime procreatis, de me et hered meis, libere, quiete, bene, et in pace, iure hereditario, &c. Reddendo inde añuatim mihi et hered meis vnū denariū ad sest̄m s̄c̄i Michis, et heriet cùm acciderit st̄m consuetud patriæ, Et reddendo inde et faciendo pro me et hered meis Dño de Berkeley ōia alia servicia inde debita et de iure consueta. Et si contingat p̄dc̄m Johem Neel sine herede de corpore suo littime procreaf obire, quod absit, tunc ōia p̄dc̄a terræ et teñta c̄m ōibus suis ptineñ mihi et hered meis integrè revertantur. Et ego verò p̄dc̄us Johes Sergeant et heredes mei ōia p̄dc̄a terras et teñta, c̄m ōibus eoȝ ptineñ, p̄dc̄o Johi Neel et hered de corpore suo legittimè procreatis in forma p̄dc̄a, contra omnes homines warrantizabimus et defendemus. In cuius rei testimonium p̄sentibus sigillum meum appofui. H[i]is Testibus, Johe Belin, Henric̄ de Egeton, Waltero Machen, Johe le hurne, Ric̄o Gilman, et alijs. Daf apud Berkeley die Jovis proẋ post sest̄m s̄c̄i Ambrosij, Anno regni Regis Edwardi tercij post conqueft̄m—xxxvi⁰

This 40: I have knowne the said Mathewe Smyth (with whom the deed remaineth), to pay more then 40. yeares, And to doe sute to the hundred Court of Berkeley from 3. weekes to 3. weekes; who hath affirmed to mee, that the estate taile created by the said Deed, as yet remaineth, not docked or discontinued. wherof I somwhat doubt: And for the penny referved I shall after write, and also for the heriot.

There is also another Deed of this land made 6. yeares before the former, in theis words, vz,

Omnibus ad quos presens scriptum pvenerit, Wiłłus Swonhunger frater et heres Thome Swonhunger de Wanesvvell, salt̄m in Dño.—Noveritis me inspexiffe quoddam

quoddam scriptm per Johem Swonhunger patrem meum factum Johi filio Isoldæ
Neel, Isabellæ et Johi filio eoȝdem, in hec verba. Omnibus xp̄i fidelibus ad
quos presens scriptm pvenerit, Johes filius et heres Johis Swonhunger salt̃m.
Noveritis me tradidisse concessisse et hoc p̄senti scripto meo confirmasse Johi filio
Isoldæ Neel, Isabelle vxori suæ, et Johi filio eoȝ de p̄dc̄a Isabella lẽtt̃ime procreat̃,
Totum illud tenementum quod Isolda Neel aliquando tenuit in Swonhunger, Habend
et tenend totū p̄dc̃m teñtum, vz. messuagiũ, Curtilagiũ, gardiñ. terras, prata pascua
et pastur̃, c̃m õibus vbiq̨ ptineñ suis dicto tenemento adiacentibus de me et hered̃
meis, p̄dc̃is Johi, Isabelle vxori sue, et Johi filio eoȝ de p̄dc̃a Isabellã legittime
procreat̃ quamdiu vixerint et vni eoȝ diutius viveñ, libere, quiete, integre, bene et
in pace, Reddend̃ annuatim mihi et hered̃ meis decem solidos argenti ad quatuor
anni terminos principales. Quod quidem scriptm et õia in eo contenta, vz, Totum
teñtum p̄dc̃m cũ õibus suis ptineñ p̄dc̄o Johi filio Johis, filio Isoldæ de p̄dc̃a Isabella
legittime pereat, | Agneti vxori eius et hered̃ de corpore p̄dc̃i Johis filij Johis filij
Isoldæ legittime procreat̃, ratifico et confirmo per presentes imperpetuum. Tenend
de me et hered̃ meis vel meis assignatis per servicia in p̄dc̃o scripto nominata ; Et si
p̄dc̃us Johes filius Johis filij Isoldæ sine herede de corpore suo legittime procreat̃,
obierit, tunc totm̃ p̄dc̃m teñtum c̃m õibus suis ptineñ mihi et heredibus meis integre
revertatur : Et ego p̄dc̃us Johes Swonhunger et heredes mei totm̃ p̄dc̃m teñtum c̃m
õibus suis ptineñ dc̃o Johi filio Johis filij Isoldæ, Agneti vxori eius, et hered̃ de
corpore p̄dc̃i Johis filij Johis filij Isoldæ legittime procreat̃, contra ões gentes
warrantizabimus et defendemus imperpetuum. In cuius rei testimonium huic
scripto confirmationis indentato sigillum predicti Johis filij Johis, filij Isoldæ, et
sigillum meum alternatim sunt appensa. Hijs testibus, Johe Sergeant, Johe Caple,
Johe Draicote, Henrico de Egeton, Thome Pain, Johe Bill, et alijs. Dat̃ apud
Berkeleie die Dominica proxime post sest̃m pasche, Anno regni regis Edwardi
tercij post conquestum, Tricesimo.

378

This is the Deed which is in force at this day, as Mathew Smyth hath said
to mee. And this, in the foresaid partition of 27. E. 3. vnder the word Hame,
(within which manor it is,) was allotted to Sergeant. [See ante, fo. 281.]

Of this land John Peers of Combe hath, in   Caroli, purchased two acres
of meadowe in Matford, of Thomas Smyth sonne and heire of the said Mathewe.

This Mathewe Smyth (nowe vpon his late death discended to Thomas his Hills place
sonne and heire,) hath also one other ancient messuage in the hamblet of Halmer, in Halmer.
within

within the manor of Hame, with divers lands belonginge therto, called Hills place, nowe decayed and become pasture ground, which hath continued and runne alonge the former lyne as aforesaid, but originally distinct from the foresaid messuage called Smythes place.

Inqu: 21º mēij. 15. Rē Caroli p̃ mortem Mathei Smyth, (qui obijt 7º Octobr̃. aº p̃d,) findeth this messuage and all the lands therto belonginge very pticulerly in Wanifwell, to bee holden of the lord Berkeley as of his Mañor of Hame, by sute to his hundred Court of Berkeley from 3. weekes to 3. weekes, and by the yearly rent of 40.ˢ And by knight service : And Thomas to bee his sonne and heire. The jury were all of his next neighbours, And for most part such as had lands of the same, and of the same tenure ; And is the first leadinge office of this land. |

379
Wikeselme.
late Buddings.
nowe Morse.

In the vtter skirts of Wanifwell towards Berkeley towne is an ancient messuage with 55 acres of land belonginge therto, late the inheritance of Thomas Buddinge high Bayly to Henry late lord Berkeley of his hundred of Berkeley, who died in 18º Rē Jacobi, sonne of John Buddinge who died 10º Eliz : ffrom which Thomas Buddinge the said messuage and lands discended to Agnes his only daughter and heire, first maried to John Mors of Came who dyed in 8. Rē Jacobi, as the Inquisicōn or office that yeare found after his death sheweth ; By whom the said Agnes hath issue Thomas Mors yet livinge, vpon whom the fee is setled : And the said Agnes was shortly after remarried to Willm Hopton, by whom shee hath issue Willm Hopton and others yet livinge, 1639, abidinge vpon this messuage : which is holden (as the rest of Wanifwell is) of the lord Berkeley, by knight service and sute to his hundred Court of Berkeley from three weekes [to three weeks,] And by the yearly rent of—11.ˢ paid to the said Lords manor of Hame wherin it lyeth ; And was severed from the capitall messuage called Wanifwell Court or manor of Wanifwell aforementioned, by a Deed made by Margaret Thorpe the widowe of John Thorpe and by Richard Thorpe their sonne, bearinge date 1º Septembr̃. aº 9º E. 4, to Willm Davis of Dursley and Margery his wife daughter of the said John Thorpe and sister of the said Richard, whervpon was a rent of—11.ˢ reserved to bee paid to the said Manor of Hame, paid at this day, as is aforesaid.

And (as if the meaninge of some of those parties had byn mistaken), a newe deed was made the 21ᵗʰ day of the said September, aº 9. E. 4. p̃d, by the said Margaret the widowe of the said John Thorpe and by Richard Thorpe their eldest sonne,

Wanswell

fonne, to the faid William Davis of Durfley and Margery his wife daughter of the faid John Thorpe, and to the heires of their bodies, Rendringe to the faid Richard Thorpe and his heires one pound of Comin, and heriot after every deceafe for ever. Which William Davis and Margery had iffue John Davis who died , and left iffue John Davis th'elder of Durfley aforefaid, who dyed in 27. H. 8. as the office or Inqu: found that yeare after his death doth fhewe: And howe hee left the fame to Nicholas Davis his grandchilde, fonne of John, fonne of him the faid John Davis th'elder, faid therin to bee holden of the Manor of **Berkeley** by 11ᵈ yearly rent for all fervices, And that the faid Nicholas was then but 15. yeares old; After the death of which Nicholas it came to Anfelme Davis, who by Deed in 1° Eliz: and by a fine in Hillary Terme 2° Eliz: fold the fame to John Buddinge aforefaid; By whofe death in 10. Eliz: pᵈ, the fame difcended to the forefaid Thomas his fonne, father of the faid Agnes, firft maryed to Mors and after to Hopton as above is written.

And this meffuage and land was in 32. H. 6. purchafed by the faid John Thorpe of Nicholas Stanfhawe and Margery his wife, and are mentioned to lye in Berkeley, Wike, Hinton, Lawrenge, Hame, Walingafton, Alkington, and Halmer, (all places neere adioyninge,) And which the faid Nicholas Stanfhawe and Margery recovered againft Wiłłm Browne and Agnes his wife in 7. H. 5. by the name of one meffuage 40. acres of land and 9. acres of meadowe in Berkeley: ffor which fee the Records in Michas terme 7. H. 5. Rot. 6. in banco. And Hillary Terme after. Rot. 43. in banco pīſo. |

And (for the antiquity of the name of Buddinge in this hundred of **Berkeley**), I will in this place note out of Deeds in Berkeley Caftle, That the aforementioned John Buddinge father of the faid Thomas was heire male lyneally defcended from Wiłłm Buddinge, to whom Adam the fonne of Nigell of Swonhunger in the time of kinge R. 1. gave in frankmariage with Alice his fifter, the 4ᵗʰ part of one yard land in Bevington; Which Wiłłm Buddinge and Alice had iffue John Buddinge, from whom was John Buddinge, from whom was an other John Buddinge, from whom was William Buddinge who lived in the time of kinge E. 3. from whom was John Buddinge in the time of R. 2. from whom was Wiłłm Budding livinge in 1. E. 4. father of John Buddinge; To whofe daughter and heire called Margaret maryed to Thomas Dagge of Harryftoke neere Briftoll, this land difcended by force of the forefaid frankmariage, and not to the brother of the faid John: Which Thomas Dagge and Margaret had iffue William Dagge, father of Wiłłm, father of Samuell.

380 Buddings name & difcent.

Samuell, who in 30º Eliz: (the yeare after the death of his father,) was hanged at Ilchester in the county of Somset, for felony by him comitted in the life of his father, wherby this 4ᵗʰ part of the said yard land escheated to Henry then lord Berkeley, Of whose Manor of Hame the same was holden; And is nowe, aº 1639, in the tenure of James Atwood for his life at—10ˢ rent: And hath for many yeares past byn called Gennes house, or Dags land: Howbeit the posterity of the younger brother of the last mentioned John Buddinge is blessed with a larger portion of livelihood, and more successefull, as before appeares.

Of this name and kindred lived Wiŧɫm Buddinge in 8. H. 7, and Thomas Buddinge of Wike, And John Buddinge of Bradston in 10. H. 8, And John Buddinge, and John his sonne in 1º Mariæ, in this hundred, as divers Court Rolls doe shewe.

Butlers lands somtimes Oldlands.

Ɯeere alſo in Wanifwell are divers lands and Tenements called Butlers, containinge 80. acres of land meadowe and pasture, and 2. groves of wood of 5. acres, which Nicholas Thorpe father of George Thorpe by deed dated 18º Octobr̃ 14º Eliz: R̃ñe, purchased of Anne daughter and heire of Thomas Butler, And wherof shortly after a fyne was levied by her the said Anne and ffrancis Butler her halfe brother, to the said Nicholas Thorpe, in Easter Terme after aº 15º Eliz: p̃d. Which said Anne had two other brothers (of the wholl bloud,) Henry, who died 1º Eliz: and Wiŧɫm who dyed 11º Eliz: both of them without issue: And were the children of Thomas Butler who died in 4ᵗᵉ Marĩ R̃ñe; And which the said Thomas in 14. H. 8. p̃chased of John Oldland, sonne of Thomas Oldland, sonne of John Oldland who dyed seized of theis lands in 1ᵐᵒ R. 3. And were before the lands of John Sergeant of Stone, who by his deed in 37. E. 3. granted the same to Walter Oldland, and to the heires | males of his body, reservinge the yearly rent of 20ˢ and an heriot after every deceafe, And doinge the services due to his cheife Lord therof, by the name of Totum capitale messuagium meum apud Wanswell, cum crosto, bofcis, terris, &c. quæ mihi accidebant iure hereditario post mortem patris mei; And are not the lands called Oldlands place formerly mentioned in Halmer fol: 223.

Ɲote further, that the said Wiŧɫm Butler brother of the said Anne was an Ideott from his birth, And soe found by two Inquisitions in 9. et 15. Eliz: seized of 85. acres of land (inter alia) holden of the lord Berkeley in soccage by the yearly rent of—17ˢ 10ᵈ ob: for all services; And was brother and heire of Henry, who died ten yeares before the said William. Which Inquisition in 9ᵐᵒ Eliz: mentioneth
all

Wanswell

all theis lands in pticuler, and findeth some of them to bee holden of the said Nicholas Thorpe, whose purchase therof abovementioned destroyed his mesnalty, and foe came to bee holden as Wanfwell Court it selfe: And the Inqu: 16ᵗ Eliz: p' morte Willm Butler is more plaine and perticular in all the premisses, wherto I referre you.

In Wanfwell also is another ancient messuage with divers lands therto belonginge, the inheritance of John Ricards of the Bay, sonne of John Ricards who died   , sonne of Willm Ricards who died   , brother and heire of John Ricards who died 30. Eliz:, sonnes of John Ricards who died in 6ᵗ Eliz:, sonne of John Ricards who died in 1ᵒ Eliz:, sonne of John, who died   , sonne of Willm who died   , sonne of that John Ricards who by his deed in 2. H. 7. (the yeare hee dyed) entayled this messuage and land vpon the said William his sonne: In which sirname of Ricards als Richards, (distinguished from another family of the same name by a Bay tree at his doore, That other from a vine, called Richards of the vine.) theis lands have continued since the time of kinge E. 2. at the least: And are holden of the lord Berkeley as of his manor of Hame, by sute to his hundred Court of Berkeley from 3. weekes to 3. weeke, The yearly rent of —4ᵈ But whether in socage or by knight service I have not observed, of old: But by a faire Court Roll in 30. Eliz: written and engrossed with the proper hand of Humphrey Alsop then high Steward, they are holden by knight service: And foe also is the Court roll of Hame in paper 29. Eliz: |

Richards lands of the Bay.

Deere also is a messuage and 53. acres of land in Wanfwell, holden of George lord Berkeley as of his Castle of Berkeley hernes in socage by fealty only, as is found by an Inquisicōn after the death of Sir James Stumpe in 5ᵗ Eliz: Rñe, pars. 1. And that Elizabeth the wife of Sir Henry Knevet was his daughter and heire, then 20. yeares old. ffor more Records heerof see fol: 258 in Lorrenge.

382 Stumpes land nowe

And theis lands are nowe the inheritance of |

383 } blank
384 }

Warth: See in Slimbridge. fol: 329.
Weston: See Kingfwefton. fol: 255.
Westridge wood: See in Wotton. fol: 403.
Whiteliffe parke: See in Hame. fol: 210.
Wickstowe: See Hame. fol: 214.

Worthy

3 D VOL. III

Worthy parke: See in Hame fol: 210. And in Alkington, fol: 30.
Wortley, an hamblet of the Manor of Wotton. See fol: 419.
Wolpen. See Owlepen. fol: 309.
Witney meadowe, als **Whitney mead**: Slimbr̄: fol: 325.
Wike iuxta Arlingham. See Arlingham fol: 56.
Wike Court, See Bainham, fol: 71. See Pedington, fol: 313. And in the backe of this leafe.
Wike als Goldeswike. See Alkington, fol: 30. and after.
Wike als Dangervils wike: See Alkington, fol: 30, and after. |

386   **Wike Court**: Of the name of Wike are divers ancient meſſuages and hamblets within this hundred, As Wike iuxta Arlingham, often written Arlingham Wike, wherof before fol: 56. And Wike als Goldefwike, wherof before fol: 30. &c. And Wike als Dangervils Wike, wherof before fol: 30. &c. And alſo the little village or hamblet in Alkington tithinge, neere vnto Nibley, wherof before fol: 33. &c. And Wikefelme in Wanifwell neere Berkeley in Hamsfallowe. Of one ancient capitall meſſuage or manor houſe wherin called Wike Court, I write, the inheritance of John Turner, whoſe father John Turner, who died in   Rē Caroli, did in Jacobi purchaſe the ſame of ffrancis Dingley, ſonne of Henry Dingley, ſonne of John Dingley; To which John and the heires males of his body kinge H. 8. 12° ffebr̄: aᵒ. 9°. r̄ni ſui, by his Lr̄es patents of that date, gave the ſame, togeather with the ffarmes capitall meſſuages or little manors of Bainham and Pedington, which ſee before fol: [71, 313]

And vpon the ſales therof there mentioned made by the ſaid ffrancis Dingley, ſoe ſcattered all his lands anciently to this meſſuage belonginge, lyinge on that ſide the pariſh of **Berkeley**, that not above 12. acres of ground is now remaininge to this ancient meſſuage called Wike Court, which is holden of the kinge in capite by knights ſervice.

Of this ſee before fol: 71. et fol: 313. |

387   **Woodford**.

Woodford: It is one of the hamblets wherof the manor of Alkington conſiſteth: wherof ſee before fol: 30.

The

Woodmancote

The Saxons our anceſtors endeavoured to faſhion their names of places after a certaine naturall force and reaſon taken from the ſcituacion of the place it ſelfe, moſt comonly, vt fons, vt nemus, (as heere), vt campus placuit, as Tacitus ſaith of the old Germanes, whoſe ofspringe wee are. This terminaćon endinge in (**forb**), manifeſtly declaringe the paſſage which heere is over the river, by the ſide of the wood heere called Michaelwood. |

Woodmancote.

Woodmancote: Anciently written **Wodemancote**, is an ancient manor within the pariſh of Durſley holden of George lord Berkeley as of his manor of Berkeley, by halfe a knights fee and ſute to his hundred Court of **Berkeley** from 3. weekes to 3. weeks; And before the ſhatteringe therof by ſeverall ſales as followeth, extended into Woodmancote, Durſeley, Came, Nybley, Wotton, Stancombe, Goldeſwike, Dangervilſwike, and Slimbridge, as followeth amongſt the purchaſors therof,

The ſcituation of the Capitall meſſuage and manor houſe of this village or Townſhip of Woodmancote, aſſureth vs from whence the name is derived: As that it was the Cote or dwellinge houſe of the Wood-man or Woodward wholly almoſt incloſed with the woods of that manor, and of the manor of Durſeley lyinge to-geather: As alſo did ſpacious woods of other manors to them alſo adioyninge.

For the old ancient owners of this Woodmancote, from the time of Willm the Conqueror or before vntill the time of kinge H. 3. I referre you to what I have formerly written of Draiſies land, als Donyngs, in Nibley, fol: 286. And in that kings raigne it was the land of Otho als Otto, the ſonne of William; and of Willm the ſonne of Otto; I ſuppoſe that two of that name ſucceeded one the other; And after of Thomas the ſonne of Otto, who dyinge in 2. E. 1. left it to Otto his ſonne, then but nyne yeares old, as an Inquiſićon found after his death in that yeare ſheweth: ffrom whom it came to Robert de Swineburne, who dyinge in 19. E. 2. left the ſame to his ſonne Thomas de Swyneburne; And after it came to Margery Swyneburne, vpon whoſe death in 16. E. 3. controverſy aroſe about this Manor, And Warren fitz Warren (who dwelt where I nowe doe,) crept into the poſſeſſion therof, who after, with Thomas his brother and Katherine their ſiſter, in 25. E. 3. aforeſaid,

aforesaid, released all their interest to another Robert de Swyneborne and his heires; ffrom whom by his Deed inrolled in the Court of Comon pleas the said 25. E. 3. Rot. 2. it came to William de Cheltenham and William de Westhall, and their heires, who beinge two servants in the house of Thomas lord Berkeley the third of that name, accordinge to the Trust in them reposed, conveyed the same to the Lady Katherine then the second wife of him the said Lord Berkeley, and to Maurice their sonne (then very younge,) and to the heires males of his body, with divers other remainders over, As by the Deed in Berkeley castle appeares: By which purchase and entayle this manor came vnto and setled in Sir John Berkeley, brother and heire male of the said Maurice, for that the said Maurice in his minority dyed without issue; Which Sir John Berkeley, after the death of the said lady Katherine who dyed in 9. R. 2, held this Manor and dyed seized therof to him and the heires males of his body in a° 6. H. 6. leavinge issue Maurice Berkeley, father of Maurice and | Edward; Which Maurice had issue William; Which Wiłłm dyed without issue male, And the said Edward was his vncle and heire male by force of the foresaid entayle: which Edward had issue Thomas and William: The said Thomas had issue John, who dyed without issue male of his body, And the said William was his vncle and heire male by force of the said Entayle: Which Wiłłm dyed in 5. E. 6. leavinge issue John Berkeley, who in Easter terme a° 9°° Eliz. sold this Manor of Woodmancote to Richard Lambert a marchant of London; By whose death in 30. Eliz: it discended to Winifride his daughter and heire, whose mother was remaried to Sir Henry Winston knight; And the said Winifride was for this Manor in ward to Henry lord Berkeley, who dyinge in her minority without issue, the same discended to her vncle Edmond Lambert (often written Edward,) brother of the said Richard the purchaser; Which Edmond, after in his life time in the time of kinge James, And his feoffees in trust after his death, (who dyed in 7° Jacobi,) for the raisinge of portions of his daughters, foe scattered almost all his lands of this Manor by their severall sales in temp: Jacobi p̄īt, to perticuler men, That it is nowe, a° 1639. 15° R̄ Caroli, the inheritance of theis 38. severall ffreeholders; vz,

Of my selfe and of you my sonne, who hold

John Trotman of Came who holds the house called Nasse court wherein hee dwelleth, of whom and it see before in Came, fol: 131.

Bromwich

Woodmancote

Bromwich gent who laft of all others purchafed of the faid feoffees what was left vnfold, As the Leet, Waft grounds, and |

Edmond Parrott and Robert his brother, are nowe in fute one with the other, **391** for 4. meffuages a cotage and about 15. acres of land meadow and pafture and one acre of wood, which they clayme from Robert their father, who by deed dated 1mo Marcij. a° 7mo Jacobi, purchafed the fame of Edward Lambert, and of Richard Swaine and John Lambe Efq^r.; which were parcell of this Manor of Woodmancote; As alfo were a meffuage and 4. other acres of wood which the faid Robert the father demifed to this Edmond for 1000. yeares.

The ffeoffees of the Maior and Cominalty of the Citie of Briftoll.

Robert Purnell of Nibley

Thomas Pitt

Chriftopher Jobbins fonne of Ambrofe Jobbins holdeth |

John Hardinge brother and heire of William, fonnes of John, fonne and heire **392** of Willm Hardinge the elder, holdeth

which the faid Willm the elder purchafed.

Thomas Purnell of Milend in Nibley.

Samuell

Samuell Bridger

William Workman

Edmond Estcourt Esq. |

Alexander Roach

Henry Ady the elder

Jesper Estcourt of Rodborrowe gent, sonne of Richard,

George Chilton

Thomas Watkins |

Nicholas Smyth

Richard

Woodmancote

Richard Partridge of Cowley, holdeth one acre lyinge in which hee purchafed of Nicholas Smyth

James Adeane

Thomas Hore

John Tilladam

John Williams |

Richard Webbe

Nicholas Trotman, fonne of Edward Trotman of the Stepps in Came, holdeth

Thomas Merfer, fonne of Thomas,

John Trotman, fonne of William Trotman, called of Trollies houfe

John

John Purnell of Wike, sonne and heire of Thomas Purnell of Nibley, who died in 20. Jacobi (as his office found the same yeare sheweth,) seized of a cotage and 2. acres of arrable land, 4. acres of pasture, and one acre and an halfe of wood, in Northnibley, late parcell of the Manor of Woodmancote, and given to Christopher his sonne in fee, holden of the Manor of Berkeley by knight service; And also of 3. other messuages, 3. acres and halfe of arrable, and 41. acres of pasture in Northnibley and Berkeley, parcell of the said Manor of Woodmancote, and holden as aforesaid, which discended to the said John in fee, who was in ward for the same.]

396 Christopher Purnell of Nibley

William Curnocke of Burrowes Court in Nibley

Robert Perrott, sonne of Robert; See before vnder the name of Edmond Perrott [Parrott, fo. 391]

John Welsteed

Henry Ady the younger |

397 John Plomer

Thomas Parsloe of Eweley

Richard

Woodmancote

Richard Merricke

Nicholas Plomer, fonne of John.

Edward Lambert, fonne and heire of the faid Edmond |

ffor the yeares of the feverall deathes of all thofe remarkeable gent of the family of the Berkeleys, called of Beverston, from the firft of their poffeffion of this Manor in 25. E. 3. vntill their alienacōn therof in 9º Eliz: See before in Beverfton, fol: 97. 98.

Duringe whiche terme of 216. yeares, the eftate taile to the heires males continued, not difcontinued or docked, vntill the forefaid fale to Richard Lambert in 9º Eliz: ffrom the firft wife of which Thomas lord Berkeley is the faid George nowe lord Berkeley difcended, And theis of the fecond wife as aforefaid, And as in Beverfton appeares, fol : jd.

But fith this Manor is not named in the booke of Domefday, either as a member of the Manor and Barony of Berkeley or as parcell of the ancient poffeffions of the Berkeleys of Durfley, wherin all their lands in this county are fet downe, as in the faid booke appeareth : nor in the Certificate of Roger Berkeley made to kinge H. 2. of the lands that hee and his Anceftors held, which fee in fol : 175. et 177. I cañot refolve otherwife but that it was a freehold in the hand of one ancient Saxon or other, holden of the Lady Abbeffe and Nunnes of Berkeley, vnles I fhould fay it is in Domefday booke comprehended vnder the Manor of Came ; wherof fome Inquificōns finde it to bee holden, And an hamblet therof ; wherto I doe encline.

Though the inhabitants in this Manor of Woodmancote claime to have a Leete or Lawe day amongft themfelves, yet the Tithingman therof with fome of this manor or Tithinge of Woodmancote appeare twice by the yeare at the Leete or

Leete

Law

Law day holden at Berkeley for the hundred of **Berkeley**, and present, as to that Court appertaineth. |

399
ffifteene.

The payment of the ffifteene or Kingsilver goeth with Ewley in one some togeather. The onus or charge wherof in the Excheq^r. is—3^{li} 14^s 7^d. The deduction is—10^s 8^d. The Remanet paid into the Exchequer for both is 3^{li} 3^s 11^d.

Subsedy.

In the last Subsedy in 5to Caroli were 10. subsedy men in this township of Woodmancote, who paid—3^{li} 16^s.

Able men.

Of able men for the warres betweene 20. and 60. yeares old, were in a^o. 6to Jacobi, 57. who appeared before Henry lord Berkeley lord Leiutenant.

Souldiers.

And now of trayned Souldiers vnder their Captaine Thomas Veel Esquire, are , wherof corsletts and musketts.

Rates.

And if the whole divition of Berkeley, accompted a 4th pte of this County, bee in any tax rated to pay—100^{li}. This hundred of **Berkeley** paies therof—33^{li} 3^s And this of Woodmancote—10^s And after that rate, bee the tax more or lesse.

In the time of kinge H. 6. arose a question betweene the inhabitants of Woodmancote and such of the inhabitants of Nibley as are called Warrens Tenants, about payment of the ffifteene or Kingsilver, whether

Freeholds within the tithinge or township of Woodmancote, vz,

Cliffords lands.

Heere are divers lands and tenements called Cliffords lands somtimes the lands of ffonte, in some records and evidences called a Manor, holden of this Manor of Woodmancote, now the inheritance of certaine sfeoffees to the vse of the Citie of Bristoll, who by their Atturney doe sute to the hundred Court of Berkeley from three weekes to 3. weekes, and pay the yearly rent of 4^d to the lord Berkeleis manor of Came. Touchinge which lands, see an Inqu^n: after the death of Alexander Bradway in 19. H. 7. And another after the death of James Clifford in 37. H. 8. And another after the death of Henry Clifford in 1°. Eliz : who left issue James Clifford, who in   Eliz : aliened the same ; And are mentioned therin to bee 8. messuages

meſſuages and 192 acres of land, meadowe and paſture, in Woodmancote neere Durſeley, holden of that Manor by 17ˢ rent: And of divers other lands and tenements in Durſeley holden of Durſley manor. |

More of this Manor of Woodmancote is to bee read in theis Records and Deeds, viz,

Rot. Clauſ. 18. Rͤ Johis. membr̃. 4.—p ſerviͨ mĩt.
Inqu: 2. E. 1. pᵗ mortem Thome filij Ottonis,—p ſerviͨ mit.
Inq: 3. E. 1. pᵗ mortͤ p̃dͨi Thome.
Rot. finium. 9. E. 1. membr̃. 16.—per ſerviͨ mĩt.
Inq: 19. E. 2. pᵗ mortͤ Robti de Swinburne.—p ſerviͨ mit.
Rot. finium. 19. E. 2. membr̃. 6.—per ſerviͨ mĩt.
Comp̃us Hampton Eſcaetor̃ in baga in ſc̃io. 20. E. 2.—mit ſerviciũ.
Inq: 16. et 17. E. 3. pᵗ mortͤ Margerie de Swinburne, ad requiſicõem Warini fiᵗ Warini.—per ſerviͨ mit.
Rot. finium. 15. E. 3. membr̃. 2. per ſerviͨ mĩt.
Rot. pateñ. 16. E. 3. ps. 1. in dorſo.
Rot. Clauſ. 23. E. 3. ps. 1. membr̃. 24. in dorſo.
Carta 25. E. 3. in caſtro de Berkeley.
Carta 25. E. 3. Rot. 2. in cõi banco, Term̃i Triñ.
Inqu: 37. E. 3. de feodis de Berkeley in ſc̃io.—per ſerviͨ mit.
Inq: 6. H. 6. pᵗ mortͤ Johis de Berkeley.
Inq: 38. H. 6. pᵗ mortͤ Mauricij Berkeley.
Inq: 14. E. 4. pᵗ mortͤ Mauricij Berkeley.
Inq: 7. H. 7. pᵗ mortem Willi Berkeley.
Michas Rec̃. 7. H. 7. Rot. 34. in ſc̃io c̃m Rem̃ Theſaur̃.
Paſch: rec̃. 16. H. 7. Rot. 9. ibm̃.
Inq: 21. H. 7. pᵗ mortͤ Edw: Berkeley.
Inq: 1. H. 8. pᵗ mortͤ Alicie Berkeley viᵈ.
4. cartæ irroᵗ in cõi banco Term̃i Michis 30. H. 8. inter Bowſer et Davis.
Inq: 6. E. 6. pᵗ mortͤ Willi Berkeley.
Inq: 30. Eliz: ps. 2. pᵗ mortͤ Ric̃i Lambert.
Inq: 15. Jacobi pᵗ mortͤ Robti Purnell de Nibley.
ffinis in banco Term̃i Michis, 8° Jacobi, inter Bolton et Lambert, &c.
Inq: 20. Jacobi, pᵗ mortͤ Thome Purnell.—per ſerviͨ mit.
Inqu: 7. Caroli, pᵗ mortem p̃dc̃i Thome. per ſerviͨ mit.
Booke of Wardſhips and Releeſes, fol: 4. 23. 32. with mee.

The

The 2. Indentures of Lamberts and Mercers wardſhips, 31º. Eliz : et 10º. Caroli.
Court roll of Came, 7º. Jacobi, p̄: mortē Edm : Lambert — per ſerviciū militare.
Inq : 16. Carͬ. p̄: mortē Wiłłi Curnocke—per ſerviē mił.
Inq : 17. Carͬ. p̄: mortē Joħis Smyth authoris huius libri—p ſerviē mił.
Inq : 17. Carͬ. ſup Mel : inquirend p̄: mortē Joħis Purnell— p ſerviē mił.

𝔅𝔶 Inquiſicōn 6. H. 6. p̄: mortem Joħis Berkeley miltis, Nibley is found to bee an hamblet belonginge to this Manor of Woodmancote, holden of James lord Berkeley as of his Manor of Came, but by what ſervice the Jury knewe not. |

401 } blank
402 }

403

Wotton.

Wotton : In Domeſdei booke written Vittune : And in the next age after written Wittune : And in the time of kinge John, Wttoñ, without (o) in the firſt ſillable : An ancient pariſh and manor, nowe, as alſo longe agone, diſtinguiſhed into the Townſhips or hambletts of Wotton burrowe, als Wotton intrinſeca, als Wotton market towne ; and into Wotton fforren, or Wotton ſorinſeca ; conſiſtinge of the hamblets or villages of Sinwell, Wortley, Combe, Bradley, Nibley, and Huntingford. In this manor of Wotton, kinge Edward the Confeſſor had, as domeſdei booke ſheweth, ffifteene hides of land in demeſne : And is nowe the inheritance of George lord Berkeley, holden of the kinge by knight ſervice in capite ; A principall part of his Barony of Berkeley.

This Manor and pariſh of Wotton was by kinge H. 2. in the firſt yeare of his raigne granted (amongſt many others) to Robert the ſonne of Hardinge, a yonger ſonne to the kinge of Denmarke, and his heires : By which grant alſo the ſaid Robert was made a Baron and Peere of the Realme of England : ffrom which lord Robert, who dyed in 17. H. 2, it came to the lord Maurice his ſonne and heire, who died in 1. R. 1. And from him to the lord Robert his ſonne and heire, who dyinge without iſſue in 4. H. 3. left it to the lord Thomas his brother and heire, who dyinge in 28. H. 3. it diſcended from him to the lord Maurice his ſonne and heire, called Maurice the ſecond.

This

This is that lord Maurice who in 36. H. 3. obtained a grant to him and his *Wotton market* heires from that kinge to have a market each friday at Wotton, And a faire each *and ffaire.* yeare to bee there holden, vpon the Even the day and the morrowe of the exaltacōn of holy croffe, with all liberties and free cuftomes which to a market and faire doe appertaine : And for the holdinge therof did out of his faid Manor of Wotton, which (as is abovefaid) then confifted of the hambletts of Synwell, Wortley, Combe, Wotton, Bradley, Nybley, and Huntingford, felect the faid hamblet of Wotton wherof the whole parifh and manor had the name ; And this is it which at this day wee call the Burrowe towne, or Burrowe of Wotton, or the market towne of Wotton ; or the Newe towne of Wotton ; which alfo in divers deeds after was called novus burgus, the newe towne of Wotton ; All which doe foe continue to this day, 1639.

And this alfo is that lord Maurice who vpon his marriage with the lady Ifable that kings neece, was fuppofed to have entayled in this time of kinge H. 3. his five manors of Wotton, Simondfall, Cowley, Came, and Hineton, to himfelfe and his faid wife, and to the heires of their two bodies ; wherby vpon a fuppofed **Remitter** in Maurice his great-great-grandchilde, (whofe father the lord Thomas in 23. E. 3. had entayled the fame Manors, with others, to himfelfe, and the heires males of his body, whereof read before fol : [7. 77. 78,]) arofe that great and longe perplexed title, which before it was fetled continued above 150 yeares, wherof to write I forbeare in this place, | haveinge in my three hiftory bookes of that family of the 404 **Berkeleis** blotted more then 20. fheetes of paper with the laborinthes and toiles therof, therin delivered in perticuler.

The forefaid Lord Maurice by the faid lady Ifable his wife had iffue Thomas, father of Maurice, father of Thomas, father of Maurice, father of Thomas and James ; which Thomas in 5. H. 5. died without iffue male of his body ; And the faid James had iffue James, who had iffue William, created Marques Berkeley, and Maurice, (of others I fpeake not in this place,) which William dyed without iffue ; And the faid Maurice had iffue Maurice and Thomas, which Maurice died without iffue ; And the faid Thomas had iffue Thomas, father of Henry, father of Thomas, father of the faid George nowe lord Berkeley. 1639. Of which difcent, with the yeare wherin each of them dyed, See before fol : 7. et 77. 78.

In one of the woods in this parifh in the hamblet of Nybley, vpon the browe *Beckettſ-bury.* of a fteepe hill, is an ancient fortification of a Campe, with double trenches broad and

and deepe, called at this day Beckettſ-bury : but whether caſt vp in the time of kinge H. 2. in ayd or favour of Thomas Beckett Archbiſhop of Canterbury who fell vnder that kinge, as the name of Beckettſbury feemeth to import, or before in the times of the Danes invations, I know not ; wherof read before, fol : 72.

Streetes. — The Burrowe or market towne containeth about 60. acres ; And confiſteth of theis ſtreetes and remarkeable places, vz, High ſtreete, Sow lane, the Chepinge or markett place, Chepinge lane, Bradley ſtreete, Haw ſtreete, Church lane, Sym lane, and

Conduit. — In the yeare of our redemption. 1630. nyne yeares now paſt, at the charges of Sir Richard ffenne and Hugh Perry his ſonne in lawe, two worthy Aldermen of London, both of them borne in this Towne, was the ſpringe of water brought vnder ground from the place called the Conduct in Edbroke feild vnto the market croſſe in Wotton, where a conduct by them was beautifully erected to the great benefit of the inhabitants, with this Inſcription ingraven theron ; This Conduite was erected and the water brought into this place at the proper coſts and charges of Richard ffenn ats Ven, Alderman of London, and Hugh Perry of London, Eſq, who were both borne in this Towne :—Thus the inſcription : ffrom which the waſt and ſpare water is ſince derived vnder ground to ſome houſes belowe in the ſame ſtreete.

Almeſhouſe. — The ſaid Hugh Perry by his laſt will dated [20ᵗʰ April, 1630] tooke care for the erectinge of an Almeſhouſe, in this towne, and for the maintaininge of [ſix poore men and ſix poore weomen. Teſtator ſtates that he was born in the town of Wotton under Edge, and directs that the mayor of that town, and his brethren and their ſucceſſors ſhall "diſburſe yearly for ever £8 for apparailling, with gowns, ſhoes, ſtockings, ſhirts, and ſmockes" as far as the ſaid money would go, the ſaid ſix poore old men and ſix poor old women that now are, and hereafter ſhall be, remaining in the Almſhouſe at the ſaid town, which I have willed to be built, in equal portions upon the feaſt day of All Saints commonly called Allhallowday, and £5 more for wood and coals to be equally diſtributed among the ſaid poor Almsfolk at the aforeſaid feaſt ; and each of the ſaid poor Almsfolk to have 20 ſhillings a piece in money at the four the moſt uſual feaſts in the year by even portions yearly for ever.

He

He alfo bequeaths to the Mayor and his brethren the fum of £300, therewith in the names of themfelves and their fucceffors, and of the Parfon and Churchwardens of Wotton for the time being, as feoffees in truft, to purchafe a convenient plot of ground near the church, and to build a convenient houfe thereupon for the fix poor men and the fix poor women laying a garden thereunto with other conveniences.[1]]

The fcituation, afwell of this Burrowe or market towne of Wotton as of the parifh church, vnder the edge or browe of the great hills adioyninge, hath doubtleffe given in the name of Wotton fubedge, or Wotton vnderedge, as alwaies almoft of late yeares it hath byn called and written: A fpatious parifh, that befides the hamblets formerly mentioned, comprehendeth the hambletts alfo of Simondfall, the Ridge, and Nynd.

The Church is faire and beautifull, dedicated to the protection of the bleffed virgin Mary, efteemed the tutelary faint therof: wherin the bodies of Thomas lord Berkeley the 4th lord of that name, who died in 5to H. 5, and of the Lady Margaret his wife daughter and heire of Gerard Waren Lord Lifle and Tieis, (who died before her hufband,) lye vnder a faire marble fquare tombe, wherin noe tres of any fuperfcription have for many yeares paft beene to bee read.

Church.

This Burrowe or market towne of Wotton hath a Leete or Lawday belonginge vnto it of all the Refiants within the fame, wherin confifteth the goverment; Taken out of the great Leet of the hundred of Berkeley in 37. H. 3. (a courfe in thofe old dayes vfuall with great lords, both in this hundred and elfwhere in this and other Counties,) what time the faires and marketts were firft obtained from that kinge: which yeare alfo, Maurice lord Berkeley, the fecond of that name and the Lady Jone his mother, (who then held this manor in Joincture,) granted by Deed to the faid Inhabitants to have fuch liberties vfages and cuftomes in fuch fort as was then vfed in Tetbury, (a Market and Burrow towne fix miles of.) which alfo was confirmed by Thomas lord Berkeley the fecond of that name in 10. E. 1. two yeares after the death of the faid lord Maurice his father: And in 1. E. 3. the Jury had leave at the Leet or Lawday holden at Michaelmas yearly, to choofe one out of their number of Burgeffes to bee the | fupreame governor amongft them till that time

Leete or Lawday

---

[1] The will is a very long one, and contains a great deal more refpecting this Almfhoufe, but we have extracted as much as feemed neceffary to fupply the information wanting in the text. It was proved in the Probate Court of Canterbury, with a Codicil, dated 25th July, 1634, on the 23rd December following. (108 Seager.) [ED.]

time twelve month, and till his Succeſſor ſhould bee ſworne, And to call him a Maior; which courſe holdeth to this day, 1639: whoſe cuſtome alſo is, (the ſelfe ſame is vſed in Berkeley, as is ſaid before fol: 77.) And as is vſed in Tetbury, well alſo knowne to mee, having likewiſe byn Steward there full 40. yeares; (Of which townſhip I have alſo wrote the hiſtory from the Norman conqueſt to theis daies;) That at the Leete holden next after Michas day, the Jury, who for that Leete are impanelled and ſworne, doe preſent in writinge three names to the Steward for their Maior for the yeare next followinge, vz, their old Maior and two others; Of which three the Steward chooſeth one, whom hee pleaſeth, either the old Maior to ſerve againe for another yeare, or which of the other two hee will: Which done, the newe elected Maior is called and ſworne: The old Maior then riſeth, leavinge his ſilver guilt Mace before him vpon the table where hee ſate with the Steward, And then comēth the newe Maior and ſitteth downe in the old Maiors place, And there chooſeth one of thoſe two to bee his ſericant for the yeare followinge, whom the ſaid Jury have likewiſe ſet downe in their ſaid preſentment, who is preſently alſo ſworne; And then the ſaid Sericant, (called in the Court rolls ſerviens ad clavem,) the court beinge ended, taketh vp the Mace and goeth before the newe Maior home to his houſe, whom all the other Burgeſſes attend. And the ſaid Sericant by the ancient cuſtome of the ſaid burrowe towne is bound to gather the Lords rents and profits of the ſaid Burrowe for that yeare then followinḡ, and to accompt for the ſame without fee or recompence from the Lord for the ſame: which if hee faile to doe, and eſpetially to pay and make even his Accompt before the Lords Auditor, the Maior is anſwerable for the ſame; Againſt whom (in Berkeley,) I have twice in my time of Stewardſhip knowne an Accōn of Accompt to bee brought, and the Maior there to have thervpon ſatiſfied what was vnpaid, either quarterly or at the yeares end, eſpecially vpon his accompt before the Lords Auditor; And alwaies about a weeke after the election of the newe Maior, hee holdeth a Maiors Court, (vſed eſpecially and conſtantly in Berkeley burrowe,) where the Accompt is taken of the receipts and payments of the ſaid Maior for the yeare paſt, And ſuch newe ordinances eſtabliſhed for the yeare followinge as they agree vpon for the better government of the towne.

At the Leet for this burrowe towne holden at Michas 1639. A° 15. R̄ Caroli (as I was in reveiwe and in writinge of this towne,) the Jury preſented the 3. names of Willm Younge their old Maior, and of Richard Poole and John Leigh, for mee (then preſent) to make choice of one of them for the yeare then and yet followinge, what time Richard Poole whom I firſt made choice of, refuſed, and thervpon vnder-
went

went the fyne of -10^s which I impofed: Alfo John Leigh whom I next made choice of, refufed alfo, and vnderwent the ffyne of -6^{li} 13^s 4^d. Neither of whom, had formerly borne any office in the burrowe; And vpon queftion that was thervpon moved, the Jury did vnanimoufly prefent, That by the cuftome of | the Burrowe they might nominate and returne for the office of Maior any inhabitant that had dwelled a yeare and a day in the towne, although hee had not formerly borne any other office, as indeed neither of them two had done; And to confirme the fame vouched one or more prefidents and a former prefentment heertofore made at a former Leete; And prefented further, That if the two named with the old Maior refufed, and did vndergoe their fynes (as nowe), That then the old Maior muft continue, and they of the Jury not to name or prefent any other. And thervpon the old Maior, after longe refufall, was content to ferve the office, efpecially when hee was remembred of his firft oath, vz, To ferve the kinge and the lord of the burrowe for the yeare then followinge, and vntill another fhould bee fworne ; And then, after a newe oath given vnto him for the yeare followinge, made choice of a newe Sericant, who alfo was fworne. And for this manner of their proceedinge in each refpect, vouched two late prefidents in Berkeley burrowe, which my felfe knewe to bee true. It was at this time alfo queftioned, That if the Maior fhould have finally refufed, what then fhould have become of the office of Maioralty.

And further it was moved, That wheras one John Smith a fhoemaker died not 2. yeares before whileft hee was Maior, That if all thofe 3. men (prefented for choice of Maior at Michas Leete followinge,) fhould have refufed, as they might, and have vndergone their fynes, (noe oath formerly taken tyinge any one of them,) what then fhould have become of the office? If then, perforce to a newe election? A difference alfo was taken betweene the Act of God, in the death of a Maior, as before, And the Act of the party, as vpon a refufall; Which are heere in this place remembred for direction to them that fhall come after.

In the vtmoft fkirt of this Burrowe or market towne, or rather in Synwell (as fome will,) one of the hamblets of the manor called Wotton fforren, (which in this place doe adioyne,) ftandeth a free grammer fchoole, founded in 8° R. 2. by Katherine Lady Berkeley, the fecond wife and widowe of Thomas lord Berkeley the third of that name ; of whofe further piety I have before written in Berkeley, fol : 77 : endowinge it with competent poffeffions for maintenance of a mafter and two poore fchollers to live collegiately togeather. And in the ordinances and ftatutes for regulatinge of the faid fchoole, the faid Lady and her feoffees ordained (amongft other

Wotton fchoole

other things) that the schoolmaster should daily pray in the church of Wotton for
408 the soules of her selfe | her father mother husband and of others; wherby through
the Statute of 1. E. 6. for dissolucōn of Chantries, this was supposed to come to the
Crowne; wherevpon divers patents were in the raigne of Queene Eliz: and of kinge
James, passed of the Schoolhouse and lands, as concealed; wherby much trouble and
expence was occationed: which soe continued till by the sole pursuite of my selfe,
tenant to such part of the schoolhouse lands as lye in Nibley, with my expence of—
700^{li} at least, as is knowne to you, the same was quieted by a Decree in Chancery
in the end of kinge James his raigne; And the schoole of newe encorporated, with
ordinances and Statutes for the regulatinge therof fittinge the present time and the
doctrine of the Church of England; In which condition it flourisheth at this day,
1639: wherof I doe here write the lesse, referringe him that desireth more to the
Records themselves, And to a sentence given in the Starchamber in the time of
kinge Charles, against one Beniamin Crokey, almost ever since a runigate in Ireland,
in avoidance of the shame and punishment which was by the sentence of that Court
to have byn inflicted vpon him for his wicked libleinge and falshoods; And lately
taken at Bristoll vpon his returne from Ireland, at this time a prisoner in the fleete
at my suite, as both of you doe knowe. October. 1639.

Of the Advowson or ius patronatus of which schoole, a fyne was levied in
Easter Terme A^o 3° Eliz: betweene Martin Petit and others p^{lts}, and Henry lord
Berkeley and others, def^{ts}.

By an Inquisicōn after the death of Sir John Berkeley knight, in 6. H. 6. it
is found, that hee dyed seized in fee of the advowson of the Chantry and Schoolhouse of Wotton subedge, que nihil valet per añū: And that Maurice Berkeley
knight was his sonne and heire. 30. annos. |

409 **Freeholds** in this Burrowe or Market towne of Wotton, aswell
ancient as of late granted in fee farme, and as lye adioyninge
to the towne, granted in the same deeds with the Towne
houses; vz,

Osbornes land. In this market towne of Wotton Henry lord Berkeley by his Deed the 13th
of November A^o 8° Jacobi R^c. granted to Walter Osborne and his heires, One
messuage or burgage house, orchard, garden, and barne adioyninge, To hold vnder
the yearly rent of 17^s 8^d And also three other burgages vnder one roofe in High
streete, and 3. gardens adioyninge, To hold vnder the yearly rent of—19^s And also
3. acres

3. acres of pasture ground adioyning to the said messuage and garden, And also 2. acres in the feild called the Middle, in Sinwell, vnder the yearly rent of—12ᵈ with sute of Court, or 4ᵈ for every default, to the burrow of Wotton. Howbeit the tenure is of the kinge by knight service in capite, beinge part of the said Lords burrowe and manor of Wotton, and held by copy of Court roll, vntill they were severed by the said grant: And is nowe the inheritance of Willm Osborne, sonne of Thomas Osborne, sonne and heire of the said Walter, Aᵒ 1639. Howbeit the said Walter the grantee made a Lease of the same to Walter his younger sonne, for sowerscore and nyneteene yeares, who hath since assigned the same to Richard Huet, Ralph Willett, Willm Leigh, gent. and |

Also the said Henry lord Berkeley by his deed dated. 1ᵒ Decembr. aᵒ 9ᵐ Rᵉ Jacobi, granted to Robert Dawe and his heires, One burgage in High streete in Wotton, vnder the yearly rent of—6ᵈ payable quarterly, and sute of Court, or—4ᵈ for every default. Howbeit, the tenure is by knight service in capite of the kinge, and was held by Copy of Court roll accordinge to the custome of the said Burrowe, till severed by the said Deed; And is yet held by the said Robert, who hath lately brought downe part of the wast water from the foresaid conduite to the doore of the said Burgage, where it falleth into a stone cisterne. _{410 Dawes land}

Also the said Henry lord Berkeley by his Deed dated 13. Nov. aᵒ 8ᵒ Rᵉ Jacobi, granted to Thomas Hunter als Perry and to his heires, Two burgage houses with two small gardens and one orchard adioyninge containinge one Rood, in the old towne, vnder the yearly rent of—3ˢ 4ᵈ And also one acre in the feild called Edbrooke, vnder the gravell pitts, in the manor of Wotton fforren, vnder the yearly rent of —8ᵈ and sute of Court to Wotton burrowe, as other customary tenants doe, or 4ᵈ for every default. Howbeit the tenure is of the kinge by knight service in Capite, beinge part of the said lords manors of Wotton burrowe and Wotton fforren, as aforesaid, before the said grant, which are soe holden; By the death of which Thomas Perry 22ᵒ Decembr aᵒ 14ᵒ Rᵉ Caroli, the same are given by his will vnto Samuell Perry and his heires, beinge his eldest sonne by a second venter. _{Hunter als Perryes lands}

By Inquisicōn taken at Cirencester 12ᵒ Julij. 15ᵒ Caroli, where this Will and guift is found, but as to the tenure, de quo vel de quibus vel per quæ servicia Juratores ignorant.

Also the said Henry Lord Berkeley by his Deed dated 20ᵒ Aug: Aᵒ 9ᵐ Rᵉ Jacobi, granted to Robert Smyth and to his heires, one messuage or burgage in the highstreete, _{Smithes land}

highstreete, with a stable, orchard, and garden ground therto adioyninge, And also one other messuage or burgage with a garden ground and barne in Bradly streete, And also one close of pasture at the vpper end of Bradley streete, called little Wadsam, containinge halfe a Rood, vnder the yearly rent of—13ˢ 8ᵈ, and sute of court to Wotton burrowe, as other customary tenants doe, or 4ᵈ for every default; Howbeit the tenure is of the kinge by knight service in Capite, being part of the said Lords manor of Wotton burrowe before the said grant, which is soe holden: By the death of which Robert Smyth in aᵒ 13ᵒ Rᵉ Caroli, the same are |

411
Vens land als
ffenns in Wotton
and Sinwell.

Also the said Henry lord Berkeley by his Deed dated 12ᵒ Aug : aᵒ 9ⁿᵒ Rᵉ Jacobi, granted to William Ven of Wotton, one Toft, messuage, and tenement, barne and outhouses, and a pasture or meadowe ground called Court meadowe, divided into three closes, containinge in the whole 20. acres, in Synwell : And 4. acres and 3. quarters of an acre in sundry feilds in Wotton fforren, vz, 2. acres in Edbrooke, and one acre in the feild called the Midle, and one other acre in the feild called Mare haven ; vnder the yearly rent of—3ˡⁱ 16ˢ And 2ˢ payable to Wotton fforren.

And also further granted to him a messuage burgage or tenemᵗ, with a stable, garden, and orchard, in Hawe streete within the burrowe towne ; vnder the yearly rent of—10ˢ

And also further granted a messuage burgage or tenemᵗ in Highstreete in Wotton towne, neere to Sym lane, under the yearly rent of—10ˢ 1ᵈ And for heriot to bee paid after the decease of every one dyinge tenant to the premisses or to any part therof, the some of—3ˡⁱ 6ˢ 8ᵈ And sute of court to the Manors of Wotton fforren and Wotton Burrowe as customary tenants there doe, or 4ᵈ for every default. Howbeit, the tenure is of the kinge by knight service in Capite, beinge part of the said Manors before the said grant, which are foe holden.

After the death of which William Ven the same discended to John Ven his sonne and heire, who dyed the kings ward of theis lands, then in his minority : wherby the same discended to William his brother and heire, who also died in his minority, and the kings ward ; wherby the same discended to his brother and heire Richard, who nowe holdeth the same, Aᵒ 1639. |

Also

Also the said Henry lord Berkeley by his Deed dated 30º Maij Aº 9ᵗᵒ Jacobi. 1611. granted to Thomas Adams and his heires One Messuage or Comõn Inne in the High streete in Wotton, then the signe of the goate, nowe of the White Lyon, with the garden and outhouses therto belonginge, then held by him by copy of Court roll according to the Custome of the said burrowe, at the yearly rent of 6ˢ 8ᵈ.

412
Pooles land late Braches. before, Adams. nowe Pooles. Wilkens. Heskens. Oldisworthes.

And also by the same Deed granted one acre neere vnto Bourn streame 7ᵈ and also one other acre in Bournfeild, and one other acre in the feild called Edbrooke knowne by the name of freindlesse acre, 6ᵈ held likewise by copy, at the yearly rent of—13ᵈ

And also further granted by his said Deed one other burgage house with the appurtenants, then in the tenure of Robert Hickes in right of Margaret his wife, held by copy of Court roll accordinge to the Custome of the said burrowe towne, vnder the yearly rent of—13ˢ 4ᵈ. All payable quarterly; And also 13ˢ 4ᵈ in name of an heriot, after the death of every tenant dyinge in possession of any part of the said burgages, or lands; And sute of Court as other Customary tenants doe performe, or 4ᵈ for every default. Howbeit the tenure is of the kinge by knight service in capite.

Of which premisses none at all remaine to the posterity of the said Thomas Adams: ffor Richard Poole of Wortley hath the Comõn Inne, which hee purchased of   Brach of London, And hee of Thomas Adams; And paies the said rent of—6ˢ 8ᵈ

And Eliz: lady Longe, first maried to Edward Oldisworth sonne and heire of Arnold Oldisworth, late of Bradley, who have issue Robert Oldisworth, (shee after remaried to Sir Walter Longe lately deceased,) who hath the said acre by Bournstreame, and the acre in Bournfeild. rent 7ᵈ Which the said Arnold had of the said Adams.

And Nicholas Hesking hath the fee of the acre called freindlesse acre, from Robert Smith, whose daughter hee maried, And hee of the said Adams. rent. 6ᵈ

And John Wilkens of Nibley hath the fee of the burgage house with the appurtenants, late in the tenure of the said Robert Hickes in right of Margaret his wife. rent—13ˢ 4ᵈ which hee purchased of |

Also

Hundred of Berkeley

413
Daunts lands.

Also in this burrowe or market towne are divers houses and lands the old inheritance of the Daunts, whose first ancestor in this place which I have observed was Thomas Daunt who held the same in the raigne of kinge E. 2. After whom was Nicholas, father of John and Nicholas: Afterwards of John Daunt; and after of Simon Daunt, and John his sonne: And after of John Daunt, who lived in the time of kinge H. 7. and after of John Daunt, and others, beinge for most part yonger brothers: which said John Daunt sonne of Nicholas, by his maryage with Margery daughter and heire of Robert de Owlepen, brought into his family that land, as there appeares, fol: 309, 310, whose issue hold the same and alsoe this land in Wotton, to this day, A^o 1639. where their later discents are to bee read: stiled by the name of gentlemen from the foresaid time of my first observation of them. As very many deeds and Leases made by them to others, and by others to them, doe witnesse. Of theis their lands a fyne was levied in Michas terme 21. H. 6. Inter Nichum Daunt, de tentis in burgo de Wotton, Wotton fforren, et in Bradley.

Stantons land in Sinwell nowe Webbs.

Also the said Henry lord Berkeley by his Deed dated 1mo Julij A^o 9no R^e Jacobi, granted to John Stanton Clerke and to his heires, A messuage and halfe an acre, (the scite place of the ancient manor house) with the pigeon house and porters lodge, and three cottages adioyninge, and three acres parcell of the court orchard, all lyinge togeather in Synwell, within the Manor of Wotton fforren, reserving the yearly rent of—13^s. And—20^s. in the name of an heriot, after the decease of every one dyinge tenant to the premisses, or to any part therof; And sute of Court twice by the yeare, or 2^d for every default. Howbeit the tenure heerof, is of the kinge by knight service in Capite, beinge part of the said Lords Manor of Wotton before the said grant, which is soe holden. And this is nowe, A^o 1639. the inheritance of Robert Webbe, wherin hee dwelleth; who in 21° Jacobi, purchased the same of John Stanton sonne and heire of the said John Stanton clerke, who dyed the yeare before. As an Inquisicon then found the yeare hee dyed, doth shewe.

414 blank

415
ffifteene.

The payment of Kingsilver, or ffifteene when it is granted by Parliament, in this burrowe or market towne, is—4^s. ob. without any deduction: And in the manor of Wotton fforren—13^s. 11^s. 4^d. without any deduction.

Subsedy.

In the last Subsedy in a^o 5° R^e Caroli were 18. subsedy men in this burrowe or market towne, who paid to the kinge—8^h 8^s.

Able men.

Of able men for the warre betweene 20. and 60. yeares old in anno 6° R^e Jacobi, which at a generall muster appeared before Henry lord Berkeley, then Lieutenant of the County, were—146.

Of

Wortley

Of trayned Souldiers vnder Thomas Veel Esq. their Captaine, are vz,   Corsletts, and   musketts.   *Souldiers.*

And of Subsedy men in aº 5º Rº Caroli, were in the Manor of Wotton fforren, —40, vz, in Nibley—18. who paid—7ˡⁱ 6ˢ: In Combe—7. who paid—3ˡⁱ 4ˢ; In Wortley—6. who paid—3ˡⁱ 4ˢ; In Synwell with Bradley—7. who paid—5²ˢ 8ᵈ; And in Huntingford—2. who paid—14ˢ 8ᵈ.   *Subsedy men in Wotton fforren*

If the whole Division of Berkeley accompted a 4ᵗʰ part of the County of Glouc̄, bee in any tax for kinge or Com̄on wealth rated at—100ˡⁱ. Then this hundred of Berkeley paies therof—33ˡⁱ 3ˢ. And this Burrowe towne of Wotton—8ˢ, Synwell with Bradley—15ˢ, Wortley—15ˢ, Nybley—25ˢ, Combe—   , And Huntingford—5ˢ, as before in fol: 239.   *Rates or Taxes*

In this wholl parish of Wotton in aº 6º Jacobi p'd, were of able men fit for the warres betweene 20. and 60. yeares old, who appeared at a generall muster—428. vz, In the burrowe towne of Wotton—146, vt supra: In Synwell and Bradley —71. In Wortley—43. In Nybley—126. In Simondsall and Combe.—38. And in Huntingford—4.   *Able men in Wotton parish.*

416 ⎫
417 ⎬ blank.
418 ⎭

Wortley.

419

Wortley: This is one of the hamblets or little villages that makes, or lately did make, the manor of Wotton fforren, and is within the parish of Wotton, holden of the kinge by knight service in Capite.

George Lord Berkeley and the lady Eliz: his mother, by their Deed inrolled in Chancery dated, 28º Novembr̄. Aº 7º Rº Caroli, sold this hamblet or village for 1500ˡⁱ to Richard Poole gent and his heires, by the name of a Manor, naminge in whose possession each parcell was: Of which severance I leave this protestation behinde, that I was, and spake, more against it to the said Lady, (shee then, when shee contracted, abidinge at the Lodge in Whitcliffe parke, and my Lord her sonne in ffrance,) then was fittinge in com̄on discretion to have done, even to the angringe of her selfe towards mee, vsinge more reasons to have disswaded her, then this leafe of paper would containe; But vnder the maske of raisinge of monies to pay

my

my lord her sonnes debts, (which to doe shee had his estate then by his Conveyance in her hands,) shee vayled her owne ends; And partly to leave a banke for M.r George Berkeley her grandchilde, that lords second sonne, (shee then entendinge him her Executor, which shee after by her Will performed,) And partly to put out at interest for her owne better maintenance, which with marvailous privacy to severall scryveners, each vnknowne to other in their imployments, shee did; And partly to give, and to have by her will to give, to kindred, freinds, and servants; Shee drewe by sale of this hamblet and of other lands and by makinḡ of Leases and Copies to his Lo:rp tenants, the greater part of—11000.li, never by her accompted for, or knowne to her sonne till after her death, that by my speciall meanes it appeared; from whom her care was to conceale all shee could in this kinde, especially after I had soe earnestly disswaded this, and some other the like; I then knowinge how shee entended to 2. woemen her kinswoemen—3000.li, which after shee performed, to one of them in her health And to the other in her last sicknes with all the seerecy shee could.

Chantry. In 20. E. 3. Thomas lord Berkeley founded a Chantry in this hamblet of Wortley, and endowed it with a messuage and one yard land and 50.s rent p añū in Wotton for a Chaplein and his successors, Divina singulis diebus celebratura in Capella de Wortley, licensed by the kinge and confirmed by the Bishop of the Dioceffe, then of Worcester, Dedicated to the honour service and protection of S.t John Baptist.

If you desire to read more of this Chantry, I referre you to what I have written in the life of the said lord Thomas, called Thomas the third, vnder the title of his Almes and devotions, in the second volume of my history of the lives of this Berkeleian family: And to the Inquisic̄on found in 5. H. 5. after the death of another Thomas lord Berkeley; And to the Inquisic̄on found in 7. E. 4. after the death of Margaret Countesse of Shroewsbury, grandchilde of the said Lord. And somwhat heerof before in Ouselworth, fol: 305. 306.

Souldiers Of Trayned Souldiers vnder Thomas Veel Esq.r theire captaine, nowe are |

Horses for Trained Band

The persons charged to finde horses for the trayned band vnder Sir Gabriell Lowe knight, the Captaine, in Anno 1626, in this Hundred, were theis, vz.

Curassiers,

    Sir William Hickes of Beverston, knight.
    Thomas Chester of Almondsbury, Esq.
    William Basset of Ewley, Esq.

Dragoones.

    Sir John Bridgeman of Nimesfeild, knight.
    John Smyth of Nibley, Esq.
    Thomas Yate of Arlingham, Esq.
    Thomas Bicke of the same, gen̄.

    John Trotman of Came gen̄ } betweene them.
    Thomas Tyndall of Stinchcombe g̃

    fortune Came of Wike, widowe } betweene them.
    Thomas Came, her sonne

    John Trotman of Stinchcombe, gen̄
    Humphry Browne of Elberton, gen̄.
    John Browninge of Cowley, gen̄.
    Thomas Walter of Horseild, gen̄.
    Edward Greene, Viccar of Berkeley, Clerke.

    Lawrance Bridger, parson of Slimbridge, clerke, } betweene them
    Willm Hopton of Wanswell by Berkeley, gen̄

    Anthony Kingescote of Kingescote, gen̄ } betweene them.
    Thomas Clarke of Newton bagpath, gen̄

    Mathew Smyth of Wanswell, gen̄ } betweene them.
    William Bower of Hurst, yeoman.

    William Bye of Kingsweston, } betweene them.
    Edward Haynes of the same
        In toto. 18.

And

And nowe, in A°. 1639. 15. R̃ Caroli, at the clofinge vp of this Defcription, in this hundred of Berkeley, are vz,

Curaſſiers,
S̃ |

422 blank

423   **For Conclufion**: Though by likelihood I have omitted many perticularities of fundry kindes in this hundred, yet it fufficeth mee to thinke That I have pretermitted little that is mentioned in fuch Records or bookes of hiftory as are eafily come by, or obtayned: Howbeit, I doe willingly acknowledge to have paſſed by divers incertainties, leaſt I might feeme to have scattered any feed of diffention or of envy, by difclofinge fecrets, in fervinge the curiofity of I knowe not whom that (befides your felves) may read heerin.

     This knowe affuredly, That whatfoever I have written in the defcription of this Hundred, is proved either by Evidences in Berkeley Caftle, or by the Records heere mentioned in the kings Courts; Or by Deeds in the private poffeffion of the ffreeholders themfelves which I have feene, Or elfe remaine in my owne Cuftody. |

424 blank

425   **After** many daies failings I am nowe arrived at the haven which I longe defired to fee: I have nowe ended the taſke which many yeares fince I impofed vpon my felfe. Soe, fonne and fervant, with my double falutation, I bid yee All haile, and farewell: And as yee conceive or delight heerin, foe cenfure mee and theis my recreations; finiſhed accordinge to the comon accompt of vs Hundredors in the yeares, vz,

        Since our goeinge to Bellein with Sir Anthony Kingſton our high Steward, in 37. H. 8. ... ... } 96.

        Since the change of the Lawes in 1ª Eliz: ... ... 82.

                                                                                                 Since

Conclusion

Since Queene Eliz: was at Berkeley, in the 15th yeare of her raigne.	67.
Since the great ffrost, in 14° Eliz:	68.
Since the first great floud of Severne in 7° Eliz:	75.
Since the last great floud (which I beheld), in 4to Jacobi, that overflowed the lower Countrey.	33.
Since the fall of the great Elme at Hams greene	64.
Since the Lord Berkeley kept his great Xmas at Berkeley Castle in 2° Jacobi	36.
Since our goeinge to Tilbury Campe in 88.	51.

But more seriously, In the yeare of our Lord—1639. 21. Decembr. Anno 15to Regni R͡r Caroli, Et anno ætatis meæ—73. currente.

And farewell also to all my 20. other bookes, the recreations of my last 50. yeares, vz.

1. 2. 3. The history of the lives of 21. Lords of Berkeley, in three large volumes.
4. The booke of Terrars, or boundaries of each particuler peell, of each tenant, holdinge for yeares or lives, by Copy or at Will, which the Lord Berkeley hath in this county of Glouc̃, in folio.
5. 6. The 2. bookes of Survey or of perticulers, parted into six columnes, contayninge each tenants name, what lives or yeares are in beinge; The quantity of acres foe held; Rent reserved; value above that rent; with what heriot, Capons, hens, or rent corne, such tenants yearly pay, in folio. In 12. et 22. R͡r Jacobi.
7. 8. Two bookes in folio, the one in parchment the other in paper, of all the Lord Berkeleis Tenures by knight service, with the proofes that are either with or against such knight service Tenures. |
9. A booke in velome, of all Wardships and knight service Releefes, which have happened to the lord Berkeleys in any county in the last 55. yeares of my service vnder this family. in 4to
10. A wood booke of each tree, whether timber or firewood, growinge vpon each tenants lease land, or copihold land of the lord Berkeleies, with their kindes, and values, in folio.
11. 12. Two bookes of Rent rolls in folio; what rent each ffreeholder or other termor, for yeares or lives, by Copy or at Will, yearly pay to the lord Berkeley.

13. A

13. A fute roll in parchment, in folio, of all ffreeholders which owe fute to the three weekes Court, or Court of pleas, holden each Munday 3. weekes at Berkeley, And for what lands they owe fuch fervice.

14. 15. 16. Three bookes in folio, containinge the names of each inhabitant in this county of Glouc̄, how they ſtood charged with Armor in aº. 6ᵗº Jacobi, And who then was Lord or owner of each Manor or Lordſhip within the County ; which you may call my Nomina villarum.

17. A booke in a large folio, how each man in this hundred, and in the whole divition of Berkeley, hath byn for divers yeares paſt, and yet is, charged in the fubfedy Rolls in the kings Exchequer.

18. A booke in a large folio, of all paſſages in the office of Lieutenancy from 1º to 11º. Rͤ Jacobi, whileſt Henry lord Berkeley was Lieutenant, who died in the faid 11ᵗʰ yeare.

19. A booke in folio of all offices or Inquiſic̄ōns poſt mortem, and of Ad quod damnum, in the county of Glouc̄ from 10. H. 3. till 28. H, 8. in which yeare I leaſt of my further fearches therin ; As I did in 1ᵐº Jacobi. in the office of the Lord Treaforers Remembrancer in the Exchequer.

20. A booke in folio what each Townſhip paieth to the ffifteenth or Tenth to the kinge, when it is granted by parliament.

21. Alfo this booke in folio, of this defcription of the hundred of Berkeley and of the Inhabitants thereof ; The laſt of all : which, as the laſt, I reioice to behold, the labour beinge ended.

26. And if you my fonne John, pleafe to accompt theis, the number will bee—26 ; vz, That of my life in 4ᵗº dedicated to your felfe, The hiſtory of the Burrowe and Manor of Tetbury dedicated by mee to one of your brothers. The hiſtory of the Manor and hundred of Boſham in the county of Suſſex, dedicated to Mr George Berkeley, when it became to bee his vpon his purchafe from his father in anno 13º Caroli. 1637. The like hiſtories of the honour and Manor of Melton Mowbray in the county of Leicr, And of Bitton in the county of Glouc̄, of all which I have beene Steward.

INDEX TO SUBJECTS

Note.—That in this and the following Indices no attempt is made to diftinguifh the different individuals or places of the fame name, or the different mode of fpelling them, and that one reference only is given, notwithftanding the name may occur more than once on the fame page.

Arlingham, Vicar of 68	Caftle Gard, Berkeley Caftle 371
Afaph, St., Bifhop of 52	"Cementarius," meaning of ... ... 69 n
Afhelworth, derivation of name 72	Chantries—
Auguftins, St., Briftol, Abbots of, 6; fucceffion of, 52, 53, 54, 55, 73, 82, 87, 96, 142, 143, 161, 167, 198, 201, 223, 228, 229, 233, 260, 262, 263, 372	Arlingham 68, 69
	Berkeley ... 90, 91, 98, 99, 232
	Bradfton 116, 117
Barns, Tithe 36, 90, 113, 209, 362	Brokenbury 55, 56
Bath, Prior of 149	Cambridge 159
Becketfbury Camp 397, 398	Cirenceller 333
Berkeley, Burgeffes of 84	Hill 225
" derivation of name 1, 95	Newport 38, 39
" law fuit 397	Nibley 278, 292, 293
" M. and H., devolution of, 7, 8; Domefday record of ... ... 8—9	Slimbridge 329
	Stone 51, 358, 363, 365, 369
" Vicars of 95, 99, 409	Wortley 408
Blood-wort, tradition concerning 329	Wotton 401, 402
Bluemead Sunday, at Stinchcombe hill, games at 349, 350	Chapels, 38, 55, 86, 87, 92, 116, 123, 225, 233, 251, 260, 261, 286, 372
Bondmen or Villans 43	"Charibdes," meaning of ... ... 344 n
"Borachias," meaning of ... ... 344 n	Charters, original, 70, 71, 87, 129, 134, 182, 184, 200, 204, 325, 326, 326 n, 353, 380, 381
Bretcorn 68	Chertfey, Abbot of 188
Briftol, Bifhopric of ... 161, 197, 232, 233	Combe, derivation of 146
" Bifhops of ... 71, 72, 161, 165, 197, 223	"Conuzee," meaning of ... ... 330 n
" Dean and Chapter of ... 61, 89, 108, 109	Copyhold lands, cuftoms of ... 16—22
" Deanery of 179, 198, 233	"Cote," derivation of 120
" Mayor and Commonalty of 389	Courts, Hundred, 10, 11; procedure in ib. ... 16
" St. Auguftin's Abbey, fee Auguftins	Cowley Fair 151
	" Sports 151
Came Church, Lamp lands ... 136, 170	Cuftom of Election of Mayor of Wotton 399, 400
" Rectory of 87	Cuftoms, Manorial, 16—22, 150—151, 197, 226, 321, 322, 324, 334
Camps 146, 193	
Canterbury, Archbifhops of ... 77, 398	Cuftoms of the River Severn ... 321, 322

INDEX TO SUBJECTS

Dedication of the Work ... 33
Documents, original, 70, 87, 129, 134, 147, 172, 182, 183, 200, 201, 223, 242, 266, 267, 268, 275, 279, 280, 281, 288, 289, 311, 325, 326, 326 *n*, 327, 350, 351, 352, 353, 380, 381
Domesday Records, 8, 51, 58, 71, 81, 99, 121, 149, 161, 170, 207, 300, 306, 323, 396
Durfley, Deanery of ... 10, 170
" derivation of name ... 170

"Eigne," meaning of ... 264 *n*
Elizabeth, Q., her vifit to Berkeley ... 411
Elm tree, at Ham Green, fall of ... 411
Eveſham, Abbot of ... 187
Eweley, various ways of ſpelling the name ... 180
Exeter, Biſhops of ... 52

Fairs ... 39, 82, 151, 164, 397
Fees, Steward's ... 16
Filton, Rectors of ... 233
Fiſh, deſcription of different kinds found in the Severn ... 319
Flaxley, Abbot of ... 61
Franchiſes, ſee *Liberties*
Free Warren ... 7, 164

"Gainagium," meaning of ... 182 *n*
Gale fiſhing in Severn ... 321
Glaſtonbury, Abbot of ... 320
Glouceſter Abbey, 66, 67, 68, 87, 102, 122, 123 *n*, 158, 193, 258, 302
Glouceſter, Abbot of ... 76, 146, 150, 151, 193, 308
" Archdeacon of ... 202
" Biſhop of ... 202, 265
" Biſhopric of ... 122
" Deanery of ... 70, 72
" Earls of ... 171, 187
" Hoſpital of St. Bartholomew ... 313
" St. Oſwald's Priory ... 334
Glouceſterſhire, Sheriff of ... 320
Granges of Kingſwood Abbey ... 121
"Gurgites," meaning of ... 344 *n*

Hame, definition of name, 207; devolution of, 208
Hereford, Canons of ... 142
Hide of land, area of ... 2

Horfield diſafforeſted ... 237
Horſes for trained band ... 409, 410
Hoſpitals ... 50
Houſes, Religious remarks upon ... 260
Hurne, derivation of ... 105, 230
Hurſt, derivation of ... 241

Katherine, St., Hoſpital, Bedminſter ... 50
"Kedellas," meaning of ... 344 *n*
Kingſwood, Abbots of, 75, 76, 81, 106, 121, 142, 147, 272, 308, 309, 317, 323, 324
Knight family, abnormal formations ... 329

Lampreys, Royal appreciation of, 319, 320; value of ... 320
Lancaſter, houſe of ... 152
Lands, peculiar reaſon for ſelling ... 252
Land, William, Biſhop ... 201
Lantony, Prior and Convent of ... 154, 297
Liberties, 6, 43, 51, 64, 67, 82, 102, 143, 150, 173, 197, 371, 399
Llandaff, Biſhop of ... 52
Longbridge Priory, file of the Warden, &c., 259, 260

Markets and Fairs ... 55, 82, 102, 175, 397
Marle, in huſbandry, 40; its character, 41; its advantages ... 42, 152
"Menaltie," meaning of ... 254 *n*
Muſters, 9, 44, 55, 70, 73, 76, 89, 105, 118, 124, 165, 176, 179, 193, 198, 210, 226, 229, 233, 239, 253, 257, 269, 304, 310, 312, 394

Nibley, derivation of, 261; value of Benefice of ... 261, 262
Nibley Green, Battle, 266; the challenge, 267; the reſult ... 268

Parks pertaining to Berkeley Caſtle ... 209
PEDIGREES—
Archer ... 243
Arundel ... 329
Atwood ... 155
Bailie ... 65, 216
Baker ... 293
Baldwyn ... 197
Baſſet ... 37, 184, 292
Baynham ... 235

INDEX TO SUBJECTS 415

PEDIGREES—Continued
Bencombe, de 78
Berkeley, 58—59, 96, 147, 150, 327, 371, 388, 397
    "   of Berkeley Town 230
    "   of Beverston 100, 101
    "   of Bradley 111
    "   of Cressage 128
    "   of Dursley 171, 172
    "   of Uley 256, 257
Bicke 66
Bower 217
Bradston 114, 354
    "   of Winterborne 118
Brail 201
Bridges 147, 148
Browning 169, 302
Buddinge 383
Burchier, als Butcher 97, 116
Clavile 78
Clifford 329, 394
Codrington 160, 332
Cole 48, 49
Cooke 243
Cowley 153
Crome 166
Cromhall, de 162
Curnock 45
Dagge 383, 384
Daubeny 168
Daunt 311
Davis 47, 153, 155
Dingley 314, 315, 386
Dockett 157, 158
Dorney 166
Dosie 47
Draisey 291, 292
Draycote 125, 126, 137
Driver 63
Ellington 154, 156
Estcourt 138
Fitz Harding 147
Fitz Nicholl 224
Freame 218
Freeman 219
Fryer 65, 231

PEDIGREES—Continued
Gilman 249
Gosington 201, 202, 203, 206
Gough 221
Gray 62
Gurnay 178, 255
Hanis 243
Hardinge 127, 128, 389
Harvey 115, 117
Harvy 222
Heort 217
Hickes 98, 105, 106, 222, 236
Hodges 65
Hurne 97, 106, 230, 232
James 216
Jobbins 288, 290
Kingscote 251, 252
Kingston 61
Laverance 47
Ligon 163
Longe 148
Ludby 335, 336
Machin 145, 211
Macy 157
May 45
Millard 157
Moigne 211
Munday 299
Oldisworth 405
Oldland 222, 284
Osborne 403
Owlpen 311
Perry 232
Planche 128
Pole 368
Poyntz 224
Rochford 308
Rogers 284, 294, 295
Rolls 64
Ryvers 242
Schay 270, 271, 284
Selewine 155, 248, 249
Seliman 129
Smyth 379, 380
Stanshawe 289, 290

INDEX TO SUBJECTS

PEDIGREES—*Continued*
Stoner 115
Stourton 211
Swineburne 387
Swonhunger 287, 370, 374, 375
Taylor 139, 243, 336
Tefte 160, 332
Thorpe 85, 220, 287, 370
Thynn 305
Trotman ... 115, 116, 130, 131, 243, 244, 250
Trye 80, 81, 352, 353, 368
Turner 386
Vele 210, 235, 236
Veu, alias Fenn 404
Vincent 213
Wall 64
Walfh 177
Warner 155
Warre 153, 154
Wawton, de 162
Wentworth 354
Wikes 139, 172
Wilkens 157
Willoughbie 214
Wintour 225, 255
With 46
Yate 59, 60, 61, 62
Poitiers, Battle of 281
Proverbs and Phrafes ... ... 22—33
"Puffe Stone," defcription of 175
Purfuits, Agricultural, their advantages ... 42
"Putts," meaning of ... ... 344 *n*

"Rent feeke," explanation of ... ... 46 *n*
Riam-mead Sunday at Alkington, games at 35

Salmon, different ftages of growth ... 319
Saxony, Duke of 181, 223
Scotland, war with 187
Severn, River, defcription of tides of, 319; fifh in, 319; cuftoms of, 321—324; variation of channel, 330, 331; fordable at times, 343; great floods in 411

Shobenaffe, derivation of 229
Sirnames, remarks on 278, 279
Slimbridge, Rectors of 328
Smyth's concluding remarks, 410—412; lift of his works 411, 412
Soldiers, 9, 44, 55, 69, 73, 76, 89, 105, 118, 124, 149, 153, 165, 176, 179, 193, 194, 198, 210, 226, 233, 239, 257, 304, 310, 312, 337, 394
Sports, Cottefwold 10, 35
„ Cowley 151, 152
"Staches," meaning of ... ... 344 *n*
"Stadia," meaning of ... ... 344 *n*
Stanley St. Leonards, Priory of ... 66, 68
Stinchcombe, derivation of name ... 347
„ Hill, games at, on Blumeade Sunday 349, 350
Subfidies, 5, 6, 9, 43, 44, 55, 69, 73, 76, 89, 104, 105, 118, 124, 152, 153, 165, 176, 179, 193, 198, 209, 210, 226, 233, 239, 256, 304, 310, 312, 337, 394

Tides and Floods in the Severn ... 318
Toad, a monftrous 92
Tolceflers—a tribute to the Lord of a Manor for liberty to brew and fell Ale ... 86
Tooth, remarkable, found at Uley ... 193
Tredington, Rectors of 202

Uley, derivation of name 192

Wakes 151, 164
Wafte lands, remarks on 328
Witch, the Berkeley, tradition of ... 94
Woden's Well, legend concerning ... 372
Woodmancote, derivation of 387
Worcefter, Bifhops of, 52, 56, 68, 87, 90, 91, 98, 123, 233, 262, 300, 328, 408
Wotton, derivation of 396
„ Borough, names of ftreets, 398; Mayor and Corporation of, 399; cuftoms ... 399—400
Wotton Crofs 398
„ Rectors, and Vicars of, 87, 263, 264, 265, 266
„ *intrinfeca* and *forinfeca*, defcription of, 396
„ School, foundation of 401

York, Houfe of 152

INDEX TO NAMES OF PERSONS

Abevan, 85, 212
Ackfon, 264
Acton, de, 207
Adams, 227, 405
Adean, 391
Ady, 51, 117, 390, 392
Aillard, 71
Alba Mara, 172, 173, 357, 358, 360
Albene, de, 375
Allen, 164
Allien, 47, 213
Alfop, 385
Andrewes, 115, 119, 157, 248
Ap Adam, 6, 100, 102, 103, 178, 255, 256
Ap Ithell, 59
Archard, 33, 287, 298, 330, 337
Archdekne, l', 109, 110
Archer, 9, 107, 202, 241, 243, 244
Arnold, 163, 366
Arras, 194, 231
Arthur, 112
Arundel, 329, 330
Afhby, 135
Afhe, 53, 184
Afhton, 244
Aftmead, 127, 136, 356
Afton, 59, 242
Atford, 156
Atkinfon, 195
Atkins, 47, 97, 194, 231, 315, 366
Atwell, 163
Atwood, 96, 117, 118, 155, 215, 348, 353, 384
Audeley, 284
Aullen, 194, 195
Avene, 351
Avery, 85
Avone, de, 77, 314
Aylway, 136

Bailie, 21, 51, 65, 97, 116, 211, 212, 216, 217, 377
Baldwyn, 197
Bankes, 337
Barkly, Sir Henry, 171 //
Barnfdall, 49, 332, 333

Barre, 286, 364
Barry, 53
Baffet, 37, 78, 107, 132, 133, 153, 181, 184, 185, 192, 193, 194, 195, 280, 281, 283, 313, 379, 409
Bay, 255
Baynard, 153
Baynham, 66, 80, 126, 127, 227, 233, 339
Baynton, 37, 236, 240
Beale, 49, 111, 126, 169, 290, 291
Beauchamp, 59, 60, 61, 84, 187, 213, 266, 294
Becket, 39, 77, 398
Beconfawe, 144, 145
Bedic, 236
Bedminfter, de, 87
Belamy, 284, 285, 287, 295
Belcher, 49, 348
Bele, le, 183
Belin, 380
Bell, 140
Bencombe, de, 78, 79
Bendall, 138, 299
Beoley, 289, 352
Bere, de la, 309
Berewe, de la, 62
BERKELEY LORDS—
  Robert I., 7, 35, 57, 58, 70, 71, 72, 82, 83, 87, 88, 91, 92, 95, 99, 100, 102, 122, 142, 147, 150, 153, 161, 164, 171, 173, 177, 180, 181, 186, 197, 200, 206, 208, 218, 223, 228, 233, 241, 251, 255, 258, 260, 270, 300, 325, 326, 396
  Maurice I., 7, 50, 57, 58, 70, 71, 83, 88, 92, 102, 122, 132, 142, 147, 150, 168, 173, 180, 186, 200, 201, 208, 229, 251, 252, 258, 259, 260, 325, 327, 334, 374, 396
  Robert II., 7, 45, 50, 58, 83, 122, 134, 142, 143, 150, 180, 182, 186, 200, 201, 202, 208, 238, 251, 258, 295, 327, 328, 396

BERKELEY LORDS—*Continued*
  Thomas I., 7, 37, 50, 58, 70, 83, 106, 107, 122, 125, 134, 140, 143, 147, 150, 156, 173 *n*, 180, 182, 183, 186, 187, 195, 208, 217, 221, 229, 231, 232, 241, 242, 251, 258, 275, 276, 288, 309, 313, 316, 323, 324, 327, 370, 373, 396
  Maurice II., 7, 58, 59, 79, 80, 83, 106, 122, 143, 150, 155, 208, 209, 223, 230, 232, 245, 317, 323, 324, 327, 368, 396, 397, 399
  Thomas II., 6, 7, 36, 38, 40, 44, 48, 63, 80, 83, 92, 96, 108, 109, 122, 128, 129, 143, 150, 151, 174, 206, 208, 224, 242, 276, 279, 280, 281, 284, 285, 289, 324, 327, 329, 330, 350, 351, 352, 357, 363, 379, 399
  Maurice III., 8, 80, 83, 90, 102, 110, 112, 123, 128, 129, 143, 148, 150, 178, 188, 208, 313, 327, 350, 357, 397
  Thomas III., 8, 39, 46, 83, 84, 90, 92, 93, 100, 102, 103, 104, 110, 112, 116, 123, 131, 132, 141, 143, 148, 150, 154, 155, 174, 188, 208, 209, 211, 213, 225, 252, 257, 263, 264, 277, 289, 295, 297, 311, 327, 336, 341, 352, 357, 362, 363, 388, 393, 397, 401, 408
  Maurice IV., 8, 83, 91, 92, 93, 123, 150, 241, 263, 320, 327, 363, 397
  James the Welfhman, 8, 83, 123, 150, 208, 327, 397
  Thomas IV., 8, 61, 82, 83, 84, 96, 123, 141, 208, 209, 217, 219, 231, 263, 266, 327, 330, 331, 332, 375, 397, 399
  James I., 8, 56, 80, 83, 112, 123, 150, 208, 231, 263, 266, 327, 331, 353, 396, 397

3 II VOL. III

418   INDEX TO NAMES OF PERSONS

BERKELEY LORDS—*Continued*
  William Marquis, 8, 43, 57, 62, 80, 83, 92, 95, 123, 150, 208, 214, 230, 252, 263, 264, 266, 267, 268, 305, 315, 324, 327, 341, 353, 354, 370, 371, 397
  Maurice V., 8, 83, 123, 150, 208, 263, 265, 324, 327, 371, 397
  Maurice VI., 8, 56, 86, 123, 150, 208, 327, 371, 375, 397
  Thomas V., 8, 56, 83, 123, 150, 208, 327, 371, 397
Berkeley, Thomas VI., 8, 81, 83, 123, 150, 208, 327, 371, 397
Berkeley, Henry L., 8, 9, 34, 36, 44, 46, 47, 54, 55, 56, 57, 60, 70, 73, 81, 83, 89, 106, 112, 117, 123, 124, 137, 138, 145, 150, 165, 179, 193, 202, 203, 208, 209, 210, 214, 218, 226, 227, 228, 229, 253, 260, 261, 265, 269, 287, 294, 295, 296, 297, 298, 301, 304, 306, 312, 321, 327, 330, 337, 341, 360, 371, 376, 382, 384, 394, 397, 402, 403, 405, 406
Berkeley, Thomas, fon of Henry, 8, 123, 150, 208, 261, 287, 327, 397
Berkeley, George, 8, 36, 45, 47, 48, 57, 72, 78, 82, 90, 98, 105, 106, 116, 122, 123, 131, 137, 142, 149, 150, 156, 159, 160, 165, 169, 184, 186, 190, 195, 199, 203, 208, 212, 217, 218, 227, 228, 230, 231, 232, 233, 239, 240, 241, 243, 248, 251, 254, 261, 270, 279, 284, 285, 288, 293, 294, 298, 305, 312, 314, 315, 321, 322, 323, 324, 327, 329, 330, 332, 333, 335, 336, 337, 338, 341, 342, 347, 349, 354, 356, 364, 369, 370, 371, 382, 384, 385, 393, 397, 407
Berkeley, Alice, 100, 123 *n*, 125, 200
Berkeley, Alicia, 71, 112. 325, 334
  " Ann, 54, 100, 189, 228
  " Brice, 111
  " Dionifia, 280, 281
  " Edward, 100, 101, 111, 128, 388
Berkeley, Edmond, 128, 149
  " Elizabeth. 59. 63, 93, 100, 111, 112, 243, 266, 322, 407
Berkeley, Ellen, 189
  " Eva, 147

Berkeley, Felicia, 59, 63
  " Frances, 101
  " George, 408
  " Havifia. 317
  " Henry, 182
  " Ifabel, 59, 63, 353, 398
  " James, 111, 281
  " Joan, 59, 108, 109, 110, 138, 189, 214, 309, 399
Berkeley, John, 59, 60, 63, 96, 100, 101, 103, 104, 111, 113, 128, 129, 130, 131, 139, 166, 189, 230, 256, 257, 281, 292, 300, 317, 352, 368, 388, 402
Berkeley, Juliana, 109
  " Katherine, 100, 188, 256, 257, 277, 388, 402
Berkeley, Leticia, 59, 60
  " Margaret, 59, 90, 96, 101, 182, 183, 352, 363, 368, 399, 408
Berkeley, Margery, 59
  " Maurice, 100, 101, 104, 110, 113, 147, 148, 178, 179, 184, 188, 189, 200, 244, 256, 257, 276, 373, 388, 402
Berkeley, Nicholas, 138, 147, 223, 224, 300
Berkeley, Ralph, 224
  " Reginald, 224
  " Richard, 96, 110, 111, 132, 148, 178, 186, 189, 190, 191, 192, 255, 256, 257, 373
Berkeley, Robert, 58, 59, 70, 80, 122, 123 *n*, 130, 147, 177, 275, 281, 350, 351, 352, 368, 373
Berkeley, Roger, 223, 224, 373
  " Simon, 58, 59, 328
  " Theophila, 28
  " Thomas, 56, 59, 80, 96, 100, 167, 178, 179, 188, 230, 256, 257, 263, 316, 368, 388
Berkeley, Thomafia, 63
  " William, 100, 101, 104, 109, 110, 111, 128, 140, 178, 184, 200, 201, 256, 388
Berkeley of Durfley, 2, 7, 74, 75, 120, 170—175, 181 206, 262, 393
  " Alice, 395
  " Conftance, 110
  " Edmund, 75, 185
  " Edward, 394
  " Giles, 185
  " Henry, 75, 81, 171, 172, 173, 174, 182, 308, 309
  " Ida, 201
  " John, 6, 75, 76, 96, 172, 174, 175, 309, 395

Berkeley of Durfley—*Continued*
  " Maurice, 395
  " Nicholas, 172
  " Robert, 62, 124, 171 *n*, 181, 185
  " Roger, 7, 72, 74, 75, 110, 121, 123 *n*, 124, 125, 171, 171 *n*, 172, 180, 181, 200, 206, 270, 306, 308, 324, 325, 326, 326 *n*, 334
  " William, 4, 6, 62, 76, 79, 96, 129, 171, 171 *n*, 172, 173, 173 *n*, 174, 181, 185, 194, 306, 308, 324, 395
Berkeley of Beoley, 80
  " of Beverfton, 139, 166, 292, 393
Berkeley of Bradley, 111, 148
  " " Shropfhire, 75, 96
  " " Stoke, 148, 255
  " " Uley, 188
  " " Worcefterfhire, 96
Beoley, de, 352
Berley, 147
Berners, 159
Berton, 328
Beft, 232
Bett, de, 186, 187
Bettifhorne, 100
Bevington, 106
Bewdeley, 121
Bicke, 66, 68, 69, 157, 409
Biford, 334
Bill, 375, 381
Billing, 242
Bird, 111, 146, 148, 149
Birton, 287
Bifeley, 351
Bifet, 185, 194
Biffe, 215
Bitton, 286
Blanch, 163, 164
Blebury, fee *Shalingford*
Blount, 167, 198, 199
Bodle, 264
Boleia, de, 134
Bolton, 395
Bonville, 211
Bottetort, 188
Bowen, 157, 158
Bower, 28, 124, 217, 218, 244, 245, 246, 248, 334, 409
Bowler, 214, 365, 395
Boxe, de, 60
Brache, 405
Bradley, de, 108, 109, 148, 366

INDEX TO NAMES OF PERSONS

Bradſton, 53, 63, 113, 116, 117, 118, 119, 280, 281, 289, 347, 351, 352, 354, 355, 357, 360
Bradway, 394
Brail, 201
Brampton, de, 186, 187
Bramwich, 331, 332
Braoufe, 76, 308
Brayne, 135, 237, 371
Bretland, 302
Bretun, de, 308
Bridgeman, 65, 66, 67, 202, 300, 301, 304, 311, 312, 409
Bridger, 141, 145, 203, 204, 205, 242, 244, 245, 246, 249, 324, 390, 409
Bridges, 49, 136, 138, 146, 147, 148, 149, 156, 159, 172, 217, 226, 335
Brokenburrowe, 286
Bromfield, 302
Bromwich, 160, 246, 389
Brookes, 348
Browne, 361, 383, 409
Browning, 125, 126, 139, 151, 154, 156, 157, 160, 169, 184, 189, 192, 199, 224, 260, 294, 297, 300, 301, 302, 348, 409
Brumelham, de, 184
Buchard, 108
Ducklert, 260
Buddinge, 249, 376, 382, 383, 384
Bulledon, 375
Burbage, 276
Burchier, 39, 90, 97, 98, 115, 116, 293, 348, 359
Burgh, de, 182, 275, 276, 280, 281, 293
Burry, 39
Burton, 54, 228
Butler, 57, 148, 222, 384, 385
Butt, 64, 275
Button, de, 184, 352
Bycke, 62, 63, 64, 157, 158
Bye, 409

Carew, 350, 364
Ceaulin, King, 1
Cage, 64
Camden, 95
Carne, 47, 48, 49, 51, 97, 109, 116, 124, 125, 126, 127, 140, 157, 160, 182, 184, 352, 409
Camera, de, 279, 280, 281
Camerarius, 147
Cantelupe, 172, 358
Carpenter, 98, 296, 378
Caple, 381
Carſwell, 64, 157

Carter, 61, 64
Cartwight, 215
Catchmay, 135, 136
Catfon, 126
Cave, de, 201
Cemeterio, de, 183
Cerney, 53
Chaldefield, de, 280, 281
Chamberlain, 147
Champneis, 178, 289
Chaufey, 289, 290, 291, 292, 308
Cheilder, 172
Chefter, 51, 54, 55, 56, 198, 233, 257, 409
Chetwinde, 99
Chideocke, 329
Chiltenham, de, 242, 311, 388
Chilton, 390
Chin, 63, 64
Choke, 168
Church, de la, 278
Clare, de, 187
Clarke, 296, 409
Clavile, 78, 79, 86, 159, 242, 243
Clayfeild, 244
Cliffe, 132, 133
Clifford, 80, 160, 174, 216, 241, 329, 332, 394
Clutterbuck, 21, 63, 64, 203, 214, 215, 366, 377, 378
Clyvedon, 211, 293
Cob, 71
Cobham, de, 198, 199
Codrington, 160, 202, 207, 332
Cogan, de, 201
Cohull, de, 201
Coke, 28, 223,
Cole, 47, 48, 97, 144, 145, 219, 294, 366
Colines, 242
Combe, 49, 147, 149, 275, 280, 281, 335
Compton, 133, 159, 258
Cooke, 111, 159, 243, 244, 322 n, 331
Corbet, 57
Cordwainer, 256
Coriet, 128, 137, 138, 160
Cornwall, 235, 236, 240
Cotele, 149
Cottington, 159
Cotton, 94
Coveley, de, 147
Cowley, 48, 126, 134, 135, 153, 154, 172, 247, 249
Coxe, 157, 158, 336
Crabb, 215, 216
Crifpe, 339

Croft, 64
Crok', 351
Croke, 56
Crokey, 407
Crome, 46, 48, 164, 166, 167
Cromhall, de, 71, 162, 166, 167, 168, 184
Crowe, 337, 339, 345
Cuhulla, de, 373
Culverhoufe, 157
Curnock, 45, 46, 49, 270, 271, 272, 273, 275, 276, 279, 282, 283, 295, 296, 299, 336, 367, 392, 396

Dagge, 383, 384
Dalton, 193
Dancey, 185, 189, 190, 191, 192, 194, 231
Danfield, 105
Dangerfield, 191
Dangerville, 44, 48, 108, 148
Daniel, 64, 177
Dantree, 266
Danvers, 271
Darcy, 54
Daflin, 375
Daubeny, 53, 162, 168
Dauni, 133, 190, 192, 307, 311, 312, 313, 314, 406
Davis, 47, 64, 99, 140, 141, 148, 149, 153, 154, 155, 195, 204, 206, 207, 244, 246, 247, 249, 333, 334, 335, 370, 375, 382, 383, 395
Dawe, 291, 403
Deane, de, 128
Denny, 111
Denys, 145, 260
Devereux, 356
Digas, 65
Dimery, 163, 225, 225 n, 227
Dingley, 77, 314, 386
Diriatt, 348
Dirlinge, 85
Dockett, 157, 158
Dodington, 53
Dollinge, 48
Donell, 177, 219, 220
Doppinge, 331
Dorney, 163, 165, 166, 189, 190, 191, 195, 314
Dofie, 47, 48
Dounton, de, 245
Draifey, 291, 292
Draycote, 125, 126, 127, 137, 168, 169, 182, 184, 280, 381
Driver, 63, 64, 69, 338
Ducy, 161, 163, 164, 168, 303
Dudley, 36, 62, 138, 144

INDEX TO NAMES OF PERSONS

Dunninge, 111, 266, 291, 292, 298, 321, 322
Dursley, de, 182
Dursewell, de, 237
Dutton, 37, 60, 236, 297
Duneepouch, 326, 326 n

Earsfield, 101
Ecton, see *Egeton*
Edridge, 183
Edmonds, 371
Edward Conf., 2, 2 n, 82, 91, 99, 101, 194, 200, 223, 228, 232, 262, 306, 323, 344, 396
Edward II., K., 6
" III., K., 147, 177
" IV., K., 152, 271
" VI., K., 57, 83, 144, 150, 327
Edwards, 246, 379
Eeles, 359, 369
Egbert, K., 1, 2
Egeton, 176, 177, 218, 219, 221, 288, 289, 290, 345, 380, 381
Egge, 323, 324
Ekinton, de, 183
Eliott, 232, 292
Elizabeth, Q., 138, 145, 148, 161, 411
Elland, 157
Ellis, 369
Eslington, 139, 154, 156, 158, 159, 245
Estcourt, 120, 138, 170, 172, 282, 390
Estgate, de, 182, 183
Ethe, 294
Evered, see *Everod*
Everey, 357
Everod, 215, 270, 273, 366, 367, 369
Evans, 48, 283
Ewley, de, 78

Faber, 183, 280
Faire, le, 326
Feilding, 73
Fenn, or Ven, 398, 404
Fillimore, 21, 28
Filton, de, 198, 199
Fisher, 71
Fitzharding, 7, 52, 58, 87, 147, 153, 197, 200, 233, 326
Fitz Nicholl, 6, 198, 199, 213, 223, 224, 227, 228, 300, 304
Fitz Ralph, 303, 304
" Robart, 216
" Paine, 329, 330
" Warren, 213, 387, 395

Fitz William, 275, 352
Fleetwood, 101, 225
Flower, 158
Ford, 156, 286
Forrister, or Foster, 177, 202, 215
Fortescue, 115, 354, 355
Foules, 140
Fourd, 195, 369
Fowell, 36, 37
Fowler, 214, 336, 339
Framilode, 219, 332, 333, 336
Framsom, 39, 116
Frantham, 361, 362
Frape, 157, 204, 245, 249, 334, 336
Freame, 50, 157, 158, 177, 218, 219, 220, 248, 249
Freeman, 205, 219, 270, 273, 366, 369
French, 154, 189, 191
Froucester, 48
Fryer, 61, 64, 65, 66, 231
Fust, 225
Fust, 99, 106, 107, 228

Gaunt, de, 100, 101, 177, 255
Gausel, 172, 214, 373
Gayner, 287, 375
Gibbens, 39, 270, 274, 283
Gibbs, 36, 270, 274, 279, 281, 282, 283
Gifford, 162, 163, 165, 168, 233, 303, 379
Giles, 68
Gilet, 352
Gilman, 125, 249, 332, 333, 334, 380
Gloucester, de Walter, 186, 187, 188
Godwin, E., 2, 3, 91, 95, 101, 193, 262
Goldsborrowe, 202, 205, 206
Gonston, 69
Goodman, 57, 123
Goington, de, 201, 202, 203, 206, 207, 326, 326 n
Gough, 126, 135, 169, 221, 368
Grafton, 216
Graile, 37, 111, 113, 148, 236, 238, 282, 365
Grantham, 57
Graffo, 182
Grava, de, 295
Gray, 62
Green, 89, 409
Greyndour, 286, 364
Griffith, 97, 163, 211, 212, 213, 216, 378
Gripp, le, 47
Grove, 284, 295
Gueda, 3

Gulston, 203
Gunne, 265, 368
Gurney, 80, 100, 102, 177, 178, 179, 252, 255, 257
Guy, 96

Hadley, 299
Hadlow, 286
Hagely, 48
Hagle, de, 242
Haia, de, 373
Hale, 38, 113, 147, 283
Hall, 46, 89, 90, 91, 127, 128, 217, 339, 341
Hamond, 65
Hampden, 299
Hampton, 154, 394
Hanbury, 121, 299, 302
Hanis, 243, 244, 248
Harding, 35, 124, 125, 126, 127, 128, 133, 137, 139, 154, 155, 169, 238, 247, 249, 355, 389
Harold, 46, 200, 262
Harper, 56, 192, 195
Harris, 74, 211, 215, 376
Harsfield, 278
Hart, 378
Harvey, 97, 105, 115, 117, 118, 119, 145, 222
Hasele, de, 325, 326, 326 n
Hathermare, 40, 130, 352
Hatheway, 36, 221, 270, 274, 281, 282, 287, 290, 298, 357
Havard, 378
Haynes, 50, 409
Hayward, 111, 127, 270, 272, 277, 279, 296
Haywarden, 164
Hearinge, 339
Heath, 69
Heathfield, 247
Heaven, 252
Heminge, 334
Hennis, 334
Henry I., K., 171, 262, 311
" II., K., 4, 5, 7, 52, 72, 74, 91, 92, 95, 99, 122, 125, 147, 150, 153, 161, 171, 172, 174, 177, 180, 193, 223, 262, 270, 325, 326
Henry III., K., 70, 71, 125
" VI., K., 5, 152, 160, 172
" VII., K., 8, 57, 83, 92, 93, 95, 135, 150, 263, 305, 327, 341
Henry VIII, K., 158, 209, 327
Hensten, 357
Heott, 217
Herrick, 91
Herynge, 178

INDEX TO NAMES OF PERSONS

Hefkins, 45, 405
Heyward, 46, 95
Hickes, 96, 101, 105, 106, 116, 162, 163, 164, 211, 213, 222, 236, 237, 240, 339, 348, 354, 355, 359, 368, 405, 409
Hide, 94, 215, 358, 369
Hiett, 348, 377
Higs, 74
Hill, 125, 133, 136, 139, 189, 191, 202
Hilpe, 299
Hoale, 163
Hodges, 65, 66, 257, 258
Hody, 50
Holecombe, de, 173
Holfred, 226
Hollifter, 56, 265, 266, 348, 361
Holt, 267
Hooke, 177, 178, 329, 330
Hooper, 48, 87, 339
Hopkins, 284, 294
Hoppy, 159
Hopton, 22, 127, 128, 137, 139, 140, 376, 382, 383, 409
Hore, 391
Horne, 66, 202
Hort, 256
Horton, 328
Howe, 111, 339
Howell, 377
Huet, 222, 403
Hughes, 298
Hugman, 205
Hulle, de la, 183
Hulmancote, de, 140
Hungerford, 111, 238, 270, 271, 272, 273, 274, 275, 276, 298, 359
Hunt, 54, 55, 121, 284
Hunter, 111, 403
Huntley, 45, 57, 66, 97, 105, 225 n, 243, 244, 245, 303, 307, 335
Hurd, 159, 335
Hurne, 96, 97, 106, 215, 229, 231, 380
Hurft, 286, 288, 335, 364, 374
Hutchens, 132, 133, 284
Hyde, 216, 369

Incram, 91
Ingaldefthorpe, 114, 119, 354, 355, 356, 360
Inge, 187
Inwood, de, 351
Ive, 56
Ivye, 271
Iwel, de, 373

Jacelyne, de, 109
James, 135, 216
 " K., 402
Jaye, 97, 98
Jenkins, 367
Jetefbury, 110
Jewet, 147, 148
Joachim, 271
Jobbins, 48, 111, 279, 288, 289, 290, 291, 348, 389
Jocham, 189
John, K., 100, 162, 176, 177. 233, 311
Jones, 99, 118, 139, 296, 299, 377
Jopfon, 164

Katherine, Q., 224
Kedon, 134, 135
Kellinge, 378
Kemis, 322, 339
Kendall, 77, 314
Kinge, 64, 138
Kingfcote, 146, 251, 252, 254, 276, 409
Kingfton, 61, 151, 158, 241, 242, 245, 249, 258, 410
Kirle, 96, 314, 366
Knevet, 258, 259, 385
Knight, 49, 50, 64, 139, 163, 164, 227, 265, 329
Knoll, de, 53

Lambe, 389
Lambert, 388, 389, 393, 395, 396
Lamport, 356, 357
Laffeborrowe, 128
Laurd, 168
Laverence, 46, 47, 97, 98, 144, 145, 211, 376, 378
Lawrance, 116, 164, 211, 231, 232, 376
Lefromonte, 71
Legg, 48
Leicefter, de, 221, 373, 374
Leigh, 108, 111, 400, 403
Lenthall, 341
Lewes, 22, 231, 232, 246, 332, 370, 377
Lidiard, 178
Ligon, 116, 161, 162, 163, 167, 184
Limefi, de, 162, 168
Lille, 152
Lockier, 254
Loe, 9
Loffe, 375
Logge, 263
Longe, 53, 147, 148, 149, 250, 270, 272, 274, 336, 338, 405
Longefpee, 201

Longford, 134, 135, 136
Longney, 61
Lovell, 352
Lovett, 348
Lowe, 306, 307, 316, 409
Lucas, 247
Ludly, 66, 206, 244, 248, 334, 335, 336,
Lude, 108, 109, 110, 112
Luffinge, 71
Lyes, 64

Mabfon, 137
Machyn, 85, 86, 145, 211, 212, 368, 380
Macy, 157
Madocke, 155
Madrefdon, de, 242
Mallet, 87, 105, 106, 197, 226, 230, 314, 365, 366, 367, 369, 371
Malmfbury, de, 53
Manninge, 190
Mape, 2, 3, 95
Mare, de la, 149
Marina, 53, 55
Marifcus, de, 167
Martell, 227
Marten, 111, 275, 279, 290, 291, 294, 295, 296
Marfhall, 280
Mary, Q., 150, 158
Matefdon, 358
Mathewe, 233, 236, 237, 240
Mathias, 221, 374
Matfon, 265, 266, 368
Mattock, 70
Mafon, 163, 367, 376
Maud, dau. Henry II., 223
Mauduit, 74, 81, 119, 129, 146, 182
Maurice, fon of Nigell, 201
May, 45, 111, 270, 272, 273, 291, 298
Mead, 65
Melkfham, 356
Meredith, 233
Merricke, 48, 393
Merfet, 391, 396
Meffenger, 236, 302
Midleton, 66
Milt, 335
Millard, 157, 159
Mills, 69, 299
Minard, 137
Minor, 126
Minfterbrooke, 315
Moigne, 211, 213, 215
Molyneux, 66, 335
Monileux, fee *Molyneux*

INDEX TO NAMES OF PERSONS

Monmouth, 128, 129
Moody, 126, 169
More, de la, 172
Moreville, 201
Morgan, 235, 237, 339
Moore, 226, 299
Morris, 151
Morſe, 132, 133, 339, 365, 367, 369, 377, 382, 383
Mortimer, 47, 175, 183
Mull, 267
Munday, 49, 206, 274, 292, 298, 299
Munden, 246, 334, 335
Mowbray, 112

Naſon, 250
Naſſe, de, 131
Nattock, 47
Neel, 380, 381
Nelme, 111, 113, 115, 137, 163, 205, 297, 348, 358, 359, 361
Nevill, 50, 100, 114, 115, 354, 355, 361
Newbury, 53, 54, 72, 233
Newland, 54
Nibley, de, 278
Nicholas, 332
Norris, 114, 178
Norton, 286
Nubbeley, de, ſee *Nibley*

Oakes, 287
Ogan, 235, 240
Oldifworth, 91, 111, 112, 137, 233, 270, 274, 330, 345, 405
Oldland, 97, 222, 367, 384
Oldpenne, de, 182, 184; ſee alſo *Owlpen*
Organ, 115
Oſborne, 402, 403
Othe, ſee *Ethe*
Owlpen, de, 133, 182, 184, 252, 280, 281, 303, 311, 313, 352, 356, 373, 406
Owſelworth, de, 309

Packer, 164
Pall, 221
Paſt, de, 201
Paris, de, 373
Parke, 245
Parker, 21, 112
Parmiter, 365, 367
Parrott, 389, 392
Paſſlowe, 125, 127, 169, 189, 191
Parſons, 48
Paſſlowe, 317, 392

Partridge, 54, 154, 155, 159, 297, 391
Pate, 115, 119, 348
Pauncefoot, 72, 339
Paveley, 114
Payne, 85, 115, 119, 189, 190, 191, 297
Paynam, 123 *n*
Pegler, 45, 154, 158, 189, 191, 192, 247, 248, 250, 336
Peirs, 111, 270, 272, 273, 381
Penda, K. of Mercia, 1
Pennard, 71
Perry, 111, 232, 398, 403
Peter, 214
Petit, 402
Phelips, 333
Phelps, 105, 369
Phillips, 151
Pike, 164
Piſtor, alias Baker, 156, 157
Pitt, 389
Pinckett, 377
Planch, 75, 128, 172, 326, 326 *n*
Plantagenet, 62, 104
Platt, 341
Pleydell, 144, 244
Ploner, 111, 133, 392, 393
Plowmaker, 126, 127
Pockhampton, de, 230
Pole, 353, 354, 355, 357, 360, 368, 369
Poole, 114, 119, 148, 400, 405, 407
Pope, 45, 49, 125, 169, 348
Porcarius, 183
Porter, 71, 112, 376
Powell, 247, 332
Poyntz, 9, 74, 78, 79, 101, 159, 191, 192, 199, 223, 224, 225, 225 *n*, 228, 258, 293, 294, 300, 301, 302, 306, 307, 309, 334, 339
Prat, 136
Praterd, 103
Price, 151
Puncherdon, 184, 185, 194
Purlyn, 227
Purnell, 36, 44, 46, 111, 113, 117, 190, 192, 205, 270, 272, 273, 274, 282, 283, 284, 290, 291, 294, 298, 299, 389, 392, 395, 396
Purtloe, 260
Pyke, 51

Quinten, 28

Raleigh, 306
Rawlyns, 133, 159
Rede, 75

Redeburne, 289
Redinge, 158
Rees, 284, 295, 348
Reginald, E. of Cornwall, 92
Reſtall, 157
Revell, 197
Ricards, 385
Richard I., K., 162
Richards, 214, 215, 297, 377
Richardſon, 324
Richford, ſee *Rochford*
Ritch, 227
Rivet, 306, 307
Roach, 390
Roberts, 63, 64, 135, 136
Robinſon, 171
Rochford, 308, 309, 336
Rogers, 284, 294, 295, 297
Rolfe, 280
Rolls, 64
Romefden, 159
Rowell, de, 96, 186
Rudiford, 294
Ruffo, 182, 184
Rugge, 286, 299
Rupe, de, 326, 326 *n*
Ruſſell, 86
Ryvers, 243

Sackville, 50, 144, 145
Sage, 125, 160, 169, 336
Saham, 241
Saint Barbe, 153, 154
St. James, de, 183
St. Maur, 360
Salop, Alexr., Archd. of, 181
Saltmarſh, de, 87, 201, 218, 256, 326, 373
Saniger, 211, 213; ſee alſo *Swonhungre*
Sanford, 158, 339
Sanmelis, 134
Saule, 136
Saxcy, 215, 216
Schay, 270, 271, 276, 284, 292, 326, 326 *n*
Scott, 64, 85
Scryvet, 199
Segar, 178
Selewine, 155, 195, 195 *n*, 248, 249
Seliman, 129, 130
Seliman, 283, 348, 358
Seneſchal, 373
Serjeant, 98, 222, 242, 285, 286, 358, 363, 364, 365, 369, 374, 380, 381, 384
Seſhville, 110
Seward, 266
Seymour, 114, 119, 144, 305

INDEX TO NAMES OF PERSONS 423

Shallingford, 53
Shawe, 286
Sheldon, 259
Shell, 205
Shellitoe, 292
Shelton, 121
Sheppard, 246, 332
Shevely, 165, 166
Shipton, 253
Shoile, 80, 352
Shottesforc, 237
Sindleford, de, 70
Skenefrid, de, 372
Skipwith, 80
Smalcombe, de, 278
Smyth, 33, 34, 45, 47, 49, 50, 60, 97, 98, 113, 115, 116, 191, 192, 205, 211, 212, 216, 217, 237, 244, 246, 247, 249, 270, 272, 274, 282, 286, 287, 288, 290, 291, 296, 297, 298, 301, 302, 315, 328, 332, 333, 337, 348, 364, 365, 367, 369, 376, 378, 379, 380, 381, 382, 388, 390, 391, 396, 401, 403, 409
Smythes, 177
Snell, 44
Snowe, 53, 99
Snygge, 258
Somers, 128, 133, 137, 138
Sparke, 189
Spenser, 80, 258, 258 n
Spicer, 204, 283
Spratton, 243, 244
Stafford, 301, 304
Stallinge, 357, 358
Staner, de, 201
Stanes, de, 71, 351, 373, 374
Stanshawe, 112, 289, 290, 291, 383
Stanton, 126, 371, 406
Staples, 205
Stapleton, 201
Staverton, 59
Stephen, K., 3, 7, 52, 91, 92, 125, 142, 171, 180, 197, 206, 233, 262, 270, 325, 362
Stephens, 9, 76, 105, 253, 304, 312
Stinchcombe, 125, 136, 164
Stintescombe, de, 71, 81, 182, 184, 275, 281, 297, 352, 355, 373
Stone, de, 253, 280, 281, 285, 286, 287, 288, 362, 363, 364, 370, 374, 379
Stonehouse, 332, 333
Stoner, 115, 354, 355, 361
Stourton, 211, 212, 213
Strange, 271
Strangwaies, 111, 113

Streat, 111
Street, 367
Stumpe, 258, 259, 303, 385
Stut, 183, 195
Sutton, 54
Swaine, 389
Swanhunger, 130, 232, 253, 280, 286, 287, 288, 289, 303, 315, 351, 363, 364, 366, 370, 371, 374, 375, 379, 380, 381, 383, see also *Sautger*
Swineburne, de, 387, 388, 395
Sydenham, 66, 335
Sydney, 297
Symonds, 243, 244, 248, 250

Talbot, 60, 61, 62, 266, 267, 268, 408
Tame, 65, 66, 202, 301, 304
Tanner, 125, 126
Taught, 378
Taylor, 47, 48, 137, 139, 204, 205, 227, 243, 244, 246, 283, 336, 337
Tecle, 244
Tempest, 341
Testle, 166, 331, 332
Thayer, 205, 246, 348
Thornbury, 290
Thornhill, 59
Thorpe, 9, 44, 50, 70, 73, 85, 86, 89, 91, 118, 124, 144, 145, 153, 188, 210, 214, 220, 222, 226, 231, 253, 256, 287, 330, 337, 345, 360, 365, 369, 370, 371, 375, 376, 378, 379, 382, 383, 384, 385
Throckmorton, 28, 37, 54, 57, 116, 119, 161, 162, 163, 168, 228, 235, 236, 237, 238, 240, 301, 302, 307, 312, 337, 359, 369, 376
Thurston, 339
Thynne, 91, 116, 305, 306, 358, 369
Tilladam, 107, 144, 227, 391
Tindall, see *Tyndall*
Tipper, 145
Tippetts, 366
Tiptoft, 114
Tirrell, 80
Toite, 176
Toki, 308, 334
Tomlins, 126, 136
Tough, 222
Tought, 377
Tovy, 227
Toyte, 45, 47, 317
Tussley, 80

Tracy, 236, 240, 278, 291, 293
Trefray, 77, 314, 315
Trepin, 178
Trevisa, 95
Tristram, 299
Trotman, 45, 49, 111, 115, 116, 117, 120, 125, 128, 130, 131, 133, 135, 136, 137, 138, 139, 140, 155, 156, 157, 159, 204, 207, 243, 244, 245, 249, 250, 270, 273, 274, 282, 295, 296, 297, 298, 334, 348, 359, 367, 388, 391, 409
Trye, 79, 80, 81, 185, 352, 353, 354, 367, 368, 369
Tudor, 178, 189
Tulse, 121
Turner, 56, 74, 376, 386
Twinen, 156
Twyniho, 216
Twyfell, 195, 195 n
Tyler, 21
Tylladam, 215, 369
Tyndall, 50, 111, 136, 157, 211, 215, 244, 284, 348, 353, 355, 356, 361, 377, 409
Tytton, 332, 333

Uley, de, 172, 180, 181, 193, 326, 326 n, 373
Urban, Pope, 92
Usher, 177, 218, 219, 220,
Utley, 215

Valers, 132, 185, 194
Vaughan, 333
Veel, 9, 37, 140, 149, 165, 176, 179, 210, 212, 226, 233, 235, 236, 237, 238, 239, 240, 269, 335, 351, 362, 394, 407, 408
Venables, 202, 207
Venator, or Venor, see *Hunt*
Venery, 164
Vere, 161
Verney, 301
Vincent, 213, 293, 294
Vizar, 236
Vrry, 357

Wade, 56, 366
Waight, 252
Wakeman, 136
Waleis, 227
Walkeley, 125, 126, 154, 164
Wall, 64, 65
Wallington, 97, 98, 116
Wallis, 366
Walsh, 177, 219, 220, 227, 289, 304, 307

Walsingham, 69
Walter, 115, 222, 339, 409
Walton, 77, 314
Wanifwell, de, 362, 372, 373
Ward, 247, 369
Warner, 44, 154, 155, 157, 158, 259
Warre, 153, 154, 326, 326 n
Warren, 135, 277, 291, 399
Waftfield, 157
Waterton, 96, 231
Watkins, 158, 211, 301, 390
Wawton, de, 162, 167
Webb, 26, 65, 73, 113, 128, 133, 136, 138, 144, 145, 148, 159, 163, 165, 166, 172, 190, 215, 335, 367, 368, 391, 406
Weekes, 111
Weite, le, 183
Wells, 232
Welfh, 376
Welfteed, 392
Weltden, 148, 149
Wentworth, 63, 115, 119, 348, 354, 355, 359, 361
Wenzi, 373
Were, de, 255
Weft, 100, 183
Wefterdale, 369

Wefthall, de, 388
Weftmancote, 59, 60, 65
Wefton, 271
Wheeler, 164, 302
White, 39, 111
Whittacre, 151
Whittard, 191
Whittington, 235, 339
Wicliffe, 38
Wike, de, 36, 63, 280, 281, 289
Wikes, 75, 76, 139, 172, 258, 259, 376
Wildby, 309
Wilkens, 157, 190, 272, 283, 287, 295, 336, 405
William Conq., 2, 7, 8, 35, 58, 67, 82, 146, 161, 171, 179, 180, 199, 200, 207, 223, 228, 232, 251, 255, 262, 300, 306
William Rufus, 171, 262
Williams, 202, 204, 391
Willet, 298, 403
Willis, 64
Willoughbie, 213, 214, 348
Wilfhire, 145
Wilton, 59
Window, 50, 258, 259
Winiet, 339
Winfton, 216, 301, 302, 334, 377

Wintle, 61
Wintour, 177, 225, 255, 345, 364, 369
Wiplet, de, 109
Wife, 246, 365
Wifhonger, 69
With, 45, 46
Wither, 106, 107, 227, 351, 352, 356
Wolftan, Bp., 38
Wood, 191, 247
Woodend, 134, 135
Woodftocke, de, 168
Woodward, 21, 123, 153, 159, 192, 334, 335, 348
Woolworth, 133, 138, 159, 172, 335
Wooth, 293
Wor, 358
Workeman, 252, 390
Wylott, 40

Yate, 58, 59, 60, 61, 62, 63, 64, 66, 67, 69, 409
Yelverton, 202, 214
Yerworth, 154
Younge, 197, 400
Yweley, fee *Uley*

INDEX TO NAMES OF PLACES

Achinton, 45, 50, 377
Acholt M., 121, 171
Acle, 70
Aden's houfe, 250
Ailburton, 69; fee alfo *Elberton*
Alderley, 78, 95, 149, 214, 289; M., 290
Alkington, 6, 7, 9; M., 21, 35—51; Riam Mead, Sundays at, 35; affeffment to fubfidy, 43; its fervile tenantry, *ib.*; fubfidy men, 44; able men, *ib.*; foldiers, *ib.*; its freeholds, 44—51; 70, 73, 76, 90, 113, 116, 117, 142, 143, 146, 152, 177, 187; enclofed in the Caftle Park, 209, 219, 220, 229, 239, 270, 273, 279, 286, 295, 305, 350, 352, 362, 363, 369, 375, 377, 379, 383, 386
Almington, fee *Alkington*
Almondefbury, 6, 9; M., 51, 52, market and fair granted for, 55, fubfidy, *ib.*; mufter, *ib.*; foldiers, *ib.*; rates, *ib.*; 70, 72, 82, 165, 187, 197, 233, 409
Almondefbury Advow., 52, 87, 88, 179, 263
Almondefbury Chantry, 55, 56
            " Park, 4, 54
Apleridge M. or Farm of, 57, 70; 208
Arlingham, Advow., 66, 67, 87
      " 6, 79, 52; M., 58; Flaxley M. in, 61; St. Auguftins M. in, 61; Wike M. in, 61; Bradfton's lands, 63; Roberts' lands, 63; Rowle's land, 64; Wall's land, 64; Bailie's land, 65; Fryer's land, *ib.*; Hodge's land, *ib.*; Mead's land, *ib.*, 66; names of places, 67; weirs or fifhings, *ib.*; Rectory & Vicaridge 67, 68; chantry lands, 68; church rebuilt, 69; warth, *ib.*; fubfidies, *ib.*; mufters, 70; 72, 142, 143, 187, 322, 342, 345, 386, 409
Arlingham, par., 120, 202, 259, 322

Arlington, 339
Afhelworth, Advow., 52, 88, 263
      " 6, 7; M., 52, 70, 71—73; fubfidies, 73; mufters, 73; 187, 233
Auguftin's, St., Abbey, Briftol, 50, 56, 61, 72, 87, 98, 102, 108, 109, 142, 143, 164, 197, 221, 233, 345
Averie's lands, 85
Avoncourt, 48, 73, 77, 314, 315
Awre, Rectory of, 154
Axfbridge, 255
Aylberton, fee *Elberton*

Bageton Grange, 121
Baggrudge, 71
Bagpath M., 73; church, 74, 76; Turner's land, 74; Harris' land, *ib.*; fubfidies, 76; mufters, 76, 79, 190, 308, 310
Bagpath par., 120
Bailie's land, 65, 216
Bankefland, 133
Barbafter, 213
Barndewood, 374
Barrers M., 218, 220
Baffets Court, 279, 283
      " lands, 132
Bay in Wanfwell, 214
Baynam field, in Nibley, 272
Baynham, 35, 73; M., 76, 386
Beckettbury, 77
Beckhams Mead, 112
Bedminfter, 29
      " Hofp. of St. Katherine 50
      " M., 70
Beeflies, 139
Belamies, 284, 287
Belamy's Place, 285, 287
Benecombe, 77—79, 159
Beoly, 75, 353, 368
Beoly-brook, 352
Berewe, 8, 62, 63, 66
Berkeley Advow. 52, 87, 88, 89; chantries in the church, 90, 142

Berkeley Barony, 22, 35, 82, 119, 125, 149, 199, 208, 228, 241, 251, 261, 262, 270, 305, 314, 323, 342, 354, 357, 360, 362, 393, 396
Berkeley Borough, 4, 6, 7, 10, 58, 81; market, 82; fair, 82; devolution of, 83; defcription and government of, 84, 90, 92, 96; freeholds, 96, 98, 117, 122, 142, 177, 208, 214, 218, 220, 259, 322, 376, 380, 381, 400, 401
Berkeley Caftle, 2, 6, 9, 40, 54, 67, 79, 80, 81, 85, 91, 92, Chapel in, 92, 98, 101, 110, 112, 113, 129, 130, 132, 147, 152, 165, 167, 168, 174, 175, 176, 188, 192, 194, 199, 200, 202, 207, 208, 209, 220, 221, 224, 238, 214, 253, 254, 255, 260, 261, 266, 267, 268, 271, 283, 285, 288, 289, 294, 301, 306, 309, 312, 316, 317, 321, 322, 324, 329, 331, 332, 352, 358, 370, 379, 383, 388, 394, 410
Berkeley Caftle, Thorpe's Tower, 371
Berkeley Church, 96, 98; chantries, 90, 98, 117; 209, 220, 232, 251, 263, 362, 372
Berkeley Divifion, 105, 118, 153, 165, 179, 193, 210, 226, 229, 233, 239, 269, 304, 307, 323, 337, 359, 407
Berkeley Honour, 171 *n*, 208
Berkeley Hund., Parks, 4; fite, *ib.*; foil, *ib.*; precedence, 5; fubfidies, *ib.*, 6; liberties, 5, 6, 7; devolution of, 7, 8, 10; court procedure, 10—16; cuftoms, 16—22; 34, 58, 60, 64, 73, 78, 79, 82, 90, 96, 102, 103, 106, 108, 113, 118, 124, 131, 135, 143, 144, 153, 155, 160, 161, 165, 169, 174, 175, 176, 182, 183, 193, 195, 197, 198, 207, 208, 210, 212, 213, 217, 218, 220, 221, 222,

3 I VOL. III

INDEX TO NAMES OF PLACES

Berkeley Hund.—*Continued*
224, 226, 227, 229, 230, 231, 232, 233, 236, 238, 239, 241, 251, 254, 269, 270, 279, 280, 285, 293, 304, 307, 312, 321, 323, 332, 333, 335, 336, 337, 342, 347, 355, 356, 357, 360, 361, 364, 369, 371, 376, 380, 382, 384, 387, 394, 399, 410

Berkeley Manor, 3, 6, 7; devolution of, 7, 8; 9, 16, 35, 52, 57, 58, 63, 72, 73, 74, 82; churches and chapels of, 86, 87; 90, 92, 95, 102, 103, 107, 108, 115, 125, 127, 128, 134, 143, 150, 154, 160, 161, 167, 171, 173, 177, 180, 181, 187, 200, 203, 218, 220, 222, 231, 233, 239, 241, 251, 254, 255, 258, 261, 262, 270, 276, 283, 303, 324, 338, 341, 342, 344, 345, 347, 349, 359, 362, 363, 383, 392, 393

Berkeley Nuncry, 2, 3, 91, 200, 262, 393

Berkeley Par., 6, 35, 38, 40, 57, 70, 77, 79, 89; able men in, 89; subsidies, *ib.*; soldiers, *ib.*; 98, 105, 107, 142, 143, 149, 208, 209, 214, 215, 216, 217, 220, 223, 227, 228, 259, 283, 293, 314, 361, 362, 367, 369, 370, 371, 375, 386

Berkeley Tavern, 97
" Vicarage, 99

Berrymead's leis, 250
Beverston Advow., 52, 87; church, 170, 251
Beverston Castle, 100, 101, 103
" 7, 9; M., 99, and Castle 100; church, 102; market, *ib.*; free warren, 103; fair, *ib.*, 130; 139; 252, 255, 257, 409
Beverston Park, 4, 6
" Township, 105, 120, 193
Bevington, 7, 98, 99, 106, 107, 117, 208, 210, 314, 366, 383
Bevington Hamlet, 105, 143
Bewarne, House, 96
Bibury, 225
Bicke's land, 66
Bilcfwick M., 52
Binley, 298
Bircheley, 7, 269, 273, 284, 285
Bird's land, 146
Bitley, 177, 220
Bitton, Smyth's History of, 412
Blackburton, 359
Blakemore, 36
Blakencsword, 70

Blisbury, Farm, 107, 209
Boddicraft, 214
Bolgrove, 49
Borrough Hill, 274
Bosham, Smyth's History of, 412
Bosworth Field, 178, 314
Bournfeild, 274, 290, 296, 405
Bournstream, 298, 405
Bowry, 277
Boxwell, 214, 307
Bradley Hamlet, 107, 108, 396
" 7, 95, 110; M., 110; devolution of, *ib.*; 190, 269, 270, 273, 285, 290, 354, 396, 397, 407
Bradley Mead, 112
Bradston Chantry, 117
" Chapel, 116
" Hamlet, 113, 118, 119, 181
Bradston's lands, 63, 118
Bradston, 63, 99, 105; M., 115; 124, 248, 258, 347, 348, 384
Bradston Tithing, 117
Brampton M., Devon, 174
Brandwood, 241
Breach, 248
Brcht, 373
Brewesthold, 233
Brightenmead, 132
Brighthampton, 225
Bristol, 6, 7, 29, 38, 48, 49, 50, 52, 55, 61, 78, 114, 141, 142, 161, 169, 232, 233, 237, 260, 262, 284, 294, 299, 329, 337, 343, 349, 368, 375, 383, 389, 394
Broadcroft, 282
Broadmead, 205, 298
Broadruydinge, 358
Brodnam, 205
Brokenbury Chantry, 55, 56
Brokenbury M., devolution of, *ib.*
Brokend, 228
Bromwich land, 160
Brookfurlong, 282
Broom, the, 307
Bruton, Som., 215, 216
Buckover, 45, 49
Bulford M., 116, 359, 369
Burrow's Court, 275, 276, 277, 282, 392
Burrowhill, 270
Burrow's Mead, 273, 277, 279
Bushing Grove, 133
Busthorpe, als Tanhouse Mill, 169
Butler's lands, 384
Buttescrofts, 273

Calais, 110, 340
Caldecote, 74, 170, 257, 306

Caldecote Grange, 121, 324
Caldecote Farm, 120
Cambridge, 82, 117, 141 327, 329
" Chapel, 141
" Chantry, 159
Came, 6, 7, 9, 16; M., 21; 28, 39, 66, 115, 116, 117, 118, 119; M., 121; description of, 122; devolution of, *ib.*; 124-131, 132, 133, 134, 135, 136, 137, 138; Taylor's land, 139; Upthorpe, 140; Daunt's *ib.*; Bourfley, *ib.*; 150, 151, 155, 157, 158, 169, 187, 194, 195, 202, 241, 248, 258, 316, 335, 347, 355, 356, 358, 363, 393, 394, 396, 397, 409
Came, Advow., 87, 251
Came Par., 122, 124, 136, 140, 146, 168, 204, 205, 207, 259, 283, 347, 358, 375, 387, 391
Camelham, 237, 239
Campden Hill, 36
Cams field, 204, 249, 336
Camylham, 37
Cannonbury M., 47, 48, 49, 65, 90, 98, 99, 141, 143; devolution of, 144, 145; 156, 219, 227
Canonbury, 16, 108, 376
Canon Court, 108, 154, 297
Cassies Compton, 339
Castle Park, 209
Catgrove, 209, 213
Cernay, 70
Cernecote, Wilts, Advow., 104
Charelton, Midd., 376
Charfeild, 274
Charlecroft, 49
Chawfiesland, 288
Chedrington, 173
Cherry-mead, 298
Chestlhunger, 205, 241
Chosley, 132, 277
Churchend hamlet, 150, 269, 347
Cinglife, 1
Cirencester, 199; Chantry, 333
Clapton, 7, 208
Claviles Place, 77
Clayfield, 48, 272, 277, 282
Claypitts, Green, 44, 45, 47, 50
Clerkenwell, 97
Cleverton, Wilts, 227
Cleyhunger, 7, 122, 146, 204, 205, 259, 347, 351
Clinger, see *Cleyhungre*
Cobb's House, 283
Cockfhoot, 296
Colbrooke, 124
Coklaston, 339
Coldnewenton, 74, 75, 76, 170

INDEX TO NAMES OF PLACES 427

Cole's Elme, 219
" land, 48
Combe, 7, 78, 108, 146; devolution of, 147, 148, 149; 153, 251, 265, 269, 273, 323, 396, 397, 407
Comly, 209
Compton, 57
Conftantinople, 347
Corietts, 137, 139, 160
Cottefwold Hills, 10, 84
Coveley, 6, 9
Coventry, 42
Cowleazes, 185
Cowley Advow., 87, 151, 302
Cowley, 7, 16; M., 21, 66, 78, 79, 95, 120, 124; 127, 139, 140, 142, 143, 149; devolution of, 150; hamlets of, ib.; church, 151; fair, 164, ib.; Cowley's lands, 153; Effington, 154; Harding's lands, ib.; Maddenfall lands, 155; Twinen's lands, 156; Piftor's lands, ib.; Wilken's lands, ib.; Dockett's lands, 157; Effington's lands, 158; Hulmancote, 159; Millard's land, ib.; Partridge's lands, 159; Bromwich land, 160; Coriett's land, ib.; 187, 192, 194, 202, 294, 297, 300, 391, 397, 409
Cowley Par., 149, 150, 158, 159, 160, 169, 170, 181
Crabb's lands, 215
Credin's brooke, 133
Creffage, 128
Crefway, 38, 272
Cromall Advow., 52, 87, 164
Cromefland, 46, 166
Cromhall Ligon, 161
" 7, 9; M., 52, 55, 70, 161; fair, 164; rates, ib.; wakeday, 164; free warren, 164, 165; 187, 197, 233
Cromhall par., 165, 181, 237, 239
" Park, 4
Culkerton, 76; Grange, 121, 308
Culverhayes, 209
Cutcrofts, 47

Dagge's land, 384
Dallifcroft, 215
Damery bridge, 237
Dancey's lands, 194
Dangervill Wike, 35, 44, 47, 352, 386, 387
Dangerville's lands, 148
Daunt's lands, 133, 406
Davis's lands, 47
Dawe's lands, 403

Deane field, 273
Dean, Foreft of, 84, 158, 328, 337, 340, 343, 357
Dean Magna, 339
Dekin's houfe, 250
Denver, Co. Norf., 214
Dimock, 339
Dockett's lands, 157
Dodington, 139
Dorney's land, 165
Doverley Riv., 85
Downfield, 132
Doyle's lands, 215
Dreycote, 122; M., 124; devolution of, 125; 136, 137, 148, 160; 169, 180
Duddington, 173
Dumballs, 337, 338, 339, 347
Durfley, 7, 26, 45, 49, 62, 63, 72, 73, 79, 81, 82, 95, 124, 125, 129, 130, 138, 139, 155, 169, 181, 184, 194, 195, 200, 204, 206, 213, 214, 219, 249, 259, 274, 294, 306, 308, 309, 325, 362, 375, 382, 383, 387
Durfley Advow., 87, 170
" Archdeaconry of, 170
" Barony of, 173
" Church, 170
" Hermitage, 175, 176
" M., 75, 76, 120, 127, 128, 170—176; Domefday record of, 170; derivation of name, ib.; rectory, 170; caftle, 171; markets and fairs, 175; hermitage, ib.; nunnery, 176; fubfidy, ib.; foldiers, ib.; rates, ib.; 387, 395
Durfley Nunnery, 176
" Town, 6, 96, 174, 175, 176
Dyrham, 1

Eaft Greenwich M., 151, 232, 259, 359
Edbrooke field, 398, 403, 405
Edgborne, 282
Egeton, 7, 176; fee alfo Halmer
Elberton, 99, 339
" Chapel, 55, 179
" M., 102, 177—178;
Champneis's land, 178; church, 179; fubfidies, ib.; foldiers, ib.; rates, 179; 256, 409
Eldresfield, 171 n
Elfoulds, 282
Ffoclewoorde, 9
Ellewworth, 173
Ellcourt's lands, 138
Ewecombe, 71, 142
" Hill, 260

Ewelme Water, 175
Ewley, fee Uley
Eynfham, Mon. of, 265

Fairford, 202, 301, 303
Filton, townfhip, 197, 198, 199; 233, 304
Filton, 6; Chapel, 55, 56
Fiftringe, 228
Flaxley Manor, of Arlingham, 61
Fordend, 273
Forthay, 269, 273, 297, 298
Fowell's Grove, 37, 282
Frampton Church, 170
Frampton-upon Severn, 117, 160; M., 329, 330, 331, 332, 334, 347
Freame's lands, 218
Freeman's lands, 218
Frends Place, 283
Frogpit, 205, 228
Froucefter par., 150, 151, 159, 303
Fryer's land, 66

Garnweir, 68
Gafcony, 173 n
Gennes Houfe, 384
Giftingthorne, 283
Glamorgan, Co. of, 342
Gloucefter, 1, 9, 38, 71, 84, 101, 102, 141, 193, 302, 349, 368
Gloucefter, Co. of, 6, 9, 55, 70, 73, 121, 124, 143, 153, 162, 170, 174, 187, 188, 202, 208, 214, 237, 259, 264, 320, 342
Goldefwike, 35, 45, 386, 387
Goodrugge, 39
Goofmead, 282
Goington, 7, 240, 242
" M., 66, 199, 200, 201, 202, 203, 207, 328, 333
Grafton's lands, 216
Greenes, the, in Nimesfield, 301
Greenhinchcombe, 273
Greenwich, Eaft, M., fee Eaft Greenwich
Grombaldfafh, Hund., 307, 361
Gromballfhay, 105
Grove, 273, 277
Grovelands, 204
Grover's land, 287
" mead, 295

Haggeley, 36
Hall Place, 127, 140
Hall's lands, 127
Halmer, 50, 122, 138, 176, 177, 208, 210, 216, 217, 221, 222, 231, 249, 260, 375, 381, 383, 384

Hame, 6, 7, 16, 50, 66, 97, 98, 99, 109, 110, 116, 117, 142, 177, 202, 227, 286, 370
Hame Church,
" M., 57, 82, 90, 105, 106, 117, 176, 187, 207; definition of name, *ib.*; Domesday description, *ib.*; devolution of, 208, 209, 210; freeholds in, *ib.*, 212, 213; Wickstowe, 213; Willoughbie's lands, *ib.*; Crabb's lands, 215, 216; Halmer hamlet, 217; Gough's land, 221; Oldland's Place, 222; Walter's land, *ib.*; Hicke's land, *ib.*; 227, 231, 232, 314, 322, 342, 345, 361, 363, 367, 369, 370, 371, 375, 379, 380, 381, 382, 384, 385, 386
Hamesfallowe, 208, 210, 216, 386
Hampton, 301, 303
Hamstalls, 209
Hardwick, 79, 185
Harehills, 36
Harford, 215
Harley, 273
Harry Stoke, 199, 383
Harvey's lands, 118
Haselden, 76; Grange, 121; 308
Hasfield, 72
Hasilcote, 120, 253, 375
Hawe Park, 4
Hawgrove, 283
Hawkesbury, Deanery of, 164
" Par., 118
Hawthurne field, 204
Hay, 197
Heathfield, 35, 45, 50
Hedge's land, 202
Hellmill, 307
Hempton, 57
Henbury, par., 255
Hengaston, 205
Henley-upon-Thames, 343
Hereford, 349
Heskens, 49
Hewith, see *Hisefield*
Hickesland, 105, 236
Hill, 8, 28; Chapel of, 87, 99, 142, 251, see *Hull*
Hill Park, 4
Hillesley, 95, 149
Hinetall, 37
Hineton, 7, 9, 16; M., 22, 43, 54, 96, 97, 107, 117, 118, 142, 143, 177, 205, 214, 218, 219, 220, 228; fubsidies, 229; soldiers, *ib.*; rates, *ib.*; Freeholder's lands, 229; Hurne's lands, 229, 230; Dancie's lands, 231; Fryar's

Hineton—*Continued*
land, *ib.*; Thorp's land, 231; 316, 317, 322, 342, 345, 370, 374, 383, 397
Hinworthy, 205, 249
Hisefield, als Hewith, 227
Hockday Hund, 134
Hockerhill, 61
Hodge's land, 65
Holts, 35, 38, 295
Hookstreet, 215
Hopton's lands, 139
Horefield Chapel, 233
Horend, 269
Horfield, 6, 9, 339
" Advow., 87
" M., 52, 55, 70, 187, 197, 198, 232, 409
Horwood forest, 237
Howcroft, 49, 272
Howley, 273
Howmead, 215
Hull Grange, 121
" 6, 107; Manor, 107, 213, 223, 224; chaple, 225; copyhold rents, 226; fubsidies, *ib.*; souldiers, *ib.*; rates, *ib.*; Freeholds: Scotland's, 226; Purlyn's lands, 227; 300, 304, 322, 342, 363, 369
Hulmancote, 7, 71, 120, 142, 150, 156, 159
Hungrode River, 255
Huntall, 238
Hunter's lands, 403
Huntingford, 270, 285, 396, 397, 407
Huntingford, 7, 37, 111, 233, 234, 235; Mathew's land, 236: Hicke's land, 236, 237; Smyth's land, 237; Durfewell's lands, *ib.*, 238; fubsidies, 239: soldiers, 230; rates, 239; tything, 240, 269
Huntsourt, 284
Hurne's land, 106, 229
Hurst, 7, 16, 28, 66, 79, 141, 202, 203, 204, 205, 206, 207; M., 240; Freeholds: Archer's lands, 241; River's lands, *ib.*, 243, 250; Selwin's lands, 248; Gilman's land, 249; Woodward's green, *ib.*; 328, 333, 334, 335, 409
Hurst farm, 241
Hurstleis, 249
Hynamsfield, 221, 228

Ichester, 384
Inwood, 185, 317, 351, 352, 353, 368

Iron Acton, M., 225 *n*, 300

Jobbin's land, 288
John's, St., of Jerusalem, Mon. of, 97

Kingcraft, 51
Kingscote Chapel, 102, 251
" M., 251; fubsidies, 253; soldiers, *ib.*; rates, *ib.*; Freeholds: Bate's Court, *ib.*; Thorp's land, *ib.*, 254; fubsidies, 256; soldiers, 257; rates, *ib.*
Kingscote par., 120
Kingrode, 343
Kingscote, 6, 7, 9, 120, 146, 312, 375, 409
Kingshill, 228
Kingsholme M, 375, 376
Kingston, 7, 81, 187, 242, 249, 333
Kingsweston Advow., 87
" M., 6, 102, 178, 385, 409
Kingswood Abbey, 74, 107, 109, 120, 121, 142, 147, 171, 171 *n*, 172, 215, 216, 299, 306, 307, 316, 317, 324, 359
Kingswood M., 74, 120, 257
" Rectory, 121
Kinley, M., 301, 303
Kinley Chantry, 301, 303
Knap, The, 139

Lacorek, 153
Lamports Court, see *Stincheombe M*.
Landheron, 329
Lasseborrow, 74, 120, 138
Lassturrowe, M., 170
Lawrenge, 383
Lay Knap, 191
Legamton. M., 163
Lesicke, 68
Lewes, 81, 129
Ley Wood, 191
Linchfield, 204, 205, 246, 249
Lipiatt, 50, 177, 218
Littlemoor, 250
Little Park, 209
Lobthorne, 367
Lockfast Bridge, 82, 142
Lockwell, 324
London, 30, 82, 124, 128, 135, 136, 177, 204, 303, 306, 307
London, Tower of, 56, 59, 60, 70, 72, 74, 90, 91, 106, 119, 121, 127, 128, 164, 170, 186, 187, 198, 233, 303, 319, 328, 331, 354, 386, 369
Long Afston, 367

INDEX TO NAMES OF PLACES 429

Longmead, 282
Lorenge Farm, 257, 259, 385
Lorwinch, 375
Lorwinge Hospital, 258
Lurgethall, 74, 320
Lydney, 339, 345

Mabfon's lands, 137
Maddenfhall lands, 155
Malletts land, 105, 230
Manland, 258
Manmead, 209
Markam, 43
Marlborough, 74, 81, 129
Marshalls, 282
Marshfield, 339
Matford Mead, 51, 273, 381
Mathew's lands, 236
Mattefdon, 7, 228, 357
Mead's land, 65
Melkefham, 181; fee alfo *Stintef-combe* M.
Melkefham's Court, 355, 356, 360
Melton Mowbray, Smyth's Hiftory of, 412
Metrefden, 228, 357
Michaelwood Chafe, 4, 35, 36, 37, 40, 46, 51, 70, 235, 237, 238, 387
Michelhampton, 148
Middleton, 63, 67, 97, 228, 231
Milend, 369, 389
Milefmore, 138, 139
Miles Place, 136
Milkfham, 277
Millards lands, 159
Minfterworth, 96
Monmouth, 286, 375
" Co., 342
Moore, 192
Moore's Mill, 298, 299
Morend, 241
Motun's land, 45
Mundaies lands, 298
Mylend, 65

Naffe Court, 130, 131, 388
New Enclofed Grounds, 337—347
Newent, 339
Newenton, 6, 7, 73, 74; M., 75; Church, *ib.*; 170, 173, 174, 308, 309, 310
Newland, 272
Newleys, 204
Newnham, 337, 339, 345
Newpark, 4, 36, 47, 57, 82, 209, 213
Newport, Chapel of St. Maurice, Chantry, 38, 98, 117

Newport, 7, 35, 39, 49, 51, 116, 117, 214, 219, 315
Newton, Ragpath, 170, 312, 409
New Work, fee *Owfelworth Houfe*
Nibley, 7, 42, 44, 46, 49, 85, 95, 108, 111, 117, 120, 124, 126, 142, 169, 181, 237, 259, 260, 261; derivation of, *ib.*; 273, 316, 347, 358, 374, 392
Nibley, Ch., 36, 251, 260, 261, 299; value of, 262; 265, Springs, 269; fubfidies, *ib.*; foldiers, *ib.*; Freeholds : — Pitcourt, 270; Burrows Court, *ib.*; Warren's Court, *ib.*, 323; Smallcombe's Court, *ib.*; Baffet's Court, *ib.*, 279; Hunts Court, *ib.*; Bellamy's Place, *ib.*; 280, 281, 283, 284, 285, 287, 288, 289, 290; Draifey's land, 291; 292; Chantry, 292; Vincent's lands, 293; Wilkin's land, 295; Marten's land, 295; Trotman's lands, 296, 297; Purnell's lands, 299; Hamlet of Woodmancote, 300; 364, 386, 387, 397, 405, 407, 409
Nibley Green, 62; battle of, 266-268; 269, 272, 297, 298
Nibley Grove, 219
" Par., 261, 359, 387, 389, 394, 395, 402
Nimpesfield, 9, 223, 224, 226; M., 300, 301, 302; Common Inn, *ib.*; the Park, 303; Kinley, 303; fubfidies, 304; foldiers, *ib.*; rates, *ib.*, 409
Nimpesfield, par., 304
Norwich, 320
Nutgarfhall, 74
Nympesfield, fee *Nimpesfield*
Nynd, 399

Oakley Park, 4, 35, 209, 305
Oldbury, 239
Olden, 204
Oldefton, 177
Oldland, 206, 277, 384
Oldlands Place, 222
Oldminfter, 99, 142, 228
" Barn, 54
Oldifworths lands, 112
Old Warth, 205
Ofborne's lands, 402
Overend, 347
Overly, 277
Overmead, 185
Overton, 63, 65, 67

Owlpen, 7, 185, 190, 303; M., 310; derivation of name, *ib.*; 313, 386
Owlpens lands, 133
Owfelworth Houfe, 306
" Par., 309
" Park, 4
" 6, 7, 9; Advow., 76, 87; Grange, 121; 308
Owfelworth M., 306; Chantry of St. John Bap., 307; the Broome, *ib.*; 309, 316, 324
Oxford, Ch. Ch. at, 261, 264, 265
Oxford, Mad. Coll. 324

Painthurft, 98
Panthurft, 217, 218
Partridges lands, 159
Patchway, 57
Peckam, 42
Pedington, 7, 73, 77, 208, 210, 227; Manor or Farm, 314, 315, 386
Peerfcourt, 181
Pennings, 49, 273, 282
Percy Furlong, 282
Perry's lands, 403
Picote, 120
Pilwell, 296
Pinelfend hamlet, 150
Piriton Paffage, 317
Piftors lands, 156
Pitcourt in Nibley M., 181, 269, 270, 271, 275, 276, 277, 359
Planch, la, 75, 128; its devolution, 128, 316
Pockhampton, 7, 107, 142, 228, 229, 230, 231, 232; 316
Poole Court, Worc., 136
Poole's lands, 405
Portbury, 70, 200
Priors Wood, 241
Purlyns lands, 227
Purnell's land, 44

Rackcombe, 274, 277
Rackridge, 277
Ragge, 209
Rancombe, 186
Red Crofts, 253
Redfield, 272
Redford, 36
Redinges lands, 158
Redwood, 241
Reignold's Mead, 204, 205
Riam Mead, 35, 70
Riddlesford, 228
Ridge, The, 270, 316, 317, 399
Rockhampton, 50, 226

INDEX TO NAMES OF PLACES

Rodborrowe, 390
Rodegreene, 295
Rodes, 282
Rodleis Deane, 298
" Weir, 68, 71
Rolls land, 64
Roules Court, 327
Roxford, 191
Ruardean M., 357, 358
Rugbagge, 35, 76
Ruydings, 273, 282, 287
Ryam, 51
Ryver's lands, 242, 243, 244, 245, 246, 250

Sages, 16; Manor, 336
St. Leonard, 339
Sandridge, 36, 40
Schoolmaster's Grove, 290
Schay's Chantry, 292
Scotlands, 226
Seliman's lands, 129; their devolution, *ib.*; grant of, 129, 130
Selewins lands, 141, 195, 248
Severn River, 3, 5, 10, 52, 58, 60, 63, 67, 68, 69, 83, 85, 86, 225, 228, 237, 317; description of, 317; passage over, 317; tides, 318; floods, *ib.*; fish in, 319, 320, 321; customs of, *ib.*, 330; variation of the channel, 331; new grounds reclaimed from, 337—347; fordable at times, 343; 375; great floods in, 411
Sextons Mill, 142, 145
Shabhill, 279
Shepardines passage, 321, 322
Shepnash Park, 4
Shepwardend, 225
Sherncliffe Court, 279, 281, 282, 283
Shipton M., 170
Shiptons lands, in Kingescote, 283
Shirborne, 37, 236, 297
Shobenalke, 228, 229
" Parke, 229
Shokerwicke, 74
Shortworthy, 132
Simondshull, see *Symondshull*
Sindleforth, 363
Sinwell, see *Synwell*
Slades, 273, 295
Slimbridge Advow., 87, 324; Church, 170, 324
Slimbridge, 6, 7, 16, 58, 66, 67, 79, 117, 127, 131, 140, 141, 159, 160, 199, 203, 204, 205, 207, 240, 241, 242, 245, 246, 248, 250, 259, 321, 329, 331, 332, 334, 337, 387

Slimbridge M., 117, 173, 187, 200, 202, 203, 241, 243, 250, 322, 324; description of, *ib.*; descent of, 327; Frampton's rent, 329; 330; the warths, 331; Bramwich lands, 331; Barnsdale's land, 332; Lewis's lands, 333; Bottiler's lands, 334; Davis's land, 335; Ludby's land, 335; Frape's land, 336; Rowle's court, 336; subsidies, 337; soldiers, *ib.*; rates, *ib.*; new enclosed grounds, trial concerning, 337-347; 362, 409
Slimbridge street, 327
" Warth, 69, 242, 250, 327, 328, 330, 331, 334, 385
Sloo, 61, 67
Smalcombe Court, 277, 279
Smith's lands, 403
Smythe's place, 379, 382
Snitend, 122, 269, 270, 274, 293, 295, 297, 347, 358, 369
Sodbury, 76, 177, 237, 289, 308
Somer's Farm, 314
Somerset, Co. of, 255, 365, 384
Southend in Nibley, 269, 282, 287, 288, 290, 291, 295, 298, 299, 347
Southend in Stinchcombe, 244, 390
Southend in Ewley, 185
Southworthy par., 152
" field, 204, 246, 249, 327
Sparkhill, 138
Sprats, 185
Squire Acre, 250
Stancombe, 270, 387
" 7, 38, 115, 117, 129, 273, 274, 282, 295; M., 347, 357, 358, 359, 361, 409
Standish, 301
Stanley St. Leonards, 195
" " " Priory, 66, 67, 150, 151, 172, 193, 257, 258
Stanley M., 75, 95, 173
Stanshawe, 289
Stanton's lands, 406
Stantons Place, 370
Stepps, 131, 138, 139, 204, 207, 391
Stinchcombe, 116, 119, 122, 135, 369, 375
Stinchcombe Chapel, 251, 355, 356
" Chapelry, 145, 270
" Church, 115, 123
" M., 115; derivation of name, 347, 349; Beacon, 349; Bluemead Sunday, *ib.*, Pier's Court, 354; Melktham's Court, 355, 356; Lamport's Court, 356; Alba Mara's lands,

Stinchcombe—*Continued*
357; Snitend, 358; Nelme's land, 359; Stancombe, *ib.*; subsidies, 360; soldiers, *ib.*; rates, *ib.*; 368
Stintescombe, 7, 10, 38, 49, 63, 147, 181, 205, 244, 295, 369
Stitchcombe, 124
Stockes, 282
Stoke Gifford, 110, 186, 188, 232, 255, 257
Stone, 7, 51, 57; Chapel of, 87; 99, 117, 142, 208, 209, 215, 222, 251, 285, 286, 293, 353, 362, 363; hamlet, 361—370; derivation of name, 361; Tithe Barn, 362; old freeholds, 362; Stone water course, 362; bridges, *ib.*; chantries, 363; soldiers, *ib.*; old court, 364; Webb's land, 367; Stone's Inn, 368; more of chantries, 369; 374, 379, 384
Stone, Chantry of, 51, 98, 358, 363, 369
Stone lower, 374
Stone upper, 374
Stonesheath, 361
Stonehouse, 158, 339
Stouthill Place, 194
Stowell, 65
Strelly, 282
Sudely Castle, 144
Surrey, Co. of, 188
Sutton Marsh, 341
Swanhunger, 7, 71, 208, 210, 220, 223, 228, 287, 315; hamlet of, 370—371, 372, 380, 383
Swanley, 7, 35, 51, 369
Swineburne, 277
Swunhaiam, 295
Swyney, 108, 269, 272, 273, 277, 279, 280, 281, 295, 298
Symondshull, 7, 9, 30, 31, 149, 262, 265, 269, 270, 316, 317; M., 322; salubrity of, 323; 397, 399, 407
Synwell, 107, 108, 148, 265, 269, 295, 396, 401, 403, 406, 407

Tachcroft, 246
Talebrockes, 166
Tanhouse Mill, see *Baythorpe*
Tanners Croft, 139
" Mead, 112
Teinton, 158
Teile's lands, 160
Tetbury Grange, 121
" 245, 250, 301, 399; Smyth's Hist. of, 412

INDEX TO NAMES OF PLACES 431

Tetcombe, 274, 290
Tetpens, 185
Tewkesbury, 136
" Abbey, 264, 265
Thornbury, 46, 49, 118, 227, 239, 339
Thornbury Hund., 361
Throughbridge, 251
Tickruydinge, 10
Tidnams, 273, 275, 277
Tilbury Camp, 411
Tockington, 225, 367
Tortworth, 163, 222, 228, 237, 301, 308, 312, 362, 363, 376
Trollie's House, 391
Trotman's lands, 296
Turner's Croft, 282
" land, 74
Twichen, 209
Twinens lands, 156
Tykenham, 184

Uley, 6, 7, 9, 77, 78, 95, 132, 154, 186, 194, 231, 256, 257, 281, 303, 333, 392, 409
Uley Advow., 87, 193
" Camp, 194
" Church, 170, 193
" M., 159, 179-196; grants of, 182, 183; camp, 193; Church, *ib.*; subsidies, *ib.*; freeholds, 194; 394
Uley Parish, 194
" Park, 4
" White Court M., 180, 186, 192
Upthorpe, 140

Valemore, 68
Velesraydings, 237
Veleham, 210; M., 211, 212, 213
Vincent's lands, 297
Virginia, 112, 370, 376

Wakefield M., York, 39
Wales, Marches of, 10, 105, 140
Walingaston, 375, 383
Wallingford Castle, 188
Walmegaston, 143
Wanswell, 7, 29, 50, 115, 117, 180, 208, 210, 214, 215, 220, 222; M., *ib.*, 223, 232, 253, 259, 286, 287, 315, 364, 365, 367, 370, 376, 409
Wanswell Court, 50, 85, 86, 371; Chapel in, 372, 373, 382, 385, 386

Wanswell hamlet, 371; Holy Well, 372; Smythe's Place, 379; Wikefelme, 382; Budding, 383; Butler's lands, 384; Richards' lands, 285; 386
Wapley, 99
Warren's Court, 277, 394
Were, Som., 99, 255
Westbury-on-Severn, 235
Westcote, 181
Westerley, par., 260
Westfield, 270, 282
Westmancote, 120
Westnewington Advow., 76
Wetton, 9, 99
" Lawrence, 256
Westridge, 10, 29
" Wood, 77
Whetenhurst, 135
Whitecliffe Park, 4, 36, 209, 368, 385, 407
White-crofs green, 136
White Court M., in Uley, 180, 186, 192
Whitings, 105
Whitflane Hund., 329
Wickley, 291, 296
Wickstowe, 208, 213, 214, 225, 227, 385
Wickwarre, 105, 213, 339
Wike Court, 314, 315, 386
Wike M., in Arlingham, 61, 62, 67, 386
Wike, 7, 35, 36, 44, 48, 49, 50, 77, 99, 116, 208, 220, 270, 274, 282, 291, 294, 315, 375, 383, 384, 386, 392, 409
Wike's fallowe, 219
Wilkens lands, 156, 295
Willoughbies lands, 213, 215
Wilts Co., 116, 227, 359, 369
Windmilfeild, 373, 379
Windsor Castle, 320
Wingesmore, 238
Winley, 279, 280
Winterborne M., 114, 118
Withers land, 106
Withe's land, 45
Wittune M., 109
Wodemancote, 6, 120; M., 130, 131, 190, 204, 292, 298, 300, 387; derivation of name, *ib.*; court leet of, 393; subsidies, 394; soldiers, *ib.*; rates, *ib.*; freeholds, *ib.*; Clifford's lands, *ib.*
Woodalend, 269
Wood-all-ends-well, 295

Woodchester M., 3
Woodends house, 133, 136
Woodend of Hull, 213, 225, 227
Woodford, 7, 35, 36, 46, 49, 51, 108, 117, 216, 369, 379, 386
Woodhouse, 335
Woolleys, 37, 239
Woodwards greene, 241, 249, 250
Woodwards lands, 159
Woodyates, 238
Woodyeates, 37
Woollaston, 214
Worcester, Co. of, 187
" City, 302, 349
Worteley, 7, 95, 112, 265, 290, 294, 307, 386, 396, 405, 407
Worth-hayes, 283
Worthy Park, 4, 35, 36, 209, 386; see also *Castle Park*
Wortley M., 407; description of, *ib.*; chantry, 408; soldiers, 408
Wotton, 4, 6, 7, 16, 38, 67, 70, 77, 82, 107, 109, 111, 112, 116, 140, 142, 146, 152, 171, 233, 239, 265, 274, 276, 277, 287, 294, 298, 323, 387, 397, 407
Wotton Advow., 52, 87, 88, 262, 263, 264, 266
Wotton Almshouses, foundation of, 398
Wotton Borough, 16, 39, 108, 109, 396, 307, 398, 399; Leet of, *ib.*, 400, 401, 402; freeholds :— Osborne's lands, *ib.*; Dawe's land, 403; Hunter's, alias Perry's lands, *ib.*; Smith's lands, *ib.*; Ven's land, 404; Pool's lands, 405; Daunt's land, 406; Stanton's land, *ib.*; subsidies, *ib.*; 407, *ib.*; soldiers, *ib.*; rates, *ib.*
Wotton Church, 170, 251, 261, 262, 263, 265, 266, 323, 399, 402
Wotton forren M., 78, 107, 108, 112, 146, 148, 149, 168, 240, 253, 261, 269, 278, 279, 283, 284, 285, 288, 289, 290, 291, 293, 294, 295, 296, 297, 312, 313, 316, 396, 401, 403, 406, 407
Wotton M., 79, 109, 146, 148, 149, 185, 187, 266, 267, 268, 271, 385, 386, 396, 398, 399, 402
Wotton School, 401, 402

Yate, 227, 339
Youngcrofts, 283, 291

Berkeley Manuscripts

LIST OF SUBSCRIBERS

LARGE PAPER COPIES

No. 1 Guise, Sir William Vernon, Bart., F.L.S., F.G.S., Elmore Court, Gloucester
" 2 Bamford, Rev. R., M.A., Jordan Villa, St. Mary Church, Torquay, Devon
" 3 Lang, Robert, Mancombe, Henbury, Bristol
" 4 Paul, Alfred H., The Close, Tetbury
" 5 Miles, Cruger, Pen Pole, Shirehampton
" 6 Maclean, Sir John, F.S.A., Glasbury House, Clifton, Bristol
" 7 James, Francis, Edgeworth Manor, Cirencester
" 8 Niblett, The late J. D. T., M.A., F.S.A., Haresfield Court, Stonehouse
" 9 Lang, Samuel, Langford Lodge, Pembroke Road, Clifton
" 10 Kerr, Russell J., The Haie, Newnham
" 11 Fawn, James, Queen's Road, Bristol
" 12 Bruton, H. W., Bewick House, Wotton
" 13 Skillicorne, W. Nash, 9, Queen's Parade, Cheltenham
" 14 George, W. E., Downside, Stoke Bishop, Bristol
" 15 Adlam, William, F.S.A., Manor House, Chew Magna
" 16 Doggett, E. G., 31, Richmond Terrace, Clifton, Bristol
" 17 Blacker, Rev. B. H., M.A., 26, Meridian Place, Clifton, Bristol
" 18 Heane, William Crawshay, The Lawn, Cinderford
" 19 Clarke, John A. Graham, Frocester, Stonehouse
" 20 Arrowsmith, J. W., 24, Westfield Park, Redland, Bristol
" 21 Smith, R. Vassar, Ashfield, Great Malvern
" 22 Uren, The late William, Crofton House, Clifton Down, Clifton, Bristol
" 23 Baker, James, The Mall, Clifton, Bristol
" 24 Fitzhardinge, Craven Hyde, Dubbo, N.S. Wales
" 25 Baker, Arthur, Henbury Hill House, Bristol
" 26 Holland, W. H., Gloucester

LIST OF SUBSCRIBERS

No. 27 Price, William P., Tibberton Court, Gloucester
  „ 28 Philp, Capt. J. Lamb, Pendoggett, Timsbury, Somerset
  „ 29 Walker, C. B., Wotton House, Gloucester
  „ 30 Scrope, Mrs., Danby-upon-Yore, Bedale, Yorkshire
  „ 31 Blathwayt, Wynter E., Dyrham, Chippenham
  „ 32 Berkeley, Francis, Leagram Hall, Preston
  „ 33 Thorp, Disney Launder, M.D., Lypiatt Lodge, Cheltenham
  „ 34 Fox, Charles Henry, M.D., The Beeches, Brislington
  „ 35 Dent, The late John Coucher, Sudeley Castle, Winchcomb
  „ 36 Hallett, T. G. P., M.A., Claverton Lodge, Bath
  „ 37 Gibbs, H. Martin, Barrow Court, Flax Bourton, Somerset
  „ 38 Boyle, E. M., F.S.A., 14, Hill Street, Berkeley Square, London
  „ 39 Baily, W. H., 129, Dyer Street, Cirencester
  „ 40 Dancey, C. H., 6, Midland Road, Gloucester
  „ 41 Ducie, The Right Hon. the Earl of, P.C., F.R.S., Tortworth Court, Wotton-under-Edge
     42 Bazeley, Rev. W., M.A., Matson Rectory, Gloucester, *(Hon. Sec.)*
  „ 43 Witts, Rev. F. E. Broome, M.A., Norton Rectory, Gloucester
  „ 44 Giles, Oliver, Park Side, Cromwell Road, St. Andrews, Bristol

---

N.B. The other six LARGE Paper Copies, and also two SMALL Paper Copies were presented by the Society to the Right Hon. Lord Fitzhardinge, Berkeley Castle.

SMALL PAPER COPIES

Ackers, B. St. John, Prinknash Park, Painswick
Allen, Rev. William Taprell, M.A., St. Briavels' Vicarage, Coleford
Ames, Reginald, 2, Albany Terrace, Park Square, East, London, N.W.
Arrowsmith, J. W., 24, Westfield Park, Redland, Bristol

Baker, James, Serrelle Villa, Goldney Road, Clifton, Bristol
Barkly, Sir Henry, K.C.B., 1, Bina Gardens, South Kensington, W.
Bartleet, Rev. S. E., M.A., Brockworth Vicarage, Gloucester
Baynes, C. R., The Lammas, Minchinhampton
Bazeley, Rev. William, M.A., Matson Rectory, Gloucester, *(Hon. Sec.)*

LIST OF SUBSCRIBERS

Beach, The Right Hon. Sir Michael Hicks, Bart., M.P., Williamstrip Park, Fairford
Beddoe, John, M.D., F.R.S., Mortimer House, Clifton, Bristol
Berkeley, Francis, Leagram Hall, Preston
Berkeley, Rowland W., 1, Tokenhouse Buildings, London, E.C.
Bibliothèque Nationale, Paris
Blathwayt, Rev. Wynter T., M.A., Dyrham Rectory, Chippenham
Boevey, A. Crawley-, East India United Service Club, 14, St. James' Square, London, S.W.
Boevey, Sir T. H Crawley-, Bart., Flaxley Abbey, Newnham
Bourne, Rev. G. Drinkwater, M.A., F.S.A., Weston-sub-Edge, Broadway
Bowly, Christopher, Siddington House, Cirencester
Boyle, Edmund M., F.S.A., 14, Hill Street, Berkeley Square, London
Bramble, Lieut.-Col. James Roger, Cleeve House, near Yatton, Somerset
Bravender, T. B., The Firs, Cirencester
Buckley, The late Rev. Joseph, M.A., Tormarton Rectory, Chipping Sodbury
Bute, The Most Noble the Marquis of, Cardiff Castle, Glamorganshire

Caldicott, Rev. J. W., D.D., Shipston-on-Stour Rectory, Worcestershire *(Hon. Sec.)*
Cattell, The late Thomas William, Blakeford Cottage, King's Stanley, Stonehouse
Chance, T. H., *Journal* Office, Gloucester
Cheltenham Library, 5, Royal Crescent, Cheltenham
Clark, George T., F.S.A., Dowlais House, Dowlais
Clifford, The Hon. and Right Rev. Bishop, Bishop's House, Clifton, Bristol
Clough, R. L., 13, Bellevue, Clifton, Bristol
Cokayne, George E., M.A., F.S.A., Norroy King of Arms, Herald's College, Queen Victoria Street, London, E.C.
Colby, Rev. Frederick Thomas, D.D., F.S.A., Little Torrington Rectory, N. Devon
Collier, Colonel, Stanley Hall, Stonehouse
Collins, J. C., M.D., Steanbridge House, Slad, Stroud
Cooke, J. Herbert, F.S.A., Berkeley
Cooke, W. H., Q.C., F.S.A., 42, Wimpole Street, London
Cornock, Nicholas, 11, Dingwall Road, Croydon
Cornwall, Rev. Alan Kingscote, M.A., Ashcroft, Wotton-under-Edge
Cowburn, Major J. Brett, Dennel Hill, near Chepstow
Cox, Alfred, Shannon Court, Clifton, Bristol
Cripps, Wilfrid J., F.S.A., Barrister-at-Law, Cirencester
Crossman, George D., Rudgeway, Gloucestershire

LIST OF SUBSCRIBERS

Dancey, Charles H., 6, Midland Road, Gloucester
Davis, Cecil Tudor, The Court House, Painswick
Dent, The late J. C., Sudeley Castle, Winchcombe
Derham, Samuel, Henleaze Park, Westbury-on-Trym
Derham, Walter, M.A., F.G.S., Henleaze Park, Westbury-on-Trym
Doggett, E. G., 31, Richmond Terrace, Clifton, Bristol
Dorington, J. E., Lypiatt Park, Stroud
Downing, William, Springfield House, Olton, near Birmingham
Ducie, The Right Hon. the Earl of, F.R.S., Tortworth Court, Wotton-under-Edge

Ellacombe, Rev. H. T., M.A., F.S.A., The Rectory, Clyst St. George, Topsham
Emeris, Rev. J., M.A., Upton St. Leonard Rectory, Gloucester
Estcourt, Rev. E. W., M.A., Newnton Rectory, Tetbury
Evans, J. B., 6, Douro Villas, Cheltenham

Fawn, James, Queen's Road, Bristol
Foljambe, Cecil G. S., M.P., F.S.A., Cockglode, Ollerton, Newark
Forster, Right Hon. W. E., M.P., Wharfside, Burley-on-Wharfdale, Leeds, and 86 Eccleston Square, London, S.W.
Fox, Alderman Francis Frederick, Yate House, Chipping Sodbury
Fryer, Kedgwin Hoskins, Maitland House, Gloucester

Gaisford, E. Sands, 23, Bassett Road, N. Kensington, London
Gaisford, Rev. Thos. Amyas, M.A., 2, Devonshire Place, Wells Road, Bath
George, W. E., Downside, Stoke Bishop, Bristol
George, William, 3, King's Parade, Clifton, Bristol
Gibbs, H. Martin, Barrow Court, Flax Bourton, Somerset
Giles, Oliver, Park Side, Cromwell Road, St. Andrews, Bristol
Giller, William Thomas, County of Gloucester Bank, Gloucester
Godwin, J. G., 83 Eccleston Square, London, S.W.
Gosling, The late Rev. J. F., M.A., Bream Vicarage, Lydney
Greenfield, Benjamin Wyatt, 4, Cranbury Terrace, Southampton
Grist, W. C., Brookside, Chalford, Stroud
Gwinnett, William Henry, Gordon Cottage, Cheltenham

Hale, C. B., Claremont House, Gloucester
Hale, Robert B., Colonel, Alderley, Wotton-under-Edge
Hall, Rev. J. M., M.A., The Rectory, Harescombe, Stroud

LIST OF SUBSCRIBERS

Hallen, Rev. A. W. Cornelius, M.A., The Parsonage, Alloa, N.B.
Harvard College, U.S.A.
Haviland, General de, Havilland Hall, Taunton
Hazeldine, Rev. William, The Priory, Tyndall's Park, Clifton, Bristol
Heywood, The late Samuel, F.S.A., 161, Stanhope Street, London
Holford, Robert S., Weston Birt House, Tetbury
Holland, W. H., Gloucester
Houghton, The Right Hon. Lord, 1, Rutland Gardens, Knightsbridge, London, S.W.
Hudd, Alfred E., 94, Pembroke Road, Clifton, Bristol
Hutchinson, Hutchinson, 42, Lancaster Gate, Hyde Park, London
Hyett, F. A., Painswick House, Painswick

Jacques, Thomas W., Pendine, Chesterfield Road, Ashley Hill, Bristol
James, Rev. John, M.A., Highfield, Lydney
Jenkins, R. Palmer, Beechley, Chepstow

Kay, Sir Brook, Bart., Stanley Lodge, Battledown, Cheltenham
Keeling, George William, 10 Lansdown Terrace, Cheltenham
Kerslake, Thomas, 14, West Park, Clifton, Bristol
King, William Poole, Avonside, Clifton Down, Bristol

Lancaster, Thomas, Bownham House, Stroud
Law, W., Littleborough, Manchester
Leigh, William, Woodchester Park, Stonehouse
Lewis, Archibald M., 3, Upper Byron Place, Bristol
Lindsay, W. A., M.A., Q.C., 17, Cromwell Road, South Kensington
Liverpool Public Library
Lloyd, Capt. Owen, 4, Oxford Parade, Cheltenham
London Library, 12, St. James' Square, London
Lucy, William C., Brookthorpe, Gloucester

Maclaine, William Osborne, Kington, Thornbury
Macpherson, J., Invercargill, New Zealand
Manchester Public Library
Margetson, William, Brightside, Stroud
Metford, Joseph Seymour, 31, Berkeley Square, Bristol
Middlemore-Whittard, Rev. T. M., M.A., Teighmore, Cheltenham
Middleton, The late John, Westholme, Cheltenham
Middleton, J. H., F.S.A., 4, Storeys Gate, St. James' Park, London

LIST OF SUBSCRIBERS

Morgan, Sir Walter, Naish House, Nailsea, Somerset
Morrell, Frederick J., Broughton Lodge, Banbury
Mullings, John, Park Street, Cirencester

Needham, Frederick, M.D., Barnwood House, Gloucester
Niblett, The late J. D. T., M.A., F.S.A., Haresfield Court, Stonehouse
Noel, Colonel, Easton Hall, Newark-upon-Trent
Norman, George, Clarence Street, Cheltenham
Norris, Venerable Archdeacon, D.D., Lower College Green, Bristol

Oakeley, Rev. W. Bagnall, M.A., Newland, Coleford
O'flahertie, Rev. T. R., M.A., Capel Vicarage, Surrey

Palmer, Rev. Feilding, M.A., Eastcliffe, Chepstow
Perceval, Cecil H. Sp., Henbury, Bristol
Perkins, V. R., Wotton-under-Edge, Gloucestershire
Peter, Thurstan C., Town Hall, Redruth
Phillimore, W. P. W., M.A., B.C.L., 6, Quality Court, Chancery Lane, London, W.C.
Phillipps, J. O. Halliwell, F.R.S., F.S.A., Hollingbury Copse, Brighton
Playne, Charles, Theescombe, Stroud
Playne, Arthur T., Longfords, Minchinhampton
Powell, John Joseph, Q.C., Fountain Court Temple, London, E.C.
Poynton, Rev. F. T., M.A., Kelston Rectory, Bath
Prankerd, P. D., The Knoll, Sneyd Park, Bristol
Pritchett, Charles Pigott, 3, Hillside, Cotham, Bristol

Rice, The Hon. Maria Elizabeth Rice, Matson House, Gloucester
Riddiford, George Francis, Barnwood Lodge, Gloucester
Rogers, R. Rogers Coxwell-, F.S.A., Dowdeswell Court, Cheltenham
Rolt, Mrs. S., Oakhanger, Berkeley
Royce, Rev. David, M.A., Nether Swell Vicarage, Stow-on-the-Wold

Savory, C. H., St. John Street, Cirencester
Science and Art Department, South Kensington Museum, London, S.W.
Scott, Charles, 52, London Road, Gloucester
Scrope, Mrs. Emily, Danby-upon-Yore, Bedale, Yorkshire
Selwyn, Rev. E. J., M.A., Pluckley Rectory, Ashford, Kent
Sewell, Edward C., Elmlea, Stratton, Cirencester

LIST OF SUBSCRIBERS

Sherborne, Right Hon. Lord, Sherborne Park
Sibbald, J. G. E., Accountant-General's Department, Admiralty, London, S.W.
Simpſon, J. J., Lynwood, Cotham Gardens, Briſtol
Smith, Alfred Edward, The Hollies, Nailſworth
Smith, T. Somerville, Sittingbourne, Kent
Society of Merchant Venturers, Briſtol
Stanton, Charles Holbrow, 65, Redcliffe Gardens, London, S.W.
Stone, John, 12, Royal Creſcent, Bath
Stroud, Frederick, Lewiſland, Cheltenham
Swayne, Joſeph Griffiths, M.D., 74, Pembroke Road, Clifton, Briſtol
Swayne, S. H., 129, Pembroke Road, Clifton, Briſtol

Taylor, John, 37, Clyde Road, Briſtol
Taynton, Thomas, Wotton Hill Houſe, Glouceſter
Thomas, William, 7, Charlotte Street, Queen Square, Briſtol
Trinder, Edward, Perrots' Brook, Cirenceſter
Tuckett, Francis Fox, Eſq., F.R.G.S., Frenchay, Briſtol
Tudway, Clement, Cecily Hill, Cirenceſter

Waddingham, John, Guiting Grange, Winchcombe
Weſton, J. D., Dorſet Houſe, Clifton, Briſtol
Weſton, John, Leſlie Court, Barnwood, Glouceſter
Wheeler, A. C., Upton Hill, Glouceſter
Whitwill, Mark, Redland Houſe, Durdham Park, Briſtol
Williams, Rev. Auguſtin, M.A., Todenham Rectory, Moreton-in-Marſh
Williams, Adin, Lechlade
Wilton, John P., 10, College Green, Glouceſter
Wiſeman, Rev. H. J., M.A., Clifton College, Clifton, Briſtol
Witts, Rev. F. E. Broome, M.A., Norton Vicarage, Glouceſter

www.ingramcontent.com/pod-product-compliance
Lightning Source LLC
Chambersburg PA
CBHW020526300426
44111CB00008B/555